LET'S GO: ISRAEL & EGYPT

is the best book for anyone traveling on a budget. Here's why:

No other guidebook has as many budget listings.

In Jerusalem we list dozens of places offering bed and breakfast for less than $15 per night; in the countryside, we found hundreds more for much less. We tell you how to get there the cheapest way, whether by bus, plane, or thumb, and where to get an inexpensive and satisfying meal once you've arrived. There are hundreds of money-saving tips for everyone plus lots of information on special student discounts.

LET'S GO researchers have to make it on their own.

No expense accounts, no free hotel rooms. Our student researchers travel on budgets as limited as your own.

LET'S GO is completely revised every year.

We don't just update the prices, we go back to the places. If a charming restaurant has become an overpriced tourist trap, we'll replace it with a new and better listing.

No other budget guidebook includes all this:

Coverage of both the cities and the countryside; in-depth information on culture, history, and the people; distinctive features like rail, city, and regional maps; tips on work, study, hiking and biking, nightlife and special splurges; and much, much more.

LET'S GO is for anyone who wants to see the real Israel, Egypt and Jordan on an inflation-fighting budget.

LET'S GO:

The Budget Guide to ISRAEL and EGYPT

1984

Ted Osius, Editor

Written by Harvard Student Agencies, Inc.

ST. MARTIN'S PRESS
NEW YORK

Distributed in the United Kingdom by Columbus Books, Devonshire House, Bromley, Kent BR1 1LT, England

Distributed throughout the rest of the world by Fleetbooks S.A., 100 Park Avenue, New York, New York 10017

ISBN: 0-312-48221-3

First Edition
10 9 8 7 6 5 4 3 2 1

Let's Go: Israel & Egypt is written by Harvard Student Agencies, Harvard University, Thayer Hall-B, Cambridge, Mass. 02138.

Editor: Ted Osius
Assistant Editor: Susan B. Whitlock
Managing Editor: Linda Haverty
Assistant to the Managing Editor: Steven Parkey
Advertising Representatives: James Heideman, Jean Huang
Advertising Coordinator: Richard Foote
Assistant Coordinator: Pamela Stedman
Researcher/Writers:

Scott Campbell: *Israel (West Bank, Negev), Egypt (Sinai)*

Jim Conant/Juliet Floyd: *Cairo, Nile Valley, Oases, Near Cairo, Sudan*

Daniel Gluck: *Tel Aviv and Central Coast, South Coast, Haifa and North Coast, Upper Galilee, Golan, Jordan*

Chris Murray: *Alexander and Mediterrean Coast, Suez and Red Sea Coast, Abu Simbel, Faiyuum*

Gideon Schor: *Jerusalem, Dead Sea, Lower and Central Galilee*

Staff Assistants: Miriam Roberts, Kenneth Hale-Wehmann, Jenny Wittner, Elliot Eder, Rick Wertheim, Rodney Yoder
Proofreaders: J. David Bunn, John Caldwell, Debbie Friedmann, Josh Gahm, Deb Iles, Diane Klein, Matthew Kraus, Susan Peisner, Gayle Sato, Stephanie Seminara, Holly Stewart, Teresa Turvey, Rick Wertheim.
Maps: Jeanne Abboud
Legal Counsel: Harold Rosenwald

Acknowledgements

The nine *Let's Go* travel guides that emerged this year are the products of immense amounts of dedication, enthusiasm, and sheer hard work. The results are no more due to the skill of this season's staff than they are a tribute to the high standards set by researchers, writers, and editors of years past. I salute the *Let's Go* tradition of excellence, and thank our predecessors for the fine examples provided over the last two decades.

To my superb assistant editor, Susan Whitlock, I owe the greatest debt of gratitude; her unparalleled competence and perseverance, and uncanny ability to make sense out of nonsense made her the best thing that could have happened to this book. Linda Haverty, our tireless leader and confidante throughout the long and heated summer, was a constant source of inspiration, always the first to help in times of desperation; I'm proud to call her a friend.

Abundant thanks go to Jim Conant, my own *Let's Go* mentor; I'm honored that he asked me to edit this first edition of the book he envisioned, and thankful for his patience and expertise in preparing itineraries. He and Juliet Floyd provided comprehensive coverage of much of Egypt despite an illness that would have daunted most mortals, and of the Sudan, which appears here for the first time. My heartfelt thanks, although insufficient, go to the dedicated researchers who braved Israeli tourist officials, Egyptian bureaucracy, and Jordanian border crossings, all in the ferocious desert heat of the Middle East. Daniel Gluck not only researched an entirely new country, but returned to Cambridge and cheerfully devoted hundreds of hours to writing, editing, typing, and answering questions about Jordanian and Israeli history and culture. Scott Campbell edured Arabic lessons at the YMCA in preparation for his plunge into the turbulent political climate of the West Bank, and topped off his summer with original research in the Sinai. Gideon Schor provided new insight into Israeli culture, and Chris Murray forged ahead even after a bout of malaria, adding entirely new sections to the Egypt chapter.

On the home front, Elliot Eder, a holdover from an earlier *Let's Go* generation, helped whip the Jordan chapter into shape, while Kenneth Hale-Wehmann added his magic touch to the Egypt chapter. Jenny Wittner helped immeasurably on the Israel introduction, and Martha Hodes proved to be an oasis in the desert with her assistance on all fronts. Chris Caldwell, Rachel Conrad, and Mark Fishbein, the other Europe editors, provided a core of support; I enjoyed their camaraderie during the difficult hiring process and in the wee hours all summer long. Mike Della Rocca, Miriam Roberts, Steve Parkey, Rodney Yoder and Phuong Pham deserve accolades for their help typing and preparing the manuscripts for the publisher. Thanks go to Maura Gorman and Judy Solo of HSA for providing money, encouragement, and a place to put the typewriters.

The chapter on Egypt owes an inexpressible amount to Daniel Mandil, a former *Let's Go* editor, who contributed the section on the Sudan, provided housing, made numerous phone calls, and supplied helpful criticisms, and to Anne Aghion, one of the world's experts on how to survive in Cairo and enjoy it. Thanks also to Carol Bardenstein for delivering the goods to their library and half hour, and to the Dutch Institute in Cairo for access to their library and typewriter. Shawki Hussein and Sonia Guirguis of the Egyptian National Tourist Office in New York contributed to the introduction.

I also wish to thank my sister Meg, whose hospitality made possible a productive business trip to the Big Apple, and my housemates, Andy, Maja, Jenny, Linus, Daniel, Scott, and Mr. Lobster, for their patience. Finally, thanks go to my parents for their enduring love, for their wisdom in letting me choose which roads to travel, and for guiding me with gentle hands whenever a guide was needed.

—T.O.

CONTENTS

LET'S GO: ISRAEL AND EGYPT

The lands of Abraham, Jesus, and Muhammad are crowded with the holy places of three great world religions. A tumultuous past and present testify to the region's strategic position at the crossroads of three continents. Powerful loyalties and beliefs inspire the passions of the Middle East's rich ethnic mosaic. After even a brief visit here, you'll understand why. The peoples of Israel, Egypt, and Jordan forged the world's oldest civilizations against the timeless backdrop of the desert.

The timelessness of the Middle East need not leave you penniless, and that's where *Let's Go* is designed to help. Prices are considerably lower than in most European countries, and *Let's Go* directs you to the best bargains. Our researchers, traveling on a shoestring, share your concerns: how to eat, drink, get around, see the sights, and sleep in the least expensive and most enjoyable way possible.

Most tourists who visit the Middle East stick to the cities and ignore other equally fascinating parts of the region. *Let's Go* tries to take you off the beaten track, and out to scenes of isolated beauty. We cover Druze villages on Israel's north coast, distant oases of the Sahara, Nabatean ruins of Jordan, and the mighty Nile from the southern Sudan to the Mediterranean.

Let's Go will also help guide you through some of the tasks you need to do before you go. We provide cost-cutting practical information that will help you decide what kind of trip to take, and valuable introductions to life in Israel, Egypt, and Jordan. And our regional introductions try to give the flavor of the areas you might choose to visit.

Once you're there, *Let's Go* tells you some of what there is to see and do in the Middle East. The orientation and practical information sections in the larger cities and regions help you get settled more easily, if you want to stay. Our sights sections help you explore mosques, churches and synagogues, ancient ruins and bustling marketplaces of Israel, Egypt, and Jordan. We point out the finest beaches and most spectacular natural wonders, and our nightlife sections direct you to some of the best clubs and most active neighborhoods.

If you intend to visit Jordan, you must be aware of how seriously the Jordanians feel about Israel. Students in Jordanian schools are required to black out all references to Israel in their textbooks before they use the books to study; you will have to follow a similar course with your *Let's Go*. Either remove the Jordan chapter from the book and leave the rest behind you in Israel or Egypt—which will lighten your pack—or at least tear off the cover so the border guards won't find any incriminating evidence without a search.

A word of warning: healthy skepticism will serve you better than blind faith in using any guidebook. This book was researched in the summer of 1983, and since then the world has not stood still: prices have changed, hostels have moved, and restaurants have closed. Perhaps the most important advice we can give you is to put *Let's Go* aside occasionally and explore on your own. The most memorable discoveries will be those you make yourself.

Planning Your Trip

Before you go, it's a good idea to decide on a tentative itinerary, even if you discard it as soon as you arrive. Where you go often depends on how long you plan to stay and how much you plan to spend, but there's a lot to be said for following your impulses. Most novice travelers try to see as much as they can in as short a time as possible. But after twenty towns in twenty days, you'll be lucky if you can still distinguish countries. For the sake of your own tranquility, let alone money and health, be more selective initially and then spend more time getting to know the places you do visit.

A good practice when planning your trip is to vary the kinds of days you spend. Don't visit too many pharaonic ruins, religious centers, or museums consecutively—spend an occasional "day off" from sightseeing relaxing in a remote oasis or on the beach. Take the time to sit back in a cafe, watch the people go by, and enjoy your freedom.

Traveling with a companion can be rewarding. A friend can share your experiences and make discoveries that you might have missed. And a companion can shield against isolation, boost your morale, and provide security and protection that might prove valuable in a pinch, all of which may make your entrance into the very different world of the Middle East less forbidding and confusing. Women, in particular, will experience a certain culture shock, and may feel more comfortable with a fellow Westerner nearby.

On the other hand, traveling alone affords greater independence and flexibility. You won't have to argue over sightseeing itineraries or where to eat. Meeting other people will be much easier, especially if you stay in youth hostels in Israel or among the Bedouins of Jordan. And going solo can be a test of your resilience and affability. Language will be the greatest problem, except in Israel, where English is widely spoken. But natives always appreciate attempts by visitors to use their language, and if all else fails, you can usually find other English-speaking travelers to provide you with temporary companionship. Even if you travel with a friend, make a point of splitting up occasionally, both to preserve your equilibrium and to gain a new appreciation of your missing partner in adversity.

Off-Season Travel

For the natives of Israel and Egypt, there is no off-season, only two distinct high tourist seasons; while most North Americans and students travel in the summer months, many Europeans and Arabs bask in the winter warmth of these two countries. In Jordan, spring and autumn are the peak seasons. But the advantages of off-season travel apply to the winter in all three countries. If you visit between late autumn and early spring, you will find fewer of your fellow countrymen, the local residents will be more receptive, and the weather will be cooler. In addition, inexpensive airfares from North America will be easier to obtain. Most of the areas we cover remain mild throughout the winter, so that swimming is still possible on the Sinai peninsula, the Red Sea Coast, and on Egypt's Mediterranean shores. And some areas do empty of tourists: Alexandria, for instance, has two million fewer residents in winter than in summer. Though the odd hotel and hostel may close, there's always plenty going on.

Useful Organizations

The first four organizations listed below serve as warehouses of information on budget travel; you may want to use them while planning your trip. Other groups listed below provide information on more specific possibilities for travel. For addresses of embassies and consulates in the U.S. and Canada, refer to the country introductions.

Council on International Educational Exchange (CIEE): 205 East 42nd St., New York, NY 10017 (tel. (212) 661-1450). This is the main office for inquiries by mail and telephone. For in-person inquiries, visit the New York Student Center, 356 West 34th St., New York, or any of the branch offices in San Francisco, Los Angeles, Berkeley, San Diego, Seattle, Miami, and Boston. CIEE is one of the broadest ranging student travel centers, and the U.S. representative to the International Student Travel Conference. Ask for information on low cost travel, educational, and work opportunities. All the usual discount travel cards are available from CIEE, as is the International Student Identity Card (ISIC). They will send you the annual Student Travel Catalog for $1, or you can pick it up free at most student travel offices.

Travel CUTS (Canadian Universities Travel Service): 44 St. George St., Toronto, Ontario M5S 2E4 (tel. (416) 979-2406). Other offices in Victoria, Vancouver, Edmonton, Saskatoon, Ottawa, Montreal, and Halifax. The Canadian representative to the International Student Travel Conference, Travel CUTS offers discounted transatlantic flights from Canadian cities, and sells the ISIC and other discount travel passes. Their magazine, *The Canadian Student Traveller,* is available free at all offices.

Harvard Student Agencies (Travel Division): Thayer Hall-B, Harvard University, Cambridge, MA 02138. ISIC, Eurailpasses, etc. Write for their informative travel packet.

Educational Travel Centre (ETC): 438 N. Frances St., Madison, WI 53703 (tel. (608) 256-5551). ISIC, flight information. If you mention that you are a *Let's Go* reader, ETC will send you a free copy of the travel newspaper *Taking Off.*

International Youth Hostel Federation. USA: American Youth Hostels, 1332 I Street NW, Suite 800, Washington, DC 20005 (tel. (202) 783-6161). **Canada:** Canadian Hostelling Association, Place Vanier, Tower A, 333 River Rd., Vanier City, Ottawa, Ontario K1L 8H9. IYHF membership costs $20 for those over 18 in the U.S., $15 in Canada, $10 and $9 respectively for those under 18. Request the *International Youth Hostel Handbook,* Volume 1 ($7.50 postpaid) for up-to-date listings of hostels in Egypt and Israel. If you arrive without an IYHF card, you can purchase an International Guest Card from the local association or from the larger hostels.

Institute of International Education (IIE): 809 United Nations Plaza, New York, NY 10017 (tel. (212) 883-8470). Information on study and teaching opportunities abroad. Write for a list of publications.

International Association for the Exchange of Students for Technical Experience (IAESTE): c/o AIPT, 217 American City Bldg., Columbia, MD 21044 (tel. (301) 997-2200). IAESTE operates trainee programs in Israel, Egypt, and Jordan.

Nomadic Books: P.O. Box 454, Athens, GA 30603. Kevin Kelly publishes a useful free catalogue listing the most recent guidebooks to *all* parts of the world. Good if you're planning to extend the boundaries of your European trip.

Documents and Formalities

Passports

You need a valid passport to enter Israel, Egypt, or Jordan, and to reenter the United States and Canada. If you are 18 or older, you can get a U.S. passport good for ten years at any Passport Agency, clerk of court, or post office. To locate the nearest agency, check the phone book under "U.S. Government, Department of State," or call your local post office. If this is your first passport, if your current passport is more than eight years old, or if it was issued before your eighteenth birthday, you must apply in person—otherwise, you can apply by mail. You must submit a completed application (available from the above offices), proof of U.S. citizenship (a birth certificate or naturalization papers), identification (such as a driver's license), and two identical photographs (two inches square on a plain white background). A first ten-year passport costs $35, a five-year passport $20 (issued to persons under 18); both types have an additional $7 execution fee. Renewal by mail is also $35, but there is no execution fee. Processing the application usually takes from two to three weeks. If you have to leave with 48 hours, the Passport Agency provides a "rush" service while you wait, but you must have valid proof of your departure date. For more details, check with your local Passport Agency, or write to the Office of Passport Services, Department of State, Washington, DC 20524 for their free pamphlet *Your Trip Abroad*.

If you lose your passport abroad, notify the U.S. consulate and local police immediately. The U.S. consulate can issue you a new passport, usually within two hours of application. In an emergency ask for an immediate temporary passport.

Canadian passports can be obtained from the Passport Office, Department of External Affairs, Ottawa, Ontario K1A 0G3, or in person at regional passport offices, which are listed in the phone book. You'll need a completed application (available at passport offices, post offices, and travel agencies), evidence of Canadian citizenship, two photos, and $21 cash or certified check. Passports will usually be issued within three to five days after receipt of the application. Canadian passports are valid for five years only. More complete information can be found in the booklet *How to Obtain a Canadian Passport*, available free from the Passport Office.

It's a good idea to carry a second proof of your citizenship (in the form of a birth certificate, driver's license, etc.) when traveling abroad, and to keep it separate from your passport. That way, if your passport is lost or stolen, you will be able to speed up the processing of a new passport by the nearest consular office. Canadians *must* be able to prove their citizenship with a document or they will not be issued a new passport.

A special note if you contemplate traveling in the Arab world after spending time in Israel: with an Israeli stamp in your passport, you cannot enter any Arab country except Egypt. To avoid being turned back at some border after a bout of political unpleasantries, ask for a separate, detachable visa in Israel. The Israelis are sensitive to the politics and will oblige, though you may have to insist. Any other evidence of your having been in Israel, such as an Egyptian entry stamp from Rafiah or Taba, or any visa procured in Israel, will also keep you out of most Arab nations. Unfortunately, the Egyptians are not as accommodating as the Israelis in providing detachable visas or border stamps. If all else fails, it is possible to obtain a second passport for limited use (e.g., travel in either Israel or Arab countries only) in your own country or in a foreign embassy. The added expense and the miles of red tape you'll have to wade through makes this an unattractive option, but one that may prove necessary.

Visas

A visa is essentially written permission granted by a government to allow foreigners to enter a country. You do not need to obtain a visa ahead of time if you are visiting Israel; visas are issued at the port of entry, and are good for three months. A transit visa, valid for five days, can also be obtained from any Israeli consulate if you wish to stay in Israel on your way to other places. Once you've arrived in Israel, it is possible to have this visa extended to ten days.

If you plan to visit Egypt or Jordan, you should apply for a visa before you arrive. An Egyptian visa can be issued at the airport in Cairo or at the port of Alexandria, but not at the borders of Israel (Rafiah), the Sudan (Aswan), or Jordan (Suez); Jordanian visas are issued at every port of entry except the King Hussein Bridge from the West Bank. But obtaining the visa ahead of time will save you time and, in Egypt, the required $150 currency exchange at the airport. You can apply for an Egyptian visa by mail or in person at the nearest consulate (consulates are normally open 10am-7pm). Either way, you must present your passport, a passport-sized photo, and a fee of $9 ($11 for non-U.S. citizens) in cash, money order, or certified check payable to "Consulate General, Arab Republic of Egypt." Include a stamped, self-addressed envelope if acquiring a visa by mail, and allow ten days to receive the visa. If you apply in person, the process usually takes 48 hours. The visa is valid for three months of touring, and must be used within three months of the date of issue. (Visas issued in Egypt are valid for one month only.) Jordanian visas are free, and valid for twelve months (visas issued at the borders may be valid for shorter periods). Apply in person or by mail at the Jordanian Embassy or at any consulate. Neither an Egyptian nor a Jordanian visa permits the holder to work.

You will notice that your Egyptian visa states that you must register with the police within seven days of your arrival in Egypt. You risk a heavy fine if you don't comply; this is one part of the bureaucracy that runs smoothly. Ask the tourist office or your hotel manager where to go—frequently the manager will do the registering for you. The best place to register is the passport office in Tahrir Square. If you neglect to register, don't panic: the U.S. Embassy issues a letter of apology for U.S. citizens free of charge, with which you can register late at the Mugamma Building at Tahrir Square.

Extensions of visas are usually granted for six months to one year, after which you must leave the country. If you wish to stay longer, however, it may be possible to take a short sea trip (e.g. to Cyprus), stay away for a week, then return for another half-year or year. You can apply for extensions of visas in Cairo at the Mugamma Building, at the Ministry of Interior in Tel Aviv, or at the Ministry of Interior in Amman.

Customs

When entering Israel, Egypt, or Jordan you may have to declare certain items, including typewriters, cameras, portable radios, sports equipment, and, in Israel, jewelry. These items may be brought in duty-free as long as they will be in use and will be taken with you upon departure. A minimum exchange of $150 into Egyptian pounds (LE) is required by Egyptian law when you first enter the country. It is illegal to bring more than LE20 into Egypt; you can bring in an unlimited amount of foreign currency, as long as you declare it on the appropriate form (form D) when you arrive. Israel does not require you to declare your currency, whether in shekels or foreign notes.

Upon reentering your own country, you must declare all articles acquired abroad. Keep all receipts. Under the new U.S. laws, you can bring in $400 worth of goods duty-free; you pay 10% on the next $1000 worth. The duty-free goods must be for your personal or household use and cannot include more than 100 cigars, 200 cigarettes (one carton), or one liter of wine or liquor (you must be 21 or older to bring liquor into the U.S.). All items included must accompany you; you cannot have them shipped separately.

While abroad, you can mail unsolicited gifts duty-free if they're worth less than $50. However, you may not mail liquor, tobacco, or perfume into the

U.S. If you mail home goods of U.S. origin, mark the package "American goods returned." Spot checks are occasionally made on parcels, so it's best to mark the accurate price and nature of the gift on the package. If you send back parcels worth over $50, the Postal Service will collect the duty plus a handling charge when it is delivered.

Certain products can be excluded from the customs tax under the Generalized System of Preferences (GSP), a plan that is in operation until 1985 "to help developing nations improve their financial or economic condition through export trade." Israel, Egypt, and Jordan are all covered by the GSP; this means you can bring in items purchased in these countries duty-free outside the regular $400 limit. Products include cameras, jewelry, phonograph records, toys, chinaware, and more. Both products and nations covered by the GSP are subject to change depending on economic conditions; inquire at any Customs Office for details.

Canadian customs regulations are different from their American counterparts. Once every calendar quarter you can bring in goods up to the value of $50. Once every calendar year you're allowed $150. These two allowances can't both be claimed on the same trip. Anything above the duty-free allowance is taxed at 25% on the first $150, and at varying rates afterwards. You can send gifts up to a value of $15 duty-free, but again, you cannot mail alcohol or tobacco.

American or Canadian, you have to declare any items that you bought at duty-free shops abroad with your other purchases, and you may have to pay duty on them if they exceed your allowance. Remember that "duty-free" means only that you didn't pay taxes in the country of purchase. When you return from abroad, you may also run into trouble with clothing or jewelry of foreign make that you originally purchased in North America. You must be able to indicate their origin with purchase receipts or identifying marks.

According to the U.S. Customs Service official brochure, *Know Before You Go,* available from the Department of the Treasury, U.S. Customs Service, Washington, DC 20229, "A vital part of Customs' role is screening out items injurious to the well-being of our nation." Among these are non-prescription drugs and narcotics, obscene publications, lottery tickets, liquor-filled candies, and most plants. To avoid problems when carrying prescription drugs, make sure the bottles are clearly marked and have the prescription ready to show the customs officer.

Student Identification

There is no single piece of identification so widely honored for procuring discounts and services as the **International Student Identity Card (ISIC).** This card is essential if you plan to use student flights, trains, or clubs. In Israel, the ISIC can obtain discounts at museums, archeological sites, theaters, films, retail stores, and even accommodations. In Egypt, the card secures discounts on train travel, airline tickets, and national monuments—often up to 50%. Since Jordan does not belong to the International Student Travel Conference, such reductions are not usually available, although you should ask Alia Airlines about reduced fares. The ISIC can be used in both Israel and Egypt for discounts on local transportation, including ferry travel, and for Student Air Travel Association flights. El Al and EgyptAir, the countries' national airlines, offer some student discounts on flights to and from Europe—check with the airlines or a travel agent for specifics. For the $8 fee and the time spent applying, the rewards the ISIC brings are considerable. The fee also provides you with medical insurance coverage of up to $1500, plus $100 a day up to sixty days of in-hospital illness.

No application form is necessary, but you must supply all of the following information, whether you apply in person or by mail: 1) current dated proof of student status (a photocopy of your school ID showing this year's date, a letter on school stationery signed and sealed by the registrar, or a photocopied grade report); 2) a vending-machine-size photo with your name printed on the back; 3) your birthdate and nationality (xerox of birth certificate). The card is good until the end of the calendar year in which you bought it. Unfortunately for those taking a year off from school, a new card cannot be purchased in January unless you were in school during the fall semester. If you have just graduated, you may still obtain an ISIC during the year in which you graduated. If you don't qualify for the ISIC and are under 26 years of age, do not hesitate to ask about youth discounts wherever you go—your passport will be the best proof of your age.

Non-students under 26 years of age should consider buying a Federation of International Youth Travel Organization or FIYTO card. It will be good for discounts on Dan Tours in Israel, and on ferry travel between Israel, Egypt, Italy, and Greece. If you plan to travel to the Mediterranean from northern Europe, the FIYTO card will give you discounts on train travel.

Among the student travel offices which issue the ISIC are the Council on International Educational Exchange (CIEE), Harvard Student Agencies, and Canadian Universities Travel Services (all addresses listed in the Useful Organizations section above). In addition, over 375 travel offices in universities around the United States issue the ISIC. The FIYTO card is available from CIEE and from agencies within Europe.

Money

Few things cause more headaches than money, even when you have it. Carrying large amounts of cash, even in money belts, is too much of a risk—and leaving your wallet unattended invites disaster. A little forethought can prevent money nightmares from becoming realities.

Travelers checks are still the safest way to carry money abroad. They're sold by several agencies and many banks, usually at face value plus a 1% commission charge. Your best choice will be a widely-known check; some American banks offer their own checks, which may not be honored in Israel, Egypt, and Jordan. **American Express** travelers checks are usually considered the most widely recognized and the easiest to replace if lost or stolen, though other major checks are sold, exchanged, cashed, and refunded just as easily. American Express provides five services free of charge to travelers whose checks have been lost or stolen. Local American Express offices will cash personal checks up to $200 (including foreign checks), have stolen credit cards canceled, arrange to obtain a temporary I.D., help change airline, hotel, and car rental reservations, and send a Western Union mailgram or international cable to one individual. **Citicorp** travelers checks are sold in financial institutions throughout the U.S. and Europe, and can be easily replaced if lost or stolen. For refund information and assistance in the U.S., dial toll-free (800) 632-6388. **BankAmerica** travelers checks can be obtained and refunded at numerous banks throughout the States and in Europe. For claims and refunds outside the U.S., call either the San Francisco or London BankAmerica Customer Service Center collect. (San Francisco: (415) 622-3800, London: 01/629 7466.) **Barclay's,** a British bank with branches in major U.S. cities at local offices of the American Automobile Association (AAA) sells Barclay's Visa

checks without a commission, as does **Thomas Cook,** another British firm. Thomas Cook checks may also be purchased at AAA offices. Finally, **Deak-Perera,** a foreign exchange with offices throughout the U.S. and Canada, offers Thomas Cook and Visa travelers checks commission-free in dollars and a number of foreign currencies.

Buy at least some of your checks in small denominations, $10 or $20, to minimize losses if you need cash fast and have to deal with a lousy exchange rate. To lower losses another way, avoid keeping all your currency in the same place: split it up among pockets and bags or, better yet, use a money belt. Try to stash away a small amount of currency in case you stay for several days in a small town with no exchange service (especially in Jordan and Egypt).

Credit cards can be used in place of travelers checks for advances up to your credit limit. With Visa or MasterCard, you can get a cash advance at any institution that supplies the card (these will be relatively few in Egypt and Jordan), but a transaction fee is always charged. American Express offices give out travelers checks instead of cash, but will cash a personal check for cardholders in the local currency (up to $1000 in any 21-day period). An advantage of the American Express card is that it allows you to use Amex offices as mailing addresses for free (otherwise you may have to pay to pick up your mail). The Amex cards are the most difficult to get, but if your parents or a relative will sign a guarantee form, Amex will issue an extra card for $25. But Visa, MasterCard, and American Express are mostly a form of extra insurance for the budget traveler. Most places you visit will deal strictly in cash.

Sending Money

Before you leave, visit your bank to get a list of its corresponding banks in the countries in which you plan to travel. That way, if you need to have money sent, your bank knows where to send it and you know where to pick it up. You can even arrange in advance for your bank to send money from your account to foreign banks on specific dates.

Cable transfer is the fastest way to receive money; you should have your money within 48 hours if you're in a major city, a bit longer if you're in a less central location. You pay cabling costs plus the commission charged by your bank. A cheaper but slower method of receiving money is by bank draft; you pay $3-5 commission on the draft plus the cost of sending it air mail (preferably registered). Or, an American Express cardholder can cable you up to $500 in travelers checks. The process takes one to three days, depending on where you are. Whichever method you use, make sure that both you and the sender know the exact name and address of the bank or office to which the money is being sent. The sending bank requires the telephone number of the recipient as well, so try to find it out in advance.

Finally, if you are stranded abroad with no money and no apparent way to get any, a consulate will wire home for you and deduct the cost from what you receive. They're often less than gracious about performing this service, so you should turn to them only as a last resort. If all else falls through and you need money immediately, consider selling some of your belongings. Merchants in the marketplace, people you meet, or even other travelers might be interested in buying some of your things.

Health

The simplest prescription for health while traveling is to keep your body, and anything you put into it, clean. Eat well, and try not to overextend yourself physically. Cutting out nutritious food to economize and introducing radical shifts into your meal schedule can become criminally easy while on the road. Remember that you're moving around more than usual, so your body needs fuel. Treat it kindly and it will more than return the favor.

The self-assembled traveler's kit should include soap (both mild and antiseptic), an extra pair of eyeglasses, multiple vitamins (plus iron for women), aspirin, sunscreen, a thermometer in a rigid case, something for diarrhea (like Lomotil with Neomiacin), something for motion sickness, and bandages. When you visit archeological sites, the dust of centuries might trigger allergic reactions you've never experienced before; bringing some basic antihistamine is a good idea.

If you know that you will require medication while you travel, obtain a full supply before you leave: matching your prescription with a foreign equivalent is not always easy or even possible. You should always carry up-to-date prescriptions and/or a letter from your doctor, especially if you will be carrying insulin, a syringe, or any narcotic drugs. Distribute all medicines between carry-on and checked baggage to minimize loss. Travelers with a medical problem or condition that cannot be easily recognized (e.g. diabetes, allergies to antibiotics, epilepsy, heart conditions) should seriously consider obtaining a **Medic Alert identification tag.** This internationally recognized emblem communicates vital information in emergency situations. In addition to indicating the nature of the problem, the tag provides the number of Medic Alert's 24-hour hotline, through which attending medical personnel can obtain information about the member's medical history. Membership costs $15; write to Medic Alert Foundation International, P.O. Box 1009, Turlock, CA 95381, or call (209) 668-3333.

Even the hardiest traveler may meet with an unexpected mishap while on the road. Before you leave, find out whether your current health insurance covers costs incurred abroad. Most major companies will cover these costs on a "short-term" or regular basis. Many university health plans also apply abroad, while Medicare (except for limited coverage in Canada and Mexico) does not. If your insurance does apply, you still have to pay in cash for treatment and be reimbursed later. You must keep all receipts and statements from your doctors and file an out-of-country claim with your insurance company; try to have all receipts written in English. If you find that your insurance covers only domestic health costs, we strongly advise you to acquire coverage for the length of your stay. Remember, the ISIC carries accident and sickness insurance (see Student Identification section). CIEE has a low-cost plan, as does the American Automobile Association (AAA). Or you can contact any insurance agency or your student travel office.

The best place to find a good doctor (and the psychological balm of an English-speaking one) may well be the emergency room of a university hospital. Otherwise, your best bet is to go to as large a city as possible, and hope that someone at the hospital speaks English (the odds are best in Israel). *Let's Go* lists hospitals in most cities; we try to note where you can find English-speaking doctors. American, Canadian, and British embassies and consulates, American Express offices, and the local police can also help you find English-speaking doctors in Israel, Egypt, and Jordan. All three countries have 24-hour hospitals and pharmacies in major cities; check Practical Information listings. In addition, the largest cities in Israel have an emergency medical organization, Magen David Adom, which you can reach by dialing 101. In Jordan the emergency number is 19. In Egypt, all major hotels have resident doctors: in an emergency, they may be the nearest source of aid.

Although no special immunizations are necessary for travel to Israel, Egypt, or Jordan, you should check your medical records to see that your innoculations are up-to-date: typhoid shots remain good for three years, tetanus for ten. Egypt and Jordan do require cholera, yellow fever, and smallpox certificates from travelers arriving from countries infected with those diseases. Your International Immunization Certificates will be inspected if you arrive in Egypt at the Sudanese border, and also if you arrive from Jordan by sea during the *Haj* (see Jordan Festivals). If you don't have the necessary innoculations, you *will* be put in quarantine for several days—an unpleasant experience. For your own safety, it's best to get a cholera vaccination ahead of time. If you need to get immunizations, update or replace International Immunization Certificates once in Egypt, go to the government's Public Health Unit (tel. 91 13 22), located in the rear of the lobby in the Continental Savoy Hotel in Opera Square. Take your own syringe, which may be purchased without prescription at any drug store.

Water and food should be fine in Israel and Jordan, although it's always a good idea to bring along antidiarrhetic pills or other intestinal medications (Lomotil is effective in most mild cases), as your diet will be much different from what you've encountered in North America and Europe. Food and water in Egypt are likely to cause more problems. Tap water is reputedly safe in Cairo, Alexandria, Luxor, and Aswan, but this depends on the sensitivity of your digestive system; the heavy chlorination may disturb some stomachs. Imported bottled water is expensive (LE.80-LE1), but there are a couple of locally-produced brands, most notably *Baraka,* which sells for about 35pt per liter. It's all right to eat fruits and vegetables that you peel, but everything else should be carefully washed and cooked. The food at street stalls is particularly hard on the uninitiated Western stomach.

Sooner or later in Egypt, no matter how careful you are, you will probably get traveler's diarrhea—affectionately known among its foreign victims as "Pharaoh's Revenge." If you get sick, drink plenty of liquids to keep well hydrated. Two domestic remedies are fresh yogurt and lemon or lime juice into which a small quantity of salt has been dissolved. Egypt has a comprehensive and heavily subsidized pharmaceutical industry, and a number of locally produced medicines work very well for diarrhea and nausea. They come with directions in English and require no prescription. Consult a pharmacist in Cairo and he'll sell you one of the more common ones. Avoid *Enterovioform,* which has been banned throughout Europe and the United States. Be aware of the two types of dysentary: bascillary dysentary is quick and painful, while amoebic dysentary comes on slowly but is harder to get rid of. Do not try to treat the latter yourself; it can cause permanent damage if not properly cared for. If you find yourself ill for a substantial amount of time, seek medical attention, preferably in Cairo or Alexandria.

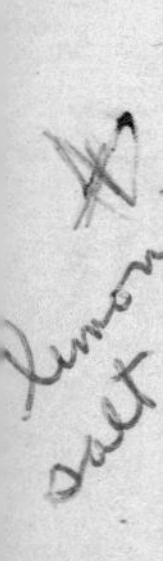

Finally, take extra precaution against infection in Egypt and the rural areas of the Jordan Valley. Cuts and bruises must be properly covered. You are also advised to take anti-malarial pills such as chloroquine, and to guard against trachoma, a contagious eye infection which can cause blindness. For anything even marginally serious, see a doctor. Above all, remember that the Nile is full of disease-carrying bugs which can cause a number of very serious illnesses. One of the most serious and most common of these is *bilharzia,* a parasite which is transmitted through the skin by small snails which live on the edge of rivers or in other stagnant waters. *Under no circumstances* should you swim in, drink from, or even walk barefoot along the Nile. There is an old saying that one who drinks from the waters of the Nile will one day return to Egypt, but it is more likely that he will never leave.

Precautions Against Heat

The hot and dry climate of the Middle East requires some special preparation. First and foremost, don't underestimate the effect the sun may have. Wear a hat to guard against sunstroke, and if you have a light complexion, use a strong sunscreen on any exposed parts of your body. Better yet, wear long sleeves and trousers; they will keep you cooler by holding perspiration close to your body. Even if you have a considerable tan, you should probably wear a shirt while swimming or snorkeling, or you may wake up with a blistering sunburn that will keep you in the shade for weeks. The desert is not the place to work on a tan.

Since heat can dehydrate you quickly and imperceptibly, drink more liquids than you think you need. Always carry a canteen filled with water if you plan to spend time outside of cities. When drinking juice, dilute it with water to avoid a reaction to the sugar. You'll have to compensate for any alcohol or coffee you drink with lots more water, since both can dehydrate you. Perspiration carries away a lot of salt, which must also be replaced. However, you should *not* bring along salt tablets. The high concentration will upset your body's balance and accelerate the dehydration process. Salting your food should be adequate.

The Sinai Peninsula is one of the hottest places on earth, with summer temperatures occassionally reaching 120 degrees Farenheit. Summer travel in the area is foolhardy. The Bedouins who live here routinely perform tasks which seem—and are—impossible for others; someone used to another climate walking in 120-degree heat would last only about two miles. Do *not* exert yourself excessively, and *never* travel alone in this region. Heat is not the only potential problem: winter nights can be well below freezing at higher elevations, even with afternoon temperatures in the 60s or 70s.

Finally, if you're traveling by car in the desert (the Sinai, or between oases), carry plenty of extra water for the radiator as well as for drinking. Don't attempt to walk for help in case of a breakdown; stay put and wait for a passing motorist. Distance and incline can be deceiving—you might not realize you've been driving up a steady incline until you look backwards at a valley several hundred meters below. To avoid overheating, turn off the air conditioning. if your engine does overheat, put it in neutral and gun it periodically.

Packing

First, and most importantly, be sure to pack lightly. A good rule of thumb is to settle on all the items you might need to bring, and take only half of them. Since you'll have to carry your belongings from the station or ferry to a youth hostel, hotel, or campground more often than you may realize, walk a mile or so with your loaded pack before you leave to see how easily it carries. If you can't manage comfortably, unload some things—the convenience of an easily transportable pack, suitcase, or duffel bag far outweighs any disadvantages of a limited wardrobe. And the more luggage you carry, the more you'll look and be treated like a tourist. Besides, you'll need room for any gifts or other purchases you bring back.

Whether or not you use a backpack depends on the kind of traveling you'll be doing. If you intend to visit mostly cities and towns, you might want to consider a light suitcase. If you're going to be covering a lot of ground or camping out, it's more efficient to carry a backpack. A small daypack will come in handy for carrying a lunch and poncho; for unobtrusive travel choose a large shoulder bag that zips or closes securely.

The hot weather in these countries demands that you wear light clothing. Because of the heat, bring lightweight shirts and pants, and plenty of cotton underwear. Laundry service can be expensive, so take permanent press or wrinkle-free clothes. Best of all, do as the locals have done for centuries—wear long, pale, gauzy things, whether shirts or skirts, in preference to typically American bright, tight T-shirts, tank tops, or shorts. Especially in Jordan and Egypt, both men and women should keep their knees and shoulders covered to avoid offending local standards of modesty (which might otherwise prevent your admission to places of worship).

Imitating native dress will keep you cooler and more comfortable, as well. Footwear is the crucial item on your packing list. An oft-worn pair of sturdy lace-up, rubber-soled walking shoes or well-cushioned running shoes will do for longer hikes, but you'll want a pair of lighter shoes, such as sandals or espadrilles, or even thongs, for everyday wear. Bring along a few pair of socks and a can of foot powder—both will keep your feet fresh and prevent blisters.

To avoid being robbed and left with nothing, don't pack everything in the same large bag. Instead, you should have some kind of pouch or money belt to hold your money, passport, and the articles you'll want with you at all times. A small notebook for writing down addresses, phrases, directions, or whatever else you discover or need during the perambulations of your day will prove useful.

In addition to the hat, sunscreen, and canteen already suggested in the Health section, you should also include a flashlight, toilet paper, first-aid kit, petroleum jelly, needle and thread, and a portable alarm clock. A rain poncho and sweater are also a good idea, whether for off-season travel or the occasional cool night. Rubber bands and plastic bags serve a myriad of purposes

while on the road. You don't have to pack a summer's worth of toiletries such as aspirin, razor blades, or tampons, but make sure you're adequately stocked before exploring less populated areas of Egypt and Jordan.

The standard electrical outlet in Israel, Egypt, and Jordan produces 220 volts AC, though in a few areas of Egypt it is 110 AC. North American appliances are usually designed for 110 volts AC. If you want to use your own appliances in these countries, they must be dual-voltage appliances, or else you will need both a converter and an adapter. (An adapter alone changes only the shape of the plug—in most areas they're three-prong; in the U.S., the norm is two-prong.) You can get adapters in department and hardware stores. Converters cost about $26. To order a converter by mail, write to Franzus Company, 352 Park Ave. South, New York, NY 10010. Ask for a copy of their pamphlet, *Foreign Electricity Is No Deep Dark Secret*.

If you decide to bring a camera, be sure to register it with U.S. customs at the airport before leaving or you might have trouble bringing it back. You can protect your film from airport x-rays by buying a special lead-lined bag from any photo shop. If you don't mind the extra bulk, buy all your film before you go—it's much more expensive abroad.

Drugs

Although the Middle East may evoke images of hashish for the having, cast them out of your mind. In Israel, Egypt, and Jordan, as in most other European and Middle Eastern countries, possession of drugs is a serious offence. If you're lucky, you'll be kicked out of the country—otherwise, you could find yourself conducting extensive research on foreign penal codes and prisons. Jordan enforces drug laws very strictly. In some areas, you will find the Muslims even look down on drinking, although it is legal throughout the country. (Note: alcohol is illegal in Saudi Arabia—don't try to carry it across the border.) Avoid buying drugs in any country unless you know the seller, since he may be a police informer.

Never bring anything across borders. International express trains are not as safe as they might seem: you and your belongings may be searched thoroughly while on board. The assistance available from the U.S. consulates to anyone arrested is minimal. Consular officers can visit the prisoner, provide a list of attorneys, and inform family and friends. They cannot obtain any more lenient treatment than that dictated by the laws of the country you are visiting, no matter how innocently you may have become entangled in drug trafficking.

Security

The theft of one's belongings while abroad is one of the greatest potential setbacks of a trip. A significant loss can often force a bitter, premature return. Thieves who prey on backpackers are exceedingly clever; the techniques employed are variegated, and crowded youth hostels and overnight trains are favorite hangouts for petty criminals. While you sleep or see the sights, a local pilferer may be rifling through your things.

Prevention is far more effective than mistrust, and a healthy, cautious attitude should carry you safely through your travels. Always keep your money and valuables with you, preferably in a money belt, and especially while sleeping. If you plan to sleep outside, try to store your gear in a safe place at a train or bus station.

The following firms offer insurance against theft or loss of luggage:

Tour Master Travel Insurance, c/o the Edmund A. Cocco Agency, 75 Federal St., Suite 1012, Boston, MA 02110 (tel. (617) 426-0652). Offers the cheapest baggage-only protection, as little as $1 per day for $1000 worth of coverage.

The Travelers Insurance Co., 1 Tower Square, Hartford, CT 06115 (tel. (203) 277-0111). Also has baggage-only policies, but at steeper rates.

Tripmaster Insurance, c/o CNA Insurance, 100 Newport Ave. Extension, Quincy, MA 02171 (tel. (800) 343-5601) or CNA Plaza, Chicago IL 60685 (tel. (312) 822-5000), also has baggage-only protection.

Carefree Travel Insurance, c/o Arm Coverage, Inc., P.O. Box 247, Providence, RI 02901. Offers more comprehensive travel insurance which includes loss of luggage. Over $2 per day for coverage which includes $1000 worth of baggage coverage.

TravelSafe, Inc., 300 71st St., Suite 520, Miami, FL 33141 (tel. (800) 327-9966 or (305) 866-7233). Similar coverage to that of Carefree at nearly $3 per day.

No firms cover loss of travel documents (passport, plane ticket, railpass, etc.), and claims can only be filed upon return to the United States. Claims must be accompanied by a police report of the incident.

Special Travelers

Women

Visiting the Middle East often poses difficulties for women traveling alone. Although women have moved into the work forces of Israel, Egypt, and Jordan, and more pursue higher education every year, society and social encounters are still male-dominated. If you look like a foreigner, especially if you're fair in a land where everyone else is dark, you'll almost certainly be harassed by curious and unwanted admirers. Common sense and sensitivity to the culture you are visiting can help prevent threatening situations from arising. In Egypt, Jordan, the West Bank, and Gaza, women are expected to conform to established norms of modesty. They never wear shorts, low-cut blouses, or T-shirts, and they rarely sit alone in cafes. Outside the major cities, you will attract particular and possibly hostile attention if you violate dress codes. Moreover, you will certainly be denied admission to sacred sites. Imitate the dress and behavior of local women as far as you can comfortably. You might want to carry a shawl with you; men seldom bother a women who wears one, and laying one over your hair will effectively discourage the attentions of those who do approach you. In any of these three countries, avoid riding alone in train compartments, especially at night. If a man starts to bother you, your best answer at first may be no answer, since any kind of response may be interpreted as an encouragement. Of course, you should not hesitate to be rude if the situation becomes threatening. A harsh scolding in any language, especially in the presence of onlookers, should cool the pursuit. In real emergencies, scream for help. *Let's Go* lists emergency, police, and consulate phone numbers in every city. Though not a pleasant thought, Israel, at least, has a Feminist Movement Rape Crisis Center, which you can reach at (03) 23 48 19.

Though it may be difficult, remember that not all interested males are dangerous. Israelis and Arabs of both sexes tend to be more physical than their North American counterparts; this is no reason to ignore them. For those who dislike Middle Eastern attitudes and behavior, a warning: you can't hope to change an entire culture in one short visit, and you shouldn't spend your time trying. Most men won't even understand your annoyance with them. If it will make life easier, find a traveling companion. Above all, try not to let unfamiliar social norms and your reactions to them spoil your trip.

Disabled Travelers

Israel, Egypt, and Jordan are beginning to respond to the needs of disabled travelers. Dr. Sami Bishara runs a special travel agency in Cairo which advises handicapped travelers and organizes tours (see Cairo Practical Information listings), and Mrs. Sadat heads a program for the handicapped within the country. The Queen Alia Welfare Fund, established in 1978, is a similar program in Jordan. Israel has several travel agencies which specialize in tours for the handicapped. But for budget travelers, advance research is particularly important. The following organizations can provide you with information:

Mobility International, founded to promote travel exchange among the disabled and the able-bodied, has contacts in 25 countries and offers advice and assistance to would-be visitors. For information on travel programs, accommodations, access guides, and organized tours, write to Mobility International USA, P.O. Box 3551, Eugene, OR 97403.

Moss Rehabilitation Hospital provides free help in planning trips and obtaining information about particular countries and cities. Write to Travel Information Center, Moss Rehabilitation Hospital, Twelfth St. and Taher Rd., Philadelphia, PA 19141 (tel. (215) 329-5715).

Rehabilitation International USA (RIUSA) is a federation of national and international organizations providing information and services for the disabled in more than 130 countries. Write to the Travel Survey Department, Rehabilitation International USA, 1123 Broadway, Suite 704, New York, NY 10010 (tel. (212) 620-4040).

Pauline Hephaistos Survey Projects publishes an access guide to Israel for the handicapped. To obtain a copy, write to Pauline Hephaistos Survey Projects, 39 Bradley Gardens, West Ealing, London W13, England.

History

Note: Since the events described in this book pertain to *three* major social and religious systems, each of which uses a different dating system, dates are given throughout using "C.E." (Common Era) and "B.C.E." (Before Common Era) rather than the more common "A.D." *(Anno Domini)* and "B.C." (Before Christ).

At the intersection of three continents, the lands of the Middle East have always been at the crossroads of civilizations. One hundred centuries ago, the first agricultural settlements sprang up along the banks of the Euphrates, Jordan, and Nile Rivers, and trade routes began to develop throughout the Middle East. More than five thousand years ago, the first Pharaohs established their dynasties along the Nile, and built the awe-inspiring monuments that stand today as relics of their three-millenia rule. Always at the center of traffic from Asia, Africa, and later, Europe, the peoples of the Fertile Crescent turned to commerce and prospered.

At the dawn of the Iron Age, Abraham, father of all the Semitic peoples, ventured into the land of Israel. In a time of famine, his descendants were forced to go to Egypt, where they were sold into slavery. Moses led the exodus of the twelve tribes of Israel, who cut a swath through the lands of Arabia as they conquered Jericho on the Jordan River and the Philistine cities along the Mediterranean Coast. After the reigns of Kings David and Solomon, a civil war broke out between portions of the Israelite kingdom. Assyrians from the north overran the weakened Palestine, pushing forward even as far as Egypt.

A century later, the Persian Nebuchadnezzar sacked the cities of Palestine and Arabia, and took the Israelites off to slavery in Babylon.

When Alexander the Great wrested the Middle East from the hands of the Persians in the fouth century B.C.E., he expanded the influence of Hellenic culture as far east as India. After Alexander's death, General Ptolemy founded a dynasty in Egypt which lasted three centuries; in the rest of the Empire, the leadership gap could not be filled as easily.

The advent of the Roman Empire brought a measure of peace to the region. Christianity followed Judaism as one of the great world religions, then Byzantium followed Rome as the capital of one the great Empires. But by the seventh century, yet another religion was born. The ardent followers of the prophet Muhammad spread Islam from Arabia to Europe, India, and North Africa. When the dust settled, Islam and the Arabic language had bequeathed a measure of cultural unity previously lacking in the Middle East. The Arabs have inhabited the land now without a break for thirteen centuries.

Always a meeting ground between East and West, the Holy Lands became a battleground for Christian Europe and the forces of Islam during the Crusades. In the sixteenth century, the Ottoman Turks began their four-century rule, and the lands of Israel, Egypt, and Jordan became Ottoman provinces ruled by pashas who spoke Turkish and remained aloof from their Arab subjects.

The West once again established a presence in the Middle East at the end of the eighteenth century, when Napolean invaded Egypt and Palestine. Under the leadership of rebel Pasha Muhammad Ali, Egypt withdrew from the Ottoman sphere of influence. The Arab Revolt of Sherif Hussein in Arabia further revealed that nationalism could be as potent a force in the Middle East as it was in Europe. But with the final collapse of the Ottoman Empire after World War I, Egypt, Palestine, and TransJordan were carved up under the British mandate.

Zionism, also a product of European forces, intensified when anti-Semitic persecution turned Jewish immigration into a matter of survival. Arab leaders and Jews fleeing European Nazism each pursued nationalist interests by denying the Middle East to the Axis powers. The Jews who survived the Holocaust looked to Palestine for a home. The Arabs, too, sought to make good on British promises for an Arab state in Palestine. When the State of Israel was proclaimed in 1948, the Arab armies immediately united in opposition.

Since the 1948 war, foreign intervention, Arab disunity, and incessant Arab/Israeli conflict have kept the Middle East at the center of world attention. Israel, Egypt, and Jordan have been scarred by the common heritage of war during the last three decades. In the 1967 war, the Israelis trounced the Arabs, seizing the Sinai, West Bank, and Golan Heights, and displacing hundreds of thousands of Palestinians. A Palestinian nationalism arose, which had lain dormant as long as hopes of Arab unity still endured. The last fifteen years have seen civil wars in Jordan and Lebanon, the fourth and fifth major Arab/Israeli wars, and countless aborted attempts to find peace for the world's most troubled region.

Although modern communication and transportation networks have diminished the importance of the ancient caravan routes at the crossroads of three continents, the conflict between the Jewish and Arab descendants of Abraham persists. And so the balancing act continues; alliances are made, broken, evolving; and peace in the Middle East remains as elusive as ever.

Getting There

In recent years, due to the strength of the dollar abroad, transatlantic tourism has increased at a feverish rate. As a result, new companies and cut-rate offers have sprung up, insuring steep fare competition. With a little effort and advance planning, you can find economical ways to get to Israel, Egypt, and Jordan. As we go to press, it is impossible to predict future rates, or even to say with certainty which types of inexpensive flights will be available. We can, however, offer valuable suggestions about the sort of transatlantic packages that will be worth investigating during 1984.

As it stands now, travelers to Israel, Egypt, and Jordan have many options. Sixteen major airlines fly from the U.S. and Canada to these countries; there are also boats, trains, and flights from Europe. How you choose to go depends on your budget, time restrictions, and your interests. The following section deals strictly with direct flights. For all other aspects of travel, including intra-European flights and overland trips, see the country introductions.

Some general rules are good to keep in mind. Off-season travelers will enjoy lower fares and face much less competition for inexpensive seats, but you don't have to travel in the dead of winter to save. Peak-season rates are generally set on either May 15 or June 1 (departure) and run until about September 15 (return). If you can arrange to leave in May and return in late September, you can travel in summer and still save. The budget flight options outlined below differ from one another in economy, flexibility and security. The simplest and surest way to decide among them is to find a travel agent who keeps abreast of the chaos in airfares and who is committed to saving you money. Don't hesitate to shop around—travel agents are by no means the same. Commissions are smaller on cheaper flights, so some agents are less than eager to help you find the best deal. The travel section of the Sunday *New York Times* or another major newspaper is a good place to start looking for bargain fares, but be sure to read the fine print on restrictions and cancellation procedures. Start looking early; some popular bargain fares are fully booked by April.

Charter flights have expanded tremendously this year, and should continue to be an economical option for a transatlantic crossing. Rules governing charters have been liberalized, so you can often book up to the last minute, although most flights fill up well in advance of the departure date. Regular charter tickets do not permit flexibility; you must choose your departure and return dates when you book your flights. Some companies allow you to book a one-way flight, but most do not. If you cancel your one-way or roundtrip ticket within three weeks of your departure date, you lose most or all of your money. With some companies, however, you can alter the ticket (date of return, etc.) by paying a $50-$75 penalty fee. In addition, charter companies reserve the right to change the dates of your flight, cancel the flight, and add fuel surcharges after you have made your final payment. Beware of fares that sound too good to be true, as not all companies are honest or reliable. Even some of the most well-known charter groups, such as CIEE, have inconvenienced many passengers with mechanical failures (remember, charter companies do not have back-up planes—you're stuck on the one they have). Flight changes and delays are the rule rather than the exception. A good travel agent can help you choose a charter wisely, but once you sign the charter contract, no one can offer you full protection against a cancelled flight or a last-minute change of date.

The **Advanced Booking Excursion Fare (APEX)** is the most flexible of the reduced fares—it provides you with confirmed reservations and is not as restrictive as charters in terms of cancellation penalties and adjusted travel dates. The "open-jaw APEX" will even allow you to return from a different city than the one into which you originally flew. However, APEX does have drawbacks: you must fly back within a specified period of time, usually 7-60 or

22-45 days after leaving; payment is due three to five weeks in advance; and APEX fares are considerably higher in peak-season. In 1983, fares to Tel Aviv, Cairo, and Amman all averaged between $699 and $900. Somewhat cheaper "super APEX fares" available on some routes, work in the same way. A $50 cancellation fee applies for both APEX and super-APEX. Book APEX flights early; by early June you may have difficulty getting your desired departure date.

Another option is to investigate unusual airlines that try to undercut the major carriers by offering special bargains on regularly scheduled flights—and to watch for those major carriers who fight back by offering special bargains of their own. Most of these special fares are in effect for short periods only, so watch for advertisements in the pages of major national newspapers. And, as with charters, be wary of the truly incredible fares; the dubious dealings of some companies could make you painfully aware of the risks of economizing too far.

If you cannot find an economical direct flight to Tel Aviv, Cairo, or Amman, you might want to fly into Northern Europe, and from there on to the Middle East. Fares to London can be very cheap—in 1983, **People's Express** offered a one-way ticket for only $149. **Capitol Airways, Metro International,** and **Icelandic** traditionally offer cheap fares from New York to the Continent, but check with a travel agent for the current bargains. Since the demise of the original Laker Airlines (the newer version is a regular charter), **standby** fares have risen substantially, and some carriers no longer offer the service. But you can still save some money and retain your flexibility by buying a standby ticket on those lines that sell them.

Once you're in Europe, there are flights to Middle Eastern capitals from many major cities. Although the number of student flights within Europe is rapidly decreasing due to so-called "camping flights," a new form of roundtrip charter, the London-Tel Aviv connection (via Athens) remains popular. In 1983, the one-way ticket for students under 30 cost approximately $200. Student/youth fares from London to Cairo ran at $229. Although there are no student flights to Jordan from within Europe, you always have the option of flying to Cairo first, and from there to Amman. Yet another route would be to fly from New York to Athens, either by charter or regular service, and then connect with a flight to any of the Middle Eastern cities. **Olympic Air, EgyptAir** and **El Al** (Israeli Airlines) all offer discounted fares to students on flights between Europe and their respective countries. **Alia Airlines** (Royal Jordanian Air) is reportedly working on a student discount plan, but has as yet none in effect. Finally, if you fly into a Northern European city, watch for special package deals to Egypt and Israel. These packages, offered by travel agents or

Helping Let's Go

Each year hundreds of readers send us suggestions and corrections—from two-word postcards to ten-page letters. These invaluable suggestions are often used in our next edition. To share your discoveries with our readers, and to help us improve *Let's Go,* please send the tear-out postcard in the back of the book (or a letter) by December 31, 1984. Mail it to *Let's Go* Staff, Harvard Student Agencies, Thayer Hall-B, Harvard University, Cambridge, MA 02138.

advertised in the newspapers, often prove the least expensive intra-European flights available, even if the fare includes a few nights in a hotel.

The days when you had to travel to New York City for a cheap flight are over, although it can still be more economical to change planes in New York, particularly for those flying from Canada and the west coast. But direct flights to Europe are available from nearly twenty gate-way cities across the U.S. Inexpensive flights are also available from some major Canadian cities: Canadian students should be sure to consult with Travel CUTS (see Useful Organizations section above for address).

ISRAEL

$1 = 81.19 shekels **$.0123 = 1 shekel**

Each of the ancient biblical prophets had a unique divine revelation: Ezekiel witnessed a valley filled with dry bones come to life, Amos envisioned hills dripping with wine, Jeremiah spied a seething pot in the distance. So it is with Israel; the land is a vision for all of its people, though a different one for each.

For Israel's Jews, the land symbolizes a process of redemption begun a century ago, when great waves of immigrants arrived at the port of Haifa. In resettling their ancient homeland, the Jews feel they have redeemed themselves, and have fulfilled a great and noble dream. For the Palestinians, however, the vision of the land is remarkably different. Theirs is often the experience of disenfranchisement, of second-class citizenry, and for some, of homelessness and exile. The Palestinian question—what is owed to the Arabs living in Israel and the occupied territories and to those living elsewhere—has contributed to the outbreak of five wars (1948, 1956, 1967, 1973, and 1982) and to countless other acts of violence.

Israel has endured the conflict, along with growing pains and the strains of integrating into its midst Jewish refugees from Nazi Europe, Muslim Asia, and the Soviet Union, but the price has been high. Everywhere you turn you'll see uniformed Israeli soldiers carrying guns, a situation you may find disconcerting at first. The costs of maintaining such a large army have sent Israel's economy reeling into triple-digit inflation. That hardship, coupled with mandatory military service, has taken its toll on the population: immigration is down sharply, emigration is on the rise. The tension also shows in the frenetic pace of life. Many Israelis find release through fast driving, heavy smoking, and a raw attitude toward sex that may leave foreigners (especially women) frightened and disturbed. Meanwhile the social and economic rifts between the "first Israel" (Jews from Eastern and Western Europe and America) and the "second Israel" (Jews from North Africa and Asia) have only recently begun to close up.

In the years since its birth in 1947, Israel has raised more questions than can ever be satisfactorily answered—moral questions about the nation's responsibilities to the displaced Arabs; intellectual questions about whether "Judaism" must now be defined in national, religious, and/or ethnic terms; and practical questions about the extent to which Israel should be governed by traditional Jewish law. But whatever your opinions on these questions and their importance, Israel will intrigue you with its almost unbelievable ethnic, geographical, and national diversity. Patriarchal tombs, Roman forts, Crusader castles, and mosques all stand within miles of modern factories and universities. Their fascination is surpassed only by the land itself, from the deserts of the Negev and fertile fields of the Galilee to sun-flooded beaches and even a snow-capped mountain.

Orientation

Useful Organizations

Tourist information offices in Israel will supply you with free maps, schedules of events, and advice. The **Israel Student Travel Association (ISSTA),** with offices in Tel Aviv, Jerusalem, and Haifa (addresses listed under respective cities), can help you with tours, student discounts, identification, and the like. If you wish to learn more about travel possibilities in Israel before your arrival, the following organizations provide both general and specific information:

Israel Government Tourist Office (IGTO). US: 350 Fifth Ave., New York, NY 10118 (tel. (212) 560-0650); 6380 Wilshire Blvd., Los Angeles, CA 90049 (tel. (213) 658-7462); 5 South Wabash Ave., Chicago, IL 60603 (tel. (312) 782-4306); 4151 Southwest Freeway, Houston, TX 77027 (tel. (713) 850-9341). **Canada:** 102 Bloor St. West, Toronto 181, Ontario M5S 1M8 (tel. (416) 964-3784). **U.K.:** 18 Great Marlborough St., London W1V 1AF (tel. 01/434 6351). Visit or write for tourist literature, including the helpful *Visitor's Companion.*

Society for the Protection of Nature in Israel (SPNI; in Hebrew, *Hahevra Lehaganat Hateva):* 13 Helena HaMalka St., P.O. Box 930, Jerusalem 91 008 (tel. 02/24 95 67). Walking tours within cities and guided hiking trips (in English) to all parts of the country, as well as special study tours for student groups. Also maintains thirty Nature Study Centers. Write to the office in Jerusalem, or ask for information from the IGTO. Local addresses: 4 Hashfela St., Tel Aviv (tel. 33 50 63/5); 8 Herzelia St., Haifa (tel. 51 14 48 or 53 12 70).

National Parks Authority: 4 Rav Alluf M. Makleff St. (P.O. Box 7028) Hakiryah, 61 070 Tel Aviv (tel. 25 22 81). Material on parks and historical sites. Also sells a fourteen day ticket ($5) covering admission to all sites. Ticket available in Tel Aviv and at major sites.

Israel Youth Hostel Association: 3 Dorot Rishonim St., P.O. Box 1075, Jerusalem (tel. 22 16 48 or 22 59 25). Operates thirty hostels. Organizes 7-, 14-, and 21-day package tours called "Israel on the Youth Hostel Trail," including accommodations, dinner and breakfast, unlimited bus travel, and entrance to National Parks.

Israel Camping Union: P.O. Box 53, Nahariyya (tel. 04/92 33 66). Write for information about organized camping tours and a full list of camping sites.

Embassies of many English-speaking countries are listed in the Tel Aviv Practical Information listings. To obtain technical advice before you reach Israel, contact the nearest Israeli embassy or consulate. Embassies:

U.S., 3514 International Drive NW, Washington DC 20008 (tel. (202) 364-5500).

Canada, 410 Laurier Ave. West, Suite 601, Ottawa, Ontario K1R 7T3 (tel. (613) 237-6450).

Australia, 6 Turrana St., Yarralumla, Canberra, A.C.T. 2600.

Consulates:

New York. 800 Second Ave., New York 10017 (tel. (212) 697-5500).

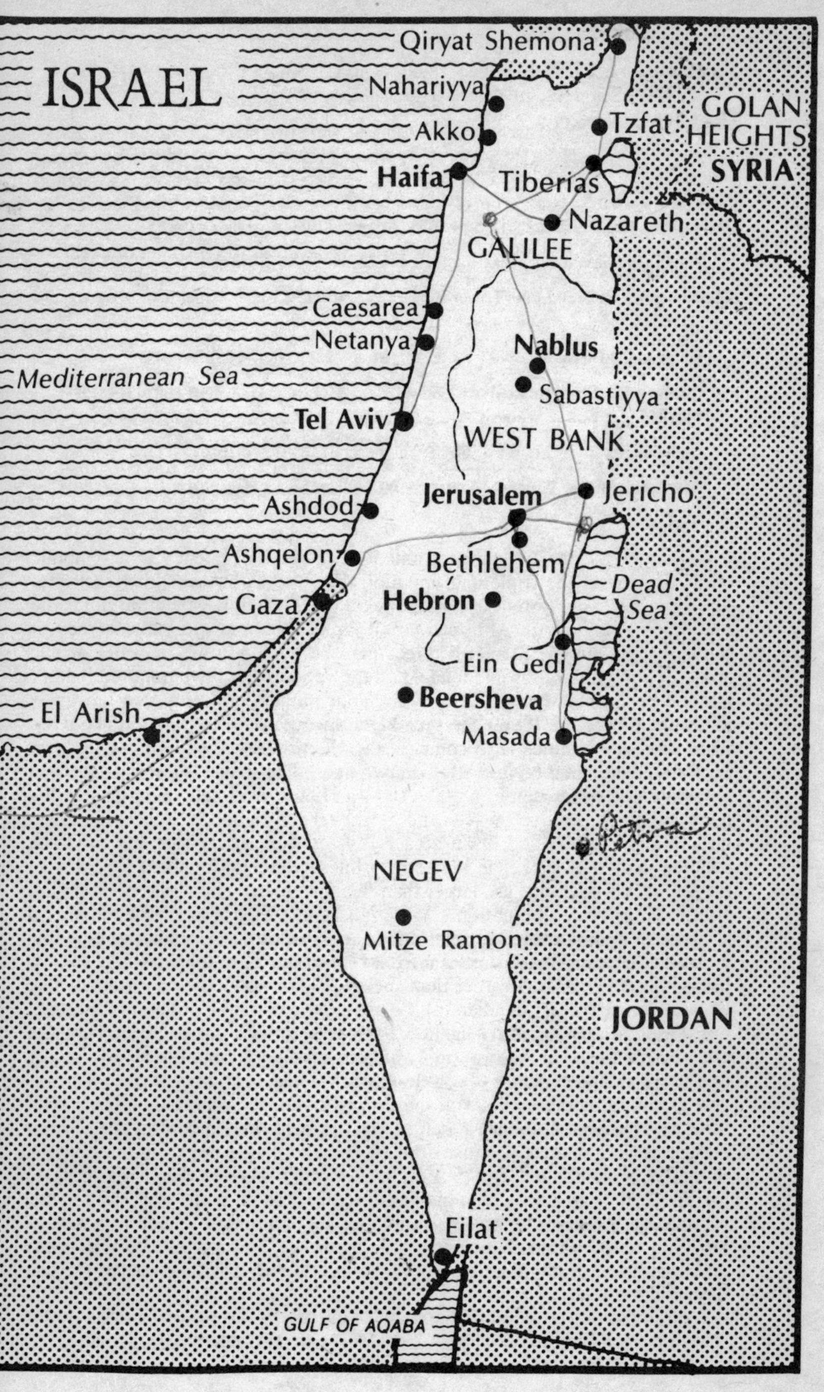
ISRAEL
Qiryat Shemona
Nahariyya
Akko
Haifa
Tzfat
GOLAN HEIGHTS
SYRIA
Tiberias
Nazareth
GALILEE
Caesarea
Netanya
Nablus
Sabastiyya
Mediterranean Sea
Tel Aviv
WEST BANK
Jerusalem
Jericho
Ashdod
Ashqelon
Bethlehem
Dead Sea
Gaza
Hebron
Ein Gedi
Beersheva
El Arish
Masada
NEGEV
Mitze Ramon
JORDAN
Eilat
GULF OF AQABA

California. 6380 Wilshire Blvd., Suite 1700, Los Angeles 90048 (tel. (213) 651-5700); 693 Sutter St., 4th floor, San Francisco 94102 (tel. (415) 775-5535).

Illinois. 111 Wacker Dr., Suite 1308, Chicago 60611 (tel. (312) 565-3300).

Massachusetts. Park Square Building #450, 31 St. James Ave., Boston 02116 (tel. (617) 266-3800).

Georgia. 805 Peachtree St., Suite 656, Atlanta 30308 (tel. (404) 875-7851).

Texas. One Greenway Plaza East, Suite 722, Houston 77046 (tel. (713) 627-3780).

Pennsylvania. 1720 Louis Tower Bldg., 225 South 15th St., Philadelphia 19102 (tel. (215) 546-5556).

Florida. 330 Biscayne Blvd., Suite 510, Miami 33132 (tel. (305) 358-8111).

Quebec. 550 Sherbrooke West, Suite 1675, Montreal H5A 1A0 (tel. (514) 288-9277).

Ontario. 102 Bloor St. West, Suite 780, Toronto 181 (tel. (416) 961-1126).

New South Wales. Westfield Towers, 100 William St., Sydney 2011.

Currency

In May, 1980, the Israeli government devalued its currency in a symbolic effort to combat the triple-digit inflation that wreaks havoc with Israeli life. The new currency system uses the Shekel (1S), which is worth ten times the old Israeli Pound *(lira)*. Although you'll rarely encounter the old currency, it remains legal tender. Standard prices may be quoted in lira in some Arabic areas. If you go to buy some felafel and the vendor says "two hundred," don't assume he means shekels—if you do, your money will disappear ten times faster than it should. If you can't read Hebrew, the simplest way to tell old lira from new shekel notes is to compare the Hebrew denomination: on the new notes the denomination is written on two lines. The shekel is a simple decimal currency and notes come in 500-, 100-, and 50-shekel denominations; coins have begun to replace the 10- and 5- shekel bills, though some are still in circulation. Shekels and lira are each divided into 100 *agorot*, but anything smaller than one shekel is almost worthless. Except for the one and five pieces, all the old coins are larger than the new ones.

For the traveler, the nation's 150% inflation rate isn't as problematic as it sounds: the relationship between prices and U.S. dollars (or any other stable currency) remains nearly constant from year to year. For this reason, *Let's Go* lists all prices in dollars rather than shekels. Some services and products may be paid for in U.S., Canadian, and Australian dollars, or in Pounds Sterling, but shops are under no obligation to accept foreign currency and are not always able to do so. Keep a supply of Israeli money for out-of-the-way places and small establishments. If you do pay in foreign currency (travelers checks and credit cards included), you may receive change in shekels; always save your most recent exchange receipt from the bank as a record of the current exchange rate. When you use foreign currency, you are exempt from the domestic Value Added Tax (VAT) on goods and services. Since many shops include it in listed prices, you may have to insist to get it discounted. You can also get VAT refunds by presenting all receipts of purchases made with foreign currency at any airport bank upon your departure. You will be refunded in the currency used; if the bank cannot make the refund, it will be mailed to your home address.

You may bring an unlimited amount of currency, foreign or Israeli, into the country in any form. You must change currency at authorized banks, at a 2½% commission. On departure, you may take up to $15,500 with you, and may change up to $3000 worth of shekels back to your currency. It's a good idea to exchange all your shekels before you leave Israel, since their value is always falling and few banks are willing to buy them. Remember, however, to bring the airport tax of $10 with you in any currency.

Business Hours and Holidays

Business hours in Israel are difficult to pinpoint: because of the variety of religions that coexist in the area, shops close on different days. Most shops, offices, and places of entertainment close early Friday afternoon until after sundown on Saturday (the duration of the Jewish Sabbath). Jewish-owned public transportation also closes down throughout the country except in Haifa, where the local ruling coalition does not include the religious party. Arab buses continue to run, primarily to the West Bank. Arab-owned concerns close on Fridays (the Islamic Sabbath), and Christian businesses on Sunday. Usual shopping hours are Mon.-Thurs. 8am-1pm and 4-7pm, Fri. 8am-2pm. Banking hours are generally Sun.-Tues. and Thurs. 8:30am-12:30pm and 4-5:30pm, Wed., Fri., and eves of holidays 8:30am-noon.

Jewish holidays, like the Sabbath, begin and end at sundown. Because the Jewish and Muslim calendars are lunar, their holidays fall on different days each year with respect to the solar Gregorian calendar we use. Major holidays include Rosh Hashanah, Yom Kippur, Simhat Torah (each in September-October), Independence Day (April-May), and Shavuot (June-July). During Succot (Sept.-Oct.) and Passover (March-April), each of which lasts seven days, shops close entirely for the first and last day and are open until early afternoon during intermediate days. Other, lesser holidays are marked by early closing only.

The major holiday observed in the West Bank, Gaza, and other predominantly Muslim areas is Ramadan, a month in summer when Muslims fast during the day (for details, see Festivals section in Egypt Introduction). Although the exact dates of Ramadan change every year, in 1984 it will run from early June to early July. Some restaurants close for the entire month, and many others close during the day, but otherwise there are few disadvantages to visiting these areas during Ramadan. Shops close at 3:30pm during Ramadan and reopen from 8-11pm.

Telephones, Telegrams, and Mail

The best place to find a working phone is the post office; next best are Egged stations and hotels. To make a local call you must buy tokens *(asimonim)*, which are available for 5-10¢ at the post office and most hotel reception desks. Stock up on them whenever you can, as they are sometimes hard to find. For directory assistance, dial 14. You can dial direct overseas from central post offices in major cities; you save both time and money by not using an operator. Dial 00, then the country code, area code, and telephone number. For collect and credit card calls, dial 18 for the overseas operator. If you call the Tel Aviv operator at 03/63 38 81 you're more likely to get through.

You can phone telegrams by dialing 171. Otherwise, post offices and hotels will send telegrams for you. Telex service is available in Tel Aviv at 7 Mikve Israel St. (7am-11pm, tel. 03/61 57 09) and in Jerusalem at the Central Post Office.

Post offices are open 8am-12:30pm and 3:30-6pm except Wed. (8am-2pm) and Fri. (8am-1pm), closed Sat. and holidays; in the larger cities some offices may keep longer hours. To receive mail in Israel you have three options. *Poste Restante* functions here as elsewhere, but you must ask repeatedly to get all your letters. Have tellers check under both first name and surname, and, if possible, check yourself. Always bring your passport or other proper ID. American Express and some ISSTA offices will also hold mail. Lines at American Express are short and employees often let you check the letter pile. ISSTA lines, however, are longer than Israel itself. Mail to Israel from North America can take up to three weeks; mail sent from Israel to North America is slightly faster. If you need to mail something to North America within 72 hours, the Central Post Offices in Jerusalem, Tel Aviv, and Haifa offer **International Express Mail** service.

Language

Language in Israel will present few problems to the English-speaking visitor. Most, if not all, Israelis speak some English, and many signs are written in Hebrew, Arabic, and English. It is a good idea, however, to learn a few Hebrew phrases. *Shalom* means peace, also hello and goodbye. *Bevakasha* is please, *todah* thank you, and *slicha* sorry or excuse me (use this phrase when pushing your way through a crowd). Streets are usually labeled *Rehov* (street), *Sderot* (boulevard), *Derech* (road) or *Kikar* (square). Since many Israelis immigrated from Eastern Europe and North Africa, German or French may also be helpful. The best phrasebooks are the Dover publication *Say It in Hebrew* and the Berlitz *Hebrew for Travelers;* both contain handy phrases and their correct pronunciation (available in most bookstores for under $2). If you intend to spend any time in the Arab towns of the West Bank or the Galilee try learning the Arabic numerals so you can find the right bus, and a few Arabic phrases (see Egypt introduction). We have included a table of Hebrew letters in the Appendix to help you decipher signs.

To and From Israel

By Air

Plane fares from Europe to Israel are surprisingly inexpensive. A one-way ticket on El Al between Athens and Tel Aviv costs only $107 if you buy it in Tel Aviv ($123 in Athens) for youths under 26 or students under 31. The London-Tel Aviv youth fare is available to those under 26 or students under 28 and costs $210, $255 in summer. The Tel Aviv-London ticket costs $238, $288 in summer. Occasionally, during off-season, El Al offices in Europe offer greatly reduced standby fares from many parts of Europe to Israel. The SATA student charter flights are even cheaper, but they did not run in 1983 because of legal problems, and no one knows if flights will resume in 1984. When operative they were available in Israel through the ISSTA student travel organization and in Europe at SATA offices. Students up to 35 were eligible. Prices in 1982, when they were last quoted, were: Tel Aviv to or from Athens $89, London or Paris $189, Copenhagen or Zurich $199. Travelers to and from Greece should realize that it's cheaper to buy Athens-Tel Aviv air tickets in Israel, despite claims to the contrary by student travel offices in Greece. Whatever your destination, be sure to save $10 in any major currency for the airport tax.

By Ferry

Israel is no longer frequently serviced by boat connections from Greece, Italy, and Cyprus. Only three boats now make the crossing. The *Vergina,* run by **Stability Lines** (in Piraeus: 11 Sachtouri St. (tel. 41 32 392/5); in Brindisi: Italmar, corso Garibaldi, 96/98 (tel. 29 77 12 or 22 21 29); in Haifa: Mano Lines, 39 HaMeginim St. (tel. 53 21 02); and in Tel Aviv: Mano Lines, 114 HaYarkon St. (tel. 24 66 01)) sails weekly from Piraeus to Haifa March-Dec., stopping in Iraklion, Crete, and Limassol, Cyprus. Student fare from Haifa is $38 to Limassol, $60 to Crete or Piraeus, including tax. **Sol Maritime Services** (in Athens, 4 Filellinon St. (tel. 32 33 176); in Rhodes, 11 Amerikis St. (tel. 22 46 0); in Limassol, 1 Irene St. (tel. 57 00 0); in Haifa, Jacob Caspi Ltd., 76 Ha'Atzmaut St. (tel. 67 44 44)) operates two boats to Israel. The *Sol Phryni* shuttles weekly between Piraeus and Haifa. One way student deck class fare is $56, plus $10 per stopover. The *Sol Olympia* sails from Venice to Haifa every ten days, except in July and August, when service accelerates to every eight days.

Overland

There are two overland routes to and from Israel—into Egypt and into Jordan. The crossing into Jordan is discussed at length in the Jordan introduction. Border crossings in the Middle East are highly sensitive to political currents; the information we provide may easily become obsolete in the coming months. Check with travel agents, tourist offices, and other travelers for the most up-to-date details.

At present, there are two border crossings between Israel and Egypt: at **Rafiah** on the Mediterranean Coast, and at **Taba,** 8km southwest of Eilat on the Gulf of Aqaba. Note that if you enter the Sinai from Israel with a tourist visa, you must leave by the same port, or from Cairo or Alexandria. You cannot, for instance, enter at Rafiah and leave at Taba. Two types of visas for travel in Egypt are available, one for the entire country, and one for the Sinai alone. The latter is valid for one week only, and involves no currency exchange requirement, but restricts you to the Aqaba Coast and the Mt. Sinai area—the Suez and Mediterranean coasts are off-limits. To get a Sinai visa, simply go to the Taba border station with a valid passport, and pay the standard "tourist fee" of LE4.10 ($5). To enter Egypt proper, you must secure a full visa, either in the U.S., at the Egyptian Embassy in Tel Aviv (54 Besel St., tel. 03/22 41 52; take bus #5 from the Central Bus Station) between 9-11am, or at the Egyptian Consulate in Eilat (34 Deror St., tel. 059/76 11 5). The consulate is open Sun.-Thurs. If you drop your passport off between 9am and noon, you'll be able to get your visa by 2pm the same day. Americans and Canadians pay US $7 plus $2.50 in Israeli currency. One warning: if you intend to travel to Jordan or most other Arab countries, you must obtain your Egyptian visa outside Israel, or you'll have to buy a new passport in Egypt. In addition, note that an Egyptian entry stamp from Rafiah or Taba is an equally clear indication that you've been in Israel, and thus precludes your entering other Arab nations.

Possibly the simplest way to navigate the whole border affairs is to let **Egged, Galilee Tours,** or **VIP Tours** (130 HaYarkon St., Tel Aviv (tel. 03/ 24 41 81/2) make all the arrangements from Tel Aviv or Jerusalem to Cairo. The charge is $25 one way, $40 round trip ($23 and $37 for students) from either city. These tours often include overnight accommodations in a Cairo hotel, which may exempt you from the $150 currency exchange requirement at the border. Verify this with the tour operator. Normally, tours do not exempt you from the LE4.10 entry fee.

Making the crossing on your own is not difficult, and can save you about 50% over the tour prices. You will have to convert your money, though confusion and hard bargaining will sometimes persuade Egyptian border officials to drop the requirement, especially at Taba. It is impossible to buy back your dollars once they're changed, unless you can prove that you've spent $30 per day in Egypt. To Rafiah, take bus #362 from Tel Aviv ($2.70); to Taba, take bus #15 from Hatmarim Blvd. in Eilat.

If the direct Egyptian bus to Cairo has left when you reach Rafiah (leaves at noon; LE5.25), take a shared taxi to El Arish (LE2), and get a new taxi there for Cairo (LE5). Direct taxis from the border to Cairo cost a staggering LE10. Only one bus per day travels from the Taba border crossing, leaving at 1pm Israeli time for Sharm el Sheikh (LE3), where you'll have to spend the night.

You can avoid all these hassles and keep your passport clean by flying between Tel Aviv and Cairo: Air Sinai daily flights cost LE95 one way. If you have previously obtained an Egyptian visa, you will not have to make the currency exchange at Cairo Airport. For information on travel from Egypt to Israel, see the Egypt Introduction.

Getting Around

Bus

Buses are the most popular and the most convenient means of traveling around Israel. Except for the Dan Company in Tel Aviv and the Arab buses serving the West Bank and Gaza, **Egged** holds a monopoly over bus service in the country. With over five thousand buses in its fleet, Egged services nearly every city and town; its signs can be seen almost everywhere. The buses are for the most part modern, air-conditioned, and inexpensive to ride. ISIC holders receive 10% discounts on all bus fares. Egged offers a special discount deal called the Roundabout ticket. These tickets, issued for 7, 14, 21, and 28 days, permit unlimited travel on any of Egged's buses, and give you a 10% discount in Egged restaurants. In addition, Egged issues a day ticket for unlimited travel on buses in Jerusalem. To be worthwhile, both of these offers require far more bus riding than any sensible traveler should do. Since Egged fares are very inexpensive, skip the deals, walk a little, and ride as much as you please.

If you plan to travel by bus, familiarize yourself with the bus system. Egged runs several non-stop and local buses between the major cities each day; non-stop buses usually fill up quickly. If you plan to travel long distances, especially during the summer, it is advisable to reserve a seat in advance. When planning your itinerary, remember that only Arab buses run during the Jewish sabbath from mid-Friday afternoon to Saturday after sundown.

Many tourists prefer to travel on Egged's tour buses. Egged offers over a hundred excursion tours to various regions in Israel. Egged tours into the Sinai desert and along the Red Sea are particularly popular (they're cheaper than the tours run by the Society for the Protection of Nature, though not nearly as good). For more information, check with Egged tour office in the U.S. by calling (212) 598-0993 or writing to their head office at 15 Frishman Street, Tel Aviv (tel. 24 22 71).

Train

Rail service in Israel, though limited, is often convenient for travel between major cities. **Israel Railways** runs a line from Nahariyya to Beersheva and Dimona in the south that passes through Haifa, Tel Aviv, and major towns along the North Coast. Another line from Haifa to Jerusalem passes through the Judean wilderness, some of Israel's more scenic countryside.

Like buses, trains cease operation during the Sabbath. Avoid traveling on Friday afternoons since the trains are crowded with people returning home early in its honor. It's safest to reserve seats in advance at any time. Fares on the train are comparable to those for buses, but Israel Railways does not offer any extended travel passes. Students with ISIC can obtain a 50% reduction on the fare.

Sherut

The fastest way of getting around is in a shared taxi or sherut. Certain taxi companies operate sherutim seven days a week. Individual seats are sold at fixed prices, with up to seven persons sharing a cab. A sherut costs as much as 20% more than the same trip on a bus.

Most sherutim leave as soon as they fill up. The locations of the main sherut stations are listed in *Let's Go* under the particular cities. Make sure that the car you get is a sherut and not a regular taxi, which charges a great deal more (if the car isn't full or the driver turns on the meter, you know you're in the wrong place). Sherutim operate on Saturdays and late at night when the buses aren't running, but be careful that the price isn't inflated over 20%. Also, if you want to get from the airport to Jerusalem, ask the fare first—this route is often a price-gouger's free-for-all.

Car

Because public transportation in Israel is extensive and efficient, a car seems an unnecessary luxury. Nevertheless, a car does afford certain freedom of movement and the ability to reach out-of-the-way places. You can drive in Israel if you have a valid national or international driver's license. Roads are paved and well-marked, and maps are available at all tourist offices. Israelis drive on the right side of the road. **Hertz, Avis,** and **Thirfty Rent-a-Car** are among the major rental companies in Israel, with offices in all larger cities. The cheapest rentals run about $10 a day, plus $.22 per kilometer, or $32 a day with unlimited mileage. Watch for special deals; **Eldan,** among others, occasionally offers cutrate prices. But don't try to save money by not buying insurance: you'll regret your frugality should you have an accident.

Hitching

Hitchhiking in Israel is widespread and accepted, though not always easy. Soldiers get first priority. Try to wait alongside them; often you will be picked up with them. Don't stick your thumb out in the *Let's Go* style—use your index finger to point out to the side. If you hitchhike in the Negev or the Golan, make sure your ride is going all the way to your destination. The best area for hitchhiking is along the North Coast and from Tel Aviv to Haifa, but public transportation in these areas is so good that you might as well take a bus. While rides are easy to catch in the Arab territories, especially in Gaza, it is not safe for women to hitch alone here.

Life in Israel

Accommodations

In Israel, the availability and type of budget accommodations varies radically from city to city. While Jerusalem is packed with hostels (both official and unofficial) and a few cheap hotels, the North Coast, Galilee, and Dead Sea have almost no inexpensive hotels but offer fine IYHF Hostels and a few campgrounds. Haifa and Tel Aviv offer cheap hotels as well as hostels. In

Eilat, Tzfat, and Ashqelon, cheap rooms to let abound. Finally, in the Negev, the most inexpensive option is to camp, or to stay at the Mitzpe Ramon Youth Hostel.

Youth Hostels

Although often crowded in summer, Israel's thirty IYHF-affiliated youth hostels are usually clean and close to historic sites and scenic areas. They have no age limit, but a few have a maximum stay of three nights. At most hostels, overnight fees in 1983 were $5.30 for members, $6.70 for non-members; breakfast is obligatory at many hostels and costs about $1.80 extra. Some hostels still follow an old rate structure, charging $5-6 for individuals under 18, $6-7 for those over 18. IYHF members get approximately 10% discount on all rates. Hostels rarely offer lunch but many have supper for about $3. Unfortunately, what you save in money you may lose in convenience. Most hostels have an 11pm curfew, although you can sometimes obtain an extension in city hostels by special permit. In addition, most hostels follow a strict schedule. They are open 5-9pm for check-in and 7-9am for check-out, and are closed the rest of the day. There are many unofficial hostels and pensions in Israel besides the IYHF; whether affiliated or not, hostels are not known for safety. Don't leave valuables lying about, especially while you sleep.

For information on the "Israel on the Youth Hostel Trail" package deals, write to the Israel Youth Hostel Association (see Useful Organizations section for address).

Hotels

Hotel accommodations are usually too expensive for the budget traveler. Still, cheaper hotels exist. In any case, the time will come when you may want to splurge and stay in a more comfortable place. The Ministry of Tourism rates hotels on a five star basis, with five stars signifying the highest quality and most expensive hotels. Budget travelers will occasionally find reasonably priced one- and two-star hotels in the larger cities; a few have doubles for $12-16 per person. But most hotels cost more. When business is slow you can often bargain prices down substantially. Tourist offices throughout Israel distribute a booklet called *Israel Tourist Hotels,* but this does not list many of the cheaper concerns. Ask instead for the booklet *Israel: A Youth and Student Adventure.*

Christian Hospices and Kibbutzim

If you plan to stay in Bethlehem, Nazareth, or Jerusalem, the three most important Christian sites in Israel, then you might consider staying in one of the many Christian hospices located in those areas. Hospices are also located on Mt. Tabor, Tiberias, and Tel Aviv. Officially, these hospices, most of which are old monasteries or Franciscan settlements, are designed to help Christians on pilgrimages to the Holy Land find board and accommodation at a reasonable price. All of the hospices we have listed, however, welcome tourists and pilgrims alike.

The 39 hospices in Israel are run by organizations representing various Christian denominations and a host of nations. Though prices vary quite a bit, bed and breakfast costs $15-18 per person at most places. Bed only in dormitory rooms can run as low as $3. Though spartan and austere, they are usually quiet, clean, and comfortable. In addition, most serve cheap, filling meals, and are located in important religious centers. Unfortunately, rooms are very limited and hence difficult to obtain in the tourist season. For a list of these hospices, write to either the Israel Government Tourist Office or the **Israel Pilgrimage Committee,** P.O. Box 1018, Jerusalem 91009 (tel. 02/24 01 41).

Some kibbutzim also offer accommodations, but these are generally out of the range of budget travelers. These "Kibbutz Guest Houses," as they are called, are usually extremely comfortable, equipped with showers, restaurants, and swimming pools.

Camping

Camping is in many ways the most economical way to see Israel. Most camping areas are conveniently located outside major cities or near scenic national parks, easily reached by public transportation, and equipped with all the amenities. Better yet, the price is right. During July and August, most camping places charge $4 per night for adults ($2.50 in the off-season). For $4.50 ($3.50 in off-season) you can get a bed in a hired tent; another option is to rent a bungalow with either two, three, or four beds. This will cost $8 per person ($6 in off-season). For more information, write to the Israel Camping Union (see Useful Organizations for address).

As in other warm countries it may be tempting to pitch your tent for free in areas not officially designated for camping. Think twice, however, before you unroll your sleeping bag. Certain stretches of beach are off limits for security reasons (the Mediterranean coast north of Nahariyya), and others have a high incidence of robbery (near Haifa, Tel Aviv, and Eilat). You'll be safest on the more secluded North and South Coast beaches near the Sea of Galilee, and police are rarely a nuisance, since camping on most public beaches is legal. If they hassle you, it's usually just to move you to a legal spot.

Private rooms

In some cities, such as Tzfat and Eilat, the cheapest and most interesting alternative to camping or a youth hostel is to stay in a private home. The IGTO, and sometimes even private travel agencies, can arrange accommodations for $26 and up per person. The more inexpensive alternative is to find a place on your own: it's rarely a problem. Just hang out at the bus station with your bags and someone is bound to find you. Prices should be no more than what you would pay at the local hostel.

Food

In the tug of war between Occident and Orient, Israelis lean gastronomically toward the West, though the raw materials are stubbornly Middle Eastern. Given the quality of meat, Israelis rely to a large extent on dairy and vegetable products, especially salads and yogurts (try the sweetened fruit yogurt called either *preely* or *yogli*). The most popular fast food is *felafel* (pita bread stuffed with balls of ground chickpeas fried in oil, plus salad, topped with white *tahina* sauce); pizza (generally mediocre to poor, especially that served by *Rimini,* the leading pizza chain) is a close second. *Hummus* (mashed chickpea, garlic, and lemon dip served with pita) is a light alternative, and *schwarma* (chunks of roast lamb and salad wrapped in pita) is a staple among Arabs and Oriental Jews. The typical Israeli eats a large breakfast, goes home for lunch, the big meal of the day, and eats a light late supper.

Preparing your own food is very cheap, especially during the summer months when fresh fruits and vegetables flow in from the kibbutz harvests. Groceries can be easily obtained at very inexpensive prices at the local outdoor markets in some cities, at the neighborhood *mahkolets* (small grocery stores), or at the western-style supermarkets in large cities. Market prices for tomatoes get as low as $.40 a kilogram, $.75 a kilogram for apricots *(mish-mish)* and peaches. In addition, the government subsidizes many staple foods. On hot summer days you'll see street vendors selling what look like hand grenades. Don't worry. These are *sabras* (prickly pears) that are quite edible, although the seeds inside may not agree with some people. (As a matter of interest, native-born Israelis are also called sabras—tough and prickly on the outside, tender and sweet within.)

If you wish to eat out, Israel has an impressive variety of restaurants. There are eleven daily newspapers published in eleven languages in Israel, and the array of cuisines represented in its restaurants is even greater. You should be aware that some establishments follow Kosher dietary laws, which means that they serve exclusively meat or dairy dishes at a given meal. There are artificial "dairy" products to accompany a meal with meat in kosher restaurants: unless you're prepared for this, it can be a rude shock to discover that your ice cream isn't what you were expecting.

To avoid single-handedly subsidizing the Israeli soft drink industry, always carry a canteen with you. In the first few weeks, however, you should be wary of the water, which may cause the painful form of diarrhea known in Hebrew as *shilshul*. There are two fruit drinks sold everywhere which are cheaper than soda and safer than water: *tapuzim* (orange drink) and *eshkoliot* (grapefruit drink, the better and more popular of the two). If you ask for "soda" you'll get club soda. For a 7-Up equivalent, ask for *limonada;* for orange soda, ask for *orangeada*. The ice cream in Israel is predictably lousy, though the Israelis love it, and whatever you do, don't order anything billed as "American pancakes."

In all cities except for Tel Aviv and Jerusalem, the best food bargain, except for the supermarket, is the **Egged Self-Service Restaurant** at the Central Bus Station. The help is always surly, but a full breakfast goes for $1.75, and a full lunch for $4. You will soon discover that the cheap sit-down Arab restaurants are no great shakes. $3 may seem cheap for a *kebab,* but dishes at these places are as à la carte as you can get, and the meat is of surpassingly low quality. Check our listings for exceptions to this rule.

Study

The Israelis give high priority to their educational system, and as a consequence, the country enjoys an extraordinarily high literacy rate. Israel presently operates seven institutions of higher learning, with universities based in Tel Aviv, Jerusalem, Ramat-Gan, Haifa, and Beersheva, and technical and scientific institutes in Haifa and Rehovot. Programs for foreign students range in length from a summer to four years. Most programs are limited to or very strongly emphasize the Hebrew language and Jewish studies, and provide unique opportunities to learn about Jewish culture. A full year course of study usually includes an *Ulpan,* an intensive study of Hebrew lasting from four to nine weeks.

One option is to pursue a full-time degree at an Israeli university, on either the undergraduate or graduate level. Admission to undergraduate bachelor programs requires proficiency in Hebrew and at least one year of college. High school students with exceptional backgrounds are also admitted. Another option is to take a one-year intensive program *(Mechina)* in Hebrew and Israeli culture before entering the undergraduate program.

Both Tel Aviv University and the Hebrew University of Jerusalem currently operate overseas student programs. You must apply directly to the university of your choice through its New York office. The **Hebrew University** program lasts a full year; you must apply by April 1 of the year in which you intend to enter. The University also offers one-year programs for graduate study. **Tel Aviv University** offers both single-semester and full-year programs for overseas students; the application deadline is June 1 for fall semester or year programs, December 1 for the spring semester. Academic years for the universities begin in late October and run through the month of June; the year is preceded by an Ulpan. For information on programs and application forms for the Hebrew University of Jerusalem, write to the Office of Academic Affairs, American Friends of the Hebrew University, 1140 Avenue of the Americas, New York, NY 10036 (tel. (212) 840-5820); for Tel Aviv University, write to the Office of Academic Affairs, American Friends of Tel Aviv University, 342 Madison Ave., Suite 1426, New York, NY 10017 (tel. (212) 687-5651). Tuition fees are moderate, and a fellowship can ease the burden of expenses. Ask at your university careers office, or write to the Institute of International Exchange (see the Useful Organizations section of the General Introduction) for their free pamphlet *Scholarships and Fellowships for Foreign Study: A Selected Bibliography*. The various Friends Committees mentioned above also offer scholarship assistance to needy students. Guaranteed Student Loans may be applied to study in Israel.

Summer courses in archeology, Hebrew, or Jewish history are offered by Hebrew University of Jerusalem and Tel Aviv University. The summer courses are about a month long, and cost about $400 to $500: room fees included. The Hebrew University offers two sessions. Apply to the various offices of academic affairs or call the Hebrew University Summer Course Department at Mt. Scopus (tel. 88 26 02).

A number of shorter-term study possibilities are also open to foreign students. The **Ulpan Akiva Netanya,** an international Hebrew center based in Netanya, has a series of four, six, eight and twenty-week programs in Hebrew language, but costs are steep and the students are usually over 35. Contact the Ulpan directly at Ulpan Akiva Netanya, P.O. Box 256, Netanya 42100, for more information. Ulpanim run by the Jerusalem municipality are cheaper and, in some ways, better. For information, contact the Ulpan office in Beit Ha'am, Bezalel Street, Jerusalem (tel. 02/22 41 56).

Further sources of information on study opportunities are the Institute of International Education (see General Introduction), and the Office of Academic Affairs at the New York consulate. To obtain a student visa, you must submit a visa application along with a letter of acceptance from the institution you plan to attend, medical forms, two photos, and a $3 fee to any Israeli Consulate.

Work

Employment opportunities for U.S. citizens in Israel are limited, although knowing Hebrew fluently helps. American companies with branches in Israel are one possible source of employment. If you obtain paid work you must secure a work visa from the government through your employer. The visa costs $3.

Two organizations sponsor traineeships, for both undergraduates and graduates, with science and technical firms abroad. Israel is a member country of both the **International Association of Students in Economics and Business Management** (known by its French acronym, **AISEC**) and the **International Association for the Exchange of Students for Technical Experience (IAESTE).** Both organizations operate exchange programs lasting anywhere from eight weeks to a year, and living expenses are provided. Applications for the AISEC program are accepted in early January only from AISEC members at participating colleges and universities. For more information, write to AISEC-

US, 622 Third Ave., New York, NY 10017. For the IAESTE program you must apply by December 15 for summer placement, or six months in advance for long-term and non-summer placement. The application fee is $50. For more information write the IAESTE Trainee Program, c/o Association for International Practical Training, 217 American City Building, Columbia, MD 21044 (tel. (301) 997-2200). The ability of either program to offer placement in other countries depends on the number of American companies with openings for interns. You will be expected to help secure job openings.

During the summer, it is often possible to work as a volunteer at one of Israel's youth hostels, IYHF or unofficial. The jobs are usually menial, including cleaning or cooking, but you'll get free room and board in return, and often a small stipend. The advantages of such work are obvious: all of the hostels are full of young travelers and they are located at or near Israel's most famous tourist sites. Since volunteers are chosen on a first-come first-served basis, there is no way to secure a job in advance. Another source of employment is the Society for the Protection of Nature in Israel—try volunteering at one of their Nature Study Centers. You can sometimes get work soliciting boarders or booking guests in the budget hotels which cater to foreigners. Wages tend to be low, but room and board may be included. Jerusalem, Tel Aviv, and Eilat are the best places to look for such positions. Finally, it is possible to volunteer for work on a kibbutz or a moshav (see below).

Archeological Digs

Working on a dig is another popular way to earn your keep, learn something completely new, and meet people. It is not for everyone, however. The work is hard and often monotonous. Digging pits and shoveling shards are only occasionally interrupted by an exciting moment. Your individual experience depends on your interest in archeology, the quality of the findings, and how much the leaders of the dig care whether you have an idea of what's developing.

In January, the **Israel Department of Antiquities and Museums** (affiliated with the Ministry of Education and Culture and located in the Rockefeller Museum, Jerusalem), P.O. Box 586, Jerusalem 91104 (tel. 28 51 51) makes available a list of excavations that are open to volunteers during the summer months. You must be at least 17, in excellent physical condition, and able to work a minimum of two weeks. The work offered is difficult manual labor. Many of the excavations require payment to cover the cost of accommodations and food, but some provide your accommodations and food for free. Once you acquire the list, you must apply to the specific dig you would like to work on: the Department will not find you a position. Another program is provided through ISSTA (see Useful Organizations), which has arrangements with Tel Aviv University for students who are interested in working on digs. They stress that the work is long and hard, and really only for those interested in the field. Another drawback to this program is the cost—over $100. **Project Expeditions, Ltd.**, an organization based in London, places people 18 or older on two-week digs at varying prices. Fees include airfare, room and board. For information, write to Project 67, 36 Great Russell St., London WCI B 3PP. Other available options are to contact the Pilgrimage, Youth, and Student Division of the IGTO, the Dig for a Day Program, and the programs offered at the Archeology Department of the Hebrew University, all in Jerusalem.

Kibbutzim and Moshavim

One of the best places to find work is on a kibbutz. Israel's kibbutzim are experiments in collective living. Their roots reach back to the communist dreams of early Zionists who came out of Russia and Poland in the years just before and after the Russian Revolution and immigrated to Palestine in the Second Aliyah (second wave of immigration). These determined, practical and virulently secular idealists were determined not to make the mistakes of the settlers of the First Aliyah from Germany who had essentially stayed in Palestine's cities and exploited cheap Arab labor. Committed to the ideal of "Jewish Labor" and a return to the land, the early kibbutzniks purchased land and established collective farms where all labor and all profit were shared more or less equally among the members. Even the care and upbringing of children was a communal undertaking—young ones lived together in dormitories from early infancy. Though the kibbutz movement did play a part in the often disturbing history of Israeli land appropriation, it nevertheless is the shining symbol of what the Zionist dream is all about: a dream of human redemption through redemption of the land.

The kibbutz movement has changed. The percentage of the population which lives on a kibbutz was never large; today it is smaller than ever: less than 4%. Many kibbutzim have become extraordinarily wealthy by means of highly mechanized agricultural techniques as well as diversification into industry. Many have become large to the degree that they engender anonymity and acquisitiveness. Not all are secular any longer; a number of religious collectives have been established. Children often live with their parents rather than in separate dormitories. Some kibbutzim now hire cheap Arab labor to do menial field work. These changes have created a far more variegated picture than existed previously, making it difficult to generalize and harder to forecast the future. Whether the kibbutzim will continue to be a symbol for the Israelis (and for many people around the world) depends, of course, on both—the kibbutzim and the Israelis.

The only way to get a feeling for kibbutz life is to work on a kibbutz for yourself. This involves a commitment to at least one month of hard work and early hours. The work, usually agricultural but increasingly industrial, is eight to ten hours a day, six days a week. In exchange, the volunteer receives room, board, work clothes, sundries, pocket money, and occasional tours of the region. The most memorable thing about volunteering is not always your contact with kibbutz life (which depends on your initiative), but the acquaintances you make with the other volunteers, who are usually the most geographically diverse people one could put together.

There are several ways to apply for a position on a kibbutz. In Israel, you can apply directly to the office of the appropriate Kibbutz Association in Tel Aviv (bring two passport size photos as well as your passport). Each kibbutz is aligned along political/ideological lines, with every Kibbutz Association under a different political party. **Kibbutz Artzi,** at 13 Leonardo da Vinci St. Tel Aviv 64733 (tel. 25 31 31) is affiliated with the left-wing party; **Kibbutz Hadati,** 1 Dubnov St., Tel Aviv 64732 (tel. 25 72 31), is affiliated with the National Religious Party; **Kibbutz HaMe'uchad,** 27 Soutine St., Tel Aviv 64184 (tel. 24 52 71) and **Ihud Hakerutzot Ve'Haikibbutzim,** Bet Hamerkaz Hahaklai (tel. 25 02 31) have united in one movement, affiliated with the Labour Party. Unfortunately, you may have to wait a long time for an opening to become available.

You can plan a kibbutz visit in advance by contacting the **Kibbutz Aliya Desk,** 27 West 20th St., New York, NY 10011 (tel. (212) 255-1338). They have representatives throughout the U.S. and Canada who will discuss various options with you, arrange for health insurance, and advise you on travel arrangements. Placements are possible all year round, though summer is more difficult to arrange. Finally, **Project 67,** 36 Great Russell St., London WC1 B 3PP (tel. 01/636 1262) places people in both kibbutzim and moshavim for varying lengths of time. Write for more information. You must be between 18 and 32 and have a medical certificate stating that you are in good health and capable of doing agricultural work in a hot climate.

Before you commit yourself, do some advance intelligence work. Kibbutzim have various physical facilities: there are many suburban-type kibbutzim featuring swimming pools, theaters, and factories, while some newer kibbutzim, housed in pre-fab huts, are probably more like the pioneer settlements you've read about in books. Most importantly, different kibbutzim accord different treatment to their volunteers: some will make a real effort to introduce you to kibbutz life, while others will treat you as a free source of manual labor. So be inquisitive, both at the enrollment offices and when you meet ex-volunteers. One very good source of information is the book *Kibbutz Volunteers* by John Bedford ($7.95; available from Writer's Digest Books, 9933 Alliance Rd., Cincinnati, OH 45242), which discusses over two hundred kibbutzim. You can also go to the Israel Government Tourist Offices for advice. The Kibbutz Associations will do their best to accommodate your preferences, but they must work with the openings available. You do have a good chance of being placed in a preferred part of the country. In any case, plan ahead and apply early.

If you're interested in working on a kibbutz and learning Hebrew at the same time, sixty kibbutzim offer a six-month work/study program called *ulpan*. For the most part, ulpanists are treated better than the average kibbutz volunteer since many are newly arrived immigrants and potential kibbutz members. Participants are required to work half a day and study half a day and applicants must be between the ages of 18 (or a high school graduate) and 35. There is a $50 non-refundable registration fee.

Approximately 5% of the Israeli population live on **moshavim,** agricultural communities where virtually all farms and homes are privately owned and operated; members cooperate in the purchase of a few large pieces of machinery, and in marketing. Volunteer work on a *moshav* is similar to that on a kibbutz, except that on a *moshav* your contact will be less with other volunteers, and more with the *moshav* members themselves. Contact the Volunteer Department of any Jewish Agency in Israel or abroad; the Tel Aviv Jewish Agency is at 19 Leonardo da Vinci St. (tel. 25 84 73). Alternatively, you can visit or write Steve Jaffe at **Unitours,** 90a HaYarkon St., Tel Aviv (tel. 24 62 61).

History

Ancient Israel, linking the African and Asian ends of the Fertile Crescent, has been settled since the dawn of civilization. The Bible speaks of numerous tribes who already occupied the region when the first Israelite tribes migrated there from Mesopotamia early in the second millenium B.C.E. During the Patriarchal Age recounted in the Book of Genesis in the stories of Abraham and Sarah, Isaac and Rebecca and Jacob, Leah, and Rachel, the Hebrews lived the semi-nomadic life of a large, extended family in Canaan. They shared and fought over the land with neighboring Canaanite tribes, and occasionally traveled to Egypt to escape the famines that ravaged the land (see Genesis 12:1Off). At some point during the fourteenth or thirteenth centuries B.C.E., one such famine caused a significant portion of the Hebrew tribesmen to settle in Egypt where for a time they appeared to have gained a certain prestige (see the story of Joseph, Genesis 37–48). Eventually political upheaval ("Now there arose a new king over Egypt who knew not Joseph." Exodus 1:8) reduced the Hebrews to petty servitude and persecution in Egypt.

Under the leadership of Moses, these Hebrews as well as many other refugees ("mixed multitude" Exodus 12:38) were able to escape Egypt across the Sinai Peninsula on their way to Canaan. Even very early written accounts of this period (for example, the Song of the Sea in Exodus 15) indicate that these wandering people were developing a conception of a national god, Yahweh, who had saved them from the Egyptians and struck an agreement with them—its terms expressed embryonically in the mountainous wilderness of the Sinai (see Exodus 20).

Early Israelite religion groped its way toward monotheism, after losing itself in the various cults of its Canaanite, Egyptian, and Babylonian neighbors, only to resurface as a diffuse cult practicing sacrificial rites. By the beginning of the first millennium B.C.E. the growing national unity of the Israelite tribes had enabled them to gain supremacy in the region. The reigns of Kings David and Solomon saw the Israelites at the height of their political strength. Solomon built a Temple in Jeruselem, centralizing the priestly class and the sacrificial cult and bolstering the position of Yahweh as the sole god of the Israelites. Much of the Old Testament appears to have been written and compiled during the centuries after the Temple was built. Large portions of the text clearly reveal priestly preoccupation with the sacrifice, the laws of cleanliness, and the treatment of the priests by various kings.

With the division of Solomon's empire shortly after his death in the ninth century B.C.E. the onset of civil strife in the land, and the growing might of neighboring powers, the prophets began to challenge the position of the priestly class and the value of the sacrificial cult. The message of the prophets emphasized that the moral and ethical character of the body politic, more than the performance of sacrificial rites, determined the healthy life of the nation. In the process they revolutionized the conception of Yahweh—by emphasizing that Yahweh was the source of a moral world order as well as the author of the national ritual that celebrated his sovereignty. The prophets universalized Yahweh, fostering what we understand to be monotheism today. The ascent of Yahweh in the prophetic mind is implicit throughout the writings of the prophets in the Old Testament: the tiny book of Jonah is its most simple and gracious expression; the fourth chapter of Micah, its most famous.

The Prophetic Age ended some time after the Babylonians sacked Jerusalem in 586 B.C.E., destroying Solomon's Temple and exiling the Israelites. Thereafter Palestine passed from hand to hand like a geographical basketball: from the Babylonians it went to the Persians, Greeks, Greco-Syrians, Judeans, and in 37 B.C.E., to the Romans. Many of the archeological sites you will encounter in Israel, including Caesarea, Avdat, Herodian, and Sabastiyya, date from this period.

As far as social historians have been able to determine, a desperate and often apocalyptical world view pervaded the Palestine of the Roman period. Roman rule was harsh, rebellions frequent and fruitless. The introduction of Hellenic thought and Roman religion into Palestine shook the foundations of the priestly cult and factionalized Jews into many different sects. Some clung to the old sacrificial ritual, some pursued the development of the new system of law and ritual, unencumbered by the Temple rites, and some embraced the prophetic tradition that envisioned individual spiritual salvation in a world to come rather than the present health of the nation. Oppressed by the tyranny of Herod the Great and Roman rule, the Jews dreamed of David and Solomon and anticipated the appearance of a descendant of David who would be anointed and rehabilitate the nation. (The book of Matthew begins with just such a genealogy of Jesus.) Eventually the concept of the Messiah, the anointed one (*mashee'ak* in Hebrew), was stripped of its national garb, revealing a savior for all the world's meek and down-trodden. It is this vision of the

Messiah and his role that Jesus preaches on the Mount of Beatitudes (Matthew 5). The messianic vision evolved one further step after Jesus' death into a mortal incarnation of God. Unlike a human savior whose success could only occur through life and action, the Messiah would bring salvation to humankind by accepting the most universally human fate: death.

Several self-proclaimed messiahs followed in the next one hundred years, still clinging to a concept of a this-worldly political and military leader. Many provoked further Jewish revolts, which in the early second century C.E. were crushed so severely by Rome that Jewish leaders afterwards refused to support any messianic figures and Judaism became a scholarly and intellectual rather than a politico-military way of life.

Conquering Rome and Byzantium, Christianity made Palestine its most holy outpost. It was here that the Church of the Nativity, like the Star of Bethlehem before it, was raised to mark the birthplace of Jesus. The cross that Jesus bore down the Via Dolorosa came to rest where the Church of the Holy Sepulchre now commemorates his martyrdom.

During a century of holy war and sweeping expansion, the followers of the prophet Muhammad carried the Islamic faith to Palestine and beyond. Crusaders dominated the Holy Land during the thirteenth century and left behind castles like Montfort in the Upper Galilee, subterranean passages in Akko, fortifications in Caesarea, and churches throughout the land. But Muslims continued to occupy Palestine from the seventh to the twentieth centuries. Palestine was a crossroads, this time of the Islamic world. The broken Caliphate, the Egyptian Fatimids, the Mamelukes, and the Turkish Ottomans successively conquered and possessed the land (see History section of Egypt Introduction). In 1917, the Ottoman Empire fell, the sun was still rising over the British Empire, and Palestine catapulted into the twentieth century.

Palestine, Zionism, and Israel

Theodore Herzl, a Viennese journalist convinced by the Dreyfus trial that the Jewish people could be safe only in their homeland, founded modern Zionism in the 1870s. Spurred by late nineteenth-century nationalist and socialist ideals, the early Zionist pioneers established trade unions and agricultural settlements that later became the institutional basis of the Israeli state. In order to receive help in defeating Turkey during World War I, Britain made promises both to these Jews and to Arab nationalist leaders in Palestine. The 1915 **McMahon Letter** promised Husain ibn Ali, Sherif of Mecca, that the British would establish an independent Arab state in the Levant. Though the Churchill White Paper of 1922 denied that this state was to include Palestine west of the Jordan River, the Arabs insisted that had been its intent. The 1917 **Balfour Declaration** promised Chaim Weizmann, then a leader of the Zionist Organization, that the British would support the establishment of a "national home for the Jewish People in Palestine." Though the Passfield White Paper of 1930 made a distinction between a national home and a sovereign state, the Zionists insisted that the meaning of the document had been to establish a sovereign state.

Jews, primarily from Eastern Europe, fleeing pogroms and filled with a dream of establishing a homeland for the Jewish people came and settled among the Arabs of Palestine. These Arabs, having been subjected to three centuries of debilitating Turkish rule, also dreamt of national independence and renaissance in the region. As the twenties, thirties, and forties passed, these dreams confronted one another with increasing irreconcilability; recriminations, riots, and general strikes broke out periodically during the 25-year British Mandate. The rise of anti-Semitic fascism in Europe during the thirties brought more and more Jewish immigrants to Palestine until the British White Paper of 1939 seriously restricted Jewish immigration and land purchases. Jews resented British enforcement of this policy at a time when Hitler's persecution forced many to flee Europe. During the war the rejection and subsequent death of many refugees further damaged relations. When the Second World War ended, the Zionists determined to establish a sovereign Jewish State regardless of British intent. The Arab nationalists were equally intent upon preventing it.

On November 29, 1947, the United Nations voted to partition Palestine into an Arab state, a Jewish state, and an international Jerusalem. Civil war broke out in Palestine; Arab and Jewish militia fought throughout the country. On May 14, 1948, the British mandate over Palestine ended and the Jewish Agency declared the independence of the State of Israel. During the civil war and the international war which followed the declaration of independence, thousands of Palestinian Arabs left their homes and farms and fled to neighboring Arab states. In the spring of 1949 an armistice was signed by Israel and the Arab states—Jordan had swallowed the original Arab state of the partition and had taken half of Jerusalem. Israel took the other half.

Since the creation of Israel the country has fought wars with its neighbors in 1956 (the Suez Campaign), 1967 (The Six-Day War), 1973 (the Yom Kippur War), and 1982 (in Lebanon). In the 1967 War Israel occupied territories belonging to Syria (the Golan Heights), Jordan (the West Bank), and Egypt (the Sinai Peninsula and the Gaza Strip) and once again many Palestinian Arabs left their homes and moved to neighboring Arab countries.

In recent years Israel has come under more and more international pressure to solve the "Palestinian problem" in some way. Accompanying this international pressure has been the growing feeling among most European, Asian, and African nations that the Palestine Liberation Organization (PLO) led by Yasir Arafat is a legitimate representative of the Palestinian people. Israel and its allies abroad, however, maintain that the PLO is a terrorist organization having no legitimacy and requiring no recognition. The PLO with equal aplomb refuses even to recognize the existence of the State of Israel, preferring phrases like "occupied" or "usurped" Palestine.

Arabs resent Israel as a symbol of Western imperialism and as an obstacle to Arab geographical and political unity. But while Arab countries sympathize with the Palestinian cause and give it symbolic support, few are willing to go to great lengths for the Palestinians and only Jordan gives citizenship to Palestinian exiles.

Jewish settlement in the West Bank remains among the most provocative issues. While the actual settlements have little economic value for Israel, they serve as a symbol of the permanence of Israeli life and culture. Control over the entire West Bank is valuable to Israel, however, both militarily and economically. In Israel's eyes, a Palestinian state on the West Bank would certainly prove a threat to Israel. Perhaps more importantly, Israeli control over the area provides a major source of cheap Arab labor. Despite a broad-based peace movement that opposes Israeli policy in the West Bank, tensions continue in part due to hesitancy on either side to make peace for fear that domestic religious and class conflict will then surface.

The 1979 Camp David Accords between Israel and Egypt, while defusing tensions between the two countries, have thus far been unable to untie the Palestinian knot. Events since then have only served to aggravate problems in the region. The Israeli bombing of an Iraqi nuclear power installation in June, 1981, the assassination of Egyptian president Sadat, the continued building of new settlements in the occupied territories, and the 1982 invasion of Lebanon have not only made future prospects for peace in the region even more remote than in years past but have created unprecedented strains in Israel's relationship with the U.S. Traditionally an unqualified supporter, the U.S. has attempted to extract concessions that it feels will not significantly weaken Israel while trying to strengthen the position of pro-American Arab countries. The resignation of Prime Minister Menachem Begin may result in a significant shake-up of the Israeli leadership.

Arab-Israeli tensions do not directly affect tourists unless they are traveling in sensitive areas of the West Bank or Gaza Strip, where it's wise to check up on travel conditions continually. One thing you will have to get used to is the tightness of security. Soldiers walk the streets everywhere in the country and Israeli customs and post office officials pay close attention to packages or other potentially dangerous objects. But above all remember that though Arabs and Israelis aren't on the best of terms, if you are sensitive to their political convictions they will welcome you warmly.

Literature

If you haven't read the Bible recently, you probably don't remember how great much of it is, and there is no better way to appreciate the holy sites, as well as the land itself, than to read the appropriate biblical passages as you tour. While you're in Jerusalem, for example, read Lamentations; if you visit Ein Gedi, read Song of Songs; at Jacob's Well in Nablus try John 4, which retells Jesus' encounter with the Samaritan woman; and, of course, read Matthew 5 upon the Mount of Beatitudes.

A number of modern authors have written fascinating accounts of their experiences in Israel. Saul Bellow's *Jerusalem and Back,* a chronicle of the author's visit to Israel in the early 70s, is a veritable feast of insights and anecdotes. Elie Wiesel's fiction, while often overwrought, casts a ghost-ridden and indispensable perspective on Israel's existence. The two-book "series" *Night* and *Dawn* is especially valuable in this regard, while *Souls on Fire* is a good introduction to Hassidism. For a survivor's view of the Holocaust, read *The Age of Wonders* or *Badenheim 1939* by Aharon Appelfeld. The author escaped from a concentration camp at age eight and wandered the forests for three years until the Red Army found him and put him to work on a food line. He soon made his way to Italy, reaching Palestine in 1946 at age fourteen. Israel's Nobel laureate, S.Y. Agnon, devotes much of his work to the problem of spiritual void resulting from challenged traditions and religious scepticism. You might also consider reading *Exodus* by Leon Uris—it's crass and blatantly anti-Arab but parts of it are entertaining. Two more substantial historical novels are Chaim Potok's *Wanderings* and James Michener's *The Source*. For insight into life in Palestine during the days of the Greeks, try *As a Driven Leaf* by Milton Steinberg. Fawaz Turki's *The Disinherited* offers a thoughtful yet angered autobiography of a Palestinian Arab. For historical background on the land and the people of Israel, the works of Solomon Grayzel are both authoritative and elegant. For a more complex socio-cultural analysis try Raphael Patai's books *The Jewish Mind* and *The Arab Mind*. Any of the historical works by Josephus Flavius, especially *The Jewish Wars,* provides an interesting though somewhat distorted primary source covering of the time of the Roman Conquest. An account of the Arab Israelis can be found in the dense but provocative *The Arabs in Israel* by Sabri Jiryis. Finally, *Voices Within the Ark* by Howard Schwartz and Anthony Rudolph is an anthology of twentieth-century Jewish poetry, much of which comes out of the Israeli experience.

If you plan to visit many archeological sites, Vilnay's comprehensive *Israel Guide* leaves no stone unturned. It is designed, however, for motorists; if you don't have a car, you'll find the organization puzzling. For a complete (and we mean *complete*) listing of places in Israel, featuring dry historic accounts and lists of vital statistics, try the large red book called *Israel Tourguide* (although it is difficult to find in bookstores).

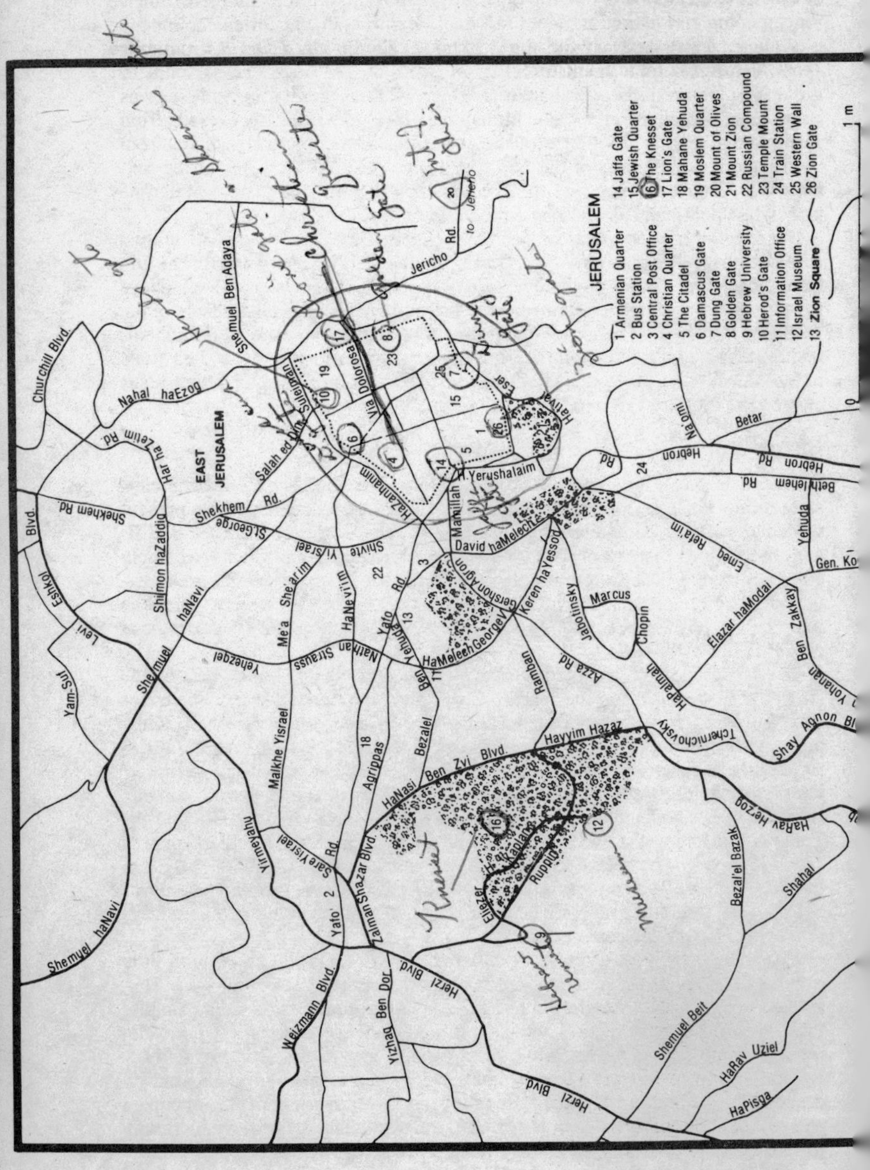
JERUSALEM
1 Armenian Quarter
2 Bus Station
3 Central Post Office
4 Christian Quarter
5 The Citadel
6 Damascus Gate
7 Dung Gate
8 Golden Gate
9 Hebrew University
10 Herod's Gate
11 Information Office
12 Israel Museum
13 Zion Square
14 Jaffa Gate
15 Jewish Quarter
16 The Knesset
17 Lion's Gate
18 Mahane Yehuda
19 Moslem Quarter
20 Mount of Olives
21 Mount Zion
22 Russian Compound
23 Temple Mount
24 Train Station
25 Western Wall
26 Zion Gate
0
1 m
EAST JERUSALEM
Churchill Blvd.
Nahal haEzog
Shemuel Ben Adaya
Jericho Rd.
to Jericho
Suleiman
Via Dolorosa
Salah ed Din
Har ha Zetim Rd.
Shekhem Rd.
St.George
Shivte Yisrael
Shimon haZaddiq
HaNevi'im
Me'a She'arim
haNavi
Yehezqel
Nathan Strauss
Yafo Rd.
HaZanhanim
H.Yerushalaim
Mamillah
David haMelech
Gershon Agron
Keren haYessod
Hativat Eser
Hebron Rd.
Betar
Na'omi
Bethlehem Rd.
Emeq Refaim
Yehuda
Gen. Ko
Marcus
Chopin
Jabotinsky
Elazar haModai
Ben Zakkay
Yohanan
Azza Rd.
Ramban
HaMelech George
Ben Yehuda
Bezalel
Agrippas
Malkhe Yisrael
Shemuel
Levi
Eshkol Blvd.
Yam-Suf
Hapalmah
Tchernichovsky
Hayyim Hazaz
Shay Agnon Bl
HaNasi Ben Zvi Blvd.
Kaplan
Ruppin
Eliezer
HaRav Herzog
Shahal
Bezal'el Bazak
Yirmeyahu
Sare Yisrael Rd.
Zalman Shazar Blvd.
Yafo
Shemuel haNavi
Weizmann Blvd.
Yizhaq Ben Dor
Herzl Blvd.
Shemuel Beit
HaRav Uziel
HaPisga

Jerusalem

Violence within and without the walls of Jerusalem has never destroyed its spirit. Time and time again, it has risen from dusty, smoky ruins, built of dreams and fey visions. Abraham offered his son as a sacrifice here; Jesus was condemned within the city walls; Muhammad rose to heaven one evening from Jerusalem's heights. Evidence of the city's importance is everywhere, from the religious monuments of the Old City to the concrete trenches of the Six-Day War. You can even feel the preeminence through the people—pilgrims pray while politicians declaim in Arab coffee houses.

Despite the myriad political questions which surround its current status, Jerusalem is above all a holy city. On Friday the Muslim merchants of the Old City close their shops and move in waves through the labyrinth of alleys towards their mosques; on Saturday the fervently religious Hasidic Jews of the Mea She'arim sector barricade their streets to guard the sanctity of Shabbat; and on Sundays the inhabitants of the Armenian quarter put down their tools to attend churches along the Via Dolorosa, the traditional road on which Jesus carried the cross to Calvary.

History

Jerusalem has a long and checkered history. It began as a Canaanite city-state on the eastern slope of the hill called the Ophel, just south of the present walled city. David conquered the Canaanite city sometime around 1000 B.C.E. and, by bringing the Ark of the Covenant to Jerusalem, established it as a holy city, the capital of a united kingdom of Israelites. David's son Solomon extended the city northward to include the present-day Temple Mount. There he built the First Temple of Israel to house the Ark and to centralize the sacrificial cult of the priestly class.

The Israelite kingdom divided shortly after Solomon's death. Ten of the twelve tribes established the Northern Kingdom, known as Israel. The tribes of Judah and Benjamin continued the Davidic dynasty in the Southern Kingdom, which retained Jerusalem as its capital. During the next four centuries the Southern Kingdom (Judea) dominated the Northern Kingdom, yet bitter internal strife left the Hebrews open to disastrous incursions from the outside. In 586 B.C.E., Nebuchadnezzar, King of Babylon, burned Jerusalem and the Temple and forced the Jews into exile. Work to rebuild the Temple began in 536 B.C.E. with the return of some Jews to Israel under Cyrus the Great of Persia. The Second Temple was completed in twenty years, but Jerusalem was not restored until the court official and prophet Nehemiah rebuilt the city walls in 445 B.C.E. and repopulated the city.

Alexander the Great's conquest of Jerusalem in 332 B.C.E. met with little opposition from the inhabitants; much of the population was thoroughly Hellenized. Following a brief period of Egyptian domination, the Seleucid Empire took Jerusalem in 198 B.C.E. Thirty years later, the remaining religious elements, disturbed by the increase of paganism introduced by these Greco-Syrians, revolted against King Antiochus IV Epiphanes, who retaliated by desecrating the Second Temple. The rebels, led by Judah Maccabee, occupied and resanctified the Temple in 164 B.C.E. and established a priestly hierarchy to rule the city. (The Jewish holiday of Hanukkah commemorates this event.)

In 64 B.C.E., the Roman general Pompey took the city, ushering in several centuries of Roman rule. The Romans installed a native son, Herod the Great, son of a Jewish father and Arab mother, as King of Judea. During his 33-year reign (37 to 4 B.C.E.), Herod rebuilt the Temple, creating the famous Western Wall as a supporting structure for the enlarged Temple Mount. The achievements of Herod the Great were undermined by his not-so-great son, Herod Archelaus. In 6 C.E., the Romans turned the governance of the province over to a series of procurators. It was the fifth procurator of Judea, Pontius Pilate, who ordered the execution of Jesus. In 66 C.E. the Jews revolted against Rome. Four years later, the Roman commander Titus succeeded in crushing the revolt, destroying the Second Temple, and razing Jerusalem.

For years, Jerusalem existed only as a Roman army camp, but by 135 C.E., Emperor Hadrian had built a new city upon Jerusalem's ashes in the hopes of establishing a Roman colony. The present-day Old City retains the plan of Hadrian's city, called Aelia Capitolina, in the two major roads which divide into four quarters and in its north-south orientation. During the period of Roman domination, Jews were not allowed to enter the city, but a Christian church was active. Upon Constantine's conversion to Christianity and his mother's travels to the Holy Land, the sites sacred to Christianity were identified and consecrated. Subsequent Christian Roman rulers dedicated themselves to building basilicas and churches to glorify the Christian heritage of the city.

After brief Persian rule in the early seventh century, Jerusalem was taken in 638 C.E. by the Muslim Caliph Omar; the city is considered to be the third-holiest city of Islam after Mecca and Medina. The Dome of the Rock was built in 688 C.E. on the Temple Mount, over the rock on which Abraham was to have offered Isaac to God (or Ishmail, in the Islamic version of the story) and from which Muhammad was believed to have ascended to heaven. The Muslims tolerated both Jews and Christians, with whom they claimed a common religious heritage and whose holy places they also revered. Unfortunately, the period of peaceful coexistence ended in the tenth century when Jerusalem passed into Egyptian control. The Fatimid despots destroyed all synagogues and churches in the city; their policy of persecuting non-Muslims passed on to their successors, the Seljuk Turks. The closing of pilgrimage routes inflamed western Christian resentment and prompted the Crusades, a series of invasions by European armies that culminated in the capture of Jerusalem in 1099. Muslims and Jews were slaughtered indiscriminately. The Latin kingdom lasted almost ninety years, during which time churches were built or rebuilt, and hospices, hospitals, and orders such as the Knights Templar were founded. In 1187 Saladin expelled the Crusader armies and allowed the resettlement of the city by both Muslims and Jews. Jerusalem became a center for Muslim scholarly study from the thirteenth to the fifteenth century under the Mamelukes, who built a number of edifices that still stand today.

In 1537, the Ottoman Emperor Suleymein the Magnificent set out to rebuild the walls of the city on the plan of the old walls. The task took four years, and the planners deviated somewhat from the older design, leaving Mount Zion and King David's Tomb beyond the walls. Enraged with their negligence, Suleymein had the two planners beheaded. Their graves, ominous reminders of the Sultan's absolute power, can still be seen just inside of the Jaffa Gate to the left. The walls surrounding the Old City and the Damascus Gate today are Suleymein's as well.

The West made its way into Jerusalem again in the nineteenth century, beginning with the reign of Muhammad Ali of Egypt (1832-1840) and the opening of a British Consulate in 1835. With the issue of the Edict of Toleration for all religions by the Sultan of Turkey in 1856, Jews and Christians were once again encouraged to settle within the city. In the 1860s, Sir Moses Montefiore, a British Jew, made several trips to Palestine and founded the first Jewish settlements outside the city walls, thus initiating Jerusalem's New City. Montefiore's windmill and some of the houses in the areas he built at Yemin Moshe were recently restored and opened to the public.

The increasing British presence in Jerusalem became an object of fierce resentment for both Jews and Arabs. During World War I, the British made declarations to both Zionists and Arab nationalists implying that each would eventually gain sovereignty over the city and thus securing both Arab and Jewish aid in the British fight against Ottoman rule. By the end of the war, Palestine had become a British protectorate under the auspices of the League of Nations. Unfortunately, the British mandate created more problems than it solved. Their inability to honor conflicting promises to Jews and Arabs exacerbated political tension in the region.

As World War II approached, the British began to resist Zionist efforts to establish a Jewish state, and proposed the formation of a Palestinian state run by both Jews and Arabs. A Zionist resistance movement, including several terrorist groups, was determined to block British policy. One of the most dramatic terrorist attacks occurred in Jerusalem in July of 1947, when Zionist extremists bombed the British government and military headquarters in the King David Hotel. The British decided to withdraw from Palestine and called upon the newly-formed United Nations to resolve the situation. The U.N. voted to partition Palestine into a Jewish and Arab state and make Jerusalem into an international city. In the ensuing War of 1948, however, the Israelis captured the New City of Jerusalem and King Abdullah of Jordan took East Jerusalem and the Old City. The divided city, separated by a no-man's land which began at the traffic light on Jaffa Rd. near the Old City, became Israel's official capital (though many governments recognize Tel Aviv as the capital).

During the Six-Day War in 1967, Israeli forces captured Jordanian Jerusalem. Since then the city has been ruled by the Israeli government and recently it was annexed into the State of Israel itself. In 1980, Israeli control of Jerusalem was once again called into question in the Egyptian-Israeli peace negotiations. The Israeli government clearly indicated its intent to stay by reaffirming Jerusalem as the capital of Israel, and former Prime Minister Begin supported this policy by moving his offices to East Jerusalem. This policy, though it caused tension, has underscored the Israelis' belief that national security rests on a unified Jerusalem.

Orientation

Jerusalem is divided into three main parts: East Jerusalem, the walled Old City, and the New City (West Jerusalem). East Jerusalem is all Arab, the Old City predominantly so. The New City, part of Israel since the founding of the state, is Jerusalem's administrative and commercial center, and the seat of the national government. "Main Street" of New Jerusalem is Jaffa Road (pronounced "Yafo"), stretching, for our purposes, from the **Central Bus Station** at the west end to Jaffa Gate, the main entrance to the Old City from West Jerusalem. Midway between the Bus Station and Jaffa Gate is the triangle formed by King George, Jaffa, and Ben Yehuda Streets—the city center, known in Hebrew as *merkaz ha'ir*.

The **Old City** is still divided into the four quadrants laid out by the Romans in 135 C.E.—the Christian Quarter in the northwest, the Muslim Quarter in the northeast, the Jewish Quarter in the southeast bordering the Western Wall and Temple Mount, and the Armenian Quarter in the southwest. The market runs throughout the Old City, but mainly down the middle and near Damascus Gate. Most of the important historical and religious sites are located in and around the Old City, but shopping, business, and nightlife center in West Jerusalem (the New City).

Fast, frequent, and inexpensive Egged buses run from the Central Bus Station to all parts of Israel. Jerusalem-Tel Aviv costs only $1.40, Jerusalem-Haifa $3. An International Student Identity Card (see ISSTA below) will get you an additional 10% discount on all inter-urban lines, if you present it at the ticket window and again when you board the bus. The staff at Egged information (tel. 52 82 31) speaks English but is rushed and rarely helpful; the same applies to the general information window located to the right of the ticket counters in the station. Fortunately, lists of destinations and fares are posted between the cashier windows. The Israel Government Tourist Office (see below) posts a schedule of major buses from Jerusalem; they have less information, but more patience. In general, buses run 5am-11:30pm. On Fridays, the eve of the Jewish Sabbath, you need to be especially careful checking schedules since buses stop running two to three hours before sunset and begin again only after sundown on Saturday. This limited schedule also applies to the eve of all Jewish holidays. Within the city, all bus drivers sell 25-ride tickets for about $3.50. If you will be in town for more than a week, buy it since the tickets represent a 20% discount on individual fares. A single ride costs 15-20¢.

You can leave luggage at the Central Bus Station while hunting for a room. The baggage and parcel office charges $1 per piece per day, and is located seven stores up the hill from the station itself. The office is open Sun.-Thurs. 6:30am-7pm, Fri. till 3pm. Hours sometimes vary, so check before you leave your bag. Most of the places we list are open during the day to receive guests, but may be closed in the early afternoon (noted in listings).

There are also two Arab bus stations in East Jerusalem. While the one on Sultan Suleiman St., between Herod's and Damascus Gates, services the south (Hebron, Bethlehem, Mt. of Olives, Jericho, Bethany, Abu Ghosh), the one up Shekhem (Nablus) Rd. services the north (Mt. Scopus, Ramallah, Atarot (airport), and other smaller Arab towns in the north). On Saturdays, the Arab buses are also useful for traveling within Jerusalem. There are two routes which begin outside the Old City: one goes up Nablus Rd. (to Mt. Scopus, Ammunition Hill, etc.) and the other goes down Hebron and Bethlehem Rds. (to the Railroad Station area, Talpiyyot, and Ramat Rachel). Unlike other bus lines, if you see one you want outside the bus station, hail it to stop.

A much faster but more expensive way to travel is by *sherut*, or shared taxi. *Moniot sherut* run from Jerusalem to Tel Aviv, Haifa, Beersheva, and Eilat seven days a week along three popular routes within the city: from Jaffa Gate down Hebron Road, from the center of town down Emek Refaim and Yochanan Ben Zakkai Sts., and from Jaffa Road down Herzl Blvd. and Henrietta Szold Rd. For interurban travel on Friday nights or Saturdays, take a *sherut* from the corner of Jaffa Rd. and HaRav Kook St. (**Habirah Cab Co.**,tel. 22 45 45) to Kikar HaMoshavot in Tel Aviv, where you can connect with *moniot sherut* to most major cities in Israel. On weekdays, **Kesher/Aviv,** 12 Shammai St. (tel. 22 73 66/7/8) also runs frequent service to Tel Aviv, and to Haifa and Tiberias via Tel Aviv. If you're traveling to Beersheva or Eilat, you'll need to call **Yael Daroma Cab Co.** (next door to Kesher/Aviv, tel. 22 69 85) in advance, since reservations are a necessity. There is also a sherut stand **behind the Central Bus Station** at 226 Jaffa Rd. (tel. 53 33 33 or 52 22 77) which goes to Tel Aviv and Ashdod. Walk through the main entrance into the station and bear left (towards the Ram Hotel), and you will soon see the taxis.

The sherut that you are most likely to take from Jerusalem is the one to **Ben Gurion International Airport.** Make a reservation in advance (be sure to confirm it again the night before) with **Nesher** at 21 King George St. and Ben

Yehuda (tel. 23 12 31 or 22 72 27). The price is $4.50 from in front of the Nesher office, $7 from your hostel or hotel. **To get to Jerusalem from the airport,** take the bus which leaves every half hour from the parking lot just in front of the main terminal. If you have a lot of luggage, you can get a sherut to Jerusalem from the area to the right as you walk out of the main terminal. Be sure you aren't overcharged—the price should be about $4.50.

If you decide to take the beautiful train ride through the Judean Hills up to Jerusalem (Israelis always speak of "going up" to Jerusalem) from Haifa or Tel Aviv's South Station, you will come to the **Railroad Station** just southwest of the Old City at the foot of King David St. (information tel. 71 77 64). One train leaves each day to Tel Aviv (7:30am), and to Haifa (4pm; 11:30am Fridays only). There are no trains on Saturday. The ride to Tel Aviv costs $1.25, to Haifa only $3, and an International Student Identity Card brings a 25% discount on all tickets. From the railroad station in Jerusalem, cross the street in front and catch bus #5, 6, 7, or 21 to the center of town.

Your Jerusalem, available free in tourist offices and hotels, gives a schedule of daily events in Jerusalem, and also includes a map and a list of **city bus routes.** Though the system would baffle Solomon, remember that most bus routes include either the Central Bus Station or the city center in their courses. To get to the New City from the Central Bus Station, cross the street (via the tunnel) and catch bus #6, 12, 13, 18, or 20—get off on Jaffa Rd. at King George St. or Zion Square (where Ben Yehuda and Jaffa Rd. meet). The most important bus for traveling from the Central Bus Station (and from the New City) to the Old City (Jaffa Gate) is bus #20. Other important city bus routes: bus #1, which connects the Central Bus Station, Mea She'arim, Jaffa Gate, Mt. Zion, and the Western Wall, and buses #12 and 27, which travel to the New City from Damascus Gate and East Jerusalem. Egged has also recently introduced bus #99, which goes to 33 of the major tourist sights in the city. There's one bus an hour 8am-5pm. A single journey for any length of the route costs $.50, one-day unlimited travel costs $4, two-day costs $6.

The Ministry of Tourism map of Jerusalem has a list of sights with the appropriate bus connections on the back. The map itself has very few street names on it, however, so keep your eyes open for Gabrieli's *Map of Jerusalem* and Yoel Ben Natan's map of the Old City. Unfortunately, these excellent maps (which also happen to be free) are becoming almost impossible to find. If you can't get your hands on any of these, try the Department of Surveys, 1 Heshin St., around the corner from the Municipal Tourist Information Office (open Sun.-Fri. 9am-noon), which sells excellent maps of all sorts (about $1.50 each).

Closing hours in Jerusalem are tricky and take some getting used to. Most of Jerusalem closes up or at least slows down between noon and 4pm each day. Churches, banks, hostels, offices, and shops close for the traditional big lunch and afternoon nap. As in the rest of Israel, banks and post offices close on Wednesday and Friday afternoons, so be sure to leave yourself enough shekels for these times. But unlike the rest of Israel, most businesses and shops in Jerusalem stay closed Tuesday afternoons rather than Wednesdays. Generally, the safest approach is to get all essential business done in the morning. In addition, remember that New City shops close Saturday, Muslim shops close Friday mornings, and Christian shops close on Sunday. By 1pm Friday, Jewish businesses close until Saturday night—which, by the way, is also the party night for Jewish youth since nothing is open Friday night.

Money can be changed during off-hours in most hotels or restaurants or at "Money Changer" booths in the Old City, but these places usually offer a lower exchange rate. A good strategy is to save your most recent receipt from currency exchanges at the bank in order to argue for a fair rate. Jerusalem banks are just as slow and inefficient as banks in the rest of Israel: for slightly better service try the **American Israel Bank** on Jaffa Rd., 1½ blocks towards the Old City from King George St.

According to Jewish law, all cash transactions are prohibited on the Sabbath. As a result, museums, concert halls, and even some restaurants circumvent this law by selling Saturday's tickets in advance. Advance tickets to museums, concerts, theater, and other events may be obtained from one of three major ticket agencies in Jerusalem: **Cahana,** 1 Dorot Rishonim St. (tel. 24 45 77 or 22 28 31); **Ben Naim,** 38 Jaffa Rd. (tel. 22 40 08); and **Klaim,** 8 Shammai St. (tel. 24 08 96 or 23 40 61). All three agencies add an 11% service charge to the price of each ticket.

The Jerusalem Post, Israel's English newspaper, has a magazine supplement on Fridays covering "What's On Around Town" for the week including movies, concerts, and special events. If you are near a telephone you can find out almost anything you want to know by calling one of the tourist information offices listed below. Otherwise, check *This Week in Jerusalem, Your Jerusalem,* or the posters lining the city's streets.

Practical Information

Israel Government Tourist Offices (IGTO): 24 King George St. in the New City (tel. 24 12 81/2). Open Sun.-Thurs. 8am-6pm, Fri. 8am-3pm. Branch office inside Jaffa Gate in the Old City (tel. 28 22 95/6). Open Sun.-Thurs. 8am-6pm, Fri. 8am-3pm, Sat. 10am-2pm. Both offer a 30% discount on admission to several major sights.

Municipal Information Office: 34 Jaffa Rd. (tel. 22 88 44). Much less crowded, more helpful and friendly than the above two offices. Sometimes has the Gabrieli map of Jerusalem. Ask here about the free Saturday morning walking tours. Open Sun.-Thurs. 8am-6pm, Fri. 8am-1:30pm.

Israel Student Travel Agency (ISSTA): 5 Eliashar St. (tel. 22 52 58 or 24 87 86). Turn left up Eliashar St. at the bright yellow ISSTA sign just below Zion Square toward the Old City—one block on the left. ISIC costs $6. Bring proof of student status and photo from shop around corner on Jaffa Rd. Services include cheap flights to major destinations in Europe, buses and flights to Cairo, car rentals, Eurail passes. Open 9am-1pm and 3-6pm. Closed Wed. and Fri. afternoons and all day Sat.

Christian Information Center: inside Jaffa Gate and to the right (tel. 28 76 47). Often more helpful than the Tourist Office. Open Mon.-Sat. 8:30am-12:30pm and 3-6pm (in winter 3-5:30pm).

American Express (Meditrad, Ltd.): 27 King George St. (tel. 22 22 11). Open Sun.-Fri. 8:30-1pm and 3:30-6pm except Wed. and Fri. afternoons.

Post Offices: Central Post Office, 23 Jaffa Rd. (tel. 24 47 45 or 24 84 02). Main section open Sun.-Thurs. 7am-7pm, Fri. 7am-2pm. Parcels office around the corner on the west side of the building, open Sun.-Thurs. 7:45am-12:30pm and 3:30-6pm, except Wed. 7:45am-2pm; Fri. 7:45am-1pm. International Calls desk open Sun.-Thurs. 7am-9pm, Fri. 7am-2pm; Telegrams desk in adjacent storefronts at the back (Koresh St. side) of the main building open Sun.-Thurs. 6am-10pm, Fri. 6am-3:30pm. In addition, the information desk is open 24 hours for sending telex, telegrams, and express letters—all at a hefty additional charge. If you come after midnight, it may take a while for someone to wake up and serve you. **Branch**

Offices: New City: Mordechai Ben Hillel St. between Hillel St. and Shammai St. Old City: inside Jaffa Gate and to the right opposite the entrance to the Tower of David. East Jerusalem: intersection at Suleiman and Salaheldin Sts. opposite Herod's Gate. Rehavia: Keren HaKayemet St. one block from intersection with King George St.

Police: Russian Compound, off Jaffa Rd. (tel. 100).

Medical Emergency: Dial 101. Near the Central Bus Station, and near Dung Gate in the Old City. Newspapers list hospitals and pharmacies on duty for emergencies. **Jerusalem Rape Crisis Center:** Dial 81 01 10. Open 24 hours.

U.S. Consulate: Main Branch on Shekhem (Nablus) Rd. and Kikar Pikud HaMerkaz in East Jerusalem (tel. 28 22 31/2). Open Mon.-Fri. 8:30am-1pm, except local and American holidays. In case of extreme emergency, call the duty officer at 23 42 71. The branch at 18 Agron St. in the New City is for ceremonial purposes only.

English Bookstores: For guidebooks and historical texts, the best store is at the **Society for the Protection of Nature,** 13 Helena HaMalka St., off Jaffa Rd. east of Zion Square. **Bestsellers,** on the ground floor of the CLAL center shopping mall on Jaffa Rd., also has a wide selection of English language books. **Sefer Vesefel,** 2 Ya'avetz St. off the corner of 49 Jaffa Rd. (third door on the right and up the stairs) is open all afternoon; you can read English books, magazines, and newspapers in the tearoom on the porch. Also try the **Bookstop** at 6 Nuwas St.

Laundromats: All charge about $2.50 for washing, $.40 for five minutes of drying, and $.50 for soap. All close early on Fri., stay closed Sat. **Superclean Geulah,** 1 Ezer Yoldot St., is closest to East Jerusalem. Walk west from the intersection of Mea She'arim and Strauss; the laundromat will be in the first alley on the left. Open Sun.-Thurs. 9am-6pm, Fri. 8:30am-1pm. **Superclean Rechavia,** 26 Ussishkin St., is open Sun.-Thurs. 6:30am-7:30pm, Fri. 6:30am-1:30pm. **Washamatic Ramat Eshkol,** Paran St. shopping mall, is open 9am-6pm, Fri. 8am-noon.

Swimming Pools: The best list of pools is published in the free *Kol Ha'ir* newspaper, unfortunately in Hebrew. The list at the IGTO is not reliable; call before you go anywhere. The cheapest pools, charging $3.50 weekdays, $5 Sat., are **Beit Taylor** (tel. 41 43 62), open every day 9am-5pm, in Qiryat Yovel (buses #18 and 24); **Jerusalem Swimming Pool,** at Emek Refaim St. (tel. 63 20 92), open every day 8am-5pm (buses #4 and 18).

Camping Equipment: Orcha, 22 Nahalat Shiva (tel. 22 66 65), in the alley off 27 Yoel Salomon St. Sales and rentals of camping and diving equipment. Two-man tents rent for $15 per week, snorkel and mask sets for $8 per week.

Telephone Code: 02. For the overseas operator, dial 18, or dial via the larger Tel Aviv office, (03) 62 28 81.

Accommodations

Although to many first-time visitors Jerusalem seems large and disoriented, it is in fact fairly small and disoriented. Fortunately, all of the places listed below are no more than a ten-minute walk from either the New City center, where nightlife and good eating spots abound, or the Old City, where history and religion draw attention. Most young travelers stay in the Old City because prices there are lower. Student hostels and hotels in the Old City or in East Jerusalem have the most colorful atmosphere, though usually atmosphere just means dirt and crowds. In addition to price and comfort, curfew times should be a major consideration in choosing a lodging. An active cultural center, Jerusalem has many cafes, music spots, and general hangouts. To enjoy this nightlife, you need at the earliest an 11pm curfew, and West Jerusalem locations are nearer.

It is also possible to get private accommodations in Jerusalem. Some locals may approach you in the street, but be aware that they may ask exorbitant prices. A better alternative is to call **Renting Room, Ltd.** (tel. 63 35 63)—an agency which specializes in finding private accommodations for tourists. For up to one week's stay, they can arrange a room for $14 per night single or $20 per night double. Longer stays are also possible. Those staying for over two months might consider short-term rental of apartments, especially during July and August when many Israeli students are on vacation. A single room in a shared flat should cost between $80-$100 a month. The best source of information is the classified section of *Kol Ha'ir,* a free Jerusalem weekly—get a friend to translate and perhaps put in an ad of your own requesting a flat, since classifieds are free. Also thorough but more expensive, the **Sheal** service, 3 Hillel St., grants two months of access to its voluminous listings (in English) for $4. Open Sun.-Thurs. 8:30am-1pm and 4-7pm, Fri. until noon. Occasionally helpful are the notice boards in Richie's Pizza on King George St. and those throughout Hebrew University.

The New City

For nightlife and comfort, the best place to stay is the New City. Modern conveniences are close by, and the streets moonlight as one big smorgasbord of eating places, movie theaters, and cultural centers. Unfortunately, inexpensive places to stay are in short supply. All places listed, except for the Hotel Zefania and Amsterdam Hostel, are about a ten-minute walk from the Old City.

Edison Youth Hostel, corner of Yeshayahu and Belilius Sts. (tel. 23 21 33). From Jaffa/King George intersection, walk one block up Strauss, take the first left onto HaNevi'im, first right up Yeshayahu; the hostel is around the second corner on the right, opposite the Edison Cinema. An airy, comfortable place in an excellent location. Clean bathrooms with hot showers. Free use of refrigerator, luggage storage $.50 a day; good felafel store and pastry shop downstairs. The friendly, relaxed management helps travelers find temporary jobs. Closed Sat. 10am-4pm. Midnight curfew. $4.50 per person plus $.60 extra for sheets. Doubles available for $13 a night. Breakfast $1.25 extra. If you pay in advance for six nights, the seventh is free. Prices almost halve in winter.

Hotel Zefania, 4 Zefania St., Geulah (tel. 28 63 84 or 27 27 09). From Jaffa Rd. walk up Strauss Rd. to Mea She'arim Rd. (where Strauss turns into Yehezqel St.) then three blocks more to Zefania. Or take bus #4 from the town center or bus #27, 35, or 39 from opposite the Central Bus Station; get off on Yehezqel St. at the Zion Orphanage. A converted three-story apartment building located in a safe and interesting neighborhood; management requests modest dress in hotel vicinity (Mea She'arim). Clean and pleasant with lots of refrigerators but a run-down kitchen. Large dining area doubles as a sitting room. No curfew. Prices range from $3 per person in a dormitory to $8 in a single. Doubles available for $10. Reservations often necessary in summer.

Amsterdam Hostel, downstairs at 4 Binyamin Metudella St. (tel. 63 96 04). Take bus #9 from the Central Bus Station, #19 from the center of town. Clean, and in a quiet residential neighborhood. The only drawback is the size—though not crowded, it is often full. Closed daily 9am-1pm; no curfew. $2.50 for the first night, $2 subsequent nights. Breakfast $.60 extra.

King George Youth Hostel, 15 King George St. (tel. 22 34 98), half a block from Ben Yehuda St. Wigged out and wild, man. Full of '60s throwbacks, druggies, and weirdos. The location for nightlife is unbeatable. The problem is the management packs 'em in tighter than a sailor on his first day ashore. Free storage of valuables. Open for dinner, often with live music; no curfew. $5 a night including sheets.

Bernstein Youth Hostel (IYHF), 1 Keren Hayesod, at the corner of Agron St. (tel. 22 82 86), near the Plaza Hotel. A ten-minute walk south along King George St. from the center of town; or take bus #7, 8, or 14 from the Central Bus Station. Facilities include reading room, all-day coffeehouse, courtyards, and an air-conditioned dining room serving large, kosher meals. Luggage check-in during the day in the coffeehouse. Booked solid by groups during July and the first half of August. 11pm curfew with twenty-minute grace period. IYHF members $5.30, non-members $6.30, including breakfast and sheets. Work volunteers receive free room and board plus $10 a week (six hours of work per day, one week minimum).

Hotel Eretz Yisrael, 51 King George St. (tel. 63 90 71). Between Bernstein IYHF and the center of town. Run by a religious Jewish couple, the Barmatzes, who take pride in their hotel's reputation as the cleanest inexpensive establishment in Jerusalem. Excellent mattresses. Free luggage storage and refrigerator use. Absolutely no unmarried couples. $10 per person, but quite bargainable when business is slow.

Hotel Kaplan, HaHavatzeleth St., just off Zion Square (tel. 22 45 91). Excellent location in the center of town on a quiet side street. Very clean, comfortable rooms. Free luggage storage and refrigerator use. No curfew. Singles $10, doubles $15 and $17.50. Try bargaining, or, if you're traveling alone, ask to share a room with someone else.

Hotel Klein, 10 King George St. (tel. 22 89 88). Half a block up King George St. from the intersection with Jaffa, on the right. Small place on the fourth floor of an office building, run by an elderly Orthodox Jewish woman. Excellent location. Use of hot water kettle and refrigerator. No singles; doubles $14. Try bargaining, especially if you're staying more than one night.

Hotel Nogah, 4 Bezalel St. (tel. 66 18 88; ask for Mr. Kristal). Only five rooms, but good facilities—refrigerator, gas, utensils, hot shower and bath. Owner lives elsewhere (at 7 Ben Maimon St.). $16 per double room.

Hotel Migdal, 11 HaHistadruth St. (tel. 22 47 49), off Ben Yehuda St. Unbeatable location, lots of rooms, very clean, and helpful owner. Up a few flights of stairs. Singles $12, doubles $20, but try bargaining.

The Old City

Whatever amount of time you plan to stay in Jerusalem, the experience of spending at least one night in the Old City should not be missed. Although safety and cleanliness are more of a concern here than in the New City, the exotic fascination of the markets and the powerful aura of religious and historical sights nearby is more than ample compensation. Accommodations in the Old City vary tremendously depending upon which area you decide to stay in, so look closely before choosing. Each hostel has a distinctive character ranging from the friendly Swedish Youth Hostel to the intensely Middle Eastern Al Arab and Al Kamal to the austere, almost monastic Armenian hospices. Lodgings in the Old City cluster near the Jaffa and Damascus Gates; the Jaffa Gate area is generally cleaner, safer, and more accessible from the New City than its Damascus Gate counterpart. Walk down Jaffa or Agron St. to the end or take bus #1, 19, or 20. The hotels and hostels located in the Damascus Gate area are usually dirtier and less safe for unescorted women, but are cheaper and interesting because of their proximity to Arab markets, mosques, and bakeries. In many of these places, bargaining still remains the rule rather than the exception, so always haggle for a lower price. The Damascus Gate can be reached by walking down to the end of HaNevi'im St. or by taking bus #12 or 27. To avoid any problems, women travelers should be especially careful not to wander around the Damascus Gate area alone after the markets close. Since this area is predominantly Muslim and Muslim women rarely wander outside unescorted, you will be considered fair game. Regardless of whether you decide to stay in the Jaffa or the Damascus Gate area you should be exceptionally cautious about leaving valuables and luggage unattended. Rip-offs are quite regular except in the most fort-like hospices.

Jaffa Gate Area

Christ Church Hospice, El Khattab Rd. (P.O. Box 14037, tel. 28 20 82). Enter Jaffa Gate and take the first right toward the blue "Poste" sign. Gate is on the left before the post office. Owned by the Anglican Church and run by Britons. Great location and spotless; surrounded by pleasant open courtyards. Lovely lounge with self-serve tea and coffee, books, and a piano. Fresh linen daily, laundry sinks, scrupulously clean showers and bathrooms. The Church itself was built in 1840 and was the first Anglican Church in the Middle East. Probably the best and safest place to stay in the area. Rooms and reception closed 9am-4:30pm; reserve a place early in the morning to beat the rush. 11pm curfew. Dorm beds $5, hearty breakfast included.

Swedish Youth Hostel, 29 David St. (tel. 85 49 80). Enter Jaffa Gate and cross the open area to David St. (the start of the market); hostel is on the left right before the Ramsis Restaurant. Small—one room for women (the nicest), one for men, and one co-ed. Abdul, the Arab owner who studied in Stockholm (hence the name), is extremely warm and concerned; he often gives short tours around the city walls and Mount of Olives. In return he asks for help in keeping the hostel clean. Free tea served all the time, free hot showers. Closed 10am-3pm; 11pm curfew in summer, 10:30pm in winter. $2 per night; stay six nights and the seventh is free.

Lutheran Youth Hostel, St. Marks Rd. (P.O. Box 14051, tel. 28 21 20). Enter Jaffa Gate, cross the square, turn right onto El Khattab and left onto Maronite Convent Rd.; at the intersection of St. Marks Rd., turn right and the hostel will be on your left. Spotless, in a great location, and beautiful: a gorgeous central courtyard with palm trees and fountain (unfortunately off-limits to guests). Best facilities in the Old City. Strict "early to bed, early to rise" policy: 9:45pm curfew, lockout 9am-noon. $3.20 a night.

Old City Youth Hostel (IYHF), 72 Ararat St. (tel. 28 86 11). Turn right at the intersection near the Lutheran Hostel on St. Marks Rd., then right again for about seventy yards. A good place to escape the general craziness of the Old City. Large, clean, and in a safe neighborhood. TV and lounge, but no kitchen. Usually crowded with school groups and soldiers; if you look like a student, you won't need a hostel card. 9-12 beds per room. Check-in 5-9pm, closed 9am-5pm; firm 11pm curfew (10pm in winter). $4 a night, including breakfast, supper, sheets and hot showers.

Petra Hostel, at the beginning of David St. (P.O. Box 14030, tel. 28 23 56). From Jaffa Gate, walk along to the left till you reach the Petra Moneychanger in the entrance to the hotel. (The moneychanger offers ridiculous rates, but can be convinced to give you the correct amount by a sternly raised voice.) Excellent location, but the dormitory rooms are up four flights of stairs. Somewhat dirty, very noisy, and unhelpful management. Flexible 11pm curfew (knock loudly anytime). $2 for a bed in the hall; private rooms $6 per person. Prices quoted may be twice as much as those listed here; bargain furiously or you'll be ripped off. Important variables are how good business is and how long you plan to stay (the longer, the better).

New Imperial Hotel, near Jaffa Gate (tel. 28 22 61). Enter Jaffa Gate and take the second left—you'll see the sign. A big, airy old place with Persian rugs, large sitting rooms, and comfy chairs. Arabian Nights-style bar. Plenty of privacy. Rooms with or without bath; reservations taken. No curfew. $12 per person, including breakfast, but bargainable.

Mr. A's, St. Girges St. From Jaffa Gate take a left onto Greek Patriarch Rd., then a right onto St. Girges. Mr. A's is a small, unmarked brown door on the right, just past Mahari Tailor Shop. Quiet hostel with a tiny courtyard. Laundry sink, hot showers, meager kitchen, and free use of refrigerator. Closed 8:45am-1pm; strict 9:30pm curfew (although longer stays sometimes get keys). $1.50 a night.

Lark Hotel, Latin Patriarchate Rd. (tel. 28 36 20). Above an expensive Armenian restaurant. Suitable for the savvy and skilled; the management will try to overcharge at every turn. Comfortable rooms, many with private bath. Flexible closing times. Don't pay more than $9 for a room; good haggling could get you $7 (initial quotes $10-15).

Alice's Youth Hostel, 42 St. Marks Rd., on the way to the Lutheran Hostel. Only for the desperate: cramped bedrooms, toilet, shower, and kitchen. Dejected flophouse atmosphere. Keep your wallet under your pillow in this place, folks. 11:30pm curfew. $3 per night.

Damascus Gate Area

Al Ahram Hostel, El Wad Rd. (tel. 28 09 26). Enter Damascus Gate and bear left onto El Wad at the fork; hostel is opposite the Government Hospital of Jerusalem and station III, Via Dolorosa. A fairly clean hostel with nice management and good location for the area, but often crowded. Free use of refrigerator. Hot showers, but Turkish, squat toilets. Some double rooms. Open 5am-midnight; strict midnight curfew. $2.20 per person, $1.40 to sleep on the roof. Breakfast $1.40.

JOC Inn and Teahouse, 21 Al Khanka St. (P.O. Box 14036, tel. 28 28 65). From Damascus Gate, bear right onto Suq Khan Ez-Zeit, then turn right onto Al Khanka St. Pretty stone architecture and open central courtyard above the tearoom. Watch your step—turtles often roam about. Moody manager. Small but clean rooms with 10-12 beds. Noisy during the day; the tearoom plays loud medleys of popular American tunes until 11pm curfew. $2.40 per person.

Armenian Catholic Patriarchate, El Wad Rd. at station III, Via Dolorosa (P.O. Box 19546, tel. 28 42 62). On the left at Station III through the heavy iron doors next to the marble frieze of Jesus. Very clean, plain, safe, and well-kept. Luggage storage for several days while you travel. Strict 10pm curfew. $5 a night.

Ecce Homo Convent, Eastern Via Dolorosa (tel. 28 24 45). Turn left onto Via Dolorosa just before the Armenian Catholic Patriarchate; Ecce Homo will soon appear on your left. Women only. Beds in semi-private cubicles with wooden partitions and curtains. Deep reverberating chords of organ music often resound through the stone hallways. $2.60 a night, including shower.

New Hotel (Hashimite Youth Hostel) 73 Khan Ez-Zeit Rd. (tel. 28 44 10). Carpeted and generally immaculate. Bathrooms have glistening, spotless porcelain. Quite a little haven in turbulent seas. $7 a night, $5 a night for longer stays. Breakfast $2.

Tabasco Youth Hostel and Tearoom, 8 Aqabat Et-Takiyeh. Et-Takiyeh is the first left off Khan Ez-Zeit after the Via Dolorosa. Plain, whitewashed dormitory rooms contrast harshly with the funky tearoom decor downstairs. Location (in the middle of the market) may be unsafe for unescorted women. Free tea downstairs and free showers, but meager kitchen. Loud music until midnight curfew. $2 a night, $1.10 to sleep on the roof.

Al Arab, Khan Ez-Zeit Rd. (tel. 28 35 37). From Damascus Gate, bear right onto Khan Ez-Zeit; on the left. Same neighborhood as Tabasco but on the main street. Ratty beds make sleeping bags a good idea; bathrooms are usable. On the whole, it could be much dirtier. Midnight curfew. $2 per night, sometimes more in summer. A few small rooms for $6 per person, but can be bargained down to about $5.

Al Kamal Youth Hostel, 23 Khan Ez-Zeit Rd. Al Kamal ("the camel") is dirtier than Al Arab, but has an eating area and a filthy kitchen for guests' use. Stone interior, large hallway, occasionally hot showers. Liveable, but barely. Midnight curfew. $3 a night, but try bargaining.

East Jerusalem

Lodgings in this section of town enjoy neither the interesting surroundings of the Old City nor the safety and convenience of the New City. Prices reflect these facts and are generally lower than elsewhere, but the sad condition of most of these places merits their bottom-dollar rates as well. Women should be careful in this all-Arab area: expect hassles. To get there, take bus #12 or 27 to Damascus Gate or walk (about fifteen minutes) from Zion Square up Harav Kook St. to HaNevi'im St., take a right, and follow it all the way down.

The first four hostels are listed in progression as they appear along the first block of Ha Nevi'im St. just outside Damascus Gate. During the early summer months, a large all-night watermelon market occupies the other side of the street, and there are many excellent Arab bakeries in the immediate area as well. These four hostels are all right near each other; check each of them yourself before you choose.

Faisal Youth Hostel, 4 HaNevi'im St. (tel. 28 21 89). All in all the best of the lot. Recently repainted and relatively clean, but the mattresses have seen better days. Great view of the city walls from the balcony of their ad hoc restaurant, which sells cheap coffee and beer. Stay away if you don't like Reggae. Young but spaced-out management. Separate dorm rooms for men and women, but couples can take a double for $8 a night. 11:30pm curfew. $2.40 per bed.

Palm Hotel, 6 HaNevi'im St. The state of this hostel depends very much on its current manager. Once a bordello, the place was run for a while by a cool American named Rick, more recently by a Frenchman named Jean-Luc. Similar to the Faisal: teahouse, music, crowded living quarters. Very hip. Doubles and dorms. Free tea and coffee. Midnight curfew; if you want to stay out late, ask in advance for an extension. $2.40 per bed.

New Raghadan hostel, 10 HaNevi'im St. (tel. 28 27 25). Only for the desperate—unquestionably the worst place in the city. Often completely booked during summer months by Arab groups (why is a mystery). The halls smell of urine and the fly-infested bathrooms are disgusting. The management is surly, too. $4 per bed; try to bargain the prices down (mention other hostels).

Jerusalem Student House (Ramsis), 20 HaNevi'im St. (tel. 28 37 33). High-ceilinged rooms with hard beds. Nice shower and adequate toilets. Free storage of valuables and luggage, refrigerator. You may wake with a few chunks of ceiling plaster on your blanket. 10am checkout, 11pm curfew. $2 per bed.

Cairo Youth Hostel, 21 Shekhem (Nablus) Rd. (tel. 28 68 26, but frequently out of order). One very long block up Shekhem Rd. from Damascus Gate, on the left. Very sordid-looking from the outside, but room quality as good as if not better than Faisal's. Terrible location past bus station, and dirty bathrooms. Poor English spoken. Midnight curfew. $3 per bed; stay six nights and the seventh is free.

Jerusalem Hotel, 4 Antara Ben Shaddad St. (P.O. Box 20606, tel. 28 32 82). From Damascus Gate, walk up Shekhem (Nablus) Rd.; on the first corner to the left, immediately past the bus station. Luxurious modern rooms, all with private bath. Pleasant courtyard and exceptionally friendly management. Luggage and valuables can be left for several days while you travel. Occasionally booked by groups in the summer; try to reserve in advance. If you are referred to the New Jerusalem Hotel, don't go—it's not worth the price. No curfew, but tell the manager if you plan to return late. $12 per person including breakfast.

Outskirts

If you want a quieter, more scenic refuge there are several pleasant IYHF hostels and camping grounds in the hills surrounding Jerusalem. Lodgings listed here are fifteen to thirty minutes by bus from the center of town.

Louis Waterman Wise Hostel (IYHF), 8 Pisgah Rd., Bayit Ve Gan (tel. 42 33 66). Take bus #18 or 20 to Mt. Herzl. A large (250 beds), beautiful hostel with a well-established reputation, though fairly new. Clean, and located in a safe neighborhood. Kitchen, but no utensils. Kosher dinners available for $2 dairy, $3 meat (very good food). 11pm curfew. Members $5.30, non-members $6.70, including breakfast.

Ein Kerem Youth Hostel (IYHF), off Ma'ayan St. (P.O. Box 17013, tel. 41 62 82). Take bus #17 to Ein Kerem, turn left on Ma'ayan St. and walk up the path. Smaller than Waterman Wise (90 beds), but in one of the most beautiful neighborhoods of Jerusalem. You'll be lucky to find a bed here in the summer, but it's worth a try. No curfew, but buses stop running at about 11:20pm.

The camping sites around Jerusalem are all beautifully situated and have excellent facilities, but they're also rather expensive ($4 per person if you have your own tent). All campgrounds have hot showers and telephones. 2-4 person bungalows are also available for about $8 per person. Although none of the campgrounds have kitchens, all will let you use a camp stove without charge.

Ramat Rachel Camping, 2km from central Jerusalem (P.O. Box 98, tel. 71 57 12). Take bus #7. Owned by Kibbutz Ramat Rachel; if you stay here you get a 50% discount on admission to Ramat Rachel swimming pool (open 8am-5pm, normally $5). Camping $5, $3 for students.

Bet Zayit Camping, Mobil Post Harei Yehuda (tel. 52 79 29), 6km west of Jerusalem. Take bus #51 from the Central Bus Station to Bet Zayit (ask to be let off near the Shekem department store). Free use of refrigerator; swimming pool admission $1.75 per day. Camping $5, $3 for students.

Mevo Beitar Camping, Mobile Post Ha'ela (tel. 91 24 74), 15km southwest of Jerusalem. Take bus #93 or 96 from the Central Bus Station (7-8 trips a day). Owned by Mevo Beitar Moshav. Small *mahkolet* (minimarket) on site and restaurant open all day. $.50 surcharge for use of pool (per day) in July and August; pool free at all other times. Camping $4 in July and August, $2.50 the rest of the year.

Food

Jerusalem may not be a gourmet's delight, but it offers a large enough selection of restaurants and shops to satisfy any taste. Vegetarians needn't worry, either: since Jewish Law forbids the eating of meat and dairy products together, vegetarian restaurants have always enjoyed a wide popularity. The only sad part is price: full restaurant meals cost an arm and a leg if you're resilient, and may even cripple your budget for life. Prices tend to be lower in the Old City, but the quality varies tremendously. Look closely before you choose. As in most Israeli cities, the most economical way to satisfy your hunger is to purchase your own food at outdoor markets and in large supermarkets. In the Old City, two huge Crusader rooms on the left side of David St. going down from Jaffa Gate house a thousand-year-old fruit and vegetable market. But the cheapest food is sold at **Mahane Yehuda Market**, between Jaffa Rd. and Agrippas. Fruit and vegetable stands line the streets and *mahkolets* (small grocery stores) with rock-bottom prices are everywhere. The Yemenite section, through the alleys leading east from Mahane Yehuda St., is the cheapest for produce, and the stalls along Ez HaHayyim St. sell the best *halvah* (a kind of sesame candy) you'll ever taste. On Agrippas, near the intersection with Mahane Yehuda St., three mahkolets specialize in canned goods. For those on the tightest budget, try coming to the market at closing time (around 7pm) when merchants lower prices shekel by shekel to sell off the day's goods. Those preferring a more suburban atmosphere can shop at **Super Sol,** on Agron St. near King George, or **Super Shuq,** 46 Jaffa Rd. In the basement of the Israel Land Development Square is another large market which, judging by the crowds battling inside, is terribly popular with Jerusalemites.

If you're in the Old City near Jaffa Gate and want a cold drink or a beer, walk out of the gate and half a block up Mamillah St. (directly across from the gate) and you will come to a little mahkolet on the left which sells drinks at prices much lower (about half) than the places inside the walls. For inexpensive and delicious fried meats, turkey roll, and salami, head for **Merkaz HaNakinik** on Dorot Rishonim St. off Ben Yehuda St. near Zion Square.

Fast food is ubiquitous in Jerusalem and tends to be both cheaper and healthier than the corresponding Western fare. The best deals are found at self-service felafel places where you can stuff your pita with as much salad as you want. Most of these places are easy to find and many are located in the New City on King George St. between Jaffa and Ben Yehuda. Felafel connoisseurs should try the tiny **Yemenite Falafel** at 48 HaNevi'im St. (no English sign). Some claim it's the best in Jerusalem. *Shisklik* (cubes of meat on a spit), *kebab* (ground meat also on a spit) and *shwarma* (roast lamb on a spit served in pita) all cooked over a grill are also easily found, but watch the quality of the meat in the Old City and Mahane Yehuda. Two of the best and cheapest places for shwarma in the New City are **Merkaz** (no English sign), on the corner of King George and Agrippas Sts. in the center of town, and **Melekh HaShouarma,** (no English sign either) on Agrippas St., right next door. Both of them charge about $1.40. If you miss cheap American burgers, stock up at the **Burger Ranch** halfway down Shelomzion HaMalka St.

Although popular, pizza is generally overpriced and rarely good. **Richie's Pizza,** on King George St., is a famous hangout for Americans, but the **Beit HaMa'aphian** (no English sign—across King George St. and to the right down Agrippas) has cheaper "pita pizzas" with a variety of toppings. Many travelers prefer **Pizzeria Rimini** to either of these; to sample the people's choice, stop in at the Rimini on King George St. or Jaffa Rd. Cheese, potato, and spinach *borekas* (triangular, savory filo-dough pastries) are the chief commodity at **Sami Borekas,** a restaurant chain labeled by many as Israel's McDonald's. One convenient Sami is at 44 Jaffa Rd., another is midway along Mahane Yehuda St. Even better, home-made borekas can be bought from a small smoked glass window (no sign; look for the Camel cigarette sticker) underneath Houminer's Department Store at 5-9 Bezalel St.

Jerusalemites take their *hummus* as seriously as they do their borekas, and everyone has his own favorite place. **Ta'ami,** 3 Shammai St. serves fine kebabs, steaks, and Turkish moussaka, as well as some of the best hummus in the city (open during lunchtime only, till about 4pm). **Rachmo** in Mahane Yehuda (up Ha'Armonim St. from Agrippas St.; corner store on right), also has excellent hummus, as does **Melekh HaHummous,** 6 Mordechai Ben Hillel St, which is closest to the center of town.

In the Old City, try your hummus with *fuul,* (another bean paste) or pine nuts at **Abu Sukri** on Al Wad Rd. (on your left, coming from the Damascus Gate, three hundred yards beyond the Armenian Catholic Patriarchate).

Israeli ice cream is probably a bit different from what you're used to; still, on a hot day its quite refreshing. In Jerusalem, the best flavors are found at **Kapulski Brothers,** downstairs in the Clal Center (97 Jaffa Rd., open till 9pm), while **Manolito's,** 36 Jaffa Rd., vends the creamiest (and most expensive) product. The two borekas stands which face each other across Jaffa Rd. at #44 and 45 also have good ice cream and remain open till late in the evening.

One warning: all Jerusalem restaurants close early Friday afternoon (around 2pm) and remain closed through Saturday, unless noted otherwise in the individual listing.

New City

The places listed below all offer full meals for about $5 and are all within a ten-minute walk from the center of town. One piece of advice: order water with your meal. At $1 a shot, soda or juice will wreak havoc with your budget without satisfying you.

Le Souffle, 5 Yedidiya St., off Koresh St. (tel. 22 55 51), around the corner from the Central Post Office. 33 different kinds of souffles, including artichoke, camembert, and brandy orange. Ask which vegetables are fresh that day. Large souffles are a bargain at $4; mini souffles cost $3. Fabulous desserts. Try their special "Paradise Cake" of thick chocolate mousse and whipped cream. Open Sun.-Thurs. 11am-10pm, Fri. 11am-2pm. Sat. night the restaurant opens two hours after sunset.

Sova, 3 HaHistadruth St. (tel. 22 22 66) is a perennial favorite. Zero atmosphere but great food. Huge meat meals, vegetarian meals even cheaper. Self-service policy allows you to eat on any budget. The gefilte fish appetizer is tasty, and if you're really hungry, try the chickpea-potato-meat-and-vegetable stew called *cholent* or *khamin.* Buy tickets in advance for Saturday and holiday lunches, or for Friday dinner (served until 8pm). Open Sun.-Thurs. 11am-4pm, Sat. 11am-2pm.

Bunny's Best Burger, at the top of Agron St. near King George. Mouth-watering hamburgers to give even the strictest vegetarians a run for their money. The special sauces, especially the garlic, will turn you into an addict. Bottomless salad bar can be combined with a burger for about $5.50, and the huge tuna platter will fill you up for half that price. Open till 11pm, Fri. till 3pm. Sat. opens 7:30pm.

Rosemary Vegetarian Restaurant, 9 Ezrat Yisrael St. (tel. 23 13 02), corner of 58 Jaffa Rd. Prettiest place in the area, with a beautiful enclosed garden on its streetfront. Delicious salads and savory pies ($3.50), also macrobiotic dishes and homebaked bread and cakes. Excellent value. Open Sun.-Thurs. noon-11pm, Sat. 7pm-midnight, closed Fri.

Heppner's Deli, 4 Lunz St. (tel. 22 17 03), just off Ben Yehuda. Inexpensive Jewish-American food, amusing decor. The chicken snitzel platter ($4.50) is particularly recommended. Open Sun.-Thurs. 10am-9pm, Fri. 10am-3pm.

Hameshek Restaurant, 14 Shelomzion HaMalka St. (tel. 22 62 78). The oldest and possibly the best of the city's natural foods restaurants, though no longer the cheapest. Excellent salad bar (comes with bread and various *garni*). Scrumptious home-baked cakes. Friendly, English-speaking service. Open 10am-10pm.

Tuv Taam Cafe, on King George St. next to Steimatsky's, not far from Jaffa Rd. Basically a Jewish diner, right down to the decor. Serves blintzes, fruit, omelettes, and the like, but the *piece de resistance* is the noodles and cheese with pineapples and raisins ($3.50). Open for breakfast. Closes Sun.-Thurs. at 11pm, Fri. at 3pm.

Ha-Ba'it (Home), 59 HaNevi'im St. (tel. 24 09 75). From Jaffa Rd. go up Nathan Strauss, take the first left and walk another seventy yards. Dairy and vegetarian restaurant serving luscious crepes with a wide variety of savory fillings for $4. Salads are also excellent. Large but attractive dining room with a few tables outside in the small surrounding garden. Open till 10pm.

The Little Gallery, 10 Bezalel St. (tel. 22 40 49). No English sign—look for a carved wood shingle. Crepes, soups, casseroles, and fruity desserts. Overpriced, but the wooden furniture and abundant plants offer some compensation.

Rasputin's, 6 Rivlin St., down from Jaffa Rd. on the right-hand side. Limited menu, but good fare. Cheese fondue for two $7, chocolate fondue for two $4. Mediocre chili at $2.75; the pasta is a bargain.

Tavlin, 16 Yoel Salomon St. (tel. 24 38 47). Soup, salad, bread, and butter for $4. Good pot pies and other dishes ($5). Food is fresh. Sometimes serves pecan pie with fresh whipped cream. Piped-in classical music and a wood-and-stucco interior create a cultured, well-seasoned atmosphere. Open Sun.-Thurs. noon-midnight, Fri. noon-3pm, Sat. 7pm-midnight.

A full meal at the following restaurants will probably cost $6-8, although the **Pie House, Zorba the Buddha,** and **Hevel HaValim** may be more expensive. All serve tasty, carefully-prepared meals and, despite the cost, are excellent values.

Mama Mia's, 18 Rabbi Akiva St. (tel. 24 80 80). Rabbi Akiva St. runs off Hillel St. opposite the Jerusalem Towers Hotel; turn right to Mama Mia's before you reach the end of the street. The best Italian restaurant in Israel has just found itself a larger and more beautiful home. Especially recommended: the delicious fettucini a la Mama Mia (about $5). Great homemade ravioli. Very popular place with a pleasant atmosphere. Open 11am-midnight.

Poire et Pomme Creperie, 7 HaMa'alot St. (tel. 22 19 75). One block from King George St. near Independence Park. A popular restaurant with seven tables, magnificent food, good prices, and a pretty decor. Always crowded. Open Sun.-Thurs. noon-midnight, Fri. noon-3pm, and Sat. 7pm-midnight. Fight the crowd for a roquefort cheese with nuts souffle crepe ($4) or a chocolate mousse dessert crepe ($3).

Mamma Leone's, 5 Hillel St. (tel. 24 27 67). Italian food in a quiet setting, for once. Portions won't make you burst, but you can order a variety of sauces on a variety of pastas.

Zorba the Buddha, 9 Yoel Salomon St. (tel. 22 74 44). Extremely unusual spiced vegetarian food. Don't be surprised to find a fried banana sitting alongside rice cooked in odd juices. Open Sun.-Thurs. 6pm-midnight, Sat. sunset-midnight, closed Fri.

Hevel HaValim (Vanity of Vanities), 34 Bethlehem Rd. (tel. 71 27 87). Serves both Israeli and North African dishes. You can sit at small tables in the garden, or on couches and cushions in the lounge. Expensive, but lovely. Try the tasty Moroccan *couscous* for $6. Plate of mixed starter salads $2.50. Music varies between oriental and jazz. Take bus #5, 6, or 21 until it first turns onto Bethlehem Rd. Open Sun.-Fri. noon-midnight.

The Pie House (HaTsrif), Eliashar St. near Zion Sq. (tel. 24 24 78). Go where the ISSTA sign points then up the stairs at the end of the street. Dinners cost $7-9 but are well worth the price. Vegetarian or meat dinner pies, fresh lemonade and juices, and salads. Bohemian atmosphere with taped jazz and folk music. Unfortunately the service is slow and they are occasionally intolerant of low-spenders. Open Sun.-Thurs. 8am-2am, Fri. 8am-5pm, Sat. 6pm-2am. Crowded by 8pm.

Old City and East Jerusalem

Uncle Moustache, in the Old City, left from Herod's Gate. Legendary as a hippie hangout. A cheap-eats place and not bad at that. If you've been here before, you're bound to note a slight decrease in standards. Still, for $3.25 you can get a full single-plate salad, rice, and meat dinner, and sit with some well-worn travelers. The legend began when Uncle Moustache had a shop and invited several long-haired youths in for tea. They turned down the invitation for lack of money, but when Uncle Moustache found out they were broke, he offered them a meal. Well, word got around. Open Sat.-Thurs. 8am-9pm, Fri. 8-11am.

Arches, 38 David St., straight down from Jaffa Gate and on the right. Call it "Old Reliable." Where else can you be sure of getting a traditional Middle Eastern meal for $5? The *mensaf,* a conglomeration of lamb, rice, and pastry, will transport you. You can get it every day 7am-9pm.

Abou Seif and Sons (Seven Seas Restaurant), Latin Patriarchate Rd., right near Jaffa Gate (tel. 27 16 97). Eat hummus with meat for $2.50 amidst stimulating aquatic scenes. Another traditional Middle Eastern restaurant. Open every day 10am-11pm.

The Quarter Cafe, above the corner of Tiferet Israel and HaShoarim Sts. (look for the sign overhead). Thanks to the miracle of self-service, you can eat Greek moussaka while gazing at the Mount of Olives without spending a fortune. Open Sun.-Thurs. 8am-6:30pm, Fri. till 3pm, closed Sat.

The Green Door. Not the real name, but coined by students to identify the place. A bakery run by Mr. Muhammad Ali (not the boxer). To get there, go through Damascus Gate, and take a sharp left up an alley at the point where the main road forks. You will find a small, bright green door opening into a dirty, cavernous room. Mr. Ali makes pita bread and does the baking for the whole neighborhood in his huge oven. He will make you a pizza with eggs, cheese, or whatever else he has that day. If you bring vegetables or meat, he will throw that on too—all for $1. He also sells soda for $.50. Open 4am-11pm.

Philadelphia Restaurant, East Jerusalem on Az-Zahara St., off Salah Ed-Din (tel. 28 97 70). Downstairs in a small mall, Phili serves reliably clean food. Meat dishes and kebabs for $5, or make a meal of 3-4 starter salads ($.75 each, $.50 extra for olives and pickles). Poor English.

Patisserie Joseph. Look for the sign inside Jaffa Gate. Inexpensive place for cokes, beer, fresh juice, and pastry. Their fresh pastries are great—make sure to find out what was made that morning. In the winter they serve *sahlab*, a homemade, hot pudding. Open Mon.-Sat. noon-9pm, Sun. 4-7pm.

Sights

Jerusalem's sights are rarely breathtaking, but they are rich in historical, archeological, and religious significance. You will find it worthwhile to do some advance reading and to seek out advice before sampling Jerusalem's many offerings. Go for guided tours when possible (many are free) and if you choose to explore on your own, pick up a good guidebook.

The **Jerusalem Plaza Hotel** (tel. 22 81 33) offers free walking tours in English daily: morning tours run Sun.-Fri. at 9am and Sat. at 10am; afternoon tours Sun.-Thurs. at 3pm. Pick up a schedule at the front desk. Meet in the lobby and from there you will share a taxi with others to the starting point (about $1). Tours last about two hours. The Plaza, on King George St. near Agron St. is easy to find.

Every Saturday at 10am (4pm also, in summer) the Jerusalem municipal government sponsors a free—and excellent—**Shabbat Walking Tour.** These tours have been held for many years now, and the guides are extremely interesting and well-informed. Meet at the Municipal Tourist Office at 34 Jaffa Rd. near Zion Square. *This Week in Jerusalem* lists the areas to be toured. Tours last about two and a half hours.

The **Society for the Protection of Nature in Israel** offers both free and paid tours daily. SPNI tours usually cost between $1.50 and $5.00 for a full day of hiking in the Judean hills or along unusual routes within the city. The guides on these "Off-the-Beaten-Track Walks" are excellent, making these perhaps the most interesting tours offered in Jerusalem. Details and a schedule of tours are available at the Society's offices, inside the compound at 13 Helena HaMalka St. (tel. 22 23 57). The office is open Sun.-Thurs. 9am-3:45pm, Fri. 9am-12:30pm.

Baruch Levin has long been known to young travelers as an excellent source of information on cheap food and accommodations. He also gives free tours of Jewish historical and religious sites. Meet him in the plaza before the Western Wall at 2:15pm Mon.-Thurs, or at 10am Sun., for an informative and fast-moving tour of the Western Wall, including its continuation into the Muslim Quarter and the excavations under Wilson's Arch. Baruch also leads Sabbath and weekday tours of Mea She'arim and arranges Shabbat meals for Jewish visitors. Call for details (tel. 28 61 42 or 53 21 31 ext. 1172—leave a message) or look for him at the Western Wall between 4pm and sunset (ask around—everybody knows him).

Two groups offer complete see-everything-of-note-in-four-hours tours. If you feel you must take one, **Walking Michael** leaves Christ Church (just down the street from the Christian Information Center) at 8:30am every morning except Sun. and charges $4. The **Jerusalem Through the Ages** tours begin Sun.-Thurs. at 9:30am and Sun., Mon., and Thurs. at 2pm in the courtyard of the Citadel. The tours have well-informed guides and are organized according to the period or subject of the sites. $7 per person, $5 for students.

It may sound strange, but Israelis often describe archeology as their national hobby, and **Dig for a Day** gives you a taste of what it's all about. Their programs (in English) are expensive but great: a day-long dig (on Herodion or at the Citadel) and day-before seminar costs $15, $12 for students. A full day seminar (no dig) costs $12, $9 for students. They are very popular with students and groups, so reserve a place in advance (tel. 24 75 25). For a very thorough tour of the Jewish Quarter, follow David St. (the shuq) from Jaffa Gate and make a right onto Jewish Quarter Rd. On the right you'll see an arcade and beyond that a sign posting times and prices of the tours.

The most interesting, unusual, and easy-to-follow guidebook is *Footloose in Jerusalem* (about $6.50) by Sarah Fox Kaminker. In addition to several detailed walks in the New and Old Cities, the book has excellent maps, good descriptions, important historical backgrounds, and illustrations. For a more humorous look at Jerusalem, buy **Marty's Walking Tours of Biblical Jerusalem** (about $4.50). The author, Marty Isaacs, outlines two itineraries which accurately reflect his extensive knowledge of the city, one on the Mt. of Olives, the other through the city of David. You might also want to take a look at *The Jerusalem Guide* by Giora Shamis and Diane Shalem or Niza Rosovsky's *Jerusalemwalks*. The novel *O Jerusalem* is both gripping and memorable, and will give you a feel for the attachment that some people have for this special city.The bookstore at the **Society for the Protection of Nature** is by far the best source of guidebooks for Israel and Jerusalem. Although ninety percent of their stock is in Hebrew, look carefully and you'll find the English language books. Or browse in **Bestsellers** and **Sefer Vesefel** for a good guidebook.See Practical Information for hours and addresses.

Free maps and pamphlets are available at the IGTO and at the Municipal Information Office. Also pick up a list of biblical references for visiting the holy land for $.20 at the Christian Information Center. The list is incomplete, but a good start. Also carry a small Bible with you; reading the Bible with respect to the places you visit may help you understand why they are so important to people.

When you enter holy places, you may be approached by guides who offer their services and expect a fee. To save arguments, set a price first—$.50 should be the limit. The best strategy is to wander over to a group that has its own guide and listen in. Tour guides do not mind this and usually appreciate interested listeners, so feel free to ask questions.

Most of the holy places in Jerusalem require modest dress. For women, this means knees and shoulders should be covered. The best solution is to carry a light blouse and skirt at all times which you can slip on over your shorts and T-shirt as needed. Women should also dress modestly in the markets to avoid being pinched. Many holy places, notably the Church of the Holy Sepulchre, also require men to wear long pants.

It pays to be adqequately prepared for the hot sun and the cool wind; the combination can dehydrate you and make you ill without your realizing it. A few walking tours cover areas with no drinking fountains or merchants—a canteen is helpful. Otherwise be sure to buy drinks along the way. A hat will also keep you cool, and prevent sunstroke. Get a cheap one in the market.

We have divided the many sights of Jerusalem into specific areas that are related historically or culturally. Sights are also grouped together according to their general location. You can buy a ticket book at the IGTO that cuts the prices of visiting the following five sights in half: Israel Museum, Rockefeller Museum, Holy Land Model, Tower of David, and Solomon's Quarries. Although these sights should probably be included in any visit to Jerusalem, the $4 book is uneconomical for students, who get reduced admissions anyway.

The Old City—Inside the Walls

Although the ancient walled city is but a small part of modern Jerusalem (only a square kilometer in size), its holy places, excavations, marketplace, and beauty make it Jerusalem's chief attraction. Wander in the windy, mazelike streets of the Old City—you'll make discoveries that are just as important as what you'll learn by taking tours. Try to get hold of Yoel Ben Natan's map of the Old City or at least Gabrieli's map of Jerusalem at one of the tourist information offices.

Jerusalem was originally a mountain city, but time and countless rebuilding have filled in the surrounding valleys and changed its boundaries. The city built by David thousands of years ago now lies almost entirely outside of the present walls. The Temple area, on Mt. Moriah, used to be protected on both sides by deep valleys. The valley of Qidron is still outside the east wall between Mt. Moriah and the Mt. of Olives, but the Western Wall plaza area is now located where the Cheesemakers' Valley once separated the Temple from the Upper City and Mt. Zion.

The present walls were built by Suleymein the Magnificent in 1542. There were once eight gates: one, the Golden Gate, has been closed since 1530 and is thought to lie over the Closed Gate of the First Temple, the entrance through which the Bible claims the Messiah will some day pass (see Ezekiel 44:1-3). Since the seven other gates open onto completely different parts of the city, be sure to pass through each one during your stay. **Jaffa** and **Damascus Gates** are the main ones: Jaffa Gate is the usual entrance from West Jerusalem and Damascus Gate serves Arab East Jerusalem. East of Damascus Gate is **Herod's Gate,** and even farther east, around the corner, **St. Stephen's Gate (Lions' Gate),** the beginning of the Via Dolorosa.

You can walk on all parts of the wall except for the sections between Herod's Gate and Damascus Gate and between Dung Gate and St. Stephen's Gate. Besides providing a great view of the Old City, this walk will give you an idea of the walls' military importance. The Jaffa Gate-Damascus Gate stretch of the City Walls are open daily 10am-4pm, sometimes longer (admission $.50, $.25 for students). Be sure to visit the new excavations near the Damascus Gate, which have uncovered one of two first century Roman Gates used for chariots (note the two small "ramp stones" on the threshold). The Damascus Gate itself was originally much taller, reaching down to the level of Hadrianic paving stones you see at the excavations. These form the beginning of the Cardo Maximus (see Jewish Quarter, below). Inside the Damascus Gate is a huge garrison hall with stairs leading up to the top of the walls. If you got on the walls at the Jaffa Gate, look for the tiny door labelled "Roman stairway" which leads into the excavations. When you walk along the walls, be careful of loose stones.

An excellent place to orient yourself is the **Citadel,** also known as the **Tower of David,** just on the right inside Jaffa Gate. Here you can see a beautiful thirty-minute audio-visual review of Jerusalem's history, a great introduction to the city (screenings in English Sun.-Thurs. at 9am, 11am, 1pm, and 3pm; Fri. at

9am, 11am, and 1pm). Afterwards, leave some time to climb the to (great view) and explore the conglomerate of structures from various pe in history. Open Sun.-Thurs. 8:30am-4:30pm, Fri. 8:30am-2pm; admission $1 $.65 for students (sometimes the student ticket is sold only at the entrance to the Citadel, and not at the slide show).

The Markets

The Old City's markets (*shuq* in Hebrew, *suq* in Arabic) offer everything from archeological artifacts (often phoney) to Bedouin clothing. The **Arab Market** begins inside of Jaffa Gate and extends throughout the Muslim Quarter. Its main thoroughfare is David St. About halfway down David St. on the left, are two cavernous rooms, the site of a fruit and vegetable market dating back to the Second Crusade. It's an excellent place to buy cheap produce.

At the end of David St., in the very middle of the Old City, is the three-laned **Armenian market.** It was once a single Roman avenue called **Cardo Maximus** but was later divided into three store-lined alleys by the Crusaders. Continuing north from the center street is **Suq Khan Ez-Zeit,** the **Olive Oil Market,** where spice, meat, and vegetable stalls provide a refreshing change from the usual tourist junk. Sweet shops abound on Khan Ez-Zeit Rd. The market continues all the way down Khan Ez-Zeit. If you turn right onto the Via Dolorosa (the Way of the Cross), you will come across small ceramics shops. Supplying all these shops with their wares is **Jerusalem Pottery,** an old company run by Armenians who make many of the beautiful ceramic street signs you see in the Old City. They make personalized plaques or door plates to order at reasonable prices, generally less expensively than any of the stores they supply throughout the Old City.

There are shops all along El Wad Rd. leading from Damascus Gate, and on HaShalshelet St. (the continuation of David St.). In fact, you will find shops all over the city, even in the Jewish Quarter. A large covered market selling old and exotic clothing lies right in front of the Temple Mount area on Suk-El Qattanin St. off of El Wad Rd. To see an old-time animal market, go to the northwest corner of the Old City on Friday mornings.

Rarely will you find genuine native handicrafts in the markets. Most of the goods sold are poorly-made souvenirs for tourists, although some beautiful, handcrafted products like inlaid backgammon sets, ceramics, olive-wood sculpture (be discriminating), pipes, and metal work are available. Be sure to bargain over everything: it is the way of the market. Almost all items can be found in several different places, so ask around to get a general idea about the price before you buy. Don't feel pressured if you think something is too expensive; you can almost always find it somewhere else. Don't bargain, however, if you don't intend to buy—you will be thrown out of shops or spat at. Also, try not to bargain for items that you're only half interested in. The merchants are masters at getting you hooked on an item by arguing over it. Merchants usually start by giving you a price two or three times above the sale price (although first quotes of eight to ten times an item's true value are not unheard of). As soon as you hear a price, contort your face to express amused disbelief, and state your own figure (a third to a half of his). When the seller tells you to forget it, walk out of the store; if you are not called back, either the salesman has spotted someone else, or your bluff has backfired—hardly a problem since ten other shops are bound to sell the exact same item. The secret is to be very firm and to avoid becoming overly attached to any one object. Above all, never let yourself be intimidated by the shopkeepers; they are professionals and will do almost anything to close a sale. Remember also to pay in exact change if

… a large, inlaid backgammon set is $13; for one of the … erywhere, $4. The "rare antiquities" sold in the mar- … orthless no matter how authentic the merchant claims … ey've been made to look. Don't buy drugs—dealer and … same person.

… and Western Wall

… **Wall** is part of the retaining wall that Herod built to support an en… ie Mount when he rebuilt the Second Temple around 20 B.C.E. The W… often called the Wailing Wall because Jews have come to this sacred plac… for centuries to mourn the destruction of the First and Second Temples and to tuck written prayers into the crevices of the Wall. The Wall can be reached by foot from Dung Gate, HaShalshelet St. (the continuation of David St.), or El Wad Rd. (during the day). About eight feet off the ground, a grey line marks what was the surface level up until 1967; about sixty feet of Herodian wall still lies underground. You can identify the Herodian stones by their carved frames or "dressing"; the stones that lie above were added by the Crusaders and by Moses Montefiore, the British Jew who tried to build up Jerusalem in the 1860s. Pre-1967 photos show Orthodox Jews praying at the Wall in a crowded alley; after the Six-Day War, the present plaza was built as a national gathering place.

The prayer areas for men and women are separated by a screen, as prescribed by Jewish law. The Torah scrolls are kept in an opening in the connecting building on the men's side of recently-excavated sections of the Wall. **Wilson's Arch,** located inside this large arched room, was once part of a bridge that spanned Cheesemakers' Valley, allowing Jewish priests to cross from their Upper City homes to the Temple (the arch is named for the English archeologist who discovered it). A peek down the two illuminated shafts in the floor of this room will give you an idea of the height of the wall as it originally stood. If you walk to the far end of the large vaulted chamber under the arch, you'll find a black door with a slit in it through which you can see more of the Wall disappearing into the darkness. The Wall continues in this direction through closed tunnels for over half a kilometer. Women can see some of these sights by entering a small arched doorway to the left at the start of the aisle leading down to the men's section of the wall and then winding their way through the excavated passageways (thought to have once connected the Citadel and the Mount) to the few stairs opening to Wilson's Arch. Women cannot, however, enter this room. The passage is open Sun., Tues., and Wed. 8:30am-3pm, Mon. and Thurs. 12:30-3pm, and Fri. 8:30am-noon. Enter through the archway parallel to the row of metal slats, which is in turn parallel to the wall.

Another way to see the excavations, along with sections of the Wall still in Muslim hands, is by taking Baruch Levin's daily walking tours (free—see Sights introduction). He sometimes even gets women into the Wilson's Arch room. Whether you go alone or with a group, remember it is strictly forbidden to smoke or photograph in the vicinity of the Wall during Shabbat (Fri. sundown to Sat. night).

Bar Mitzvahs occur at the Wall on Mon. and Thurs. mornings—often five or six at once—and are quite a sight, with the women keeping up a steady clamor of clucking and cheering at the railings and the divided screen. The crowds and dancing which bring in the Sabbath at sundown on Friday should also not be missed. Try to come at least once at night, when the Wall is brightly lit, the air cool, and the area quiet.

The recent excavations at the Southern Wall of the Mount the most important digs in the world. Archeologists have m from almost every period of the city's history. These excavati seen on a guided tour, so check the Plaza Hotel schedule (free) for the Protection of Nature tours (fee required). You can also v try to slip in with a tour group at the entrance by Dung Gate.

On a hill overlooking the Old City, the **Temple Mount** is a Christians, Jews, and Muslims alike. A little explanation can hel out the hodgepodge of religious sites. Christians regard the Temple Mount as the backdrop to the Passion. For Jews, it is significant as the site of the two great Temples of Israel. A sign at the entry ramp near Dung Gate warns Jews not to enter the Mount so as to avoid walking on the long-covered inner sanctum, the "Holy of Holies" forbidden to all save the High Priest, who entered only once a year to ask forgiveness for himself and for the Jewish people. Actually, no one is quite sure where the Holy of Holies stood within the walls, but since there's a chance of stepping on it, Jews avoid the area. (For the history of the First Temple and its destruction, see I Kings 5, 6, 8, II Kings 11, 12, 22, 25, and Lamentations.) The Second Temple, according to tradition, was exactly the same as its predecessor (except that no miracles were performed there). Each temple lasted only a few hundred years; each was destroyed on the ninth day of the Jewish month *Av*. The Talmud remarks of the Second Temple that "he who has not seen the building of Herod has never seen a handsome building in his life." A large, beautiful scale model of the Second Temple and the surrounding city on display at the Holy Land Hotel today serves as the next best thing to seeing the Temple itself (see New City sights below).

At present, two grand mosques dominate the Temple Mount: Israel's holiest, the silver-domed **Al Aqsa,** and its most magnificent, the golden **Dome of the Rock.** A feast for mind and eye, the complex is considered one of the three most important Muslim religious sites. The Dome of the Rock enshrines the rock upon which Abraham was to have offered Isaac, and from which Muhammad ascended to heaven at the end of his mystical Night Journey, recorded in the Qur'an. Both the Dome of the Rock and Al Aqsa were first built near the end of the seventh century, although Al Aqsa has been completely rebuilt several times (earthquakes). The beautiful tiles covering the walls of the Dome of the Rock were affixed by Suleiman the Magnificent, the same Sultan who built the city walls in the sixteenth century. Between the two Mosques lies a fountain called El Kas, where Muslims must wash before prayer. Built in 709 C.E., the fountain is connected to underground cisterns with a capacity of ten million gallons. On the right as you enter the Temple Mount from the ramp is the **Islamic Museum,** which houses a collection of relics taken from the mosques as they were restored (admission 30¢). Ahead on the right is a booth where you can buy an entrance ticket good for both mosques—admission $1, $.50 with student ID. At time of publication, visiting hours were restricted to Sat.-Thurs. 8-11am, due to the tragic shooting of several Arabs by a crazed ultra-nationalist Israeli soldier. Regular hours (in summer Sat.-Thurs. 8-11:30am, 12:15-8pm, and 4-5:30pm; winter 8-11am, 12:15-2:15pm, 3-4pm) may be restored in the near future. Closed Friday year round (all hours subject to change during Ramadan and other Islamic holidays).

The Mount is supervised by Arab policemen who speak neither English nor Hebrew, and who are annoyed by behavior inappropriate to their holy site. Avoid holding hands with members of the opposite sex, and remember to dress modestly. Also be aware that many sections considered off-limits by the police are not marked as such.

The Jewish Quarter

Before 1948, the Jewish Quarter contained numerous beautiful and ancient synagogues of great historical and religious importance. Unfortunately, during the six-month siege by the Arab League during the 1948 War, the synagogues, along with the rest of the buildings in the Jewish Quarter, were largely destroyed. Restoration work began with the unification of Jerusalem in 1967 but has since been slowed by the archeological discoveries made at virtually every turn of the shovel. Guided tours of this area are especially valuable, since the landscapes and sights change as reconstruction progresses. While the living areas in this quarter may seem sterile, you can get a feel for how well the style of the Old City has been preserved by wandering in and out of alleys and courtyards. (And you may get lucky and be invited in to see a home and its view of the Temple Mount.)

An excellent and worthwhile book providing a full historical account of each synagogue in the Quarter is *Synagogues of the Jewish Quarter* by Shimon Ben-Eliezer. The thin paperback also contains photographs of the synagogues before they were destroyed and is full of fascinating legends surrounding the sights.

The Jewish Quarter is in the southeast Quadrant of the Old City—the site of the Upper City during the Second Temple era. Although the Quarter can be reached either by entering Jaffa Gate and heading down David St. until you reach Jewish Quarter Rd. (take a right) or by climbing the stairs diagonally across the plaza from the Western Wall; once inside there is no easy way to navigate. Habad St. and Jewish Quarter Rd. (also called Street of the Jews) run north-south, flanking the site of Cardo Maximus, one of two main arteries through the Roman-built city. At the southern end of Jewish Quarter Rd. is a small square graced by a carob tree and an upturned grinding stone which marks the site of some of the bloodiest hand-to-hand combat in the 1967 war. Beit-El Rd. runs off east from here, winding its way along to *der Deutscher Platz* or **Kikar Ha'ashkenazim,** a street of rowhouses built by Dutch and German Jews in the 1800s. The most outstanding building on the street is the House of Rothschild, built by the Austrian Rothschilds in an attempt to reinvigorate the Jewish Quarter. The Rothschilds invited Jewish families to come and live here, but never more than three years. Now architects work within, rebuilding and redesigning the surrounding neighborhoods.

Back on Jewish Quarter Rd. you'll see an arcade of ritzy shops and, farther on, a colonnade of restored pillars to the right. The **Cardo Maximus,** Jerusalem's main drag in ancient times, is now undergoing restoration and drawing quite a bit of archeological attention. Across the way stands the so-called Broad Wall. Because so many buildings were uprooted here in the Six-Day War, archeologists had a field day poking around the sector some fifteen years ago. One of their great finds was the remnants of an ancient Jewish fortification. Some say it's so old it proves the Hebrews inhabited the area long before any other people. A single white stone arch soars above the ruins of the **Hurva Synagogue.** Once the focal point of the Jewish Quarter, the Synagogue was destroyed during the 1948 war and subsequent Jordanian occupation. The white arch that now marks the spot expresses the hope that this temple will rise again. For a more intact ancient building, try next door (and down the stairs) at the **Ramban Synagogue,** named after its thirteenth-century founder, who was expelled from Spain after winning a debate with a cleric set up by the Catholic Church on the relative merits of the two religions. A letter written by Ramban (displayed in the Synagogue) describes the state of the Jewish community in 1267, the year he arrived from Spain: "Only two Jews, brothers, dyers by trade, did I find." The Synagogue is open daily for mornin evening prayer.

Perhaps the most successful restoration in the old Jewish Quarter can be found at the old **Yishuv Courtyard Museum,** 6 HaHaim St. (cross Jewish Quarter Rd. from the Ramban Synagogue, go up the stairs, then look left for the tan and brown sign pointing the way). The Museum is set up like a house; each room exhibits an aspect of life in the Jewish Quarter before its destruction in 1948. Open Sun.-Thurs. noon-4pm, closed Fri. and Sat.; admission $.80, $.60 for students.

The **Four Sephardic Synagogues,** including the Synagogues of Rabbi Yochanan Ben Zakkai and of Eliyahu HaNavi, should not be missed. At the time they were built, Muslim law forbade the construction of synagogues taller than the surrounding houses. To attain the loftiness befitting a synagogue, these ancient places of worship were built in large chambers under the ground. Today the synagogues are still the historical and spiritual center of Jerusalem's Sephardic community, and religious services are held early every morning and evening. Of special note are the beautiful Spanish Torah arks carved from wood, and a chair supposedly used by Elijah the Prophet, both in the Eliyahu HaNavi Synagogue. You can reach the Sephardic Synagogues by walking south along Jewish Qtr. Rd. to the parking lot, turning left and then left again, and walking down the wooden staircase. (The synagogues are open to visitors Sun.-Thurs. 9am-4pm, Fri. 9am-1pm., $.25 donation requested.)

Also visit the picturesque ruins of **Tiferet Yisrael Synagogue**—if you can find it (look for red signs pointing the way near the Ramban Synagogue)—and some of the small synagogues and *yeshivas* (places of religious study) tucked away in alleys and courtyards throughout the entire Jewish Quarter. Young men and, in a few places, young women, live, pray, and study in these academic institutions for many years as they pursue Judaic learning. Several yeshivas, however, have begun encouraging Jews with little or no religious background to come for short stays. Try stopping in at **Aish HaTorah**—the guys at this yeshiva are mostly American and very open to visitors dropping in, even for only one class. To get there from the Western Wall, walk up the stairs to the Jewish Quarter and take your first left onto the street before the covered arcade (Beit Ha Sho'eva Rd.) All expenses are paid by the yeshiva for those who study.

The Christian Quarter and Via Dolorosa

In the northwest quadrant of the Old City, the Christian Quarter surrounds the Church of the Holy Sepulchre, which marks the place of Jesus' crucifixion, burial in the grave of Joseph of Arimathea, and subsequent resurrection. Many small chapels and churches of various Christian denominations, all claiming to be biblically significant, extend in all directions from the Church of the Holy Sepulchre.

The **Via Dolorosa** (the Path of Sorrow) is the route Jesus followed from the site of his condemnation to the site of his crucifixion. Each of the fourteen stations along the route—not all of them on the Via Dolorosa—marks an event which occurred during Christ's final walk: the last five stations are in the Church of the Holy Sepulchre. Although millions of pilgrims have come to Jerusalem to walk this very path, the stations are still poorly marked. The doors of the holy institutions responsible for maintaining the stations are generally closed, but as Matthew 7:7 advises, "knock, and it will be opened to you." Donations are frequently solicited for the upkeep of the grounds. On Fridays at 3pm, a procession of priests and pilgrims meets at St. Stephen's

...olorosa begins, to follow Christ's route and offer pray-... r a superb view of that area of the old city as well as of ... d Mount of Olives, turn onto Burj Laklak Rd. inside St. ... limb the stairs to the top of the city walls.

... Dolorosa, start inside of St. Stephen's Gate. On the right ... **Anne,** a twelfth-century Crusader church honoring Mary's ... vely grounds. (Open in summer Mon.-Sat. 8am-noon and ... till 5pm; closed Sun.) The Via Dolorosa begins under the **Chu... ...ters of Zion,** where excavations have revealed a large chamber thought to ... ontius Pilate's Judgement Hall. This is the first station; here Jesus was condemned to death by the Roman tribune. Herod's fortress, **Antonia,** is the second station, where Jesus received the cross. Others place the second station, probably correctly, where the **Chapels of the Flagellation and Condemnation** now stand (open in summer every day 8am-noon and 2-6pm, in winter till 5pm). Across the street, in the El Omariye School's courtyard, would be the first station. The other stations before the Church are located by signs on walls along the route. At station III, Jesus fell to his knees from exhaustion. He met his mother at station IV. These two stations are separated by a short strip of El Wad Rd. Simon the Cyrene helped carry the cross at station V. At station VI, Veronica wiped Jesus' face with her veil. (The Greek Orthodox Patriarchate has this veil on display—just find the street with the same name.) Jesus fell a second time at station VII. At station VIII, he consoled the gathered women, and at IX, he fell for the third time. The path then enters the Church.

The **Church of the Holy Sepulchre** marks the traditional site of Jesus' crucifixion (known as Golgotha). The location was first determined by Helena, Emperor Constantine's mother, during a pilgrimage in 326 C.E. Her clue was the Temple of Venus the Romans had built to cover the site. Excavations soon uncovered the tomb of Joseph of Arimathea and three crosses which, she surmised, had been hastily left there after Christ's crucifixion as the Sabbath approached. Constantine built a magnificent church over the site that was later destroyed by the Persians and then the Turks. The present building dates from Crusader times, though parts of the foundations are from the original fourth-century church. In 1852, after centuries of inter-faith conflict, the Ottoman rulers divided the Church among six Orthodox groups—the Protestants were left out—all of whom jealously guard their territorial rights. (By the same decree, two Muslim families still hold the Church keys by hereditary rights.)

The Church, one of the most revered buildings on earth, is also one of the most confusing. The diversity of the keepers lends the Church some of its fascination and color, but it also keeps the building in shambles and perpetually under construction; the large-scale repair work which needs to be done would entail a level of cooperation and even a pooling of resources which the denominations have been unable to achieve. The Church of the Holy Sepulchre is presently divided into two main parts—the rotunda under which the tomb lies, and the Greek Orthodox Cathedral—with many side chapels. There are two chapels below the ground level, one dedicated to Queen Helena and one at the point where the crosses were found.

Once in the Church, you can continue along the Via Dolorosa. Just inside the entrance door and up the stairs on the right is the **Franciscan Chapel** of station X where Jesus was stripped of his clothes. The next three stations on the Via Dolorosa are also at this level—the supposed site of Golgotha. The final station (XIV) is in the tomb. In the courtyard of the Church there are many small chapels of different denominations to explore. Guards at the Church of the Holy Sepulchre are especially strict about immodest dress. Men wearing short pants will be refused admission; women, as always, must keep their legs and shoulders covered. Open in summer every day 4am-8pm, in winter 4am-7pm.

The Christian Quarter has a few other interesting sights. **St. Alexander's Church** along the Via Dolorosa houses the Russian mission in exile; they hold prayers here for Czar Alexander III every Thurs. at 7am (the only time the church is open). Come see the excavations downstairs, open Mon.-Thurs. 9am-3pm; admission $.60 (ring bell). Across the street, with its entrance on Muristan St., is the **Lutheran Church of the Redeemer.** (Open daily 9am-1pm and 2-5pm. Closed Monday afternoon and Sun.) Head up the narrow spiral staircase to its bell tower for an incredible view of the city. Finally, for something completely different, take a left from the Russian mission onto Khan Ez-Zeit and you will find the two-tiered stairway leading to the **Ethiopian Monastery.** At the top of the stairs, go straight and enter the gray door with the green beam over it. You will find an Ethiopian village of mud huts and a small courtyard. The courtyard is located over part of the Church of the Holy Sepulchre. The Monastery is open all day.

The Armenian Quarter

Lying on the northern slope of Mt. Zion next to the Jewish Quarter, the Armenian Quarter seems like the mythical town of Brigadoon, a village unaffected by the forces of modernization. In the **Syrian Orthodox Convent** on Ararat St., the ancient language of the Talmud, Aramaic, is spoken both during services and in casual conversation. The Syrian Church believes this spot to be the site of St. Mark's house and of the Last Supper, while most other Christians recognize the Cenacle on Mt. Zion as the hallowed place. To get to the convent, enter Jaffa Gate and go right along the Citadel onto Armenian Patriarchate Rd. Take a left at St. James Rd. and another left onto Ararat St. The convent is down Ararat a bit on the right. (Open daily 9am-noon and 3:30-6pm; if closed, knock.)

The **Armenian Compound,** down Armenian Patriarchate Rd., past St. James Rd., is a city within a city where about one thousand Armenians live, learn, and pray. Once a large hospice for the reception of pilgrims, the quarter became residential after 1915, when refugees from the Turkish massacres settled there. The compound itself has schools, two libraries, a soccer field, a printing press (Jerusalem's first, dating from 1833), a cathedral, and a monastery. The gates to the compound close at 10pm each night and do not reopen until 6am, just as the Old City of Jerusalem was locked each night for security many years ago. The building over the Armenian Patriarchate Rd. is part of the Patriarch's residence. The church treasure is a famed collection of manuscripts, relics, and art that have been donated over hundreds of years by Armenian pilgrims. Sadly, the collection is rarely shown. Instead, visit **St. James Cathedral,** a fantastically ornate twelfth-century Crusader structure built over an eleventh-century Georgian church and an even more ancient structure beneath this. Inside are beautiful ceramic tiles—the Armenians make the new tiled street signs for the whole city—and scores of chandeliers, hanging lamps, and censers. In the courtyard before the entrance, be sure to notice the votive crosses. Pilgrims left these as gifts and according to convention each had to be different. Look closely and you'll see that each is unique, though more than two hundred decorate the walls of the compound. The oldest dates from the twelfth century. (Open for services Mon.-Fri. 3-3:30pm and Sat. and Sun. 2:30-3:15pm.)

You can enter the compound through the door on the left past the Cathedral heading down Armenian Patriarchate Rd. The library (open Mon.-Fri. 3:30-5:30pm) is on the left after you enter and the newly renovated **Mardigian Museum** is on the right. The exhibits are well-displayed in 40 rooms that are used to house seminary students. (Open daily 10am-5pm except Sunday; admission $1).

The Old City—Outside the Walls

Throughout the ages, the Old City of Jerusalem has taken many forms, from the Canaanite City of David, entirely outside the present-day Old City walls, to the large sprawling Jerusalem of Jesus' time, which covered an area containing both David's city and the present-day Old City. No visit to Jerusalem is complete without visiting the many historical and religious sites which lie outside the city walls. A walk down the **Mount of Olives,** preferably early in the morning or late in the afternoon, when the sun lights up the Old City, is a must. The journey is marked by many churches commemorating Christ's life (Mary's Tomb, the Garden of Gethsemane) and by a large Jewish cemetery. A visit to the old **City of David,** where archeological remains of early Jerusalem can be seen, is also fascinating. West of the City of David is **Mt. Zion,** the place of worship for Jews when the ancient temples were destroyed. **East Jerusalem** also has its share of antiquities; the Rockefeller Archeological Museum; another possible site of Golgotha called the Garden Tomb; and finally, an interesting underground set of tombs owned by the French.

The City of David

The City of David, the original Jerusalem of Canaanite times, lies on the ridge called the Ophel, south of the Temple Mount. The city was inhabited and called the Lower City until the destruction of the Second Temple in 70 C.E. King David conquered the Canaanite city by leading his army through the underground course of the Gihon Spring (Jerusalem's main water supply at that time) and then scaling the wall that leads to the inside of the city. In 701 B.C.E. King Hezekiah devised a system to prevent a recurrence of David's feat: he built a tunnel to bring the Gihon waters into the city walls and store them in a pool, thus hiding the entrance of the spring and keeping invaders such as the Assyrians from finding water as they camped outside the wall.

II Chronicles 32 describes the building of the tunnel and the subsequent siege of Jerusalem by Sankheriv, King of the Assyrians. According to the account, while Syrian armies advanced on the outlying towns and settlements of Judah, laborers in Jerusalem dug hurriedly from opposite sides of the tunnel in order to save time as the Assyrian army approached. They had no way of knowing whether the two tunnels would actually meet. Minutes before the arrival of the enemy, the laborers heard the picks and voices of their companions on the other side just a few meters off the mark. Although the joining place of the two tunnels cannot actually be seen (it's about half-way through the shaft) a guide can point it out to you. **Hezekiah's Tunnel** is open for those who wish to slosh through with a flashlight. Bathing suits or shorts will do—the water is rarely higher than 1½ ft. Sneakers or waterproof foot-covering is also a good idea. The wading takes about half an hour. Start at the Gihon Spring source on Derech HaShiloah, or Shiloah Way. Shiloah Way branches to the right from Jericho Rd., as you walk down into the Qidron Valley from the bottom of the Mt. of Olives. The tunnel ends at the Pool of Shiloah. You can then walk back to the road to your left and catch an Arab bus up the valley. (Open Sun.-Thurs. 8:30-3pm, Fri. 8:30-1pm, closed Sat.)

The City of David contains many archeological remains, consisting mostly of ancient tombs. All of these are spectacularly lit-up at night a great view from Ophel Rd., which hugs the outside of the Old Ci ern part. Churches and temples don't conveniently mark all the places here. If you follow Shiloah Way all the way down into the Kidron, you will find four tombs on your left dating from the Second T period. The first tomb seen is **Absalom's Pillar** which, by legend, is the tom of David's favored but rebellious son (II Samuel 15-18 has the story). Behind this tomb and to the left is the **Tomb of Jehosaphat.** A dirt path on the left as you head into the valley leads on to more impressive rock-hewn tombs. To appreciate the tombs and the remains of the city, you may require a guide. The Society for the Protection of Nature runs excellent tours of the entire City of David area (including Hezekiah's Tunnel) every Friday at 10am (about $1.50) and the Plaza Hotel brings slightly older groups here for free. If you decide to tour the area alone, at least take along a copy of *Marty's Walking Tours* (see Sights introduction).

The Mount of Olives

The Mount of Olives seems inappropriately named: only a few olive trees grace the slopes of the hill that rises across from the Eastern Wall. But the religious significance of this place has made the name endure. Beautiful churches now dot the slopes of the Mt. of Olives, marking the sites of Christ's triumphal entry into the city through the Golden Gate, of his teaching and betrayal, and of his ascension. That the Mt. of Olives has three gardens of Gethsemane (one Catholic, one Greek Orthodox, and one Russian Orthodox) brings into question the accuracy of these biblical sites, but does not detract from their beauty.

A walk down the Mount, with stops at the many churches, tombs, and gardens, is most enjoyable in the morning, when the sun shines at your back and permits clear views and pictures of the Old City. Since most churches are closed on Sun. and in the afternoon from about noon to 3pm, mornings are also the most practical time to come. You can take Egged bus #42 or 43 from Damascus Gate or Arab bus #75 from the station across the way to the top of the Mount. Get off at the Intercontinental Hotel (if you took the Arab bus walk five minutes from the last stop in the same direction the bus was going) and enjoy the incredible view of the Temple Mount—this view is especially spectacular at night, when Jerusalem truly deserves the sobriquet "the City of Gold."

One of the most impressive sights on the Mount is the **Russian Orthodox Church,** with its dominating Bell Tower of the Ascension (the highest point in Jerusalem). It is not generally open to the public—you can try to get permission to enter at the Russian Mission near the Old City (tel. 22 25 65). Winding your way north and up the hill you will come to the combined entrance gate for the **Church of the Eleona** and the **Church of the Paternoster.** (Open Mon.-Sat. 8:30-11:30am and 3-4:30pm, closed on Sun.) Both were founded by Queen Helena in the fourth century. The Church of the Eleona stands where Jesus revealed the "inscrutable mysteries" to his disciples. Destroyed over the years, the Church was reconstructed after archeologists uncovered the foundation in 1910. The Church of the Paternoster commemorates the first statement of the Lord's Prayer ("Our father who art in heaven . . ."), which is written in many languages inside the Church. The Chapel of Christ's Ascension is further north along the road.

Two paths lead down the Mt. of Olives, but the one that descends from near the Intercontinental will lead you to most of the important sights. As you descend, on your left you will first see the **Tombs of the Prophets** Malachi, Haggai, and Zechariah, open daily 9am-3pm, closed Sat. and holidays (the groundskeeper can show you around for a fee at other times), then the **National Cemetery,** and the **Common Grave** of those who fell fighting for the Jewish Quarter during the 1948 War (the ages of the boys who died are not in Hebrew). Behind and below them stretches an immense **Jewish Graveyard,** the oldest in the world, as well as a resting place for many modern and ancient Jewish heroes.

On the right side of the path are several interesting churches. The magnificent tear-shaped **Basilica of Dominus Flevit,** meaning "the Lord wept" (Luke 20:41), is open daily 8-11:45am and 3-5pm, though a priest may come to let you in at other times if you ring the bell-rope. Excavations of early Canaanite tombs are on the grounds. Further down, on your right, stands the impressive **Russian Church of Mary Magdalene,** with its seven golden cupolas. Built by Czar Alexander III in 1888, this church is open only Tues. and Thurs. 9am-noon and 2-4pm ($.30). If you continue along the same path, you'll come to the **Church of All Nations;** the garden inside the iron door is one of several claiming to be the Garden of Gethsemane. This is purportedly where Jesus spent his final days in prayer and was ultimately betrayed by Judas (Mark 14:32-42). The huge, beautiful mosaic on the facade of the church shows Jesus bringing peace to all nations of the world. (Open April-Oct. 8:30am-noon and 3pm-sunset; Nov.-March 8:30-noon and 2pm-sunset). A quick right at the foot of the road directly ahead of the church leads to the **Tomb of Mary.** This eerie tomb receives light only from the door and candles. Greek Orthodox, Armenians, Syrians, and Copts all share in the upkeep. (Open 6:30am-noon, 2-6pm, closed Sun.)

Mt. Scopus, called in Hebrew *Har HaTzofim,* lies north of the Mount of Olives and is home of both the Hebrew University and the famous Hadassah Hospital. Between 1948-67, Mount Scopus remained a garrisoned Israeli enclave in Jordanian territory. Its summit offers magnificent panoramic views not only of Jerusalem but also of Jordan, which lies to the east.

The Rockefeller Museum, Three Tombs, and the Biblical Zoo

The **Rockefeller Archeological Museum** (tel. 28 22 51) records the history of Palestine by exhibiting relics from each major period in chronological order. For those interested in volunteering for one of Israel's many digs, try mumbling "archeology, volunteer, dig" to the gatekeeper at the side entrance to the museum, who'll probably respond by giving you a list of digs with application procedures. The person to contact for detailed information is Mrs. Marta Retlig (tel. 28 51 51), but she is only in the Museum during the morning hours. (Haya Fisher at the Pilgrimage, Youth, and Student Division of the IGTO (tel. 23 72 11) is also an invaluable source of information on archeological digs and other student work and study programs). A library and pleasant garden are within the museum complex. The Museum is on Suleiman St. east of Herod's Gate. Open Sun.-Thurs. 10am-5pm, Fri. and Sat. 10am-2pm; admission $2, $1.50 for students. Every Friday at 11am you can take a guided tour of the complex.

If you leave Damascus Gate and head half a block up Shekhem (Nablus) Rd., you will see a sign leading to the **Garden Tomb.** The Garden is considered another possible site for Golgotha because of a tomb found there and the skull-like look of the hill it is built on (Golgotha means skull in Hebrew). But no matter what you believe, you will en... the tomb and the courtesy of the inte... (and humorous) free tour during the sum... 12:30pm and 2:30-5:30pm; closed one hour...

If you continue walking on Nablus Rd., p... to the right) and the intersection with Salah E... French sign indicating the gate of the **Tomb o...** thought that the Judean kings were buried here, ... that the tomb was built by a Mesopotamian queen f... to Jerusalem. Enter the huge forecourt and then head... the burial chamber. Inside, you can buy a candle and e... though the inner maze is hardly as large as you might e... ...ooms are plain and uninteresting. The Tombs are open daily 8:3...

As if you'll ache for more after crawling around these tw... ...bs, take bus #2 or 39 to the north of Jerusalem and get off at Sanhedriyya. Nearby, halfway up HaSanhedrin St. off Yam Suf St., you'll find not only a pretty park, carpeted with pebbles and pine needles, but also the **Tombs of the Sanhedrin.** In ancient times the Jewish people established a high court/senate composed of esteemed sages and leaders. The body, known as the Sanhedrin, ruled on all sorts of grave legal matters and even reviewed the case of Jesus. Since membership in the senate conferred special prestige, separate burial areas were designated for the corpses of the great men. The tombs are more finely carved than the Tomb of the Kings, but are similarly arranged as catacombs. You'll see several tomb-like facades in the park, but the main one has a triangular pediment above and is close to Yam Suf St. Open Sun.-Fri. 9am-sunset. If you continue up HaSanhedrin St., turn right onto Bar-Ilan St., and walk up several blocks, you'll come to the **Biblical zoo** on the right. For a city the size of Jerusalem, it's a large collection of exotic animals, many of which are mentioned in the Bible—the appropriate passages are posted on each cage. Open every day 8:30am-sunset (buy tickets for Saturday in advance); admission $2.50, $1.50 for students.

Back near the Old City walls (midway between Damascus and Herod's Gate) are **Solomon's Quarries**—a great place to escape the midday heat. In these cool caves, extending about 250 yards under the Old City, workers are thought to have quarried limestone for the building of ancient Jerusalem. (Open Sun.-Thurs. 8am-4:30pm, Fri. 8am-2pm; admission $.50, $.25 for students.)

Mount Zion

Mount Zion sits outside of the city walls opposite Zion Gate and the Armenian Quarter, although it has been inside the city walls at various times since the Second Temple era. From 1948 to 1967, it was part of the no-man's land separating East and West Jerusalem; the bombshell-marked gate and buildings indicate that peaceful contemplation of the divine has not been the only activity on the Mount. Mt. Zion has long been considered the site of the Last Supper and the Tomb of David (though recent archeological evidence suggests otherwise). To reach these sights, leave the Old City through Zion Gate. Go straight, bearing right at the double door marked "Custodia Terrae Sanctae," and at the fork in the road, go to the left. The entrance to **David's Tomb** is on the other side of the building (bear left at the "Custodia Terrae Sanctae" door). Under the **Coenaculum** is the study room of the **Diaspora Yeshiva.** The scholars are always happy to discuss their life at the yeshiva as well as the importance

…oks of Moses) and Talmud (a compendium of Jewish law). …ricans. Every Saturday night singing and live music in **Asaf's** … the entrance to David's Tomb, mark the end of another Sabbath; all …rs are welcome (see Nightlife).

When you enter to visit David's Tomb, an Orthodox Jew may start guiding you around the whole complex of sights, expecting 50 cents to a dollar at the end. Tell him you are a poor student, but give something if you use his services. Although important for religious reasons, the tomb is essentially an empty room. Above the red velvet-covered tomb in the small cave, silver crowns (not always displayed) represent the number of years since Israel has gained independence. A new crown is added each year. For a fabulous view of the Old City, walk straight through the greenish courtyard, turn left, and take the stairs up to the top of the minaret. David's Tomb is open Sat.-Thurs. 8am-6pm, Fri. until 2pm; in winter closed an hour earlier each day.

The **Chamber of the Holocaust,** directly opposite the entrance to David's Tomb, commemorates the many Jewish communities destroyed during World War II. Slideshows (at 11:30am, 1:30pm, and 3pm) document more recent manifestations of Anti-Semitism (open Sun.-Thurs. 9am-5pm, Fri. 8am-2pm; admission free to museum, but slideshow costs $.75). The **Palombo Museum,** also nearby, displays the work of the famous sculptor (open irregular hours, but usually in the morning; admission is free).

The huge **Basilica of the Dormition Abbey** lies off the right fork of the road leading to the Coenaculum. This massive structure has a beautiful floor mosaic depicting the prophetic tradition. Descend to the crypt, where the artwork in the niches is striking (especially that given by the Ivory Coast Republic) and the figure of Mary sleeps peacefully in the center. (Open 7am-noon and 2-7pm). Guided tours of Mt. Zion will open up the vast history and meaning of the area to you. The historical sights by themselves are not very exciting. Buses #1 and 38 run between Mt. Zion and Jaffa Gate (#1 goes through Mea She'arim to the Central Bus Station, #38 goes to the center of town).

The New City

Since the first Jewish pioneers moved timidly outside of the protective walls of the Old City in 1860, a burgeoning modern city has taken hold in the west of Jerusalem. Despite large-scale immigration resulting in the city's rapid growth, a decree insures that all its buildings are still faced with the golden Jerusalem stone and the old neighborhoods together with the new make for a pleasant and cool modern city. One of Jerusalem's features is its highly international composition. As you explore, you'll encounter entire neighborhoods of Moroccans, Russians, Yemenites, Germans, and Americans.

One of the outstanding sights in Jerusalem is the **Israel Museum** (take bus #9, 16 or 24). The museum is actually a magnificent collection of different museums. Start at the **Archeological Museum,** a beautifully laid-out guide to thirty thousand years of human habitation in the Fertile Crescent—the area between ancient Mesopotamia and Palestine. The exhibit will explain much of the ancient history of the area. Proceed next to the **Art Museum** which has an excellent collection of ancient and modern art, including works of the Impressionists and Dutch masters, reconstructed synagogues, typical Venetian and English parlors, and an anthropological exhibit of South Sea culture. The **Judaica wing** displays Torah scrolls, menorahs, and other interesting ritual objects from Jewish communities throughout the world. Outside, the **Billy Rose Sculpture Garden** contains the sculpture of such modern masters as Moore and Picasso; try to come on a Tuesday night when the exhibit is il-

luminated. Be sure to pick up a schedule of
Museum so you can enjoy the garden without
at the **Children's Museum;** it's a fascinating plac

Above all, do not miss the **Shrine of the Book,** w
remarkable archeological finds of our day: the De
the building resembles the covers of the pots in whi
two thousand years in the Caves of Qumran nea
Wilson's book *The Dead Sea Scrolls* gives a matc
covery and significance of the scrolls. Dating from the
to 70 C.E. and belonging to a mystical, ascetic cult calle
the scrolls contain sections of the Old Testament almost ... oks
that came down through the hands of countless Jewish sc ... scrolls are made more significant by the belief that John the Baptis... perhaps Jesus belonged to the Essenes sect. Unfortunately, the exhibit is marred by poor lighting, poor explanation, and the tendency not to mark clearly which scrolls are originals and which are copies. The Israel Museum is open Sun.-Thurs. 10am-5pm, except on Tuesdays when the main building is open 4-10pm and the Shrine of the Book is open 10am-10pm; Fri. and Sat. open 10am-2pm. Free general guided tours of the Museum in English are on Sun., Mon., Wed., and Thurs. at 11am, Tues. at 4:30pm. There is also an in-depth tour Mon. at 3:30pm. Admission is $3.50 for Museum and Shrine, $2 for Museum only; $1.50 student admission is good for both Museum and Shrine. $2.25 student annual membership gives you unlimited entrance to Israel, Rockefeller, Tel Aviv, and Haifa Museums, as well as discounts on programs at the Museum. Tickets for Sat. and holidays must be purchased in advance. For museum information call 63 62 31.

A five-minute walk from the Israel Museum is the **Knesset,** Israel's Parliament. If you wish to see the Knesset in session, come on Mon. or Tues. 4-9pm or Wed. 11am-1pm. Make sure to bring your passport to get in. The debates are in Hebrew or Arabic. On Sun. and Thurs. 8:30am-2:30pm, you can take free tours of the Knesset building, which include an explanation of the Israeli system of government and a look at the Chagall tapestry and the mosaics adorning the building. Take bus #9 or 24.

Beyond the Knesset to the southeast lie four sights that, taken together, express much of the history and beauty, horror and hope that provide a backdrop to the modern state of Israel.

Furthest away are the **Chagall Windows,** depicting the twelve tribes of Israel in enchanting, stained-glass designs based on Genesis 49 and Deuteronomy 33. The windows, housed in the Hadassah Medical Center (not to be confused with Hadassah Hospital on Mt. Scopus), each contain rich symbolism and history. Take the free guided tours offered daily except Sat. at 8:30am, 9:30am, 10:30am, 11:30am, and Sun.-Thurs. at 12:30pm (meet at the Kennedy Building, (tel. 41 63 33). To get to the windows, take bus #19 or 27.

Yad Vashem (tel. 53 12 02) is the most interesting and powerful of Israel's Holocaust museums. You really shouldn't leave Israel without seeing it. Designed so that the facts and events of the Holocaust follow the chronology of World War II, the Museum exhibit ends in a simple and moving memorial (housed in another building). The surrounding gardens were planted in memory of non-Jews who risked their lives to save Jews during World War II. (Open Sun.-Thurs. 9am-5pm, Fri. 9am-2pm; admission free). Take bus #18, 20, or 39.

The **Holy Land Hotel** has a scholarly and dramatic model of the Second Temple. It offers a good perspective on the Old City sights you have seen. (Open daily 8am-5pm, one hour less in winter; admission $1, $.50 for stu-

Mt. Herzl, located near Yad Vashem, is a pretty park and ... the founder of modern political Zionism, Theodore Herzl. The ... useum contains documents and records of early Zionism. (Open Sun.-...s. 10am-5pm, Fri. and Sat. 9am-1pm, longer hours in summer, admission ...ree.) Bus #12, 13, or 21 will take you to Mt. Herzl and nearby Yad Vashem, but only bus 21 goes to the model.

Much of the enchantment of Jerusalem derives from the character of its individual neighborhoods. **Mea She'arim** is the world's only remaining example of the Jewish *shtetl* communities which flourished in Eastern Europe before the Holocaust. Its inhabitants still dress in the East European garb of two centuries ago. In the old section, around the eastern part of Mea She'arim St., the houses are arranged in blocks facing inward around central courtyards, originally for purposes of defense and community insularity. Unfortunately, this limits what the casual tourist can see. Consider taking the free tours given by Baruch Levin (see Sights introduction).

Mea She'arim is probably the cheapest place in the world to buy Jewish books and religious items. Bargaining is the rule for religious objects; try the stores on the easternmost stretch of Mea She'arim St. For books, however, you'll want to look in the small, untouristed shops selling exclusively literature. One such store, **Pe'er HaTorah** (no English sign), is on 7 Mea She'arim St., just east of the intersection with Strauss Rd., and has absurdly low prices on Hebrew-only prayer books, Bibles, and other books of Jewish Law. By the way, Mea She'arim also has some of the best bakeries in the city; most remain open all night on Thursdays, baking *challah* and cake for the Sabbath. The bakery next to the Pe'er HaTorah book store has excellent apple strudel while the one at 15 Rabbenu Gershom St. (off Yehezgel) bakes great *borekas* and chocolate rolls.

The people of Mea She'rim are very religious and devote their whole lives to studying the Torah and living according to its laws. Although most are poor and live in crowded conditions, they are remarkably hospitable, and will often invite strangers into their apartments for Sabbath dinner. But Mea She'arim also has its extremists, and although few in number, they are vocal and receive a good deal of publicity. Two sects in particular, the Neturei Carta and the Satmar Chassidim, oppose the current Israeli government on the grounds that it violates Jewish law, based on traditional religious doctrine. In Mea She'arim, one famous and recurring piece of graffiti states, "Judaism and Zionism are diametrically opposed."

Women must dress modestly in Mea She'arim (as the Torah requires); as always, arms and knees should be covered. Men must wear long pants. Courtesy demands that visitors respect these requirements. Always ask before you photograph; religious law forbids the practice, and often the residents of the Mea She'arim consider photography a serious invasion of their rights and privacy.

The neighborhood of **Zichronot,** just south of the Mahane Yehuda market, is also crowded, poor, and religious. Its residents, however, rather than being immigrants from Eastern Europe, are Sephardic Jews, from Yemen, Persia, Turkey, and Morocco. In contrast to the bookstores and silversmiths' which line the streets of Mea She'arim, here you'll see barber shops, blacksmiths, and sandal-makers.

If Yad Vashem has the final word on the Holocaust in Europe, the **Museum of the Potential Holocaust** spells out anti-Semitism in the United States and discusses the possibility of similar annihilation in America. Brought to you by the Jewish Defense League, or at least assorted members, the museum presents the problem by leading visitors on a guided tour through its collection of racist and anti-Semitic literature. Located at 33 Ussishkin St. (tel. 69 05 55), around the back. Tours Sun.-Thurs. 1pm, 2pm, 3pm, and 4pm; admission is $1.20, $1 for students.

In the southern part of town across from Mt. Zion and the Armenian Quarter of the Old City is the restored neighborhood of **Yemin Moshe,** also known as Mishkenot Sha'ananim. It was here that Sir Moses Montefiore, a wealthy English Jew, first managed to convince a handful of residents from the Old City's overcrowded Jewish Quarter to spend occasional nights outside of the city walls. In order to strengthen the settlers' confidence, Montefiore built a small compound with crenellated walls resembling those of the Old City and a stone windmill, both of which can still be seen today. Inside the windmill a small, free museum is dedicated to Moses Montefiore for his persistent efforts, which eventually initiated Jerusalem's New City. (Open Sun.-Thurs. 9am-4pm, Fri. 9am-1pm.) This beautiful neighborhood is now one of the most exclusive in the city, and has become somewhat of an artists' colony. The **Wien Gallery,** 18 Malkhi St., is particulary good (open Mon.-Thurs. 11am-1pm and 4-7pm, Fri. 10am-3pm). Browse through works of Israeli artists and the great masters, which sell for thousands, and perhaps ruminate over the masters' unsigned, limited edition works, which sell for one hundredth the price of the others. The gallery can be reached by bus #6, 18, or 30 and is only a short walk from the Jaffa Gate. A short walk from Yemin Moshe is the West Jerusalem YMCA, with its museums, athletic facilities, and panoramic view of Jerusalem from the tower.

Before the Six-Day War, **Ammunition Hill** was Jordan's most fortified strategic position in the city, commanding much of northern Jerusalem. Taken in a bloody battle by Israeli commandos, the Hill now serves as a memorial to those soldiers who died in the 1967 conflict. The somber, architecturally-striking museum, housed in a reconstructed bunker, gives an historical account of the 1967 battle for Jerusalem using maps, photos, and a Hebrew-English text. (Open Sun.-Thurs. 9am-5pm, or until 7pm during July and August, Fri. 9am-1pm; admission $.35; accessible to the handicapped). Buses #9, 25, and 28 let you off at the foot of the hill. There is a great view of the city at the top.

If Israel's modern struggles interest you, there are two more sights you should visit. The **Hall of Heroism** museum, inside the Russian compound, commemorates the work of Israel's underground movement in the pre-1948 struggle against British domination. Most of the figures lived and died in violence, illustrating both their fierce commitment to building a Jewish state and the iron hand with which the British ruled. In fact, the hall itself was converted by the British from a Russian building erected by pilgrims to Jerusalem's desolate main prison. Open Sun.-Thurs. 9am-4pm, Fri. 10am-1pm; admission $.60, $.40 for students. Enter through Heshin St., just off Jaffa Rd.

Slightly less compelling but more relevant, the **Tourjeman Post** museum recounts Jerusalem's history from its wrenching division in 1948 to its dramatic reunification in 1967. The building, once called the Tourjeman Post, somehow withstood severe shelling during the War of Independence and became an Israeli command post when the Jordanian border ran across the street from 1948 to 1967. Nearby stood the now-dismantled Mandelbaum Gate, the only passage across the old Jordanian-Israeli border. Open Sun.-Tues. and Thurs. 9am-3pm, Wed. 9am-1pm and 4-7pm, closed Fri. Follow Shivtei Israel St. away from the old city and turn right onto Hel Handassa St. (the continuation of Shmuel HaNavi St.). The museum will be on your right.

Nightlife

Jerusalem's magic does not stop at sundown. In the evening, especially in summer, the New City pulsates with excitement as crowds of students, tourists, artists, and citizens mingle in the streets and in the town's many cafes, theaters, and concert halls. The sights dominate the visitor's perspective during the day, but the personality of this special city comes out at night as people relax and folk culture bursts out all over the city. Find a hostel with a midnight curfew or later, and explore.

Every night, the sixteenth-century walls of the Old City are lit to a golden hue, transforming it into a medieval fantasy world. A walk along the walls between Zion Gate and Dung Gate can be spectacular at night, but the path is uneven and you must be careful even when there's a full moon. The bar at the Intercontinental Hotel on the Mount of Olives offers a mountain-top view of the walls, the Temple Mount, and the surrounding sprawl of the New City lights (take bus #42 or 43). The terrace of the grand King David Hotel offers another lovely view of the walls (King David St.)

The cultural fare, like the city, is diverse without being overwhelming. The **Jerusalem Symphony** performs frequently at the plush **Jerusalem Theater** on Marcus David and Chopin Sts. (tel. 66 71 67). The theater also hosts numerous cultural events such as plays, dances, lectures, concerts, and a weekly film festival each Friday afternoon at 2:30pm (tickets only $2). Similar events are also held at the **Israel Museum** (tel. 63 62 31) and at the **Hebrew University** campuses of Mount Scopus and Givat Ram. Built by the Turks in the 1880s as a caravan stop, **the Khan,** across from the railway station, houses a small, intimate theater, an art gallery, and an immensely enjoyable nightclub. It's rarely frequented by tourists, but its concerts and plays are well known among local residents. Finally, if you have the opportunity, attend a rock, jazz, or classical performance at the **Sultan's Pool**—a beautiful outdoor amphitheater named after Sultan Suleymein the Magnificent, the Ottoman ruler who repaired the ancient aqueduct in 1536. Your best guide to all Jerusalem cultural events is the entertainment supplement to Friday's *Jerusalem Post*. Also contact the various tourist information offices; most have free publications which list the city's various evening activities, such as *Your Jerusalem, This Week in Jerusalem,* and *Hello Israel.*

Ballet and Israeli folk dancing convey more of the city's cultural rhythms; you can either watch or dance almost every night. The following four places offer folk dancing free or for a nominal fee (about $.50): **Moadon 12½,** amidst the Resnick dorms of Hebrew University's Mount Scopus campus, has open dances on Sunday nights (tel. 88 26 70, bus #9 or 28); **International Cultural Center for Youth** (ICCY), 12a Emek Refaim St., offers dancing events every Wednesday evening at 8pm (tel. 66 41 44/5/6, bus #4 or 18); the **House for Hebrew Youth** (YM-YWHA), 105 HaRav Herzog St., conducts classes on Thursdays and dances on Saturday nights (tel. 66 61 41, bus #19); and free outdoor dancing takes place in the **Liberty Bell Gardens** on Saturday nights in summer beginning at 8:30pm.

Some other night spots are:

Tzavta, 38 King George St., behind the parking lot (tel. 22 76 21). A small music-theater club with nightly programs in English. See the schedule of events out in front or ask in the IGTO. Friday evening screenings of repertory films (buy tickets in advance). Tickets $2-5, depending on the event, but there is always a sizable student discount. Visiting musicians and experienced actors are invited to audition.

Pargod, 94 Bezalel St. (tel. 23 17 65). A very small club also offe entertainment. Wed. nights and Fri. afternoons are devoted to live jazz. . open most nights 9pm-12:30am, with a $3 cover charge, and also Fri. afterno 5:30pm with no cover. Buy tickets before Fri. night. All in all one of the best cl in Jerusalem. Unfortunately, at the time of publication, it was closed for some unexplained reason. It should reopen in 1984.

Asaf's Cave, Mt. Zion Cultural Center, near David's Tomb (tel. 81 08 56). Each Sat. night a celebration occurs (at 9pm) signaling the departure of the Sabbath and the start of a new week. The Diaspora Yeshiva Band, with roots in R&B (as well as in the Talmud), performs in a mixture of English, Hebrew, and Yiddish. Admission $6, $3 for students. Also performances of jazz-fusion most Tues. nights in summer (call to check); admission $2.50, no student discount. Bus #1 and 38 stop nearby.

JBR Club, corner Agrippas and Messilat Yesharim St. (tel. 22 77 70). Somewhat rowdy music-dance club run by Americans with a heavily collegiate atmosphere. Open nightly except Friday 9pm-midnight, with live rock each Wed. Try to come toward the end of the week when it's more crowded. $2.50 admission includes free first beer.

Although Jerusalem cafe-setting is not quite up to Tel Aviv's high standards, for tea, dessert, and taped music in a laid-back atmosphere there are several excellent and expensive places lining Ben Yehuda St.'s pedestrian mall. **Cafe Atara,** which attracts a younger crowd, has excellent dessert pancakes, marzipan pastries, and some of the best Turkish coffee in the city. Not far away, on Rivlin St., choose between **Rasputin's** (see Food section), **Chocolate Soup,** where they serve good crepes, and yes, a delicious chocolate soup of grains, nuts, fruit and milky chocolate, and the elegant **HaSha'on** ("The Clock"). **Chocolate Soup** also has live music on Mon. and Wed. The **Don't Pass Me By Pie House** is on Nahlat Shiva St., through the alley beside 33 Jaffa Rd. Also in the center of town are **Le Souffle, The Pie House,** and **Poire et Pomme Creperie** (see Food section for addresses). All of these tea houses close Fri. afternoon for Shabbat, and reopen Sat. an hour or two after sunset. Street musicians, some of them quite good, dot Ben Yehuda St., singing hippy music and general songs of protest.

Unfortunately, most of the Old City cafes close with the *shuq* at about 6pm. The **Danish Tea House,** open until about midnight, will play from their American music collection on request. Ask to see the list and then choose. The Danish Tea House is down David St. from Jaffa Gate, and then left on Muristan Rd. Like the other places in the Old City (Tabasco and JOC Inn—see Accommodation section for details), the Danish Tea House is a pick-up joint for Arabs, so women should be discreet.

Drinking spots come in several shapes and sizes. **The Tavern** on Rivlan St. is a predominantly English-speaking pub with a dart board in the back and live music every Thursday night starting at 10pm. **Champs Pub** on Yoel Salomon St. (near Zion Sq.) is a crowded nightspot. **The Little Pub** and others around it serve expensive, lousy food, but remain popular spots for meeting travelers. It is in a courtyard off Jaffa Rd., just east of Rivlan St.—look for the sign. **Charlie's Pub** evokes a Greenwich Village bohemian atmosphere, with its movie posters on the walls and '60s American music in the background. It is in the Jerusalem Towers Hotel at 23 Hillel St. (open Sun.-Thurs. 1pm-2am, Fri. from 8:30pm, and Sat. from sundown to 2am).

The twelve movie theaters around town provide a good chance to catch

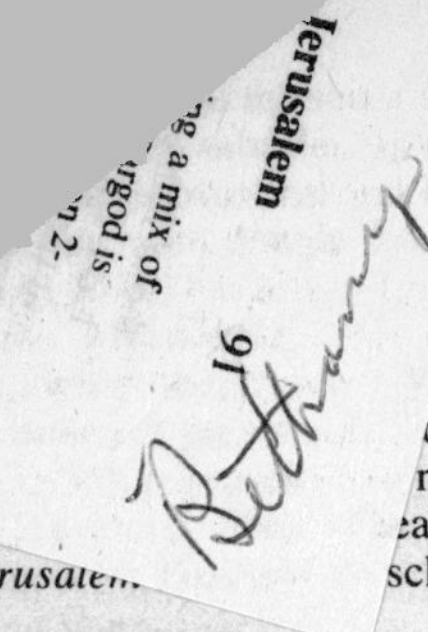

years ago. Most films are in English and if not ...tion to the regular cinemas and the films shown ...vta mentioned above, three places screen foreign ...es. **Cinema One,** Qiryat Yovel (bus #18, 19, 20; ... programs but is infamous for the poor quality of its ...bove) has English movies every Mon., Wed., and ... is in season. The real gem, however, is the new ... on Hebron Road in the Valley of Gehinnom (tel. ... repertory films nightly and on Friday afternoons (no ...eaters charge between $1.50-3.00, and the Friday *Jerusalem* ... schedule of movie listings. Bring your student ID.

Near Jerusalem

Bethany (El-Azariye)

For a pleasant half-day excursion from Jerusalem, take either Egged bus #43 or Arab bus #36 and get off in the town of Bethany, 4km east of the city. If you feel energetic, you can easily walk, taking a short cut over the Mount of Olives (twenty minutes). A relatively prosperous Palestinian village, Bethany was once the home of Lazarus and his sisters Mary and Martha. It was in this home that Jesus is believed to have stayed when he visited Jerusalem and a **Franciscan Church** built in 1954 now marks the spot. The church features several impressive mosaics including one illustrating the resurrection of Lazarus. Three earlier shrines, the earliest built in the fourth century C.E., have been excavated nearby. South of the church, you'll find the remains of a vast abbey built in 1143 A.D. by Queen Melisende. Note the enormous olive oil press in the monastery's cavernous interior.

Bethany still contains the first century **tomb of Lazarus** which was first enshrined in the fourth century; when the Crusaders arrived, they built a church over it, a monastery over Mary and Martha's house, and a tower over Simon the Leper's (the last was another resident of Bethany who was cured by Jesus). In the sixteenth century, the Muslims erected a mosque over the grotto, and in the following century, Christians dug another entrance to the tomb, so that they could also worship in the grotto. If you are shown the tomb by one of the local guides, he may treat you to a dramatic re-enactment of the story, crying out: "Lazarus, come forth," as some hapless tourist emerges from the low entrance to the tomb. Be sure to tip the guide a few shekels since he is paid nothing by the government. Admission to the tomb is $.15. Above the tomb is a small Greek Orthodox church, also dedicated to Lazarus.

Abu Ghosh

Thirteen kilometers west of Jerusalem lies the Arab village of Abu Ghosh, whose inhabitants aided the Jews in the war of 1948 and who speak both Arabic and Hebrew. In the seventeenth century, Sheikh Abu Ghosh required pilgrims to pay a toll here as they traveled to Jerusalem. The spot is revered by Jews and Christians alike as the original site of the holy Ark of the Covenant that was moved by King David to Jerusalem. The **Notre Dame de L'Arche d'Alliance** (Our Lady of the Ark of the Covenant) was built on the site of the ark—it cannot be missed, since it's topped by an enormous statue of Mary holding the infant Jesus.

Below the sacred hill stands a magnificently preserved **Crusader Church** (open 8:30am-11am and 2:30-5:30pm, except Sun.), built like a fortress in 1142 and acquired by the French government in 1873. It now houses six French Benedictine monks and, in an adjacent building, the same number of nuns. The impressive church where they worship was built above the site of a Roman castle and a natural spring, which once filled bathing pools for the Roman conquerors of the Holy Land. Excavations beneath the church have uncovered relics dating back to Neolithic times.

If you're at all curious about the Benedictine order, the church is a good place to inquire. Your friendly hosts can explain the importance of the Jewish tradition in Catholic doctrine. Though the liturgy is in French and Latin, monks and nuns study the Bible and Psalms in Hebrew. The Benedictines carry out their daily offices as described in the *Rule* of St. Benedict, starting with *matins* at 5am, *ludes* at 7am, a two-hour break for personal prayer and study, mass at noon, manual work in the afternoon ("if you don't work, you don't eat"), vespers at 6pm and *complis* after dinner. And, of course, they practice Gregorian chants, claiming that the melody corresponds to the meaning of the language of Scripture. The monastic life disappeared from the French Catholic tradition from the time of the French Revolution until the late 1800s, but it was not until after World War II that the abbots decided to de-emphasize apostolic action in favor of the contemplative life. A small *hostelerie* in the monastery is available for those interested in sharing the monastic life (tel. 53 97 98).

A **War Memorial** has been erected at **Qiryat Anavim** near Abu Ghosh in memory of the Palmach soldiers who fell fighting on the road to Jerusalem during the 1948 War of Independence. In this Jewish settlement you'll find the **Haezrahi Youth Hostel** (tel. 53 97 70); members $4, non-members $5, breakfast $2 extra. Five kilometers down the road towards Jerusalem is a **campground** (tel. 53 77 17) run by the moshav at Bet Zayit, open all year round.

To reach Abu Ghosh, take an Egged bus to Qiryat Ye'arim, near the Our Lady Church, or to Qiryat Anavim. Sheruts traveling between Jerusalem and Tel Aviv also stop at Abu Ghosh.

Latrun

Located on Israel's vital lifeline, halfway between Jerusalem and Tel Aviv, Latrun was the site of fierce fighting during the 1948 War of Independence. The Arab Legion held this crucial junction against numerous Haganah onslaughts, as the desperate Jews tried to relieve their besieged comrades in Jerusalem. During World War I, the British fought here under General Allenby, and in earlier times, Crusaders, Arabs, Greeks and Romans also assembled legions here in preparation for their respective assaults on the Holy City. The coveted fort guarding the junction now stands as a reminder of the strategic importance of the area.

Across the road from the fort is the **Monastery of Latrun,** built in 1927 by the French Trappist Order on the ruins of a twelfth-century Crusader fortress. The site is presently being excavated and the remains of a Crusader basilica have been unearthed. The trip is also worth it for the wine you can purchase at the monastery—it is made by the monks from the local vineyards. This is said to be the site of the home of one of the thieves crucified by the side of Jesus, hence the name Latrun (Home of the Good Thief).

On the other side of the Tel Aviv-Jerusalem highway is a monastery now used by the French Prehistorical Research Center as its base for archeological digs. Below the monastery are the ruins of the **Emmaus basilica** (open 9am-noon, but hours are flexible). According to Christian tradition, Jesus appeared to two of his disciples here after his resurrection.

Canada Park, one of the numerous spots in Israel forested with the help of the Jewish National Fund, is on the edge of the West Bank just north of Emmaus, and contains numerous archeological remains. A well-preserved Roman bath can be found at the side of the road near the basilica; it was built around 640 C.E. and hints at the prosperity of Emmaus during the Roman-Byzantine period. Water holes, conduits, and the remains of an amphitheater can also be found in the park. Read the sign overlooking the West Bank Valley of Ayalon—it warns of the precarious security conditions in "Judea and Samaria," or the Occupied Territories.

Continuing north along the edge of the West Bank, you come to Modiin, another interesting archeological site which features the **Tombs of the Maccabees** (Qubar el Yahud). The hilltop ruins have been declared a national monument. Every year on the first night of Hannukah a team of runners carries a torch lit near the tombs to Jerusalem where it is used for the ceremony of lighting the Hannukah lights. Latrun can be reached by taking bus #402 or 433, passing between Jerusalem and Tel Aviv every half hour.

Avashalom Stalagmite Cave

Some of the first speliological structures in the Middle East are found 19km northwest of Jerusalem next to the village of the Ness Harim, at the Avashalom Stalagmite Cave. Even the ridiculously large numbers of tour groups that converge on this place won't overshadow the intense beauty of these caverns. If you've never seen a stalactite cave or ache to see a beautiful natural sight rather than the many manmade ones around, then a visit is a must. Take bus #43 or 418 from the Central Bus Station to Ness Harim (about seven daily), and walk from there to the cave (2km). Admission price includes a mandatory slide show and guided tour (tel. 91 11 17).

Ein Kerem

Once a small Arab village, Ein Kerem, on the outskirts of Jerusalem, is traditionally regarded as the birthplace of John the Baptist. Historians couldn't have chosen a more beautiful spot. Come here for an afternoon, and wander through the village's tiny alleys and streets. You can visit both the Church of St. John and the lovely Church of the Visitation. Mary's Well, an ancient spring, is a small stone trough beside the Youth Hostel (see Jerusalem Accommodations). The two or three cafes in Ein Kerem are expensive for meals but are worth a quick stop for coffees and small snacks. To get there, take city bus #17 from the Central Bus Station which runs every 20-30 minutes.

Galilee and Golan Heights

The Galilee is the land of the Bible, but it belongs very much to the twentieth century. Old Testament battles are periodically retraced by modern war maneuvers; New Testament miracles, like the multiplication of the loaves and fishes, are reflected in the superabundant agricultural production of the kibbutzim. The valleys and fertile green hills surrounding the shores of the Sea of Galilee (Yam Kinneret), once the site of Jesus' wanderings, are now lush farm lands fed by the sweet waters of the Jordan River.

The Galilee is bounded by the Mediterranean coast to the west, the West Bank to the south, the Golan Heights and Jordan to the east, and Lebanon to the north. The material riches of the landscape have inspired artists, poets, and philosophers for centuries. The great rabbinical sages of Tiberias produced the two great commentaries on the *Torah,* the *Talmud* and the *Mishnah;* and in Tzfat, they added a touch of mysticism to their speculations and contributed the *Cabbala* to the canon of Jewish literature.

If the Galilee's potent sense of history should lull you into spiritual contemplation, the roar of Phantom jets flying overhead will shock you back to the present day. The jets fly east in formation to defend the beautiful—and controversial—**Golan Heights,** once Syrian territory. After Syrians lobbed shells and showered rifle fire on the farming kibbutzim of the Galilee, Israel captured the Heights in the Six-Day War, and annexed it in 1982.

Getting Around the Galilee

Buses run into the Galilee from the coast through Afula, Haifa, and Nahariyya or from the south through the spectacular **Jordan Rift Valley.** Hitching is possible and quite common, but can be very frustrating for men since women and soldiers are the first to get rides. Fortunately, most sights are easily accessible by public or tour buses from one of the major transportation centers: Afula serves the Lower Galilee, while Nahariyya and Haifa serve the Sea of Galilee area.

Lower Galilee

Important historical sights and pretty national parks fill the Lower Galilee, making it marvelous touring country. Afula is the transportation hub for the various sights in the middle of the Lower Galilee, but you probably won't want to stay there since it offers little itself. Many of the buses to sights in the area run infrequently, so check schedules before you reach Afula to avoid spending the night there.

Megiddo (Armageddon)

In ancient times, the fortress town of Megiddo bordered the crucial route between Egypt and Mesopotamia which became the Roman Via Maris. Its strategic significance explains why it was inhabited from 4000 B.C.E. to the Greek period of the fourth century B.C.E. Until recently, excavations had uncovered finds dating only as far back as King Solomon's day (970-930 B.C.E.) when it was a chariot town and home of the cavalry used to collect Solomon's heavy taxes. Then, a few years ago, an exploration trench revealed another fifteen layers of civilization beneath Solomon's city, indicating that Megiddo had been the site of twenty different cities in all.

The archeological site is dramatic in its age, extent, and its view over the whole Jezreel Valley (or Emek Yisreel). A small **museum** near the entrance has exhibits explaining the various layers of excavations and a model of Solomon's chariot town. One of the most intriguing aspects of the site (pointed out in the museum) is the tunnel built to hide the city's water source from invaders and to make the water accessible from inside the city walls (much like Hezekiah's Tunnel in Jerusalem). You can walk through this tunnel to the outside of the site. The museum also has a helpful list of biblical references to Megiddo. Among the many citations, Revelations 16:16 is perhaps the most dramatic: it forsees the final battle between good and evil occurring here in the Valley of Armageddon (the Christian name for the town, coming from "Har"—Hebrew for "mountain"—and "Megiddo"). Try to see the museum between tour groups.

From the observation point on the site, you can look out over the **Valley of Jezreel,** the site of the bloodiest battle mentioned in the Old Testament. Most of the valley was swampland until 1920, when Jewish immigrants drained the land and turned it into Israel's most fertile valley. The round mountain standing in the distance by itself is Mt. Tabor, where Deborah amassed the Israelite troops to conquer the rival Canaanites (Judges 5), and where Jesus talked with Moses and Elijah in the Transfiguration (Luke 9).

Megiddo, like all the National Park sites, is open daily 8am-5pm, Fri. until 4pm; admission $1.20, $.65 for students. You can buy a booklet for $.10 describing the site. You should only consider buying a 31-sight ticket ($5; good for two weeks) if you plan on extensive and rushed sightseeing in the parks. Bus connections to the site itself are infrequent—about every two hours. But you can get on and off buses at a junction halfway between Tel Megiddo and Gvat Oz, about 1 km from the site. Buses to Afula stop on one side of the road, buses to the Coast and Tel Aviv on the other, both about every twenty minutes.

Beit Alpha, Gan HaShlosha (Sachne), Beit She'an

Heading southeast out of Afula you'll find **Beit Alpha,** the kibbutz where the beautifully preserved mosaic floor of a fifth- or sixth-century synagogue was found (open daily 8am-5pm, Fri. until 4pm; admission $.60, $.30 for students), The frequent tours through the synagogue provide an explanation of the building's layout, and the enclosed site gives a good idea of what early synagogues looked like. The Afula-Beit She'an bus can take you to Beit Alpha—look for the orange sign.

Southeast of Beit Alpha, the lovely park of **Gan HaShlosha** (also called Sachne) dates back to Roman times and features resplendent waterfalls and swimming holes full of refreshingly crystalline water. Gan HaShlosha can be reached by taking the Afula-Beit She'an bus and is definitely worth an afternoon excursion (open daily 10:30am-1pm; admission $.60, $.40 for students). Bring a picnic lunch (there is also a snack bar and restaurant) and enjoy. Belongings can be left under the lifeguard's chair for safekeeping.

Continuing southeast of Sachne, you'll come to an unreconstructed **Roman amphitheater** in **Beit She'an.** The amphitheater was built in 200 C.E. to accommodate five thousand spectators. Designed for dramatic performances rather than gladiatorial combat, the stage area of the amphitheater is virtually intact. The site is open daily 8am-5pm; admission $1.10, $.55 for students. The town of Beit She'an also has a little-known but fascinating **museum** just 200m from the bus station. Open Sun.-Thurs. 8am-2:30pm, Fri. 8am-12:30pm; admission $.40, $.30 for students. Ask at the museum about other archeological sights nearby. Beit She'an itself is not a very pretty town, having been bombarded by the Syrians as late as 1975—note the square bomb shelter rooms added onto every house.

If you want to camp out in a place rich in biblical history, stop at the **Ma'ayan Harod campsite** (tel. 81 60 4), which lies between Afula and Beit Alpha, 1 km from the road. The facilities are adequate, the grounds are rarely crowded, and best of all, it's the place where Gideon defeated the Midianites (Judges 7).

The Tiberias-Beit She'an bus will take you to **Belvoir** (or **Kokhav HaYarden,**) an immense Crusader fortress with a spectacular view. You're better off if you have private transportation, however, because the bus will drop you 10km from the sight, and it's a tough uphill climb.

Nazareth (Nazerat, Nasra)

Nazareth is no longer the quaint town that Jesus grew up in, but a rather unappealing collection of tourist shops and a few churches. It is worth a visit, though, for the beautiful **Basilica of the Annunciation,** one of the most moving and unusual churches in Israel. Nazareth also has an interesting melange of religions and cultures: the town is half Christian and half Muslim, with an adjoining Jewish settlement.

Orientation

Nazareth consists of the old Arab town, where the Basilica and other Christian sites are located, and the new or upper city, called **Nazerat Illit,** where Jews have built a thriving community. If you arrive by bus, get off at the intersection of Casa Nova St. and Paul VI St., the main thoroughfare in Nazareth, and walk along Casa Nova St. to the **Israel Government Tourist Office** (open Mon.-Fri. 8am-4pm, Sat. 8am-3pm, closed Sun.). They are very helpful and will give you a guide to sights and a map. If the IGTO is closed, try **Abu Nasser's Restaurant** next door. Mr. Nasser can give you any information you need (resturant open daily except Sun. 8:30am-5:30pm) and usually knows the latest concerning cheap accommodations. He can also offer you a good meal at a reasonable cost. Those who plan to spend time in Nazareth sightseeing, but aren't staying the night, can leave their packs at the **Egged Station** a block down from Casa Nova St. on Paul VI Road, across from the Paz gas station. The baggage room is open Mon.-Sat. 7am-3pm, Sun. until 2pm, and charges $1.10. For $.75 you can leave your luggage with **Taxi 27** just up the street from the tourist office (open daily except Sun. 7am-6pm).

To get information for bus departures from Nazareth, call Egged (tel. 70 04 0). When you are ready to leave, go down Casa Nova Street and take a left on Paul VI Road. One block down, you will find the bus stops—buses for Haifa or Tel Aviv on the left and for Tiberias on the right.

Accommodations and Food

Try and avoid staying overnight in Nazareth: the city closes down at 7pm and there is little to see. If you do find yourself in need of a place to stay, two places offer budget accommodations. The **Religieuses de Nazareth** (tel. 54 30 4, P.O. Box 274) is a clean hospice where dorm beds cost $3 a night. To get there, go up Casa Nova St. and take a left after the Casa Nova Hospice; it will be on the right at #306. If you're unlucky enough to arrive when the sisters are on one of their retreats (usually at the end of July or the beginning of August) call the **Freres de Betharram** (tel. 70 04 6), who offer dormitory beds for $6 a night. More expensive is the **Greek Catholic St. Joseph's Seminary** (tel. 70 54 0), where beds are $13 per person. Open in summer only, it is located next to the "Grand New Hotel" and can be reached on bus #1. If all else fails go to Tiberias, where accommodations are cheaper and more plentiful.

You can get cheap meals at a couple of places in addition to **Abu Nasser's.** The **Nazareth Restaurant** across from the bus station is a no-frills establishment serving no-frills meals at no-frills prices. A few blocks down from the bus station on Paul VI towards Casa Nova St. is the **Al-Amal** restaurant which is cleaner, serves better food, and offers a greater variety of dishes.

Sights

Nazareth is undeniably a city of churches. This wealth of churches is the result of the city's religious importance: Nazareth became a center of Christian pilgrimage when it became known as the site of the Annunciation, where the Archangel Gabriel is said to have appeared before Mary to announce the birth of Jesus. The most historically and religiously significant of the churches is the **Basilica of the Annunciation,** a complex of two different modern churches built in 1966 over the remains of older structures and maintained by Franciscan monks. The result is a fascinating mixture of modern and ancient architecture, which most visitors find either utterly repulsive or brilliant. If you're lucky enough to visit the church during a service, notice how the eerie, high-pitched music from several different parts of the basilica resonates through the immense concrete structure. The artwork in the courtyard was donated by many different countries; be sure to examine the huge bronze doors of the basilica which depict the crucial events in the life of Jesus, surrounded by the great prophets and other Biblical figures. The entry level is built on the site of Mary's house, where the Annunciation took place. Inside, the new altar lies before the remains of three early churches. To the left of the cave you'll find excavated ritual baths from a third-century Christian church. Next to the railing is the line of a fourth-century Byzantine church wall. Finally, the back wall of the building is from a twelfth-century Crusader church.

The stairs to the right of the church entrance feature a series of mosaics depicting Pope Paul VI's visit to the Holy Land. The second level contains some of the most intriguing art in the church: a series of international artists' interpretations of the Annunciation, and ceramic reliefs of the stations of the cross molded by Arab Christians.

The excavations of the ancient town of Nazareth lie in an archeological garden underneath the plaza that opens from the upper floor of the church. Find a monk inside the church and ask if he can show you around the excavations. Across the plaza (follow the signs) is **St. Joseph's Church** where you can look down on the cave thought to be Joseph's house. Remnants of an older church lie beneath, and stairs lead down to caves where grain and oil were once stored.

The **Greek-Catholic Synagogue Church** in the center of the Arab market is not a combination synagogue-church as its name implies, but rather the site of the ancient synagogue where Christ is believed to have preached as a young man. The other church worth a visit in Nazareth is the **St. Gabriel Greek Orthodox Church** on the road to Tiberias. This dark and almost Oriental-looking church stands over the original water source of the town, known as **Mary's Well**—the well is still there and working. Many believe the water has magical healing powers, but it would be hard to judge from its stale taste. If you have extra time, follow the signs to the Maronite Church; the **Mensa Christi Church** next door allegedly marks the place where Jesus shared a meal with his disciples after the Resurrection.

All of the various churches in Nazareth are open in summer 8:30-11:45am and 2-5:30pm, in winter 9-11:45am and 2-4:45pm. Remember, Sunday mornings are reserved for services, and shorts are not allowed in any of Nazareth's churches at any time.

Nazareth has a lively Arab market. If you want to buy goods here, bargain the price down to at least half if not a third of the original quoted price. For a lovely view over the Galilean hills, hike up to the rim of the amphitheater in which the old city sits. You will also get a look at the hidden side of a modern Arab town.

Kfar Kanna, a little town to the north of Nazareth, was the site of Jesus's first miracle, the transformation of water into wine at the wedding feast (John 2:1-11). The town contains a Franciscan Church built in 1881 to commemorate the event. Buses leave for Kfar Kanna every 45 minutes from Mary's Well in Nazareth, or you can take bus #431 (to Tiberias) and ask the driver to let you off at Kfar Kanna. It leaves every forty minutes from the main bus station.

Central Galilee (Sea of Galilee)

The Galilean hills are beautiful, but the Sea of Galilee is entrancing. Whether you take the dusty ride through the West Bank, descend from the mountains of Tzfat, come rolling across the hills from Nazareth, or emerge from the fertile Jordan River Valley, the Sea (known by Israelis as the Kinneret) will appear an almost miraculous sight in this dry and arid land, with its coast of banana groves and palm trees and the bluish haze of the Golan Heights in the distance. The Sea has its share of important history: Christ performed miracles here and taught in the villages along these coasts. Moreover, Jewish sages assembled the Mishnah and Jerusalem Talmud and established the vowel system for the Hebrew language here.

The hills and fields surrounding the **Mount of Beatitudes** and the coast around **Capernaum,** where Jesus preached to the fishermen possess an ageless serenity, contrasting sharply with the nearby trenches of Deganya A, where settlers struggled to establish the first kibbutz in the area under the pressure of Syrian bombardment from the Golan Heights. Since the taking of the Heights by Israeli troops in 1967, the Sea of Galilee has become a popular winter resort because of its mild climate and hot mineral baths; it is also quite crowded during the summer with families and young tourists. You can avoid both the heat and other tourists at air-conditioned youth hostels and kibbutzim or in a shady campsite by the water. Although tourism has raised prices in the Sea of Galilee, it has also encouraged good fish restaurants on the water's edge and a weekend nightlife of discos and cafes.

Tiberias

Tiberias (Teverya in Hebrew) is the only major city on the Sea of Galilee, and an ideal central touring base for the area. Some visitors feel Tiberias is too built-up and touristy while others think it too sleepy. Neither view is fair to the city. Tiberias may not have Tel Aviv's nightlife or Jerusalem's historical offerings, but it is a fine place to relax and move at a slower pace. Tiberias offers quiet camping, beautiful beaches all along the sea, a few interesting ruins, some nightlife, and the chance to visit a kibbutz.

Orientation

Tiberias has three levels. The old city is on the water, the new city (Kiryat Shmuel) is up the hill (take bus #1 or 5 from the bus station), and the "uptown" is on top of the hill (buses #7, 8, or 9 from the bus station). There is little reason to venture above the old city except to see a movie. **Rehov HaGalil,** running parallel to the water, is the main thoroughfare in Tiberias.

Israel Government Tourist Office: 8 Al Hadef St. (tel. 20 99 2). Head towards the sea from the bus station and turn left on Al Hadef St. A daily schedule of events is posted inside. Open Sun.-Thurs. 8am-6pm, Fri. 8am-2pm.

Central Post Office: along Rehov HaYarden (tel. 21 51 5). Take a right as you exit the bus station onto Rehov HaYarden; the Post Office will be on your left. Open Sun., Mon., Tues., Thurs. 7:45am-12:30pm and 3:30-6pm, Wed. 7:45am-2pm, Fri. 7:45am-1pm. Also has public phones and places overseas calls.

Bus Station: Rehov HaYarden. For information call 91 08 0.

Emergency: Police (tel. 92 44 4). First Aid (tel. 20 11 1 or 91 01 1). Open 24 hours.

Hitching: For points south and west: the main intersection at HaYarden and HaBonim Sts. For points north: one block further down towards the water.

Accommodations

Meyouhas Hostel (IYHF), HaYarden St. (tel. 21 77 5). Near Great Mosque. Comfortable and safe. TV/writing room. Dinner a good deal at $2-$3.25. $5.30 for members, $6.30 for non-members, in 4- to 8-bed rooms, plus an obligatory $.50 extra for air conditioning May-Sept. (you'll need it). Breakfast included. Open for reception daily 1pm-midnight in summer, 4pm-midnight in winter. 12:45am curfew, midnight in winter.

Maman Hostel. From HaYarden St., turn south on HaGalil, then bear right on Tavor—the hostel is on the first street to your right (tel. 92 98 6). Friendly management, no curfew, and a nice balcony with a bar and modest restaurant. $6.50 per person including breakfast and air conditioning.

Nahum Hostel (tel. 21 50 5). Just around the corner from Maman. Kitchen facilities and a great view from the roof, plus it's been newly expanded and renovated. $5.50 per person including breakfast. Unfortunately, those planning to stay Fri. night must pay for Sat. night as well.

Castle Inn Hostel. Next to the Plaza Hotel (tel. 21 17 5). Right on the wharf, with a fantastic view of the sea from the terrace. Hostel residents are entitled to a discount on admission to the disco downstairs during the weekdays (men $1, women allowed in free). Closed 1-4:30pm. Kitchen facilities. Flexible 11:30pm curfew. $4.50 per person, and an extra $.80 charge if you use their sheets.

Paz Hostel. On Tavor St. just before Maman (tel. 20 42 2). Refrigerator and cooking facilities. 5-bed dorm rooms with no bunks. A bit dirty. $4 a night, $2 for breakfast. $12 for a double.

Terra Sancta. On the wharf amidst the fish restaurants. (tel. 20 51 6). Built in 1100 C.E., and little has changed since—including the plumbing. Dirty and primitive, but liveable on the whole. The cheapest place in town at $1.80 per person.

The Church of Scotland Hospice. Just behind the Meyouhas Hostel (P.O.B. 104; tel. 90 14 4). Private rooms in a lovely setting in the old city. Large private rooms with bath and overhead fans, superb facilities, beautiful garden and private beach.

Nice management. Check in anytime. Written reservations without deposit accepted. Bed and breakfast $19.50 per person, $13 for students. No curfew.

Camping

Though the best way to escape the heat and prices of the city, camping, at least in summer, will bring you closer to the crowds. Many of the campsites on the lake are full during July and August; staying there is akin to seeing the average Israeli at home. Of the four campsites near the Sea of Galilee, **Ein Gev** is the most popular (tel. 51 16 7 or 51 17 7). The campsite is a 2km walk along the road south of Kibbutz Ein Gev (take the boat from Tiberias). During July and August, there are sometimes as many as four boats a day, but call in advance to check since departure times change daily. Tickets and information can be obtained at the **Kinnereth Sailing Company** on the wharf near the Plaza Hotel (tel. 21 83 1; open 8am-4pm), $5 round trip, $4 one way. Buses #18 and 21 run from Tiberias to Ein Gev ten times a day ($.50), the last one leaving 7:30pm, 2:30pm on Fridays (buses don't run on Saturdays). Hitching can be very slow. The campsite has a clean, open beach area, a small supermarket, and shower/toilet facilities. Day use is $2.25, but there is a comparable free beach just south of the campsite. A bed in a bungalow for two, three, or four costs $6-8 per person in high season. An air-conditioned holiday caravan for six costs $85. Tent space costs $4.50 per person. Water, electricity, and hot showers are all provided, and you can rent a refrigerator for $2.75 a day. To make a reservation for the high season write 3-4 months in advance to Ein Gev Camping, Jordan Valley, Israel.

Further south on the east side of the Sea of Galilee, are the **Ha'on** (tel. 51 14 4) and **Ma'agan** (tel 51 36 0) campsites. Ha'on does not have bungalows, but does rent tents. The prices are approximately the same as those at Ein Gev. Two kilometers southwest of Tiberias lies **Kfar Hittim** campsite (tel. 92 91 1) in the Hittim Valley. No holiday caravans are available, but tents and bungalows can be rented. Ein Gev and Ma'agan are open all year while the others are open May-Oct.

Though private beaches line the sea, interspersed among them are stretches of open shoreline for free camping. The government has conveniently put some jiffy johns and trashbins at a few of these points. Bring your own food, water, and insect repellent. Take the Ein Gev bus from Tiberias and get off when you see a campsite or walk south along the coast past the Tiberias hot springs. About ½km farther, steps to the left lead down to a particularly nice beach for camping.

Food

Tiberias offers a variety of alternatives for cheap meals. You can buy produce at the market on Rehov HaGalil (open Sun.-Fri. afternoons) or pick up a light lunch or dinner at one of the innumerable felafel stands on HaYarden St. (they close around 7pm). The seafood restaurants along the waterfront offer romantic candlelit settings. A good dinner of St. Peter's fish (the kind of fish that Peter caught) costs about $6. For slightly less, you can have a quarter-slice of watermelon or an ice cream sundae. Be sure to check the prices before ordering. A cheaper option is to patronize the cafe/restaurants on HaGalil and HaBonim Streets and the squares in between (where you can buy pizza). A brand-new supermarket just opened up in the Great Mosque Plaza, across from the Meyouhas Hostel.

Egged Bus Station Restaurant. The best deal for a complete meal. Open daily for breakfast and lunch except Sat.

Avi's Tea House, Kishon St., between HaGalil and HaBanim Sts. a few blocks up from the plaza. Also **PiziGal,** which will have moved up the street by 1984. Both offer pizza for $2.25-3.00. PiziGal has very good vegetarian dishes, such as asparagus crepes, *moujadara* (lentils, rice, and mushrooms), and yogurt soup. Both open noon-2am.

Biko's Restaurant, off HaBonim St., next to the Great Mosque. The U.N. Soldiers eat fish here, and they are as realiable a source as truck drivers.

The House Chinese Restaurant, opposite the Lido Kinneret. For a hot date or just a real treat. Take the left fork on Gedud Barak Rd. after Meyouhas Hostel as you head toward the sea. Reservations needed for weekend nights, but it's worth reserving a terrace table on any day (tel. 20 22 6). The food is great, the setting lovely, and the background music tasteful. Entrees are about $9, and completely a la carte—tea is $1 extra. A full meal is about $12 per person. The bar is comfortable and incredibly expensive. Open every day 5pm-midnight, Sat. opens at 1pm.

Sights

Tiberias, one of Israel's four holy cities, was founded around 20 C.E. by Herod Antipas and named for the Roman Emperor Tiberius. Throughout the Roman period, it remained a quintessentially pagan city—a center for Roman hedonism, according to Josephus—and during the Jewish Rebellion against Rome in 66 C.E. Tiberias sided with the Romans. By the third century, however, Tiberias had become the center of Jewish life in the Holy Land. It was here that the *Mishnah* (a collection of Jewish law forming part of the Talmud) was codified (in 200 C.E.), here the Palestinian *Talmud* was edited (in 400 C.E.), and here the vowels were added to the Hebrew alphabet. During the Byzantine period, it was to Tiberias that Jews from Persia and Babylonia came on pilgrimages; even today, legend has it that the redemption of Israel will begin in Tiberias.

Like most of Israel, before the twelfth century Tiberias was conquered by the Muslims, the Crusaders, and then the Muslims again. By the end of the twelfth century, the battered city was little more than rubble. But Tiberias later flourished and grew under Muslim rule, especially that of Daher el Omar in the mid-eighteenth century. In 1837, Tiberias, along with most of the north of Israel, was devastated by an earthquake. Not until the turn of the century did Jewish immigrants begin to resettle the area; in 1912, the first suburb was built outside the ancient city walls. By 1948, Tiberias had over 12,000 people, half of them Jewish. Tiberias was taken by the Israelis very early in 1948—weeks before the state of Israel was declared.

The old city has been destroyed by conquerors and earthquakes and only fragments of the old walls remain. To get a feel for its former glory, attend the free walking tour offered by the **Tiberias Plaza Hotel** (tel. 92 23 3) on Saturday at 10am (call the Plaza or the IGTO first to check times). A seventh-generation Tiberian gives the ninety-minute tour, pointing out the more obscure sights that tell much about the city's past.

When you get off the bus on Rehov HaYarden, you will be near the **Tomb of Maimonides,** or, as he is known in Hebrew, "Rambam." Maimonides was born in Córdoba in 1136 and died in Egypt in 1204; his attempt to wed Aristotelian and Arabic philosophy with the study of religion sparked a controversy in Jewish thought analogous to that sparked by Aquinas concerning the use of reason in matters of faith. According to legend, a donkey carried his coffin to

Tiberias without instruction. The tomb is plain and marked only by Hebrew signs. To get there, walk two blocks east along HaYarden St. towards the water, then turn left up Y. Ben Zakkay St. for two and a half blocks. The tomb will be on your right.

Tiberias is the site of one of the earliest known **hot mineral springs.** Even today, many people flock to Tiberias to use the mineral waters as therapy. Numerous legends have arisen concerning the hot springs. Some maintain that they originated in the time of the flood when the insides of the earth soared upwards; others contend that the springs were originally cold, but that Solomon forced a group of demons to heat them from the bowels of the earth to cure his subjects. Solomon then made the demons deaf so they could not hear of his death and would continue to heat the springs forever. If you want to lounge in a warm mineral pool by the sea near Tiberias, walk 2km south of Tiberias on the coastal road or catch bus #5 or 2 from the front of the central station or from HaGalil St. Both buildings at the site house mineral pools; for $6.25 you can lie in the pools and take a cleansing shower afterwards. The pool is too slimy for serious swimming, but very relaxing. For another $9, you can have a massage as well. Or, take a bubble bath for $4 extra. The old building, called **Tiberias Hot Springs** and meant for people with serious health problems, is open Sun.-Thurs. 7am-1pm, Fri. 7am-12:30pm, closed Sat. The new building, called **Tiberias Hot Springs Spa,** is open Sun.-Thurs. 8am-8pm, Fri. 8am-3pm. Sat. 8:30am-8pm.

Near the springs, just south of the old building, are some excavations of ancient **Roman Baths.** The second-century **Hamat Synagogue,** with a beautifully preserved mosaic floor, was found on the site. Open Sun.-Thurs. 8am-5pm, Fri. 8am-4pm, closed Sat.; admission $.55, no student discount.

On the waterfront esplanade sits the **Franciscan Terra Sancta Church,** just north of the Plaza Hotel. Built in the twelfth century to commemorate St. Peter's role in the early church, the edifice features a Latin transliteration of the Apostle's Hebrew name—Simon Bar-Yonah.

Many tourists come to Tiberias for the recreational offerings, particularly swimming and waterskiing. The private beaches right in town are much nicer than the string of places to the south. (The beaches south of town have bungalows, but even these are overpriced and smelly.) For still better beaches, take a bus south until you see an enticing spot or go to Ein Gev campground (the guest beach at the Ein Gev kibbutz is not worth the $2 admission fee). The private beaches just on the northern end of the old city near Meyouhas Hostel are another good alternative. The **Lido Kinneret** is the first you come to if you take the left fork after the hostel (admission $3). You can water-ski here for $20 per fifteen minutes. **Shell Beach** next door charges the same prices, as does the misnamed **Quiet Beach. Blue Beach** has a big swimming area, but is always packed with tour groups eating lunch at the expensive restaurants, and it charges $4.

If you've come for sailing, you're apt to be disappointed. Sailboats are not rented because the sea can get rough unexpectedly and very quickly. You can rent kayaks ($3 per hour) and windsurfers ($6 per hour) at **Ein Gev** campground. Waterskiing is popular and expensive, though with a little effort you might be able to find a cheap entrepreneur who will underprice the hotels and private beaches.

Nightlife

Tiberias has plenty of entertainment, if you're willing to seek it out. Two of the beaches (Quiet and Blue) have outdoor discos with disco dancing alternating with folk dancing every hour or so. **Quiet Beach** opens the disco every night at 9pm in July and Aug., and on Fri. and Sat. nights only the rest of the year (admission $2). **Blue Beach** is open from 9pm every night in the summer (admission $4). Bring your bathing suit to swim between dances. The **Castle Inn** wins points for ingenuity (if not aesthetics) for its disco in an old Greek Orthodox monastery complete with flashing lights, tile floors, and stone arches; admission is $2 and the bizarre setting is worth it. (Open Fri. and Sat. nights from 9pm).

There are three moviehouses in town and the restaurants along HaGalil Street show videotaped movies at their outdoor cafes; you can see an old James Bond flick for the price of a beer. The **Tiberias Plaza** has sunset cocktail cruises on Mondays and Thursdays at 5pm—you must ask if they have room for non-guests and purchase tickets beforehand at the Plaza. They also have a quiet but expensive bar that often features live music. The House Chinese Restaurant has a lovely bar; drinks start at $4.

The IGTO sponsors Wednesday night **folk dancing** and Saturday night folk song and dance performances in the open air. Ask at the office for information and schedules. During Passover, Ein Gev is the site of one of Israel's largest **music festivals.** You can get information about tickets at the IGTO.

Near Tiberias

Near the spot where the Jordan River flows out of the Sea of Galilee is Israel's oldest cooperative settlement, or kibbutz. Founded in 1910, **Deganya** was the first Jewish settlement in the Jordan Valley, and the birthplace of Moshe Dayan. On May 19, 1948, a few days after the State of Israel was declared, the Syrians took the nearby town of Semakh and, armed with tanks, tried to overrun Deganya. The settlers, with only small-caliber rifles and Molotov cocktails, held them out until one tank broke through the perimeter. It was stopped by a Deganya settler using a home-made grenade—the other tanks retreated and never returned. The destroyed Syrian tank resting at an angle on the lawn of the kibbutz still witnesses Deganya's exciting past.

Like many other kibbutzim, Deganya is now a wealthy, industry-oriented community (most of its income is generated by a diamond-tool factory). Deganya can be reached by buses #18 or 21, or any of the buses headed for Beit She'an and the Jordan Rift Valley.

Northern Coast

For Christians, the Sea of Galilee is most significant as the setting for many of Christ's miracles and much of his teaching. At the northern end of Galilee are four of the most important sites—the Mount of Beatitudes, Tabgha, the Church of the Primacy, and Capernaum. If you don't mind doing a good deal of uphill hiking, you can reach the sites by taking bus #459 (connecting Tiberias and Tzfat) to the Capernaum junction, marked by a small traffic island and a sign reading "Capernaum 3km." The youth hostel is straight down the road; the turn-off for Tabgha's two churches and Capernaum is a left halfway down this road. Unfortunatey no buses run to any of the actual sights, and hitching is slow.

About 1.5km east of the Capernaum junction lies the **Mount of Beatitudes,** where, overlooking sea, field, and town, Jesus spoke the famed words of the Sermon on the Mount: "Blessed are the poor in spirit, for theirs is the kingdom of heaven" (Matthew 5:3). Today, the Mount is one of the most serenely beautiful spots in Israel. The peace is interrupted only infrequently by a tour group—even then, the power of this setting seems to instill quiet among the visitors. A church, built by Mussolini in remembrance of the sermon delivered here, now stands on the Mount—the balcony is always cooled by a brisk wind, and is a quiet spot in which to read, write, and think. (Open everyday 7am-noon and 2-5pm.)

Taking the well-worn path down from the Mount to the coastal road, you'll find the ancient town of **Capernaum** about 1 km to the east. Here Christ performed two of his miracles: the healing of Simon's mother-in-law and of the Roman Centurion's servant (Luke 4:31-37 and 7:1-10). The Franciscans now guard some of the ruins of the ancient city. You must be modestly dressed to enter Capernaum and the church at Tabgha—no shorts, and women must cover their shoulders and arms. Open daily 8:30am-4:15pm, admission $.40. The bus passes the Capernaum junction about once an hour to both Tzfat and Tiberias. During the summer, a boat leaves daily (in the morning) from Lido Beach (tel. 21 53 8) to Capernaum; round trip fare is $6, but call ahead, because the skipper won't go unless there are enough people.

Two kilometers east of Capernaum, you'll find the first of **Tabgha's** two churches. Called the **Church of the Primacy,** it marks the spot where Jesus made Peter "Shepherd of his People." After the Resurrection, Peter led the rest of the apostles on a fishing expedition a hundred yards from Tabgha. In the morning, a man on shore shouted to them, "Friends, have you caught anything?" When they said they hadn't the man said, "Throw your nets over the starboard side—you're sure to catch something." The instant the nets hit the water, more fish swam into them than they could possibly carry. Jumping off the boat and swimming to shore, Peter found Jesus there cooking fish for twelve, and when the others sailed in Jesus conferred the primacy on Peter, charging him to look after his people with love and care. The twelve celebrated with a feast. The Church of the Primacy was built around a rock said to be the table (mensa) of this feast, though the building itself dates only to the 1930s. On the seaward side of the church stand the steps from which Jesus called out his instructions, and right on the shoreline is a series of six double or heart-shaped column bases, built by the early Christians and called the "thrones of the Apostles."

Just west of the Church of the Primacy along the northern coast of the sea lies the **Church of the Multiplication of the Loaves and Fishes.** A mosaic inside tells the story of how Jesus fed four thousand pilgrims who had come to hear him speak with only seven loaves of bread and a few small fish (Matthew 15: 29-30). The site is open April-Sept. 7:30am-6pm, Oct.-March 8am-5pm; the church is open 8:30-5pm.

About one kilometer further east (make a left where the road ends) is the **Karei Deshe Youth Hostel (IYHF)** (tel. 20 60 1). A lovely place to stay before or after seeing the sights, it comes complete with campsites, swimming areas, and peacocks set in a park of eucalyptus trees and rocky coast. Rooms are air-conditioned. Bring your own food; the hostel food is substandard and there are no markets or restaurants nearby. Dorm beds are $4.30 for members under 18, $4.60 for non-members; $4.80 for members over 18, $5.40 for non-members. Beds in family rooms are $5.50 for members, $6 for non-members. Bungalows are $6 for members and $6.25 for non-members, and camping is available at $5 per person. Dinner costs $3.20 for members, $3.70 non-members. Prices include air-conditioning in summer ($.50) and kitchen use.

Halfway between Tiberias and the Capernaum junction is **Migdal,** the birthplace of Mary Magdalene. Although Migdal (or Magdala) was a flourishing metropolis during the period of the Second Temple, today only a tiny white, domed shrine marks where the city once stood. Northeast of Capernaum, where the Jordan River flows into the Sea of Galilee, is **Jordan Valley Park,** a JNF site with beautiful watermills and lush greenery.

An excellent way to explore the north coast is on horseback. The next bus stop after Capernaum junction towards Tzfat leaves you on the road to Korazim, in front of a riding stable called **Vered Hagalil.** A half-day ride through the Galilean hills down to the sea and then up to the Mount of Beatitudes costs $16 per person. To cut costs, the American expatriate owner, Yehuda Avni (from Chicago), will let you camp free on the grass and use shower and toilet facilities the night before your ride if you call and ask first. There is also a nice bunkhouse where bed and American breakfast cost $16. The restaurant is quite reasonable and the food is great. The stables offer many different kinds of rides. Experience isn't necessary, but remember that saddle sores are an inevitable hazard of riding. For reservations write to Vered Hagalil, Korazim (tel. 35 78 5).

Tzfat

Set on Mount Canaan, overlooking the Galilean hills and the Sea of Galilee, Tzfat is a city of the spirit. Wake up for sunrise on a clear crisp morning, with the fog rising from the valleys to the west—you'll see why Tzfat became a center of Jewish mysticism in the sixteenth century, and one of the four Jewish holy cities.

Although Jewish settlement in Tzfat dates back to the time of the Second Temple, the Jewish presence has been far from continuous. Plundered first by the Romans (66 C.E.), and later by the Crusaders (twelfth century), Tzfat was left deserted in their wakes. A thriving Jewish community reemerged in the Middle Ages, when Spanish Jews (refugees from the Inquisition) began to build the synagogues of today's "Spanish Quarter." Other mystical sects came to Tzfat to settle, the most famous being that of Rabbi Isaac Lourie Ashkenazi, known to his followers as *Ha-Ari,* the Lion. By the late nineteenth century, after Arab riots and an earthquake, the town became predominantly Arab, and in the 1948 War of Independence Tzfat was bitterly contested due to its strategic position at the center of Northern Galilee. In recent years, Tzfat's beautiful surroundings and temperate climate have made the city a popular summer resort among Israelis and foreigners alike, but its peaceful, serene atmosphere remains unaltered.

Orientation and Practical Information

Bus #459 travels between Tiberias and Tzfat. The trip takes about an hour—buses run every hour or two. If you're coming from Jerusalem you can either take a direct bus, or the bus to the Qiryat Shemona (change at nearby Rosh Pinna). Once you are in central Tzfat, everything of importance can be reached by foot. The city is arranged in circular terraces of streets descending from the castle ruins in the center. The main street is **Rehov Yerushalayim,** which makes a complete circle around **Gan HaMetzuda** (the Park of the Citadel). Beginning opposite the Central Bus Station and later crossing over Rehov Yerushalayim on a quaint stone arched bridge is a second important street—**Rehov HaPalmach.**

Israeli Government Tourist Office: 7 Rehov Yerushalayim (tel. 30 63 3). Just north of Central Bus Station. The free map is a necessity in Tzfat. Open Sun.-Thurs. 9am-1pm and 4-6pm, Fri. and the day before a holiday 9am-1pm.

Central Bus Station: Kikar Ha'Atzmaut, (tel. 31 32 2 or 31 12 3). Parcel storage (for your pack) open Sun.-Thurs. 7am-4pm, Fri. 7am-2pm; $1.20 per day.

Central Post Office: next to a radar dish visible from corner of HaPalmach and Aliyah Beit Streets. Branch office at 37 Rehov Yerushalayim. Open Sun.-Tues. and Thurs 7:45am-12:30pm 3:30-6pm, Wed. 7:45am-2pm, Fri. 7:45am-1pm. Closed Sat. Branch office closes at 12:30pm Wed. and Fri.

First Aid: Magen David Adom, Rehov Aliyah Beit, near the central bus station (tel. 30 33 3 or 101).

Police: tel. 30 44 4; for emergency dial 100.

Telephone Code: 067.

Accommodations and Food

Tzfat has an accommodations situation unique in Israel. The **IYHF Youth Hostel** is well-equipped and only a short ride away from the bus station. But the residents of Tzfat provide inexpensive accommodations in spare rooms within their own apartments, and in separate flats altogether. Most of the pensions are comfortable, with hot showers, living rooms, and separate kitchens for guests. The best way to find one of these places is to let them find you. Just walk around the Central Bus Station holding your luggage and it shouldn't be long before you are approached. But don't pay until you see the place, and ask if it has the amenities you require (e.g., hot showers, clean sheets). If you get to town after the buses stop running, sack out in the park of the citadel above town. Be warned, though, that the gardeners turn on the sprinklers at 6am.

Searching for a place to stay on your own (especially during the summer tourist season when trade is brisk) is a waste of time as nearly all pensions are run as second businesses and the owners are rarely present during the day. If no one approaches you at the station, ask at the tourist office or try:

Shoshanna Briefer, two large apartments off HaPalmach St. Follow Rehov Yerushalayim clockwise until you pass under a bridge. Take the stairs up to the bridge and cross over, heading away from Gan HaMetzuda. Turn off at the first alleyway to your right and take the alley that runs diagonally in the same general direction as the road. At the bottom of the alleyway on the left you will see a large, green metal door: the entrance to the second apartment. First apartment is in the same alley, a grey door on the right, ⅔ of the way down. Good toilet and shower facilities, small kitchens with refrigerators. Several pleasant doubles and triples. One apartment has better rooms and a larger kitchen; the other has a small, shaded courtyard. Both places about $4 per person without breakfast.

Beit Binyamin IYHF, near the Amal Trade School, in South Tzfat (tel. 31 08 6). A twenty-minute walk from the bus station. Bus #2, 2a or 6. Large, well-equipped hostel with a brand-new kitchen and dining room, serving all meals upon request. Unfortunately, the recent rash of thefts should make you tie your bags to your toes before you bed down.

David Ohana, on Javetz St., off the corner of 16 Rehov Yerushalayim (tel. 30 73 4). Take the first left off Javetz, make a right after the yard through the stone arch and go up one flight of stairs. Airy though not overwhelmingly clean rooms, not far from the tourist office. Shower and kitchen facilities. More privacy than Shoshanna's. $6.50 per person, no breakfast. Other places on this street rent rooms too.

Malkah Pinto, 100 Rehov Yerushalayim. Near the bridge, just a little way back toward the bus station. Through the red doors and left up the stairs. Charming.

The stretch of Rehov Yerushalayim north of the bridge (to #48) is lined with good, cheap felafel stands and expensive sit-down restaurants. There are two exceptions: the **HaMifgash Restaurant** opposite the small observation point and park and the **Milu Restaurant** at the corner of Alya Bet St. both serve good Oriental food at fair prices. Milu is open daily 8am-midnight, Fri. till 4pm. The **Steakia HaSelah** (no English sign), a tiny grill two doors west of the bridge, has some of the best *shwarma* in the country, served in a pita pocket with do-it-yourself salads ($2). Take the stairs up to the bridge and walk away from Gan HaMetzuda (southward) to reach the fruit and vegetable **market** held from dawn until dusk every Tuesday and until noon on Wednesdays (in front of the Central Post Office). There is also a brand new **supermarket** on HaPalmach St. above the bus station.

Sights

Tzfat's small size makes sightseeing fairly easy, as long as you keep asking directions. Unfortunately, the older sections are so intricate and poorly marked that giving explicit sightseeing directions is well-nigh impossible. You may find it helpful to think of Old Tzfat as divided into three semi-distinct sections: the **Park Area,** at the top of the mountain (ringed by Rehov Yerushalayim), the **Artists' Quarter,** southwest of Rehov Yerushalayim, and the **Old City** or Synagogue Quarter, immediately to the north of the Artists' Quarter on the other side of Ma'alot Olei HaGardom.

The meager ruins of a twelfth-century Crusader fortress which once commanded the main route to Damascus grace **Gan HaMetzuda**—a cool, wooded park which is now an excellent spot for a picnic. At the summit stands a monument commemorating the Jews who died here during the 1948 war. A convenient entrance is near #41 Rehov Yerushalayim, across from the **Davidka** monument, which commemorates a weapon used in the War of Independence because of the frightening noise it made.

Just north of the park, along the same road as the Ron Hotel, is the **Glickenstein Museum.** Though dedicated to the sculptor of that name, it houses works of other artists as well, including the masters. The building itself was constructed in 1911 as the official residence of the Turkish Pasha. It then changed hands from Turkish to British to Arab, and finally to Israeli. The Israelis turned it into a museum in 1953. Best of all, the overseer of the museum, originally from French-Canadian Minnesota, can give you a fascinating overview on life in Israel. Open June-Oct., Sun.-Thurs. 9am-noon and 4-6pm, Fri. 9am-noon, closed Sat.; admission $.20, $.10 for students.

The **Shem Va'Ever Cave,** one of several sacred caves in the region, is believed to be the burial site of Noah's son and grandson, Shem and Ever. Located near the top of the bridge off HaPalmach St., the cave is kept by an elderly Jewish man who will light a small candle for you and say a prayer before requesting a small donation.

Nearby, at the intersection of Rehov Yerushalayim and Arlosoroff St., a forest of English signs directs you down the hill to the *General Exhibition* (open Sun.-Thurs. 9am-6pm, Fri. 9am-4pm, closed Sat.; in winter open only Sun.-Thurs. 9am-5pm. It's a good place to start your tour of the Artist's Quarter. Wherever you begin, however, you'll find the most interesting work and the prettiest galleries on the smaller streets, further south. Many of the galleries are run by the painters themselves, so hours vary. In general most studios are open daily (including Sat.) 10am-1pm and 4-9pm. Not surprisingly the galleries with large displays fronting the street are the most touristy, while the better ones don't always have large "Welcome. Entrance Free" signs.

If you find navigating in the Artists' Quarter confusing, the **Old City,** also known as **Qiryat Batei HaKnesset** ("The Synagogue Quarter"), will be an outright labyrinth. The best way to see the area is to give up before you start; just resign yourself to getting lost and set aside an hour for hiking around. The two most famous synagogues in the city are the **Caro** and **Ha'ari Synagogues.** To reach them, take Ma'alot Olei HaGardom St. off Rehov Yerushalayim and make a right onto Beit Yosef St. The Caro Synagogue will be straight ahead. For the Ha'ari (Ashkenazi) Synagogue, follow Beit Yosef until it becomes Alkabetz St. Make a right up a stairway, above which are several stained-glass stars of David, and continue straight under the stone arch. To the right, on Rehov Najara, is the synagogue. The Caro Synagogue has a remarkable set of old books and Torah scrolls (ask to see them). Here the Cabbalist Rabbi Joseph Caro, author of the vast *Shulkhan Arukh* (a guide to nearly all the practical, day-to-day aspects of living according to Jewish law), studied and prayed in the sixteenth century. Just downhill are the **Abuhav** and **Alsheich** synagogues, off Abuhav St. in the "Spanish Quarter." Take a left off Beit Yosef St. onto Alsheich St. and then a quick right; both will be to your right. The light blue walls of this section are repainted annually before the holiday of *Lag ba'Omer,* and are believed to ward off certain evil spirits. At each of the little synagogues you will be discreetly asked for a contribution. Virtually all these synagogues are open to visitors, though even the tourist office readily admits they're more often closed than open; if you happen to come during a prayer service, wait outside for it to end. Unless it's Sabbath or early morning, the service will not last more than fifteen minutes. One peculiarity about all the synagogues here: since Tzfat is to the north of Jerusalem, the synagogues' holy arks are all on the southern, rather than the eastern, wall. Nearby, up the stairs, you'll find the **Tifferet Gallery,** featuring the artwork of Hassidic Jews.

On the outskirts of the old city, off Rehov Ha'ari, are located three adjoining **cemeteries** (if asking directions in Hebrew, say "Batei Ḥakvarot"). The oldest contains the graves of the most famous Tzfat Cabbalists, as well as a domed tomb built by Karaites (a medieval group of Jewish heretics) of Damascus in the fifteenth century, and said to mark the grave of the biblical prophet Hosea. (For more information on the Karaites, see Ramla section.) On the wall inside the tomb you'll find an article posted about an eighth-generation Tzfat resident named Moshe Shebabo. Originally a none-too-religious gym teacher, he began having recurring dreams in 1980, in which an old bearded man begged him to restore the badly neglected graves. Shebabo quit his job, became religious, and single-handedly undertook the restoration of the graves. Any visible grave on the site is the result of this man's work. Nor is it hard to see why such work would be important. The Cabbalists believed that because of the pure air in Tzfat, the soul of any person who dies here will enter Paradise immediately. The Cabbalist Ari (Luria) once said that the number of "righteous men, martyrs, and geniuses" buried at Tzfat is equal to twice the number of Jews who went out of Egypt in the Exodus—a rather self-serving remark, since the Ari himself, is, of course, buried here. Legend relates that under this same hill lie Hannah and her seven sons, whose martyrdom at the hands of the Syrians is recorded in the Book of Maccabees; supposedly you know you are walking over their hidden graves by a sudden feeling of fatigue.

If you are stranded in town on Saturday and neglected to take your *mikvah* (ritual bath), try the lovely swimming pool and leisure center (open in summer only) just off Derekh Ha'atzmaut, behind the Central Bus Station. The first buses pull out on Saturday at 3pm.

Near Tzfat

Each year during the holiday of *Lag ba'Omer,* thousands of pilgrims converge on the tiny village of **Meron,** site of the tomb of Rabbi Shimeon Bar Yokkai, the great second-century Talmudic scholar who composed the *Zohar* while hiding in Peki'in (see "Near Nahariyya" section). The Cabbalists hold that Bar Yokkai once vowed to God that the Jews would never forget the importance of the Torah. Mindful of this vow, the Tzfat *chassidim* dance and sing their way to his tomb in a joyous procession, accompanied by an ancient Torah scroll from the Bana'a synagogue (in the Spanish Quarter). Contact the tourist information office in Tzfat for further details.

Meron is also the beginning of a gorgeous 6km hike through **Wadi Ammud.** You can descend into the Wadi along the winding track which begins near the bottom of the cemetery, or hitchhike a few kilometers out of town and descend from there. Be careful: the depth of the Wadi not only guarantees a difficult climb at either end, but also intense heat. Be sure to take along a couple of litres of water per person and try to begin your hike as early as possible. The walk takes about three hours; you can take a bus back to Meron. The truly adventurous can try scaling the highest mountain in Galilee, **Har Meron** (1208m). It towers over the village of Meron and offers, at different points along its ridge, views of both the Mediterranean Sea and the Sea of Galilee. You can pick up the trail for this steep climb on a dirt track starting just west of the village.

Upper Galilee

The Upper Galilee is the forested source of the entire Galilee region's natural wealth. The almost tropical water sources of the Jordan River carve up the lush **Hula Valley** into numerous nature reserves. **Metulla,** on the Lebanese border, is Israel's northernmost point. From **Qiryat Shemona,** the principal town of the Upper Galilee, it is possible to tour the area by public transportation. Qiryat Shemona is easily reached from Tiberias, Tzfat, or Afula as well as Haifa, Tel Aviv, and Jerusalem. The **Tel Chai Youth Hostel (IYHF)** is a convenient rest stop, while the campgrounds at **Chorshat Tal** are sheltered by a forest canopy.

Qiryat Shemona

Orientation and Practical Information

A small town filled with refugees-turned-immigrants from the Arab states of the Persian gulf and Northern Africa, Qiryat Shemona is the administrative and transportation center of the Upper Galilee. The town's history is interesting, but there's nothing much to do here.

In 1920, Halsa and other nearby Bedouin villages attacked Metulla, Tel Chai, Kfar Giladi and other Jewish towns, accusing them of aiding the French, who were claiming control over the Bedouin lands. Yosef Trumpeldor tried to defend the towns by letting the Bedouins into Tel Chai to disprove their accusations. However, the Bedouins attacked, killing Trumpeldor and seven others. These six men and two women were buried in **Kfar Giladi,** where the lion in the Cemetery of the Shomerim now stands. In honor of the eight heroes, the town built on the ruins of Halsa was named Qiryat Shemona, "Town of the Eight."

The **Central Bus Station** in Qiryat Shemona is on Sderot Tel-Chai; the only eateries in town are bunched up near the intersection of Tel-Chai and Tchernikovsky. The telephone code for Qiryat Shemona and the surrounding region is 067.

Near Qiryat Shemona

Just south of Qiryat Shemona is another of Israel's Galilee wilderness parks, the **Hula Nature Reserve** (tel. 37 06 9). Here, in addition to the wondrous landscapes, there is a myriad of wildlife. The pelicans and herons are easy to spot; the water buffalo are hard to miss. Sunday, Tuesday, Thursday and Saturday there are free guided tours in English. To see the wild boars or the mongoose, get there at dawn and hope for the best. Visiting hours are Sun.-Thurs. 8am-4pm, Fri. and holiday eves. 8am-3pm, Sat. 9:30am-1pm.

To the west of Qiryat Shemona lies **Tel Chai.** First established in 1918 as a military outpost after the withdrawal of British forces from the Upper Galilee, Tel Chai has grown to be a symbol of Israel's early pioneer movement. A monument to Yosef Trumpeldor, the famous one-armed founder of the Zion Mule Corps, stands on the outskirts of town. The original watchtower and stockade settlement, destroyed by Arab nationalists in 1920, has recently been turned into a small museum (open in summer Sun.-Thurs. 8am-1pm and 2-5pm, in winter Sun.-Thurs. 8am-4pm, Fri. 8am-noon, Sat. 8am-1pm; admission $1.20, $.80 for students). They'll screen an excellent slide show in English for a small group of people. Tel Chai is also the home of Israel's northernmost **Youth Hostel** (tel. 40 04 3). Just off the main Metulla-Qiryat Shemona road, it is served by buses from both towns—tell the driver you want the youth hostel instead of the archeological site. Beds are $3.60, two go for $7, and quads are $12.84. The dining room is filthy but friendly. Breakfast $1.15, lunch $2.20, supper $1.30.

Buses #25, 26, and 36 from Qiryat Shemona all travel east through the **Chorshat Tal Nature Reserve.** Buses run every hour or so, making this an excellent spot to stop for a picnic. Huge oak trees, some of them nearly two thousand years old, can be found throughout the forests here. Such trees do not survive anywhere else in the Holy Land. According to an old Arabic legend, the trees have been preserved because ten messengers of Muhammad rested here. Finding not a single tree for shade nor a hitching post for their camels, they pounded sticks into the earth to fasten their mounts. Overnight the sticks sprouted and the holy men found themselves in a gorgeous forest by morning.

Further along the road is the **Chorshat Tal Camping Ground** (tel. 40 40 0), on the banks of the Dan River. Tent sites are available for $4.50 ($2.80 in the off-season), three- and four-person bunks for $24 and $30, respectively ($18 and $24 in the off-season). Caravans for four cost $36 ($28 off-season), for six cost $45 ($34 off-season). The campground is an easy jumping-off point for the rest of the Galilee, despite an 11pm curfew; campers must clear out by 1pm.

Just down the road is the kibbutz **Sha'ar Yeshuv,** which hosts one of the SPNI's Field Study Centers. Accommodations are rarely available here, but you can sometimes listen in on the tour group's lectures when they're in English. The next kibbutz to the northeast is **Kibbutz Dan,** in the midst of the Hula Valley's lushest nature reserve. The waters come from the **Fountain of Dan** at the foot of the large Tel Dan, still being excavated (open in summer Sun.-Thurs. 8am-5pm, in winter 8am-4pm). Unfortunately there is no swimming here. The kibbutz museum of the valley flora and fauna was renamed **Bet Ussishkin** after the death of the Jewish National Fund director of that name. Open Sun.-Thurs. 9am-noon and 2-5pm. The real treat, however, is the nature reserve all around.

Just south of Metulla, set back from the road, the cool mountain air is pierced by the mist from the **Tanur Waterfall.** After the 18m drop, enough mist is created to suggest the name *tanur* or "oven." The Ay'un River later joins the Jordan on its way south. The water is not hot; if you are, jump in. Bus #20 from Qiryat Shemona is the local bus and will drop you off close to the falls if you ask.

The border town of **Metulla** is unremarkable, but popular with tour groups. Just west of town, the **Good Fence** refers to an opening in the border fence between Israel and Lebanon where Israel has allowed Lebanese Christians to pass through and obtain free medical attention from an Israeli clinic. Politically, Metulla's significance lies in the image the "Good Fence" gives the Israelis: kind-hearted samaritans who love to help poor, needy Lebanese. Few propaganda sites are as easy to manipulate as this one—the Lebanese here are Christians fighting Lebanese Muslims for Israel. At present, the Israeli Defense Forces hold both sides of the border and the novelty of the Israelis' aiding the Lebanese Christians has worn off. Soldiers have replaced most of the tourists and the sandwich stands and war memorial flea markets are sure to follow.

Although there should be no reason for it, if you need to stay in Metulla overnight there are several alternatives. Since the tourist market is depressed, you can bargain the fancy hotel prices down to your level. The **Ha Mavri Hotel** (tel. 40 15 0) and the **Arazim Hotel** (tel. 40 01 5) charge between $7 and $15 per person depending on the size of the room. Both are on the main street near the bus stop. If you backtrack towards the beginning of the town along the same street, the last two houses on the right are boarding houses. The elderly owners of each are wonderfully friendly and will talk non-stop in almost any language but English. Expect to pay $3-5 per night.

Golan Heights

The Golan Heights stretch from the alligator ponds on the **Yarmukh River** in the south to the snow-capped heights of **Mt. Hermon** on the Lebanese-Syrian border. They include the land east of **Lake Tiberias** on a high escarpment stretching west to the Syrian city of **Quneitra.** The region is one of diverse natural beauty, but over the millennia armies have struggled over it for reasons other than its scenery. The heights above the fertile Jordan valley have held special strategic significance for many civilizations. In order to secure absolute superiority over the Golan, the Romans fought relentlessly to take the town of Gamla, resulting ultimately in the death of all but three of its citizens.

Unfortunately, the glorious battles of yesterday are the political nightmares of today. In the 1967 war, Israel occupied the Golan Heights after a two-day campaign. As a result, the Hula Valley agricultural settlements were spared the light-arms fire and occasional shelling of the Syrian troops that had been based there. In 1973, Syrian troops pushed Israeli forces back almost to the pre-1967 borders, only to see Israel reconquer this territory (and more) the following week. As part of the 1973 peace treaty, Israel returned both this newly-conquered territory and part of the land captured in 1967. But in 1981, the Israeli Parliament *(Knesset)* voted to annex the Golan, arousing a storm of international protest as well as unrest among the Golan's sizeable Druze population, who were required to carry passes indicating their Israeli citizenship. For the most part, the annexation has been merely symbolic, and the controversy—both political and military—remains. From Syria's point of view, the land was seized by an illegal act of aggression. Israel, on the other hand, claims that Syria's possession of the Heights posed intolerable threats to northern Israeli settlements, pointing to the pre-1967 attacks on Ein Gev as but one example. From the eastern escarpment you can now look down on Syrian Quneitra in a zone administered by the United Nations; from the western cliffs you can see the bunkers and trenches from which the Syrian armies watched large Israeli communities; and from the southern slopes down to the Yarmukh River you can see the peaceful hills of Jordan.

Orientation

It is possible to tour most of the Golan by public transportation, but infrequent services along sparsely-traveled roads make careful planning a necessity. In general, buses to sites near to and east of the Sea of Galilee leave from the **Central Bus Station** in Tiberias, passing **Kibbutz Sha'ar Ha Golan** (Gateway to the Golan). The Upper Galilee, Hula Valley and Northern Golan are served by buses from Qiryat Shemona and occasionally from Tzfat as well. The bus from Tzfat crosses an important Gate to the Golan, the **B'not Ya'akov Bridge** over the Jordan River, some 10km from Katzirin. According to legend, this is where Jacob passed with his family when his daughters predicted that they would sell their brother into Egypt. The name B'not Ya'akov (daughters of Jacob) actually comes not from this story, but from a Crusader nuns' order of the same name. From the bunkers and trenches of **Mitzpeh Gadot,** Syrian armies once looked down on the strategic bridge, 1km to the west. At the point where the Jordan Valley opens up into the Hula Plain, you will see some three-girdered structures. They are tank stoppers, repainted by the Israelis after 1973 to complement the large memorial to fallen Israeli soldiers.

Since relatively few cars traverse the Golan, hitching requires extreme patience and preparedness. If you do set out on your own, be sure to take a good map, a *kal-kar* (water bottle) and at least a day's worth of food, since eateries are few and far between.

Organized tours of the area are faster, more convenient, and sometimes even cheaper in the long run. However, they can be rushed and usually preclude hiking and swimming. **Egged** offers full-day tours of the region (three days a week), leaving from Haifa ($29), Tiberias ($22, $20 for students), or Tel Aviv ($30). The Tiberias tour, which is more comprehensive, runs on Tuesdays, Thursdays, and Saturdays, and manages to provide an excellent overview of the Upper Galilee and Golan Heights region. In addition, **Oded Shoshan** in Tiberias (tel. 21 81 2) owns several minibuses and taxis and is very knowledgeable about the Golan. For $14 he will take you on a personal tour of the area. The best tours, however, are the two- to four-day camping trips organized by the **Society for the Protection of Nature in Israel.** Although they are quite expensive, the trips may visit otherwise-inaccessible spots, are always led by knowledgeable guides, and often include special treats like inner-tubing on the Jordan River.

The only other option is to rent a car. If you have enough people, this is an excellent way to tour the area. (See Israel Introduction for addresses and rates.) You can cover the Golan and Upper Galilee in a day by starting early, but this doesn't leave much time to hike into Gamla or swim in the pools and falls.

The Golan is no longer subject to curfews, and you do not need a travel permit. However, the frequent military maneuvers in the Golan may restrict your movement. Roadblocks are usually lifted in a matter of minutes, so ask how long it will be. In the areas closest to the border, pay strict attention to the requests of soldiers and stay on the paved roads away from leftover land mines.

Sights

On the same bus line from Qiryat Shemona as the Dan area in the Upper Galilee is the **Banyas,** source of the Hermon River. The "source" is a gushing rock wall at the site of an ancient Greek sanctuary dedicated to Pan, the god of nature and shepherds. Since classical Arabic has no equivalent to the p-sound, the Arabic version of "Pan's Place" is "Banyas." Herod built a temple to Pan here which was enlarged by his son Philipus, who named it Caesarea (after his emperor, Augustus Caesar). It was called Caesarea Philipus to distinguish it from the coastal Caesarea, and Philipus's successor added Neronis to the name, in honor of Emperor Nero. It was here also that Jesus chose Simon as his first disciple and renamed him Peter. The Hebrew prophet Elijah, called *El Khadar* (the Green One) by Muslims and St. George by Christians, also had a shrine by the cave of the Banyas. This church was converted into a mosque, which is still visible today. Finally, this same spot is sacred to the Alauwy, an Islamic sect whose members live on the banks of the nearby Hatzbani River. Only 1km from the old Syrian border, the area was used as a staging point for attacks into the Hula Valley until 1967.

After taking a brisk walk around the Banyas—don't even bother to stick your toes in like everyone else—either head off over the creek to the nature reserve to enjoy the jungle or trek about 1km down the road (towards Qiryat Shemona) to the **Banyas Waterfalls.** This resort, the largest waterfall in the region controlled by Israel, is also overcrowded, but the water is beautifully chilling and the crashing falls drown out most of the unpleasant commotion. These falls are rarely as gentle as those at Ein Gedi so take a hardhat or take care.

Only 1½km from the Banyas, visible through the trees, is **Nimrod's Castle.** After building Babylonia, Nimrod, called the "first mighty man on earth" (Gen. 10:8), constructed this huge fortress high enough so that he could shoot his arrows up to God to prove his strength. A plaque above one of the many gates reads in Arabic: "God gave him the power to build this castle with his own strength." Nimrod's slaves' strength must have been phenomenal as well, judging from the enormity of the stones they dragged up the steep cliffs. In Nimrod's later years, when he had turned away from Allah, a fly was sent down from heaven into the great man's nostril to eat away at his brain until he died a painful death. The fortress is sometimes called *Qalat Zuveira* after the Hebrew or Arabic word for fly, *zevuv*.

Despite its size and cliffside approach, Nimrod's castle was conquered only 25 years after it was completed. After a succession of owners, the castle was taken by the Hashashein, Muslims who have gone down in legend as a group of fanatics that turned ferocious under the influence of hashish. We still speak of their deadly prowess when we use the English word, assassin. The view from the top of the fortress is unrivaled anywhere in the Upper Galilee or Golan. Har Hermon is to the north, the Hula Valley to the southeast, and small, predominantly Druze villages sleep below it. You can see the small shepherds' shacks perched on the mountainside, waiting for their Majdal Shams Druze owners to return for the three-month grazing season. Keep an eye out for the many opossum that play and hide among the fallen stones. The approach to the castle, from which you can see clearly right into the tiny Druze village of En Kinya, lies just off bus routes #55 (between Qiryat Shemona and Katzirin) and #51. Tell the driver you want to climb up to the castle.

Because of the large number of Israeli visitors to this area, as well as the local Druze population, it's not difficult to hitch rides between the castle (a difficult climb) and the picturesque Druze villages of En Kinya, Mas'ada, and

Majdal Shams. **Majdal Shams,** about 5km to the north of the others, is the largest town in the Golan. Its name means "Tower of the Rising Sun." There is little to do in town besides chat with the friendly locals. The *shiruelas,* or low-hanging baggy pants worn by the men, date from Ottoman Turkish times. Since the Qur'an describes Muhammad's re-emergence in the world as coming through the "bowels of a man," the devout Turkish Muslims wanted to make sure the reborn prophet had enough room in case he should arrive unexpectedly. Unlike the Druze on Mount Carmel near Haifa, the Golani Druze have experienced little westernization of customs or commercialization due to tourism. Down the road to the south is tiny **Mas'ada,** a village where Israeli flags and pro-Israeli murals have been encouraged by the government during the demonstrations following the annexation. The village is next to a large placid lake, **Birkat Ram.** One thousand meters above sea level, the lake was formed in the mouth of an extinct volcano and is therefore almost perfectly round. There's no swimming, since the lake is used as a reservoir. You'll know you're at the lake when you see the parking lot of the two-story **Birkat Ram Restaurant.** The restaurant is crowded and, worse, completely surrounded by fences to prevent you from getting any closer to the lake or even from getting a good look except from the restaurant porch. The Druze owners are polite, but extremely possessive of the lakeview. If you set off to explore the fields around the lake, remember they are owned by Druze citrus farmers who live in nearby villages. If you walk out of the parking lot and turn right, you'll see a picture-postcard view of an immaculate Druze mosque beneath snowy Mt. Hermon.

Bus #51 from Qiryat Shemona passes by the Druze villages on its way up to **Moshav Neve Ativ,** which runs the winter ski slopes on the south slope of Mt. Hermon (tel. 067/31 10 3).

Although Majdal Shams is still the largest town in the Golan, Israel has chosen the Jewish town of Katzirin, founded only in 1977, as its administrative center and capital city. Bus #55 runs frequently from Qiryat Shemona; others from Tiberias and Tzfat run once a day. Hitching is quite easy in the vicinity of Katzirin. Katzirin can be a convenient base in the Golan because it has an excellent **SPNI Field Study Center** as well as some sights of its own.

Two kilometers south of the city are the remains of a synagogue from the Talmudic era. There is not much to see here or in the deserted Arab village around it, but you can appreciate the site more if you stop in at Katzirin's **Golan Archeological Museum** near the Central Bus Station. It's one of the most informative archeological museums in the country despite its tiny size. The staff (especially Uli) is wonderfully friendly if you show you're interested. They'll show you artifacts from many synagogues of the Golan and explain the meaning of the ritual symbols engraved in the stones. All of the ruins in the Golan are made from volcanic basalt rock which is very difficult to engrave. You can see actual olive pits and grains of wheat preserved over thousands of years because they were accidentally charred. These are some of the oldest pieces of evidence of agricultural communities, dating back almost to the Stone Age. Open Sun.-Thurs. 9am-1pm, Fri. 9am-noon, Sat. 10am-noon, admission $.50, $.40 students. Next door to the Museum are a supermarket and a public pool (admission $1.20).

A few kilometers north of Katzirin, the road ends in a T heading west to the B'not Ya'akov Bridge or east towards Quneitra. If you go east 2km, you can turn left towards the **Gilabon Nature Reserve** embracing the valley of the Gilabon River. Although the **Devorah** waterfall is an up-and-coming resort for Israelis, it is inaccessible except with a car—thumb or rent.

Continuing towards Syria you climb still farther to the higher levels of the

Golan. About 5km before the border are two kibbutzim, Merom Golan and En Zivan. Merom Golan means "Golan Heights" and was the first Jewish settlement erected in the Golan, a few months after the 1967 war. Near the kibbutz is **Har (Mount) Bental;** closer to En Zivan, with the radio antennae, is **Har Avital;** from the observation point here you can look down into the destroyed city of Quneitra. In 1967 Israel captured the town in fierce fighting and then returned it to Syria in the cease-fire agreement.

Once a city of 30,000 and headquarters of the Syrian Army, Quneitra is now a ghost town in no-man's land on a tense border—only an occasional UN vehicle disturbs its deadly silence. A few kilometers southeast of Katzirin, not yet served by public transportation, is the **Ya'ar Yehudiyya Nature Reserve** and the source of the **Zavitan River.** From just off the road you can hike down the river through some of Israel's most spectacular greenery. To find the starting point for the hike (which can take up to four hours), inquire at one of the Field Study Centers or ask one of Israel's most devout nature-hikers, who can usually be found here. Head downstream to the **Birkhat HaMeshushim.** These ponds received their name (meaning Hexagons) from the unique formation of the nearly hexagonal columns of rocks at the water's edge. The meshushim can also be reached by climbing upriver from the Bet Tzayda Valley (ask for Tzomet Bet Tzayda) along the Kinneret; or by walking down the path from the deserted village of Jaraba, about 13km south of B'not Ya'akov Bridge off the left side of the road. In addition to many animals, birds and much flora you'll see tracks cross the road or river at right angles so that tanks can cover these grounds in a hurry if necessary. The river basin is occasionally closed to through traffic due to military maneuvers in the area. More often temporary roadblocks are set up while tank blasts and mines go off a few kilometers ahead. You'll almost never actually see the maneuvers, but the sounds carry through the hills.

Some 15 km south of Katzirin is the Golan's most famous archeological site, the ancient city of **Gamla.** From high on the terrace you can see the two valleys carved out by the Daliyat and Gamla Rivers on their way to the Kinneret. Called by many the "Masada of the north" Gamla is nearly impossible to reach except by car or organized tour. Since most of the cars in this area are going there, however, you might want to use a placard with your destination printed on it and hitch. The name Gamla comes from the Hebrew word for camel, *gamal,* powerfully suggested by the double hump-shaped mountain on which the ancient city was built.

During Herod's iron rule over the Israelite communities in the Holy Land, three theories developed about how best to resist the Roman domination. The *Isi'im,* white-robed desert-dwellers, feared the Romans' superior strength and chose isolation, developing their communal way of life in the arid highlands. The *Metunim,* in the political center, adopted the passive approach. The *Kanayim,* the most religious of the Jewish groups, prepared to rebel with force by fortifying their city Gamla, nestled in its inaccessible terrain. You'll see that their idea was sound when you take the three- to four-hour leisurely hike down the mountainside, across the ravine, and up to the ancient ruins. But the Romans patiently concentrated their forces against this last rebellious hold-out and besieged the city for many months. When the final assault came, the outclassed defenders fled to the very top of the mountain and hurled themselves and their families off the steep northern cliffs to avoid being enslaved by the Romans. At the end, only two women survived, along with the commander of the Jewish forces, Joseph Matityahue. Joseph was converted to Christianity and forced to write a history of the Roman conquest of the Jews. His book,

The Jewish Wars, under his Christian name Joseph Flavius, has become the primary source of historical information on this period.

The site is open Sat.-Thurs. 8am-5pm, Fri. 8am-3pm; admission is $.80. Especially in the summer, the hike down is best made in the late afternoon so that the return ascent is out of the hot sun.

About the furthest point east you can visit in the Golan is the kibbutz of **Chispin.** The Field Study Center here is run by the SPNI in conjunction with the extremely religious kibbutz. It is called **Midreshet Ha Golan** and operates much like any other Field Study Center. For information call 067/63 46 1 or 63 30 5, or call Omer (tel. 63 81 9) in Katzirin. You can often stay overnight for $3-5 and meals are available during the day. Buses from Tiberias (#18,19) leave five times a day. The Midreshet also organizes informative outings to Nahal Devorah, the Banyas, Tel Dan, and Gamla; but they're very expensive unless you latch onto a group. Mitzpeh HaOn (literally the HaOn lookout point) is the best place to see just how shockingly close the Golan Heights bring you to the Kinneret settlements. The 600m drop to Kibbutz HaOn on the edge of the lake is precipitous; from the cliff you can practically hear the conversations in the valley and see Tiberias across the lake.

Buses between the Golan Heights and Tiberias pass about 1 km from the town of **Chamat Gader,** a few kilometers east of Deganya and Semakh. Here, close to where the Syrian, Jordanian, and Israeli borders meet, is the site of ancient Roman steambaths. From the third century C.E. until their destruction in the ninth century these huge sculpted baths were continually in use, drawing their heat from the naturally hot mineral springs. Even more ancient artifacts indicate that the pools were used in biblical times as well. Six of the halls have been excavated and the first two opened to the public. The government is planning to renovate the baths so they will operate as they did eleven centuries ago. Until this is completed, there are two other swimming holes. The warm, muddy one is for human beings, the other for alligators. The park is open 8am-5pm; admission $3.50, $2.50 for students. The last bus for Tiberias which leaves directly from the park departs at noon. Otherwise you can make the tortuous 1 km climb to the intersection to catch the buses from other parts of the Golan.

Tel Aviv
Jafo (Jaffa)
0
1 km
1 Bet November Square
2 Carmel Market
3 Central Bus Station
4 Central Post Office
5 Central Railway Station (El Al Terminal)
6 Great Mosque
7 Great Synagogue
8 Hamedina Square
9 Hamoshavot Square
10 Hassan Bek Mosque
11 Helena Rubenstein Art Pavilion
12 ISSTA
13 Jaffa Post Office
14 Maagen David Square
15 Malchei Yisrael
16 Masaryk Square
17 Museum Ha'Aretz
18 Old Jaffa
19 Railway Station South
20 Tel Aviv Museum
21 Tel Aviv University
22 Tel Aviv University Branch
23 Tourist Information Office
24 U.S. Embassy
TEL AVIV
JAFO (JAFFA)
Tel Aviv Port
Atzmaut Garden
Orange Beach
Clore Park
Jaffa Port
Ramat Aviv
Tel Aviv Nat'l Park
Yarkon River
Kerem Hatemanim
Neve Zedek
Shekhunat Florentin
to Jerusalem

Tel Aviv and Central Coast

The narrow, ninety-kilometer stretch of coastline from Tel Aviv to Haifa is the heartland of modern Israel. Nearly two-thirds of Israel's population and most of its major businesses call this region home. Through the ages, cities such as Caesarea and Jaffa have repeatedly been destroyed and rebuilt by succeeding empires. Their ruins present the ancient face of Palestine. A more youthful, modern visage is reflected in the steel skyscrapers, abundant night-life, and cultural offerings of Israel's largest city. The land north of Tel Aviv, once mostly barren and dry wasteland, now blossoms with the crops of prosperous kibbutzim and miles of sunny Mediterranean beaches and tanned bathers.

Tel Aviv

Although "Hill of Spring" ("Tel Aviv" translated from the Hebrew) is hardly the first image that comes to mind for visitors to Israel's latter-day boom-town, its biblical allusion is revealing. When God sent Ezekiel to guide the exiles to the town of Tel Aviv during Babylonian times, the prophet recounted a dream of dry bones coming to life again at their return to Israel. In 1909, Meir Dizengoff and his neighbors founded the city as a Jewish suburb of Jaffa, and translated the title of Theodore Herzl's utopian book *Old New Land* into Hebrew as Tel Aviv. In a period of only decades, an inhospitable stretch of desert has been transformed into one of the world's major capitals. Although many Israelis denigrate its vast landscape of skyscrapers and traffic-ridden boulevards for their cold, impersonal character, swearing that nothing could induce them to live in such a noisy nightmare of a place, the constant rebuilding, modernization and expansion of Tel Aviv is a living symbol of the determination to survive that is fundamental to the success of the Israeli dream.

Among the consequences of the rapid, relentless growth predicted by Ezekiel is the invigorating diversity of the Tel Aviv metropolis. From the spice markets of Shekhunat Florentine to the student community in Ramat Aviv, from the verdant suburbs of Savion to the glittering nightlife of Dizengoff Circle, Tel Aviv abounds in exciting surprises and more than makes up in cosmopolitan bustle what it lacks in ancient charm.

Much of Tel Aviv consists simply of identical, nondescript apartment blocks extending for miles. Even the downtown area can't shake off that drab, colorless quality indicative of a city built overnight with a purely functional intent. As you might expect, most of the interesting sights in Tel Aviv are museums. Two of them—the Diaspora Museum and the Modern Art Museum—are outstanding. Tel Aviv is also located near the old port of Jaffa, in the southern part of the modern city, where you will find the ancient walls and Muslim monuments Tel Aviv utterly lacks. Only after you have mastered the chaotic traffic, seen beyond the bland architecture, and escaped the noisy commotion, all in spite of the conspicuous lack of friendly assistance or even simple courtesy, can you begin to search for those small, enchanting neighborhoods that Ezekiel dreamt of and Herzl described.

Orientation and Practical Information

Five urban bus lines are particularly important to the visitor: #4 begins at the Central Bus Station, runs parallel to the coastline up Allenby Rd. and Ben Yehuda St. and then returns; #5 starts at the Central Bus Station, travels north along Sderot Rothschild and Dizengoff, turns around at Nordau and Yehuda

HaMaccabi (two blocks from the Youth Hostel), and then returns along Dizengoff to the Central Bus Station; #10 leaves City Hall to Jaffa along the coast and returns up Ben Yehuda; #25 begins at Tel Aviv University and goes to Haifa Rd., Yehuda HaMaccabi (Youth Hostel), the Shuq HaCarmel, Jaffa, the Bat Yam beaches and then returns; #27 runs from the Central Bus Station on Petakh Tikvah and Haifa Rds. to Tel Aviv University and the Diaspora Museum and returns.

Israel Government Tourist Office: 7 Mendele St., off Ben Yehuda St. (tel. 22 32 66). Open 8am-6pm, Fri. until 3pm. They can provide you with a city map, a listing of hotels, a calendar of events, and a bus schedule.

ISSTA: 109 Ben Yehuda St. (tel. 24 71 64 or 24 71 65). Open 9am-1pm and 3-6pm; Wed. and Fri. 9am-1pm only. Closed Sat. For ISIC cards, bring a national ID card (or a letter with an official stamp), one photo, and $6.

American Express: 16 Ben Yehuda St. (tel. 29 46 54), Meditrad Ltd. Open Sun., Mon., Tues., and Thurs. 8:30am-1pm and 3:30-6pm, Wed. and Fri. 8:30am-1pm, closed Sat.

Central Post Office: 132 Allenby Rd. (tel. 62 36 13). Open 8am-8pm. Fri. to 3pm. Closed Sat. This is the place for Poste Restante. Otherwise, Tel Aviv has numerous excellent neighborhood post offices.

Airport: David Ben Gurion Airport is 22 km southeast of Tel Aviv in Lod. El Al, the Israeli Airline, runs a steady bus service to the airport from 4am-10am every thirty minutes, and 10am-10pm every hour. For bus information, call 21 62 62: for flight information, call 62 52 52 between 7:30am and midnight. Also try 97 24 84 anytime. The El Al head Office is at the corner of Ben Yehuda and Shalom Aleichem Sts. Be prepared for a whopping airport tax of around $10.

Central Bus Station: in the southern part of town, outdoors. For information and schedules, call 33 11 32. The biggest station in Israel and a bit confusing. Most urban buses go here, including #4, 5, 26, 27, 32, 41, and 46. Intercity buses leave from the seven islands outside the information and ticket office. Those to Netanya leave from Hagra St.; those to Lod and Ramla leave from Finn St.; those to Hadera and Zichron Ya'akov leave from HaNegev St.; and those to Azor and Bat Yam leave from the field off Neve Sha'anan.

Railroad Station: Trains to Haifa and Netanya leave the Arlosoroff St. Station (tel. 25 35 48). Trains for Jerusalem leave in the morning from Bnei Beraq and the afternoon from Tel Aviv South Station. For Central Train information call 25 42 71.

Hitching: For Haifa, get on Derech Haifa. For **Jerusalem,** hitch from in front of the South Station. To hitch **south,** get on Derech Yitzchak Ben-Zvi in Jaffa.

Sherut Companies: to the suburbs and to Jerusalem from Salomon St. opposite the Central Bus Station. Cars to most other major cities in Israel leave from Allenby Rd. and Kikar HaMoshavot. These cost roughly twice as much as the buses. On Friday evenings and Saturdays the sheruts run (the buses don't) but cost about 20% more than usual. A sherut to the south is called a *servees*.

Emergencies: Police (tel. 100); First Aid (tel. 101); Rape Crisis 24-hour number (tel. 23 48 19).

U.S. Embassy: 71 HaYarkon St. (tel. 65 43 38). Ask here for medical advice.

Canadian Embassy: 220 HaYarkon St. (tel. 22 81 22).

Australian Embassy: 185 HaYarkon St. (tel. 24 31 52).

British Embassy: 192 HaYarkon St. (tel. 24 91 71).

Egyptian Embassy: 54 Basel St. (tel. 22 41 52).

Society for the Protection of Nature: see Israel Introduction.

Laundromat: 45 Bograshov St. (tel. 28 83 94). Coin operated washers and dryers. Wash $3, soaps $.40, dry $1.60. Open 8am-7pm, except Tues. and Fri. till 1pm, closed Sat. Also 51 Ben Yehuda St. (tel. 22 29 54). Same hours and prices.

Bookstores: Steimatsky's, 107 Allenby St., the largest in Israel. **Al Heh Bookstore,** at the corner of Dizengoff and Frischmann Sts., has a good selection of travel books. **Quality Books,** 45 Ben Yehuda St., has books on Israel and a few used paperbacks. All bookstores have some titles in English.

Ticket Office: For concerts, plays, etc. 93 Dizengoff St. Open Sun.-Thurs. 9am-1pm and 5-7pm. Closed Fri. afternoon and Sat.

Kibbutz offices: see Israel Introduction.

Addresses: House numbers run from the sea to the east and from south to north. They are often posted at street corners on the wall of the nearest house.

Equipment: American Bazaar, at 20 Salomon St. (tel. 33 16 38) at the Central Bus Station, sells all kinds of camping and travel equipment that is otherwise hard to find in Israel. Open 7am-8pm. U.S. prices plus.

Telephone Code: 03.

Accommodations

Most of Tel Aviv's cheaper hotels are located within two or three blocks of the beach, on or near Allenby Rd., Ben Yehuda, and HaYarkon Sts. Since these major roads are thunderous at times and busy most of the night, be especially choosy about where you sleep if you're sensitive to noise. Even in a relatively quiet hotel, ask for a room off the street. The hostels in Tel Aviv fill quickly, especially during the summer, so try to check in early.

The Greenhouse, 201 Dizengoff St. (tel. 23 59 94). Take bus #5 from the Central Bus Station. This is one of the nicest places in Tel Aviv. Clean rooms, friendly management, a central location, and no curfew. Beer for $.65 and coffee for $.30 in a pleasant T.V.-sitting room. $5 per person in 5-bedded rooms. Also rents small one bedroom flats for $110 per week for up to four people—especially suitable for couples and families. Reception open in summer 7:30-10am and 12:30pm-12:30am, otherwise 7:30-9:30am and 4pm-12:30am.

Hotel Yoseph, 15 Bograshov St. (tel. 28 09 55), off Ben Yehuda St. Take bus #4 from the Central Bus Station. Centrally located but cramped, and not especially clean. The "Voice of Peace" plays on the radio in a tiny lounge area with a table, chairs, and a bar with cold beer for $.80. The hippy hotel of Tel Aviv: when rock is on the radio there's room for four or five to dance. $4 per person; $1.20 extra for breakfast. 1am curfew.

Hotel Shalva, 14 Ha'ari St. (tel. 65 68 66), corner of Rav Kook near Kikar Magen David and Shuk HaCarmel. Take bus #4 from the Central Bus Station. Cheaper and shabbier than Yoseph, but quiet by Tel Aviv standards (except during the Sabbath). Walls are peeling, bathrooms are not too clean, but the rooms have balconies and there's a refrigerator for common use. For groups willing to bargain this can be the cheapest place in town (especially in the winter). The owner, who speaks French better than English, asks $6 for singles, $8 for doubles, $12 for triples. This does not include breakfast, but you can use his hot pots and fridge.

Bnei Dan Youth Hostel (IYHF), 32 Bnei Dan St. (tel. 45 50 42). Inconveniently located in the northern part of the city on the Yarkon River, a fifteen-minute walk from the beach, 25-minute walk from the center of town. Two blocks off the #5 bus route (get off at Yehuda HaMaccabi, and walk away from the city to Bnei Dan St.); buses run until 12:30am. The rooms are okay, but the bungalows cramped. 11pm curfew, but if you ask nicely you can usually get an extension. Excellent bulletin boards list events and bargains. Reception open 7-9am and 5-11pm. Sometimes closed during the day, other times you can leave luggage for $.20 per day. Members under 18 $5.30; non-members under 18 $5.20. Members over 18 $5.30; non-members $6.30. Some private rooms with bathroom available for $6.10 (members) or $6.60 (non-members). Prices include breakfast. It is sometimes possible to volunteer five hours per day in exchange for free room and board.

Nes Ziona, 10 Nes Ziona St. (tel. 65 65 87). Off Ben Yehuda south of Trumpeldor St. Excellent location in the center of town on a relatively quiet street, and the best deal in Tel Aviv for a hotel. $9 per person in well-kept singles, doubles and triples with private showers, $8 per person using a common shower. It's often $1 cheaper when business is slow. No curfew.

The Hostel, 60 Ben Yehuda St. (tel. 28 70 88). Between Mendele and Bograshov, around the corner from Hotel Yoseph. Take bus #4 from the Central Bus Station. Not an official hostel, despite its name. Disadvantages include unfriendly management, midnight curfew, four-flight walk-up, and the shabby effect mattresses on the floor create (no breakfast, either). Advantages: less cramped than the Hotel Yoseph, a sink in every room, refrigerator, common area with table and chairs. Check-in 5-11pm, usually closed 9am-5pm. Bed in dorm room $4, $3.60 for students, bed in double $6, triple $5.20, quad $4.80; the one single is $8.

Hotel Tamar, 8 Gnessin St. (tel. 28 69 97). More civilized than most cheap places. Near Cinema Hod: take Mendele St. from Ben Yehuda St. away from the sea. Recommended by the National Tourist Office. Homey and in a fairly quiet neighborhood. The friendly owner serves coffee, and there is a refrigerator in the hall. Singles $14, doubles $17.50 ($20 with private bathroom), triples $21. Variable student discounts.

Ha Galil, 23 Beit Yoseph St. (tel. 65 50 36). Near the market off Allenby St. #56. Singles $13.50, doubles $20. Closes at midnight, but you can get a key for the outside door if you ask.

Hotel Nordau, 27 Nahalat Benjamin (tel. 62 16 12). Lots of privacy, low on friendliness, but in a pleasant neighborhood. Singles $10, doubles $12.

Hotel Riviera, 52 HaYarkon St. (tel. 65 68 70). Near the beach. Singles $10, $14 with shower; doubles $14, $18 with shower. (Specify with or without shower.) Women under 35 can ask for a bed in a dorm room for $6. Breakfast included.

Bell, 12 Allenby Rd. (tel. 65 42 91). Singles $12-14, doubles $22-24, triples $30 (the third bed is rather small). Breakfast included. No curfew.

Immanuel House Christian Hospice, 12 Beer Hoffman St., Jaffa (tel. 82 14 59), on the corner of Auerbach and Beer Hoffman. Take bus #85 or 27 to Yerushalayim and Eilat Sts. If you're looking for a quiet place out of the hub, this is a good option. Newly renovated, it is clean and friendly. With breakfast they ask $10 per person in a room or $6.50 in a dorm. (If you're waiting to have money wired, they'll trust you for a few days.)

Except during times of increased political tensions, it is legal to sleep on the Mediterranean beaches. Those closest to the city are the noisiest and the least safe. Go north, if possible as far as the Herzliyya beaches. Just north of Herzliyya, within walking distance, there are some caves in the cliffs which are great for seclusion. As always when sand-snoozing, sleep on your wallet and be careful.

Food

As with any melting pot, Tel Aviv's immigrant diversity is most evident in its cuisine. Jewish communities have come from places as distant as South America, Siberia, India, and China. As a result, Tel Aviv has incredible international cuisine that includes such offerings as Brazilian, Russian, and Vietnamese restaurants, and, of course, kosher Jewish eateries as well as a kosher Chinese restaurant. Tel Aviv has its share of Oriental exotica, especially in food—try the neighborhoods of Neve Zedek (where the city's new Bohemians gather) and Kerem HaTemanim.

For Balkan food, try one of the Bulgarian sidewalk places on HaQishon St., off Herzl St., or one of the Rumanian restaurants on Eilat St., which is the continuation of Petah Tikva Rd. leading southwest. The **Goulash Corner,** 108 HaYarkon St. at the corner of Frischmann St., has good Hungarian food.

For a reasonably priced Italian meal, try **Cantina Pizzeria Capri** at #107 Dizengoff, or if you're in the mood for Russian food head for the restaurants at #110 and #265. The Middle Eastern cuisine at **Acapulco** on the corner of Frischmann and Dizengoff Streets is quite popular, as is the traditional Israeli food at **Batya** on the corner of Dizengoff and Arlosoroff Streets. For Chinese food, go to the small, reasonably priced restaurant on Ibn Gevirol St.; finally, for *couscous,* try the **Tripoli Restaurant** at 27 Raziel St. in Jaffa (bus #10).

The **South American Restaurant,** at 103 Yehuda HaYamit in Jaffa, has great food, but it's not authentic Latino. The same goes for the cheaper **Señor Sandwiches** that appear throughout the city. Vegetarians will appreciate **A Taste of Honey,** an American dairy restaurant with lots of Yiddish dishes at 14 Frischmann St. They'll often subtract 20% from the bill if you take out. The die-hard American who craves a McDonalds should try **McDavids** on Frishmann St. and at 22 Ibn Gevirol.

The first all-natural restaurant in Tel Aviv, **Banana,** is now open at 334 Dizengoff St.; its prices are astronomical. Not surprisingly, the old port of Jaffa still harbors the best seafood around (walk southwest from the clock tower). Try the **Little Jaffa** at 6 HaDayagim or the **Babai** (with the small porch).

All of these restaurants, however, fall in the luxury category for most Israelis. To eat cheaply in Tel Aviv-Jaffa is to follow the Israelis to one of the many neighborhoods which specialize in street food. The cheapest places to fill up are the self-service joints on Ben Yehuda St. or the innumerable felafel stands (those around the Carmel Market and along Bezalel St. off Allenby and HaMelech George are the spiciest and stay open late). Mix either (but not both) the red *harif* hot sauce or the yellow mustard sauce with lots of tahina. You can add as much sauce and greens as you want for about $1.

The Yemenite Quarter has good Oriental food between the Carmel Market and the beach. There are a few very cheap worker's restaurants on Peduim St., as well as the spruced up Zion Restaurant (28 Peduim St.), the place outsiders go when they want a Yemenite meal. For between $1 and $3 you can eat at an *a la esh* (on the fire) stand along Kanfe Nisharim St. (which runs north-south) in the Neve Zedek area. Spleen, hearts, liverwurst, and even an occasional cactus are served up in pita bread. Ask around for someone selling homemade *marak basar* (a wonderful Yemenite meat soup) or *melauach* (fried, salted dough dipped in one of several *srug,* or sharp sauces). For $1-2, either of these makes a filling meal. A family's tureens are generally empty by noon or 1pm, after which they may not be refilled for a day or two, so try to eat lunch early. If you speak any Arabic, here is your chance to use it.

Not far from the *a la esh* stands near the clocktower in Jaffa, Arabic *mamtekim* sellers hawk their Middle Eastern sweets at every few meters. These cakes and pastries, swimming in warm, sticky honey, are especially popular during Ramadan. Beware of the rainbow-colored *rabat lakum* rubbery sugar; unless you've got a sweet tooth the size of a camel, you'll never be able to finish a piece, much less enjoy it. But don't miss the *kanafe,*a salty cheese wrapped in pasta and covered with hardened boiled honey. It costs less than $1, and you'll survive the sugar rush.

Between the clocktower and the flea market two stands called **Abu-Lafiah** and **Abu-Limo** sell wonderful pita sandwiches (with meat, omelettes, or sesame sauce inside) as well as large, soft bagels dipped in *za'atar,* an oregano-like spice. The Arabs of Abu-Lafiah were so successful selling this treat that a Jewish family opened up next door. Abu-Limo's za'atar sells better than its name, a bizarre mixture of Arabic and Hebrew; but it's obvious where the crowds are.

For rock-bottom prices on food you can shop at the large outdoor **Shuq HaCarmel.** If you're farther north, the **Shuq HaTzafon** (off bus #4) is cheaper than the grocery stores but a little more expensive (and cleaner) than the Shuq HaCarmel.

No matter where you're going and what you're eating you'll need to replenish sacred bodily fluids. Thankfully, Tel Aviv is the fruit juice capital of the world. Practically anywhere in the city, 50¢ will buy a chilled glass of *meets* (fruit juice). Apples, oranges, grapefruits, lemons, bananas, grapes, and coconuts all go through the blender with water or milk. And, for a wonderful splurge, plunge into some iced coffee with ice cream.

Very fashionable these days are the blintz shops often owned by Hungarian Jews. Try the one at 35 Yermiyahu St., which fills its blintzes with cream, chocolate, cinnamon, apples, cheese, nuts, raisins, jam, spinach, *kashkeval,* eggplant, or Hungarian goulash with mushroom sauce. A serving of two blintzes runs $3-$3.50. If you're really in the mood to show off, they'll serve you a bowl with a chocolate, cream, and nuts blintz aflame in rum, right outside on the patio, for only $3.

Sights

In a country rich with ancient remains, Tel Aviv's attractions are uniquely modern.

One of Tel Aviv's more interesting quarters is the bustling **Shuq HaCarmel Market** ("shuq" means market), which specializes in clothes, footwear, and undergarments, but also features a few produce and grocery stalls. The frenzied, chaotic atmosphere will excite even the most blase of tourists. Another place to explore is **Kerem HaTemanim** (Oriental Quarter), which exudes local color despite the suspicious number of stores selling American T-shirts. The **Neve Zedek** area is quickly becoming known as the Artists' Quarter. Although the streets can be almost deserted by 7 or 8pm, during the day one can explore the studios of Israel's avant-garde and people-watch from cheap cafes.

For a more peaceful retreat head for the expansive **HaYarkon National Park,** in the northern part of the city, where you can rent a rowboat and cool off on the Yarkon River. Rentals are near the bridge where Haifa Rd. passes over the river and cost $2.50 per hour for two people and 50¢ extra for every added passenger. The two companies offering such rides are **Tikvah-Dagon** (tel. 41 29 21) and **Irgun HaYarkon** (tel. 44 84 22).

The closest thing to an historical monument in Tel Aviv proper is probably the **Great Synagogue** on Ahad Ha'am St., with its enormous dome and glossy stained glass windows. It was completed in 1926, and renovated in 1970 (almost ancient by Tel Aviv standards). On the eve of the Sabbath (Friday at sunset) throngs of the faithful make their way towards the synagogue, bringing all traffic to a halt—an impressive spectacle.

Tel Aviv's primary outdoor attraction is its vast, sparkling waterfront. The beaches are fair, though intermittently polluted, and extremely crowded in summer—many of the city's residents take advantage of every opportunity to head for a quick swim. Most of the popular beaches are adjacent to the Sheraton, Hilton, and Gordon Hotels, though the southern coastline tends to be less crowded. Avoid the grossly overpriced refreshment stands in the large concrete mall called Kikar Atarim. Ben Yehuda St., with bountiful, inexpensive food and drink, is never more than a two-minute walk from the beach. Near Kikar Atarim a marina offers wind-surfing, surfboard, and sailboat rentals. As you move from Tel Aviv's hotel beaches further to the north (but before Herzliyya), more and more young people and topless or nude bathers appear. You don't need to pay the entrance fee for non-Tel Aviv residents at the Country Club beach here. It's a mere fifteen-minute walk to the beach just north or south where you can climb down and enter free. The United bus #90 runs limited service to these beaches, even on Saturday, from Allenby Rd. or near the planetarium in Ramat Aviv. This makes a good Saturday trip when the weather is fine and there's little else to do.

Ignore all the luring advertisements for the **Shalom Tower Observatory;** the dull Tel Aviv skyline isn't worth the $1 charge to take the elevator to the top of Israel's tallest building, and the view from old Jaffa is better, anyway. The most interesting thing about the monstrous structure is that it occupies the original site of the **Herzliyya Gymnasium,** once the pride of the city because it was the first school in which classes were conducted in Hebrew. If you've never seen a wax museum the one beneath the tower is as good as any. If you've been to one, this is no better than a copy. Take bus #1, 12, 25 or 61 to 9 Ahad Ha'am St. (tel. 65 73 04). Open Sun.-Thurs. 9am-5pm, Fri. 9am-1pm, closed Sat.

Museums

Tel Aviv is a museum-goer's heaven. **Bet HaTefutzot,** or the **House of the Diaspora** (tel. 42 51 61), has become the most popular museum in the country. It is situated in the Tel Aviv University campus in the suburb of Ramat Aviv, to the north of Tel Aviv (take bus #24, 25, 27, 74, or 79). The numerous exhibits, models, and audio-visual displays all provide variations on a single theme, as the museum attempts to underscore what is common to the culture and history of Jews scattered throughout the world. The museum provides ambitious and well-thought-out documentary coverage of the Jewish experience in exile, elaborating on a host of fascinating and often horrifying historical incidents. The exhibits attempt to make an emotional impact upon the visitor, and especially on Jewish visitors.

The first floor of the museum features exhibits concerning Jewish religious traditions, such as Passover, Yom Kippur, and circumcision, that distinguish Jewish culture in the Diaspora, "the period of wandering," which refers to the dispersion of Jews throughout the world and their hope of returning to Israel. Movies, slides, maps, and artifacts tell the history of the diverse groups of

Jews in their respective countries of exile. For many, the most powerful exhibit is the "Scrolls of Fire," a collection of documents that provide a first-person perspective of the pogroms and massacres of Jews from Roman times to the Nazi concentration camps of World War II.

A visit to Bet HaTefutzot could take anywhere from four hours to two full days, depending on the extent to which you want to explore. Throughout the museum, little mini-cinemas feature a variety of documentaries, as well as numerous little telephone-like ear phones with recordings of dramatized arguments or discussions between historical personages; there is even a computer that will answer questions about Jewish history—it's a matter of how much time you want to devote to such diversions. The Diaspora Museum is open Sun., Mon., Tues., and Thurs. 10am-5pm, Wed. 10am-9pm, closed Fri. and Sat. Admission is $2, $1.40 for students. The **Chronosphere,** a multi-screen audio-visual display expanding on the same general theme as the rest of the museum, costs an additional $.60. Three buildings down from the Diaspora Museum is the Tel Aviv University Mensa offering inexpensive food. However, during the school year (which ends the last week in June) the cafe is plagued by a long wait (except Fridays) and by traditional Israeli coldness to strangers.

On the hill of **Tel Qasila,** also within the Tel Aviv University campus, excavations begun in 1948 and continuing today have revealed twelve stratae of remains dating back to a twelfth-century B.C.E. Canaanite settlement. Tel Qasila grew to be an important community under the rule of Kings David and Solomon, whose oil and wine presses can still be seen here. Entrance to the archeological exhibit is part of the fee for the extensive Ha'Aretz Museum complex.

The most famous of the eight other museums in the complex is the **Glass Museum,** containing one of the finest and most valuable collections of glassware in the world. Exhibits trace the entire history of glassmaking, from the earliest examples of the craft in the fifteenth century B.C.E., through the Middle Ages. Next door is the **Kadman Numismatic Museum,** which documents the history of Israel as it is reflected in ancient coins. Jewish religious art, ceremonial objects, and ethnic costumes are on display in the **Museum of Ethnography and Folklore.** The **Ceramics Museum** has an informative collection of pottery, especially the Gaza and Akko styles of "ibriq" pottery. They illustrate the invention of pottery, the relation between ancient and modern uses of pottery, clay and pottery as writing materials, and the religious nature of ceramics historically. The **Nechustan Pavilion** houses the rewards of the excavations of the ancient copper industries at Timna better known as "King Solomon's Mines."

In addition, the complex houses the **Alphabet Museum,** the **Lasky Planetarium,** the **Museum of Science and Technology,** and most recently a simple yet rewarding display of the tools of trade of many ancient and modern crafts. Called "Man and His Work," it covers the various smiths, the woodturner, cotton carder, potter, shoemaker, weaver, harness maker, and barber. The Ha'Aretz complex is open Sun.-Thurs. 9am-4pm, Fri. 9am-1pm, Sat. 10am-2pm; admission $1.20, $.80 for students, free on Sat. The complex is on HaUniversita St., two blocks east of Haifa Rd.; take bus #24, 25, 27, 74, or 79. The Lasky Planetarium is closed on Friday but has special sky shows Mon.-Thurs. at 10am, 11am, and noon, Sat. 10:30am, 11:30am, and 12:30pm, Sun. 11am and noon. Also, evening sky shows Tues. and Sat. at 8 and 9:30pm.

Also part of the Ha'Aretz Collection, although at different sites, are the **Museum of the History of Tel Aviv-Yafo** and the **Museum of Antiquities of Tel Aviv-Yafo.** The first, at 27 Bialik St., traces the history of the first all-Jewish city through photos, models, dioramas, and a panoramic slide and sound presentation. Not for the restless. Open Sun.-Thurs. 8am-3pm, Fri. 9am-1pm, closed Sat. The second is a portrayal of the history of the twin cities through the excavations carried out in them over the last twenty years. Open Sun.-Thurs. 9am-4pm, Fri. 9am-1pm, closed Sat. Admission to both museums is $.60, $.40 for students.

The **Tel Aviv Museum** has snazzy split-level galleries and a large collection of Israeli and international modern art. The museum is quite large—if your time is limited, head straight for Pavilion #2. In the first half, you will find a fabulous collection of Impressionist art, including canvasses by Corot, Renoir, Pissaro, Monet, and Duffy, with some works by Utrillo, and a delightful sculpture of a ballerina by Degas. The second half of the Pavilion features post-Impressionist masters such as Picasso, Juan Gris, Kokoschka, Roualt, and Matisse, among others. The modern collections tend to celebrate Israelis at the expense of quality. The Museum's specialty is its special exhibitions. Either call or try to pick up a copy of the Friday edition of the *Jerusalem Post;* it has a supplementary section which describes the museum's exhibits and special events. The Tel Aviv Museum is at 27 King Saul Blvd. (tel. 25 73 61). Take bus #18, 19, or 70. Open Sun.-Thurs. 10am-10pm, Sat. 10am-2pm and 7-10pm, closed Fri.; admission $2, $1.40 for students, but ask about the money saving year-long pass which gives you discounts on admission fees to other museums in Israel. The admission ticket for the Tel Aviv Museum also entitles you to enter the **Helena Rubinstein Pavilion,** which has changing exhibits, usually on art or history. It is just down the street at 6 Tarsat Blvd.; take bus #5, 11, or 62. To get there from Tel Aviv Museum, turn right on Saul Hanelech, left on Ibn Gevirol, right on Dizengoff, and left onto Tarsat. Open Sun.-Thurs. 9am-1pm and 5-8pm, Sat. 10am-2pm. Closed Fri.

Besides the outstanding museums listed above, you might want to visit one of the following. The **Haganah Museum,** at 23 Rothschild Blvd. (tel. 62 36 24), features a large, permanent exhibition tracing the growth of the Israeli army, beginning with the underground resistance movement against the British and including exhibits highlighting the stunning campaigns of 1948, 1956, and 1967. The **Jabotinsky Institute,** 38 HaMelech George St. (tel. 29 02 11), is dedicated to the life and thought of the Israeli revisionist Ze'ev Jabotinsky. **Ben Gurion's House** is worth visiting just to get a feel for the greatness of Israel's first Prime Minister; it is located at 17 Ben Gurion Blvd. (tel. 22 10 10), and is open Sun.-Fri. 8am-1pm, Mon. and Thurs. also 5-7pm. Admission is free.

Jaffa

Once the main port of Palestine, then a great Arab city, and now the showpiece of Tel Aviv, Old Jaffa is marvelous to stroll around in, despite its pricey restaurants, nightclubs, and tourist shops. The Crusader walls, Christian convents, and solemn mosques have all been restored, and the narrow medieval stone passageways rebuilt and cleaned; even if the old city is now a bit too polished, it is nonetheless pleasing to the eye. The easiest way to get to Old Jaffa is to take bus #10 from Ben Yehuda St. or bus #25 from north of the University and get off at Yefet St. when you see the clocktower.

Jaffa goes by many names: it is known in Arabic as Yafa, and in Hebrew as Yafo, which means "beautiful"; in the Bible it is referred to as Joppa. Even the ancient Greeks were familiar with the city and found a place for it in their mythology. Legend has it that Poseidon, the god of the sea, chained the young maiden Andromeda to the rocky reef which protects the harbor of Jaffa to this day. On the verge of being consumed by some enormous aquatic dragon, she was rescued in the nick of time by Perseus. In the right season, the constellation Andromeda can be seen above, while in the touristy markets of the old city, vendors still sell the bones of the dragon and the links of Poseidon's chain.

Even more delightful is the biblical fable connected with the city. God ordered the prophet Jonah to spread the word of His existence to the fierce Assyrians. In a fearful fit of pragmatism, Jonah fled instead for Joppa and boarded a departing ship (Jonah 1:3). He soon regretted his disobedience as a harsh storm started up and the vessel was tossed mercilessly about on the rough sea. Realizing that the entire crew of the ship faced death by drowning because of his foolishness, Jonah requested that his shipmates throw him overboard. God calmed the rage of the sea and called on a whale to swallow the disobedient prophet. After three days of prayer in this unlikely haven, he was forgiven and the whale brought him back to Joppa. In the New Testament (Acts 9:40), the Book of Acts states that the Apostle Peter came to Joppa and brought a dead girl by the name of Tabitha back to life. This miraculous event naturally helped him find some receptive ears for his teachings, so he stayed a while in the house of a tanner named Simon, who lived by the sea. Here he first received the inspiration to spread the gospel to non-Jews. What is alleged to be the house of Simon the Tanner can be visited today in Old Jaffa.

Recent archeological finds in Jaffa date from the eighteenth century B.C.E., making it a candidate for the oldest port city in the world. In 1468 B.C.E., the Egyptians conquered Jaffa by employing a cunning variation of the Trojan Horse ploy. Two hundred large clay jars were brought to the city market, each containing an Egyptian soldier. Once within the town walls, the soldiers popped out and captured the city. King David conquered Jaffa around 1000 B.C.E., and under King Solomon it became the main port of Jerusalem—a position it maintained until the rise of Caesarea under King Herod. During the twelfth century, Jaffa was taken by the Crusaders, by Saladin, by Richard the Lionhearted, by the Muslims, and finally by the Crusaders again, who then built magnificent walls and towers, some of which can stil be seen today. Nonetheless, in 1267 the Mamelukes overpowered the city, and from that time on Jaffa remained a major Arab stronghold until 1948. In 1740, the first Jewish hostel was established in what is now Kikar Kedumim. It included two *mikvas* (ceremonial baths) and a synagogue. (Libyan Jews have reopened the synagogue, which is still in use today.) Discontented with the UN resolution granting the creation of a Jewish state in Palestine, most of the Arab population of Jaffa staged a mass exodus one Passover Day 1948—seventy thousand men, women, and children left. Resettled primarily by Jews, Jaffa was officially incorporated into the township of Tel Aviv in 1948.

Above all, Jaffa is a town of spires and towers. The most famous of them is the **Clock Tower of Yafo,** on Yefet St., which marks the entrance to the city. Every Wed. at 9:30am a free tour of old Jaffa offered by the Government Tourist Office meets here. Next to the clock tower is the towering minaret of **El Machmudia Mosque,** a huge structure erected in 1812 (entrance is forbidden to non-Muslims). Down Mifraz Shelomo St. from the mosque, the **Archeological Museum** contains finds from neighboring sites in Old Jaffa. The columns and capitals dispersed around the museum's courtyard date from the first century B.C.E., and were brought to Jaffa from Caesarea during the last century. (The museum is open Sun.-Thurs. 9am-4pm, Fri. 9am-1pm, closed Sat. Admission $.60, $.40 for students.)

Behind the museum lie the grassy **Gan HaPisga Gardens,** which contain a small, modern amphitheater and a major archeological site with excavations of an eighteenth-century B.C.E. Hyksos town and a later Egyptian city. Among the finds was a thirteenth-century B.C.E. stone door on which was inscribed the name of the Egyptian king Ramses II. A strikingly ugly sculpture dominates one hill in the gardens, its three sections depicting the fall of Jericho, the sacrifice of Isaac, and Jacob's dream. From the park, a wooden footbridge leads to Kikar Kedumim, where you will find a smaller and better-preserved archeological site, several beautiful churches including the colorful Greek Orthodox **Church of St. Michael,** the Roman Catholic **Monastery of St. Peter,** a small Armenian church, and the **House of Simon the Tanner** (closed in 1983).

After the 1948 War, the numerous beautiful, abandoned Arab stone structures around Kikar Kedumin became the home of a large artists' colony. Although many of the galleries are worth exploring, the area has become quite touristy in the last few years, and good bargains are hard to find. Especially if you're just browsing, take a look in the **Ceramic House** at 16 Mazal Arie St. with its outdoor sculpture gardens. This gallery specializes in works by kibbutz women. Around the room are small ceramic boxes filled with beautiful *chatchkas* (knicknacks) of porcelain, glass mosaic and sand vases. It is open Sun.-Thurs. 10am-1:30pm and 8-11:30pm, Fri. 10am-1:30pm, and Sat. 8-11:30pm. Although Kikar Kedumim is the most touristy corner, the **Something Different Gallery** at #3 exhibits the story of Old Jaffa through slides and posters. This may be a somewhat tacky way to get you into an over-priced shop, but it works. The nearby clifftops offer some splendid vistas of the old city and the Tel Aviv beachfront and skyline. From the lighthouse a few blocks to the south you can see **Andromeda's Rock,** scene of the mythological rescue.

Shuq Hapishpisheem, the large, covered flea market of Jaffa, retains much of its Oriental flavor and old-world charm. One of the most exciting markets in Israel, the large covered complex of stalls offers endless delights: Persian carpets, leather goods, and brassware of all kinds (chalices, tea sets, plates, bells, and lanterns). Hashish connoisseurs will no doubt be delighted by the vast selection of enormous "hookahs," elaborate Middle Eastern waterpipes available here. Bargaining is a way of life here, and it is customary to cut the starting price offered you at least in half. To get to the flea market from the clock tower, continue one block south down Yefet St. and turn left. The market is sandwiched between Ziyyon and Me-Ragusa Sts.

Nightlife

Most visitors to Tel Aviv bake on the beaches during the day and wait for the evening for Tel Aviv to come alive, its streets buzzing with the frenetic sounds of nightclubs and discos. **Dizengoff Circle** has recently been spruced up with a futuristic pedestrian walkway; though the plaza now looks jazzier, it has lost some of its raw vitality. Still, this is where you will find several of Tel Aviv's most famous nightspots. Particularly spiffy is the **Peacock's Discotheque** at Kikar Namir, which boogies from 10pm to 2am. **Mandy's Piano Bar** at 317 HaYarkon St. (tel. 44 34 00) has a mellower, more relaxed atmosphere. The better nightclubs at Kikar Kedumim in Jaffa offer wonderful views of the ocean and of Tel Aviv. Cover charges can run as high as $10.

Not-so-famous nightspots include **Norman's Bar** at 275 Dizengoff (tel. 15 10 07) and **Bernie's Bottle Club** at 231 Ben Yehuda (tel. 45 16 29), which is owned by a friendly expatriate Englishman. Nearby on Trumpeldor St. is the **Bonanza Pub,** a surprisingly good imitation of a traditional English pub with backgammon, darts, poker dice, and a piano which you are welcome to play if you're there early. This place doesn't fill up until late and generally hosts a largely English-speaking crowd which rarely tolerates anything but British and

American rock or soft pop. For jazz the only options are the **Jazz Cellar** at the Martef Elyon, **Bet Lessin** at 34 Weizmann St., or on occasion the **Shablul** at Dizengoff Center (enter on Tchernikovsky St.; tel. 28 84 91). Although the drinks are priced to kill, the coffee's not bad, and the acts are first-rate; you can often avoid the cover by saying you're a tourist and just want to take a peek. Once inside, they'll never find you again.

Many travelers enjoy the piano bar at the **Tel Aviv Hilton** in Kikar HaAtzmaut because the pianist enjoys taking requests from foreigners. He is usually there 5-11pm. Although doors don't open until 9pm and the cover is $5 (including the first drink), the **Theater Club** sponsors fantastic reggae every Tuesday night during the summer at 7 Mendele St. (above the Tourist Office). The crowd is a great mix of young Israelis, expatriate Europeans, and African and Caribbean Blacks (some Jewish).

For those who are not into the "drink and wink" scene, Israel offers a unique alternative. Israeli **folk dances** are a remarkable combination of exuberance and elegance. Dancing is one of the best ways to meet Israelis on their own terms; you might even find them downright friendly. Beginning the last week in June, Kikar Malkhe Yisrael in front of the city hall fills every night from 8:30 to 10:30pm with people of all ages dancing Israeli-style. The music ranges from Zionist pioneer songs (actually revamped Slavic folk tunes) to westernized Arab melodies, down to good old American disco, which the Israelis dance not in pairs, but en masse in rows, according to fixed routines. To get to Kikar Malke Yisrael, take Dizengoff St. from Dizengoff Circle, turn right on Gordon St., and walk about six blocks. At Tel Aviv University, the post-army college crowd averages some 150 people four times a week. (Mon., Wed., Thurs., Sat. 7-11pm; admission $1.) Take bus #24, 25, 27, or 74 to the main gate (#8) and follow your ears. On Wednesdays the emphasis is on teaching new dances. For more information call the Student Organization at 42 05 91.

If you're in Jaffa on a Sunday night the folk dancing at **HaSimta's Cafe** in Kikar Kedumin clears the streets. It is a young 20s crowd; $.80 for each session 7-9pm and 9-11pm, but most stay for both. If you're willing to admit you are a beginner, you'll receive all the help you need to learn the simple steps. Even if you will not be cajoled into dancing, the cafe has a collection of powerfully provocative paintings on sand backdrops by Froimovici in the foyer. For other folk dance sessions at Kikar Namir, Bet Hamlin and HaYarkon Park, see the *Hello Israel* tourist publication free at hotels and tourist offices, or call the IGTO. They will also tell you about song and folklore sessions nightly at 8:30pm in Kikar Kedumim during the summer, as well as periodically in some of the ritzy hotels. They're lively but super-patriotic and corny. Unless you've got a pretty high Zionism threshhold, stick to the folk-dancing.

Tel Aviv is famous among Israelis as the most "cultural" city in Israel and, true to its reputation, Tel Aviv has an assortment of jazz and classical concerts, opera, ballet, and dance performances every night. For an extensive listing of performance schedules and variety of other activities in Tel Aviv, see the free publications *Events in the Tel Aviv Region* and *This Week in Israel,* both available at the IGTO and at several of the more expensive hotels. See Practical Information section for the main ticket office. The **outdoor theater** in Neve Zedek at 6 Yehieli St. often has concerts and dance performances not listed elsewhere. Call them for schedules (tel. 65 12 41/2).

After 10pm another unique Tel-Aviv-Jaffa alternative is to visit the bagel factories where astounding quantities of delicious *"bagelas"* (or *"bagelim"*) are made by hand on primitive equipment. If you can find the places, they're free. Don't mind the less than friendly employees; they are not tourist officials but workers. The most interesting factory (it doesn't look like a bakery) is in the Neve Zedek area just west of the Shalom tower. Take Montefiore St. southwest past the tower to the end, then turn left onto HaShachar. Bear right (not the sharp right) to the end of the block and turn right onto Yavniel St. for a half kilometer until the first stop sign. The second house on the right past the street to the right is the bagel factory. The two bagel barns in Jaffa are a bit more touristy because they're just beyond the old Clock Tower (on the right if you bear left onto Bet Eshel). For 30¢ you get an evening's entertainment and a bagel.

Near Tel Aviv

Tel Aviv, like most major cities, is ringed by a number of smaller suburbs. Most of them are modern, clean, attractive, and boring. **Herzliyya** and **Bat Yam** are both seaside resorts, with alluring beaches and painfully expensive hotels. **Petakh Tikvah, Ramat Gan,** and **Holon** are purely residential, while **Bnei Beraq** is a modern Me'a She'arim.

Bus #200 takes you to **Rehovot** (22km south of Tel Aviv), stopping a hundred yards from the gate of the world-famous **Weizmann Institute of Science,** named for Israel's first president, Chaim Weizmann, also a research chemist. In many ways, the Institute is symbolic of the Israeli dream: once a barren stretch of scrubland, the Institute grounds are now covered with beautifully manicured lawns, woods, and gardens. The Institute (tel. 054/83 59 7) is open to the public Sun.-Thurs. 8:30am-3:30pm and Fri. 8:30am-noon with no admission charge, while the **Weizmann House,** set in a particularly beautiful corner of the grounds, is open only Sun.-Thurs. 10am-3:30pm, admission 25¢. The free documentary slide show at the Wix Auditorium (screened at 11am and 3:15pm) is tedious and uninformative; pick up a pamphlet in the library across the street.

Rehovot itself is just a nice, peaceful, completely residential town. Its main avenue, Herzl St., is lined with felafel shops and inexpensive restaurants. Those at Manchester Square (a ten-minute walk south from the institute) are cheap and self-service. The main gate to the Weizmann Institute is at the north end of Herzl St., a twenty-minute walk from Bilou St., Manchester Square and the Central Bus Station. Also on Bilou St., you'll find Rehovot's main fruit and vegetable market; one stall, in the far right-hand corner, sells delicious olives and smoked white fish and mackerel (a ½lb. fillet will cost about $.90). The trip to Rehovot does not require a night's stay but if you must, try the **Margoa Hotel** at 11 Moscovitz St. (tel. 054/51 30 3), which will give you bed and breakfast for about $20.

Rehovot's older sister settlement, **Rishon Le Tzion,** as its name signifies, was one of the first Jewish settlements in Zion. Baron Edmund de Rothschild, the patriarch of the settlement, gave the money for its creation amidst the newly planted vineyards in 1882. While Rehovot declined the aid of the Baron Rothschild, Rishon Le Tzion might not have survived without it. After planting vineyards from Bordeaux, Burgundy, and Beaujolais in 1887, he built the winery that is still used by the vineyards of both cities. The winery can be visited Sun.-Thurs. 8am-3pm (tel. 03/94 20 21). Call for the schedule of tours in English, which compare favorably with the Carmel Oriental wine you can buy at a discount after the tour. From the Central Bus Station the Rishon Le Tzion winery is the huge building to the south.

Ramla

Ramla ("Said" in Arabic) was built by the Arab Caliph Suleymein in the years 714-717. (It is the only city in Israel to have been founded and originally developed by Arabs.) Though the centuries have left few traces of the three hundred years when Ramla was the capital of the Muslim community in Palestine, all evidence points to its having been a major center, both in population and wealth. This was due to the important role played by Ramla in the long contest between Muslim Shiites and Sunnis, and to its strategic position on the road connecting Damascus and Baghdad with Egypt. Ramla was the capital of the Sunni Umayyad rule while the more fundamentalist Shiite center of power was the Arabian peninsula. While the Sunnis were more flexible, the Shiites refused to recognize the oral tradition, proclaiming the supremacy of the Qur'an or "Written Law." Also, around the eighth century C.E., in the same area, a similar split within the Jewish community saw the isolation of the Karaites, who refused to recognize the Talmud (the Rabbinic commentaries on the Bible) or the oral law, insisting on devotion to the Mikra or Old Testament.

With the Bedouin looting in 1025 and the devastation wrought in 1033 and 1067 by earthquakes, by the time the Crusaders took Ramla in 1099, the city was in ruins. The Crusaders thought that Ramla was Arimathea, the home of St. Joseph of Arimathea, who buried Jesus. In 1187, the Muslim Saladin conquered the city. Five years later, he and Richard the Lionhearted signed a treaty in Ramla by which the Crusader kingdom was allowed to keep the coastal strip. In 1267, Ramla was captured by the Mamelukes, under whose hands the city prospered until the seventeenth century, when the Turks took over and Ramla again fell into decay. The settlement was gradually revived by Jews escaping persecution in Jerusalem, and by Christians serving in the monastery of St. Joseph of Arimathea. Ramla became an important stopping point for pilgrims on their way to Jerusalem, and Napoleon stayed in the St. Joseph monastery before his ill-fated attack on Akko.

In the twentieth century, Ramla was once again inhabited mostly by Arabs; it had the first paved road in Palestine, and during World War II, it was the site of the British war cemetery. In 1936, anti-Zionist riots caused the Jewish population to flee, but in 1948, the Israelis attacked Ramla and the town surrendered immediately, with all but 1500 of the local Arabs fleeing for good. Today, Ramla's 37,900 inhabitants are mostly Jewish, and include three thousand Karaites.

Orientation and Sights

The Ramla Bus Station fronts Sderot Herzl, the town's main drag. Of the four major sights in Ramla, three can be found by chasing steeples. Just north of the bus station is the **White Mosque,** with its slender white minaret, built in the twelfth century as a Crusader church. Because it has remained in constant use ever since then, it is remarkably well-preserved. The changes effected by the Muslims have been minimal, confined mostly to the outer courtyard, as well as the *mirhab,* the traditional niche in the direction of Mecca which Muslims face as they pray.

Further along Sderot Herzl, past the open-air fruit and vegetable market, you'll see the square, pointed tower of the **Church of St. Nicodemus and St. Joseph Arimathea.** (Open Mon.-Fri. 9-11:30am, but the hours are irregular). Though parts of the Church were built in the sixteenth century, most of it was completed in 1902. Ring the doorbell, and somebody who speaks no English and little Hebrew will answer. He will show you the main praying area; ask him for "Napoleon," and he'll show you a second story room with "Napoleon" written on the door. Turn the latch and go in. This is where Napoleon had his staff headquarters in 1799 when he unsuccessfully attempted to seize Palestine from the Turks.

The third and final tower, the square, flat-topped **Tower of the Forty Martyrs,** stands alone at the end of Danny Mass St., which branches off Sderot Herzl farther north. If you're lucky, the tower gate will be open; if not, you'll have to find the Arab guard and pay him a few shekels to let you inside. The inscription over the entrance to the tower says that it was built by Muhammad Abu Kalaon in 1318. In the past, the tower was the site of many festivals and pilgrimages, so many, in fact, that according to local legends, the people of Lod grew jealous and plotted to steal the tower. Armed with "miraculous" rope given them by a local wise man, the Lodites harnessed themselves to the tower and pulled; as they pulled, the ropes (made of rubber) stretched so that the Lodites thought the tower was actually moving. More reliable than this story, perhaps, are accounts that the tower was used as an observation post. To the west of the tower is a small building where, according to some Muslim traditions, the prophet Salah is buried. In the surrounding fields, farther in from the road, you will see the ruins of the **Jamal el Abias Mosque,** for which the tower originally served as a minaret.

From the mosque, you can make a short walk to the **Pool of St. Helena.** Walk back to Sderot Herzl and turn left at the large police station to HaHaganah St. Make a right; the pools are on the right side of the street, opposite the **Haganah Gardens.** The little building on the left has an entrance going down to the pools. The Pool of St. Helena is an artificial rain reservoir built in the eighth century and named after the mother of Constantine. In Arabic it is called the Pool of El Anazia and in Hebrew it is the Pool of the Arches ("Berekhat Hakeshatot"). The pool is neither particularly large nor deep; rowboats can be rented for a short ride at $.25.

If you are for some reason stuck in Ramla for the night—and we advise against it—try the **Hotel Eden,** 99 Herzl St. (tel. 96 11 98; from the bus station turn left). They have rooms for between $6 and $12 per night; expect to bargain. Cheap felafel stands can be found along Herzl St., as well as a few not-so-clean looking street-meat counters. The *couscous* sold in these shops is generally dry and bland.

Netanya

The most famous and the largest of Israel's Mediterranean resorts, about 20km north of Tel Aviv on the Sharon coast, Netanya is blessed with good weather year round and a long strip of beautiful beach. An extensive park layout with paths, benches, and picnic tables makes Netanya a pleasant if expensive spot for a beachfront vacation, and popular with Israeli and recently French tourists.

But despite its natural beauty, Netanya is just another Mediterranean resort town, with an unattractive, dull modern city to the east, and countless restaurants, hotels, tourist shops, and tourists along the coast. The city has little that is peculiar to Israel, and unfortunately all too much that is typical of characterless, high-priced retreats that cater to the newly-wed and retired. Though pretty and polished, Netanya has little for tourists to do (in all, there are three cinemas, a second-rate orchestra, and a batch of third-rate nightclubs). The beaches, though breathtaking, are quite over crowded, and the cafes and restaurants are shamelessly overpriced. You may want to stop off here for an afternoon on the beach, but in the final analysis, Netanya is neither peaceful enough to provide release nor sophisticated enough to provide excitement. Furthermore, the hotels are expensive, and there are no cheap student accommodations.

Orientation

The **Central Bus Station** is located on Benyamin Boulevard, which turns into Weizmann Boulevard further north.From the bus station, walk north to Herzl St.—the town's main shopping avenue—turn left, and after four blocks you'll arrive at Ha'Atzmaut Square, a very attractive park complete with fountain, and the center of Netanya's tourist district. Near the bus station, Sha'ar Hagay St. cuts diagonally across from Benyamin Blvd. to Herzl St., and has less ostentatious shops, cafes, and bakeries (and a good fruit stand). The **Tourist Information Office**—a small building with tinted windows—is at the far end of the square. Right next to it are the steps leading down to the main beach; the beaches in Netanya are all free. Those slightly to the north, under the small cliffs, are least crowded in summer. The Tourist Office can provide you with a pictorial map of the city, a list of hotels with ratings and prices, and various weekly calendars of events. The **railway station** is on HaRakevet Rd. (tel. 23 47 0), outside the town proper. The taxi service to Tel Aviv is located on Herzl, off Kikar Tzion.

Practical Information

Israel Government Tourist Office: Kikar Ha'Atzmaut (tel. 27 28 6). Very helpful and friendly. Open in summer Sun.-Fri. 8:30am-2pm and Sun.-Thurs. 3-6pm; in winter Sun.-Fri. 8:30am-2pm.

Main Post Office: 59 Herzl St. (tel. 36 47 3). Open daily 7:45am-12:30pm and 3:30-6pm, Wed. 7:45am-2pm, Fri. 7:45am-1pm. Branches (same hours) at 15 Herzl St. and 8 Ha'Atzmaut Sts.

Central Bus Station: 3 Sderot Benyamin (tel. 37 05 2). Buses to Tel Aviv every ten minutes. Last bus to Tel Aviv at 10:30pm. Last bus leaves Tel Aviv for Netanya at 11pm. Full schedule for all buses is posted on the wall to the left of the information window.

Emergencies: Police (tel. 100). First Aid, Magen David Adom (tel. 23 33 3). Laniado Hospital, Divrei Chayim St. in the northern part of town (tel. 36 07 1).

Pharmacy: Terufa, 2 Herzl St. (tel. 28 65 6).

Early Closing Day: Tuesday. All shops closed on Tuesday afternoon.

Bike Rentals: Rent-a-Bike (tel. 28 80 5), at 12 Nice Blvd. (pronounced Nitza) rents bikes for $3 per half-day, $5 full-day, and $25 week. A $5 deposit is required.

Laundry: on the corner of Smilanski and Reures Sts.

Telephone Code: 053.

Accommodations and Food

Hotels in Netanya are all quite expensive; below are listed the cheapest of the lot, with all prices including breakfast except where otherwise indicated. Many places lower their prices by 10-15% from November to February. Be sure to bargain whenever possible, and make it clear that there are many other hotels and you are just a "poor student." You can try camping on the beach, but chances are you'll be kicked off by the military police patrolling the area at night.

Dekel Hotel, 3 Ben Yehuda St. (tel. 22 06 5). Faces the pretty Sara Sq. Relatively new building with lovely double rooms, although not particularly clean. Toilet and shower in every room, but not air-conditioned. $13 per person, but the manager may ask $15 if the place is crowded. The owner knows he's the cheapest in town so don't try bargaining. No curfew.

Orit, 21 Sderot Chen (tel. 23 46 5), in the southwest corner of town. Once a small and cozy hotel, now a hostel for Swedish groups who fill it completely during spring (mid-March to May) and autumn (mid-September to early Dec.). At other times, the young, friendly management opens the scrupulously clean, airy doubles (each with private shower and toilet) to all. Lovely dining room and lounge. Free use of refrigerator and small library (mainly in Swedish, but they also stock the current *Jerusalem Post*). Singles $15, doubles $13 per person. No bargaining.

Daphna, 29 Rishon LeTzion (tel. 23 65 5). Accommodations not deluxe, but very clean, and the old woman who runs it is a doll. Private bathrooms, not air-conditioned. Pleasant little garden. Singles $16, doubles $20. No curfew.

Ofakim, 67 Dizengoff St. (tel. 23 18 8). Large and pleasant hotel with nice lounge, but without air-conditioning. Doubles cost about $16, but breakfast is not included. No point in bargaining during the summer months.

Hotel Atzumaut, 1 Ussishkin (tel. 22 56 2). Fancy place on the fourth floor with expensive bar and lounge. Singles $14, doubles $28 including private showers. Try bargaining if you're staying more than one night.

Hotel Ruben, 25 Ussishkin (tel. 23 10 7). Cramped, cramped, cramped. Private bath. $17 single, $25 double; $20 single, $30 double in July and August. Bargain with the cranky owners and don't be intimidated.

Unfortunately, food prices in Netanya are higher than elsewhere in Israel. Avoid the pricey cafes and restaurants around Ha'Atzmaut Square. On Sha'ar Hagay St. just off Kikar Tzion, **Broadway Pizza** (tel. 22 70 0 to order pies) serves slices that taste remarkably like the stuff back home. Topped with olives is a novel but pleasant variation. **Don Pegro's,** off Dizengoff St., serves sightly cheaper pizza, but it's not as good. In the same area, you will also find a number of stalls featuring felafel and other quick and inexpensive edibles. On Herzl St. just east of the intersection with Dizengoff you will find the **American Dream Ice Cream Parlor** which, for 70¢ a cone, serves some of the best ice cream in Israel (though it's still a far cry from even Baskin Robbins). The patisserie at 6 Eliyahu Krause St. (one block south of Herzl St. off Smilanski St.) sells fresh *challahs* and luscious cream-pastries at slightly lower prices than their tourist-district counterparts. The **Tamar Cafe** on Smilanski St. off Herzl has diabetic macaroons at about 1¢ apiece. One of the cheapest places to eat is the **Burger Ranch** on Herzl St., one block from the bus station. Burgers of various kinds are about $1.50 and shakes $1.20. At the far end of the square the **Apollo** game room (with pool table and outdated video games) sometimes sells sandwiches for $.75.

The mini-market **groceries** on either side of the Baruch gallery (at Harav Kuk St.) sell cheap food and liquor as well. The best food values, however, are at the Oriental Shuq centered on Zangwill St., two blocks east of Weizmann Blvd. near the center of town (closed Tues., Fri. afternoon). Sometimes on summer evenings, kids sell whole coconuts on the street at Benyamin and Halutzim Sts. near the bus station.

Sights and Activities

Before anything else, be sure to go to the Tourist Office and pick up the biweekly *Programme of Events in Netanya,* which has listings of concerts, folk dancing, and a host of other activities. While you're there, also ask about visits to diamond-cutting factories and a citrus-packing house (Dec.-April only). Take bus #601 (the Tel Aviv local) to the New Industrial Center. Sun.-Thurs. at 1pm, the nearby **Beer Factory** offers free guided tours of the brewery and packing plant. At the end of the tour, you can buy the brewery's products at a specially discounted price and get wasted.

On Monday evenings during the summer, there is free **folk dancing** in the square, if you don't mind throngs of onlookers. Tuesday evenings, the **Netanya Philharmonic Orchestra** practices its limited repertoire either in the square or in the amphitheater at Gan HaMelech (King's Garden) just to the north of the square.

Netanya's three art galleries are the **Baruch,** 2 Herzl St., the **Blue Bay,** in the Blue Bay Hotel at 37 HaMlachim, and the **Netanya Art Gallery,** on HaMa'apilim St. sea-side of the King Solomon Hotel. Blue Bay also has an especially nice nightclub and discotheque which makes a worthwhile splurge ($5 entrance fee).

Near Netanya

Between Herzliyya and Netanya there are two interesting beaches easily accessible from the coastal road. The seaside cliffs near **Kibbutz Ga'ash** reach to some 200 feet where, during the summer, Israelis not off risking their lives in a war often risk their lives hang-gliding. Nearby, though not on any map, is the area known as **Sydneyalia.** Set back about ½km from the beach are the remains of an old church or monastery. Closer to the small cliffs you can pick up shards of strange blue glass from an ancient Roman glass factory. About 2-3km closer to Netanya, where the Poleg River meets the sea, is the beautiful **Poleg Nature Preserve.** A walk upstream takes you past eucalyptus trees (planted during the last century to dry up the swamps that once dominated the Sharon Plain), beautiful flowering plants, and perhaps a colorful kingfisher or *bulbul,* easily recognized by its big black head and bright yellow chest.

Eight kilometers north of Netanya off the coastal road is **Kfar Vitkin,** one of the largest *moshavim* in Israel. The Israeli army has now taken over most of the buildings and facilities of the adjoining **Emek Hefer Youth Hostel** for a training camp. If you don't mind the company, Yosef, the enormous warden, will let you stay in one of six single-sex bunks. Bed charge is $3.50 for IYHF members, $4 for non-members, with no meals served. Yosef will sometimes let you use the kitchen when the khaki shifts have finished. For food, try the reasonably-priced supermarket just outside the moshav. A short walk along the highway to the north of the hostel you'll find a Milk Bar and a truck-stop cafeteria, both open until midnight. Aside from the plethora of assault rifles, the atmosphere is very casual and relaxed; there are no curfews. The only drawback is that the moshav turkey coops nearby attract flies during the day and when the wind is right, make the whole place smell unpleasant. However, the turkeys have another role to play. Young moshavniks have figured out that throwing dead turkeys into Alexander's Stream (*Nahal* in Hebrew) attracts turtles from the sea some 2-3km away. You can sometimes see these creatures from **HaAvim (Turtle Bridge)** about ½km past the train tracks on a dirt road east of the moshav. Some of them are two to three feet long.

Kfar Vitkin is on the Netanya-Haifa seaside highway, a five-minute walk from beautiful free beaches on the Mediterranean. There are frequent buses along the highway; take a local bus if you wish to get off near the hostel. To get to Haifa from the hostel, take a local to Giv'at Olga, where you can catch an express to Haifa. You can also hitch either north or south from in front of the youth hostel. It's both illegal and difficult to hitch on the newer Derech Haifa.

Caesarea

On the site of a small anchorage named Strato's Tower, Herod the Great built this city for his emperor in Rome at the end of the first century B.C.E. The extensive ruins of the ancient city now constitute one of Israel's finest archeological sites and major tourist attractions. Unfortunately, despite the difficulty of reaching the site without a car, the ruins are being commercialized at a frightening rate. Already the Crusader city is marred by a dozen tacky cafes, gift shops, a beach club, and even a disco among the ruins. A shopping mall is planned outside the town, which further threatens its once secluded charm. Nothing, however, can deprive Caesarea of its inherent fascination; it will always remain a short but mandatory stop for every traveler to Israel.

First used as a port in the fourth century B.C. by the Phoenicians, Caesarea was the site of Strato's Tower, after which the city was originally named. In 25 B.C.E., Herod decided to turn Caesarea into one of the great metropolises of the East and ordered the construction of a large hippodrome, theater, and agora, as well as an aqueduct that carried fresh water from Crocodile River to the north. The entire project was designed to curry Roman favor, and with this end in mind, Herod named the new city after the Roman emperor Caesar Augustus. By 6 C.E., Caesarea had become the capital of the Roman province of Judea, and it remained the seat of Roman power in the area until the downfall of the empire.

Caesarea has a number of historical connections for Christians. Most importantly, it was here, in around 30 C.E., that the Roman Governor Pontius Pilate ordered the crucifixion of Jesus Christ. Not surprisingly, the first historical proof of the personage of Pontius Pilate, outside of the testimony of the Gospels, was also found here during excavations in 1961. An inscription on the theater mentions Pilate, who apparently was the Roman Prefector in Caesarea from 26 to 36 C.E.

Caesarea has seen brutal times. It was the Jews here who raised the standard of rebellion against the Romans in 66 B.C.E. After the Romans successfully squelched the Jewish Rebellion four years later, they celebrated by publicly sacrificing thousands of Jews in the hippodrome in Caesarea. Sixty years later a second Jewish uprising, the Bar Kochba Rebellion, was also brought to a brutal end. This time the Romans were more selective—ten Jewish sages were slowly tortured to death in the arena at Caesarea, among them the beloved wise man of Israel, Rabbi Akiba.

The Archeological Site

The ruins at Caesarea consist of a hodgepodge of remains from different historical periods. The most substantial chunks are actually the remains of the Crusader city. Four hundred years after the Arab conquest of the Byzantine city, the Crusaders arrived. They captured Caesarea in 1101, lost it to Saladin in 1187, and retook the city during the third Crusade under Richard the Lionhearted. In 1254, Louis IX of France strengthened and expanded the city's fortifications, and it is to him that we owe most of the massive ramparts and battlements, including the impressive moat, all of which are still in excellent condition.

What makes the situation confusing are the remains of a fourth-century C.E. synagogue that archeologists have uncovered, and the slender minaret of a Turkish mosque that rises in the midst of the Crusader walls and Roman ruins. Ironically, very little remains of the Roman city—this is largely because Caesarea's magnificent structures were constantly pillaged and plundered by neighboring towns. Some of the most impressive remains of the Roman city of Caesarea can now be seen at Akko or Ashqelon.

To the right as you approach the ticket booth is the dry protective moat, into which part of the guard tower has fallen. The city was further protected by a drawbridge, an iron gate whose grooves you can still see in the stones, and a wooden gate with a pole holding it shut; look for the large holes in the entranceway walls where the pole was inserted. People didn't enter the Crusader city walking in a straight line, as should be apparent, but had to turn two corners instead. This, too, was to prevent a charging attack. Note also the windows above the entrance areas where archers were stationed to pick off interlopers.

The rest of the site is well-marked; there are, as you will note, relics from the Roman period (the main road, several statues), the Arab period (granaries and residences), and, of course, the Crusader period (the walls and churches). If you take the dirt road about midway between the entrance gate and the beach, to your right as you enter the site you will reach first a church and then the guard tower and outer walls of the Crusader settlement. The beach, which is to your left as you enter the city, is beautiful and very calm.

Although the main body of ruins lies within the Crusader walls, the three most interesting Roman remnants all lie outside of the site proper. Adjoining the cafe, near the admissions booth to the main site, is a small excavated area that contains two of the most famous finds—the two colossal second-century C.E. Roman statues, one of red porphyry and the other of white marble. They were discovered by kibbutzniks from Sdot Yam when they were ploughing one day. Continuing south along the road or the waterfront about 1 km, you come to the enormous but excessively restored **Roman theater.** After 1700 years, the reconstructed theater is now used for concerts and dramatic performances. Ten years after excavations began in 1951, the theater opened with a performance by Pablo Casals. Continuing north along the beach about 1 km, you will come to the town beach in front of the modern village of Caesarea, which is the site of the excellently preserved **Roman aqueduct.** An admission ticket entitles you to entrance to both the theater and the site, so hang on to it. (Open daily 8am-4pm, Fri. until 3pm; admission $1, $.50 for students.) If you get to the ancient city very early in the morning, the fishermen leave the gates open and you can enter for free. Behind the fortress remains on the peninsula, you can see small fish (used for bait) washed up onto the rocks where the fishermen stand.

Turn right at the main road, walk about ten minutes, and you'll see on your left the archway with a cross that leads to the area where the Roman hippodrome used to be. This race track could, in its heyday, accommodate 20,000 spectators, and measures 1056 by 204 feet. The archway is not from Roman times, but was built long afterwards. If you don't go to the beach, and want to see the aqueduct and hippodrome, simply walk down the main road from the Crusader city, looking for the hippodrome on your right, then turn left at the intersection which says "This is the site of the new Caesarea Shopping Center" and follow the signs to the aqueduct.

All of the beaches around Caesarea have large "No Bathing" signs posted on them. No one seems to pay heed to them, however. Although the posted signs warn of the strong undertow there is a problem even if you merely traipse the sands: the tar from the oil tankers at the offshore station can only be removed from your feet with cooking oil. So keep your shoes on. The two hotels on the beach are extremely expensive; head south toward Netanya or Kfar Vitkin for cheaper accommodations. The beach and the aqueduct are about ½km from the modern town, and the archeological site and the theater 1 and 2km respectively further south along the coast. Many visitors to Caesarea simply unroll their sleeping bags on the beach, but devotees of organized camping can walk south from the theater (about 1km) to **Kayet veShait** resort village and occupy a small sandy corner of their campground. Neither option is truly safe as this seems to be a popular area for sneak-thieves. Keep your valuables extra-secure.

If you're hitching to Caesarea, get off the Haifa Rd. about 2km north of the Caesarea-Afula interchange as the highway passes over a small road. Although there is no highway exit, you can easily climb down the trestle. To the east is Or Akiva, to the west about 1 km is Caesarea. Leaving Caesarea, the Haifa Rd. is not so easy to hitch on; continue 1-2km further to the east where the parallel older coastal road, also known as the Haifa-Hadera Rd., is excellent for hitching. The roads intersecting this one at Ma'agan Mikhael, Zikhron Ya'akov, Dor and En Hod are even easier to hitch as they are frequented mostly by the kibbutzniks in the area.

Near Caesarea

Between Caesarea and Ma'agan Mikhael on the old coastal road (7km south of Zikhron Ya'akov, just outside of Benyamina) is Moshav Bet Chananya. Just outside the moshav are two well-preserved Roman aqueducts, believed to have brought water from the Shuni springs northeast of Benyamina down to the ancient city of Caesarea. North of the moshav is **Tel Meborakh,** where excavations are continuing after several important Roman artifacts were found. Two of several marble sarcophagi found in the ruins of a Roman mausoleum can be seen in the Rockefeller Museum in Jerusalem.

Kibbutz Ma'agan Mikhael is one of the largest and most beautiful kibbutzim in Israel. Its grounds are easily recognized by the pine trees—a rare sight in this part of the world—that line either side of the coastal highway. Part of the kibbutz serves as a wildlife preserve and features a fabulous bird observatory. To the north you can see acres and acres of neat rectangular fish ponds. The various archeological finds are housed in the kibbutz' own little museum. The preserve runs along the banks of Nahal HaTaninim ("Crocodile River"), supposedly the only unpolluted river on the Israeli coast. Unfortunately, there are only two places to stay in the immediate vicinity. The guest house run by the kibbutz is extremely expensive, although you can stay for free if you can manage to get yourself invited by a kibbutznik. The Field Study Center (Bet Safer Sadeh) generally accommodates only pre-arranged tour groups, but they may let you stay if there's room. From the road walk west to the kibbutz entrance and then south, staying close to the highway, to the Bet Safer Sadeh Nature Preserve. At the Crocodile River running just south of the kibbutz, the large sea turtles mentioned above (see Near Netanya) can sometimes be seen.

The archeological site and beach at **Dor** are best reached by walking 5km north along the beach from Magen Mikhael. Dor's calm, lovely beach is protected by four small rocky islands, each a bird sanctuary, which you can explore at low tide. The **Tel Dor** archeological site is on the hill at the far northern end of the beach; you'll need shoes to walk on the rusty wire-and-sand road. The site seems to have been founded in the fifteenth century B.C., but Dor's most important remains are from the Hellenistic and Roman periods; temples dedicated to Zeus and Astarte were discovered here, as were the ruins of a Byzantine church. According to Josephus, a Jewish temple existed in Dor before the destruction of the Second Temple.

Near the south end of the beach is a **campsite** (tel. 063/99 01 8) run by the Dor Moshav, which was built on the ruins of the Arab village of Tantura, once a center for dye-making. Open April to October only, they have three-bed bungalows for $20, while tentsites go for $2.50 per person, or $3.50 in July and August. The beach is often still called Tantura. The caves and ruins make this a great beach to camp on if you're careful. Dor and Tantura beach can be reached by getting off the highway at the Kibbutz Nachsholim sign and walking towards the sea.

On a hill overlooking the fertile coastal plain sits Zikhron Ya'akov, founded by Rumanian Jews in 1882. The early settlers fought against malaria-infested swamps until the Baron Edmond de Rothschild came to their aid. The town's name means Ya'akov's Memorial; it was named in honor of the Baron's father. Today travelers remember it better as the home of the **Carmel-Oriental Winery** founded by the Baron. One hundred years old, the winery now produces almost all of Israel's domestic wine, as well as a large stock for export. Free cellar tours are given Sun.-Fri. every half hour from 9am-3pm (tel. 063/ 88 64 3). At the end of the tour you can sample the finished product.

The decrepit structure off the shore is the glass factory built by the Baron and managed by Dizengoff, later the mayor of Tel Aviv. It used the white sand of the coast to make the glass bottles in the Baron's winery in Zikhron Ya'akov. Obviously, the winery did better than the glass factory.

The **Rothschild Family Tomb** is a short distance away, as is the **Aaronson Museum,** commemorating NILI, an early Zionist paramilitary intelligence unit.

Between Dor (and the beautiful beaches of Nachsholim) and the Prehistoric Caves by Ein Kerem one can turn off the old coastal road to the east to **Moshav Kerem MaHaRal.** It's named after the sixteenth-century Rabbi Judah Lowe of Prague who was called the MaHaRal as the legendary creator of the "Golem" (or Homunculus). From the moshav, walk west to a peacefully beautiful forest spotted with unmarked ruins.

Haifa and North Coast

Now Israel's third largest city, only one hundred years ago Haifa was just a small community of houses. At the turn of the century, the railway to Damascus was completed and the British finished dredging the harbor, allowing Haifa to become a major seaport. When waves of immigrants started to make their way to the Holy Land, most of them arrived at Haifa, and it was here that many of them stayed. Haifa is now a flourishing city of 250,000, and although it technically dates back to Crusader times, virtually all of the city was built during the last few decades to accommodate the boatloads who came from Europe. Haifa's scenic offerings are therefore considerably more modern than the ancient ruins of other cities in Israel. Even the prophets in Haifa are modern: well before today's skyscrapers and mountain subway appeared, Theodore Herzl called Haifa the "city of the future" in his 1901 utopian novel the *Old New Land*.

But accuracy of vision alone has never secured popularity for a prophet—or for the subject of his prophecies. Although Israeli pride in Haifa is obvious, foreigners do not always share their enthusiasm. They see Haifa as another large, crowded urban sprawl, not unlike many American metropolises, and not particularly interesting at that. So don't be surprised if many of your fellow travelers advise you simply to avoid Haifa, and spend your precious time elsewhere.

From Akko, the only living Crusader city, to the white cliffs far beneath Rosh HaNikra, the North Coast is called the *Sulam Tzor* or "Ladder of Tyre." Although it does not cover a very large area, travelers can pass quickly from ancient ports to modern beaches, from white cliffs to mountain vistas. Despite the psychological strain of a constant stream of nervous soldiers going to and from the adjoining territory in Lebanon, this is an easy region of Israel to travel in. Plans are underway for development of the tourist attractions on the North Coast; perhaps the Israelis won't sacrifice the simple, ancient, or untouched for the modern commercial tourism.

Haifa

While it is true that little tangible evidence remains here of the great empires of the past, Haifa does reveal a unique and intriguing history. The city has long harbored political and religious minorities, both individuals and whole sects. Excavations on the Carmel have uncovered caves which, first inhabited in prehistoric times, later became a refuge for the prophet Elijah, who fled there to escape the wrath of King Ahab. Elijah was followed through the years by other outcasts until the beginning of the second millenium C.E., when invading Crusaders built the first of several monasteries above the cave; the Carmelite Order still operates one there today. Other minorities have found peace and support in and around Haifa in the past two centuries. The German Templars brought new industry and prosperity to the area in 1869; Islam gave to Haifa three of its more interesting offspring, the Druze, the Baha'i, and the Akhmadiya, all of whom exist today.

With the building of a railroad in 1905 and the opening of the port in 1933, the Jewish face of Haifa emerged. The often illegal immigration of the Second Aliyah provided the workers who came to dominate all sectors of the economy during the Arabs' 1936-39 strike against the British. The Jewish Haganah built up the city's fortifications with British assistance, preparing Haifa to be the last holdout against the Nazis if they should conquer Egypt and lower Palestine. With this preparation the predominantly Jewish city was the first territory secured after the Israeli Declaration of Independence in 1948.

Today, the clean streets and stately residential neighborhoods do not constitute tourist attractions, and if you are looking for exotic Middle Eastern atmosphere the city has virtually nothing to offer. But there are a number of places of interest to those who wish to learn about the modern state of Israel, in particular two of the country's leading universities and the massive Dagon. Moreover, since Haifa has been carved out of the steepest face of Mt. Carmel, it offers outstanding views from the heights separated by forested, green valleys and public gardens. With this natural backdrop to a modern city with a lively history, it is no wonder that residents call Haifa the most beautiful Israeli city after Jerusalem.

Orientation

Haifa divides into roughly three levels. In ascending order of altitude, they are: the downtown or **port area,** a raucous neighborhood where the bus and train terminals are located; the **Hadar area** (Hadar HaCarmel means "Glory of the Carmel" in Hebrew), where you'll find many middle-class businesses, hotels, and restaurants; and finally, **Carmel,** which contains the most expensive homes and hotels. In the higher parts of the town, most of the avenues run parallel to the water, with very few perpendicular streets. These main avenues are connected by numerous narrow staircases which are often likened to the twisted, craggy trunks of the wine grape trees you see on the south slope of Mt. Carmel; indeed, "Carmel" comes from the words "God's Vineyards." The alleys can be perfect thoroughfares for exploring the heights. Don't hesitate if you seem to be walking through someone's backyard. You are, but that's okay.

Haifa has excellent public transportation, including Israel's only subway, the Carmelit, which connects all three of the town's main areas. To get to the suburbs, you'll have to take a bus. Revealing its liberal and secular tradition (for many years now, Haifa's has been the only local government that is not in coalition with the Jewish religious parties), many of Haifa's municipal buses run on Saturdays, although the Carmelit does not. Take advantage of the excellent public transportation in Haifa—what looks like a short walk on your map may involve arduous and time-consuming up or downhill hiking. A ride on the subway costs $.17. Bus fares are higher: $.17 or $.30, depending on the distance of the ride.

Practical Information

Israel Government Tourist Office (IGTO): 18 Herzl St. (tel. 66 65 21 or 66 65 23). Employees here are competent and helpful. Information on currently scheduled events, including films and concerts, as well as train timetables and an excellent free map. Take bus #10 or 12 from the port area or #21 or 28 from the Central Bus Station. Open Sun.-Thurs. 8am-3pm.

Municipal Information Offices: Central Bus Station, ground floor (tel. 51 22 08); 23 HaNevi'im St. near intersection with Herzl St. in the Hadar district (tel. 66 30 56); 119 Sderot HaNassi, opposite Gan Ha'Em and the uppermost Carmelit station (tel. 83 68 3); 14 Hassan Shukri St., in the City Hall, lower Hadar district (tel. 64 53 59 or 64 07 75). They also have a map and can be helpful, but lack the patience and experience of the IGTO. Hours at Har HaCarmel and C.B.S. locations are Sun.-Thurs. 9am-4pm, Fri. 9am-1pm. Hours for HaNevi'im St. Sun.-Thurs. 8am-7pm, Fri. 8am-1pm. Hours at City Hall Sun.-Fri. 8am-1pm.

ISSTA: 20 Herzl St. (tel. 66 08 39). Three doors to the left of the IGTO, upstairs in room #245. Open Sun.-Thurs. 9am-1pm and 3-6pm, Wed. and Fri. 9am-1pm only.

American Express (Meditrad Ltd.): 2 Kikar Khayat (tel. 64 22 67) Entrance in alleyway next to Steinmatsky's off Ha'Atzmaut St. just west of Khayat St. Open Sun.-Thurs. 8am-4pm, Wed. and Fri. 8am-1pm, closed Sat.

Central Post Office: in the port area at 19 Sderot HaPalyam (tel. 64 08 91/2). The place for overseas calls and Poste Restante. Open Sun.-Thurs. 7am-6pm, Fri. 7am-2pm. A large, far more convenient branch is located on the corner of Shabbtai Levi and HaNevi'im Sts. in Hadar. Open Sun.-Thurs. 8am-8pm, Fri. 8am-2pm. There is another large branch in the Central Bus Station.

Central Bus Station: For information (tel. 51 52 21). On Derech Yafo at the start of the main road to Tel Aviv. Buses south leave from here only; buses to the north and southeast (Nazareth, Druze Villages) generally stop in Hadar as well. In the evening, and very infrequently on Saturday, buses #251 to Akko and #271 to Nahariyya (via Akko) leave exclusively from Daniel St., off HaNevi'im St. in Hadar. To Nazareth, the Arab bus #331 leaves from the Kikar Paris more frequently than the Egged bus #331 from the Central Bus Station. Central Bus Station baggage check is opposite platform 10 and is open until 3:15pm, 2pm on Fri.

Railway Station: next to and connected by tunnels with the Central Bus Station. For information, call 53 12 11. Also on Ha'Atzmaut St. next to the Dagon grain silo at Kikar Plumer. The scenic ride to Jerusalem is slow but highly recommended.

Carmelit: runs every ten minutes from Kikar Paris downtown to Gan Ha'Em uptown with stops near Khouri, Shabtai Levi and Arlosoroff.

Sherut Companies: Kavei HaGalil (tel. 66 44 42)—very frequent cars to Akko and Nahariyya from 16 HaNevi'im St. in Hadar in lot on left just down from Herzl St., and from Kikar Plumer in port area. Aviv (tel. 66 63 33)—to Tel Aviv, Jerusalem, and Tiberias from 10 Nordau St. in Hadar. Cars to Jerusalem leave on the hour Sun.-Fri. 6am-5pm, Sat. 6am-2pm. Reservation needed for cars to Jerusalem. Aryeh (tel. 67 36 66)—to Tel Aviv from 9 Beerwald St. in Hadar. Amal (tel. 52 28 28)—to Tel Aviv from 157 Derech Yafo next to Central Bus Station.

Emergencies: Police, 28 Derech Yafo (tel. 100); First Aid, Itzhak St. (tel. 101).

Rape Crisis Center: (24 hours) tel. 88 79 1.

U.S. Consulate: 37 Ha'Atzmaut St. (tel. 67 21 67). Open 8:30am-12:30pm and 3-4:30pm. Closed Sat., and Wed. and Fri. afternoons.

Hitching: Hitching to and from Haifa is easy. To go south, get on the coastal highway by the Bus Station or to the west of it. To go north or east (a bit harder), stand across from the Bus Station, the Dagon, or near Haifa University (best bet to get to Druze villages).

Books: Beverly Book, 7 Herzl St., ½ block from HaNevi'im St. (tel. 93 32 17). A great place with a fine selection of fiction and non-fiction books, both used and new, average price $1. Old comics too. Beverly, who is usually inside, will buy or exchange your used books "if they're good." Open Sun.-Thurs. 9am-1pm and 4-7pm, Tues. and Fri. 9-1pm only. Steimatsky bookshops are located at 82 Ha'Atzmaut St., near Khayat St.; 16 Herzl St., near the IGTO; and in the Central Bus Station arcade. New books, also a selection of travel guides. Also sells the excellent 1:250,000 Ordnance Survey Map of Israel, available in both English and Hebrew. Two-set sheet a steal at $3.50.

Society for the Protection of Nature: see Israel Introduction.

Swimming Pools: The **Macabee Pool,** on Bikurim St. in Central Carmel (tel. 80 10 0) is open-air in summer, heated and covered in winter; admission $2.50, $2 for students. Nearby but less popular is the **Galei Hadar Pool,** 9 Rapoel St. (tel. 66 78 54); admission $2.25, $1.50 for students. Both pools are open every day, but close early Fri. afternoon. If you're staying at the Technion, you can use the excellent pool there.

What To Do in Haifa: 24 hr. recording in English (tel. 64 08 40).

Telephone Code: 04.

Accommodations

Haifa is short on the budget hotels and pseudo-hotels that flourish in Jerusalem. Its youth hostels and camping sites, while not centrally located, are in beautiful spots close to the sea. Hotels in Haifa, as in most parts of the country, are expensive. Singles start at $12 and doubles at about $18. Most places prefer that you pay in foreign currency, which will save you the 15% value-added tax. The **Hadar district,** where the cheapest hotels are located, is convenient but noisy. The best nightlife is concentrated in the Carmel, where the hotels are plush, new and expensive.

International Tourist Hotel, 40 HaGeffen St. (tel. 52 11 10), just a few blocks west of the Haifa Museum. Used to be called the Bethel Hostel. Take bus #22, 40, or 42 from the Central Bus Station. Heavy Christian emphasis, but all are welcome. No food allowed in the rooms, but there are tables in the courtyard and a snack bar that sells breakfast. Air-conditioning. Triple bunk-beds at $3.25 per person with your own sheets, $4 without. Rooms closed 8:30am-5pm; Friday registration only 4-7:30pm. Strict 10pm curfew.

Technion University—HaFun program, Kiryat HaTechnion in the Carmel district (tel. 29 22 87 or 23 41 48). Take bus #19 from the Central Bus Station or from Herzl St. to the new campus ("Technion City"). Call first; keep trying if no one answers. A special hostel primarily for foreign students with comfortable three-bed dormitory rooms. Minimarket, laundry machines, and free use of dormitory kitchens. Access to Technion's extensive athletic facilities as well as organized activities and excursions. No curfew, but buses stop at about 11:30pm. Excellent program, but three-day minimum stay. Open mid-July to early Sept. $9 per night; $7 for students.

Carmel Youth Hostel (IYHF), 4km south of the city at Hof HaCarmel (tel. 53 19 44). Closest of the three IYHF hostels, but still inconvenient. Take local bus #45 from the Central Bus Station to the main road below the hostel. 20-min. walk up a side road to the hostel is dangerous; recommended only for groups and those who will not return after dark. Brand new, 400 beds. Splendid view and near a free, uncrowded beach. No restaurants or food stores nearby, but the overpriced hostel cânteen (open 7-10pm; dinner $3) has good food. To get to town, take bus #43 from in front of the cemetery. Rooms and reception closed 9am-4pm. Standard IYHF price of $5.60 for members and $6.50 non-members; members under 18 $4.80, non-members $5.10. Prices include breakfast.

Qiryat Tivon Youth Hostel (IYHF), 12 Alexander Said St. (tel. 93 14 82), 12km southeast of Haifa, off the road to Nazareth. Take bus #74 or 75 from the Central Bus Station, or bus #331 from Kikar Paris. Informal, pretty hostel with a small garden and goats. Spacious kitchen, but poor cooking facilities. Near Beit She'arim, site of an ancient synagogue. Reception open all day; no curfew at night. $5.30 members, $6.70 non-members, including breakfast.

Kitman House, 40 Geula St. (tel. 66 08 29). A private apartment in a tall building. Access to kitchen, TV, radio, and stereo. $18 per room (doubles and triples).

Nathan's Youth Hostel, 13 Akiva St. (tel. 66 08 29). Just around the corner from Kitman, under the same management. Two quads at $3.50 per person. No curfew, but a small key deposit.

The Eden, 8 Shemaryahu Levin St. (tel. 66 48 16). In the Hadar district. Grungy, but could be worse. Make sure to ask for a towel before you pay. Expensive for what you get. Singles $13, doubles $20 without breakfast.

Talpiyyot, 61 Herzl St. (tel. 67 37 53/4). Very clean, and in an unbeatable location. Buffet breakfast on the balcony included. Highly recommended. Singles $16 with private shower, $14 without; doubles $25 with shower, $23 without.

Nesher Hotel, 53 Herzl St. (tel. 64 06 44). Similar to Talpiyyot, but a bit somber. Small lounge. Singles $15 and up, doubles $31.50 and up, triples $47 and up; some rooms have private shower. Breakfast included.

Ophir Hotel, 1 Shimshon St. (tel. 24 23 35). Slightly out of the way (except for nightlife), but pleasant. Tricky to find: take the ramp on the left-hand side of the sidewalk, then go down the stairs to the left of the first building. Quiet neighborhood. The only affordable place in the Carmel. Singles $12.50, doubles $20.

Appinger Hotel, 28 Ben Gurion St. (tel. 51 54 84). A beautiful old building with singles for $6-10, doubles $15-20; 10% student discount.

Daphne Hotel, 31 Nordau St. (tel. 66 29 93). $6-8 per person with breakfast.

Young Judea Youth Hostel (IYHF), 18km east of Haifa in the village of Ramat Yohanan (tel. 44 29 76). Take bus #66 from the Central Bus Station to Kfar Atar (buses run until 8pm). Primarily for youth groups, which completely book it June-Sept. Be sure to call ahead. Standard IYHF prices.

Campground: at Kibbutz Neve Yam, 18km south of Haifa (tel. 92 22 40). Just off a beautiful beach, and near the ruins of the Crusader fortress of Atlit (closed to tourists by the military). Excellent facilities, including a small store for provisions. Open all year. $4 per person, $2.50 off-season.

Food

Haifa specializes in good felafel—HaNevi'im St. is nicknamed felafel row, and HeChalutz St., running perpendicular to it, has an equally large selection of good, cheap felafel and sandwich stands. Some places also sell corn-on-the cob (in Hebrew, *tiras*) from large street-side vats. The felafel stands and cafes along Sd. HaNassi on Mt. Carmel are open Friday nights and Saturdays, as are some of the HeChalutz St. places.

Balfour Cellar, 3 Balfour St. (tel. 66 53 00). One of the few remaining luncheonettes in the world where the mashed potatoes are made from real potatoes and fresh butter. A sizeable meal in the outer section costs $2-3, more in the waitress-service section in the back. Open Sun.-Thurs. to 10pm, Fri. to 2:30pm. Opens Sat., after Shabbat, at about 6pm.

Farm Foods, 30 Herzl St. Inexpensive dairy restaurant, crowded at lunchtime. Blintzes, fish, dairy dishes $1-1.75 each. Open until 8:30pm. until 1:30pm Friday. Closed Sat.

Betteinu, 29 Jerusalem St. Inside the William Green Cultural Center. Similar fare to the student restaurants below, but a bit more expensive. On a beautiful street in the Hadar district. Full meals with meat are $5. Open for lunch only.

Bet HaPri (House of Fruit), Shemaryahu Levin and Herzl Sts. (No English sign; look for the "Whitman" snowflake logo across from the HaMashbie dept. store.) Any combination of fruits or vegetables will be turned into a great shake for $.50. Good selection—be creative.

Technion University, Beit Ha-Student (Student House Cafeteria). Inexpensive, but the food doesn't warrant a special trip (unless you miss your own college dining hall). The women behind the counter are very nice but speak English poorly, so point to what you want and smile. Open all year during meal times, except Sat. and holidays. Full meal of salad, main course, side dishes, bread, and juice for $1.75.

Haifa University. Similar to Technion. Meals $2.

Although not worth a special trip, if you happen to be at the lowest Carmelit station with a few spare minutes on your hands, there is an inexpensive outdoor fruit and vegetable market just west of the Kikar Paris station between Nahum and Nathan Sts. If you walk east on Nathanson from here, you will find a shop at #777 which sells Arab delicacies. Although the (cow's) spleen is a bit expensive at $6, the ox testicles are a mere $2—best price in Israel. Adjacent to the fruit market on Nahum St. is the **Shichmona restaurant,** with some of the best meat prices in the city.

Sights

The **Haifa Tourism Development Association,** 10 Achad Ha'Am St. (tel. 64 58 07) offers several tours of sights in the Haifa area. Depending on the group that assembles, the tours to the Druze Villages, Ein Hod, Mukhraqa, and Kababir can be excellent; some of them are free. In addition, the Association conducts a highly recommended free walking tour of Haifa's main museums and sights every Saturday morning. The tour leaves from the observation point on the Carmel at the corner of Sha'ar HaLevenon and Yefe Nof Sts. at 10pm and lasts until about 1pm. One note: many Haifa museums are closed on Fri. and open on Sat. In such cases, Sat. admission is usually free.

The **Baha'i Temple** is probably Haifa's most interesting sight. It was built as a memorial shrine to the Persian Mirza Ali Muhammad, the forerunner of the eclectic and rapidly growing Baha'i religion. In 1844 Muhammad declared himself to be "El Bab," the "Gateway to God." Before his execution in 1850, he heralded a new religious teacher who would be the messenger of God. After El Bab's death, his student, Mirza Husein Ali (also known as Baha-u-Illah), was exiled to Akko, where he preached the unity of all religions. He is revered today, along with El Bab, by the world's three million Baha'i. Baha-u-Illah is buried in the Baha'i gardens in Akko, whereas the Bab's remains, brought to Haifa in 1909, now rest in the Persian gardens next to the Temple. The palm, olive, and eucalyptus trees growing here are particularly impressive in the dry Israeli climate.

The temple itself combines Eastern and Western architecture; perhaps this reflects the multiple origins of the Baha'i faith. The large golden dome distinctly resembles those of Baroque Christian cathedrals, but it perches above unmistakable Moorish archways. Before entering the temple, remove your shoes, and ask for one of the pamphlets explaining the Baha'i religion. As a measure of courtesy, don't turn your back on the sanctuary inside as you leave; walk out the doorway backwards. The temple, located on HaTsionut Ave., can be reached by taking either bus #22 from the Central Bus Station or bus #23, 25, 26, or 32 from HaNevi'im St. near the Municipal Information Office. Open 9am-noon, gardens open until 5pm; admission free.

Near the temple on HaTsionut is the **Baha'i Archives Building,** a handsome structure completed in 1957 and modeled after a classical Greek temple. The interior of the building is not open to the general public.

The Baha'is are not the only interesting minority on the Carmel: the **Akhmadiya,** adherents to a little-known Muslim pacifist sect, have also survived in a high corner. They are followers of Akhmed El Kadiani, who proclaimed himself *Mahdi* (the Muslim Messiah) in India in 1889. His message criticized proselytization by force, a traditional practice in Islam. The members of this peaceful missionary sect settled in Haifa's Kababir district uphill from the Baha'i Temple, where they now have a mosque and a publishing house. The area is served by bus #34.

Most of Haifa's museums are close to the Baha'i Temple in the **Carmel district,** which anyone will tell you is the most beautiful part of the city. Although few government offices or public buildings are located here, it is called the *Merkaz* or "center" of the city. Carmel is modern Haifa's classy upper city, with ritzy hotels and luxurious homes. The earliest known biblical reference notes that the land allotted to the tribe of Asher was at the spot where "Carmel touches the sea." The three hundred-meter peak still offers a gorgeous view of the sea north all the way to the white cliffs of Rosh HaNikra, and south to the ancient fortress of Atlit.

The easiest way to get to the Carmel district is to take the Carmelit up to the last stop, Gan Ha'Em (named after the splendid Gan Ha'Em Gardens, which adjoin the subway station). The uptown leaves from Paris station (in Kikar Paris, which is named for the collective French builders of the Carmelite) about every ten minutes and costs under $.20. Alternatively, you can take bus #21, 22, 23, 27, or 37 to Gan Ha'Em.

At **Gan Ha'Em** ("Mothers' Park," literally; also "Picnic Paradise"), you can relive some childhood experiences on a walk through the small municipal zoo. It's not exactly an African game reserve, but you will be surprised by some of the beasts indigenous to this small country. The zoo (tel. 81 88 6) is open Sun.-Thurs. 8am-4pm (6pm in July and Aug.), Fri. 8am-1pm, and Sat. 9am-4pm (6pm in July and August). Across the park at 124 HaTishbi St. are three museums which offer another perspective on the flora and fauna of northern Israel. The **Prehistoric "M. Stekelis" Museum,** the **Natural History Museum,** and the **Biological Museum** are all open Sun.-Thurs. 8am-2pm, Fri. 8am-1pm, Sat. 9am-4pm (tel. 85 83 3).

The **Mane Katz art museum,** 89 Yefe Nof Rd., popularly called HaPanorama Rd. (tel. 83 48 2), is one block west of the Carmelit subway line. It displays sculptures and canvases by Mane Katz, a member of the Paris group of "Jewish Expressionists" that included Modigliani, Chagall, and Cremegne.Open Mon.-Thurs. 10am-2pm and 4-6pm, Fri. 10am-noon, Sat. 10am-3pm, closed Sun. One block further west, the **Tikon Museum of Japanese Art,** 89 Sderot HaNassi (tel. 83 55 4), another tiny, delightful museum, sells exquisite high-quality posters for $2-4. Open Sun.-Thurs. 10am-1pm and 4-7pm, Sat. 10am-2pm, closed Fri. Near the intersection of HaPanorama and HaTsionut, opposite #135 HaTsionut, you will find a garden of striking bronze sculptures by Ursula Malkin. The garden also offers great vistas and near-idyllic prospects for picnics.

Further down the slope, beyond the Baha'i Archives, a staircase-alley along Beit She'arim St. leads to the Haifa Museum, a largely unsuccessful attempt to integrate ancient and modern art. When visiting this museum, proceed straight to the top floor where the archeological displays far surpass everything else in the museum. The exhibit includes beautiful mosaic floors from **Shikmona,** the archeological site on which the ancient city of Haifa was probably located, and an extensive collection of sculptures and figurines from Cana'anite (eighteenth century B.C.E.) through Greek and Roman times. Particularly noteworthy are the informative labels on the exhibits: a full account is given of the special powers, mythological history, and supernatural relatives of many of the ancient deities on display. The highlight of the exhibit is *The Fisherman,* a small masterpiece of Hellenistic sculpture from the second or third century B.C.E., which is housed in the room to the right as you leave the stairs. The Haifa Museum is at 26 Shabbtai Levi St. (tel 52 32 55 or 52 32 58) and is open Sun.-Thurs. 10am-5pm, Sat. 10am-2pm, closed Fri. Admission is $.50, $.25 for students. Special guided tours are given on Sun., Thurs., and Sat. at 11:30am.

Half a block past the museum at the intersection of HaTsionut Ave. and HaGeffen St. there are two art schools which have small galleries: The **Artist's House** at 21 HaTsionut (tel. 52 23 55), open Sun.-Thurs. 10am-1pm and 4-7pm, Sat. 10am-1pm, closed Fri., and **Beit HaGeffen Arab/Israeli Cultural Center** at the very beginning of HaGeffen St. (tel. 52 52 52), open Sun.-Thurs. 10am-1pm and 4-7pm (4-9pm in winter); Fri. and Sat. 10am-noon only. Admission to both galleries is free.

Below this cluster of art centers lies the old Arabic quarter, *Wadi Nisnas.* Between the fork of Wadi Nisnas and Yohanan HaKodesh Sts. on Nathanson St., the dirt-cheap Arab fruit market does a small but lively business. This bustling area below the Haifa Museum also serves as a gateway to the Hadar district. Two museums in Hadar cater to special interests. The **National Museum of Science and Technology,** opposite 15 Balfour St. (tel. 67 13 72) contains a varied collection of working models. Though the exhibits are heavily biased towards those with some connection to Israel, the "touch and try" policy could make a visit amusing. Open Sun., Mon., Wed. 9am-5pm, Tues., Thurs. 11am-7pm, Sat. 10am-2pm, closed Fri.; admission free on Sat. The **Music Museum** at 23 Arlosoroff St. displays ancient and modern folk instruments, ostensibly from all over the world. In fact, only the biblical world is represented, but the reconstructions are worthwhile. Open Sun.-Thurs. 10am-1pm, Sun. and Wed. 4-7pm, Fri. 10am-noon, closed Sat.

On Ha'Atzmaut St. near Kikar Plumer lies the **Dagon Silo** (tel. 66 42 21), certainly one of the most remarkable buildings ever constructed for the purpose of storing wheat. This curious modern edifice, whose asymmetrical twin towers dominate Haifa's waterfront, looks like some strange latter-day version of a Crusader fortress. Sunday to Friday at 10am, guides conduct a free and entertaining half-hour tour in the silo's museum, which contains interesting archeological displays about the history of grain storage and ingenious models of the Dagon Silo in action. The museum is closed to the general public at all other times.

Farther north along the coast a number of beaches look inviting on a blistering summer day. **Hof HaShaket,** the most convenient, costs $.50; the swimming here is good, and rafts can be rented for use along the breakwater. **Hof Bat Galim,** near the Central Bus Station, is rocky and unpleasant, and the Olympic-sized pool there has been closed indefinitely. If you don't mind traveling, take bus #44 or 45 to free Carmel Beach. On Saturdays the northern beaches are so packed that it might be worth hitching to the south, where the beaches are nicer and you can glimpse the sand between the sunbathers.

Elijah's Caves and the Carmelite Monastery

Throughout history, the slopes and grottoes of Mt. Carmel have been inhabited by hermits and ascetics from all three of Israel's major religions. The tradition supposedly began in the ninth century B.C.E., when the prophet Elijah used one of the caves to hide from an enraged King Ahab and wife Jezebel after Elijah had defeated the four hundred and fifty prophets of Ba'al (see I Kings 17-19). Both the caves and the prophet Elijah are revered by Muslims, who call the latter El Khadar, the "green prophet" of the green mountain. According to Christian tradition, the same cave became a refuge for the Holy Family on their return from Egypt. Later, many generations of Christians used the area as a shelter from persecution. The caves have recently been renovated and should be open to the public by the summer of 1984.

Directly above Elijah's cave, the **Carmelite Monastery** sits on a promontory with breathtaking views of Haifa Bay. The Carmelite Order, founded in 1150 by a Latin monk named Berthold, has been forced to move the site of its monastery throughout the centuries by Muslim persecution and various conquests. The monks now live in a relatively new church and monastery complex called **Stella Maris,** built in 1836 on the ruins of an ancient Byzantine chapel and a medieval Greek church. The church is adorned with lovely paintings and stained glass windows depicting Elijah rising in his Chariot of Fire, King David playing his harp, numerous other prophets, and the Holy Family. Conservative dress is required for entrance (no shorts or bare shoulders). If you arrive at the same time as a group or if you start a conversation with one of the monks, you may get to see the small museum which contains ruins of former monasteries on Mt. Carmel from Byzantine and Crusader times. The monastery is open daily except Sun. 8:30am-1:30pm and 3-6pm; admission free. To get there, take bus #25 or 26 from in front of the Baha'i Temple on HaTsionut Ave. or from HaNevi'im St. to the corner of Tchernichofsky and E. Fleg Sts. The convent of the female order of the Carmelites, up the hill from the monastery, is closed to the general public.

To get to the larger caves below the monastery, you can either walk one kilometer west along the road from the Central Bus Station (buses #3 or 5) or take bus #26 from Edmund Fleg St. near the monastery, or #43 or 44 from the Hadar district. For the more adventurous, a path leads down the mountainside from the monastery, beginning near the elbow in the road, just to the left of the fence with the "No photographing" sign. The monks themselves use it for an annual visit. The hike takes about twenty minutes and offers gorgeous views all the way down. The caves are open daily 8am-5pm (Fri. until 1pm); admission free.

Below the caves lies the **National Maritime Museum,** 198 Allenby Rd. (tel. 53 66 22), whose well-documented collections cover only a limited range of concepts and history. However, the special exhibitions of marine art give a colorful glimpse beneath the Mediterranean waves. Open Mon.-Thurs. 10am-5pm, Fri. 9am-3pm, Sat. 10am-2pm, closed Sun.; admission free. Nearby at 204 Allenby, the old ship *Af-Al-Pi* now contains the **Clandestine Immigration and Naval Museum** (tel. 53 62 49), an excellent presentation of the techniques and the humanity of the Ha'Apala, the smuggling of immigrants into the Holy Land during the British mandate. The ship's plank is down Mon., Wed., Thurs. 9am-3pm, Sun. and Tues. 9am-4pm, Fri. and holidays 9am-1pm, closed Sat.

The Universities

At the opposite end of the Carmel ridge, Haifa's two major academic complexes survey the slopes below. The architectural pride of the **Haifa University** campus, designed by the renowned architect Niemeier, is a large 25-story building known as the "White Elephant." As the focus of student activities, the building, whose proper name is the **Eshkol Tower,** always contains art exhibits; from its observatory, Israel itself becomes a work of art. On a clear day, the astounding view encompasses most of the country from the Lebanese highlands to the smog-scrapers of Tel Aviv. Notice in particular the Druze Villages on the south slope of the Carmel. Free guided tours of the campus are conducted by students from 9am-2pm (until noon on Fri.), starting from the Main Building. (For more information, call 24 00 95 or 24 64 45). To reach the university, take bus #24 or 37 from Herzl St., or bus #92 from the Central Bus Station. For the tower, get off at the next to last stop.

A visit to the new campus of the **Technion,** Israel's high-powered scientific pantheon, is worthwhile primarily for its campus life and hostel (see Accommodations and Nightlife). The Technion is divided into two campuses: the older, more interesting one on Balfour and Herzl Sts. in Hadar houses about one-tenth of the students; the newer Qiryat HaTechnion (Technion City), on Mt. Carmel, houses the rest. Altogether, the school has an enrollment of about eight thousand, with a faculty of fifteen hundred. Call 29 23 12 for information on occasional guided tours of the new campus. Take bus #17 from the lower town, #31 from Central Carmel, or #19 from the Central Bus Station or Herzl St.

Nightlife

Asked once about the city's sparse entertainment, Haifa's first socialist mayor is reputed to have pointed to the city's round-the-clock factories and said: "There is our nightlife." Although still a relatively quiet metropolis, there's plenty to do—if you go to the right places. The IGTO should be your first source of information. A most memorable evening activity in Haifa is to walk along Rehov Yefe Nof or Panorama Road (take the Carmelit to Gan Ha'Em) for a view of sparkling city lights that is both expansive and intimate. Less expansive but more intimate is the Bat Galim Promenade along the shore behind the Central Bus Station. The best time is dusk. There is always a lot of activity in and around Gan Ha'Em, with occasional free summer concerts. Be sure to pick up the free weekly publication *Events in the Haifa and Northern Region* at one of the tourist offices for a complete day-by-day listing of concerts and special events, or call 64 08 40 after 4pm. If you don't mind more tourists and higher prices, hike up to the Carmel, a popular shopping district. For a rawer, more driving atmosphere, walk along Ha Nevi'im St.

The **Haifa Çinematique** located at 104 HaNassi St. (tel. 82 74 9), a few blocks from Gan Ha'Em, has three to four English movies every night of the week except Friday. Right next door is the Haifa Auditorium, a beautiful hall where the Israel Philharmonic and distinguished musicians perform concerts regularly.

There are also a few good nightspots hidden away behind the furious, felafel-eating mask of nighttime Hadar. There are evening shows as well as chamber music Saturdays at 5pm at **Zavit Cafe Theater** (tel. 25 36 41), tucked away on beautiful Jerusalem St., down the stairs to the left at #23. Nearby, in the Benyamin Gardens, is an expensive restaurant. Don't be tempted: the atmosphere does not warrant the prices. Just enjoy the classical or soft-rock music from the bright-red, cast-iron kiddie carousel in the park. Further down, near the port, the **London Pride Pub,** 85 Ha'Atzmaut St. (tel. 66 38 39), at Kikar Khayat is a raucous pick-up joint frequented by many of the port's sailors. Cover is $3 weekdays, $5 Fri. and Sat., with the first drink included. Open at 9pm. A more posh pub-disco is the **Club Amsterdam** at 124 HaNassi (tel. 25 69 28), with a cover charge of $3.50 on Fri. and Sat. (including one drink), no charge weekdays. **Exotica,** at 22 HaTsionut Ave., is a fairly seedy night-club/restaurant, a hangout for the local *chackchakim* (riffraff). The **Club 120** (called the *Mo'adon 120* in Hebrew), at 120 Rehov Yefe Nof (tel. 82 97 9), is a bit more civilized but there's always a cover (usually $2-4). Weekends it's filled to capacity. On weeknights they'll often give a 25% student discount; women enter free on Mon. and Wed. nights.

A good way to meet young Israelis is to attend some special activities at the Technion and Haifa University. They frequently offer dances, coffeehouses, and movies, especially during the school year. In July and August, the Technion holds nightly dances, and foreign students are welcome. For further information, call 23 41 48/9, and remember to bring along a student ID and your passport.

On Sunday evenings during the summer, there is often free disco dancing outdoors at Dado Beach, 8pm-midnight. On Mondays, look for a rock concert at Gan Ha'Em at 5:30 pm; the fee varies between $.50 and $6. On Tuesday evenings Bat Galim Promenade hosts a free outdoor flea market from 5-11pm. More disco dancing takes place on Wednesday evenings outdoors at the Carmel Center, 8-11pm. On Thursday evenings on Hassan Shukri St., near Gan HaZikharon, street performers do their tricks by a flower market, 5-11pm. At the Rothschild Center (142 HaNassi) folk dancing begins at 8pm. You can folk dance on Friday nights, too, at the Technion in Neve Sha'an at 8:30pm, and see films too good to be shown all over Israel. Call 82 74 9 for information and schedules. Finally, on Saturday evenings there's a free art bazaar near the Dan Hotel on Rehov Yefe Nof.

Near Haifa

The Carmel mountain is actually much larger than the boundaries of the city of Haifa. The name "Haifa" may derive from the Hebrew *Hof Yaffa* ("beautiful coast"), but "Carmel" is taken from *Kerem El* ("Vineyards of God"). Many of the areas finest grapes today can be found not on the coast, but on the inland slopes (e.g. En Hod, Daliat El-Karmel, Osfia), on the plain of Sharon (e.g. Atlit, Neve Yam, Dor, Zikhron Ya'akov, Ma'agan Mikhael), in the Jezreel (e.g. Qiryat Tivon, Beit She'arim) or Zevulun valleys (e.g. Kfar HaMaccabi, Akko, Nahariyya, the Achzivs).

Beit She'arim. Only twenty years ago, excavations at Beit She'arim, 19km south of Haifa, revealed the remains of an ancient synagogue and an impressive network of catacombs. In the second century C.E., this was the site of the Supreme Rabbinical Council—the *Sanhedrin*—which presided over all of the world Jewry. During the third and fourth centuries it became the central necropolis of the Jewish world; archeologists have uncovered a vast complex of twenty caves with numerous handsomely adorned sarcophagi, including one of Rabbi Yehuda Hanassi—the founder of the Sanhedrin. Beit She'arim became the sacred burial place during the first few centuries of the Common Era because Jerusalem was closed to Jews. Inscriptions and engravings indicate that the coffins found in the catacombs came from all parts of the ancient world to this enormous secret Jewish cemetery in the Holy Land.

The archeological site and a museum are located in a park near the town of **Qiryat Tivon** (½ hour's walk, or try hitching). Hours for both are Sat.-Thurs. 8am-5pm, Fri. 8am-3pm; admission is $1.35, $.70 for students. Between the synagogue and the catacombs, you'll come to a turn-off for the Alexander Zaid statue—a more recent construction—which offers a superb panorama of the surrounding hills. Zaid was the guardian of these hills during the 30s until his death in the 1936 uprisings. Because of his good reputation with local Arabs, he was and his sons now are the main mediators between the Arab *chanullas*, or extended families, of the area. Qiryat Tivon also has a lovely **Youth Hostel** (see Haifa Accommodations), and a swimming pool open every day 9am-4:30pm, with a poolside disco on Fri. nights. To get to Beit She'arim, take bus #75 from the Central Bus Station or from Herzliyya St. in Haifa to Qiryat Tivon. The site is a ten-minute walk from there.

En Hod. In the early 1950s, a group of artists settled in a small deserted Arab village on a picturesque hill on the western slopes of Mt. Carmel and named it En Hod. The village has subsequently grown into a well-known artists' colony, filled with workshops and studios and offering everything from traditional folk crafts to ultra-modern painting. Many Israelis come here to study ceramics, weaving, or drawing. Some of the old Arab homes are still intact, lending the community an Eastern flavor. Although the studios are closed to casual visitors, the large **En Hod Gallery,** run by two friendly, English-speaking women, exhibits works by the En Hod residents (open daily including Sat. 9:30am-5pm, Fri. till 4pm; admission $.20). Across from the gallery is the very pretty, but somewhat expensive, **Artists' Inn Cafe** and nearby is the site of En Hod's new **museum,** which exhibits works by Marcel Janco, one of the founders of the Dadaist movement, as well as other artists. Admission $1, $.75 for students. Although Dada is explained in four languages, the art of clear presentation of confusion has not yet been mastered in the museum. But the works stimulate a good deal of discussion, for which there are wonderfully soft chairs. From the top floor porch you can look down the mountain through the valley to the ancient port of Atlit, now encircled by a military camp and hence inaccessible. Just up the main road is the settlement of Yamin Orde, from which the view is even better. If, in walking around, you can artfully avoid the visitors (foreign and Israeli) and engage the artists themselves, then indeed En Hod has the atmosphere of a true artists' colony. During the summer, more of the artists are in residence—but so are more tourists. En Hod is 14km south of Haifa. To get there, take bus #202, 203, or 222 heading south along the old Haifa-Hadera road. From the junction where the bus lets you off, En Hod is a twenty-minute walk uphill. Hitching is relatively easy due to the large population in the area.

Druze Villages. Another of the religious minorities in the Haifa area is the Druze sect. Two Druze villages, **Daliyat al-Carmel** (25km) and **Isfiya** (21km) are within easy reach of Haifa. Daliyat al-Carmel is perhaps the more interesting of the two, and with a population of 7500, it is one of the largest Druze villages; both towns are a delight to wander in.

The Druze religion was founded in 1017 by an Egyptian chieftain who drew on the various beliefs then current in the Islamic world. The Druze are very secretive about their faith; conversion to the Druze religion is not allowed. They believe that God's will can only be revealed to a very few, and hence even most Druze are ignorant of the greater part of the Druze doctrine. Sir Lawrence Oliphant, one of the few outsiders close to the sect, was a Christian mystic and a strong supporter of Zionism in the late nineteenth century; he and his wife lived in Daliyat el-Karmel for five years. For part of that time, Oliphant's secretary was the Hebrew poet Naftali Hertz Imber, who later wrote *Hatikva*, accepted as the Israeli national anthem after independence.

The Druze are easily recognized by the mens' thick greying mustaches under their flowing white "kaffiyehs", and by the women's black robes with white shawls. The Druze are ruled by a hierarchy of elders, whose respective positions are determined by the extent to which they have been initiated into the well-concealed secrets of this mysterious religion. An elder, or "Michubad," does not wear a kaffiyah but rather a tightly-wrapped white cap and a blue-black robe. One of the few things known about the religion is that the most holy prophet is Jethro, Moses' father-in-law. Elijah and hence the Carmel region also play an important role. (See Haifa Sights.)

At one time the Druze kingdom, under the Emir Fakhr al-Din, stretched from Lebanon to Gaza to the Golan Heights. Since their defeat at the hands of the Turks and Bedouins, the Druze have never again ruled their own territory. An unsuccessful rebellion against the Egyptian Pasha in 1830 led to the destruction of the Druze villages on the Carmel and elsewhere. When in the 1860s the Turks were anxious to see the Druze as a buffer against the Bedouins and the Christians were looking for potential converts, the Druze were welcomed back to two of the villages they had founded on the Carmel.

For nine hundred years, the Druze have managed to preserve their ethnic and religious identity, even though they speak Arabic and have always lived near Arab Muslims and Christians. A people without their own land, the Druze generally give allegiance to the nation in which they live. The Israeli Druze, in particular, have long supported the State of Israel. The community insists that its sons serve in the Israeli army so that they can enjoy the same rights as Jews, and they have especially distinguished themselves as soldiers and as officers of the highest ranks. Since 1980 the Defense Ministry has been paying for the restoration of Oliphant's house on the outskirts of the town. It is now a memorial for the many Druze soldiers killed in Israel's wars. Although the street names are not used, everyone knows where the "Beit Oliphant" is, so ask. The villagers are proud of the memorial and often sit in its gardens.

The Druze are supremely hospitable and welcome visitors to their towns, especially in recent years, as the bazaar in Daliyat el-Karmel has attracted more and more tourists, bringing increased revenues to the village. The bazaar is most lively on Saturdays (the Druze do not keep the Jewish Sabbath), but if you wish to see and speak to the Druze, it's better to come during the week. The Saturday prices are much higher, as well. You should bargain, though it may be difficult; the Druze know they can get high prices from most tourists. Don't feel badly if you don't purchase anything—most of the clothes and handicrafts are imported from India, while the furniture comes from Gaza.

The only reasonably priced accommodations in the villages are in Isfiya at the **Stella Carmel Hospice** (P.O. Box 7045; tel. 22 26 92), which has bed and breakfast doubles for $12 per person, or bed and three meals for $16.Try to call first, as the Hospice is very popular. Nearby, through a maze of valleys, lie the ruins of a fifth-century synagogue with a tiled floor depicting a candelabra and the Hebrew inscription "Peace upon Israel." If you ask for "Rosh HaCarmel," you will be led uphill 2km to the highest peak on Carmel. The view of the many ridges and great forests that spread into the Zevulun valley will dazzle you. Bring some food to this picnicker's paradise.

The Druze villages make an excellent daytrip, even on Saturday. From Haifa, buses #92 and 93 from the Central Bus Station and the Hadar district stop in both villages on weekdays. Sheruts from Elyahu St. near the Zim building or from Shemaryahu Levin and Herzl Sts. on Sat. cost under $1 each way. If you're hitching, start on Sderot Abba Khoushy, which passes Haifa University. From the Haifa-Nazareth road, you must go south at Nesher. The most scenic way to return to Haifa is to hitch in the direction of Kibbutz Bet Oren and the sea. From Daliyat el-Karmel the road passes Isfia, then forks right to Haifa and left to Bet Orea. If you go left and left again at the next fork, the road will take you through the beautiful winding valley down to the old coastal road near Atlit. Going south a few kilometers, En Hod is up the next left and the beautiful beach **Neve Yam** is after that on the right.

Just south of En Karmel, visible from the highway, are the **prehistoric caves** known as the *Mearot Karmel.* To get here straight from Haifa, take the local Tel Aviv bus and plead to be let off at the caves, as there really isn't a stop. If the driver refuses or (more likely) forgets, get off at Geva Karmel and walk back a kilometer or so. From the road you can see the three large caves in the cliffs facing the ocean through the banana fields. The largest is called the *tanur* because it resembles an oven with its chimney. An English sign recounts the story of the twelve 130,000-year-old skeletons of Neanderthal humans found along with paleolithic tools and the bones from sixty other animal species. Among these were the elephant and rhinoceros which were indigenous to the Middle East before either Arabs or Jews. The artifacts are no longer in the caves (although you can see them in the Rockefeller Museum in Jerusalem). You can, however, learn of the similarities between bats and pigeons: their droppings are indistinguishable even in larger quantities. The caves are open every day 24 hours.

Up the road from Daliyat el-Karmel away from Isfia (bear left at the only fork along the way or you'll go to El-Yakim) is the site of Elijah's defeat of the four hundred fifty priests of Ba'al. **Mukhraqa,** the Arabic name, refers to the "sacrifice" or "burning" that Elijah offered to God from an altar here (see I Kings 17-40). After the victory, Elijah's servant saw a rain cloud come from this mount to break the long drought. The Carmelites see in the clouds a symbol of the Virgin Mary, to whom, along with Elijah, they are especially devoted. In 1886 they built a small monastery here, which is now open Sat.-Thurs. 8am-noon and 1-5pm, Fri. 8am-noon only, closed Sun. From the roof, the **Jezrael Valley** spreads out before you; on a clear day the snow-capped Mt. Hermon lies on the horizon. If you happen to be hitching to Nazareth or Afula, you can see the tiny Arab tent communities between El-Yakim and Yokne'am on the way. Egged buses #37 or 39 from Haifa stop at Mukhraqa eight times a day in the summer, less in winter. Check the schedule in the Central Bus Station before you go.

Akko

The old town of Akko is a compact gold mine of historical monuments, and one of Israel's most striking cities. Its motley collection of Islamic minarets, Turkish walls, Napoleonic cannons, and Crusader fortifications combine to create a thick, exotic atmosphere of medieval adventure and old-world charm. Akko, like Jerusalem, is really two cities: the entirely Arab old town and the mixed Arab and Jewish new town. The contrast between the two is striking—despite an occasional Western bed or electric fan in some houses, the lifestyle of the Arabs who dwell in the labyrinthine streets of the old town remains fundamentally unchanged, while the high-rise apartment buildings and broad shopping avenues of the new town are a testimony to the prosperity of Israel's Jewish population.

Some of the Arab residents of the old city are very warm and out-going towards tourists, while others are not—you may find yourself torn by different emotions as you walk through the old town, greeted alternately with friendly smiles and jeers. During the summer, when schools have vacation, you may also find yourself awarded a very informative, if somewhat tiresome, self-appointed guide. He will probably not be interested in a tip, and may well be insulted if you offer one. The young men who so boldly approach you in the street are often only interested in practicing English and impressing their friends. Women, however, even those with male companions, should tread carefully, for the hospitality is seldom directed towards them without expectations. Many of the local men consider picking up foreign women a full-time sport. What begins as a pleasant conversation may turn into a dangerous encounter. It is also not advisable to buy or try any drugs offered to you on the streets—the local police keep a remarkably close watch on the dealers and usually throw foreign offenders into the local prison for several very unpleasant days before expelling them from the country.

The city may be ancient (some of the houses have been occupied steadily since the Crusaders built them), but it has a vibrant spirit. Since Akko was obviously intended for the pedestrian, give yourself some time to walk around and explore.

History

Akko (or "Acre," as it is often written in English) has witnessed a long and colorful history, and still retains many of the artifacts to prove it. During its first millennium, it changed hands in rapid succession among the Romans, Christians, Jews, and Muslims. Akko's history does not become truly distinguished until 1140, when the Crusaders took it from the Muslim Caliph. The Hospitaller Knights, a division of the Order of St. John named after the Hospital of St. Mary, renamed the city St. John d'Acre and made it the chief Crusader port in the Holy Land. Akko was conquered by Salahdin in 1187, but Richard the Lionhearted retrieved it in the name of the Church in 1190. During the thirteenth century, Akko was the capital of the Crusader kingdom, and the fortresses of Montfort and Gadin were built to protect it and supply it with agricultural products. The Mamelukes conquered and destroyed Akko in 1290, and the site remained desolate until the Bedouin Sheikh Daher el Omar rebuilt the city in the 1740s on top of the extensive foundations provided by the Crusaders. During his reign the city was once again made the undisputed capital of the Holy Land. Daher's fortifications form the inner walls of present-day Akko. The Sheikh's successor was a ruthless but successful Albanian Muslim named Ahmed. Called "Al-Jazzar," the butcher, he built the great mosque that now bears his name, as well as the Khan el-Umdan, the aqueduct north of the city, and the steam-baths in it. With some aid from Britain, he successfully resisted Napoleon's two-month siege of the city in 1799, so that Napoleon was forced to withdraw his eastern campaign back to Egypt and then to France. Akko's port declined when the new steamboat traffic needed the deeper harbors of Haifa and Beirut, and the city languished until the British used its prisons for members of the Jewish resistance. Soon after the Irgun prison break in 1947, the Israeli Defense Forces and the State of Israel were born.

Practical Information

Most of the city's services are in the new town; the one exception is the old city branch of the **Post Office** at the entrance to the Crusader city. The ticket booth at the entrance also serves as the town's **Municipal Information Office** (tel. 91 02 51). If they have no pamphlets, go to the office of the director of the Municipal Museum. The **Central Post Office** is in the new town off Ben Ami St., by the corner of Yehosafat St. The **police** can be reached by dialing 91 02 44; for **First Aid** call 91 02 33.

To get to Akko from either Haifa or Nahariyya take bus #251 or 271, leaving every fifteen minutes, **Kavei Hagalil** sherut company has frequent cars to Haifa and Nahariyya, leaving from the parking lot on Yehosafat St., near the corner of Ben Ami St. (tel. 91 01 1).

The **telephone code** for Akko is 04.

Accommodations and Food

The **Akko Youth Hostel (IYHF),** just across from the old lighthouse, has clean, spacious rooms in a two hundred-year-old building, once the palace of the Governor when the Holy Land was a province of the Ottoman Empire. Located in the Crusader city itself, it is one of the finest urban hostels in Israel, and is rarely full. A very good dinner is served for $3.30 members, $4 non-members; use of the kitchen costs $.40. Cold soft drinks and beer are available at standard prices, and the enterprising manager even sells a map of the Old City for about $.10 (a necessity). Rates: members $5 under 18, $5.60 over 18, nonmembers $5.55 under 18 and $6.70 over 18. Prices are the same for 4-person rooms, but these are reserved mostly for families. All rates include breakfast. To get to the hostel from the bus station, walk out and turn left, then right at the first corner onto Ben Ami St. Follow Ben Ami to the seashore, turn left onto HaHaganah St. until you reach the lighthouse and take the alleyway to the left; the hostel will be on your left just past the arch. The **Abu Cristal** restaurant nearby (under the lighthouse) has tables overlooking the water and is a very pleasant place to go in the evenings. However, be sure you know what you've ordered before you begin your meal—they've been known to rip off unsuspecting tourists. Around the corner from the hostel, heading away from the lighthouse, is a **Pitah Bakery** where you can buy piping hot pitah bread straight out of the oven in the mornings for 7¢ apiece.

Even cheaper than the hostel is **Avraham's Guesthouse.** Avraham, a friendly and hospitable Arab who cannot resist smothering foreign female guests with kisses, provides comfortable mattresses on his living room floor for $4 per person, and a sumptuous breakfast you would be foolish to refuse for another $1. Unfortunately, the place is quite noisy and the doors don't open until 5 or 6pm. Finding Avraham's abode is a bit tricky, since it is totally unmarked. He is located on Salah-a-Din St., next to the Land Gate. Next door to the **Ali Baba Restaurant,** you will see steps leading up to the Burj Nightclub—turn right at the top of the steps and you are there. Believe it or not, there is no place else to stay in the old town, and no place as cheap in the entire area. The tourist authorities are still drawing up plans to renovate the old Muslim *caravanserais* to accommodate modern pilgrims. Because of Akko's proximity to fancy coastal hotels to the south and new city developments to the north, beach camping is not as acceptable here as elsewhere.

Sights

From the bus station go towards the left down Weizmann St. to get to the old city. The Municipal Information Office will be on your right, the Elie Cohen Park on your left. As you pass the Al-Jazzar wall you can see the moat beneath the Burj el Kommander to the left. The entrance to the Mosque of Al-Jazzar is just to your right on Al-Jazzar St.

The third largest mosque in Israel, and the most important one outside of Jerusalem, the **Mosque of Al-Jazzar** dominates this city of monuments with its large green dome and tall, sleek minaret. Ahmed Al-Jazzar ordered its construction in 1781 on what is believed to have been the site of San Croce, the original Christian cathedral of Akko. As you step through the entrance to the mosque, you will find yourself in a beautiful courtyard with Roman columns which were taken from Caesarea. The western end of the courtyard rests upon the cellar of a Crusader fortress. The surrounding structures are lodgings for students of the Qur'an and personnel of the mosque. The small building in front of the mosque houses the sarcophagi of Ahmed Al Jazzar and his adopted son, Suleiman Pasha. The tower was destroyed by an earthquake in 1927, but promptly restored; the rest of the complex is in magnificent condition.

In front of the mosque is an octagonal fountain where the faithful wash their heads, hands, and feet before entering the holy sanctuary. From here, they continue barefoot along the wooden walkway. You will probably be asked to remove your shoes and certainly should not set foot on the grass mats (in summer) or the wooden walkway (in winter) that adorn the floor of the Mosque's interior. Inside in the green cage on the balcony up to the right is a shrine that contains a hair from the beard of the prophet Muhammad. Services are conducted in the mosque five times a day, but the original caller has been replaced by a loudspeaker which can be heard throughout the city. The mosque is open daily 9am-noon, but you can often enter in the afternoon as well; admission is 25¢, no student discount. Blouses and skirts are provided so that women can cover exposed skin. Well-informed guides will also provide you with a short tour of the mosque, in return for which they request a small donation. Be sure the guide you get is the one who speaks English—the other will just mutter incoherently as he leads you around and then takes your money.

Across from the mosque on Al-Jazzar St. you will see a restored white stone gate. This is the entrance to the **Subterranean City of the Crusaders.** What remains is actually not the entire city, but only the area that was known originally as the "Hospitaller's Quarter" (the government prohibited further excavations for fear that the Arab village above it might collapse). In the entrance halls you will see three enormous pillars surrounded by a variety of architectural styles—generally speaking, anything decorated with pictorial representations (flowers, human forms) is Crusader work; the more abstract embellishments and the Arabic writing are Ottoman additions. The neighboring halls date from the original twelfth-century Crusader city, and were probably part of a hospital complex. If you look carefully, you will realize that the arches all project suddenly out from the floor, indicating that the floor today is some four meters above the halls' original level. (The barrels and girders you see throughout the complex were placed there recently to support the original walls.)

The complex is quite extensive, and contains several sections. From the entrance halls proceed to the courtyard, where you can see part of the fortifications built by Daher el Omar. Turn left, and enter the **Hospitaller's Fort** through the imposing Turkish gate, directly underneath which stands the original Crusader gate. If you then turn right, you'll be in the center of the original Crusader complex. These halls are used for occasional concerts by the Haifa Symphony Orchestra, as well as the annual **Akko Underground Theater Festival.** The Festival, a week-long celebration in mid-October, attracts small theater groups from all over Israel. Unfortunately, only a small number of the performances are in English.

Back across the footbridge, you can follow the halls around and down to the famous **Refectory,** also called the **Crypt of St. John.** This lowest portion of the complex was actually never used as a grave, but functioned rather as a dining hall and reception area.

By the third column in the crypt a staircase leads to the long underground passageway from the crypt to the area called **Al Bosta.** The passageway may have been dug originally by the Crusaders as a hiding place in case of attack. It was carefully restored by Al-Jazzar to serve as a means of escape if Napoleon penetrated the city walls. Al Bosta consists of six connected rooms opening out into a central courtyard, and was probably the final defensive outpost of the Crusader complex. The rooms also served as a hospital for wounded knights. The Turks used it as a post office, naming it al-Posta.

When you pay admission to the Crusader city ($.55, $.45 for students), hang on to the ticket: it is also good for the adjacent **Municipal Museum** (just to the right of the Crusader city exit). The museum contains four small exhibits covering archeological finds around Akko, Crusader weapons, the folklore of the area, and Islamic art and culture. Until 1947 the building was a Turkish steam bath built by the Old Butcher. The Crusader city and the museum are open Sat.-Thurs. 9am-4:30pm, Fri. 9am-12:30pm.

Turning left down the stairs when you leave the museum will take you through the Oriental Market, itself not the least of the charms of the old town. The market (*suq* in Arabic) is a bustling hubbub of butchers, grocers, bakers, and fruit, vegetable, and pastry vendors. Copper, brass, and leather goods are also plentiful. Little eating places, scattered throughout the suq, offer shish kebab, felafel, and sandwiches of various sorts. The first caravanserai (in Arabic, *khan*) you come to is the **Khan el-Afranj** on the left. During the Muslim occupation of the city, three caravanserais were constructed to lodge travelers and their animals. Near the el-Afranj are the **Khan el-Umdan** and the **Khan el-Shawarda,** flanked by the **Jamin el Raml Mosque** (open 4-6pm; admission $.20). The most impressive of them is the Khan el-Umdan, the Inn of the Pillars, just past the Isnan Pasha mosque and the Arab fishing port. The magnificent structure of the Khan is notable for its handsome two-tiered colonnades. Al-Jazzar, the reigning chief of Akko, built this caravanserai towards the end of the eighteenth century for Turkish merchants selling goods. The lower stories of the courts served as stalls for horses, camels, and other animals, while the upper galleries served as boarding rooms. The Khan is marked by a tall, slender square clock tower with the Turkish symbol of a half-moon and a star, built in 1906 to celebrate the jubilee of the Turkish sultan Abdul Hamid, who ruled Palestine from 1876-1918. The clock is now gone, but you can climb up the slippery narrow staircase to a stunning view of the city. The tower is open only irregular hours (sometimes the old city ticket booth will know).

Through the Khan el-Umdan going inland is the Khan el-Shawarda and a block or so further the western seawall. A quick walk north (to the right) from here should convince you of the strength of this Crusader stronghold. The market is in swing between 7am and 7pm.

Nearby is the **old Arab fishing port,** still in use. During July and August the Arab fishermen take tourists out in boats for lovely tours of the seawalls, and fabulous views of the city. Set a price before you go, not more than $1-$1.50 in a boat with other tourists. Often they will try to sell you "special" private cruises, quoting prices of up to ten dollars, but you can bargain them down considerably. If you decide to take one, watch carefully what kind of boat they bring up (if it's a rowboat pulled by children, simply walk away in disgust).

Just before you reach the Burj Kurajim on HaHaganah St. the **citadel** commands your attention. Housed in this huge Turkish fortress (which was used by the British as their central prison) the **Museum of Heroism** is a moving testimonial to Israeli resistance organizations. The citadel was erected in the late 1700s on Crusader foundations of the thirteenth century, and used as a prison by the Turks. The most famous inmate during the Turkish rule was Baha-u-Illah, founder of the Baha'i faith, who was imprisoned in the second story in 1868. During the British Mandate period, members of the Jewish underground were imprisoned here, including Ze'ev Jabotinsky in 1920. Jabotinsky had organized the Jewish Resistance Movement during the earlier part of this century, long before Israeli independence became an active issue for most Jews.

One particular resistance group, Menachem Begin's Irgun, provided the prison with its most dramatic moments. Eight members of the Irgun were hanged from the citadel's gallows in the years 1938, 1946, and 1947. The **Gallows Room,** now the museum's most sobering exhibit, still has the noose in place and photographs of the eight victims on the wall. The Irgun retaliated by hanging a British officer, an act for which Margaret Thatcher has reputedly never been able to forgive Begin. On May 4, 1947, the Irgun outwitted its British captors by staging a spectacular prison break that freed eleven of its members and 255 other inmates. (The Haganah, contrary to many sources, took no part in the break, and its members stayed in prison.) The event provided material for the escape scene in the movie *Exodus,* which was filmed here. At the time, the prison housed about 560 inmates under the guard of about half that many British soldiers. The museum is open Sat.-Thurs. 8:30am-5pm, Fri. 8:30am-12:30pm, admission $1, $.90 for students. Although it adjoins the Crusader city, the entrance to the citadel is on Haganah St., opposite the western seawall.

Renowned throughout history as the most impregnable port in the East, Akko remains above all a city of battlements and bastions. Akko's reputation in recent centuries has rested squarely on the hefty **Al-Jazzar Wall,** extending along the northern and eastern sides of the city and surrounded by a moat of sea water. The best place from which to view the wall is the **Burj el Kommander,** an imposing Crusader bastion along the northern corner. To enter the watchtower, climb the steps that begin where Weizmann St. crosses the wall. The long, slender cannons along the wall are of French design, and are popularly known as "Napoleon's cannons," but inscriptions on some of the barrels indicate that they could not have been brought to Akko before the middle of the last century. The square mortar-like cannons are of Turkish origin and were for shooting rocks rather than cannonballs. They were, in all probability, used to defend the city during Napoleon's siege in 1799.

The city walls originally encompassed the entire harbor, but all that remains of the harbor walls is the ruined **Tower of the Flies,** the site of the original lighthouse, standing by itself in the middle of the bay. The original fortifications were toppled by a devastating earthquake in 1837, and for some time fishermen were forced to keep their boats on the patches of sand at the edge of the city until the present breakwater was built. At the eastern corner of the walls, near the shoreline, is the so-called **Land Gate,** once the only entrance to the city. The top of the gate affords a fine panorama of the bay. At the northwestern corner of the city opposite the Museum of Heroism is the **Burj Kurajim** (The Fortress of the Vineyards), commonly referred to as the British Fortress despite its Crusader and Turkish builders.

The New Town

The only part of the new town of Akko of particular interest to tourists is **Hof Argaman** (which means "Purple Beach" despite its remarkably white sands). Some claim that this is the finest beach in Israel now that the Red Sea beaches have been returned to Egypt. Although that assessment is questionable, the beach is definitely popular and quite crowded in summer (admission $.50). To get to Hof Argaman, follow Jonathan HaHashmonai St. out from the Land Gate along the coast for about ten minutes. Dominating the beach are the new town's only hotels, the Argaman and the Palm Beach, both very expensive. Past the Palm Beach Hotel is a free beach of the same caliber as Hof Argaman. Just outside the Land Gate is **Walls Beach.** Though not as attractive as the others, it has a few special features. You can rent windsurfers here for just $2 an hour; sailboats go for $4 an hour and small motorboats (with even smaller motors) go (slowly) at $5 an hour. Although the signs say "Bathing prohibited" in three languages, if you let that stop you, none of the several hundred swimmers will ever know. There's a place to change through the low door across from the beach entrance.

The main shopping avenue is Ben Ami St., lined with stores providing every kind of modern convenience, and offering a stark contrast to the stalls of the old town's bazaars. A number of inexpensive felafel stands arc to be found around the corner of Weizmann and Ben Ami St. Further from the old town but substantially better are the food stands on Yehosafat St., off Ben Ami St.

Near Akko

Lohame HaGeta'ot, a kibbutz founded in 1949 entirely by rebels from the ghettos of Poland and Lithuania, is famous for its **Holocaust Museum,** dedicated to the memory of the Jewish resistance fighters and ghetto rebels of World War II. Although perhaps a less moving monument to the Holocaust than Yad VaShem (in Jerusalem), Lohame HaGeta'ot is more descriptive and documentary—a place to learn what actually happened. Changing exhibits often include artwork by inmates of the ghettos and concentration camps. The museum is open Sun.-Thurs. 9am-4pm, Fri. 9am-1pm, Sat. 10am-5pm. Admission is free, but a small donation is requested.

The **Roman aqueduct,** just outside the museum to the south, is very well preserved—not so surprising given that it's not a Roman aqueduct. The Turks of Al-Jazzar built it in 1780 to carry water the 15km from the Kabri springs to their stronghold in Akko.

Two kilometers south of the kibbutz are the beautiful **Baha'i Gardens,** arranged in traditional Persian style. The gardens are the site of the villa and tomb of Baha-u-Illah, founder of the Baha'i faith (the name means "Glory of God"). The villa contains a small collection of religious articles. The villa is open only Fri.-Mon. 9am-noon, but the gardens are open every day until 5pm; admission free. Both sites lie just off the main Akko-Nahariyya road, accessible by the very frequent bus #271 (make sure, however, that it is not an express).

Nahariyya

Nahariyya is a particularly pleasant version of the typical Israeli coast resort, with a fair beach, shady park area, tree-lined streets, luxury hotels, and lots of modern buildings. The name comes from the Hebrew word for "river," since Nahariyya was built over the small Ga'aton river. The town is understandably a popular retreat for native Israelis as well as wealthy French tourists, but has few historical or cultural offerings. Nahariyya's beaches are better than average for Israel, if somewhat crowded, though you can avoid the people by heading north along the coast towards Achziv and avoid the small beach fees by moving 1 km or so south.

Practical Information

Municipal Tourist Information Office: in the main Egged Bus Terminal building fronting Ga'aton Blvd. (tel. 92 61 25), four blocks up from the water. Open Sun.-Thurs. 9am-1pm and 4-7pm, Fri. 9am-4pm, closed Sat.

Central Post Office: 40 Ga'aton Blvd. (tel. 92 35 55). Open Sun.-Thurs. 8am-12:30pm and 3:30-6pm, except Wed. 8am-2pm, Fri. 8am-1pm.

Railway Station: Ga'aton Blvd. at the far (east) end of the Central Bus Station.

Central Bus Station: Ga'aton Blvd. (tel. 92 34 44 for information) Nahariyya can be reached from Akko or Haifa by buses #270 and 271.

Emergency: Police (tel. 92 03 44); first aid (tel. 92 33 33); hospital (tel. 92 21 01).

Bicycle Rental: Speed, Shevil HaGanim St., off the corner of 26 Ga'aton (tel. 92 19 65). No English sign. $5 a day for a well-kept bike.

Telephone Code: 04.

Accommodations, Food, and Sights

Nahariyya's cheapest hotel is not cheap. The **Beyt Erna** at 29 Jabotinsky St. (tel. 92 01 70) has singles for $14, doubles for $24, $2.50 more in July and Aug. (Jabotinsky St. is one block up from the waterfront). The following four are more expensive: **Kalman,** 27 Jabotinsky St. (tel. 92 03 55), singles $15 ($13.50 in off-season), doubles $25 ($23 in off-season); **Karl Laufer,** 31 HaMeyasdim St. (tel. 92 01 30), singles $16, doubles $27, no air conditioning. July and Aug. add 20%; **Nof Yam,** 14 HaMapilim St. on the waterfront (tel. 92 00 59), singles $15, doubles $26; **Rosenblatt,** 59 Weizmann St. (tel. 92 34 69 or 92 00 69), singles $16, doubles $27. All prices include breakfast. Cheaper accommodations can be found at the **Youth Hostel** at Gesher Haziv and the campgrounds at Achziv and Kabri (see below).

The **Kabri Campground,** once managed by nearby Kabri Kibbutz, is now simply an abandoned site, without facilities, and you can camp for free. To get there, take one of the frequent Ma'alot buses to Kabri junction, or walk 5km east along Yehi'am Rd. (the continuation of Ga'aton). Turn right at the junction (the road on your left heads into the kibbutz itself) and the campsite will be about 1km on your left. The kibbutz asks all campers to take their garbage with them when they leave.

Although there are dozens of little restaurant/cafes along both sides of Ga'aton Blvd., they all offer the same mediocre food at the same high prices. Nahariyya's beaches and peaceful gardens make it a delightful place for picnicking; a reasonable supermarket can be found on the corner of Ga'aton and Herzl St.

Nahariyya has little in the way of sights. As if to foreshadow its popularity as a honeymooner's resort, a four thousand-year-old **Canaanite Temple** dedicated to Asherah (Goddess of Fertility) was accidentally discovered in 1947 on the hill next to the shore of Nahariyya. The municipality building near the bus terminal contains a **modern art museum** (fifth floor) with very little modern art, some archeological finds of the area, and a cute malacological section for pretty seashells. The roof of the building offers a fine view of the area.

Saturday walks with the **Friends of Nature** are a pleasant way to spend a day when there is little else happening. Call 92 02 46 or 92 19 23. Or you can try horseback riding for $3-4 an hour; call Bakals (tel. 92 05 34).

Near Nahariyya

Rosh HaNikra

Although it is the United Nations checkpoint on the Israel/Lebanon frontier, Rosh HaNikra is best known for its beautiful white chalk cliffs. The waves that have pounded against the cliffs for centuries have carved fantastic sea caves into the chalk walls. These natural grottoes were enlarged when a tunnel, originally intended for the passage of a train between Haifa and Beirut, was dug through the cliffs. The Israeli government, astutely perceiving Rosh HaNikra's potential as a tourist attraction, blasted additional tunnels through the rock to improve access to the sea caves, and topped the cliffs off with an observation point and cafeteria that command a spectacular panorama of the northern Israeli coastline.

Since the highway from Nahariyya ends at the observation point, the only way down to the caves is by cable car, which costs $1.75 round trip, $1.25 for students (be insistent, and show them your card). The cable car runs seven days a week between the hours of 8:30am and 5pm (3:30pm in winter). Try to come early since the afternoons are often packed with coach tours and youth groups. The worse the weather, the better the show at Rosh HaNikra—the waves splash dramatically around the natural caverns, forming powerful cross-currents and whirlpools, and echoing thunderously through the subterranean tunnels. On calmer days, the show is not quite as impressive, but that is amply compensated for by the excellent swimming (technically illegal, but nonetheless popular) in the deep waters at the base of the dazzling white cliffs. Be sure not to venture out into the waters to the north; the Lebanese border guards have no sympathy with even the most innocent and ill-informed of illegal immigrants. Incidentally, don't try photographing the border crossing, unless you fancy having your camera seized.

Montfort

Although there are many excellent nature trails in the Western Galilee, few are accessible without a car and an ordinance-survey map. If, however, the northern border is quiet, it is possible to make a beautiful half-day trip to the Crusader fortress of Montfort. The main structure was built by the Knights of the Order of the Templars in the twelfth century and was partially destroyed by Saladin in 1187 during his march on Akko. Rebuilt by the Hospitaller Knights in 1230, the fortress was enlarged and strengthened; the knights named it *Starkenburg* (meaning "strong castle" in German), or *Montfort* in French. The impressive 18m tower and 20m main hall, along with the remnants of the fortress complex, can still be seen. The northern approach is via a dirt path leading off the east-west road between the settlements of Elon and Goren. Two kilometers on the way, you'll reach a small junction with a picnic site, from which a steep and winding trail leads down to the fortress.

Near Kibbutz Goren are dozens of beautiful and well-marked nature trails, most of which pass the Mitzpeh Goren, where the view of the castle is best. On the southern approach, the road from Mi'ilya leads north for 2½km, then turns into a footpath for 1½km more (bear right wherever the trail forks). Since buses run only 4-5 times a day along the northern road, and every half to full hour along the southern road (through Ma'alot to Mi'ilya and Nahariyya), you might wish to enter from the north and leave by the south. While you're there, the little Christian Arab town of Mi'ilya is a convenient diversion. In the village center lie the ruins of a twelfth-century French family's fortress. The family name, de Milly, stuck.

Both Montfort and **Gadin Castle** in Yechiam, 8km to the west, were built to protect Akko, the Crusader capital. Though destroyed by the Mameluke Sultan Baibars in 1265, the ruins are still quite impressive, and offer yet another view of the Sulam Tzor—Western Galilee highlands. The Castle is open Sun.-Thurs. 8am-5pm, Fri. and holiday eves 8am-4pm; admission $.60, $.30 for students.

Peki'in

Although technically part of the Central Galilee, Peki'in is best reached from Nahariyya. The village is known as the spot where Rabbi Shimeon Bar Yokkai and his son, Eleizer, fled from a Roman decree prohibiting individuals from studying the Torah. For thirteen years, the learned pair hid in a small cave in the hillside, sustained by a miracle which caused a spring to flow and a carob tree to bear fruit, right beside the mouth of their cave. During this time they composed the *Zohar,* the single most important text of Kabbala, or Jewish mysticism. To reach the cave, which is considered by Jews a holy place, take the road which winds up to the top of the village from the bus top. When you see a marking stone on your right (faintly engraved with a Hebrew map) head downstairs, turning right again through a gap in the stones. If you continue down the steps, then choose the downhill roads at every intersection, you'll come to a pool fed by Bar Yokkai's spring (which now trickles from a small pipe by the fence). From the spring, take the road that runs between the twin "no entry" signs, and turn left when you see colorful flags painted on the right-hand wall. The synagogue on this site, which stood in the days of Shimeon Bar Yokkai and his son, is now a small museum. If the synagogue gate is closed, knock on the door (just opposite the gate and upstairs) and ask to be let in. Although the museum is technically free, you should probably leave $0.50 or so in the small box on the table with the prayer books.

Back near the bus stop, you'll find a tiny Arab cafe (only one table and some chairs) known to residents of the surrounding settlements for its tasty *pita* baked in the tiny shack off to the right. If you ask for *pita-eem-lebene,* the proprietor will spread a piece with olive oil, dillweed, and a very sour, fermented white cheese called *lebene,* then fold it over ten times into a delicious multi-layered sandwich. Before you buy one, go over to the little shack and watch the woman bake the huge pita over the primitive dome-shaped hearth, as she has for thirty years. The whole show plus lunch costs $.50-$.60; she prefers that you pay in American currency.

Bus #44 from Nahariyya makes the round trip to Peki'in six or seven times a day; be sure to ask the driver to let you off at Peki'in Atika (Old Peki'in) not Peki'in Chadasha (New Peki'in), which is one stop earlier on the same line. If you ask nicely, the bus driver will drop you off about 3km past Old Peki'in at Tzomet (junction) Bet Jan. A 2½km walk or hitch will bring you to a small, peaceful Druze village. Much less commercialized than Daliyat el-Karmel or Isfia, **Bet Jan** is a relaxing place where it is easier to strike up conversations than in most other areas. The view of the valley is beautifully serene and silent.

Achziv

The name Achziv refers to a stretch of coastline beginning about 4km north of Nahariyya. It's historical heart is the **Achziv National Park,** with its beautiful lawns, sheltered beach (complete with showers and changing rooms), and eighth-century remains of a Phoenician port town. (Open daily in sumer 8am-5pm, Fri. till 4pm; 3pm in winter; admission $1.75 for persons over 18 and $.90 students, and $.40 for persons under 18.) Abutting the park on its northern boarder is **Achzivland,** a self-proclaimed independent state founded in 1952 by Eli Avivi, who leased the land from the Israeli government. **Eli's Museum,** housed in a deteriorated but beautiful Arab mansion, exhibits his esoteric collection of implements, statue fragments, and maps—mostly from the Phoenician period. (Open 24 hours; admission $0.75, $.50 for students).

The small building behind the museum is Achzivland's exceedingly primitive guesthouse, where $4 will buy you a slab of foam rubber and $2, a spot on the tiny lawn outside. More attractive by far are the campsite and hostel, a short distance up the road. Along the way you will pass **Gesher Haziy,** one of eleven bridges blown up on the evening of 16 June 1946, "the night of the bridges," to protest the British government's closure of Israel's ports to all Jewish immigrants. The graves of thirteen members of the Haganah Resistance movement, killed in an ensuing skirmish at the bridge, ring the small monument beside the bridge.

The **campground** at Achziv (tel. 92 17 9; off-season 92 33 66) is pleasant and, thankfully, enormous. It has 150 tent sites, which cost $2.75 per person, $3.75 in July and August, while two-, three-, and four-person bungalows are $17.50, $23, and $27 respectively. Although it's frowned upon, there's room to get lost and spend a night under the stars.

Yad Le Yad Youth Hostel (IYHF) is half a kilometer further north along the main road (tel. 92 13 43). Named "Memorial for the Fourteen" after those killed in a coastal raid a number of years ago, the hostel is huge and rarely full despite its excellent location next to the beach. The hostel charges $4.50 for members, $5.60 for non-members ($4 member, $4.25 non-member if under 18), without breakfast. Meals can be bought at the wimpy bar next door, or cooked in the hostel kitchen for $.45. Although the gates are shut at 11pm sharp, you can stay up as long as you want, since each hosteller gets his own room key.

Negev and South Coast

Contrary to Hollywood-fed expectations, all deserts are not endless plains of sand scorched mercilessly by the sun. Take the Negev Desert, for instance: after Jerusalem, the Negev is considered by many to be the most fascinating place in Israel. The Negev has rugged and mountainous terrain, is dotted with Bedouin camps and ruins, and even gets cool at night. If you persist in believing that deserts cannot support life, you will be astounded when you set eyes upon the fertile green fields of a moshav or kibbutz that has somehow been cultivated in the midst of this arid wasteland.

The word *negev* means "dry land," and indeed the main obstacle to Israel's ambitious plan of settling and civilizing the desert, which makes up over half this country, is the lack of water. A pipeline has been constructed bearing water from the Mediterranean in order to irrigate fields, but although the occasional patches of green are an impressive tribute to Israel's determination to achieve the seemingly impossible, for now at least, most of the Negev remains as wild and uncivilized as ever.

Unfortunately, from the tourist's point of view, the Negev is not all that it is made out to be by the glossy brochures and alluring posters. The **Negev Mountains,** in the southwestern part of the desert bordering on the Sinai, offer the most dramatic scenery, but are almost completely uninhabited. The Negev's most striking features are its three enormous craters—**Qatan, Gadol,** and **Ramon;** however, you can see only Ramon without taking an outrageously expensive organized tour (more than $100). The best and cheapest way to see most of the natural features of the Negev is to join a **Society for the Protection of Nature in Israel** tour (see Israel Introduction).

You can reach the various archeological sites, which are sure to please anyone with a lively interest in the subject, on your own, but the Negev will mainly be of interest to people who want to see the Israel of today: a young, struggling nation employing the labor of a dedicated population and the aid of modern technology to come to terms with nature and make the most of what little land it has. A more demanding tourist who is pressed for time and eager for flashier, more dramatic attractions is bound to be disappointed, however, with the Negev's austere landscape, nondescript towns, and stifling heat.

At the western edge of the Negev is Israel's South Coast, offering five good beaches at Bat Yam, Palmahim, Ashdod, Nizzanim, and Ashqelon. To the south of Ashqelon lie the city of **Gaza** and the **Gaza Strip,** a small stretch of land along the coast under Israeli military administration since 1967. Summer visitors to the South Coast should be aware that its lowland proximity to the sea causes this region to be one of the most humid parts of Israel, a stark contrast to the dry, arid climate just a few miles inland. The area contains several sites of historical interest, especially at Ashqelon and at the city of Gaza.

When in the desert or in the heat of the South Coast, follow these simple rules and no problems should arise: drink at least a gallon of liquid daily, wear a hat, get an early start, and try to avoid physical exertion between noon and 3pm. See Health section of the General Introduction for information on travel in the desert. Partly because of the climate, but mostly because of the political tensions near the occupied Gaza Strip and the scarcity of cars in some areas, this is one of the more difficult areas for hitchhikers. Sheruts, however, are very common, running all the way from Ashqelon to Gaza. Beach-bumming, except very close to the cities of Ashqelon and Ashdod, is definitely out. Military patrols comb the beach at night. Especially in the south, they often rake the full length of the beach at night and later check the sand for footprints. Buses to the Negev and South Coast, particularly to Beersheva, Ashqelon, and Arad, leave frequently from the Central Bus Stations in Jerusalem and Tel Aviv.

Beersheva

A perfectly pleasant town with numerous public gardens but nothing very exciting to see, Beersheva has tried unsuccessfully to make itself into a tourist attraction. What is most impressive about Beersheva is how totally urban and ordinary it is, considering the extremely inhospitable desert from which the new capital of the Negev has sprung. But once you've verified this for yourself, you may not feel inclined to linger any longer. Try to come to Beersheva on a Thursday morning to see the colorful Bedouin market; if you are going to or from Eilat on a Wednesday, break your journey by stopping in Beersheva. Stay for the market, and then continue your trip—Beersheva has plenty of buses going in both directions.

Beersheva has been held in high esteem by the Jewish people since Abraham dug a well here which Abimelech, King of Gerar, promised not to use (the name Beersheva means "the Well of the Oath," Gen. 21:22-24). Often called the City of the Patriarchs, it has had a small but continuous Jewish population for 2500 years. In 1907, the Turks revitalized the town by establishing a police outpost from which to keep an eye on the Bedouin tribes in the area. When the Israeli army wrested the city from Egyptian occupation in 1948, it was actually a village of less than two thousand people. Since then, it has mushroomed into a formidable metropolis of over 130,000 inhabitants. Most of the city's immigrant population now lives in large, drab apartment buildings that lack the aesthetic appeal of Israel's more ancient cities.

Orientation and Practical Information

The **Central Bus Station** (tel. 74 34 2) in Beersheva is next door to the municipal market on the eastern edge of the downtown area. Across the street from the main entrance to the bus station is the **Government Tourist Office** (tel. 36 00 1; open Sun.-Thurs. 8am-5pm, Fri. 8am-1pm). They can give you a map of the city and information about accommodations and events in the area. To get downtown, take any municipal bus from in front of the bus station until the last stop. You will arrive at a little bus terminal in the heart of the city, just off the corner of Ha'Atzmaut and Herzl Sts. If you walk up to the corner of Histadrut and HaDassa Sts., you'll find the Post Office (tel. 32 51 0; open Sun.-Thurs. 7:45am-12:30pm and 3:30-6pm, Fri. 7:45am-1pm); branch office across from the Central Bus Station. If you go north along Ha'Atzmaut St., on your right you will pass the attractive old Town Hall (where you can get an excellent map of the city for $.20) and a mosque that now houses the **Negev Museum;** about 500m farther along on the left is the **Youth Hostel.**

Bus service to Beersheva is excellent. Buses run hourly between Beersheva and Jerusalem, and four times a day between Beersheva and Eilat (except Fri. and Sat.). #371 (express) and 351 (local) run every fifteen minutes from Tel Aviv between 5:30am and 10:30pm, bus #354 runs twice daily from Haifa, #385 four times a day Sun.-Thurs., three times a day Fri. from Ein Gedi and Masada, #388 every half hour from Arad, and #363 every hour from Ashqelon. In the Beersheva bus station, the information window is on the east side of the terminal under the arcade. If you want to take a sherut to Eilat, Jerusalem, or Tel Aviv, go to Yael Daroma on Keren Kayemet l'Israel St. near the intersection with Herzl St. (tel. 39 14 4).

For **First Aid** in Beersheva, call Magen David Adan at 40 Binlik St. (tel. 78 33 3). For **police,** dial 100.

Accommodations

The least expensive beds in Beersheva are at the **Bet Yatziv Youth Hostel (IYHF)** on Ha'Atzmaut St. next door to the Bet Yatziv Biological Institute. The hostel (tel. 77 49 0 or 77 44 4) has 300 beds, and is never close to reaching its capacity. The cost is $6.30 for members over 18, $5.80 under 18. For non-members, $7.50 over 18, $6.20 under 18. A room in the adjoining guest house is $19.20 for a double, $13 for a single. Excellent breakfast is included in all prices. Dinner is $3.80 ($4.40 non-members) and is the best meal in town—reason enough to stay there. (Non-guests are not permitted to eat at the hostel.) The pool, open 9am-5pm, costs $2. The office is always open, and there's no curfew.

For more private accommodations, try the annex of the **Hotel HaNegev** 26 Ha'Atzmaut St. (tel. 77 02 6), where well-kept doubles go for $8. The **Hotel Eshel** on Histradut St. (tel. 77 91 7) just up from Keren Kayemet l'Israel has less desirable rooms with fans for $10, whether occupied by one or two persons.

Food

If you decide not to eat in the hostel, the best source for a hot meal is the **self-service cafeteria** in the bus station; a healthy-sized dinner or lunch with a meat dish is $4, and breakfast is $1.80. For something lighter, the **snack bar** at the corner of Keren Kayemet l'Israel and Hehaloutz St., two blocks south of Herzl St. in the Old Town, offers a variety of meat and pita sandwiches for $1.20. This neighborhood also abounds in felafel stands, but the best place for felafel, sandwiches, produce, or vegetables is the municipal market, next to the bus station (open until about 6pm). A fantastic bakery, serving fresh pastries at all hours of the day and night, is on Sara St., just behind the police station in the Old Town. In the evening, Beersheva's liveliest avenue is **Smilanski St.,** four blocks west of Ha'Atzmaut, where bars, cafes, souvenir shops, and art galleries all stay open until about midnight.

Sights

The main attraction in Beersheva is the **Negev Museum,** which features archeological finds from all over the desert, but primarily from the ruins of ancient Beersheva, just 5km outside the city. Excavated from 1969 to 1976, the site holds artifacts dating from as far back as the eighth century B.C.E. Above the remains of the prehistoric city were uncovered remnants of a Roman bathhouse that was once part of a Herodian fortress/palace. The prize of the museum is the **Animal Mosaic,** a beautiful sixth-century C.E. floor depicting animals woven together in an intricate geometrical design. A collection of medieval maps of the Holy Land and exhibits on Bedouin culture are found here as well. During the daylight hours, you can climb the mosque's tall minaret for an excellent view of Beersheva. (No cameras allowed because of the military installations underneath.) Open Sun.-Mon. 8am-1pm and 4:30-6:30pm, Tues. 8am-1pm, Wed.-Thurs. 8am-4:30pm, and Fri. 8am-12:30pm; admission $.20, $.10 for students. Sometimes the museum closes at odd hours for no apparent reason.

You may want to visit the archeological site of **Tel Sheva,** the impressive hilltop remains of ancient Beersheva. (Before you visit, examine the models and explanations of the site's layout in the Negev Museum.) Next door, past and present intermingle in contemporary Tel Sheva, a village of Bedouins who have been induced by the Israeli government to abandon their nomadic lifestyle and join the Beersheva community. The Bedouins retain their ancient customs and wear traditional clothing, and many of the women still cover their faces in public. A museum devoted to the life of the Bedouin, called "Man and the Desert," has recently been completed. Open Sun.-Thurs. 10am-1pm and 4-6pm, Sat. 10am-1pm; admission free. To get to Tel Sheva, take bus #81 from the bus station. The only other worthwhile historical attraction in Beersheva is **Abraham's Well** which, unfortunately, was dug only a few years ago, on the corner of Ha'Atzmaut and Hebron Sts. at the southern end of town.

If more modern things grab your attention, take a look at the new **Town Hall.** The pride of Beersheva, this building has an oddly-shaped tower that dominates the town's horizon. Even more ultra-modern in architecture and atmosphere is the campus of **Ben-Gurion University,** founded in 1969, in the northeastern corner of the city.

Perhaps the most unusual sight in Beersheva is the avant-garde **Memorial of the Negev Palmach Brigade,** located on the eastern outskirts of the city, dedicated to the soldiers who fell in the 1948 campaign to capture the desert. Unless you can read the Hebrew inscriptions, it's difficult to understand what it's all about. Try to get someone knowledgeable to explain the significance of each of the immense concrete shapes. Some of the more apparent shapes include that of a watchtower and aqueduct, fought over and protected by the Palmach Brigade, a lacerated snake representing the defeated enemy forces, and the perforated and split Memorial Dome. Admission to the park and structures is free.

Most tourists come to Beersheva for the well-known **Bedouin market,** which takes place just south of the municipal market and the bus station on the road to Eilat Thursday mornings from 6am-1pm. Hundreds of Bedouins, both the semi-settled from around Beersheva and the nomads from deep in the desert, gather in the area around Hebron St. to sell sheep, goats, clothes, cloth, jewelry, and whatever else has come into their hands. By all means get there early and bargain vigorously, or bring some jeans and offer to swap. Try to wade through the plastic garbage and trinkets and seek out some of the beautiful Bedouin crafts that can be obtained here, such as beaten copperware, delicate jewelry, irresistible embroidered camel bags, and handwoven rugs. The appellation Bedouin is sometimes misleading as Israelis can also be seen selling T-shirts touting American pop culture.

The **municipal market,** easily identified by its strange, arched rooftops, is primarily a wholesaler's market and all sorts of odds and ends can be purchased here, most of which are of little interest to the tourist. A number of stalls do deal in Bedouin crafts, and Bedouin women in their beautiful black velvet robes like to come here to do their shopping.

Near Beersheva

Arad

Halfway between Beersheva and Masada, Arad serves as a transfer point for buses running to the Dead Sea area. Founded as a residential settlement in 1961 for laborers from the Dead Sea Works, Arad has suddenly grown in importance since the discovery of natural gas in the surrouding area. As the bus approaches, Arad appears to leap forth from the encircling, barren desert. The **Tourist Information Office,** in the town's commercial center (tel. 98 14 4), can supply you with information about the Dead Sea and other nearby areas of interest. The center of town also contains the **Blau-Weiss Youth Hostel (IYHF)** (P.O. Box 34; tel (057) 97 15 0) with dorm beds; members $5.60, non-members

$6.50. The hostel is clean and has a kitchen for members, but there is no air conditioning.

Arad has tried to make a major tourist attraction out of the archeological site of **Tel Arad,** the ruins of the biblical city of Arad conquered by Joshua, but the ruins are 10km out of town and not worth the trek. (Site open April-Sept. 8am-5pm, Oct.-March 8am-4pm, closed one hour earlier on Fri.; admission $.75, $.50 for students.) The town of Arad itself is mostly residential and offers little to see. It has frequent bus connections to Beersheva, Masada, and Ein Gedi, and since only three buses make the through-trip daily from Beersheva to the Dead Sea, you may find yourself changing buses here.

Sede Boqer

One of the most beautiful kibbutzim in the Negev, Sede Boqer is truly an oasis in the desert. It rains apricots, kiwis, sheep, goats, and chickens. The kibbutz is famous as the home of David Ben-Gurion and his wife, Paula. Ben-Gurion loved the Negev, hated to be torn away from it to serve as Prime Minister, and died here on his beloved kibbutz. His home, only slightly larger than the residences of his less famous neighbors, has been left almost exactly as it was when he and his wife lived there (except for the addition of annoying glass doors separating visitors from the living room and library). Open Sun.-Thurs. 8:30am-3:30pm, Fri. 8:30am-1pm, Sat. 9am-1pm; admission free. Fruits of the kibbutz can be purchased near the entrance of Ben-Gurion's house. Be sure to walk by the kibbutz zoo, which is full of Negev deer, swans, flamingos, etc.—an oddly-placed tropical paradise. Sede Boqer is easily accessible by the frequent buses running between Beersheva and Mitzpe Ramon or Eilat.

Shivta

One of the Negev's most outstanding archeological sites is at Shivta, a first-century B.C.E. Nabatean city. In the sixth century C.E., Byzantine monks erected several churches of which some impressive remains can be seen. Unfortunately, Shivta is about 50km southwest of Beersheva in the middle of nowhere, and can be reached only by car or tour bus. Open April-Sept. Sun.-Thurs. 8am-5pm, Fri. 8am-4pm; Oct.-March the site closes one hour earlier. A similar Nabatean city with Byzantine churches is at **Mamshit.** Open daily 7am-6pm; admission $1.30, $.65 for students. Less interesting than Shivta, Mamshit is located next to the modern Israeli settlement of Dimona, which has frequent bus connections to Beersheva. Dimona is the home of an unusual sect of "Black Hebrews" who are neither Jewish, Christian, or Muslim, but some combination of the above.

Avdat

Fifteen kilometers farther south is Avdat, the magnificent ruins of a first-century B.C.E. Nabatean city. On the crossroads of the caravan routes from Petra and Eilat, Avdat thrived as a stopping point for travelers, and the Nabateans were notorious for marauding caravans, since they could see them from as far away as Mitzpe Ramon or Sede Boqer. The Nabateans farmed extensively, using sophisticated irrigation techniques which have been adapted to modern-day use by two experimental Israeli farms. (You can see the farms from the site.) Romans captured the city in the first century B.C.E., used it as a garrison, and exploited the agricultural skills of its former masters. The city flourished again during the Byzantine period; a large portion of the visible ruins date from this time. Seventh-century Islamic marauders protected the Roman baths, but not much else.

The archeological site consists of Nabatean remains of an altar and necropolis, enormous water cisterns, Roman baths, most of the columns of a fourth-century Byzantine church, and the original walls of the city, still in excellent condition. Open daily 7am-6pm; admission $1.30, $.65 for students. Meals at the roadside restaurant cost a hefty $6. Make sure the bus driver lets you off at the archeological site and not at one of the two turn-offs for Ein Avdat, a mid-desert oasis.

Mitzpe Ramon

Dangling on the precipice of the Maktesh Ramon (Ramon Crater), the small community of Mitzpe Ramon, 86km south of Beersheva, lies in the heart of the desert. The Ramon Crater, largest of three craters in the Negev, is an awe-inspiring spectacle. The road runs along the upper edge and then descends into the basin of the 300-square-kilometer canyon. The area is soon going to be made into a nature reserve, complete with a huge visitors' pavilion and an archeological/geological/ecological park in the center of the crater.

The town of Mitzpe Ramon began as a support unit for the observatory that crowns a hill to the south. Its srategic and military value became of greatest importance to Israelis after 1948; it was then developed to house married soldiers. Now Sephardic and Eastern Jews, and English, South African, American, and European Jews comprise its growing population. Since the return of the Sinai to Egypt, Mitzpe Ramon's importance as a southern tourist and military outpost has been enhanced.

The **Bet Noam Youth Hostel** (tel. 88 04 3) always has plenty of room. It's a bit primitive, but the management is friendly and clear, cool nights make for good sleeping. $3.50 for members, $3 for those members under 18, $4.40 for non-members, $3.30 for non-members under 18. Dinner costs $2.-2.20 and this is, in fact, the only food in town, unless you plan to do your own cooking ($.35 for use of kitchen). Kosher meals are cooked at the hostel, but only if you call and order in advance. The town has a public swimming pool (open Sun.-Thurs. 8am-5pm, Fri. 10am-4pm, Sat. 9am-5pm; entrance $1.20) and a one-room **museum** exhibiting a small collection of geological specimens and artifacts.

Eilat

Until 1959, Eilat was little more than a military outpost far from the growing cities of the north. Eilat's only distinction lay in its being the southernmost point of the young nation of Israel. Known to its residents as "the end of the world," Eilat even boasted a popular bar by that name. The port began to grow when the 1956 war forced Israel to develop it as a southern port; later, the capture of the Sinai gave the city enough elbow room to become Israel's major resort. In the past ten years, dozens of luxury hotels, restaurants, and tourist shops have sprouted along the beach, which boasts year-round swimming. With the return of the Sinai in 1982, Eilat is once again at the end of the world—but only if your world extends only as far as Israel's border. Eilat is now a convenient jumping-off point for excursions into the Sinai Desert and is a point of entry for Egypt.

King David established his southernmost defense outpost in the Negev at Eilat. But it was his son, King Solomon, who first realized Eilat's potential as a port for Far East trade. Eilat flourished from Solomon's time until the end of Byzantine rule when it was conquered by Saladin in 1167. Under Muslim control, it dwindled to an insignificant oasis as the well-fortified Aqaba, just across the gulf, replaced it as the vital link to the Red Sea and the Indian

Ocean. Eilat was just a few run-down Turkish shacks known as Um Rashrash when the Israeli army captured the oasis and revived its biblical name in 1948. While they were at it, they renamed the Gulf of Aqaba the Gulf of Eilat, so the broad finger of the Red Sea which extends between the Sinai and Saudi Arabia is now known by two names. The neighboring ports of Eilat and Aqaba have maintained a surprisingly peaceful relationship since 1949, despite the enmity that persists between their two governments. Even in 1967, when Israel and Jordan were at war, the ports exchanged no fire.

Orientation and Practical Information

Using the sea as a reference point, it's easiest to divide Eilat into three major sections: the town itself, on the sloping hills above the sea; **Lagoon Beach,** below to the east, lined with luxury hotels and including a public beach area; and to the south, the ancient and modern ports. Farther south lies the Egyptian border, and beyond that, the Sinai.

If you plan to take a bus to Jerusalem or Tel Aviv, you probably can't count on getting a seat without advance reservations, but buses to Tel Aviv and Beersheva run frequently enough (ten times daily to Tel Aviv and four times to Beersheva) that it is usually possible to reserve a seat a couple of hours in advance. Be aggressive in line and in claiming your seat—otherwise you may stand for five sweaty hours.

If you're not up to the aggravation of the Israeli bus system, you can travel from Eilat to Beersheva, Jerusalem, and Tel Aviv by sherut with **Yael Daroma** (tel. 72 27 9), located on Hatmarim Blvd. at Almogim St. Cars leave about four times a day, and fares are only slightly higher than what you would pay on a bus.

Baggage can be a big problem in Eilat, where it's too hot to exert yourself much. Since all you will need are shorts, a shirt, a bathing suit, face mask, snorkel, and a canteen, you might consider leaving your pack in the parcel storage in the Egged Bus Terminal while you tour the area. This is an especially wise investment if you plan to sleep on the less-than-safe beach. The charge is $.85 per bag for every 24 hours, and the luggage room is open Sun.-Thurs. 7am-6pm, Fri. 7am-2pm.

Before you hit the beach or head south, equip yourself with covering for your head and a canteen or two; the dry heat here can dehydrate you very quickly. Soft drinks in Eilat are very expensive, averaging $1.20 for a can of Coke; drinking water is not always readily available, so you should always have some with you.

Israel Government Tourist Office: on Hatmarim Blvd. (tel. 72 26 8 or 76 73 7), half a block towards the waterfront from the post office. One of the most helpful tourist offices in Israel, they can provide you with maps, brochures, and transportation schedules. They even provide information about crossing the border into the Sinai. Open Sun.-Thurs. 8am-6pm, Fri. 8am-1pm.

Post Office: Hatmarim Blvd., in the Commercial Center. Open Sun.-Tues. and Thurs. 7:45am-12:30pm and 4-6:30pm, Wed. 7:45am-2pm, Fri. 7:45am-1pm.

Police: Sederot Avedat at the eastern end of HaTivat HaNegev (tel. 72 44 4 or 73 55 4). They probably won't want to hear about your stolen pack.

Hospital: Yotam Rd. (tel. 72 30 1 or 73 15 1). The first aid station is on Hatmarim Blvd. (tel. 72 33 3).

Egyptian Consulate: 34 Deror St. (tel. 76 11 5). Walk south on Elot St., go right at the Mor Center, take the first left, and look for the flag. Open Sun.-Thurs. 9am-2pm. Visas issued on day of application.

Car Rental: Hertz (tel. 76 68 2), Inter-Rent (tel. 74 89 3) and Kopel Rent-A-Car (tel. 74 10 5) are all in the New Tourist Center on Yotam Rd. Avis (tel. 73 16 4) is next to the airport. Budget (tel. 76 13 9) is under the Etzion Hotel on Hatmarim Blvd. All places have a minimum age requirement of 21. Prices are uniformly outrageous, starting at $15 per day, plus $.20 per km, or $50-70 per day for unlimited mileage. Insurance is an additional $6 per day. You cannot bring a hired car into Egypt.

Self-Service Laundry: on Hatmarim Blvd., the first shop inland from the Elot St. intersection, on the beach-bound side of the street. Washing $2.40 per load (up to 8 kilos), soap $.60, drying $2.30 per half hour, but use the sun instead—it's free. Open Sun.-Thurs. 9am-1pm and 4-8pm, Fri. 9am-1pm.

To get to the Egyptian border, take bus #15, which runs every hour on the hour, from a stop across the street from the central bus station and from stops on Hatmarim Blvd. and Arava Rd. The bus goes all the way to the Sonesta Hotel, but you'll want to get off just before at the Israeli checkpoint, to get your exit visa. Remember that only one bus a day serves the Sinai; it leaves from the border at 1pm, Israeli time.

Accommodations

The cheapest air-conditioned accommodations in Eilat cost around $6 per person. The question is whether you want to stay in a hostel for that sum or in a pension or private room. Most people would choose the latter, but the problem is that the cheapest rooms can only be obtained from people who let rooms temporarily as a sideline. The best way to find such deals is to stand around with your pack as you get off the bus from Jerusalem or Tel Aviv and look for someone who is soliciting boarders. Chances are that they'll find you as soon as you step from the bus; you won't have to search very hard (if at all). You can get some pretty good deals this way, despite the Tourist Office official line that these places are not recommended (the Office says they've had complaints from people who have stayed in private rooms. Look the place and the owner over before you spend the night and use your own judgment.) If for some reason you can't find a place (or they can't find you), go to any of the travel agencies in town and they'll find you a private room. For more standard accommodations, try:

Youth Hostel (IYHF), at the corner of Elot and Arava Sts. (tel. 72 35 8), across from the Red Rock Hotel. Not amazingly clean, but air-conditioned and a good place to meet people (if it's not filled with Israeli school children). $6.90 for members, $6.40 under 18, $8.10 non-members, $6.80 under 18. Closed 9am-5pm, midnight curfew. Vegetarian dinner $4-4.40, 15% less for non-Israelis.

Max's Youth Hostel, Ofarim St. (tel. 71 40 8). From the bus station, walk on Hatmarim Blvd. across HaTivat HaNegev, take the first right, and turn left just before the end of the street. The next left is Ofarim. Much cleaner and brighter than any other place in Eilat, and quite friendly as well. Cooking facilities, two refrigerators. Max, a Welshman, sings (or groans) each morning at 7am to wake you up. $4 a night plus $1 for an optional, excellent breakfast. Early-arriving couples should ask for one of the few double rooms (same price). Closed 9am-11am for cleaning, midnight curfew. Reliably air-conditioned.

Nophit Hostel, at the corner of Arava and Elot Sts. (tel. 74 70 9), next to the Youth Hostel. A dump. Cheaper, noisier, and shabbier than its official neighbor. $4 a night in a dorm room.

Eilat Hostel, Faran St. (tel. 72 86 2). From Elot St., walk inland on Jerusalem Rd. and take the first left. Also a dump. Refrigerators, but no cooking facilities; sometimes no reception staff. Inconvenient to the beach. $7 per person for a bed in a small, grimy room.

Beit Eshel Hostel, off Rehov Barnea (tel. 72 73 7). Walk inland on Jerusalem Rd. and turn right on Roded St. Fairly clean, crowded. No cooking facilities. $5 per person for a room with 4-5 beds.

Camping

There are two alternatives: official and expensive, and unofficial and free. The latter is by far the more popular. During July and August, literally hundreds of young people sleep out on the public beach in front of the city. No one seems to pay any attention to the "No camping" signs, so don't you worry about that either. Though obviously the cheapest bed in town, the beach does have its drawbacks. First there are thieves—try not to sleep alone. Women should join up with a reliable party, and personal possessions should *never* be left unguarded. Second, there are rats on the beach near the major hotels, attracted by the garbage areas. To avoid both problems, go towards the Jordanian border (east of Sun Bay Camping) or south of the Red Rock Hotel. Sleeping on these beaches is even legal, as is tent-pitching (strictly forbidden on the public beach). Despite the signs to the contrary, there are no usable toilets on any of these beaches.

By far the best place to camp free is on the beach at Taba, 8km south of Eilat on the Egyptian border (take bus #15 to the last stop). It's safer than the town beaches; toilets and outdoor showers are actually functional, and tent-pitching is possible.

For official camping in town, try **Sun Bay Camping** (tel. 73 10 5), which has an enclosed area of bungalows and camping facilities on the beach 750m before the Jordanian border (served by bus #1A). $3.50 per person for a tent site. Bungalows are an exorbitant $25 for two, $30 for three, and $35 for four, but the management hopes to have dormitory-style accommodations for $5 per person by the summer of 1984. Far cheaper is **Bedouin Camping** across the street from the Coral World Underwater Observatory (take bus #5 to the last stop). Bungalows and facilities are spartan, but the fees are only $2 per person for a tent site, $5 per person for a bungalow ($6 if you want a single).

Food and Nightlife

The only Israeli cuisine to be found in Eilat is felafel, but the array of international restaurants should distract you from this standard fare. None of Eilat's restaurants, however, is both memorable and cheap. The closest approximation of these two conditions comes about at the **Shrimp House,** just off Hatmarim Blvd. on Edom St., where all the fish, chips, salad, bread, and hummus you can eat are only $6. They don't grumble after serving the second or third helping. Vegetarian dishes figure prominently on the menu of the restaurant at the **IYHF Youth Hostel,** theoretically open only to guests ($4-4.40 for dinner).

Those homesick for the sugared splendors of IHOP may want to dine at the **Pancake House** in the New Shalom Shopping Center ($2 for two pancakes). A **delicatessen** in the New Tourist Center sells fantastic sandwiches for $1.20 (cheap by Eilat standards); look for a sign reading "American Sandwiches."

Several outdoor restaurants along the waterfront serve fresh fish from the Red Sea. The local bounty from the gulf is delicious, but the only catch is that the seafood is expensive.

Since many accommodations in Eilat provide cooking facilities, one of the best and most convenient ways to eat well and inexpensively is to put a meal together yourself from the voluminous offerings of the **supermarket** at the corner of Elot St. and Hatmarim Blvd., three blocks inland from the bus station. (Open Sun.-Mon. and Wed.-Thurs. 7:30am-1pm and 5-7:30pm, Tues. 7:30am-2pm, and Fri. 7:30am-2:30pm.)

Eilat has one moviehouse, Cinema Eilat, next door to the post office; it usually features year-old Hollywood fare.

Discos abound in the major hotels, but the liveliest, cheapest, and most international place to park one's elbow is at the **Peace Cafe** (commonly known as the "Piss Bar"), a popular outdoor hangout at the corner of Almogim and Agmonim Sts., around the corner from Max's Hostel (see Accommodations). N.B.: the place serves as a makeshift job market every morning. A bar with no name is in the basement of the Center Apt. Hotel, behind the bank Hapoalim at the commercial center on Hatmarim. They specialize in "local" Israeli alcohol and will play whatever music you request. Pretty spaced-out crowd.

Sights

Eilat's number one sight is underwater. Not only will all the super-hotels be out of view, but you'll find yourself in an incredibly colorful world of corals and exotic fish, the likes of which you never imagined you would encounter outside of an aquarium. All you have to do is stick your head in the water and watch the flamboyant array of butterfly fish, emperor fish, clownfish, lionfish, and many other brilliantly-colored species parade by.

The best place to snorkel and rent equipment in Eilat is at **Coral Beach,** an underwater nature reserve 5km south of Eilat (take bus #5 headed towards the sea in front of the Central Bus Station). Open daily 8am-5pm; admission $1.40, $.80 for students. Mask, snorkel, and fins can be rented for $1.40, $1, and $1.60 respectively. If you are certified and have a buddy, full scuba gear can be hired for $26 per day at **Aqua Sport,** next to the Reserve (tel. 72 78 8). And if you're not certified but have been inspired to learn to dive, Aqua Sport also runs short, intensive courses for $120. These holiday courses, however, are not as thorough and comprehensive as the longer ones offered in North America and Australia. Coral Beach is the most crowded reef territory on the Red Sea, and you can do much better for isolation and beauty if you head south along the Sinai coast.

A judicious first stop would be at the spectacular **Coral World Underwater Observatory and Aquarium,** the last stop for bus #5. The main attraction is the underwater observatory, one of five like it in the world: a glass-walled chamber 100m out and 5m below the surface of the water that allows you to examine the coral reefs and incredible fish from up close. The aquarium tanks, in the front part of the complex, will be of interest to divers—they contain a fabulous collection of fish native to the Red Sea and will allow you to identify specimens and learn the names of many of the creatures you will meet in your underwater explorations. You'll also get a good hard look at your future enemies, such as stonefish, scorpion fish, lionfish, rays, and Moray eels. Open Sat.-Thurs. 8:30am-5pm, Fri. 8:30am-3pm; the admission could submerge your money supply: $5, $4 for students.

If you intend to spend a lot of time underwater, *The Red Sea Fish Guide* is indispensible and has waterproof pages which identify dozens of species, including those which are poisonous (available for $12.25 at most bookstores and dive shops). Cheaper and more compact is *The Red Sea Fishwatcher's Guide,* a one-page, submersible card available for $3.25.

The bus stop just before Coral Beach is the pier for the popular glass-bottom boats. A two-hour cruise is $3.50 and not very exciting, but the half-day excursions include a snorkeling stop at Coral Island. The island has been returned to Egypt, but Israeli boats are allowed to unload snorkelers into the waters. Since the price of $7 includes equipment, it's not such a bad deal.

The beach at **Taba,** just before the Egyptian border, is the nicest of the non-coral beaches and is less crowded and safer for sleeping than the town beaches.

The **Hotel Sonesta,** adjacent to the beach, made international headlines during the Sinai turnover in 1982, since both Egypt and Israel claimed that the structure was within their negotiated borders. It's actually between the two checkpoints on a stretch of land the Israelis have managed to secure. From the hotel and the beach, you can see four countries—Israel, Egypt, Jordan, and Saudi Arabia.

Breathtakingly rugged desert scenery awaits you to the north of Eilat at **Red Canyon,** a gorge accessible only by organized tour (about $21). From Red Canyon, tours continue to a lookout above **Moon Valley,** a somber, lunar canyon now controlled by Egypt, and to **Amram's Pillars,** some unusual mid-desert rock formations.

Twenty-five kilometers north of Eilat is **Timna Valley,** a small national park that preserves something of the region's Bronze-Age history. The 6000-year-old Timna Copper Mines, in the southeast corner of the park, reached their height during the Egyptian period. Ruins of eleventh-century B.C.E. workers' camps and cisterns evoke this vital industry. The area still holds significant copper deposits, and drilling has been carried on since 1955.

King Solomon's Pillars, also in the park, are a number of sandstone pillars as high as 50m presiding over the desert. Nearby, stop to look at the fourteenth-century B.C.E. **Temple of Hathor,** the remains of an Egyptian sanctuary.

Organized tours operate to Timna Valley; hitching is also possible—have the bus driver let you off at the sign for Alipaz (*not* at the Timna Mines signpost 2.5km farther south) and walk towards the entrance 2km away. The park is always open, though not always attended; admission $1.

Farther north along the main road from Eilat and also hitchable is the **Hai Bar Biblical Nature Reserve,** a wildlife park constructed to repatriate animals native to the region in biblical times. The reserve contains freely roaming gazelles, donkeys, ostriches, and other animals, mostly imported from Africa. Open 7:30am-1:30pm, but the best time to get a look at the animals is 8-10:30am when they are being fed; admission $1.40, $.80 for students. Only closed vehicles are allowed to enter. The entrance to the park (where you can wait for an entering vehicle) is 1½km from **Yotvata Kibbutz.** Here **Y'elim Camping** (tel. 74 36 2) has tent space for $5 per person all year round. All of the above sights are interesting, but hardly worth the hefty sums charged by tour operators ($20-40). If you still want to try out an organized tour, contact **Johnny's Desert Tours,** in the New Shalom Shopping Center (tel. 72 60 8 or 76 77 7), **Yaalat Tourist Services,** in the New Tourist Center (tel. 72 16 6), or **Egged Tours,** in the Central Bus Station (tel. 73 14 8).

Ashqelon

For several centuries, Ashqelon flourished as an important center for the Philistines, those Old Testament arch enemies of Israel. The prophet Zephania predicted, however, that one day it would become a great Israelite city. Modern residents of Ashqelon like to point to their city as the fulfillment of Zephania's prophecy, and they have even named the city's main square in his honor. In 1972, just before the big drive to make Ashqelon a major tourist resort, the Roman Mausoleum near Afridar's beaches was discovered. The vault of the tomb depicts the face of Demeter, the goddess of antiquities and mystical religions; the antiquities abound in and around Ashqelon, but the mystical religion of the city is now unquestionably Tourism.

Although there is much to see here, the tourist atmosphere can be rather oppressive, especially in the summer. Still, if Ashqelon is not your first priority on a trip to Israel, it should not be your last. Israel's southernmost Mediterranean city has miles and miles of sandy beaches, all uncommonly clean and unreasonably beautiful, and a very pleasant National Park complete with archeological ruins and camping site. Ashqelon's weather is so reliable that its hotels have put together a "rain insurance" scheme, providing a "rain check," good for a free night in a hotel for every day it rains on their guests. You will meet a large number of American, Canadian, Russian, African, and European *olim* ("immigrants") here; Ashqelon has one of the most important, and probably the most deluxe, *Merkazei Kleetah* ("absorption center"), where immigrants are given special apartments and attend special orientation classes during the first three months of their residency in Israel. If you are fluent in Spanish, German, or Russian, you'll certainly be able to use it here. Many *olim* are a little homesick, most are nervous, excited, and enthusiastic, and all have hilarious stories to tell about adjusting to life in Israel. Watch for them: they're the ones trying desperately to look Israeli.

Orientation and Practical Information

Ashqelon is actually a union of five smaller townships, set in a lush fertile plain on the southern coast. Each of the neighborhoods retains its own individual flavor, from the old Arab town of **Migdal** to the snazzy commercial center of **Afridar,** originally settled by South Africans, to the two flanking residential suburbs of **Barnea** and **Shimsom** and the industrial area of **Ramat Eshkol.** Although the bus station is centrally located, it is far from any of the major tourist attractions. It is impossible to travel around Ashqelon without relying very heavily on the municipal bus system. Buses #3, 11, and 13 connect the Central Bus Station with the beach (only during the summer); buses #4 and 7 serve both Afridar and Migdal, and bus #5 serves Barnea. All transportation comes to a grinding halt during Shabbat and holidays, so try not to arrive in Ashqelon during these periods. The information booth in the Central Bus Station can provide you with a printed bus schedule of any bus that runs between Ashqelon and any other major Israeli city. Bus #437 leaves Jerusalem about every hour for Ashqelon (and vice versa); the trip takes about an hour and a half. Bus #301 leaves every twenty minutes for Tel Aviv, but if possible you should plan to meet the less frequent express bus, #300. Bus service to the Gaza Strip is rapidly improving; bus #20 now makes at least four trips per day all year round. You can use the baggage check in the Central Bus Station every day 7am-4pm for a small fee.

Especially if you happen to be in Ashqelon for the weekend, planning to camp and capture rays, you may need to rely on sheruts. In Migdal the station is at Herzl and Zahal Sts. (tel. 22 33 4); in Shimson, on Kerem Kayumet St. (tel. 22 26 6/7); and in Barnea it's at Bet HaMishpat St. (tel. 25 55 5 or 22 28 2). Rides within Ashqelon are usually under $.50, although between Ashqelon and nearby cities fares can reach $2.50. Because so many young people use sheruts between townships, some of them are very small and may ask you to buy two seats, one for your pack.

Buses #4, 5, and 7 will all let you off at **Zephania Square** in the heart of Afridar, Ashqelon's geographical and administrative center. You know you have arrived when you see the handsome clock tower of the town's **Tourist Events Center,** an attractive complex of neo-Romanesque architecture built with donations from South African Jews. Directly across Ben Yehuda St. from the clock tower is the **Government Tourist Office** (IGTO). There are several grocery and fruit stores near the center; halfway between Zephania Square and the Central Bus Station on Hasneg St. is a huge supermarket. You can buy pizza around Zephania Sq. for about $.95. Inside the Tourist Events Center is the **Post Office,** next to the entrance to the Roman Sarcophagus (open Sun.-Thurs. 7:45am-12:30pm and 3:30-6pm, Fri. 7:45am-1pm, closed Wed. afternoon).

The name Asqelon comes from the old Hebrew unit of weight as a money measurement—the shekel. As the shekel has made its resurgence as the new currency in Israel, Ashqelon has been reviving its historical sights and putting its name on the tourist map. As a result, almost everything costs a sugar shekel (akin to a pretty penny). Be creative and plan well for accommodations, schedule your day to avoid too many bus trips, carry water if possible, and buy food in Migdal.

Israel Government Tourist Office (IGTO): Afridar Center, diagonally across from Rachel Cinema (tel. 32 41 2). To get there from the Central Bus Station, take a bus to Afridar Center. Ask for Reynor Rosenberg; she speaks fluent English, can answer all your questions, and will supply you with the essential *Ashqelon Pictorial Map*. Also recommends doctors and dentists. Open April-Oct., Sun.-Thurs. 9am-1pm and 3-7pm, Fri. 9am-3pm; Dec.-March, Sun.-Thurs. 9am-1pm and 2-6pm, Fri. 9am-3pm.

Central Post Office: Rehov Herzl in Migdal. Open Sun.-Thurs. 8am-7pm, Fri. 8am-1pm. You can make international phone calls from here. Post offices also in Afridar Center, Shimshon Quarter, and Givat Zion.

Bus Information: Call 22 91 1 or 23 80 7.

Police: Emergency (tel. 100). Information (tel. 34 22 2 or 24 14 4). Located on the corner of HaNassi and Eli Cohen Sts.

First Aid: Call 23 33 3.

Telephone Code: 051.

Accommodations

The only cheap accommodations in town are the campground and bungalows in the **National Park** and private rooms, which can be arranged through the IGTO in Afridar. If you take bus #11 or 13 (during the summer only), get off just before the beach, and walk about five minutes to the south, you will come to the entrance of the National Park. Alternatively, take bus #9 or 3 to a footpath which allows you to enter the park by passing the front gate, which has a steep admission fee of $1.70, $.80 for students. The campground (P.O. Box 5052; tel. 25 22 8), run by the National Parks Authority, offers a variety of lodgings and services. By foot, it is about fifteen minutes from the entrance of the park, to the left. A splendid camping ground, it is usually quite full, mostly with vacationing Israelis. If possible, call and reserve in advance. Since it is inside the National Park, there are beaches, archeological sites, snack bars, restaurants, and lots of picnic space and facilities right on the premises. Camping facilities are under the management of the Israel Camping Union, so prices are standard: $4.50 for adults ($2.75 off-season), $2 for children under 13 ($1 off-season). Bungalows for two people are available for $18 ($13 off-season), for three people $24 ($18 off-season), and for four people $30 ($24 off-season). A bed in one of these bunks costs $9 per person per night. Renting a whole caravan is also very reasonable, if you can get together enough people you like. A caravan with four beds costs $36 ($27 off-season), with six beds $44 ($33 off-season). Air-conditioning is available at $10 a day, and a fridge at $3 ($2.50 off-season). On Saturdays you may be able to rent space only in a bungalow; call ahead to avoid problems. Try not to leave the camp on a Saturday evening; wait until Sunday morning to pay, or pay ahead of time. You can often get away with camping in the park for free, as it is large and usually crowded. The **Ashqelon Holiday Village,** near the entrance to the park, is unbelievably expensive, but if you look as if you belong (it's a private club), you might be able to slip past the guards and use the pool free of charge.

The IGTO arranges rentals of private rooms in homes around the city. The charge is usually $6-8, not including meals. The cheapest hotel is the **Ashqelon Hotel** at 82 Dram Africa Blvd. in Afridar (tel. 34 75 9) with singles for $15, doubles for $26. From the IGTO, walk through the National Gardens and turn left on Dram Africa. Across the street at 38 HaTamar St. is **Samson's Gardens** (tel. 34 66 6), a similar hotel with slightly more expensive rooms ($30-35 for doubles). Both places are clean and include breakfast in room prices. Location is none too central. If business seems slow, try bargaining down the prices. Samson's Gardens can be a good deal if you convince them to let you put a third person in the doubles without extra charge.

Occasionally, people solicit boarders at the bus station; the system is not as developed as it is in Tzfat or Jerusalem, so play it by ear. They may begin by asking as much as $18 a night, but if you mention camping, prices will quickly plummet to $4 or $5. These rooms are often in Migdal, hard to find and unmarked. The quality varies widely, of course.

Unlike much of the south coast, the beaches near Ashqelon are not forbidden to campers. As with so much else in Israel, however, this depends on the current political situation. If you try to camp out, the worst that can happen is that the military police will chase you up to higher ground. Try not to be too close to the sand, avoid the "separate" beach just north of Delilah beach near the Roman Tomb, don't build fires, and clean up after yourself. The northern beaches might be a little safer, but be wary of thieves on the entire stretch of beach.

Sights

Strategically situated on the Via Maris Road connecting Egypt with Syria, Ashqelon has had a long history of conquest, destruction, and rebuilding. The many civilizations who created Ashqelon's history have indeed been generous to today's visitors.

Ashqelon's seaside **National Park** (tel. 22 04 4) is one of the most popular in Israel. It was built on the site of four thousand-year-old Canaanite remains buried under the ruins of Philistine, Greek, Roman, Byzantine, Crusader, and Muslim cities. The ruins offer extensive evidence for Ashqelon's claim to be one of the oldest cities in the world (competition for the title is fierce throughout the Middle East). Ashqelon was one of the principal cities of the Philistine heartland on the Mediterranean coast. The saga of Samson (Judges 14-16) exemplifies the hundreds of years of strife in the region between Philistines and the Israelites.

The most extensive ruins both in the park and outside it are from the Roman era, thanks to Ashqelon's native son, Herod the Great, who enlarged and fortified the city which Alexander the Great left behind. The most compact part of the modern site, situated in the center of the National Park, features an imposing Roman colonnade and a haphazard collection of Hellenistic and Roman columns, capitals, and statues, including two magnificent Roman statues of Nike, the winged goddess of victory. The first section of antiquities you'll see will be the **Bouleuterion** (marked by a sign with explanations), which was the Council House Square of Ashqelon when it was an autonomous city-state under Severius in the third century C.E. Afterwards, there is a sunken area with descending steps on the right, resembling a courtyard. This is actually the inside of a Herodian building. There are a number of statues and columns standing or lying about. You'll see three major pillar reliefs, two of Nike, on a globe supported by Atlas, and one of the goddess Isis with the child-god Horus. These statues were made of marble imported from Italy, and were executed between 200 B.C.E. and 100 C.E.

Along the southern edge of the park are segments of the walls of the twelfth-century **Crusader city.** The most peculiar part of the site are the Roman columns sticking out of the ancient Byzantine seawall on the beach. It is believed that they were inserted into the wall like cannon-barrels in order to scare off invaders from the sea.

Outside of the park on the other end of the beach, not far from the stop for buses in the summer, is the splendid **Roman Tomb,** believed to have contained the remains of a wealthy Hellenistic family of the third century C.E. The frescoes that adorn its interior are in remarkable condition. The paintings on the walls represent scenes from classical mythology. One can see Pan playing his pipes, Demeter, and the snake-haired Gorgons, whose portraits were supposed to protect the family from evil. There are also human scenes representing the hunt and the grape forest, under which are abstract squiggly lines intended to imitate the look of marble. The tomb was discovered in 1937; you will have to unbolt a waist-high red iron door to get in. (Don't forget to close it on your way out; otherwise sand from the beach will corrode the paintings.) The tomb is open daily 9am-1pm, Sat. 10am-2pm.

The main attractions in the Afridar section of town are the two stunning **Roman Sarcophagi,** enclosed in a courtyard of their own along with some other Roman sculptures. They both date from the third century C.E. The first depicts the abduction of Persephone by Hades, the god of the Underworld. Their two-horse chariot is being guided by Hermes past Cerberus, the three-headed canine guardian of hell. To the left is the basket of flowers Persephone had been picking. On the lid of the sarcophagus (distinguished from Persephone's grieving parents) are a faceless couple, which were to be completed when the sculptor could carve the visages of those to be buried. The second sarcophagus depicts the battle of good versus evil. The clad, helmeted Greeks are clearly triumphing over their naked enemy barbarians. The courtyard containing the treasures is open Sun.-Thurs. 9am-4pm, Fri. 9am-3pm; admission free.

Ashqelon's northern and most recently settled sector, **Barnea,** contains two significant historical sights: the ruins of a sixth-century Byzantine church, and next to it, a beautiful fifth-century mosaic floor. These contrast with the Hebrew tablets and other ruins of Jewish synagogues of the Byzantine era that can be seen in the park. The best way to get to the Barnea ruins is to take bus #5 bound for Barnea from either Afridar or the Central Bus Station, get off at

Shimshon Blvd., and walk half a block to Zvi Segal St. The #4 bus lets you off one block further south at the corner of Shimshon and Bar Kochba Sts.

The somewhat shabby but colorful old town of **Migdal** (*Majdals* in Arabic) has its own interesting history. The Arabs who lived here before 1948 had inhabited the city since Turkish times. After the Sultan King Bibarus (the Mameluke) conquered and destroyed Crusader Ashqelon in 1270 C.E., the city was neglected for several centuries until, in the nineteenth century, Lady Stanhope claimed to know of a treasure buried here. The ruling Turkish Pashas of Akko and Jaffa brought Arab slaves to dig for the riches. Although the treasure was never found, the Arabs remained while the huge stones they excavated were shipped to build up Akko and Jaffa. When the new state of Israel captured the town in 1948, almost all of the Arab population fled to Egyptian Gaza where they now live in refugee camps. Its old stone houses huddled close together, Migdal contrasts sharply with the spacious suburban atmosphere of Ashqelon's other districts. It is now the main shopping quarter of town, and features a lively vegetable market, and, on Wednesdays and Thursdays, a fruit market. Besides the inexpensive produce, you will find very cheap sandwiches and snack bars—felafel often costs as little as $.40 here. Try to look for the shops with the thickest white tahina sauce. Walk north on Herzl Street just past Zahel Street, and you will see the market in the narrow passageway to your left. Whatever you do, don't try to walk to Migdal; though your map may not show it, it is separated from the rest of Ashqelon by a large open field.

The long sandy beach that extends the full 12km length of the city, although rocky in places, is one of the finest in Israel, with plenty of spots for quiet reflection or camping out. Just north of Delilah beach is the "separate" beach where religious bathers are separated by gender on weekdays. A few kilometers south of Ashqelon is the Kibbutz Zikim, which used to have a non-religious nude beach. The kibbutzniks prefer that you do not camp out on their beaches. You can see the floating dock where tankers unload their "dirty gold." Unfortunately, this is the source of the south coast beaches' one bane—when the tankers clean their holds with sea water (illegally) rather than with chemicals (expensively), a tar-like substance washes ashore, sticking to bathers' feet. To get the black spots off, use turpentine or cooking oil.

Nightlife

Movies, the beach, people-watching, and the wonders of nature comprise Ashqelon's nightlife. The **Rachel Cinema** at Zephania Square plays English-language films every night at 7:30 and 9:30. **Esther Cinema** in the Givat Zion district (renamed to spite the U.N.'s resolution equating Zionism with apartheid) also plays films in English. In the evenings some of the fancy hotels sponsor discos or other activities, although the clientele is downright boring. Instead, courteously stop in at the studio of Ilana Shafir, 2 Kapstat St. in Afridar. Her exquisite mosaics, paintings and drawings are exhibited Sun.-Thurs. 6-9pm.

Near Ashqelon

Yad Mordechai

Perversity triumphs over taste at the **Kibbutz of Yad Mordechai,** 16km south of Ashqelon, where you'll find one of the more bizarre monuments to Israeli military victories in the country. In 1948, members of the kibbutz withstood a fierce attack by the Egyptian army, providing precious time for defense forces to regroup in Tel Aviv. An enormous model of the battle, covering several acres, has been constructed, complete with dummy soldiers, tanks, planes, and all sorts of weapons. A recorded explanation in several languages recounts the battle and elucidates various parts of the colossal reconstruction of the event. The kibbutz also contains a museum dedicated to the activity of the Jewish resistance movement, covering the period from the Warsaw Ghetto Uprising until the 1948 War. Open daily 9am-4:30pm except for Yom Kippur; admission $.80, $.70 for students. You can take bus #30 from Ashqelon but unless this sort of thing thrills you, don't bother.

Ashdod

The Book of Joshua refers to the ancient town of Ashdod as a "city of Giants"; unfortunately, no giant-sized ruins remain. Alexander the Great seized the city from the Persians, but neither left any monuments. Close to the beach, you can see the remains of a synagogue from Roman times and one corner tower of the Beroart Crusader fortress. From the Ashdod bus station, you must either walk south along the beach or hitch to get to the ruins. The coastal route will show you most of what Ashdod has to offer. The few hotels are not worth the exorbitant rates they charge; if you want to spend the night in the area, you're better off on the beach, though you should be wary of the fast-approaching high tide. Five kilometers southeast of Ashdod is the deserted Arab village of **Isdud,** where daring Israelis sometimes camp despite police disapproval. If you choose to follow suit, bring lots of water since the desert encroaches very quickly and there will be no one near to help you.

Bet Guvrin, Tel Maresha, and Tel Lakhish

About 22km east of Ashqelon and easily accessible from Tel Aviv and Jerusalem, **Qiryat Gat,** the capital of the Lakhish region, is the jumping off point for several important sites. Tel Gat, the hill to the northeast, was formerly believed to be Gath, one of the five major Philistine cities and the birthplace of Goliath. However, excavations in 1959-61 failed to turn up any evidence of an ancient capital around the Arabic holy tomb Sheikh Erani, so Gath remains lost. Since excavations have been discontinued, there isn't much to do in Qiryat Gat; your best bet is to visit the three sites nearby.

Bet Guvrin, a modern kibbutz, was built in 1949 on the ruins of the deserted Arab village Bit Jibrin. The surrounding region is characterized by huge outcroppings of cactus and fig trees hiding some four thousand caves. Some of the caves were carved naturally as water carried away the soft limestone. Others were carved by the Phoenicians, who cut round holes in the earth, scooped out the limestone, and used it for the construction of their great port at Ashqelon. Thus, many of the caves have vast bell-shaped rooms with sun roofs.

Although the Romans fortified the ancient city and renamed it Eleutheropolis (City of Liberty), the Talmud refers to the inhabitants as *Bene Chorim* (Sons of Holes) or as *Bene Chorin* (Sons of Liberty). Later, the caves became natural sanctuaries for hermits and monks of the Byzantine period. St. John and others came seeking solitary meditation, and often carved crosses and altars into the walls. At a nearby tel, called Sandahanna after the Arabic Saint Hanna (Saint John), excavations in 1921 uncovered beautifully-preserved, ornate Byzantine mosaics of colorful birds and flowers. These mosaics, which served as floors in fifth- and sixth-century churches, can be seen near the top of the tel, protected by small sheds. Recently a Roman mosaic floor, in even better condition, has been unearthed. Other finds, such as stones with Hebrew inscriptions from a third-century synagogue, Crusader artifacts, and Greek objects of art, are on display at the Rockefeller Museum in Jerusalem.

Since the sites are unmarked and the tel is quite large, you may need to ask the assistance of one of the kibbutzniks from modern Bet Guvrin, a twenty-minute walk down the hill. Even young children seem to be well-acquainted with the area and accustomed to serving as guides.

To get to Bet Guvrin may take some doing: there are only two buses a day from Qiryat Gat, at around 8am and 5pm. Some of the Qiryat Gat-Hebron buses pass right by Bet Guvrin. Be sure to ask the driver if he will let you off there since there is no regular Egged stop. If you miss the morning bus, try hitching—there are many moshavim and kibbutzim in the area. Either hitch from one block south of the Qiryat Gat bus station or walk ten minutes south until you come to a T. Catch cars going or turning to the left. Taxis run from the Central Bus Station to Bet Guvrin or Tel Maresha ($10), and to Tel Lakhish ($6). To get to the caves, walk north from the front of the kibbutz to the paved road opposite. The first fork bears left to the largest of the Bet Guvrin bell caves; the right fork leads to Tel Maresha. The magnificent view from this place makes it worth the trip even if you're tired of ruins. On a clear day, you can see Tel Aviv and the Mediterranean to the west, and the Jordanian hills and the Dead Sea to the east. All around, ancient ruins poke out of the ground defying the cactus.

The ruins at **Tel Maresha** include several Phoenician bell caves, one of which has a stone calumbarium with thousands of niches carved into it, two decorated graves, and a Crusader basilica nearby. The sixty caves around the ruins contain colorful wildlife drawings—lions, giraffes, and elephants (oh my!). Try to latch onto a tour group to help you locate the occasional artifact on the large tel.

Tel Lakhish is just north of the moshav of the same name, 2km south of the Bet Guvrin-Hebron road. Although archeologically more important, Tel Lakhish is not as interesting as Tel Maresha. Because of its strategic location at the intersection of the road to Egypt and the approach to Jerusalem, it was often a scene of conflict in ancient times. Excavations in the 1930s revealed nine levels of settlements dating as far back as the third millenium B.C.E. Since it is almost inaccessible without a car and most of its artifacts have been removed to museums in Jerusalem and Britain, Tel Lakhish is no longer irresistible. Because of this area's isolation, climate, and proximity to the West Bank, local moshavniks strongly discourage camping out in these hills.

Gaza

The Gaza Strip is a thin plain stretching from the Mediterranean to the sandstone hills inland and from the Shiqma River in the north to the Besor River (often called the Azza River) at the Egyptian frontier to the south. The most important fact about the Strip, both to its inhabitants and to tourists, is its status under Israeli military occupation. Many Middle Eastern cities delight visitors with histories of various conquerors and remains of civilizations come and gone. Gaza frightens us with its modern equivalent: the conquerors are still in residence. Although it contains few "sights," Gaza is definitely worth a visit. Though you'll see Palestinians hard at work at all hours of the day, it's impossible not to recognize the crushing poverty of Gaza's inhabitants. Israelis tell many horror stories about what has happened and can happen in Gaza; given the Israeli military occupation and the diverse and sometimes unpredictable Palestinian response, their fear is understandable.

Gaza can be friendly to foreigners, however, especially to men or mixed groups. Although most men in Gaza seem to have learned that foreign women are not acceptable targets for their overtures, problems occasionally arise. You may see unescorted foreign women working for the relief agencies, but most women traveling alone are advised not to venture into the Strip.

Security is tight, but rarely affects tourists. There is little crime on the Strip, perhaps because the Palestinians know that the Israelis have little patience with them and even less mercy. The Palestinian police monitor traffic and not much else; the Israelis are responsible for law and order. Although there are both civilian and military police patrols the distinction is meaningless as both are uniformed, armed, and Israeli. Since disturbances in the Strip tend to be political rather than criminal, your experience in Gaza rides on the current political situation—be aware of recent happenings.

Gaza's fortunes through the ages have been determined by its position as "the Guardian of Africa, the Gate of Asia." Four thousand years before Napoleon used these words to gloat over his most recently conquered city, the Egyptians were using Gaza as the staging point for their attacks into Asia. Thousands of years later, the Hyksos returned the compliment, after which the city became the capital of the Philistine empire. For the next several centuries, the early Israelites fought a losing battle with the Philistines who drove "chariots of Iron" (Judges 1:16-30). Later, Samson proved his might by humiliating the Philistines in Gaza. For desecrating the city's gates, the Philistines captured Samson (with Delilah's aid), blinded him, and forced him to prance about in public in the Temple of Dagon. Samson brought the Temple down, killing himself and his captors. According to Arab tradition, Samson lies buried under the site of today's Great Mosque along with Muhammad's great-grandfather and uncle. Samson was known as Abu el Azam or Father of Might and Gaza was called Azza (as it is today in Hebrew) meaning "Might." Respectful of the skilled artisans and knowledgeable traders of the area, the Greeks changed the name to Gaza (Treasure).

The Crusaders took Gaza in 1150 and built a large church which the Mamelukes later turned into the Great Mosque. By the turn of this century, the city was predominantly Muslim. When the United Nations called for an end to the 1948 War, most of the Egyptian army found itself sitting on the Gaza Strip. Hundreds of thousands of Palestinians abandoned their homes in cities all along the coast and followed the Egyptian army southward during its retreat before superior Israeli forces. When peace was established in 1949, most of these Palestinians were also trapped in the Strip, unable to return home. The territory remained under Egyptian control until 1956, when it was temporarily recaptured by Israel and then returned along with the Sinai. During the Six Day War of 1967, Israel again captured the territory and since then has had the difficult task of governing the refugees. Israeli military rule has brought an end to the guerilla activity in the region. But, though the administration has improved medical facilities and created a modicum of prosperity, it has not succeeded in substantially alleviating the poverty of the half-million refugees living there, nor has it done little more than submerge the feelings of bitterness and hatred toward Israel. Those feelings have a way of extending to tourists who step out of their comfortable lives to look at the refugees for an hour or two as an interesting curiosity. Gaza, then, is a place to visit not only for its sights and beaches, but also for its sobering witness to the realities of Middle Eastern politics.

Language should not present a problem in Gaza. Most of Gaza's Arabs are eager to chat in English, French, or even Hebrew (unless they are politically inclined, in which case this is taboo). School children often study English (although sometimes you'll wish they didn't—their incessant shouts of "What time is it? How are you? How old are you?" can be quite annoying). Near the Islamic University on Al Azhar St. (Thalatine St.), you can easily hook up for a few hours with one of the religious students, who will be more than willing to practice his English. Be careful when spending money in Gaza; the Palestinians often quote prices in the old Israeli lira rather than the new shekels.

Orientation and Practical Information

A convenient daytrip from Ashqelon, the city of Gaza can be reached by bus #20 (twice a day) from Ashqelon's bus station or by sherut from Ashqelon's old town of Migdal in the area east of Herzl St. and south of Zahal St. Once in the Strip, you'll find buses both infrequent and irregular. All go to and from the city of Gaza and all are locals; take #30 to Bet Lahia, #31 to Jabalia, #32 to Khan Yunis, #33 to El Maghazi and El Braij (El Bererj), and #35 to El Arish through Rafiah. Sheruts within a town generally cost under $.50; between towns or refugee camps expect to pay about $1.25. Although Israelis may tell you it's dangerous to hitch in Arab areas, especially occupied territories, Palestinians will tell and show you otherwise. However, hitching is rarely necessary, for the sheruts are cheap and common. (They honk at you when they have an empty seat—wave if you want it.)

Buses and sheruts enter the Gaza Strip on the only road that runs its entire length, Saleh el Deen. The Gaza bus station is at the first traffic circle, **Palestine Square.** The city's main street, **Omar el Mukhtar,** leads to the center of town, **Gaza Square.** Everything in Gaza city is on or just off this thoroughfare. Omar el Mukhtar connects Saleh el Deen with the sea; you can walk its length in about an hour. Just south of Gaza Square is the main food market or *suq.* Between the two is the sherut stand. Most Palestinians call sheruts *servees.*

Just outside the market are the moneychangers who will offer to buy dollars from you at discount rates. But don't be too sure about who's getting the discount; the exchange rate is no longer artificially supported. The **Post Office** and **police station** are just before Palestine Square on Saleh el Deen. The post office is open Sun.-Thurs. 9am-noon and 3-5:30pm, Fri. 9am-noon (tel. 25 12 5). The **telephone code** for Gaza is 051.

The *Shorafa* Tourist Office at 922-100 Omar el Mukhtar claims to handle tours within Israel and provide flight information. However, they speak little English, have no map of Gaza, no written handouts, no information, and little desire to help you. The Palestinian newspaper *Al Fajr* has an English edition, a good source of information which will alert you to specific events of interest. Any curfews in effect will be announced here. Although the paper is often censored, most information relevant to tourists is not. Pay careful attention since the Israeli military makes no curfew exceptions for tourists. A dusk-to-dawn curfew is always enforced along the entire beach area, often including the small coastal road.

The **UNRWA Field Office** is a pastel-blue building off Thalatine St., which intersects Omar el Mukhtar a few blocks toward the sea from the Municipal Park. If you call ahead, the UN is sometimes willing to organize a guided tour of the refugee camps. Call Mr. Filfel, the Director of Public Relations (tel. 61 19 5/8), at least three days in advance. He may give you a large map and a packet of boring statistical fact sheets.

Accommodations and Food

The city of Gaza has two rather expensive hotels and a number of more affordable, less luxurious establishments. Bargaining is often possible as Gaza is not yet the tourist trap some of the hoteliers would like it to be.

El Walid Hotel, across from the Municipal Gardens on Omar el Mukhtar (tel. 61 23 4). A neat, clean place with old, small beds which cost $6 per person in doubles or dorms. Breakfast not included.

Cliff Hotel, slightly to the left of the intersection of Beach St. and Omar el Mukhtar (tel. 61 35 3). Singles $15, doubles can be bargained down to $20. Nearby are the fancy Loveboat and Smour restaurants which feature double-digit dining.

Marina House. A bit difficult to find but easy to ask for since everyone knows the name. Head towards the sea on Omar el Mukhtar, turn right just past the new Cultural Center, pass the alley to your right, and take the next right. The hotel is 50m down on your left. The woman who owns it will often give students a "discount" (she detests bargaining) but the basic prices are $25 for a single, $35 for a double, breakfast included. Lunch and dinner prices hover around $10.

Hotel Gold, on Omar el Mukhtar just after the road divides for a few blocks as you are going northwest. Only exhibits an English sign "Hotel." Next to a large hardware store. The three floors of this place are kept remarkably clean by a large family. Good conversation, coffee, and a soft bed start at $5 a single, $8 a double.

Like everything else, most of the restaurants and street stands are on Omar el Mukhtar. Salads, corn, hummus, roasted or skewered beef and lamb, and sweet, muddy Arabic coffee are the standard fare. Expect to pay about $2 for a full meal without meat, $3-5 with. Fish, in season, is the local delicacy and is mostly sold at the two or three small restaurants along Beach St. During Ramadan, many restaurants are closed. The **Al Farous** restaurant next to the UN Beach Club remains open and is a good splurge at $5-8 per meal. Also, during Ramadan, the dishes served at the street stands tend to be overly sweet desserts the Muslims use to break the daily fast. *Gitaief* is the most popular—sugared nut filling inside a fried dough pancake dipped (until dripping) in honey. This stuff should cure any sweet tooth. The blue-green fish stand near the Cliff Hotel has salted eels in season. Most of the Palestinians won't touch them, but those that do swear by them.

By far the cheapest place to shop for food is the *suq* just northwest of Gaza Square off Omar el Mukhtar. If you'd rather pay for a good deal more cleanliness, try the **supermarket** to the right of Omar el Mukhtar, two blocks towards the sea past the Municipal Park. Ramadan is not the best time to visit Gaza (or other heavily Muslim areas). Few stores are open during the day and the evening feasting is generally a family affair. If, however, you are invited, don't miss it!

Sights

The extreme political conditions of the Gaza Strip are mirrored in its people. While thousands live in the squalid refugee camps with no hope of a better life, artists of more fortunate means use their talents to make statements which they hope will change the course of the bitter stream in some small way. Israelis and Palestinians argue over the provenance of a mosaic in some ancient ruins, managing to turn what would be an urbane disagreement anywhere else into an ideological confrontation. The Islamic University of Gaza has been the scene of riots between students and Muslim Brotherhood Fundamentalists. The dense population, both in the city and in the refugee camps, serves only to heighten the air of frenzy. Tourists are not spared this pervasive tension, and must step more gingerly here than they are perhaps accustomed to. Here in Gaza, the sights are not, for the most part, of the ordinary museum/temple/harbor cruise variety; rather, the tourist is struck by the sight, and the feel, of many people with divergent political stances living in very close quarters.

Fortunately, there are a few sanctuaries. In the middle of the noisy *suq*, look for the **Great Mosque** (Jammal el Ikbeer), a place of worship open to non-Muslims whenever one of five daily prayer sessions is not in progress. (Remember to remove your shoes upon entering.) The **British War Cemetery** is also quiet, although ominously so, considering the region's militarism. This expanse of gravestones and neatly-kept gardens is maintained by the British Consulate. Indian soldiers who died in the service of the British Armed Forces have a memorial that is inscribed with passages from the *Bhagavad Gita*. If you're discreet, you can camp in this safe area, but get going early—they water the grounds around 7am. The Cemetery is marked by an unobtrusive gate along Saleh el Deen, at the entrance to the Strip. A 7-Up factory stands across the road. In town, the **Municipal Park and Gardens,** on Omar el Mukhtar near the sea, may also provide a needed respite.

The most pleasant part of a visit to Gaza may be in getting acquainted with the local artisans and their work. The cane furniture industry for which Gaza is famous has its center in Palestine Square, while carpet sellers vie for your attention in Gaza Square. The alley opposite the Municipality in Gaza Square leads to the pottery factory *(fawakhyr)*. Ask to be shown the subterranean studios where potters turn the wheels by treadle and use kilns of ancient design.

Much of the jewelry used as currency by Palestinians (who distrust Israeli currency) emerges from the gold cellars on Omar el Mukhtar, seaward from the *suq* and on the opposite side of the street. Nihad Sabassi, Gaza's best-known artist, has his studio in this area as well. His paintings and woodburnings hang in the government building and in some hotels. Also on Omar el Mukhtar is the UN's **Gaza-Embroidery Gift Shop** (open Sat.-Thurs. 9am-4pm, closes earlier during Ramadan). Many of the paintings and wood engravings seen around the city are the work of Ghalil Badah, whose studio is near Beach St.

The disputed remains stand near the beach, about 1 km south of the UN Beach Club (see below). Israelis claim that this was a Byzantine (sixth-century) synagogue. The mosaic floor is offered as evidence, and stones with Hebrew inscriptions are alleged to exist. Palestinians, however, point to the representations of animals in the stones as very unlikely in a synagogue. Don't bother taking sides in the debate; the ruins are not particularly striking.

Except for the tar from the tankers near Ashqelon, Gaza's **beaches** are delightful. They are not the cleanest on the Mediterranean coast, but they are among the most accessible and least crowded, especially during Ramadan. You'll notice something peculiar about the beaches—there are only men and children swimming. Because of Islamic rules forbidding married women to appear attractive to men, the rare woman who enters the water does so fully clothed and at her own risk. Foreign women must keep Islamic customs in mind at all times, especially at the beach. Fortunately, the **UN Beach Club,** a few blocks southwest of where Omar el Mukhtar meets the beach, maintains a section of its beach for UN staff and visiting UN forces, mostly from Lebanon. Although you cannot use the indoor facilities at the Club, you can swim in front of their lot, near a ten-year-old shipwreck. Even here, women should be careful; the Palestinians' curiosity about women's bare legs and shoulders is a nuisance, but cannot simply be ignored.

Moonlight strolls on the beach are *verboten*, owing to the dusk-to-dawn curfew. The Strip's small fleet of fishing trawlers must also stay offshore until dawn, so one can see a thin, bobbing necklace of yellow lights reflected in the swells. If you get too close to the beach, the military police are likely to train their huge spotlight and automatic weapons on you, spoiling an otherwise lovely scene.

Safer forms of entertainment are not easy to come by. The **cinemas** in Gaza show Egyptian films in Arabic, and are so rowdy that only men attend, except for one night a week set aside for women and children. Lecture rooms, theaters, and game rooms are among the facilities promised at the **Cultural Center of Gaza,** if it ever opens. The facility, off Omar el Mukhtar, cost scads of money to build but remains dark, since the Gaza municipality has yet to secure Israeli assurances that the Center will be allowed to open. The wedding processions down Beach St., almost every Friday afternoon except during Ramadan, are festive and free.

Near Gaza

Although most of the activity and general spirit of the Strip can be sampled from Gaza city, a few sidetrips are worthwhile. The eight refugee camps, while hardly pleasant sights, do bear witness to the misery wrought by war. The nearest, Beach Refugee Camp, is north of the intersection of Omar el Mukhtar and Beach St. The two largest are at either end of the Strip—Jabaliya near Gaza city, and Rafiah by the town of Rafiah. Closer to Egypt are Bureij and Nuseirat. Dayr el Balah and Maghazi are the smallest camps, and Khan Yunis is outside the town of the same name.

The area of the Rafiah camp, ironically, was used in the 1940s by the British as a detention camp for captured members of the Jewish resistance. Both Khan Yunis and Rafiah should be visited on those days when the Bedouins set up their markets—Wednesday and Thursday in Khan Yunis, and Saturday and Sunday in Rafiah. A carnival atmosphere accompanies intense bargaining over food staples, animals, clothing, and household goods.

Dead Sea

The Dead Sea, Israel's largest lake and, at 1200 feet below sea level, the lowest point on earth, was given its somewhat gloomy name by Christian pilgrims who were disconcerted by the complete absence of any form of life in its waters. Its Hebrew name, Yam HaMelach, which means "the Salt Sea," is certainly more appropriate, since the lake has a salt concentration eight times that of the Mediterranean, Atlantic, or Pacific. The high salt concentration has its good points and its not-so-good points. On the positive side, swimming in the Dead Sea is like nowhere else in the world. The high salinity dramatically increases the buoyancy of your body; you can float effortlessly on the surface of the water, and read a book while you're at it. It actually requires a great deal of exertion to submerge yourself, making the lake ideal for non-swimmers (as long as they stay on their backs). However, the high salt content is not particularly good for your hair and if you open your eyes under water, you will be in for at least several very painful minutes of blindness (if that should happen, wash them out immediately with fresh water; the main beaches all have freshwater showers). Since you will want to wash the salt off as soon as you get out of the sea, you may want to stick to the popular resort beaches where showers are readily available. These resorts are, from north to south: **Qulya, Ein Feshka** (Enot Tzukim), **Ein Gedi, Ein Boqeq,** and **Newe Zohar.** (Water is not potable.) Finally, don't expose any cuts or bruises to the water, which will probably seep into a few minor scrapes you didn't even know you had. Smaller cuts shouldn't prove too painful, and may even heal faster because the salt cleanses the wound and kills off bacteria.

Fewer tourists come to the Dead Sea than to other, more northern resorts because of the harsh climate; desert temperatures are barely tolerable during the summer, when it is extremely humid. The Dead Sea is actually evaporating at an incredible rate, and every year the water level recedes a bit. This accounts for the constant haziness that obscures what would otherwise be a spectacular view of the basin, for the scenery couldn't be more breathtaking: a jagged wall of cliffs rising dramatically up along both the Israeli and the Jordanian coast (only 1½ miles away). It was this ruthless environment with its hidden caves and isolated mountaintops that religious ascetics and political fugitives chose as an ideal hiding place in ancient times. The remnants of these refuges at **Masada** and **Qumran** are perhaps the most famous archeological sites in Israel today. All things considered, the Dead Sea is a beautiful and unusual place to visit.

A highway, completed in 1970, runs directly along the Israeli side of the sea and is serviced by bus #486, which starts from the central Egged terminal in Jerusalem. For those planning to hop on and off the buses, Jerusalem-Qumran fare is $1.20, Qumran-Ein Feshka $.25, Ein Feshka-Ein Gedi $1.05, and Ein Gedi-Masada $.50. If you are on a tight budget and are planning to stay in the Dead Sea area a while, you might consider stocking up on some food. There are no inexpensive grocery stores here—only tourist resorts and kibbutzim. Also remember that the same rules apply here as in the desert: bring along a water bottle, drink plenty of fluids, and keep your head covered.

If you really want to get out into the desert, you might consider taking an organized tour. One such program, offered by the **Metzoke Dragot Desert Tour Village,** takes you to major sights as well as rugged desert terrain, all with a full dose of hiking and outdoor life. For more information, call in Jerusalem (02) 22 23 08 or at Kibbutz Mitzpe Shalem (057) 84 34 0.

Masada

The huge fortress at Masada, built as a hideaway by King Herod on a lonely plateau 20km south of Ein Gedi, was the final scene of the great Jewish rebellion against the Romans from 70 to 73 C.E. For three years, one thousand Jewish defenders held out against Roman attack. Rather than surrender, the defenders committed mass suicide, thereby becoming an important symbol of the Jewish struggle for freedom. Today, Masada is the site used for swearing in members of the Israeli army. No visit to Israel would be complete without a stop at this legendary clifftop with its magnificent view of the Dead Sea.

History

Masada's high, rocky plateau is an ideal site for a fortress; encircling cliff walls protect it from easy attack. The first citadel was built on the mountaintop in the second century B.C.E. by Jonathan, brother of Judah Maccabee. Towards the end of his rule, Herod, fearing rebellion, had a luxurious palace built at Masada to be used as a hideaway, not realizing that several decades later Jewish rebels would turn his grand construction to their own advantage.

Starting in 55 C.E., a number of Jewish groups revolted against Rome and scored significant victories in Palestine. One of the first came in Masada when a band of Jewish zealots captured Herod's palace and transformed it into an invincible stronghold. The Romans, however, made steady inroads on the Jewish settlements, and in 70 C.E. they managed to capture Jerusalem, destroy the Temple there, and seemingly bring to an end the Jewish rebellion. But they soon realized that the stubborn band of zealots at Masada were refusing to surrender and planned to continue their resistance. As more families joined the zealots, the Romans feared another massive uprising and so began their siege of Masada, a siege that lasted three years.

With little food and no real prospect of survival, the rebels, under the leadership of Elazar Ben Yair, turned back numerous Roman attacks. The Romans responded by surrounding the mountain with eight camps connected by a wall, to insure that none of the zealots would escape alive. The Roman General Silva, with a troop of 15,000 men under his command, undertook one of the great tour-de-forces of the day by erecting an enormous stone and gravel ramp leading up to the summit of the sheer cliffs. By 73 C.E. the Romans had reached the top and started to demolish the fortress walls. The 967 men, women, and children of Masada, having survived three long years of hand-to-hand combat, realized that their end was nigh. On the night before the Romans prepared to invade the fortress, the rebels reached the fateful and courageous decision expressed in the words of their leader, Elazar Ben Yair: "We would rather die than be the slaves of our enemies, and we shall remain free as we leave the land of the living, we, our wives and our children." Each man burned his possessions, said farewell to his family, and put them to death. Legend has it that the men then prepared stores of wheat and water which they placed in the citadel's courtyard to demonstrate to the Romans that it was not for want of provisions that they had perished. They drew lots and ten men were selected to execute the others and check each house to make sure everyone was dead. Lots were drawn again, and one person was selected to take the lives of the other nine, and finally his own. The following morning, the Romans stormed the stronghold, expecting to meet great resistance but encountering only a deathly silence. The only survivors were two women and five children whom the Romans spared and who lived to tell the now immortal story of the martyrs of Masada.

Practical Information and Accommodations

Masada is not actually on the Dead Sea, but a few kilometers inland on the road to Arad and Beersheva. Buses go to Masada eight times a day from Jerusalem via Ein Gedi, ten times a day from Arad, and five times a day from Beersheva, but the Beersheva service is particularly unreliable. If you are thinking of continuing on the Sinai from Masada, the bus to Eilat stops by the Youth Hostel at 8:30am and 3:30pm daily, except Sat. Hitching to or from Masada, or anywhere on the Dead Sea for that matter, is quite poor since most of the cars are crowded with tourists.

As you get off the bus, the first thing you will see is the 200-bed **Taylor Youth Hostel (IYHF)** (tel. 84 34 9). While the hostel has clean rooms and air conditioning, it's also crowded and has poor food and an 11pm curfew. The charge is $6.60 for members and $7.80 for non-members. Prices include air conditioning and breakfast. Lunch costs $3.60 for members and $4.20 for non-members, supper $2.30 and $2.50, respectively. The hostel is closed from 8:15am-5pm; check-in is 5-7pm.

There is also a small guest house run by the National Parks Authority which offers a bit more privacy than the youth hostel; beds are $10 per person. The only other inexpensive accommodations within reach is the **campground** at Newe Zohar to the south and the Youth Hostel at Arad (see below). The closest hotels, for those who can afford them, are a few kilometers south at Ein Boqeq (also see below). Considering these prospects, you might want to visit Masada by daytrip from Ein Gedi.

Perhaps the most attractive alternative for those adventuresome souls eager and willing to break the law is to sleep on top of the mountain. Signs are posted all over warning that it is an illegal offense to trespass after 4pm, but it's highly unlikely that any officials will follow you up the snake path. On a summer evening, around 6pm, it's not uncommon to see ten or twenty backpackers winding up the mountain bearing food, sleeping bags, and sometimes even firewood. The ruins are wonderful to explore by moonlight (you might consider bringing a flashlight if there is no moon) and the cool mountain breeze keeps the temperature comfortable. Be sure to pack up and move off before the groups begin arriving at about 6am. You can check your luggage at the hostel or guest house for about $1 a piece.

Next to the Hostel at the base of the mountain is an assortment of outrageously expensive refreshment stands, souvenir shops, and air-conditioned restaurants. The shops all feature copies of Prof. Yadin's popular book on Masada which you can obtain for far less at Bestsellers in Jerusalem. Drinking water is available from a number of faucets and hoses: don't drink anything that is not marked as drinking water.

Sights

The present ruins at Masada were unearthed in 1963 by a team of archeologists headed by Yigael Yadin. They discovered the skeletons of some of the zealots, as well as numerous dwellings and the structure of Herod's magnificent palaces. Most tourists begin their sightseeing at the entrance to a huge **water cistern,** located to your right near the last flight of stairs to the summit. One of seven all together, it is estimated that the zealots were able to store enough water in the cisterns to last them for eight years. As you enter the site proper, to your right is the enormous **Northern Palace,** originally a three-story structure and the core of Herod's pleasure retreat. Climb up for an aerial view of the palace's impressive layout. About one-third of the ruins is actually restoration work—a black line runs along the walls demarcating the original from the reconstructed sections. The main attraction of the Northern Palace is the Roman-style **Bathhouse,** where some of the original frescoes can be seen.

At the edge of the northern cliff, with its half-circle patio, lies what archeologists believe was **Herod's Private Palace.** If you follow the steps down along the sheer walls of the cliff you will come to the lower sections of the Private Palace. In the bathhouse of the lowest section, the skeletons of a man, woman, and child were found, along with a Jewish ceremonial prayer shawl. The lower terrace contains quite a few original frescoes and columns, and affords a spectacular view of Roman General Silva's camp. Traces of all eight Roman camps, appearing as brownish rectangular enclosures, are clearly distinguishable from the mountain, and close examination reveals an outline of the wall that connected them.

Climb back up the steps from Herod's Palace and turn right as you reach the summit to reach the zealots' **synagogue,** the oldest known synagogue in Israel. Scrolls were found here containing Hebrew texts from several books of the Old Testament. Most of them are now on display in the Shrine of the Book in Jerusalem, but a few modest examples can be seen in the museum by the cable car station. Finds from around the synagogue and elsewhere on the site indicate that the zealots were devoutly religious and observed all the rituals prescribed by Jewish orthodoxy of the time, despite the hardship of being isolated on the mountain. Continuing still further along the edge, you come to the **Western Palace,** which houses some splendid mosaics dating from Herodian times, the oldest in Israel. Some of the best mosaics are to be found in the **Byzantine Chapel** near the Western Palace. It turns out that Masada was occupied for a short period during the fifth century C.E. by Christian monks who erected the chapel. Also next to the Western Palace is the **Western Gate** (you enter here if you come by the Roman path), which offers a view of the Roman ramp leading up the side of the mountain. Most of the rest of the site features watchtowers, additional fortifications, and countless zealot dwellings. Scattered throughout the site are kegs of drinking water which you should take advantage of frequently, beyond the dictates of thirst; it is surprisingly easy to get dehydrated climbing around in the desert heat.

There are three ways to get up to the ruins—by cable car or by two foot paths. The easier of the two trails, the **Roman Ramp,** starts on the west side of the mountain, on Arad Rd., and takes about thirty minutes to climb. More popular, more scenic, and more difficult is the original **Serpentine Path,** so named for its tortuous bends. The path has been fixed up a little since the zealots used it, but you still might consider starting at the crack of dawn; bring water bottles. The hike up the Serpentine Path takes just under one hour for most people, and if you start early enough, you will have a breathtaking view from the top—the sun slowly rising over the vast expanse of the Dead Sea some 1400 feet below. Don't start hiking up in the afternoon: you want not only to avoid the heat, but also to have time to tour the extensive ruins. One reasonable compromise is to hike up the mountain early in the morning and take the beautiful cable-car ride down when it starts to get hot. (It leaves from near the top of the Serpentine Path). If you come later in the day, listen in on one of the tour groups as they walk around the site.

The cable car fare is $3 one way, $4 round trip; for students $1.50 one way, $2 round trip. Admission to the site is $2, $.75 for students. The cable car starts at 8am and leaves every half hour; last cable car up is at 3:30pm, 1:30pm on Friday. The site is technically open 6:30am-3:30pm.

South of Masada

Ein Boqeq's excellent beach has made the town one of the most popular resorts on the Dead Sea. Located on the southern half of the Sea, a few kilometers from Masada, Ein Boqeq is a good place to stop off for a swim on the way to Arad and Beersheva. There are showers on the beach where you can wash off the salt immediately after swimming, as well as some hot mineral springs. Remember, the water in the springs is for swimming, not for drinking: the sulphur content would have you vomiting for days.

Ein Boqeq has two hotels, but they're unbelievably expensive. For cheaper accommodations, head further down the coast to **Newe Zohar,** where you'll also find a good beach with showers and boating facilities. **Newe Zohar Camping** (tel. 84 30 6) charges $2 a person for camping, and has bungalows to let at $6 per person. The main attraction around Newe Zohar is the fantastic salt formations, floating high, like crystalline icebergs, in the southern regions of the Dead Sea.

Traveling south from Newe Zohar, the road will drop you into searing **Sodom.** For some reason, almost everyone seems to remember something about the story of Sodom and Gomorrah: maybe it's the plot. In Genesis 18-19, Sodom and Gomorrah are described as the wicked cities of their day: not even ten righteous men dwelt among them. God naturally did not look favorably on these dens of iniquity, and rained fire and brimstone on the two towns, transforming the whole area into utter desolation. Only Abraham's nephew Lot, his wife, and their two children were spared; God sent an angel to lead them out of the havoc of destruction on the condition that they did not turn back and look upon the gruesome fate of their neighbors. Lot's wife, succumbing to sympathy or curiosity, disobeyed and was instantly turned into a pillar of salt.

Like so many places with grand biblical associations, there is very little to do in Sodom. The main reason to come to Sodom is to see the column of salt that tour guides and local residents will introduce to you as Mrs. Lot. Sodom is now the home of the **Dead Sea Works,** which extracts potash and other minerals from the Dead Sea for export. Most of the workers at the plant live at the nearby towns of Arad and Dimona, because the climate is intolerably hot in Sodom, which, according to some, is indisputable proof that it once must have rained fire and brimstone here.

Ein Gedi

Ein Gedi is the Dead Sea's most attractive spot. In addition to a good beach, Ein Gedi has a nature reserve with streams, waterfalls, and natural pools which offer refreshingly cool relief from the humid climate and salty waters of the Dead Sea. The nature reserve, a remarkably fertile oasis, features the lushest vegetation in the area and a host of rare species of desert wildlife.

Practical Information and Accommodations

Buses connect Ein Gedi to Masada and Arad eight times a day, to Jerusalem eight times a day (bus #486), to Beersheva five times a day, to Tel Aviv once a day at 2pm and to Haifa once a day (be ready at 2pm). The bus to Eilat (#444) passes through at 8am and 3pm, stopping only at the bus stop on the main road, and doesn't run on Saturday. Reservations for seats on the Eilat bus cannot be made at Ein Gedi or Masada, so you'll just have to hope. During the height of the tourist season, your chances of getting a seat, surprisingly enough, are quite good since Egged often runs two buses at a time to accommodate the high demand. If you really want to be on the safe side, reserve a seat on a bus to Eilat before you leave Jerusalem.

The prime choice for accommodations in the Dead Sea area is the **Bet Sara Hostel (IYHF)** at Ein Gedi (tel. 84 16 5). You might consider using it as a base from which to tour the rest of the area. Although the youth hostel has 200 beds, it is usually a bit crowded, and the management tends to be rather unfriendly and impersonal. The place is clean, however, the rooms are air-conditioned (between 6pm and 6am), and the cafeteria serves pretty good meals. The showers are clean and refreshing, but don't drink any of the tap water from the showers or the bathroom; use the cold water drinking fountain instead. The entire hostel is closed from 9am-5pm; if you arrive during that time, you can leave your pack in the courtyard next to the registration office, where it should be quite safe. Check-in is 5-9pm, but get there early or you'll be waiting in line for an hour or two. The charge is $6.75 for members under 18, $7.50 for non-members under 18, $7.50 for members over 18, $9 for non-members. There is a 15% discount for non-Israelis. Breakfast is included in the price; dinner is $4.50, making it the best deal at Ein Gedi. There is no curfew. Family rooms must be reserved in advance ($8.50 per person). The Hostel is right next to the turn-off for the nature reserve.

Not quite as priceworthy or as comfortable as the hostel is **Ein Gedi Camping** (tel. 84 30 3), on the beach a few kilometers south of the Hostel and nature reserve. The campground and all the other commercial enterprises surrounding it are run by the nearby kibbutz; the office next to the snack bar can provide information. The charge for camping is a bit steep at $4.50 per person, and since nights at Ein Gedi are almost as hot as the days, you might want to think twice about sleeping without air conditioning. The bungalows for let offer greater privacy with air conditioning. They are available every day for $34 for two, $46 for three, $58 for four. There is an additional 15% charge for Israelis. The campground also runs an expensive, air-conditioned restaurant.

Admission to the beach by the campground is free and worth a visit merely for its showers. Many people sleep on the beach during the summer, and although it is technically illegal, no one is likely to bother you. If you are staying at the Hostel you can shower there or at the springs, so you might consider swimming near the Hostel, where you can enjoy relative solitude, and save yourself the walk.

Sights

Israelis settled in and cultivated the area around Ein Gedi, including the nature reserve, partly because of its biblical associations. In I Samuel 23:29 it is written that David took to the lush oasis to escape the wrath of King Saul. Ein Gedi is also mentioned in the Song of Songs, where it is referred to as the "Fountain of the Kid," the name that has stuck to this day. Jewish settlers established a kibbutz a few kilometers south of the beach at Ein Gedi in 1953, which, over the years, has become well-known in Israel for its fruit and for the restored fountain mentioned by Solomon. They also cleared a path for the famous waterfall, replanted palms and reeds in the area, and started a field school for the study of flora and fauna. If you befriend a kibbutznik, you can spend a night or two at the kibbutz for free, but you probably won't be able to afford the kibbutz's expensive guest inn ($40 per person!).

Biblical references aside, the **nature reserve** is the main reason to come to Ein Gedi. If you're short on time, at least make the fifteen-minute hike up to **Nahal David,** "the waterfall of David," a beautiful slender pillar of water dropping the full length of the cliffside to a shallow pool at the bottom. Pools abound in the area; investigate the little paths that branch off the main trail and disappear into the thicket of giant reeds. From the waterfall another trail climbs up the cliffside to **Ein Gedi Springs,** where there is a nice pool, and to some ruins, including, among other things, the remains of a **Maccabean Fortress** and a **fourth-century synagogue.** Another route takes you to **Dodim Cave,** a marvelously cool niche where a waterfall flows down the cliff and water drips off the mossy roof. The climb is a bit tiring, but rewarding; you can enjoy the solitude and the chance to see a herd of ibex—a strange-looking wild goat. Also, watch out for the tiny hyrex, which can be found lurking in the reeds. It looks like a small grey badger without a tail. Strangely enough, zoologists have unconvincingly classified the 12-inch creature as a relative of the elephant. The nature reserve also contains a number of rarely-seen leopards which have a reputation for being rather unfriendly towards tourists. The reserve is open Sun.-Thurs. 8am-4pm, Fri. 8am-2pm but no entrance is permitted an hour before closing. Admission is $1; no discount for students. For the more athletically inclined, a climb along the **Nahal Arugot,** entered from 500m south of the main road, takes you to the charming hidden waterfall. It's a good hour and a half's walk from the road (look for the sign), but if you follow the course of the stream you shouldn't have trouble finding it. The pool at the end, considerably deeper than the others, amply rewards the exertion.

Next to the entrance to the nature reserve is a refreshment stand which offers delicious Ein Gedi dates at a steep price. On weekends the pools along the main stream become quite crowded with Israelis from Jerusalem. At first, foreign visitors are rather puzzled by the popularity of the pools, since the Dead Sea is so near, but not after they step into the Dead Sea's warm, viscous water.

Qumran and Ein Feshka (Enot Tzukim)

If you are coming from Jerusalem, the first major stop of interest is Qumran, the site of the discovery of the famous Dead Sea scrolls. In 1947, two Bedouin shepherds looking for a missing sheep wandered into a remote cliffside cave and stumbled on a collection of earthenware jars that contained the ancient manuscripts. The largest of the fragile parchment scrolls was a 22-foot-long text of the Book of Isaiah, written in Hebrew and now beautifully displayed in the Shrine of the Book, a subsection of the Israel Museum in Jerusalem. Encouraged by the initial discovery of the scrolls, archeologists searched the surrounding caves and began excavations at the foot of the cliffs. In 1949, they uncovered the settlement of the sect that wrote the Dead Sea scrolls.

Archeological evidence suggests that the site was first settled as far back as the eighth century B.C.E., was reinhabited in the second century B.C.E., temporarily abandoned during the reign of Herod, and completely deserted after the Roman defeat of the Jewish uprisings in 70 C.E. Historians believe that the authors of the scrolls were the Essenes, a fanatical Jewish sect which, disillusioned with the liberal faith of the Hasmoneans, took to the isolated site at Qumran in the second century B.C.E. to dwell completely in accord with Mosaic law. The Essenes believed that the forces of darkness embodied in Hellenistic and Roman culture threatened human civilization, and that in a short period of time the forces of light would prevail and they would be handsomely rewarded for their piety.

The visitor to Qumran who stumbles among the ruins or along the cliffs in the sweltering Dead Sea climate will be moved by a mixture of admiration for the Essenes and disbelief; it must have taken great religious conviction to impel these people to live under such unfavorable conditions merely for the sake of a little privacy. Fortunately for tourists, you don't have to be a religious ascetic to enjoy the sight: the main archeological site is quite compact and can be viewed without too much exertion. Start first at the **watchtower**, which affords an excellent view of the site and is well worth the modest climb. Proceed to the **Scriptorium**, the chamber where the scrolls may have been written. The more ambitious can also climb up to the famous caves themselves, but this requires a great deal of stamina and plenty of water—drinking water is available next to the site.

The archeological site is located 400m from the coastal highway, and is serviced by bus #486, which lets you off at the turn-off. Keep your eyes peeled for the sign and ring the bell for the stop. Open every day 8am-4pm, until 5pm April-Sept.; admission $1.25, $.65 for students. Nearby, on the northern tip of the Dead Sea at the junction with the road to Jericho, lies **Qulya**, formerly a luxury resort and now a restaurant and bathing spot.

Once you've worked up a sweat climbing around at Qumran, you can take advantage of the salt water and fresh water bathing at **Ein Feshka** (Enot Tzukim is the Hebrew name), just 6km south of the ruins. The small beach is usually fairly deserted, except on weekends. From the beach a dirt road leads inland to the nature reserve, where you can at least partially submerge yourself in the small pools formed by the natural springs. Rivulets lace the area, vacationers lounge about within cakes of Black Dead Sea Mud (reputed to be healthful), and showers are nearby. Open every day 8am-4pm; admission $1.60 (no student discount). For a better beach, better nature reserve, and better springs, head south to Ein Gedi, another 29km down the road.

SEND US A POSTCARD

We'd like to hear your reaction.
Did you make any discoveries?
Did we steer you wrong?

Let us know.

WEST BANK

The West Bank refers to the land west of the Jordan River which was administered by Jordan from 1948 until it was captured by Israel in the Six Day War of 1967. It is an area trapped in some form of transition: as of 1983 the status of the West Bank—that is, whether it would be granted political autonomy, returned to Jordan, or annexed by Israel—was still undecided. While many Israelis are determined to keep the West Bank under Israeli occupation, many residents of the West Bank refer to the area as Palestine, in the hope that one day it will be granted the status of an independent nation. With both sides equally adamant, the West Bank is likely to remain at the center of political and military controversy for years to come.

Despite these difficulties, the West Bank should not be written off by tourists. It is rich in biblical sites and in tradition. The ancient settlements of the West Bank, with their predominantly Muslim population, exude an exotic, Middle Eastern atmosphere, remaining far less westernized and modernized than Israel proper. Both the city dwellers and the peasants of the West Bank are, in general, considerably poorer and more tradition-bound than the Arabs in Israel. But with a little caution and a lot of common sense, you can get a feel for Palestinian culture and political views.

Before you travel in the West Bank area, inquire about security problems there, and remember that even if living conditions have improved since 1967, the West Bank Palestinians are unhappy about the prolonged occupation of their land. On the whole, anti-Israeli sentiment is quite strong and many Palestinians feel humiliated and outraged by the security precautions taken by the Israeli government. How you will be received by West Bank residents as a tourist is mainly up to you. If you act in a friendly outgoing manner, you will find that most of the Arabs in the area are amiable and hospitable hosts. However, if your manner strikes them as belligerent or in any way hostile, whether intended or not, then you will be in for a number of unpleasant experiences, not the least of which is having little children hurl stones at you. The advantage of knowing a few Arabic phrases before you visit the West Bank cannot be overemphasized. To the local resident, it demonstrates a sensitivity and curiosity for Arab culture which will go a long way in eliminating any hostility caused by the Israeli occupation. Pick up a copy of Berlitz' *Arabic for Travellers* and keep it in plain sight. Many Palestinians speak English and will be delighted to help you learn their language. If you know any Hebrew, pretend you don't. Palestinians will ask you again and again if you speak Hebrew, but it is safer not to use the language of their enemies, even if it appears to be the only way to communicate. Remember to use the Arabic name for Jerusalem: *al Khudz,* meaning "the Holy." Avoid the Hebrew *Yerushalayim*.

We try to offer some indication of what kind of attitudes you can expect to encounter in the various towns and villages of the West Bank. Naturally, some of our comments may be outdated by recent political developments. Remember that the very strong Israeli military presence on the West Bank has a purpose. Unannounced curfews can be imposed on a Palestinian town at a moment's notice, and they must be obeyed. Often the best way to tour the West Bank is by taking daytrips from Jerusalem. Hebron should only be visited on a daytrip, but Bethlehem, Jericho, and Ramallah are relatively safe.

If you remain cautious and use a little common sense, you can even stay in Nablus overnight. In some towns, however, the military authorities require that visitors leave before nightfall.

Arab buses, though not as dependable or comfortable as Egged buses, are far more colorful and offer an excellent opportunity to meet and talk with West Bank residents. Since Arabs generally avoid Egged buses and Israeli soldiers never ride on Arab buses, your mere presence on an Arab bus will usually be interpreted as a gesture of friendship and sincerity. The only major drawback is that while most Egged buses are air-conditioned, most Arab buses are not.

No matter who controls the area politically or militarily, the West Bank is predominantly Arab and Muslim. If you want to travel successfully in the West Bank, you must respect the customs and traditions of the local populace. Men should always wear long pants and a shirt; women should wear a long skirt, a light long-sleeved shirt, and a bra. In addition, women should avoid traveling alone on the West Bank.

As you might expect, Jewish holidays are not observed in the West Bank. Check the section on Muslim festivals in the Egypt chapter introduction for details on important Islamic holidays. **Ramadan** will begin in early June in 1984 and last for 28 days; it is strictly observed in many West Bank towns, so restaurants will be closed until sundown.

Hebron (El Khalil)

Already ancient at the time of the Patriarchs, Hebron is one of Israel's four holy cities (the others are Tiberias, Tzfat, and Jerusalem). Its so-called Cave of Machpelah (pronounced *Mearat HaMachpelah* in Hebrew) is the second most sacred site in Israel for Jews after the Western Wall in Jerusalem, and Muslims hold the site in reverence as well. With its brown stone houses, ancient monuments, and bustling market, Hebron is one of the most enchanting and exotic cities in the West Bank. Unfortunately, in modern times, Hebron has been plagued by Arab-Israeli tensions—it lies next to one of the most hotly-disputed Israeli settlements in the Occupied Territories. Next to Jerusalem, Hebron is probably the most intense microcosm of the Israeli experience—a priceless and hallowed antique tradition, with discord and bloodshed as the modern result.

At the present time, Hebron is predominantly an Arab town, and its inhabitants are unusual even in the West Bank for their fierce pride and traditionalism. In practical terms, this means that both Israelis and tourists encounter difficulties, for Hebron is a hotbed of resentment towards Israel—a situation not improved by the recent Jewish settlement nearby at Qiryat Arba—and some of the hostility occasionally spills over in local Arabs' treatment of tourists. Before visiting Hebron, inquire about the security situation—the tension has a way of flaring up for a short time and then receding.

History

In biblical times, Hebron was known as Qiryat Arba, "District of the Four." One legend maintains that the "Four" referred to the four giants who fell from heaven after a revolt against God. In the Book of Numbers, when Moses sent spies to Canaan to bring back a report on the conditions there, the scouts returned with wide-eyed reports of Hebron's giants. As proof, they brought bunches of grapes so large that a single cluster had to be carried by two men. Though you won't be able to verify the story about the giants, you can still check out the grapes: Hebron grapes have long been renowned throughout the Arab world and Israel for their size and juiciness.

Hebron is revered by Jews and Muslims alike for its Tombs of the Patriarchs or Cave of Machpelah. Abraham chose Hebron, the highest of the four holy cities (at an altitude of three thousand feet) as the site of his family cemetery. Beginning with his wife, Sarah (Genesis 23:17-19), all the subsequent patriarchs and matriarchs were buried in Hebron, except for Rachel, who died on the way to Bethlehem and had to be buried en route (the still observed Jewish custom of very quick burial was apparently already established). Some claim that Abraham chose the cave because he knew it to be the burial place of Adam and Eve, for there is a tradition that the Garden of Eden must be near Hebron. Consequently, many rabbis explain that Qiryat Arba refers not to four giants, but to the four married couples who are supposedly buried here: Abraham and Sarah, Isaac and Rebecca, Jacob and Leah, and—though it does seem rather far-fetched—Adam and Eve. Hebron is also mentioned in the Bible as the first site of King David's illustrious reign. He ruled here for seven and a half years before he moved to Jerusalem and made it the nation's capital.

After biblical times, Hebron followed the typical vicissitudes of cities in the Holy Land—conquest, successively, by the Romans, Arabs, Crusaders, the Arabs again, and finally the Mameluke Turks. The Mamelukes renamed Hebron Haram el Khalil, after Abraham, who is known to the Muslims as *Al Khalil er Rahman,* "the Friend of the Merciful." Accordingly, to this day the Arabic name for Hebron is El Khalil, which means "The Friend." Throughout the period of Muslim domination, the Jewish community was very small, and may have disappeared entirely for brief periods during the Middle Ages. The community was revived by an influx of Spanish Jews in the sixteenth century; they brought with them a craftsman's tradition of glass-blowing which has continued to be an important part of Hebron's commercial life to this day. Hebron's Jewish population remained small, however, until the nineteenth century, when many Hassidic and Russian Jews emigrated here.

In 1925, an entire yeshiva was moved from Russia to Hebron, and a Hadassah medical clinic was opened here. The local Arabs took offense, and in 1929 there were massive riots, in which virtually the entire Jewish community was killed or wounded. The survivors were evacuated by the British to Jerusalem. The extent of the British connivance in the whole incident remains unclear to this day. Many of the older citizens of Hebron will tell you that the British went out of their way during this period to stir up resentment and spark the still explosive tension between the Arabs and Jews in the area. After the 1929 massacre, several unsuccessful attempts were made by Jews to resettle in the holy city of the Patriarchs. It was not until after the 1967 war that a significant number of Jews returned to Hebron, settling in the new Jewish quarter, Qiryat Arba, to the northeast of town, and the nearby village of Gush Etzion (sometimes called Kfar Etzion) to the north.

Practical Information

For the past decade, Hebron has made international newspaper headlines at least a couple of times a year for some new outbreak of violence. Since the 1967 takeover, the city has been guarded around the clock by the Israeli Army. Soldiers stand watch along the streets, particularly in and around the Cave of Machpelah, to make sure that Jews can come and pay their respects without being molested by the local citizenry. The tension reached a high pitch during the summer of 1980 after an Arab attack on West Bank Israeli settlers returning from religious services left six dead and fourteen wounded. The Israeli government responded by deporting the Arab mayor of Hebron, Fahd Kawasme. Then a series of bloody clashes during the summer of 1983, sparked by the stabbing of a 19-year-old yeshiva student, left the embattled city more tense than ever, and the Israeli military imposed a curfew and prohibited all visitors from entering.

Understandably, some Israelis may advise you to avoid Hebron. But visiting Hebron isn't as dangerous as it's made out to be. First of all, the Arabs are, for the most part, careful to distinguish between Israelis and tourists, and generally welcome the latter as impartial observers and as good business. Furthermore, as one Arab shopkeeper put it: "If someone approaches you with a smile, you smile back; and if someone approaches you glaring stubbornly, you do the same." This is not to say that Gentiles alone will be welcome here, but only that Jewish visitors who wish to have an enjoyable time in Hebron should try not to antagonize the local Arabs; if you broadcast Zionist sentiments, you should know that you're asking for a confrontation. All tourists should try to be respectful of Muslim traditions. What may seem like perfectly natural behavior to you may be looked upon by some Arabs as a gesture of hostility, for they consider this their holy place, too.

One safety precaution you can take is to stick to the avenue patrolled by Israeli soldiers—if you do, generally no ill will befall you. All in all there is little reason to avoid Hebron, but it is recommended that you leave before sunset. In the Jewish community of Kfar Etzion, 22km north of Hebron, is a **Youth Hostel** (tel. 74 24 77), but individuals are discouraged from staying there, as the hostel caters to groups. The fee, too, is discouraging: $20 per person per night. By far the simplest way to see Hebron is by daytrip excursion from Jerusalem.

The best way to get to Hebron is by Arab bus #23 ($.75), leaving frequently from the main Arab bus station near Damascus Gate in Jerusalem. If you prefer the Egged buses, both Kfar Etzion and Hebron are serviced by bus #34, which leaves frequently from Gate #1 in the Jerusalem Egged Terminal. The only disadvantage is that the bus stops for a while in the uninteresting residential settlement of Qiryat Arba. Buses #440 and 443 go less frequently from Jerusalem to Hebron and Qiryat Arba, continuing to Beersheva. Bus service continues until sundown, so don't be intimidated by the Arab taxi drivers who tell you that you have already missed the last bus. One note of caution: if the situation should worsen in Hebron, bus service may be reduced.

Virtually all of the town's services are in the northwestern part of the city, on El Malik Feisal St., including the **bank, hospital** (tel. 97 61 26), **police station** (tel. 97 14 4) and **post office.** The **Arab bus station** is on Khalil er Rahman St.; the **Egged bus stop** is on the main square in front of the Tombs of the Patriarch. Occasionally, maps and brochures about Hebron are available at the IGTO on King George St. in Jerusalem.

Sights

The Hebron skyline is dominated by the massive compound standing above the caves, identified as the **Tombs of the Patriarchs, the Cave of Machpelah.** According to Genesis (49:30-31) Jacob asked to be buried in the cave, saying "There they buried Abraham and Sarah, his wife; there they buried Isaac and Rebecca, his wife; and there I buried Leah." The patch of land above the tombs has been bitterly contested throughout the course of history by Crusaders, Muslims, and Jews. Presently, it is the only religious shrine in Israel in which both Jews and Muslims worship together. The Israeli soldiers who are stationed around the site to enforce order lend an eerie tension to the hallowed precinct.

Like many structures in Israel, the colossal edifice that now stands over the Cave of Machpelah is a hodgepodge of different periods and styles; the net effect is, nonetheless, quite imposing. Both Jewish and Arab traditions attribute the original stonework of the building to King Solomon who, it is said, enlisted the help of demons to cut and move the large stones. Archeologists, for the most part, claim that the oldest surviving sections date from the times of King Herod. Many consider them to be the finest examples of Herodian architecture to be found in Israel. During succeeding centuries the building fell into disrepair, though a small synagogue was continually maintained inside the ruins. The Byzantine Christians built a chapel next door, and the Muslims added a mosque in the seventh century. In 1103, the Crusaders conquered Hebron, and, of course, promptly transformed the mosque into a church. The Crusaders lost Hebron in 1187, but regained the city again in 1192 under Richard the Lionhearted. Crusaders reputedly opened up the tomb in 1215 and discovered the remains of the Patriarchs, a feat which hasn't been attempted since. The Mamelukes, who followed the Crusaders as masters of Hebron, regarded the opening of the sacred tombs as a sacreligious act and prohibited non-Muslims from entering the shrine. That edict was enforced for the following six hundred years by the Arab citizens of Hebron. Until 1967, Jews were allowed to stand and pray, but were only permitted to ascend as far as the seventh step, which is supposed to be at the level of the holy grotto. After the war, the Israelis dug the steps away, thereby removing the symbol of their former second-class standing. On the south side of the building, however, you can still see the steps. If you look closely, you'll notice that at one point the wall has been blackened by smoke. This marks the spot of the infamous seventh step where certain Orthodox Jews still come to pray and burn candles.

The walls surrounding the tombs contain Herodian remains, as well as layers from succeeding generations. The massive stones were fitted together so neatly that no mortar was necessary. The two handsome square minarets date from Mameluke times; there were four originally. Many pilgrims who come to Hebron to pay their respects to the Patriarchs find themselves unable to locate the tombs because the structure that contains the shrine looks much more like an impregnable fortress than a house of worship. Enter the gate and walk into the courtyard, which lies over the cave itself. Male visitors should don one of the paper yarmulkahs available at the entrance at the top of the staircase—it is forbidden for men to enter the sanctuary without headcovering. A hallway leads to a chamber which has now been reconverted into a synagogue. On one side of it, behind the metal grating, are the richly decorated cenotaphs of Abraham and Sarah, and on the other, those of Jacob and Leah. A cenotaph is an empty tomb; the actual remains lie in the Cave of Machpelah below the building. Be sure to note the thirteenth-century stained-glass window near the cenotaphs of Jacob and Leah, and the *mihrab* on the southern wall (a *mihrab* is the niche found in every mosque, which faces Mecca and towards which all Muslims must face as they pray). Near the same wall is an ornate pulpit dating from 1091.

Isaac and Rebecca Hall to the south of the synagogue is the site of the **Great Mosque.** The hall is closed to non-Muslims during Ramadan. The mosque is square, in the style of Mameluke architecture, and finely decorated with inlaid wood and mosaic in the traditional Muslim style. The floor is covered with beautiful Persian rugs. Near Abraham and Sarah's chamber, in the long courtyard which serves as the women's mosque, is a small window inside of which is a stone with an imprint on it: according to legend, this is the imprint of Adam's foot. (Adam reputedly came here after his expulsion from Eden.) A small adjoining mosque contains a cenotaph dedicated to Joseph, honoring the Muslim tradition that claims that Joseph's tomb is also in Hebron. During religious services, it is strictly forbidden for non-Muslims to enter the main mosque: however, the adjoining worship halls can be passed through at any time—and Arabs are in no position to protest since the passageways are patrolled by Israeli soldiers.

The Tombs of the Patriarchs are open 7:30-11:30am (7:30-11am during Ramadan) in winter, until 5pm in summer, closed Fri. and Muslim holidays. Be sure to dress properly (no shorts or short-sleeved shirts).

Next to the walls of the Tombs is **Harat el Yahud,** the remains of the original Jewish quarter. A sixteenth-century Sephardic synagogue has been recently uncovered here and is now reconstructed, along with some of the surrounding ruins. Continuing west down the main avenue, Khalil er Rahman St., you will come to **Birkat es Sultan,** "the Pool of the Sultan." It is reputed to be the "Pool of Hebron" where David had the slayer of Saul's son, Ish-Bosheth, hanged.

Surrounding the Tombs of the Patriarchs is the large sprawling Hebron market, one of the largest and most interesting of the West Bank. Check with the Israeli soldiers before entering the market; it is usually safe for tourists. The basic structure of the main market is medieval (vaulted ceilings and all), but the artifacts sold are distinctly Middle Eastern. It would be foolish to buy any of the blown glass sold here—nothing is guaranteed to break as quickly as glassware in transit—but you will enjoy looking at the items displayed. Besides the glassware, the Hebron market is distinguished as a place where Arabs and Bedouins actually do business with each other, rather than just another tourist bazaar (though the salesmen will still overcharge tourists if they can).

Starting north of the market are the endless tunnels and arched passageways that run beneath the houses and ruins of this ancient city, forming a vast labyrinth of covered alleys. Though a delight to explore, the tunnels can be dangerous, and we strongly urge you to keep a watchful eye on anyone who seems to be following you.

At the western edge of Hebron, a little over a mile west of the Cave of Machpelah, you will find the **Oak of Abraham** ("Eshel Avraham" in Hebrew)—the purported site of biblical Mamre, where Abraham pitched his tent to welcome tired travelers, and was visited by the three angels who told him of the impending birth of Isaac. The oak belongs to the Russian Orthodox Church, which built a monastery around it in 1871. The tree is known in Arabic as "Ballut es Sebta," which means "the Oak of Rest," for the three angels, to whom the adjacent church is dedicated, supposedly rested a while in its shade. According to Christian tradition, the Holy Family also rested here on their way back from Egypt. Unfortunately for tradition, we know that the oak tree that stands now is no more than six hundred years old. Nevertheless, the tree was venerated as far back as the late Middle Ages, and a sliver from the Oak of Abraham was believed to safeguard the traveler from misfortune.

Another tradition contests the claim that the Moskobiya Monastery occupies the site of biblical Mamre, and argues instead that the oaks of Abraham referred to in Genesis actually stood at **Bet Ilanim,** to the north of Hebron, on Keizun er Rama St. Excavations of this site have uncovered enormous walls, originally erected by Herod and rebuilt by Emperor Hadrian in 135 A.D., as well as traces of Roman temples and a fourth-century Christian chapel.

In addition to the cultural interest of this Orthodox Muslim city, the streets of Hebron are worth exploring for their wealth of hidden monuments from past ages. An excellent example of Mameluke architecture not to be missed is the thirteenth-century minaret of the **Ali Baka Mosque** on El Ai Yubi St. Most of the mosque is presently under reconstruction, but that does not keep the Muslims from praying within its half-built walls. In the southwest part of Hebron are the ruins of a Crusader fort known to the Arabs as **Deir el Arbain.** The site is holy to both Jews and Muslims, for beneath the ruins are believed to lie the tombs of Ruth and her grandson Jesse, who was the father of King David. Next to it is an ancient Jewish cemetery, which features a monument dedicated to the victims of the 1929 riots (see above).

Two major Talmudic towns, **Eshtemoa** (now a Muslim village) and the ruins of **Susya,** lie 15km southeast of Hebron. Accessible by dirt road, both contain excavated remains of fifth-century synagogues. The one at Susya has been restored and features a fine mosaic floor.

Bethlehem

Bethlehem is sacred to Christians as the birthplace of Jesus Christ and to Jews as the site of Rachel's tomb. The town is a picturesque blend of old stone houses, bustling markets, and numerous churches and convents. Populated at present almost entirely by Arab Christians and other Christians from around the world, Bethlehem, like Nazareth, is distinctive in the West Bank and is reputed to be the safest of its cities.

History

The Hebrew name for Bethlehem means "House of Bread," and its Arabic translation is "House of Meat." Bethlehem is a town peculiarly rich in biblical resonances, if not in biblical sights. The first mention of Bethlehem is in Genesis 35:19-20, which notes that "Rachel died, and was buried on the way to 'Ephrat'; that is, Bethlehem." Bethlehem next figures in the Book of Ruth, as the home of Boaz, the wealthy farmer Ruth (a Moabite convert to Judaism) married, and with whom she had Obed, the father of Jesse. The seventh son of Jesse was David, the greatest of the biblical kings. He was tending sheep in his hometown of Bethlehem when he was called on by the prophet Samuel to replace Saul as the King of Israel.

It was the birth of Jesus one thousand years later that transformed Bethlehem into a target for religious pilgrimages from around the world. Jesus probably came from Nazareth, and not Bethlehem, but since the prophet Micah had predicted that "out of Bethlehem shall he come forth with Me that is to be ruler in Israel, whose goings forth have been from old, from everlasting," the gospels took pains to assert that Jesus, like David, hailed from Bethlehem. This version of the Nativity story is crystallized in Luke 2:1-7, which states that Joseph and Mary, who was "great with child," arrived in Bethlehem and were forced to spend the night in the manger of a stable "because there was no room for them in the inn." On Christmas Eve, a solemn procession goes from Jerusalem to the Church of Nativity in Bethlehem to commemorate the birth of Jesus. If you visit Israel in the winter, you'll have three chances to catch the colorful parade, since the Catholic and Protestant churches celebrate Christmas Eve on December 24, the Greek Orthodox church on January 6, and the Armenian church on January 18.

Throughout most of its history, Bethlehem has been dominated by powers hostile to Christianity, and in the past pilgrims were by no means as welcome as they are today. In 135 C.E., Emperor Hadrian erected a pagan temple in Bethlehem, and deliberately desecrated the holy grotto which early Christians revered as the site of Jesus' birth. The Emperor Constantine's mother Helena rectified matters somewhat by building a church over the spot. It was here, at the end of the fourth century, that St. Jerome wrote his great translation of the Hebrew Bible into Latin. Known as the "Vulgate," it became the standard Bible throughout the Middle Ages; it was the first book ever printed, and it remains to this day the accepted translation of the Bible into Latin for the Catholic Church.

Practical Information

Bethlehem relies heavily on nearby Jerusalem for much of its public services. Most of what you'll need in Bethlehem is located on or near Manger Square, across from the Basilica of the Nativity. The area enclosed by Najajreh and Star Sts., both of which begin at Manger Square, comprises most of the town's shopping district, including the town's open-air market.

Israel Government Tourist Office (IGTO): (tel. 74 25 91) on Manger Sq. Almost useless, but they distribute an excellent free map of the town (also available at the Jerusalem tourist office). Open Mon.-Fri. 8am-5pm (4pm in winter), Sat. 8am-1pm, closed Sun.

Post Office: Manger Sq., down the stairs in front of the tourist office. Uncrowded and efficient. Open Mon.-Sat. 8am-5pm, closed Sun.

Sheruts: all originate at Manger Sq. They stop running at about 6pm. Fare to Jerusalem is $.50.

Police Station: (tel. 74 15 81) on Manger Sq.

To get to Bethlehem, take Arab bus #22 ($.30) from the main Arab bus station in Jerusalem. The **bus station** in Bethlehem is around the corner from Manger Sq. on Manger St. The last bus back to Jerusalem is at 6pm.

Accommodations and Food

Ever since Mary and Joseph finally found their famous accommodations in town, Bethlehem has been providing overnight bedding for its out-of-town guests. Though today the city has more than mangers to offer the traveler, the rates are a lot steeper. The town has only five inexpensive beds in the **Franciscan Convent Pension** (tel. 74 24 41) on Milk Grotto St. just beyond the Milk Grotto Church. $5 per person in a dorm room, $6 with sheets, $7 including breakfast. The friendly, French-speaking nuns also have singles for $12 and doubles for $22. All rooms are extremely clean and well-kept. The cheapest hotel in town is the **Palace Hotel** (tel. 74 27 98) in front of the Basilica of the Nativity, where singles go for $12, doubles for $20, and triples for $25. **Handal's Hotel** (tel. 74 24 94) on Midan St. is cleaner, with singles for $15, doubles $25. The closest youth hostels are at Kfar Etzion ($20 per person; see the Hebron section), and for Jews, at **Har Gilo** near Beit Jala. The closest campground (tel. 71 57 12) is at **Ramat Rachel,** 4km from Bethlehem on the road to Jerusalem ($3.50 per person per night, $8 per person in bungalows).

The **Al-Amal Restaurant** on Najajreh St. just off Manger Square offers inexpensive fare. In both the **St. George Restaurant** on Manger Square and the **Vienna Restaurant** on Milk Grotto St. entrees go for $6-7.

Sights

Bethlehem's main attraction is the massive **Basilica of the Nativity,** on Manger Square. It is one of Christianity's three most sacred churches in the Holy Land, and is the oldest church in the world still in use. The first basilica was erected over the site of Jesus' birth in 326 by Constantine the Great, under the supervision of his mother Helena, but this was damaged by the Samaritans in 529. The structure was restored and enlarged by the Emperor Justinian. During the Persian invasion in 614 A.D. practically every Christian shrine in the Holy Land was demolished with the flagrant exception of the Basilica of the Nativity. It was reputedly spared because it contained a magnificent mosaic of the three wise men of the East who were depicted in flowing robes characteristic of Persian magi. After undergoing a number of alterations, the basilica was the site of Baldwin's coronation as the first King of the Crusades in 1100. The church was improved extensively by the Crusaders, but after the Crusaders' defeat at the hands of Muslims, Christian priests were allowed to serve in the Basilica of the Nativity only by permission of the Sultan. The basilica managed to escape the wholesale destruction of churches in the Holy Land by the Mameluke Turks, but by the fifteenth century it had become so decrepit that it was described as being like a "barn without hay." In addition to suffering from neglect by the Muslim rules, the basilica was beset by bloodshed among the Catholic, Greek, and Armenian Christians, all of whom sought control of the shrine. Only in the 1840s was the church restored to its former dignity, but the carving up of the edifice among different Christian sects continued, as the Franciscans and Anglicans joined the fray to lay hold of their own little enclaves.

If only the outcome of this rich history were a beautiful church. Unfortunately, the Basilica of the Nativity, though colossal and awe-inspiring, is by no means a graceful or elegant structure. It is far less moving, for instance, than its counterpart, the Church of the Holy Sepulchre in Jerusalem. Contributing to the awkward appearance of the facade are the main entrance and windows, which were blocked up during medieval times as a safety precaution. To enter the basilica, you will have to bend over and step through the narrow, appropriately-named Door of Humility—a reminder of the days when the Christians had to prevent the Muslims from entering the holy place on horseback. Orthodox Jews refuse to enter through this doorway, since it would mean bowing their heads in a "heathen" shrine.

The high point of the basilica's interior are the beautiful mosaic floors from Constantine's original church. The mosaics lie beneath the level of the marble Crusader floor, and are concealed by wooden trap doors which you should feel free to lift up. The four imposing rows of reddish limestone Corinthian columns date from Justinian's reconstruction, as do the fragments of mosaic scenes from the New Testament along the walls. The wooden ceiling of English oak was a gift of King Edward IV, while the handsome icons that adorn the altar were presented in 1764 by the Russian imperial family. (The basilica and adjoining sights are open during daylight hours.)

To get to the **Grotto of the Nativity**—the original site of the manger where Jesus was born—take one of the staircases on either side of the High Altar in the Nave on the main floor of the basilica, and follow it down to an underground sanctuary beneath the church. As you enter the grotto, you'll notice that the columns on either side of the doorway have served as the marble canvases for a unique form of graffiti—dozens of crosses have been etched into the stones over the centuries by pious pilgrims. A star bearing the Latin inscription *"Hic De Virgine Maria Jesus Christus Natus Est"* ("here Jesus Christ was born of the Virgin Mary") marks the spot where Jesus was born. The star itself has had an eventful history: first installed by the Catholics in 1717, it was removed by the Greeks in 1847, and restored by the Turkish government in 1853. The quarrel over the star supposedly helped fuel the rivalries which were to explode in the Crimean War. Don't stand in front of the star and block access to it—many pilgrims come to Bethlehem solely in order to kneel down and touch their lips to the sacred spot.

Adjoining the Basilica of the Nativity and accessible via a doorway at the top of the stairs leading from the Grotto is **St. Catherine's Church,** built by the Franciscans in 1881. Beautiful, light, and airy, St. Catherine's is a welcome change from the grim interior of the Basilica of the Nativity. Along the walls are superbly detailed wood carvings of the fourteen Stations of the Cross. St. Catherine's is primarily famous as the site from which midnight mass is annually broadcast to a worldwide audience on Christmas Eve.

A staircase on the right side of St. Catherine's leads down to the **Tomb of St. Jerome.** His actual remains are no longer here, since they were removed to the Church of Santa Maria Maggiore in Rome. The first room you enter is the **Chapel of St. Joseph,** commemorating the humble carpenter's vision of an angel who advised him to flee with his family to Egypt to avoid Herod's wrath. On a slightly higher level is the **Chapel of the Innocents,** dedicated to the victims of King Herod's drastic precautionary measure to thwart the prophecy that he would be overthrown by a newly-born Messiah. The memorial was inspired by Matthew 2:6—"And Herod slew all the children that were in Bethlehem, and in all the coast thereof, from two years old and under." The burial cave of the slaughtered children is under the altar and can be seen through a grill. To the right of the grotto entrance are rooms containing the tombs of St. Jerome, St. Paula, and St. Paula's daughter, Eustochia. Walk through this area to get to the cell where Jerome actually wrote the Vulgate as well as his translation of the *Onomasticon,* a Greek list of place names in the Holy Land.

The main daily festivity in Bethlehem is the solemn procession conducted by the Franciscan Fathers to the basilica and the underground chapels. Also adjoining the basilica and accessible by different staircases from the nave are an Armenian monastery, a Greek convent, and the Anglican Chapel of St. George, built in the thirteenth century. The basilica complex is open 6am-7pm. Proper dress is required: men must wear long trousers, women long skirts and no short sleeves.

Five minutes from the Basilica of the Nativity down Milk Grotto St. is the amusingly chintzy **Milk Grotto Church,** the cellar of which is supposed to be the cave where the Holy Family hid while fleeing from Herod into Egypt. The cave (and church) takes its name from the milky white color of the rocks. According to one legend, while Mary was nursing the infant Jesus some milk fell on the nearby rocks, turning them forever white. Open daily 8-11:45am and 2-5pm.

Around the corner from the Basilica of the Nativity, just before the Chapel of the Milk Grotto, is a Coptic Church; you will probably be beckoned into it by the officiating priest, who will heave an enormous plastic bag filled with quarters on the holy altar, undo the clasp, finger through the coins, and, with eyes gleaming, ask you for some "Change: dollar bills, fives, tens maybe?" but a few coins is all that is required and even that will be appreciated. As perhaps you might have guessed, Bethlehem is still quite a handsome city, and undoubtedly a place of great sanctity, but it has become tragically commercial. For instance, vendors sell packets of white powder supposedly made from the chalky stone of the Milk Grotto sanctuary—it is guaranteed to stimulate the flow of a mother's milk when nursing her child.

From the Basilica of the Nativity it's a twenty-minute walk along Manger St. to Rachel's Tomb. About halfway between the two sights is the **Well of David,** on the left side of the road as you head toward Rachel's Tomb, at the top of a few stairs. According to tradition, this is the well mentioned in Samuel 23, which was under the control of the Philistines during one of David's wars against them. After David complained of his thirst, three "mighty men" broke through the ranks of the Philistines and drew water for their king "out of the well of Bethlehem that was by the gate." Upon receiving the gift, David refused to drink from it, and offered it as a sacrifice to God. The three impressive cisterns which constitute the well are usually open 7am-noon and 2-7pm.

The **Tomb of Rachel** ranks as one of Judaism's most sacred sites. (Rachel is the only one of the Matriarchs and Patriarchs not to be buried in Hebron.) Throughout history Jews have come to worship at this spot, and throughout history synagogues have been built and destroyed over the site of the tomb. Apparently, the shrine was respected for a period during Crusader times, when, according to one legend, Christian monks discovered that the stones they hauled from the holy tomb across town to rebuild the Basilica of the Nativity would always reappear the following morning at their original site. The present structure, with its simple white dome, surrounded by a perpetual crowd of weeping Yemenite women, was built by the British Jewish philanthropist Moses Montefiore in 1860. Though Rachel's role in the biblical narrative is relatively undistinguished—she was Jacob's second wife and gave birth to his favorite and last sons Joseph and Benjamin—she later became a symbol of maternal devotion and empathetic suffering. She died while giving birth to Benjamin, and therefore had to be buried in Bethlehem rather than in the Cave of Machpelah along with the rest of the Matriarchs and Patriarchs. Despite Rachel's own misfortune, the tomb is particularly revered as the place to pray for a child or safe childbirth, and hence is a popular destination for female pilgrims. The tomb is often mobbed with Orthodox Jews, many of whom are far more interesting than the shrine itself, which will probably prove somewhat disappointing if you come expecting to see a grandiose structure. Men should be sure to don one of the readily available paper yarmulkahs as they pass through the entrance guarded by armed soldiers. The left side of the tomb is reserved for women and the right side for men. If you wish to watch the faithful at prayer or to pray yourself, take care to stand at the proper place. The tomb is open Sun.-Thurs. 8am-5pm, Fri. 8am-1pm, closed Sat., and is on the northern edge of town on the road to Jerusalem, at the intersection of Manger St. and Hebron Road. The bus stop for the Jerusalem/Bethlehem/ Hebron bus is directly across the street.

At the eastern edge of Bethlehem is the Arab village of **Beit Sahur,** beyond which is the **Field of Ruth,** believed to be the place where the biblical story told in the Book of Ruth occurred. But since Beit Sahur means "the House of the Shepherds" in Hebrew, another ancient tradition holds that this is the **Shepherd's Field,** where shepherds tending their flocks were greeted by an angel declaring the birth of Jesus (Luke 2:9-11). The small chapel erected on the field in 1954 has become an extremely popular destination for pilgrims. To get to Shepherd's Field, take bus #47 from the stop next to the police station in Manger Square, get off at Beit Sahur, and walk twenty minutes to the site (open 8-11:30am and 2-5:30pm). Otherwise, walk the 4km from Bethlehem. Signs will direct you—just follow Shepherd's St. starting in Manger Square in front of the Basilica of the Nativity.

The Bethlehem **market** makes little attempt to cater to tourists, but it's colorful and interesting. The Arab women wear beautifully embroidered traditional garb and the men wear kaffiyehs; business is carried on under tattered burlap and nylon to keep out the sun. Filled with the sounds of vendors hawking their wares, the market lends a Middle Eastern flavor to this otherwise primarily Christian town. The market is located up the stairs from Paul VI St., across from the Syrian Church. One block further along Paul VI St. towards Jerusalem is the fanciful **Lutheran Evangelical Church,** across from the imposing buildings of the Salesian Convent. One block down Paul VI from the market, towards the Basilica of the Nativity, is the **Bethlehem Museum,** featuring exhibits of Arab crafts and traditional costumes.

Four kilometers south of Bethlehem, just off the road to Hebron, are three large **reservoirs,** which archeologists believe were constructed several

Solomon's Pools

thousand years ago. The pools were clearly a great technological feat for their times; local tradition holds that they were the work of King Solomon. Excavations indicate that the reservoirs probably even predate Solomon. They were used by both the Romans and the Turks to supply water for Bethlehem and Jerusalem.

Near Bethlehem

One of the most impressive and least known of the archeological sites on the West Bank is **Herodion** (Har Hordus), the ruins of a magnificent palace set on top of a spectacular volcano-like peak. King Herod, who spent his life in perpetual fear of assassination, ordered the construction of the circular fortress on this sawed-off mountaintop so that he would have an impregnable hiding place. According to Herod's instructions, after his death Roman soldiers carried his body on a long procession from Jericho to the top of Herodion where the tyrant was buried. During the Jewish War from 66-70 C.E., Herodion and Herod's other citadel, Masada, were occupied by Jewish rebels. Herodion was one of the last rebel outposts to fall to the Romans; it is believed that at the last moment, the rebels at Herodion, like those at Masada, took their own lives.

Excavations began at Herodion in 1962, and are still in progress. Archeologists have already uncovered a great deal of what must have been one of Herod's greatest architectural achievements: a massive circular double wall, guarded by four evenly spaced watch towers and containing a splendid palace and bath house. Herod's tomb is believed to be located on the hilltop, but as yet has not been discovered. The view from the top is breathtaking—Jerusalem to the north, Bethlehem to the west, the Dead Sea barely visible to the east, and the desolate Judean desert stretching endlessly to the south.

The turnoff for Herodion is well-marked and is near the northern entrance to Bethlehem (ignore the orange sign several kilometers before Bethlehem which reads "Herodion 15km"). Herodion is about 11km from Bethlehem, and is not accessible by public transportation. Hitching is good, however. If you can gather six or seven people, take a sherut; round trip from Bethlehem should be about $12. The site is open Sat.-Thurs. 8am-5pm, Fri. 8am-4pm; admission $1.30, $.65 for students.

Even more remarkable and isolated than Herodion is the **Mar Saba Monastery.** Carved into the walls of a remote canyon, the monastery is precariously perched above the Qidron River. In 478 C.E., St. Sabas chose one of the numerous caves that dot the cliffs overlooking the Qidron River as a likely spot to embark on a solitary ascetic style of life. In time, however, he began to accumulate disciples with whom he erected a monastery. Sacked by the Muslims in the seventh century and the Bedouins in the last century, the monastery has been extensively restored by the Russian Orthodox church. Only fifteen monks now live in the extensive monastery complex, which at one time housed five thousand monks. The bones of St. Sabas are on display in the main church. The Saint's remains were taken from his tomb (outside in the courtyard) during the Crusader period and relocated to Venice; they finally made it back to the monastery in 1965. Women are strictly forbidden to enter, and must view the chapels and buildings from the safe distance of a tower near the monastery. Men must wear long pants to be admitted. To enter the monastery, pull the chain on the large blue door. Once inside, you'll be given a tour in English by one of the monks. The monks occasionally ignore the doorbell on Sundays and late in the afternoon, so try to arrive early on a weekday. There is no entrance fee, but it's customary to make a donation.

To get to the monastery, take Arab bus #60 from Bethlehem to the end of the paved road at Abudiye. From there, it's a 5km walk along the dirt road to Mar Saba. Sherut fare from Bethlehem direct to Mar Saba is $15-$20 round trip.

The road to Mar Saba passes by the **Monastery of St. Theodosius,** built over a sacred cave which is reputed to be both the hangout of the great fifth-century saint and the resting place of the Three Wise Men on their way to Bethlehem.

Jericho

No doubt you've heard about how Jericho's walls came tumbling down long ago. Most of the walls no longer exist, but you can still visit the ancient city and its modern counterpart, a cool shady oasis town 15km north of the Dead Sea. Set in one of the hottest spots in the world, the Jordan Plain, Jericho provides welcome relief from the relentless heat and incessant sun of the Judean desert. Among its many distinctions, Jericho is not only the lowest city in the world (250m below sea level), but claims to be the oldest as well—possibly seven thousand years old. If you have the stamina to walk or bike in the heat or the financial means for a taxi, the archeological sites to the north of the modern town are well worth a visit.

The ancient city of Jericho is well known throughout much of the western world, mainly because of the account of its capture by the Israelites in the Book of Joshua (chapters 2-6). Briefly, two Israelite spies sent into Jericho by Joshua were concealed in the house of a harlot named Rahab. In exchange for her kindness, they promised her that the house of her family would not be destroyed if it was marked by a scarlet cord. Meanwhile, Joshua ordered his army to march around the city for seven days. On the seventh day, the tribes of Israel blew on their trumpets and attacked and destroyed the city walls. The entire city was sacked, with the exception of the single house with a scarlet cord dangling from its window.

As early as 63 B.C.E., Jericho became a district capital of the Roman state of Judea. The lush oasis town was presented as a gift by Marc Antony to Queen Cleopatra of Egypt. Jesus also spent some time here, according to the Book of Matthew (20:29-31). In the seventh century, the city fell into Persian hands, and was successively conquered by Arabs, Crusaders, and Turks, until it became part of the Occupied Territories in 1967.

The palm trees and lush greenery of Jericho form an anomalous spectacle in the dry, dazzling, white Judean landscape, looking very much like your prototypical desert mirage. The present town of seven thousand Arabs is actually a couple of kilometers south of the center of the ancient city, and is only of interest to tourists for its small but interesting market and the bus stop. Probably due to the Israeli military base next to the city, Jericho is one of the safest places to visit in the West Bank.

Most of the town's services are on Amman St. in the center of town, including the **police station** (tel. 25 21). The **bus station** is farther away on Ein es Sultan St. The best way to get around town and to the nearby sights is by bicycle, if you can bear the heat. Rickety bikes can be rented for $1 per hour from one of the three shops on Muscobeya St. To get to Jericho take Egged bus #961 or #963 from the Egged terminal in Jerusalem. Jericho can also be reached by Arab bus #28 ($.60), which leaves from the main Arab bus station in Jerusalem and unloads you in the center of town. The Arab buses stop running at 4pm, but sheruts ($1.40) continue until about 6pm. **Hisham's Palace**

Hotel on Ein es Sultan St. (tel. 24 14) rents rooms for $4 per person. The place is very old and almost always empty, so insist on a good room.

Sights

The extensive ruins of **Hisham's Palace,** a splendid example of early Islamic architecture, are Jericho's most outstanding attraction. Known as Khirbet et Mafjir in Arabic, the palace was built as a winter residence for Caliph Hisham between 724 and 743 C.E., in order to provide a retreat from the relatively cool winters of Damascus. Only four years after its completion, the palace was levelled by a severe earthquake and was never rebuilt or reoccupied. An impressive aqueduct, which can still be seen today, conducted water to the palace from nearby springs at Ein Duq. Among the most famous and handsome of the numerous decorative features is a large ornamental window in the palace's central court—it consists of a large piece of stone carved into an elaborate six-pointed star and embedded within a circular casing.

The **Bath Hall** of the palace contains Jericho's finest gem: a magnificent mosaic floor, entitled the "Tree of Life," and depicting a brightly-colored orange tree under which are three graceful gazelles, one of whom is being attacked by a lion. The floor is in superb condition, and is considered by many to be one of the most beautiful mosaics in the Middle East. It is in a small building at the far left corner of the Bath Hall known as the Guest Room. Several sections of the Bath Hall floor have been uncovered, revealing a number of superb mosaics with Islamic geometrical designs. Also beautiful is the gypsum-laced stonework in the Bath Hall and other parts of the palace. Most of the other impressive finds from the palace are now on display at the Rockefeller Museum in Jerusalem. Open daily 8am-5pm in summer, 8am-4pm in winter, closes one hour earlier on Fri.; admission $1.30, $.65 for students.

Next to the palace is **Amawi Park** with a swimming pool—admission is $1, but, in the Arab tradition, only men are allowed. Hisham's Palace is about 3km north of Jericho; follow the signs to Jiflik Rd. along Qasr Hisham St., leading north out of Jericho. If you are coming from ancient Jericho, turn left as you leave the site and walk or ride along the road that runs straight through the refugee camp; it is about 2km. This route to the palace will take you past the remains of a fifth-century **synagogue,** which, though historically insignificant, houses a well-preserved mosaic floor decorated with Hebrew lettering and, in the middle, a large menorah. Watch carefully for the small, tattered sign on the right side of the road, and take the right fork as you approach the building. The attendant may be inside drinking tea when you arrive; ask anyone you see to summon him to let you in. The site is open every day 7am-6pm; admission free.

The seven thousand-year-old ruins of **Tel es Sultan** to the north of the modern city form the basis of Jericho's claim to being the oldest fortified village in the world. Some of the finds from the excavated city date from the early Neolithic period, leading archeologists to suspect that Jericho might even have been inhabited as early as 10,000 years ago. Excavations at Jericho (pronounced *Yeriho* in Hebrew) seem roughly to confirm the biblical account of the Israelites' return to the Holy Land around the fourteenth to twelfth centuries B.C.E. The site is open every day 7am-6pm in summer, 8am-5pm in winter; admission free.

From the top of the archeological site you can see a vast sea of mostly abandoned mud huts—this was one of the largest refugee camps in the West Bank, built with the assistance of the United Nations. Most of the refugees fled across the river to Jordan during the Six Day War of 1967.

Across the street is **Elisha's Spring,** known to the Arabs as Ein es Sultan, which means "the Sultan's Fountain." Jewish tradition holds that this is the fountain referred to in the Bible (II Kings 2:19-22), which the people of Jericho called upon the prophet to purify. The prophet supposedly tossed some salt into the water ". . . and said, thus saith the Lord, I have healed these waters. There shall not be from thence any more death or barren land." Apparently, Elisha knew what he was doing, since the water is still quite drinkable. Ignore the outdated sign that says: "No admittance. United Nations Property." To reach the fountain and the archeological site, follow Ein es Sultan St. to the northwest out of town. Signs clearly mark the way to the site.

As you walk another kilometer past ancient Jericho you will see an imposing Greek Orthodox monastery, built in 1895, resting precariously on the edge of a cliff. The mountainside on which the monastery is perched is believed to be the famed Mount of Temptation mentioned in the Bible. The Emperor Constantine, at the request of his mother Queen Helena, erected the first monastery on the site only 340 years after the death of Christ. The complex of buildings making up the monastery is erected in front of a grotto, the spot where Jesus fasted for forty days and forty nights after being baptized in the Jordan River by John the Baptist. Six wizened old Greek monks live in the monastery now; most of its rooms stand empty. One of them will point out the rock where Christ was supposedly tempted by the devil and served by angels. An inscription in ancient Greek over the spot describes the momentous event. The mountain itself came to have the name **Qarantal** after the Greek word for forty, "quarantena." The summit of the mountain also serves as a pedestal for the Maccabean **Castle of Dok,** beside which are the remains of a fourth-century Christian chapel. The monastery is open Mon.-Sat. 7am-3pm and 4-5pm in summer, 7am-2pm and 3-4pm in winter. However, the church containing the rock where Jesus was tempted is often closed by about 11am. Access to the summit of the hill and its ruins is officially blocked, but if you befriend the Arab attendant, he may open the door for you. To reach Qarantal and Na'aron (see below), take the turn-off to the left just before the site of ancient Jericho.

Another kilometer or so down the road from Qarantal, next to the natural springs of Ein Duq (or Duyuk), are the remains of an ancient Jewish settlement and a fifth-century synagogue known as **Na'aron,** which contains an elaborate mosaic floor. A part of the mosaic floor depicting Daniel in the company of lions was destroyed by fanatical Jews who looked on any form of pictorial representation as idol worship; several other sections of the floor seem to have suffered a similar fate. To visit the site, ask for the key in the restaurant at Casino Al-Amara in Ein Duq.

Near Jericho

About 10km east of Jericho is **El Maghtes,** the spot on the Jordan where John the Baptist is believed to have baptized Christ, thus making the river forever sacred to Christians throughout the world. A nineteenth-century Greek Orthodox monastery marks the spot where Christians come to immerse themselves. The site was under military supervision during the summer of 1983; it will probably remain off-limits to all civilians.

Although the Jordan is Israel's longest river (that isn't saying much), most visitors are disappointed by how gentle and narrow it is. Since the area along the West Bank of the Jordan came under Israeli military administration in 1967, the peaceful river has demarcated the border between the state of Israel and the Hashemite Kingdom of Jordan. The **Allenby Bridge** (called by the

Jordanians The King Hussein Bridge) is the only place from which you can cross the river and enter Jordan (see Jordan introduction for details). You can reach the bridge by the main Jerusalem-Jericho road. Palestinian women and older Palestinian men who live on the West Bank can pass back and forth freely, since Jordan still looks upon the West Bank area as part of Jordan. For young men, it is more difficult—they must secure permission from the Israeli military to leave the Occupied Territories for Jordan, and the length of their visit must be clearly spelled out beforehand (usually at least six months).

Extending from the Judean Hills to the Jordan Plain is a canyon rich in springs and vegetation. You can walk along **Wadi Qilt** river, which winds through the canyon between Jerusalem and Jericho; the 35km trek features monasteries, ancient ruins, hermits' caves, and lush oases with small waterfalls and refreshing pools, all set in a spectacular narrow gorge. Those who don't feel up to hiking all of Wadi Qilt should consider visiting the archeological site at the mouth of the river, 2km southwest of Jericho. Known to Arabs as **Tel Abu Alayiq,** the site's Hasmonean, Herodian, and Roman ruins span both banks of Wadi Qilt. Particularly impressive is the first-century B.C.E. winter palace of King Herod.

The Road from Jericho

The road from Jerusalem to Jericho cuts through the harsh desert landscape of the wilderness of Judah. A visit to Jericho is a worthwhile affair simply for the striking scenery en route. On both sides of the road are Bedouin camps with their large canopies, clusters of goats and children playing nearby, and occasionally even a camel. The road has deep religious significance. About 8km before you reach Jericho, a short distance from the road, stands the **Mosque of Nabi Musa** in the middle of the desert. This spot is revered throughout the Muslim world as the grave of the prophet Moses, and an enormous stone cenotaph marks what is reputed to be his tomb. Jews do not worship the site because of the biblical passage (Deuteronomy 34:1-6) which relates that Moses died and was buried on Mt. Nevo, some 30km away. But Islamic tradition holds that Allah carried the bones of the prophet to this spot, so that the faithful could come and pay their respects. And that is exactly what they do—once a year a large procession departs from Lion's Gate in Jerusalem for Nabi Musa. It turns out that this celebration coincides with Easter, when the Christians make a procession along the same route to El Maghtes on the Jordan River. As a result, there have been occasional conflicts and even some tragic outbursts of violence. The mosque containing the prophet's tomb is only open during Muslim prayer times—at noon, 3:30pm, 7pm, and 8:30pm, and all day Friday. During the month of April, as many as half a million pilgrims from all over the Islamic world make their way to Nabi Musa; throughout this period, only Muslims are admitted. A few kilometers before Nabi Musa is the small industrial center of **Ma'ale Adummin,** next to which are the ruins of a Crusader castle. Christians hold that the police station here occupies what was originally the site of the Inn of the Good Samaritan.

Ramallah

Ramallah has fallen victim to the tensions that pervade this region. Because of the many Palestinians refugees from Jaffa, Haifa, Ramla, and other towns that have settled in the area, Ramallah has become another hotbed of anti-Israeli sentiment. The Arabs in Ramallah are not in the least ambivalent in their attitude towards the Israeli government; they resent Israeli occupation of their city, in particular the presence of Israeli troops. The antagonism between Israelis and Palestinians was intensified in the city during 1980 when the mayor of Ramallah had his legs blown off by a bomb. Those responsible have yet to be identified.

If you are interested in the political problems of the West Bank, Ramallah is the place to get a detailed, if highly emotional, presentation of the Palestinian side of the story. The Palestinians are generally quite open and friendly to tourists, whom they generally consider neutral observers of the political situation. Occasionally, they will apply the following litmus test—they ask you "what country is this?" and you reply either "Israel" (wrong answer) or "Palestine" (right answer). No matter what your actual political leanings, Ramallah is definitely not the place to express any pro-Israeli sentiments.

On the journey to Ramallah, you will pass a number of interesting sites which tell much about the current political situation on the West Bank. The first and possibly biggest controversy surrounds the East Jerusalem office of the Israeli government. Indeed, Menachem Begin and the Likud Bloc's official annexation of East Jerusalem in 1980 was seen as an unnecessarily provocative move by many foreign observers and as an insult to the Jordanians and the rest of the Arab world. A few kilometers north of Jerusalem is **Shofat,** the largest refugee camp in Israel, housing over 20,000 displaced Palestinians. Many of the homes are quite luxurious—they were abandoned by wealthy Palestinians who fled to Jordan after the 1967 war. The region just south of Ramallah was the summer resort of many powerful Jordanians, including King Hussein—ask someone to point out his villa halfway between Jerusalem and Ramallah. It is now the headquarters for one of the Israeli army divisions occupying the West Bank.

As you approach Ramallah, you pass through an archway that says "Welcome to El Bireh," which never fails to confuse visitors. El Bireh (or Bira) is Ramallah's junior twin, located directly to the south. Ramallah itself has very little of interest for the tourist; the main reason to come to this bustling city is to see the colorful market, next to the bus station, and to observe life as the Arabs live it. Ramallah is reputed to be the richest and most beautiful town on the West Bank, and its lovely gardens and modern residences, if not as picturesque as the houses of Hebron or Bethlehem, certainly indicate a high standard of living. Having lost most of their Arab clientele since coming under Israeli military administration in 1967, the town's tourist facilities have deteriorated somewhat. The tourist office next to the bus station is permanently closed. One hotel has managed to remain open, however. The **Miami Hotel** (tel. 95 28 08) on Jaffa Rd. charges $10 per night, but is hardly worth it. The rooms are clean, but only because no guests ever stay there. Ask any local to direct you to **Na'oum's Restaurant,** a well-known Ramallah restaurant. To get to Ramallah, take bus #18 from the Arab bus station on Nablus Road in Jerusalem ($.30).

Near Ramallah

The peaceful village of **Bethel** (Hebrew Bet El, Arabic Beitil), just 4km north of Ramallah, is marked on most pilgrims' maps as Jacob's Ladder. This is reputed to be the spot where Jacob lay down to sleep and dreamed of a ladder ascending to heaven (Genesis 28). On awakening, Jacob built an altar and named the spot Bet El, the "House of God." Today Bet El is the headquarters of the Israeli "civilian" administration which governs the West Bank. Although the administration delegates limited authority to elected Arab mayors and other Palestinian leaders, in reality, all power remains in the hands of the Israeli officials of the area. The administration center itself is of no interest to tourists, but a visit to the nearby Jewish settlement of **Bet El** is worthwhile. Surrounded by tall fences and barbed wire and guarded by military forces affiliated with the civilian authorities, the settlement provides a unique opportunity to catch a glimpse of life in an armed Israeli settlement. The residents are usually quite willing to discuss West Bank politics and their role in them. Bet El is accessible by Egged bus #70 from Jerusalem or El Bireh. From Ramallah you can get there by foot, thumb, or taxi ($2 for the taxi; make sure the driver takes you all the way to the town and not just to the administrative center). Once there, hitching back to Ramallah or Jerusalem is safe and easy (stay on the access road).

Twelve kilometers northwest of Ramallah is **Bir Zeit,** home of the largest and most important university in the Occupied Territories. Its 2200 students have a history of organized opposition to the Israeli government and, whenever internal or external political turmoil forces the Israeli army to tighten security in the West Bank, the first institution to be closed is usually Bir Zeit. The old campus is on the main street near the bus stop; the best place to meet students is at its dining hall. The palatial new campus lies 2km out of town on the road back to Ramallah. The university is open mid-October through mid-February, and from early March until late June, unless political events force it to close. Bus #19 leaves for Bir Zeit from Radio Boulevard in Ramallah, just off Manarah Square. Sheruts leave from the same street.

Nablus (Shekhem)

Nablus is the largest city on the West Bank and home of Najah University, the second most important university in the Occupied Territory. Young Palestinians look hopefully upon Nablus as a possible candidate for the intellectual and administrative capital of their unborn nation. Israelis, of course, do not share this hope and prefer to call it by its biblical name, Shekhem, revered as the final resting place of Joseph.

There is not much to see in the town itself, though the bustling business district is fun to stroll around in if you don't mind being stared at. Expect to be approached countless times by Arabs who will want to know if you are Israeli, and will want to learn all they can about you if you're not. At the edge of town is **Jacob's Well,** a one-hundred-foot well still used by local residents. It is believed to date from the time when Jacob bought the surrounding patch of land as a place to pitch his tents (Genesis 33:18). Access to the Well is through the Greek Orthodox Convent, open Mon.-Sat. 8am-noon and 2-5pm. The Israelis are said to have carried Joseph's bones from Egypt and buried them on this land. Thus, a few hundred meters north of the well is the **Tomb of Joseph,** now a Muslim shrine. The crooked path to the Tomb leads through the slums of Nablus; sightseers are strongly advised to take the less-direct main roads (clearly marked). Once there, you'll see a sizeable band of Israeli soldiers at the entrance—they've been installed to protect visitors' automobiles and the adjacent yeshiva from stonings and other attacks. The Tomb is open 6am-6pm.

Mt. Gerizim, the tree-covered slope just southeast of Nablus, features an excellent view of the Shomron Valley. Since the fourth century B.C.E. it has been the holy mountain of the Samaritans, who, rejecting the traditional site of Mt. Moriah outside of Jerusalem, revere it as the spot where Abraham offered to sacrifice his son Isaac. The Samaritans are an Israeli sect who were excommunicated by the Jews in Jerusalem and not allowed to participate in the reconstruction of the Temple. In turn, the Samaritans decided to reject the bulk of the Old Testament and broke away from mainstream Judaism. They worship only the Five Books of Moses and the Book of Joshua, and to this day they are still known for their extremely literal interpretation of these texts. An interesting but gory event is the Samaritan observance of Passover. The highlight of the ceremony is the actual sacrifice of a number of sheep atop Mt. Gerizim. Tourist buses from Jerusalem and Tel Aviv bring visitors to witness the bloody rite. The hike up the mountain is a long one—taxis can be hired for about $10.

Nablus, like most northern West Bank towns, has no tourist facilities and is by no means the safest place to spend the night. The closest recommended accommodations are in the **Hankin Youth Hostel** (tel. 81 66 0) at Maayon Harod, to the north, or in Jerusalem to the south. If you're really stuck, try the **Al-Estiklal Pension** at 11 Hatin St., or the **Ramsis Hotel** around the corner at 85 Assakia St. The first is definitely the cleaner and airier of the two; the toilets at the second have probably not been cleaned since the owner lost his eyesight. Neither place has showers; both charge $3 per bed. To reach them, walk south away from the main road from the bus station, turn left on Tuari St., and left again on Hatin St.

To get to Nablus, take bus #2 from the Arab bus station on Nablus Road in Jerusalem ($1.05). The last bus back to Jerusalem from Nablus is at 5:30pm. Sheruts also run frequently from the garage at the base of Nablus Road in Jerusalem or from Ramallah ($2). If you want to visit the University, ask anyone at the bus station to point out the bus (no number) to the campus, 3km away.

If you take a bus north from Ramallah towards Nablus, the Arab bus driver may point out a settlement of pathetic-looking homes to you. This is El-Balata, a large refugee camp built to house those who fled Israel in 1948, many of them with the intention of returning in the near future—a hope they have not yet abandoned. *Balut* means oak in Arabic; the site is also identified with the Oak of Moreh (Genesis 12:6) and is, ironically, the first place where Abraham was promised Canaan for his offspring. Buses also run to Nablus from Afula and Jenin in the north.

Sabastiyya

Omri - 6th King of Is.

The West Bank's wonderful secret is the magnificent ruined city of Sabastiyya, just 11km northwest of Nablus. The ruins feature a fabulous array of Israelite, Hellenistic, and Roman ruins. The strategically-situated hilltop was first built up by Omir, the sixth king of Israel, in the ninth century, and was known both by the biblical name of Shomron, and Samaria. Under the rule of Omri's son Ahab, during which the Kingdom of Israel reached the height of its power, the city of Shomron flourished. But during Herod's time, the city was renamed Sabastiyya and transformed into the showpiece of the Holy Land. Herod had the beautifully situated hilltop metropolis built to win the favor of the Roman Emperor. The ruins are just above the present-day Arab town of Sabastiyya. At the base of the site, on the access road which bypasses the town, are the majestic columns of a colonnaded street, which offer some indication of Sabastiyya's former opulence. At the entrance to the site itself are the similarly imposing pillars of the **basilica.** The beautifully-preserved **Roman theater** further on is far more impressive than its famous counterpart at Caesarea. At the top of the hill, along with a spectacular view of the Shomron Hills, are the remnants of Israelite and Hellenistic acropolis walls, and a Roman acropolis, dominated by the enormous column bases of the **Temple of Augustus.** Adjoining the temple are the extensive remains of **Ahab's Palace,**

Sabastea

built by the unpopular tyrant in the ninth century B.C.E. The site is open 8am-5pm, until 4pm on Fridays; admission $1.30, $.65 for students. To get to the ruins, get off the bus at the first white "Sabastiye" sign (this road leads through the modern town) or at the second, yellow "Samaria/Sebaste" sign (the route past the colonnaded street) and head uphill.

The Arab village of Sabastiyya is worth a moment's attention as well, especially for the ruins of a splendid twelfth-century **Crusader Cathedral** that can be reached from the steps leading down from the main square. The cathedral was built over the remains of an earlier basilica, destroyed by the Persians in 614 C.E., which was believed to have stood over three sacred tombs—those of the prophets Elisha and Obadiah, and that of St. John the Baptist. The ruins are located within the confines of the **Mosque of Nabi Yahya,** for the spot is holy for Muslims as well. (Nabi Yahya is the Arabic name for St. John.) To get to Sabastiyya, take the Arab bus bound for Jenin from the central bus station in Nablus (fare $.40) or hail one of the numerous sheruts (fare $.60). The bus will only take you as far as one of the turn-offs for Sabastiyya, a 2km walk from the village and the site.

Jenin, 35km further north, is a large Arab town with a colorful market district, but little else of interest to tourists. The fortress that dominates the city from a hilltop to the west is disappointingly modern; it was built by the British at the beginning of this century. Buses travel to Jenin from Nablus and from the Sabastiyya turn-off ($.80). The only hotel consists of four beds ($2 each) in the back room of a grill house.

JORDAN

$1 = 0.366JD **$2.97 = 1JD**

History and hospitality thrive best in the world's hottest spots, claim the Bedouins. Jordan proves their point. Here, thousands of years of political and religious strife, fueled by the heat, have forged an unparalleled array of historic monuments, from Crusader castles to desert palaces, from Roman ruins to the rose-hued heights of Petra. And although recent tourists have tended to let the political temperature scare them away, Jordanian hospitality has always warmed the weary traveler's soul.

The cost of travel in Jordan is high, but this is a testimony to the country's economic success in the face of great obstacles. In Jordan you needn't peer through crowds of tourists just to see sights wrapped in plastic, with English labels. The country remains largely untouched by the Western wanderer: Islam in Jordan is passionate enough to be fascinating, yet not dogmatic enough to be frightening. You can travel in Jordan on the back of a camel, or swim underwater among the brilliant coral reefs of the Gulf of Aqaba. To those willing to sacrifice a few greenbacks on the altar of the Arabian desert gods, Jordan offers ruins and natural wonders as ancient and magnificent as any in the world.

Orientation

Useful Organizations

Several sources of information on Jordan may be particularly helpful to you. Before you go, you may want to consult one of the offices listed below for visa information and other technical advice.

Jordan Information Bureau: 1701 K St. NW, 11th floor, Washington, DC 20006 ((202) 659-3322).

Embassy of the Hashemite Kingdom of Jordan: U.S.: 2319 Wyoming Ave. NW, Washington, DC 20008 ((202) 265-1606); **Canada:** 100 Bronson Ave., Ottawa, Ontario K1R 6G8 ((613) 238-8090); **U.K.:** 6 Upper Philimore Gardens, London W8 7HB (01/937 3685).

Jordan Mission to the United Nations: 866 United Nations Plaza, New York, NY 10017 (tel. (212) 752-0135).

Honorary Consuls in the U.S.: Frank Jameson, 2049 Century Park East, Los Angeles, CA 90067; Jamil Diab, 6215 East Shea Blvd., Scottsdale, AZ 85254; James Kimberly, P.O. Box 351, Palm Beach, FL 33480.

Once you've arrived in Jordan, you'll want to check in with the **Ministry of Tourism and Antiquities,** the country's only public tourist office. Several other organizations in Amman will provide you with aid and information, including the **Department of Antiquities,** the **American Center for Oriental Research,** and the **U.S. Information Service** in the American Cultural Center. For addresses and hours of these offices, see the Practical Information listings in Amman.

Currency and Exchange

The **Jordanian Dinar (JD)** is the legal tender of Jordan. Each JD is divided into 100 piasters (pt) or 1000 fils. A piaster is occasionally referred to as a "girlsh," a ½pt piece as a "tarifeh," and a 5pt piece as a "shilling." Bills come in denominations of 50JD, 20JD, 10JD, 5JD, 1JD, and 500fils, silver coins in 250fils, 100fils, 50fils, and 20fils, copper coins in 10fils (1pt), 5fils, and 1fil. Denominations are always written in both Arabic and English. Prices are written in this book as you are most likely to encounter them: i.e., although the piaster is the most commonly used term besides the dinar, prices are generally quoted in dinars and fils.

The currency in Jordan is fairly stable; for many years the JD has been equivalent to just over US $3. Since the government lets supply and demand regulate the exchange rate, there isn't much of a black market. The currency exchanges on the streets are open much later than banks, often until 9pm, and charge a 2½% commission, roughly the same as the bank fee. Larger hotels can also change money at odd hours, but offer less favorable rates.

Business Hours

Jordan's business timetable has been shaped by the various natural, religious, and economic forces at work in the country: as long as the desert sun has reigned, the lunchtime hours have been a time of rest. Most stores and offices open between 8am and 9:30am, close from 1-3pm, and reopen in the afternoon. Some modern offices use air conditioning and are therefore able to remain open throughout the day. In Amman, retail stores often close as late as 8pm or 9pm, when the transportation system winds down. Banks and government offices, however, retain only a skeletal staff in the afternoon; try to do all your important business in the morning, as little can normally be accomplished later in the day.

Friday is a holiday throughout the Muslim world, although perhaps less so in the bustling economy of Amman and the resort of Aqaba, where some stores stay open seven days a week to keep up with the competition. Foreign banks and offices generally observe both Friday and Saturday as weekend holidays, though they may keep longer hours during the rest of the week. Recently many Jordanian shops and museums have chosen to make Tuesday an additional day off. National holidays are listed in the Festivals and Holidays section.

The only consistent daily schedule is the Islamic call to prayer. Five times a day, whether at home, on a bus, or on the street, the faithful turn off the material world to kneel on the prayer carpet facing the holy city of Mecca. Non-Muslim travelers should wait until after the last of the daily prayer sessions (around 8pm) before visiting a mosque, and should always enter with respect. Dress properly, approach slowly, and pause to be sure that no one objects to your presence.

Telephones, Telegrams, and Mail

In Jordan, lax child labor laws, sparse private phones and even more sparse pay phones combine to make under-age messengers more efficient, in most cases, than a telephone call. The country's phone system is functioning and automatic, but overloaded. Pay phones are particularly poor and require 10fils whether or not your call gets through. If you ask a shop owner where to find the nearest pay phone, he will in all probability invite you to use his. Though he may charge you 50fils for the convenience, you're more likely to reach your number. A third option is to use the phone in a hotel, but be sure to find out about surcharges ahead of time. In general, push-button phones are quicker

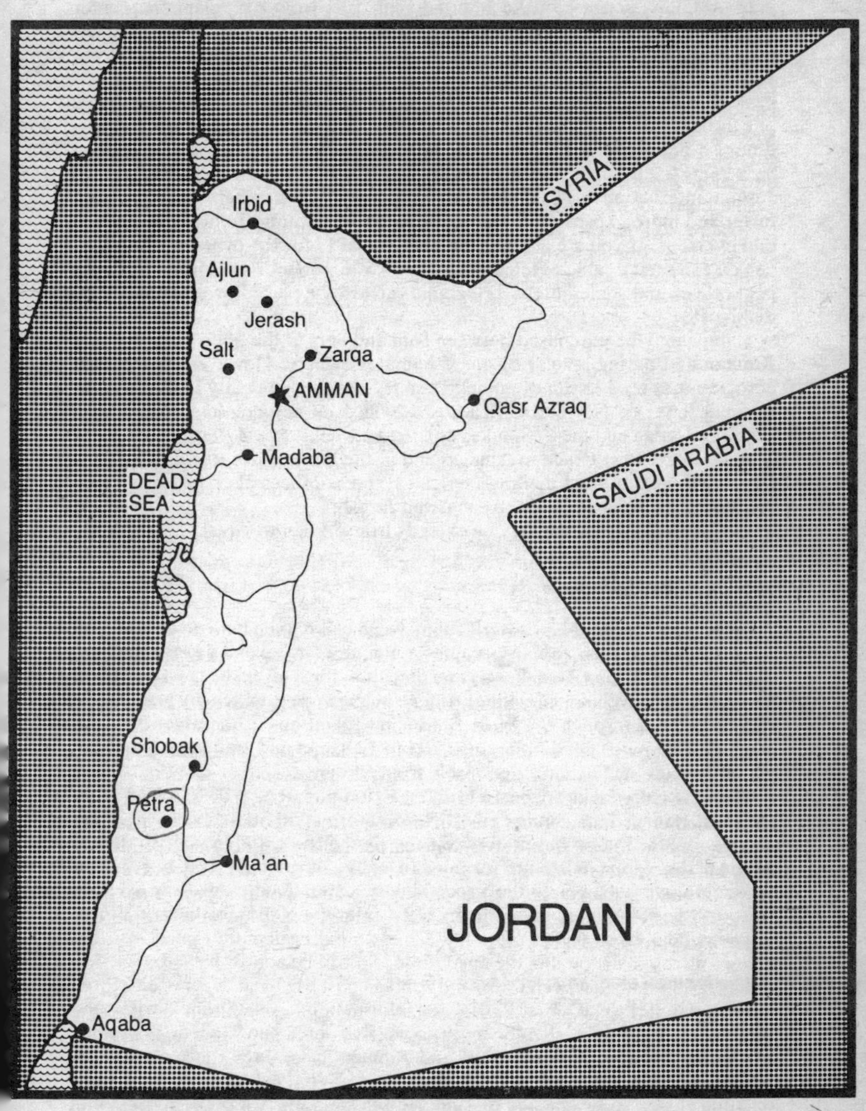
SYRIA
Irbid
Ajlun
Jerash
Salt
Zarqa
AMMAN
Qasr Azraq
Madaba
DEAD SEA
SAUDI ARABIA
Shobak
Petra
Ma'an
JORDAN
Aqaba

than rotary dials, but either should be operated slowly for the correct number to be registered. Keep trying after the first unanswered ring or busy signal.

In Amman, you can make international calls from the telephone center around the corner and up the hill from the Main Post Office on Prince Muhammad St., across from the Khayyam Department Store. When calling North America, the first three minutes will cost about $15 (5.250JD); you pay at the desk after the call is made. Count on an hour or two before the connection is put through, and bring a book. Connections, when they are made, are sometimes so poor that conversation is impossible. The telephone center is open 8am-9pm; try to arrive before 7pm to call North America. In other parts of Jordan, international calls must be made at fancy hotels, where service will be faster and more expensive. Late night and early morning are the best times to dial overseas. If you are at a private phone, dial 17 for the overseas operator.

You can send a cable or telegram to the U.S. for under 200fils from the larger post offices and some hotels. Telegrams can also be placed over the phone by dialing 18.

Stamps may be purchased between 8am and 8pm at the Main Post Office in Amman and during regular business hours elsewhere. However, stamps and aerogrammes tend to run out quickly, so try to buy them early in the day. An air mail letter to North America costs 200fils, an aerogramme 120fils; mail between Jordan and the U.S. takes one to two weeks. *Poste Restante* operates at the Central Post Office in Amman and in the larger cities (the Central Post Office will not forward mail). American Express offices also hold mail; they are located in Amman, Irbid, Aqaba, and Jarash.

Neither mail nor phone service extends from Jordan to Israel.

To and From Jordan

Although every Middle Eastern country can claim to be both an ancient and a modern crossroads, Jordan occupies a unique political and geographic spot on the traveler's map. It makes a good first stop, for it gives the most flexibility in organizing travel in the region. From Amman, Syria is enticingly near, Israel can be entered through the West Bank, and Egypt lies at the other end of a short cruise. When conditions for travel to Lebanon and Iraq improve, these countries, too, will be most accessible from Jordan.

The new **Queen Alia Airport** has information numbers at 08/53 17 2/3. Alia Airlines' reservations number is 24 13 1/4, information numbers are 92 20 5/6 and 91 49 1/8. Public buses between the new airport and Abdali station in Amman run every half hour for 50pt (usually, but not always, bus #31b). Taxis, too, will take you to the airport, but be careful: since specially licensed "airport taxis" are allowed to charge a flat rate of 2.500JD for the trip downtown, regular taxis try to offer the same deal. Legally, they must use the meter—if you insist on this the cost of the trip will be almost halved.

EgyptAir flights between Cairo and Amman cost $175 and depart Cairo three times a day (tel. 53 93 3 or 30 01 1 for information). Alia Airlines makes the same flight daily, for slightly more expensive fares (no student discount). Flights between Larnaca, Cyprus, and Amman leave three times a week for $125 (tel. 38 78 7). For information on flights to Syria, call 22 14 7.

Jordan can also be reached by land and sea from the rest of the Arab world. The **Egyptian Navigation Company** sails weekly from Suez to Aqaba. The journey takes approximately nine hours, and third-class or deck fare costs LE46. The company's Cairo office is at the corner of Kasr el Nil and Sherif Sts. The JETT bus from Abdali station to Damascus takes between four and six hours, depending on border complications, and costs 2.500JD. **Karak** buses (in Amman, tel. 25 17 4) also make the trip. More frequent service taxis *(servees)* run from the several companies on Shabsough St. near the Gold Market in Amman for 4.500JD. Service taxis and JETT both make the return trip. Remember to get a Syrian visa before attempting to cross the border (see Embassies section of Amman). Syria will only grant one if you have a Jordanian entry stamp (i.e., if you did not enter the country via the King Hussein Bridge).

Although Jordan has no relations with Israel, it is possible to travel between the West Bank of the Jordan River and Jordan proper with a little patience and political perceptiveness. If you're asked questions by the Jordanians, don't mentioned the word Israel, because technically there are *no* border connections between the two countries.

To reach Jordan from the West Bank, you must cross the Allenby/King Hussein Bridge near Jericho. Crossing the Bridge is a simple but time-consuming maneuver provided that you have no Israeli stamps on your passport, and that you have previously obtained a Jordanian visa. Israeli buses #961, 3, 4 travel to Jericho from Jerusalem, as do Arab buses #952 and 977 from elsewhere in the West Bank. Don't get off the bus until you see the large mosque in the city center. Take a right at the mosque to the square where the service taxis wait. The only taxis licensed to go all the way to the Bridge (past the first security checkpoint) are those lined up under the big blue Jericho Municipality sign. Others will drop you off at an earlier checkpoint where you'll have to wait for the rare shared taxi with an empty seat. It's hard to bargain down the price, since there's no other way to get to the Bridge, but try; you shouldn't have to pay more than $1.50-2.50 for the twenty-minute ride. Shared taxis go all the way to the Bridge from Damascus Gate in Jerusalem for under $2.

Once you reach the Bridge checkpoint, you must buy $13 worth of stamps from the Israelis to affix to the back of the visa paper. Since the government controls your right to exit, bargaining is not in order. After your luggage has been inspected, you'll have to wait for one of the approved buses. Take advantage of the time to buy Jordanian Dinars, as there is no currency exchange on the other side of the Bridge. The five-minute ride across the Bridge costs 2JD ($6) regardless of the exchange rates. It is usually cheaper to pay in dollars.

On the East Bank, you'll be issued a "permit" saying that you came over the Bridge and probably shouldn't be allowed to make the return trip. Though you shouldn't lose the evidence that you entered the country legally, you shouldn't keep it in an obvious place, as it announces that you were in the West Bank and possibly Israel. This souvenir could prevent you from being issued a West Bank permit later. If you are merely returning over the Bridge after a Jordan-based visit to Israel, your permit will just be stamped.

To visit the West Bank from Jordan you need a permit issued by the Ministry of the Interior. The Ministry is at the Gamal Abdel Nassar Circle (also known as Ministry of Interior Circle or *Duwar Dakhlia*). Fifty fils worth of stamps (which you can buy at a premium outside the Ministry) and a photo (you can buy four at Sarko's, down the block from Beefy's, for 1JD) will be affixed to your application. Take the application to Room 36 on the first floor before 1pm (closed on Fri.). The processing takes at least three days, after which you may or may not receive a permit. If you don't, try again. Preferred religions on the application are Christianity and Islam. The most difficult question is "Port of entry to Jordan." Queen Alia International Airport, Aqaba, or Ramtha (on the Syrian border) create no problems. If you say King Hussein Bridge, however, you are implying that you consider the West Bank Israeli territory, and you will be denied a permit. Write "Jerusalem," or leave the question blank, and then explain that technically you never entered Jordan, since the King Hussein Bridge is not an international border. If all else fails, you may have to fly to Cyprus or Egypt, and from there to Israel.

With the West Bank permit you can buy a JETT ticket for the bus at 6:30am from Abdali station (2.500JD). You can also take a service taxi before noon for 1.500JD. The bus, however, takes you all the way to the Israeli checkpoint, while the taxi brings you only as far as the terminal for foreigners. Occasionally, Israel will ask young travelers for evidence of financial security up to $400; they will always search your luggage thoroughly.

The King Hussein Bridge is closed Friday at noon and all day Saturday. The best time to cross is early in the morning.

Getting Around

Most visitors to Jordan stay long enough to see the major sites at Petra and Jarash, but not long enough to master the transportation system. Since organized bus tours and private taxis could easily cost $15-25 per day, you'll want to avail yourself of cheaper if slower modes of transportation. Jordan's attractions are timeless; they will wait for you.

All of Jordan's roads are currently open to unrestricted travel; travel to the West Bank requires a special permit (see above). But as long as the Middle East is a center of international attention, situations change rapidly, and it's wise to check with the Ministry of Tourism for the latest developments. In general, you should carry your passport at all times while traveling, especially in the border areas. Near Syria, all foreign passports will be checked. On the road to Aqaba, Palestinian passports are checked more carefully, but foreign passports may be given a glance. To visit the Dead Sea you need not only your passport but possibly a police permit (obtainable on the way) as well.

Taxi

Due to late hours and unspecified routes, you will probably require a taxi at least once during your stay in Jordan, if only to get from the airport to Central City in Amman (2JD). Regular taxis are marked with a yellow square on the door. Jordanian cabbies take their horns seriously, their fares a little less so and the law hardly at all, but with a few hints you should be able to emerge from a ride safe, sound, and solvent. Insist that the cab driver use the meter: it's your only protection against inflated prices, and it's also the law. If he refuses, try getting out and writing down the license number to report to the police and the Ministry of Tourism. If this fails and you need to get someplace, bargain hard. Especially at night, cabbies will often carry you only at a pre-negotiated and unreasonably high price. Neither bargaining nor the law is strong enough to protect you in this case, so either enjoy the big-spender role or walk. Drivers also tend to charge extra (illegally, again) for large amounts of bulky baggage.

Service Taxi

Shared or service taxis, identified by the white squares on their doors, run specific routes in Amman and between the central transport terminals in the larger cities. In Amman, they cost 60-100fils; a ride may cost up to 2.650JD from Amman to Aqaba. These shared taxis are the most convenient and comfortable way to travel, but they rarely run in the evenings and the long-distance ones may make only two or three trips a day. In addition, the schedules are irregular because service taxis wait until all seven seats are full to depart.

Until a new station is built for southern Amman, service taxis leave from **Wahadat station** to Madaba (300fils), to Karak (1.700JD) down the King's Highway, and to Ma'an (1.350JD) via the newer Desert Highway. At Ma'an you can transfer for service to Wadi Musa (Petra) and Aqaba (430fils and 1.300JD, respectively). The station is between the Abu Darwish Mosque on Jebel Ashrafieh and the Wahadat Refugee Camp. Service taxis to the northern part of the country depart from the **Abdali station** on King Hussein St. Service costs 420fils to Jarash, 630fils to Ajlun, 760fils to Irbid, 270fils to Salt and 1.500JD to the King Hussein Bridge. Service between Jarash and Ajlun runs infrequently for about 230fils. From Irbid, its 260fils to Um Qeis and 420fils to El Hemma.

All of these prices are government regulated, but drivers occasionally hike the fares. See if other passengers accept an impromptu increase—they won't unless it's justified. Shared taxi lines are the one place foreigners aren't given special treatment, so be prepared to push it out with the best of them. In Amman itself, your place in line might have some effect.

Bus

In Amman, public buses supplement the service taxi system. The intercity bus network is fairly sparse due to the monopoly granted by the government to the **Jordan Express Tourist Transport (JETT)** company, though private buses cover the most popular routes and private mini-buses travel to more remote areas. Most towns have one main terminal shared by all forms of transportation; Amman and Irbid have several. The JETT office is about six blocks north of the Abdali station in Amman.

Bus fares are slightly lower than service taxi rates, but buses travel more slowly. The JETT luxury coaches cost more than regular buses but are usually air-conditioned and sometimes even accompanied by a host. They also leave more or less on schedule rather than waiting for seats to be filled. Every day four buses leave Amman for the 4½-hour trip to Aqaba (3JD), at 6:30am, 9:30am, 2:30pm, and 4pm. Scheduled daytrips to Petra leave Amman at 6:30am.

Car

Some of Jordan's most interesting attractions are hardly served by the public transportation system. For groups of four to six, renting a car can be a good way to reach less accessible sights and to take in a lot in one or two days. For example, the round trip to Azraq via four or five desert castles can be done in eight to twelve hours. The magnificent Kings Highway route, served by no other mode of transport, can be seen from a private car in another full day. Petra deserves as much time as you can possibly spare; some rental agencies will let you return a car from Amman in Aqaba, after which you can get a ride to Petra for a leisurely stay.

Most rental agencies charge about 8JD per day, including insurance, plus 40fils per kilometer. The unlimited mileage deals are cheaper in the long run: $35-40 per day for three days is standard. Larger firms like **Avis, Budget,** and **Europacar** charge slightly more. **Satellite,** by the Housing Bank near Abdali and **Jorac** at Second Circle, are generally less expensive. Always ask if the car has a fire extinguisher; the desert heat may demand it. The Four Wheel Drive cars the companies push are unnecessary except to get to Qasr Touba, south of Azraq. Even at Wadi Rum, ordinary cars are adequate, and can be supplemented by Bedouin camel rides.

Hitching

Hitchhiking experiences in Jordan are varied and interesting; you'll benefit from the chance to see the country and meet its people. Among small towns there's a lot of local traffic (Jordan Valley, Amman environs, Irbid area), so rides come fast and are friendly. In the desert and the city, caution is essential. Some of Jordan's desert roads, like the Desert Highway, the Kings Highway, and the road to Wadi Rum, see a good deal of traffic, but even short waits in the sun are dangerous. Any car with space will stop, but often those that pass will be full. Bring lots of water and cover your head with a broad-brimmed hat. The road to Azraq is even more difficult. Try not to be let off where sand dunes will be your only companions. It's perfectly acceptible to ask the driver of the car letting you off at some lonely desert junction to wait around until you get another ride. In the cities (Amman, Irbid, and even Jarash and Ajlun) the main problem is that empty taxis continually pass looking for eligible passengers, and won't stop pestering you.

Because of the profusion of rich tourists and transient workers in Aqaba it is nearly impossible to hitch a ride there, unless you are a woman traveling alone. Finally, if you're hiking around in the Petra or Wadi Rum areas, rides will literally walk up to you. Generally they will have six legs, no wheels, two donkey ears and a Bedouin kaffiyeh.

Although criminal violence against strangers is practically unknown in Jordan, there's always a slight risk involved in hitching. Use common sense when getting into a car, and be on your guard. The international "Let's Go" symbol of the outstretched thumb works fine in Jordan. The art is called the "autostop."

Life in Jordan

Accommodations

Though the Jordanian government has gone to great lengths to establish adequate, regulated accommodations for tourists, especially in Amman, it has not done so with the budget traveler in mind. **Classified tourist hotels** charge prices as high as Jordan's record temperatures (Centigrade dinars and Fahrenheit dollars), and the country's one youth hostel has been closed. Fortunately, there are several options open to those with limited funds—especially men. Single women will find it particularly difficult to lodge cheaply in Jordan, but with a little planning, not impossible.

Hotels in Jordan are inspected annually and regulated according to a five-star system. Rates for the five classes are based on quality and determined by the government, so bargaining is difficult; hoteliers may be more flexible in the off-season winter and summer months. The Ministry of Tourism provides a comprehensive list of classified hotels and their prices. Below is a table of the rates set by the government.

Class	Singles	Doubles
Five-star	16-22JD	19-25JD
Four-star	8-11JD	10-14JD
Three-star	4.500-6JD	7-8JD
Two-star	3JD	5JD
One-star	2JD	3JD

Most hotels add a 10% service charge; ask if it's included in the price you are quoted.

One- and two-star hotels, as well as some of the cleaner **unclassified hotels,** are the least expensive alternatives in Amman. Some of the cheaper places charge an extra 250fils for a hot shower; most have Turkish squat toilets and frequent drainage problems, so footwear is essential. Hotel owners will often ask to hold your passport for the length of your stay; if you wish to leave your luggage and travel, especially near any borders, you must insist on getting it back. Women should avoid the unclassified hotels, which cater to Arab *men,* seasonal workers more interested in TV than a shower and snooze. Some inexpensive hotels won't even accept single women.

Couples traveling together must keep in mind that Jordanian law does not permit unmarried couples to share a room. Fortunately, most hotel owners know that Western women often keep their family name and neglect to carry marriage licenses with them on trips—in other words, you won't have trouble if you keep a low profile. Women should respect dress codes at all times, and even men should wear a shirt and long pants at night in the hotel. If a problem arises, call the Ministry of Tourism and your country's embassy *before* the police arrive, to have some support behind you.

Outside of Amman, both transient workers and their hotels are rare; the only alternatives are the sparse tourist hotels in Aqaba, Government Rest Houses in Petra, Karak, Azraq, and Dibbin National Park, camping out, and private invitations. The **Rest Houses,** clean but simple, charge a whopping 5.500JD for singles, 6.500JD for doubles. If you plan to stay at one, especially in the spring or fall, it's best to reserve a place in advance with the Hotel and Resthouse Corporation, P.O. Box 2863, Amman, Jordan (tel. 42 24 3).

Camping is possible anywhere in the country, although facilities are non-existent. Favorite sites include the beach at Aqaba, the abandoned buildings of Amman, and the Dibbin National Park. You'll need a sleeping bag even for cool summer nights; winter evenings can bring sub-freezing temperatures. Also, keep some water handy to offset the effects of the dry air. One step up from camping is to spend a night with the Bedouins. Throughout the country their black tents still represent oases in the desert and hospitality to strangers. Tea, Bedouin coffee, and meals always accompany an invitation, although showers and toilets rarely do. The Bedouins of Petra, so accustomed to visitors that many speak English, usually charge 1-1.500JD per night, but elsewhere families will refuse your cash, preferring baubles from abroad or a song or two in English.

Finally, **overnight invitations** to private homes are fairly common, especially for men traveling alone. Unfortunately, they're usually extended only after most of the cheap hotels fill up, so unless you want to risk it, locate a place to sleep as early in the day as possible.

Food

Although the Jordanian population is quite young, its cuisine has evolved through centuries of Bedouin cooking. Even a young Palestinian living in a refugee camp can accurately describe *mensaf,* the national dish: eight to ten kilos of rice on a tray at least a meter across, topped with pine nuts and the stew of an entire lamb (or goat). The Bedouins still serve the head of the lamb on top of the whole shebang, reserving the prize delicacies—eyes and tongue—for the tongue-tied and goggle-eyed guests. The right hand is used to ball the rice, and flat bread to pull off chunks of meat and dip them into the *jamid,* or sweet yogurt.

Most other dishes in Jordan come from the main ingredients of the *mensaf*. Traditional dinners, served between 2-3pm, are rarely as spicy as those in other Arab countries. They include *musukhan,* boiled chicken with olive oil and a delicious spice called sumac, served with *khoubz* (Jordanian-style pita); *yahkne,* a meat casserole with small onions, cabbage, and tomatoes; and *mahsi,* a tray of vine leaves stuffed with mincemeat, rice, and onions. *Mazza,* loosely translated as hors d'oeuvres, is actually a meal in itself, and one of the most popular for serving dinner guests. It consists of *hummus* with oil, sardines, cucumbers, tomatoes, pickles, fried eggs, and *za'atar* spice with olive oil, all presented on a tray and accompanied by tea. Luckily for those invited to join in, there is no clean plate club in Jordan; it is polite to leave some food uneaten to indicate that the hospitality has been more than generous.

Traditionally, even ritually, a guest receives *qahwa sa'ada* (Bedouin coffee) both as a greeting and as a farewell. When the guest first arrives, the roasted beans are ground in a carved wooden *mihbash* (mortar and pestle). The *mihbash* is considered a musical instrument; its strong rhythmical pounding announces to neighbors that a meal is being prepared for guests, and during the feast of Id-al-Fitr a symphony of the *mihbash* sounds through many Bedouin valleys. Once ground, the coffee beans are boiled in a large brass pot, then poured through ground cardamom pods into a smaller brass pot, and finally poured through tamarisk twigs to a third pot, from which the coffee is served. The coffee, always poured with the left hand into one of a stack of tiny cups, is gone at a sip, but you'll be offered refills; three is the polite number of cups to accept.

Outside of private homes, restaurants abound. In general, if you can read the menu you can't afford the food. Luckily, however, street food is plentiful. Kebabs and *shwarma* (spitted, skewered lamb or chicken) are known as *rosta.* Fresh *ka'ik bilsimim,* a bread ring with sesame seeds, is considered a street treat, and you'll see long lines at the market for *knaffeh,* a creamy sweetmeat that should be tasted at least once. Follow the crowds and explore.

Water in Amman is not very pure; bottled water (130fils) or iodine tablets are a good idea. As the desert recedes, more vegetables enter the country's diet, but raw salads and fruits are dangerous—peelables are best, and everything should be washed carefully, if possible with soap. Stay away from the felafel served in the streets, which is generally dry and often fried in week-old or contaminated oil. Finally, if you slip from these rules, don't worry; while minor stomach upsets may be unpleasant, more serious illnesses among tourists are rare.

Study/Work

There are two ways for foreigners to appreciate Jordan from the inside, as residents rather than tourists—to work and to study there. The latter is by far the easier option. Jordan's two universities, in Amman and Irbid, are both open to foreign students. While the **University of Jordan in Amman** has a liberal, westernized atmosphere in which North American and European students will feel at home, the new **Yarmoukh University in Irbid** is much more conservative and traditional. However, students interested in Islamic culture may enjoy the change of pace and attitude at Yarmoukh. Each school offers a wide range of courses (though at Yarmoukh University the only majors are in the sciences), and each runs a summer school. Both universities guarantee dormitory housing for women. The Jordanian Embassy or consulate should be able to provide you with further information on either school; the University in Amman has a special foreign student program—write to Hala Hourani at the University if you are interested in attending.

If you want to work in Jordan, you can approach the problem in several ways. If you speak Arabic and don't mind breaking the law, you can try to land a job once there, though technically your visa doesn't permit this. Construction jobs and other manual labor will be the most likely options. To work legally, you must acquire a permit ahead of time. You must have an offer of employment in order to apply for the permit, so try to find a job with an American or Canadian firm in Jordan. Your employer can then secure the permit for you. The **International Association for the Exchange of Students for Technical Experience** (see General Introduction for address) sponsors traineeships in Jordan. Write for information. Finally, if you want an exciting job and don't mind not being paid, think about working on an archeological dig. Volunteers are always needed. Most archeological journals list American-sponsored digs abroad; *Biblical Archeology* is perhaps the best place to begin your research. You may also write to the **Archeological Institute of America,** 15 Park Row, New York, NY 10038 (tel. (212) 732-6677) for information on fieldwork opportunities.

Festivals and Holidays

Two grand, joyous splurges punctuate the Muslim calendar, the Id-al-Fitr and the Id-al-Adha. The **Id-al-Fitr** follows the holy month of **Ramadan,** 28 days of daytime fasting. During Ramadan, shops, offices and banks keep reduced schedules, and some restaurants shut down entirely (those remaining are less crowded). Everything closes by 5 or 5:30pm, when undulating rivers of people flow methodically through the streets to their evening breakfasts. By nightfall, the flood disappears and the streets are left to the heathens. Shops sometimes open for a few more hours at 8 or 9pm. At the end of the month, the Id-al-Fitr breaks the fast with three full days of feasting.

The **Id-al-Adha,** a four-day feast, follows the return of the *Haj* (holy pilgrims) from Mecca. Although both feasts are generally private family affairs, guests are occasionally invited to join in. Abraham's religious piety in offering his son Ishmail as a sacrifice is commemorated during the prayers of the Id-al-Adha; the non-Muslim tourist will need to make other sacrifices, as almost everything closes and transportation slows.

In 1984, Ramadan will run from early June to early July. The *Haj* is eight weeks later. To find the exact dates of yearly holidays, it's best to check with the Ministry of Tourism in Amman or any Arab consulate abroad. The *Hegira,* the Islamic calendar, follows lunar periods, unlike our own Gregorian calendar. From the first year of Muhammad's flight from Mecca to Medina (622 C.E.), each lunar year has had thirteen less days than the Gregorian 365-day year. To realign the months and the seasons, an extra month is added periodically, much as leap year corrects the solar calendar every four years.

Besides the Ramadan and the feasts, the most important holidays in Jordan are **New Year's Day, Moulid el Nabi** (Muhammad's birthday), the feast of **Al Miraj,** commemorating Muhammad's visit to heaven, and **Arab Renaissance Day,** three weeks before Ramadan, marking the Arab Revolt of 1916. Government offices and banks close on the national holidays of the **King's birthday** (November 14), his **accession** to the throne (August 11), **Independence Day** (May 25), **Labor Day** (May 1), and **Arab League Day** (March 22).

For the Christian community, the **Easter Celebrations** (some following the Gregorian calendar, others the Hegira) are the most spectacular of the year. **Christmas** is a smaller feast, especially for the Coptic and Abyssinian Churches, which celebrate it during the second week of January rather than on December 25.

History

The Middle East is the perennial center of attention in a world obsessed by conflict and conquest, and the recent political history of Jordan is reflected in the faces of everyone you'll meet there. Nowhere else is ancient history more important for an appreciation of sights, and nowhere else is modern history more important for safe travel to those sights.

In Jordan, at the junction of Europe, Africa and Asia, evidence of the world's earliest sedentary communities has been found. Ancient texts from the dawn of written history describe the first inhabitants east of the Jordan River: the Edomites, Moabites, Ammonites, and Amorites. The Israelites inaugurated the Biblical Period of Jordanian history when they returned from their sojourn into Egypt. For the next centuries Israelites warred against the tribes that inhabited the area while, under kings such as David and Solomon, they nurtured a fragile monotheism. But after the death of Solomon and the division of the kingdom, the lures of Jezebel proved too much for the Israelites, who returned to paganism; Moabites, Assyrians, and later Persians subsequently overran—but failed to subdue—the twelve tribes. Only the Nabatean kingdom, safely ensconced in the capital city of Petra, wholly maintained its independence until the Roman era.

Eventually, Persian rulers granted religious freedom and local autonomy to Palestine. Peace and prosperity lasted until Alexander the Great swept into the Middle East, carrying Hellenic culture with him. Upon Alexander's death in 322 B.C.E, Ptolemy assumed dominion over Egypt while Seleucus governed Babylonia. Jordan and Palestine, once again on the trade route between two great empires, became the scene of battles and rebellions for the next three centuries.

Whereas the Assyrian, Persian and Greek occupations left little behind, the Romans, who entered Damascus in 64 B.C.E. and Jerusalem the year after, spent a good part of their four century rule building the stone cities whose remains you can visit today. Ten Roman cities banded together in a defensive pact called the Decapolis; significant remains are at Pella, Gedara (Um Qeis), Gerasa (Jarash) and Philadelphia (Amman). The independent Nabatean cities continued to flourish during this time; their unsurpassed architectural genius was eventually incorporated into the Roman Empire.

Some sixty years after the Roman occupation commenced, Jesus was born. The New Testament chronicles the struggles between Jesus' faithful and the Roman emperors; eventually, however, the Byzantine heirs of the Roman Empire adopted and promoted Christianity as well. The Byzantine era ended in 614 when Persians penetrated the desert defenses of Northern Arabia, and with the cooperation of the region's Jews, destroyed the Christian fortifications. The ensuing power vacuum paved the way for the Arab followers of the Prophet Muhammad to spread their faith.

A few years after the Prophet's death, the entire Middle East was in Muslim hands; by the next century Islam pervaded a region greater than that of the Roman Empire at its height. Jordan, which still commanded the crucial trade routes between the new capital of Damascus and both Egypt and the Arabian peninsula, remained prosperous. The first Muslim rulers, the Umayyads, were intensely devoted to the desert, and built desert hunting palaces between Amman and Azraq. But the castles were not designed with defensive purposes in mind, and eventually fell to rival Muslims. When these Muslims moved the capital from Damascus to Baghdad, Jordan's prosperity declined. In the succeeding thirteen centuries, the region has been continually inhabited by Arab Muslims.

Among the long line of Crusader fortresses built after 1099 from Turkey all the way to Aqaba, those in the Principality of TransJordan (Oultre-Jordain) were the most important. The Crusaders built their capital within the confines of the huge fortification at Karak, and built castles at Shobak (Montreal), at Wadi Musa (Le Vaux Moyse) and at Jeziret Faonon (Isle de Graye). Hostilities persisted incessantly between the Crusaders and their Muslim rivals, until 1187 when Muslims defeated the Crusaders at Jerusalem.

In the sixteenth century, the Ottoman Turks commenced four hundred years of rule. Little remains from this period, mostly because the Turks' primary interest in the Holy Lands was to safeguard the route Muslim pilgrims had to travel to get to Mecca. Along the *Darb el-Haj,* or Pilgrim Road, the scanty remains of waterhole forts remain at Mafrak, Zarqa, Qattrana, Hasa, Aqaba, and Mudawara. Today the route followed by the great caravans since the sixteenth century is the paved Desert Highway.

In the twentieth century, resistance to the corrupt Ottoman rule grew increasingly widespread. In 1916, when Turkey was embroiled in the First World War, Sherif Hussein led the Arab Revolt. At the war's end, after the troops of Hussein and T.E. Lawrence drove the Ottomans out of the Middle East, British promises of Arab independence turned to compromises; Lebanon and Syria fell under the French sphere of influence, and Palestine became subject to British mandate.

After Jordan's support for the Allies in World War II, Hussein's son Abdullah was recognized as ruler of the Hashemite Kingdom of Jordan. West of the Jordan, tremendous Jewish immigration and anti-Semitic persecution during World War II strengthened Zionist demands for a Jewish homeland. After the expiration of the British mandate in 1948, the United Nations partitioned Palestine into Jewish and Palestinian states. The Arab states allied in a war to eliminate Israel, but the Jewish State survived, and war between Arab states and Israel continues to this day.

In 1950, Jordan persuaded the West Bank Palestinians to join with the East Bank as part of the Kingdom of Jordan. Although no other Arab country was willing to assume the financial and political burden of assimilating the Palestinians, the Jordanians expected to benefit from the political prestige naturally accruing to the state that espoused the Palestinian cause—still inextricably linked with the cause of Arab nationalism—and presented it to the rest of the world.

Realizing that peace offered the best hope for Jordan, King Abdullah participated in secret talks with Moshe Dayan, emissary for Israeli Prime Minister Ben-Gurion. Other Arab governments, threatened by the overtures, let their displeasure be known. In 1951 a Palestinian youth assassinated the King in Jerusalem; the crown passed to seventeen-year-old Hussein, Jordan's present king.

Inter-Arab conflicts had only just begun. The Arab states disagreed on how to combat Israel or how to support the Palestinian national struggle; many resented Jordan's self-appointed role as representative of the Palestinians. The question was momentarily resolved when the Palestinian Liberation Organization (PLO) was created in 1964 to be the voice of the Palestinian people. But the addition of a new voice to the chorus did not prove the key to Arab harmony as the events of the late sixties soon showed. Egypt and Syria, the PLO's most forceful supporters, pitted themselves against more moderate Iraq and Saudi Arabia. Jordan was caught in the middle. While Syria shelled Israel's northern agricultural settlements and the PLO staged guerrilla attacks on targets deep within Israel, Jordan bore the brunt of Israel's military reprisals.

Jordan lost the West Bank as a result of the 1967 war with Israel. The loss of almost all of its fertile land, commercial enterprises and tourism revenues, and the absorption of some 250,000 Palestinians, devastated Jordan's economy. After the war, Iraqi, Syrian, and Saudi troops remained poised against Israel on Jordanian territory, and Palestinian organizations had become strong enough to threaten the King. Within three years, King Hussein's loyal army of Beduoins was entrenched in a civil war with the PLO. By the time the PLO was defeated, thousands had been killed, more wounded, and a new Palestinian terrorist group had been born to commemorate the "Black September" of Jordan's civil war.

The Egyptian Peace Treaty with Israel in 1979 resulted in further disintegration of Pan-Arab unity: Jordan temporarily broke off formal relations with Egypt in protest. Recently, Jordan returned to the limelight when the U.S. suggested a renewed alliance be established between Jordan and a Palestinian entity on the West Bank. While politicians and soldiers continue to wrestle with the complicated issues of land, refugees and peace, Jordanians will doubtless continue to develop the modern nation and at the same time preserve the ancient homeland.

Literature

Whether you will be uncovering the hidden faces of modern Islam, treading the stones of Roman remains, or delving into the unwritten history of the Nabatean nomads, a trip to Jordan is an excursion beyond the borders of your own culture. Cold immersion into the life and times of Arabia can be a shock to the system; a little preparation can go a long way to ease the transition. Several books may add to your appreciation of Jordan.

The *Qur'an* is an obvious place to begin. While you ponder why this collection of historical trivia, adulation of Allah, and blood-curdling threats to the infidels is the literal and symbolic foundation of Islamic Arabia, you will also learn something of the untranslatable nature of the Arabic language, in which "every word is potentially a talisman conjuring the ghosts of the entire family of words from which it comes" (Jonathan Raban). Among English travel accounts, the classics are several works written by two infiltrators of the *Haj* pilgrimage and two famous soldiers of the desert. C.M. Doughty's *Arabia Deserta* and Wilfred Thesiger's more recent *Arabian Sands* are powerful adventure stories inspired by a romanticized version of Bedouin lifestyle. (T.E.) Lawrence of Arabia's *Seven Pillars of Wisdom* contains vivid descriptions of the battles fought and the territory explored during the Arab Revolt of 1916-18; even if you won't be able to get to Wadi Rum in the Jordanian desert, you must see "Lawrence of Arabia" on the big screen. The Arab Legion chief of the 1940s and 50s, John B. Glubb, wrote several books based on his first, *A Soldier With the Arabs*. A little less adventurous, but more erudite, is Jonathan Raban's *Arabia: A journey through the labyrinth*. Unfortunately, Raban introduces you to more Europeans than Arabs, and only one chapter deals with Jordan (really, Jebel Amman).

For the more specifically archeological and historical taste, there are G. L. Harding's *Antiquities of Jordan* and Julian Huxley's *From an Antique Land*. Both are authoritative, and even absorbing when you have the sights of your itinerary before you. If you're petra-fied you'll miss some detail of the "rose-red city," Iain Browning's *Petra* is wonderfully comprehensive. And finally, Agatha Christie's *Argument with Death* makes a light introduction to the power of the setting at Petra.

Amman

Like Rome, Amman was built on seven hills, or "jebels." Unlike Rome, it *was* built in a day—or perhaps two. Before 1948 Amman was nothing but a tiny Jordanian village. Since then, on two separate occasions, Jordan's population has doubled in one week. After the wars of both 1948 and 1967, Palestinian refugees streamed across the border to claim the citizenship which only Jordan among the Arab countries was willing to extend to them. Most of the Palestinians now live in and around Amman and make up over half of Jordan's population. Each work week sees the population of Amman double as laborers invade the city in search of wages.

The result is an Arabian collage of loud, hectic markets masquerading as streets and gleaming boulevards with bureaucratic monoliths, elite housing and tourist hotels. The city is held together by roller-coaster taxi rides and the measured, almost mournful calls to prayer of each and every mosque and *muezzin*. For all the urban hustle, no one really has anywhere to go and people are more than happy to show you around. They may even treat you to meals and beverages; their generosity is a godsend in a city as expensive as it is hot. There isn't really a great deal to see in Amman, so don't sacrifice time better spent in Petra, Jarash or Jordan's other magnificent sights.

Orientation

"Center City," or downtown Amman, lies in a valley neatly framed by several jebels, or hills. You can easily walk the distance between the Al-Husseini Mosque and the spacious Roman Theater that define the boundaries of center city. The shops, as numerous as grains of sand, sell everything imaginable for negotiable prices. And although hotel prices are fixed by the government, a wide range is represented here.

On all sides, the hills of Amman train their steep faces on the downtown and slope away from the city as would the points of a star. **Jebel Amman,** along whose summit you can see the neon signatures of the fancy hotels, is the governmental and diplomatic core of the city. Its seven numbered traffic circles follow a line leading westward out of town. Sloping down to the north from Jebel Amman lies the ritzy suburb of **Shmeisani,** which also has its share of luxury attractions—both underwater in the swimming pools and after dark in the nightclubs. **Jebel Al Webdeh** is across the wadi to the north of Jebel Amman. Its quiet residential district is spotted with fine hotels but little else. Its northern slope descends to King Hussein St. where the **JETT** and **Abdali** (north) bus stations have attracted a swarm of street food stands and busy hotels. **Jebel Hussein,** up the slope to the northeast, is residential up to its northern boundary at the **Ministry of Interior traffic circle.**

Closer to the Roman Theater is **Jebel Qala'a,** where the ancient city of Rabbath-Ammon is being excavated beneath the site of the Archeological Museum. To the south in the direction of the **Queen Alia International Airport** is **Jebel Ashrafieh,** whose ornate Abu Darwish Mosque can be seen above the **Wahadat** (south) bus station and the **Wahadat Palestinian Refugee Camp.** Beyond the other residential jebels, the city slowly melts back into the desert sands that surround it.

The names of the streets in Amman are better preserved in the collective memory of the people than in Arabic script. And English transliterations are often hopelessly removed from anything the average street-walker will recognize. To find your way around, even with a good map, you will need to remember certain landmarks, in particular the various jebels themselves and the major theaters, banks and monuments on them. Bus and taxi routes, as given below, are described both by the various landmarks they pass and by the street names you see on a map. When in doubt, ask—between a street name, a landmark and people's eagerness to help, you will not only find your way but the way of Arabia as well.

Buses and service taxis to the northern part of the country leave from the Abdali bus station, on King Hussein St. in Jebel Webdeh, while traffic to and from the south is based at the Wahadat station near the Abu Darwish Mosque on Jebel Ashrafieh. For bus #31b to the new airport, you must buy a ticket in the hut in the center of Abdali station. Buses within Amman radiate from the downtown area and cost 50fils for intra-city trips. Buses #53-61 pass the Abdali station, the JETT offices, and Ministry of Interior Circle. #39 climbs Jebel Amman to the numbered circles, while #41-45 go directly to Third Circle before passing Fourth, Fifth, Sixth, and Seventh Circles. Buses #10 and 59 go to the Sports City (north of Shmeisani), and buses #10 and 53 go to the University. Bus #61 travels Jebel Hussein to Duwar Firas; buses #61-63a all pass the Archeological Museum on the Citadel. Buses #21, 23, and 24 pass the Armenian Quarter and the Abu Darwish Mosque on the way to the Wahadat south terminal station.

Service taxis provide good, inexpensive service to the various sectors of this hilly city, and are a bit quicker than buses. Identify them by the white squares on the front doors; the upper number in the square refers to the route. Note that service fare is the same no matter how far along the route you go, and that the long lines at major intersections are for these service taxis. The Center City terminus, origin/final destination for many routes, is up the staircase facing the post office and 50m to the right.

Outlined below are the seven most important routes, as well as four other routes that will prove useful.

Rte. #1: travels on Jebel Amman between Center City and Third Circle, passing First and Second Circles. 60fils.

Rte. #2: starts downtown on Basman St. (look for the Basman Theater), then travels on Jebel Amman to Malik Abd Ribiya St. between Second and Third Circles. 60fils.

Rte. #3: starts downtown on Kureisha St., then travels on Jebel Amman to Fourth Circle. 70fils.

Rte. #4: runs from Basman St. to the Al Amana Circle and gardens, passing near all points of interest on Jebel Webdeh. 60fils.

Rte. #5: from Basman St., travels up Jebel Webdeh to the Queen Alia Institute, just uphill from Abdali station. 60fils.

Rte. #6: starts downtown at terminus on Malik Razi St., better known as Cinema Al-Hussein St., then travels along Kings Faisal and Hussein Sts. to Gamal Abdel Nassar Circle *(Duwar Dakhlia)*, passing Abdali and JETT stations.

Rt. #7: starts by Cinema Al-Hussein, then runs past Abdali station to Shmeisani near the Ambassador Hotel and the Gallery Alia. 70fils.

Other routes: Wahadat station service taxi starts at Kureisha St. (a.k.a. Safki Seil St.; near Petra Bank) and passes near Abu Darwish Mosque on Jebel Ashrafieh. From the same area different service taxis head west to Middle East Circle far out in Shmeisani. 100fils. Another route starts at Shabsough St. near the Gold Market

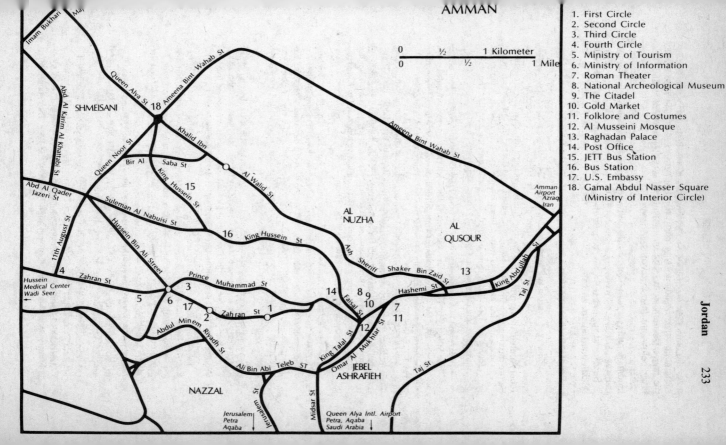

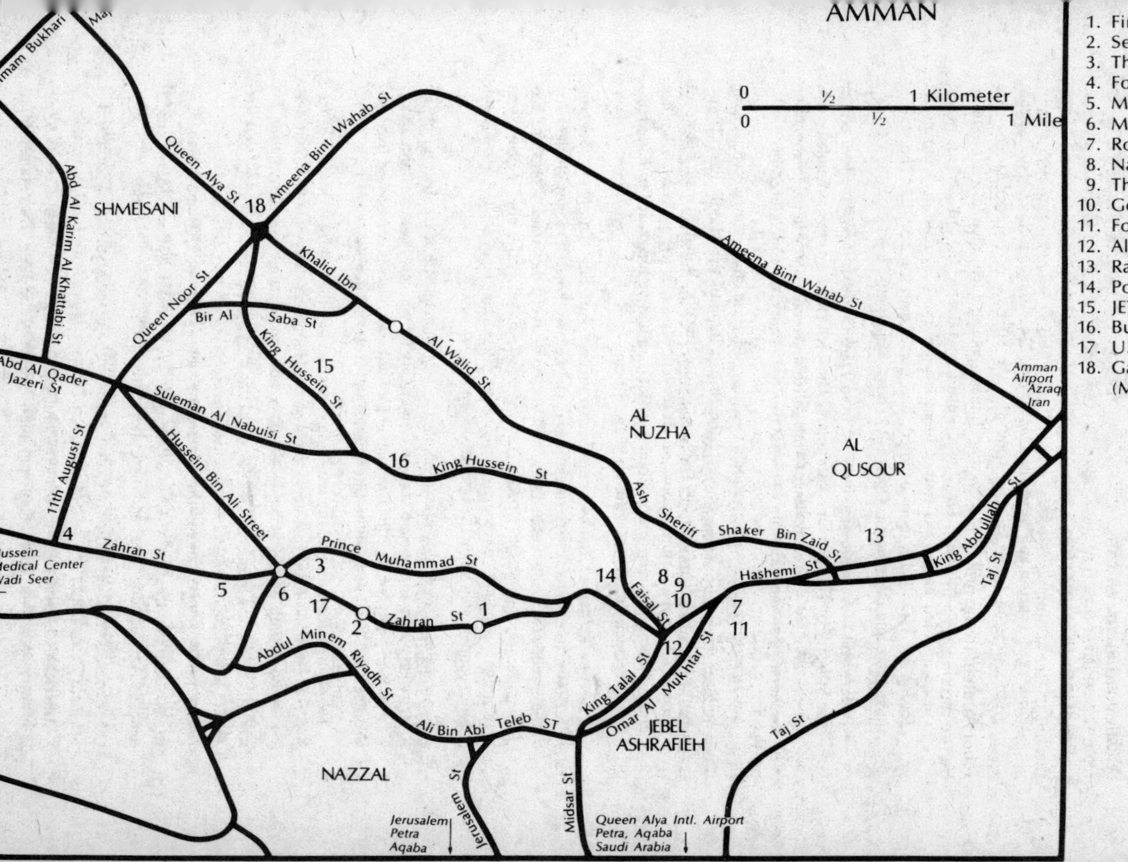
AMMAN
1. First Circle
2. Second Circle
3. Third Circle
4. Fourth Circle
5. Ministry of Tourism
6. Ministry of Information
7. Roman Theater
8. National Archeological Museum
9. The Citadel
10. Gold Market
11. Folklore and Costumes
12. Al Musseini Mosque
13. Raghadan Palace
14. Post Office
15. JETT Bus Station
16. Bus Station
17. U.S. Embassy
18. Gamal Abdul Nasser Square (Ministry of Interior Circle)
0 ½ 1 Kilometer
0 ½ 1 Mile
Amman Airport Azraq Iran
AL QUSOUR
AL NUZHA
JEBEL ASHRAFIEH
NAZZAL
SHMEISANI
Ameena Bint Wahab St
King Abdullah St
Taj St
Shaker Bin Zaid St
Hashemi St
Ash Sheriff
Omar Al Mukhtar St
Faisal St
King Talal St
Queen Alya Intl. Airport Petra, Aqaba Saudi Arabia
Midsar St
Ali Bin Abi Teleb ST
Jerusalem St
Jerusalem Petra Aqaba
King Hussein St
Al Walid St
Khalid Ibn
Prince Muhammad St
Zahran St
Abdul Minem Riyadh St
Saba St
Bir Al
Queen Noor St
Suleman Al Nabuisi St
Hussein Bin Ali Street
Queen Alya St
Abd Al Karim Al Khattabi St
Abd Al Qader Jazeri St
11th August St
Hussein Medical Center Wadi Seer
Imam Bukhari

in Center City, then passes Abdali station and Jebel Hussein to Ministry of Interior Circle *(Duwar Dakhlia)*. 60fils. Between *Duwar Dakhlia* and Third Circle, service costs 60fils. **Wadi Seer Service:** from Third Circle past Fourth, Fifth, Sixth, and Seventh Circles to Wadi Seer. 150fils.

Regular taxis, with yellow squares on the doors and a working meter on the dashboard, will take you anywhere for 150fils plus 50fils per kilometer. For tips on combatting inflated fares, consult the Getting Around section of the Jordan Introduction.

Practical Information

Ministry of Tourism and Antiquities: P.O. Box 224, Amman (tel. 42 31 1/7). From Third Circle on Jebel Amman, walk past the Ministry of Foreign Affairs. The MTA will be on your left across a field; make your first left, then turn left again to reach the front entrance. The Public Relations Office, to the left past the model village and left again, has tourist literature, an excellent map of Amman and Jordan for 1JD, and a more detailed, less useful map for 2.500JD. The staff is hospitable and informative. Open Sat.-Thurs. 8am-1pm.

Department of Antiquities: going west from Third Circle, just past the turn-off for the Ministry of Tourism and Antiquities. They sell excellent, more detailed maps of the country's three regions (Amman/Irbid, Karak, and Ma'an) highlighting archeological sights and ruins (1JD). Open Sat.-Thurs. till 1pm, closed Fri.

American Express: c/o International Traders, with main offices downtown on King Hussein St. (tel. 25 07 2), opposite the British Bank of the Middle East. If you walk uphill, you'll see it on the right just before the fork. Will hold mail, but won't answer telephone inquiries about messages left. Messages left at the branch office across from the Ambassador Hotel in Shmeisani will be forwarded to King Hussein St. Open Sat.-Thurs. 8am-noon and 3-6pm.

Currency exchange: Banks are open to change currency Sat.-Thurs. 9:30am-12:30pm; foreign banks are sometimes open later. Authorized money changers on the street give comparable rates, and are open every day until 8 or 9pm. Exchanges are open at Queen Alia Airport 7am-7pm and at the border near Syria (Ramtha) 7am-2pm. Exchange at the King Hussein Bridge, on the West Bank Side, is open only when the bridge is open.

Central Post Office: downtown on Prince Muhammad St., at the bottom of the staircase where the service taxis to Center City let you off. Poste Restante box is open 8am-8pm, but the office will never forward mail. Cables can be sent from this office. The post office at the Intercontinental Hotel is open 8am-6pm.

Telephone Office: around the left-hand corner and up the hill from the post office, across from the Khayyam department store. Open every day 8am-8pm, but may stay open until 9pm if several calls have not gone through (see Orientation for information on international calls). For telephone information, dial 122; dial-the-time is at 04.

Emergency: It's best to call the American Embassy (tel. 44 37 1) and ask them to call the police or ambulance. Official number for the **police:** 39 14 1. **Medical emergencies:** dial 19 or 21 11 1 or 37 17. For the **ambulance,** dial 75 11 1.

Pharmacies: *Your Guide to Amman,* a monthly pamphlet, lists hotels, all-night pharmacies, and all-night taxis.

American Cultural Center: just off Third Circle on Jebel Amman (tel. 41 52 0). Library open Sun.-Thurs. 8am-5pm, until 7pm Mon. and Tues. They sponsor films and lectures, hand out free translations of daily Arabic newspapers, and in general know what's going on around town.

American Center for Oriental Research (ACOR): P.O. Box 2470, Jebel Amman. From Sixth Circle, walk towards the Amra Hotel, turn right opposite the driveway, then take your first left; ACOR is on the first right after this, one block down on the right (tel. 81 49 17). Responsive staff will answer questions about Amman and Jordan. Their specialized library has information about sights to visit in Jordan. The **Friends of Archeology** sponsor brief trips throughout the kingdom twice a month. Beware of steep membership fee (35JD and photo). For lodging possibilities here, see the Accommodations section. Library open daily 9am-11pm.

Embassies

United States: midway between Second and Third Circles on Jebel Amman (tel. 44 37 1), across from the Intercontinental Hotel. An excellent resource if you have difficulties with Jordanian bureaucracy, especially regarding foreign visas and West Bank permits. Consular division open Sun.-Thurs. 8:30am-1:30pm.

Canada: off Abd Al Karim Al Khattabi St. in Shmeisani (tel. 66 61 24). Open Sun.-Thurs. 8am-2pm.

United Kingdom: Third Circle on Jebel Amman (tel. 41 26 1). Consular division open Sun.-Thurs. 8:30am-1:30pm.

Australia: Fourth Circle on Jebel Amman (tel. 43 24 7). Open Sun.-Thurs. 8:30am-2:30pm.

Egypt: one block closer to Third Circle than the U.S. Embassy. Due to prohibitively long lines of rude Egyptian guest workers, it's better to obtain an Egyptian visa upon entry at an Egyptian port. If you do make it into the embassy, you'll be treated well. No charge for visas for U.S. citizens. Bring a photo. Consular division open Sun.-Thurs. 8am-2pm.

Iraq: between First and Second Circles on Jebel Amman (tel. 39 33 1/2). Iraq currently issues no tourist or transient visas, especially to U.S. citizens; the situation may change if the current war with Iran wanes.

Lebanon: Second Circle on Jebel Amman (tel. 41 38 1). Temporarily closed to the public because of war.

Saudi Arabia: First Circle on Jebel Amman (tel. 81 41 54). Visas issued to Americans without charge; bring a photo. Open Sat.-Thurs. 8am-1pm.

Syria: up from Third Circle on Jebel Amman towards the Holiday Inn (tel. 41 39 2). Take a left at the five-way intersection, then your first right. To obtain a Syrian visa, bring 2JD and two photos. You must have a Jordanian entry stamp on your passport, and have removed all evidence of visits to the West Bank. Open for visas 9am-1:30pm.

Accommodations

Huge tourist hotels define the skylines of Jebels Amman and Hussein. The Intercontinental, Marriott, Ridgeway, and Holiday Inn are all urban reference points by virtue of their size alone. But their luxury rooms would cost you a month's allotment for food. In contrast to these hilltop palaces, Amman's street level is swimming with little hotels. Every block has three or four, every ten-foot alley at least one. But look into a few before you start to rejoice: chances are they're all-male, not too clean, a little intimidating and a lot of money for what they offer. It's not until you get into the range of 8-10JD that

Amman's hotels are dependably clean and safe. What's a budget traveler to do? Below are listed some of the safer inexpensive hotels.

Unclassified Hotels

Haifa Hotel, downtown on King Hussein St., near the large Arab Bank. Lumpy beds, and grimy rooms and toilet area. Fills early. Bed in a small dorm room 1.500JD; 1.350JD per person in a double or triple.

Grand Hotel Baghdad, across the street from the Haifa. Rooms are small and muggy, but if the hotel is full (it usually is), you can sleep on the roof for under 1JD. Otherwise, prices similar to the Haifa.

Cliff Hotel, downtown at the bottom of King Hussein St. (you may have to ask). European—not Turkish—toilets. Fills up almost every night, so bargaining is unlikely. Singles 1.500JD, doubles 2.500JD; showers 250fils extra. 10% service charge.

One-Star Hotels

Bader Hotel, Prince Muhammad St., a few blocks up from the post office towards Jebel Amman (tel. 37 60 2). A particularly safe place with friendly management. Single women will appreciate the relative privacy. Small valuables can be locked in a safe; free luggage storage. Clean rooms. Singles 2JD, doubles 3.500JD. 10% service charge.

Cleopatra Hotel, near the Abdali bus station. Accustomed to foreign students; women will be safe here. Fills up early. Same prices as the Bader.

Happy Land Hotel, King Hussein St. downtown. Looks fairly clean, but noseplugs are occasionally advisable because of the location. Upper rooms are less noisy at night. Singles 2JD, doubles 3.500JD. Negotiable, especially for women.

Two-Star Hotels

Al Monzer Hotel, practically in the Abdali bus station (tel. 38 78 1). Not as dirty and noisy as it looks. Fills up before 5pm. Singles 3JD, doubles 5JD, plus 10% service charge.

Abassi Palace Hotel, Al Amaneh St. a few blocks east of the huge Al-Husseini Mosque. Good for men, women, and couples. Hospitable owner's son speaks English well. The TV room is among the more civilized in Amman. Singles 3JD, doubles 5JD. Triples a great deal at 6.500JD.

Palace Hotel, King Faisal St. downtown, between the "Seiko fork" and Malik Talal St. Clean European toilets, hot showers. Some singles have large beds. Singles 3JD, doubles 5JD, triples 6.500JD, though the owner will sometimes overcharge. Keep asking questions and he'll come down.

Karnak Hotel, King Hussein St. (tel. 38 12 5 or 37 36 1). Same quality as the Palace Hotel. The cafe downstairs serves good coffee, tea, or juice for 100fils. Singles 3JD, doubles 5JD; they'll put an extra bed in the room for 1.750JD.

Three-Star Hotels

A few blocks from the Abdali bus station are two pleasant hotels for men and women with a good cash flow. Both are very safe, and will store your luggage if you plan to return for an extended stay. To reach the **Canary Hotel,** the nicer of the two, from Abdali, walk downtown to the fork at the base of Jebel Webdeh, bear right, then take the first right after the fork up a staircase sidewalk. Rooms are air-conditioned, and breakfast is served outside in the outdoor garden, the home—not surprisingly—of dozens of canaries. Singles cost 4.500JD, doubles 7JD, plus 10% service charge. Two blocks further up the same street, the **Select Hotel** (tel. 37 10 1/2) has darker rooms, only some air-conditioned, and nary a canary to be found. But the place is clean and very quiet, with the same prices as the Canary.

The two best (three-star) hotels downtown are located on the same street as the Abassi Palace. The **Sultan** and the **Saladin** are both pretty safe for women and couples. Singles cost 4.500JD, doubles 7JD. Also downtown, near the Roman Theater, is the four-star **Philadelphia Hotel,** the oldest and most famous in Amman (tel. 25 19 1). Though now more a landmark than a nice place to stay, it is still given high ratings by the government. Rumors abound as to when it will be knocked down, but the Nazzal family is reluctant to lower the boom. If someone offers to spring for you at the hotel of your choice, prove your devotion to Amman by suggesting the Philadelphia. Singles are 8JD, doubles 10JD.

If you want to stay in Amman's fancy new residential and hotel district, where the city's only nightspots are found (hint: they're in the hotels), try the **Omar Al-Khayyam** (tel. 66 41 37). Singles cost 6JD, doubles 8JD.

Pensions

Amman's pensions are intended for family use, and are therefore more expensive than similar quality hotels. Groups, however, can try to work out a deal. The **YWCA** at Second Circle on Jebel Amman (tel. 41 58 8) has small rooms (one or two beds) for 6JD, larger rooms (two or three beds) for 8JD. The **Lipton Pension** at Suq Assukar (tel. 37 58 0), behind the Al-Husseini Mosque downtown, has singles for 4.500JD and doubles for 7JD. You can add beds or people for a few JD extra.

For those with a special interest in archeology, the **American Center for Oriental Research** (tel. 81 49 17) has a limited number of rooms available on a first-come-first-served basis. Call or write to reserve a bed in these simple but clean dorm rooms. The large private house has a family atmosphere; English and archeology are the languages spoken. The 7JD charge includes full room and board. If you plan to stay more than a week, it's worthwhile to become a member. See Amman Practical Information listings for address and directions.

Food

Despite its rich Bedouin heritage, Amman's cooking (cuisine is not the word) hardly merits enthusiasm. It lacks diversity, and is spiced about as imaginatively as the Dead Sea. Lightly spiced and highly priced are the restaurants where the elite meet to eat with their foreign guests; cheap street stands are home to all the bacteriological life not found in the warm, stagnant waters of the Dead Sea.

To fill an iron stomach without taking a great weight out of your wallet, try the felafel and corn-on-the-cob which abound (100fils). Hummus plates and various sizes of salads cost 150fils, and the flat, yellow chickpea-like beans called *tatermos* make a good addition. Bread, however, is the essential element. Every street stand sells some: the flat-bread *khoubz* is the most convenient, the sesame rings *(ka'ik)* the most tasty. Both sell for about one piaster. Kebabs and *shwarma* are always available for about 60pt, but since they remain in the heat all day, you may be sharing them with Amman's winged or crawling residents. The **Government Vegetable Suq,** between First and Second Circles (1½ blocks south) is cleaner than the vast **Mosque and Market area** downtown near Malik Talal St. The market around the Abdali bus station is small and rather dirty; the one around the Wahadat station is enormous and equally dirty.

Amman's sit-down restaurants don't offer your food budget much leeway. The first two places we list are quite inexpensive; the restaurants following are good for splurges. Remember, a 10% service charge is always added to the final bill.

Riviera Snacks, Third Circle. Cold, rather sterile atmosphere. English spoken. Dry ham and cheese sandwiches cost about 450fils. No frills.

Gondola Cafe, just uphill from Central Bank on King Hussein St. Family-run joint where Dad taught himself English so he could scold his sons for not being industrious enough. The watery salad requires three servings of bread, but a whole meal, including tea, costs under 200fils.

Amigo Nabil. From First Circle, walk one block south to Hospital Circle and turn left to the corner. An Italian restaurant with excellent lasagne for 1.700JD and buffet salad with antipasto for 1.500JD. The only place in town that serves cappucino (350fils). Give your splurge some splash with their sangria.

India Chicken Tikka Inn, just downhill from Third Circle on Prince Muhammad St., features Tanduri chicken; half a bird costs 1.500JD. Diversify your orders, though, since many of the other dishes are also excellent.

Restaurant China and Taiwan Tourismo, both on Jebel Amman near Third Circle. Affordable restaurants with carefully-prepared dishes. The China Restaurant serves the cheapest hard drinks in town.

Abu-Ahmed (also known as the New Orient Restaurant), right around the corner from the Intercontinental Hotel. Offers *Musukhan,* an unusual, delicious Jordanian dish, big enough to split with a friend, for 2.500JD. Chinese food is served, but the Arabic fare is their specialty.

If you're in the Shmeisani district and aren't too hungry, ask directions to the **Ata Ali** street cafe. Although it's hard to find, people will direct you to the outrageous neon sign of this ice cream and sweetmeats parlor. **French Loaf Bakery,** one block south of First Circle and around the corner to the left, sells all kinds of French breads almost as cheaply as the downtown markets.

Sights

Amman is often seen as merely a transit center between Jordan's main points of interest, but it has several worthwhile sights of its own. If you remember that it was a tiny town only a few years ago, its attractions seem more significant.

The **Roman Theater,** facing the Philadelphia Hotel downtown, is Amman's best known sight; the city has grown around it for almost two thousand years. Dedicated to Antoninus Pius V, and largely constructed between the first and second centuries B.C.E., the theater still seats about six thousand at summer concerts and performances. Built into the foundations of the theater are two of Amman's three museums. The **Folklore Museum** consists of two rooms filled with mannequins exhibiting Bedouin custom and lore. If you'll be out in the desert, take note of the *mihbash,* the roast coffee grinder you'll still see (and hear) in almost every black tent. The **Museum of Costumes and Jewelry** is more interesting; unlike most museums, which strive to preserve an ancient society or age for a modern audience, this one highlights and explains current attire and jewelry in Jordan. In revealing the origins of certain regional embroidery styles, for example, it explains why the white shawl is called *Nashek Rouho,* "the Thrilling of the Soul." You'll also learn about the origins of agate, whose color soothes the desert-weary eye, and amber, a desert cure for rheumatism and asthma, made from the resinous gum of conifer trees extinct some seventy million years. The museums are open Sat.-Thurs. 9am-5pm, Fri. and holidays 10am-4pm, closed Tues.; admission 100fils to either.

On the southern slope of Jebel Qala'a is Amman's acropolis, the site of ancient Amman. You can climb up **Citadel Hill** from the Roman Theater, but go slowly, or the heat will give you a splitting headache. Don't let the mounds of backyard garbage fool you—they don't necessarily mark off a path. Taxis also make the climb, and bus #63 passes nearby. At the top, the view of the Roman Theater is superb. The wadi below and to the right is the Center City; across from it is Jebel Ashrafieh and the zebra-domed Abu Darwish Mosque. To the east, you'll see the Royal Palace at Raghadan. But you'll have to get a little closer to see the red-and-black regalia of the Circassian guards.

Apart from the panoramic view, the main attraction on Citadel Hill is the **Archeological Museum,** constructed on the site of Amman's major excavation and filled with its spoils. To the north of the site is the Umayyad Castle, built in the seventeenth century. What's left of the Roman Temple, dedicated to Hermes, still stands in the southeast sector of the site. The Castle, barely discernible yet the best-preserved of the ruins, features an Umayyad latrine just inside the North Gate. You'll recognize it immediately by its marked similarity to contemporary Jordanian toilets. The Archeological Museum contains a chronological sampling of all the finds from the different periods of Jordan's ancient history. Open Sat.-Thurs. 9am-5pm, Fri. and holidays 10am-4pm, closed Tues.; admission 100fils.

To the west of the Roman Theater in the wadi are the romantic remains of the **Nymphaeum,** on the corner of Safki Seil St. Here the Romans exchanged their marriage vows a thousand years ago.

The heart of ancient Amman was once the Citadel; today it's downtown, in and around the Al-Husseini Mosque. The Ottoman-style structure was built in 1924 on the site of an ancient mosque. Today, ancient traditions and modern innovations blend in the bustling market area surrounding the Mosque. Food and other merchandise compete for space with the children learning business administration, while the old men nearby are intent on their games of tric-trac and their hubble-bubbling *Nargileh* (water pipes). The Gold Market, between King Faisal and Shabsough Sts., is chock full of knowledgeable Saudis and awestruck tourists. You won't be able to buy, but it's fun to watch.

For a more manageable selection of indigenous products, search through the **Al-Aydi Craft Center.** Off a steep alley leading from Second Circle (follow the sign for the Babaloo Restaurant), it's a non-profit exhibition of jewelry, embroidery, caftans and pottery worked by refugees. Amman also offers an increasing number of galleries displaying national and regional artistic works. Galleries are to be found in the Ministry and luxury hotel districts.

The most impressive display of Amman's artistry however, is the **Abu Darwish Mosque.** Its striking brown-and-white checkerboard dome can be seen clearly from all six other jebels. To get there, take the Wahadat station service taxi from Kureisha St. up Jebel Ashrafieh.

Finally, if you're in Amman during the summer, you can see the world's best camel racing at the **Hippodrome** in Marka. Races are held only on occasional Fridays; the Ministry of Tourism has details. You can call the Royal Racing Club directly at 56 03 3.

Nightlife

Although the night sky over the Jordanian desert is a spectacular display, no comparable stars can be found in Amman after dark. After the last prayer session empties the mosques and the tourists leave their sunset stomping grounds on Citadel Hill, a few cafes stay open and little else. Dinner is usually served late—between 8 and 10pm—after which Amman closes its eyes on the devilish dark.

In the **Babiche cafe,** you can sense the power and social pressures of the elite Jordanian singles crowd from the way they examine each other without words. The cakes are sweet, the prices aren't, and the place closes around 8pm. The cafe is near the Shmeisani junction (tell the taxi you want to go to the *Mukhabarat* or Secret Police Building and you may not have to pay for the ride). Go under the trestle, make your first right, then left, then right. On the other side of the Shmeisani (about twice as far as the Ambassador Hotel, on the same road—a forty-minute walk) is the Middle East Hotel, which hosts an excellent disco on Friday and Sunday nights. The crowd is heavily foreign, especially black African, so the tunes often turn to reggae. You may be able to avoid the 1.500JD cover, but drinks are still 1JD each. Out by Sixth Circle, the **Amra Hotel** also has a fairly lively nightclub on Fridays and Saturdays, with similar prices. The **El Cesar Restaurant** on Jebel Webdeh (tel. 24 42 1) offers more traditional Jordanian music and dancing, but few affordable edibles.

Near Amman

Salt

In the 1940s, when Amman was still a tiny backwater village, the city of Salt was almost chosen as the capital of Transjordan. Today, Salt resembles a mini-Amman: it is a city of jebels topped by a ruined citadel. But the downtown area beneath the Citadel lacks the excitement of the larger city. The pride of Salt is a mosque on Jebel Yushah, which according to Arab legend covers the site of the tomb of the prophet Hosea. However, you can't see the tomb—only the Jordan Valley spread out below. A sleepy little town 30km northwest of Amman, Salt is almost worth visiting. Bus #57 goes there, slowly; a service taxi from Abdali costs 500fils.

Wadi Seer

To the north of Wadi Seer, a small town on the old route to Salt, lie two ancient sights with the surprising names **Araq el Amir** (the Caves of the Prince) and **Qasr el Abd** (Castle of the Slave). The hospitable Circassian villagers of Wadi Seer believe that the secret to the history of these sights is encoded in the carvings on the huge blocks of brown stone which stand between the town and the caves; the only clue offered by the caves themselves, which form two visible rows in the brown limestone mountainside, is the Aramaic inscription "Tobiah" near two of the cave windows.

In the absence of an interpreter for the markings in the stone blocks, local legend holds that the Castle of the Slave was built by a love-struck slave named Tobiah. While his master was away on a journey, Tobiah built the palace and carved lions, panthers and eagles into its walls to gain the hand of his master's daughter. Unfortunately, the master returned before Tobiah could finish the work, and the slave went unrewarded.

Historians prefer to explain the inscription and the castle remains with reference to Tobiah the Ammonite servant. Although Tobiah was a biblical priest, the name of the castle refers to his occupation as a "servant" of God. Joseph Flavius, a first-century writer, also records the wealth of the Tobiad family and the exploits of their young son Hyrcanus. Hyrcanus, a favorite of Ptolemy V and Cleopatra, was kicked out of Jerusalem by Antiochus, the great Seleucid King of Syria, when he sided with the king's rival, Ptolemy. Hyrcanus "settled in the country across the Jordan . . . where he built a strong birtha (fortress) which was constructed entirely of white marble up to the very roof and had beasts of gigantic size carved on it; and he enclosed it with a wide and deep moat." As you approach the white and rose-colored stones which make up the only remains of a Hellenistic palace in the Middle East, try to imagine the original moat, which could only be crossed by circling all the way around the palace, thereby forcing one to admire it from all angles. The area is good for camping; be sure to have a sleeping bag, for the nights are chilly even in summer. The nearby village of **El Bassa** has refreshing springs and a shop selling sweet yogurt on fresh, hot flatbread for 150fils. At the bridge below is an ancient mill and aqueduct; above the left bank of the wadi you'll see the ed-Deir (monastery).

The service taxi to the Municipality of Wadi Seer leaves from Third Circle and costs 150fils. A minibus leaves from Abdali station for the same price and will let you off either in Wadi Seer, at the El Bassa springs, or at Araq el Amir.

Ain Ghazal

At Ain Ghazal ("spring of the gazelle"), you can see a team of American archeologists digging, dusting, photographing and sorting at what many claim is the largest prehistoric site in the Middle East, more extensive even than Jericho. So far, finds have included pre-pottery Neolithic whitewash, vessels made from the calcium deposits in stone. You can check on the progress of the excavation and get an interesting introduction to the practice of archeology at the American Center for Oriental Research in Amman (see Practical Information listings). To get to Ain Ghazal, take bus #67 from Center City to Marka; get off at the stop after the First Circle in Marka *(Duwar Marka)*. Turn right at the corner by the bus stop and walk to the schoolhouse ahead on the right, the headquarters of the excavation.

Deir Alla and Shuna

Deir Alla is the spot where Jacob rested after wrestling with the angel at Phanaral; it is also the site of ancient Succoth. Although a temple and shrine have been uncovered, the ruins are sparse and not easily identified.

A service taxi from Abdali station will take you to Deir Alla for about 500fils. The trip takes one and a half hours, but service is sporadic. The driver sometimes waits across the parking lot from the Arabella office; it pays to negotiate both price and time of departure. If you're hitching, it's a long, lonely trek, as few cars pass. But you do pass through **Zai National Park,** about 5km beyond Salt, where there are perfectly good abandoned camping grounds. Two kilometers past the Ghor Canal, turn right and you will cross the **Zarqa River** (the biblical Jabbok). From there you will see Deir Alla in the distance.

A 34km hitch south from Deir Alla is **Shuna,** the last town of the King Hussein Bridge. Here Jesus exalted the budget traveler, saying "It is easier for a camel to pass through the eye of a needle than for a rich man to enter the kingdom of heaven" (Matthew 19:24).

Pella

A 30km ride north of Deir Alla lands you in biblical Pella, now called *Khirbet el Fahil*. On the way you can clearly see the Qalat Rabadh near Ajlun in the east. The ancient site of Pella extended south across Wadi Jorm to Tel el Hisn, the ancient acropolis with ruins of both a theater and a temple, and northeast to Jebel Abu el Khas and the village cemetery. Since no restoration work has been done, few tourists come here and transportation is minimal. However, despite the difficulty of reaching Pella, the archeological importance of the area shouldn't be underestimated. The serenity, natural beauty, and eerie timelessness of the ruins are best appreciated with sufficient water and a large picnic.

Petra

For more than a mile, you walk in reverent silence, preparing yourself for this holy marriage of vast nature and tireless Nabatean sculptors. Finally this narrow fault, a stark fissure carved three meters wide from the sandstone left by a receding Red Sea, is cut short. You are left defenseless, facing a towering sculpture blazing red in the sunset's fierce glow. It is raw mountains impossibly fashioned by human hands into delicate features. It is the *Khazneh,* the Treasury, Petra's finest monument to the watchful gods of the dead. And it is only the beginning.

Petra is perhaps the most astonishing and unique ancient city bequeathed to us. It's worth changing your travel plans just to explore this Nabatean death-cult city carved to match the imposing proportions of the mountains. Rock: mountain: sandstone: limestone: stone. Petra, in ancient Greek, indeed means stone.

History

The Red Sea is not red. Petra assuredly is. Whether or not the Red Sea parted, the walls of Petra's *siq* certainly did, and you can still walk through Petra's 1½-mile canyon entrance, as Johann Ludwig Burkhardt did in 1812. For seven hundred years, Petra had been lost to all the world but a few hundred Bedouins. The hostile Lyathene Bedouin tribe prevented visitors from venturing into their well-guarded treasure. The Swiss explorer Burkhardt, a recent convert to Islam and well versed in Arabic, heard some Bedouins speak of the "lost city" and determined to find it. At first he was unable to engage a guide, but he knew that if this was the Petra of legend, the biblical Sela, then it must be close to Mt. Hor, the site of Aaron's tomb. On returning from the pilgrimage to Mecca, Bedouin *Haj* visit Mt. Hor on the festival of Id-al-Adha to make a sacrifice. Impersonating a devoted follower of Islam, Burkhardt found a guide and, on August 22, 1812, walked between the cliffs of Petra's *siq*. Awestruck, and driven to sketch the monuments and write his thoughts into a journal, he aroused the suspicion of the Bedouin guide. The ancient rocks were carved by a divine magician, warned the guide, who was now urging the visitor to consummate his sacrifice and leave. Since Burkhardt left, others have never stopped arriving and slowly the mysterious story of the Nabatean City has been uncovered.

The Arabs call the area's water source Ain Musa, or springs of Moses, claiming that here was where the prophet struck the rock and requested water (Exodus 17). Recent excavations at nearby El Beidha indicate that the region was inhabited as early as the Neolithic period. By the eighth century B.C.E., the earliest farmers in the Middle East had settled in the vicinity of Wadi

Musa. By the seventh century B.C.E. the Nabateans had quietly moved in on land controlled by the Edomites and begun to profit from the trade between lower Arabia and the fertile crescent. The Nabatean kingdom flourished and grew, secure in its easily defended capital. The Seleucid heirs of Alexander the Great attacked in 312 B.C.E., but were so easily repulsed that the city enjoyed peace for another three centuries. During this era, compulsive sculptors among the Nabateans carved their huge temples out of the mountains, drawing on Egyptian, Greek and later Roman architecture for ideas. The only truly Nabatean style can be seen in the crowstep staircases that grace the foreheads of many of the monuments. In 63 B.C.E., the Nabatean King Aretas defeated the Romans of Pompey. But the Romans controlled the entire area around Nabatea, prompting the later King Rabel III to strike a deal: as long as the Romans did not attack during his lifetime, they would be permitted to enter after he died. So, in 106 C.E. Romans and Nabateans together began to improve even further on the city carved from Nubian sandstone.

At its height, Petra may have housed an incredible 20-30,000 people. But after an earthquake in 363 C.E., the shifting of the trade routes to Palmyra (Tadmor) in Syria, the expansion of the sea trade around Arabia, and then another earthquake in 747 C.E., Petra declined rapidly. It fell under Byzantine and then Arab control for a few centuries, before the Crusaders tried unsuccessfully to resurrect it by constructing a new fortress. By then it had lost so much of its importance that even its position was forgotten. Petra slowly decayed at the hands of time, earthquakes and a few remaining Bedouins. It was sought unsuccessfully by occasional explorers, but not until 1812 did the rose-red city again open its narrow entrance to Western wanderers.

Orientation and Practical Information

Although the camels amble along at the same pace as ever, it's no longer an eight-day trip from Amman to Petra. The air-conditioned JETT coaches which leave Amman daily at 6:30am for 3JD one way arrive about 3½ hours later. If the wait in Ma'an isn't too long, the service taxi from the Wahadat station in southern Amman for around 1.750JD takes about the same length of time. From Aqaba, the 1½-2 hour trip costs 1.500JD by service taxi and about 1JD by minibus.

Just outside the portico of the ancient city, at the bottom of the hill on which the town of Elji is built, is the **Petra Visitor's Center.** The tourist police here are the best trained and most helpful in the country; their expertise is rivaled only by that of the Bedouin guides you can hire for 2JD a trip. It is easy to tag along behind another group with a guide or to make a group of your own. The various guide books available at the Visitors' Center are helpful, but only the Bedouins can really show you around. One guide in particular, Muhammad Ibrahim, who wears a yellow "expert" cap, has an uncanny way of drawing you into the magic of the mountains. He will also introduce you to many of the Bedouins living in Petra who may invite you to spend the night.

Next to the Visitors' Center is the **JETT bus station,** from which buses return to Amman around 3pm (even if they claim to be ready by 1pm). In the spring and fall peak seasons, reservations are necessary; otherwise you can get a seat without them. Although you'll probably want to spend most of your time in Petra itself, the village of **Elji** is just a few minutes' walk uphill from the Visitors' Center. At the top of the hill, on the other side of the village, is the intersection leading south to the Desert Highway and Aqaba, and north up the Kings Highway back to Amman. The *Ain Musa* or springs of Moses that emerge here are so important that the village has also adopted the name of the valley they create, **Wadi Musa.**

On the other side of the Visitors' Center are the Rest House and the swinging gate at the beginning of the trail down to the *siq*. Here you can rent a horse for the short ride (1 to 2JD), but it's more interesting to walk, keeping your eyes up on the tower cliffs of Jebels Khubtha to the right and Madras to the left, and on the monuments that begin to appear all around you.

Hardly changed since Burkhardt stumbled upon it in 1812, Petra evokes a primitive atmosphere. Although cars now occasionally squeeze through the *siq,* a large restaurant grows inside Petra, and a fancy hotel is opening just outside it, to get away from the tour groups beginning to flock to the *Khazneh* and inner valley only requires a little climbing. A few of the spectacular monuments are close enough to be glimpsed on a one-day jaunt, but most, thankfully, are hidden behind a thin curtain of sweat and inspiration. It is essential to spend enough time in Petra to lose yourself in its wonders. In Petra you'll be cradled in Bedouin hospitality, the best sanctuary for a woman traveling alone. Several European women have married Bedouin men and settled in Petra, which is perhaps why the respect for women is so high here and "admiration" rarely goes beyond offering gifts.

Despite what you will hear from the government about the fragility of Petra's monuments, the most brittle link in the magical chain of spectacle and hospitality is the Bedouin people. The government is trying to evacuate them from their tents and caves in Petra to a housing project near Wadi Musa. But the living soul of Petra is a Bedouin one, and any visit to Petra must begin with a visit to the tents of its Bedouins.

Accommodations and Food

Although Jordan's tourist literature boasts about the government Rest House and restaurant at Petra, you can ignore it during a week-long stay and not miss it. Rooms at the Rest House are only sometimes clean, which is inexcusable at 5JD for singles, 6.600JD for doubles and 9JD for triples. The food is a bit more reasonable: 1.650JD is a standard price for Western, somewhat institutional food. Beer costs about 660fils a bottle. If the Rest House is worth a visit it's mostly because it was built over one of Petra's Nabatean tombs; the dimly lit restaurant is the inner chamber of that tomb.

Inside Petra, accommodations and food are the province of the Bedouins who are caught between their instinctive hospitality and burgeoning entrepreneurship. Several "Pepsi" stands sell drinks and Bedouin meals, yet it is still common to be invited back to the black tent or cave for a meal with the family. While the hospitality is complete, so is the art of business. Knowing they have a monopoly on grub in the Wadi, the Bedouins have inflated the prices of everything bought inside Petra. Higher transportation costs account for some of this increase, but much of it is pure profit search. The shop of the local sheikh Salameh Abu Saksoukah, or 'Father of the Beard,' is just beyond the Roman Theater and is the most expensive of the local joints. Others are found directly across the wadi from the theater, at the foot of Jebel Habis below the museum and in the cave across from the Ed-Deir. This last has only drinks for 150fils apiece while the others serve various combinations of bread, yogurt, rice and lamb for about .750-1JD each.

For a camping site, you have tens of thousands of vacant caves from which to choose. Those far away from the theater area are safe for stashing luggage for weeks on end. Be sure you've got water for the night, for the dry air works on your throat even as you sleep. The most interesting camping in the region is strictly a black tent invitation. They're common enough that you can politely refuse an offer such as Abu Saksoukah's; he will usually ask 1 to 2JD for the night along with dinner and breakfast. Sometimes you can get invitations in the village of Wadi Musa itself. In return for hospitality and often in place of payment, the Bedouin will accept any kind of gift from abroad, though such items are not expected.

Sights

It seems no work of man's creative hand,
By labor wrought as wavering fancy planned;
But from the rock as if by magic grown,
Eternal, silent, beautiful, alone!
Not virgin-white like that old Doric shrine
Where erst Athena held her rites divine;
Not saintly-grey, like many a minster fane
That crowns the hill and consecrates the plain;
But rosy-red as if the blush of dawn
That first beheld them were not yet withdrawn;
The hues of youth upon a brow of woe,
Which man deemed old two thousand years ago.
Match me such a marvel save in Eastern clime,
A rose-red city half as old as Time.

—Dean Burgon, Franciscan Friars' *Guide to Jordan*

The Nabateans worshipped only two gods. Dushara was the god of strength, symbolized by the hard sculptured rock; Al-Uzza (or Atargatis) was the goddess of water and fertility. A finite number of Nabatean and later Roman Kings were also revered. But the number of temples and tombs in Petra seems infinite. These, with the colors and shapes of the mountains and their caves, constitute the sights of Petra.

Even before you enter the *siq,* caves stare at you from distant mountain faces and large **Box Tombs** called *sahrij* monuments call your attention. Although it is unclear whether these huge cubes were really tombs or sacrificial altars, we know that they were carved from hills which no longer stand so close to them. On the left, built high into the cliff, is the **Obelisk tomb.** Closer to the entrance of the *siq,* **rock cut channels** once held ceramic pipes bringing the Ain Musa waters to the inner city as well as to the farm country surrounding it. A nearby modern dam had corroded until, in 1963, it burst and a flash flood killed 28 tourists in the *siq.* While designing a new dam, excavators uncovered the ancient Nabatean dam. Builders used it as a basis for the new dam.

As you enter the *siq,* walls towering 200m on either side of you begin to shoulder out the light. Niches in the rock once held idols of the gods to protect the entrance and welcome the visitor to Petra. For a kilometer and a half, your anticipation is heightened as the *siq* winds along its way and then slowly admits a faint pink glow as the *Khazneh,* or Treasury, slips in to command the exit from the *siq.* At 90m wide and 130m tall, it is the best preserved of Petra's monuments, although bullet holes are clearly visible on the upper urn. Believing the urn to be hollow and filled with some ancient Pharaoh's treasure, the Bedouins periodically fire at it in hopes of bursting this Arabic piñata. Actually, the Treasury was a royal tomb and, like almost everything else at Petra, the urn is solid rock. In the morning, the sun's full rays flood the monument and invest it with a rich peach color, while in late afternoon it glistens rose until the sun drops and an eerie display of red followed by mauve begins.

To the right of the *Khazneh,* Wadi Musa opens up and presents the large **Roman Theater,** ahead to the left and the long row of Royal Tombs on the face of Jebel Khubtha to the right. The Romans built their theater under and into the red stone Nabatean necropolis whose caves can still be seen (and slept in) above it. The Theater seats some three thousand people and is being restored to look as it first did in the second century. Appreciative audiences are returning for the first time in over 1500 years, and, after hiding for centuries in curtained chambers beneath the stage, a marble Hercules finally emerged to greet them a few years ago. Traditional Bedouin dances are slated for performance here in future seasons.

Across the Wadi are the **Royal Tombs.** The **Urn Tomb** or **Palace of Justice,** with its unmistakable recessed facade, majestically commands a splendid view of the still widening valley from a high portico. The stone steps are just a few minutes' climb. Nearby is the **Corinthian Tomb,** a close copy both of the Khazneh and, allegedly, of Nero's Golden Palace in Rome. The **Palace Tomb** is so broad that it juts out from the mountainside. The Tomb had to be completed by attaching pre-assembled stones to its upper left corner. Around the corner to the right is the **Tomb of Sextus Florentinus,** who was so enamored of these hewn heights that he requested his son to bury him in this last outpost of the Roman Empire.

Beneath and to the right of the Royal Tombs are several Bedouin tents and caves, including those of Sheikh Salameh Abu Saksoukah, his son, and his one Bedouin and two Egyptian wives. With a laugh, they will tell you of a Saudi legend to explain the "crow-step" decoration on top of each building. The crow-steps look so much like the stairways leading up to the front doors that the people of Meda'in Salih, a miniature Petra in Saudi Arabia, claim Petra was so wicked and sinful that Allah threw it upside down and turned it to stone. Whatever their origin, these crow-steps endure as the single exclusively Nabatean aspect of Petra's amalgam of architectural styles.

Around the bend to the left, several restored columns dot either side of the paved **Roman main street.** Two thousand years ago, columns lined the full length of the street, while markets and apartments emptied off it. Near the street was an ancient public fountain, suggested today by the raised **Nymphaeum** ruins near its beginning. Further on is the triple-arched **Temenos Gate,** formerly thought to have been constructed to herald a visiting emperor who never actually appeared. Recent excavations reveal that it actually served as front gate of the **Qasr Bint Faoron** (Palace of the Pharaoh's Daughter). Despite the Arabic name, the "Palace" was a Nabatean temple to honor the god Dushara. Across the road to the right, recent excavations have uncovered the **Temple of Al-Uzza-Atargatis,** also called the **Temple of the Winged Lions,** for obvious reasons. In season, you can watch the progress of the American-sponsored excavations here. The single column to the right of the road with two brothers fallen at its feet is known in Arabic as the *Zib Faoron* owing to the Bedouin penchant to attribute the magical or unknowable to the pharaoh. The name means, not surprisingly, the **Pharaoh's Phallus;** the column actually marks the entrance to the ancient Roman city.

Above the Qasr Bint Faoron, a rock-hewn staircase leads to a small **Archeological Museum** purportedly open weekdays 9am-5pm, Fri. and holidays 10am-4pm. Unfortunately, the neighboring Bedouin who unlocks the doors and collects the 100fils admission to the museum is not often around.

Especially if you're visiting during the peak spring and fall seasons, up to this point you'll have had to share the splendor of Petra with a flock of tour-group shutterbugs. Many people, content with this daytrip dosage, will go home raving about Petra's first 10%. It's only the tip of an inverted iceberg; the rest is carefully nestled into dozens of high places across a vast area. These monuments reward the climber with fascinating stone sculptures, spectacular natural beauty, and once-in-a-lifetime vistas. At least two days are necessary for the following four treks and another two or three days if you include the "Near Petra" listings, assuming you do not afford yourself the luxury of getting severely lost a few times. The Bedouins will say you must stay long enough to watch your nails grow long—to experience the redness of their dirt first-hand, as it were.

The shortest and simplest of the climbs begins to the right of the Museum and winds its way up Jebel Habis. At the top is the **Crusader Castle (Qasr Habis),** outclassed by so much else at Petra. The panorama is spectacular, though, and on the way down you can decide if the carved peak resembles an ice cream castle beginning to melt in the desert sun. If not, enjoy the colors. The return hike should not take more than an hour, depending on how many "artifacts" the Bedouins can convince you to look at on the way.

The second climb begins just to the right of Jebel Habis below the Museum. A sign points to **Ed-Deir** (the **Monastery**) and leads northwest, across Wadi Siyah to Wadi Deir, with its fragrant oleanders. As you squeeze through the narrowing canyon you confront a hole of human shape in the facade of the **Lion's Tomb.** A hidden tomb awaits the crazies who try to climb the cleft to the right of the tomb; less intrepid wanderers backtrack to the right and find it a few minutes later. On the path again, the carved block across the wadi represents Dushara, and eventually, stone steps lead you high up, past a providential Pepsi stand (150fils), to Petra's largest monument. The **Deir,** 50m wide and 45m tall, was never really completed and is less ornate than the Khazneh. On the left, a lone tree popping through a crack in the rock leads you to more ancient steps which carry on all the way up to the rim of the urn, atop the Monastery. To the west, through an opening in the mountains, you can see the Wadi Araba stretching from the Dead Sea all the way to the Gulf of Aqaba. Straight across the wadi looms the highest peak in the area, Jebel Harun (Aaron's Mountain). On top of the mountain a white church reputedly houses the **tomb of Aaron.** If you have iodine tablets and a canteen you can pull cold water out of a mountain collector well some 100m east of the monastery clearing. From the well, an elaborate system of stone pipes and ducts is visible on the facing mountain, and Bedouin voices mixed with donkey braying are audible in the lush valley below. The whole trip takes at least three hours, more if you detour into Wadi Siyah and its seasonal waterfall on the way back.

The third hike begins where the second did and winds around Jebel Habis to Jebel **Umm Al Biyara** (Mother of Cisterns), the site of Petra's original acropolis and the biblical city of **Sela.** At this point, a Judaean king supposedly threw thousands of Edomites off the cliff. Constructing your own version of the story from the myriad petroglyphs and inscriptions might drive you over the edge as well. Further south is the **Snake Monument,** one of the earliest Nabatean religious shrines. From here it's about two hours to **Aaron's Tomb** on Mt. Hor (Jebel Harun). The meandering path winds around Mt. Hor before ascending it from the south; when it disappears on the rocks, follow both donkey droppings and the scuff marks of their shoes. As you start to climb Jebel Harun you'll see a lone tent. A Bedouin inside, the official holder of the keys, will escort you the rest of the way and open the building for you to explore. The entire third trek can take 5-6 hours.

One of the most popular hikes is a circular route affording a glimpse of the **Great High Place of Sacrifice** on Jebel Al Madbah. A sign just before the Roman Theater points to a staircase. Visible near the top, **Obelisk Ridge,** the southerly peak, presents one obelisk to Dushara, another to Al-Uzza, a smaller lion fountain and a horned altar. The Northern Ridge also supports a powerful string of sites: two neatly cut altars, an ablution cistern, gutters for draining away sacrificial blood, and cliff-hewn bleachers for a bird's eye view of the slaughter. The magnificent view of the whole Wadi Musa valley should ease acrophobic nerves a bit. On the way down, the first grotto complex past the sculptured lion is the **Garden Tomb.** Below it is the **Tomb of the Roman Soldier,** a well-proportioned structure with an elegant facade and a rock triclinium which has the only decorated interior in Petra. The trail then leads into Wadi Farasa by the Katute site, the dwelling of a merchant apparently driven away by the Romans' nearby waste disposal site. Finally you leave the trail near the Pharaoh's Phallus. The circle, followed either way, takes about 1½ hours.

Near Petra

The region around Petra sparkles with lesser archeological gems, but you can only investigate places within walking or donkey distance. The problem is that all roads in this isolated area lead back to the Kings Highway, none to outlying sites. The protected position of those sites is partly a blessing, though. Outside of Petra, imported commercialism has altered Bedouin life not at all, wildlife is easier to spot, and you may well have the following places entirely to yourself.

Before the entrance to the *siq,* a trail to the left of the Obelisk Tomb climbs to **El Madras,** an ancient Petran suburb with nearly as many monuments as Petra itself. On the way there watch for the short-eared desert hare and a full spectrum of long skinny lizards—red, brown and even pastel blue. Bring plenty of water, some food and a Bedouin guide. The round trip takes 4-8 hours, depending on how much of Madras you want to see.

If you pass the Tomb of Sextus Florentinus and continue on to the *Mughar el Nasara* or Caves of the Christians, you will find a trail cut into the rock that leads to the northern suburb of **Al Barid.** A road passing the new hotel in Wadi Musa also approaches this archeological site. Al Barid is a curious miniature of Petra replete with a short *siq,* many carved tombs and caves, and inscriptions on high places. There's even a painted house, something Petra can't claim. On the return to Petra, there's a slight detour to a High Place at **Wadi Turkmaniya** where a long Nabatean passage is inscribed in Aramaic script above the tomb. Also off the new road past the hotel is **El Beidha.** Excitement runs high among the members of the excavating expedition here because they have uncovered pre-pottery Neolithic remains of a sedentary society dating back to the eighth century B.C.E. This finding would make it one of the earliest known farming communities in the Middle East, along with Jericho on the West Bank of the Jordan. A Bedouin guide can lead you here over an easy trail taking about three hours each way. Again bring food, water, and an extra 1-2JD, harmonica or frisbee as payment.

Aqaba

The setting is perfect. A sweeping natural amphitheater beneath a backdrop curtained with rugged brown hills, Aqaba is Jordan's sole access to the sea. And what a world awaits you there beneath the water: legions of brilliantly colored fish species romp through a fantasyland of coral, each a different shape and psychedelic hue. The marriage of port and resort has proved something less than perfect for budget travelers in Aqaba, however.

Aqaba the Swinging Resort is the darling of Arab elites who need a periodic escape from their dry, overly clad cityscapes. Aqaba the Strategic Port has been the ace-in-the-hole breadwinner for some of the world's most rich and powerful rulers. And the blow-by-blow account of this urban prizefight is rather intriguing. Aqaba's commercial potential has been known since biblical times, when Solomon's ships laden with copper sailed for Ophir from the port of Etzion-Geber. The Romans stationed their famous Tenth Legion here, the Crusaders fortified the port and little Isle de Graye, 7km off the coast, and the successors of Saladin built the fort whose remains shield the modern Visitors Center. In 1917 Faisal and British officer T. E. Lawrence captured the port from the Ottomans during the Arab Revolt. In 1965 King Hussein pulled a master stroke by trading Saudi Arabia six thousand square kilometers of southeastern desert for thirteen coastal kilometers. He proceeded to develop Jordan's new armpit on the Gulf of Aqaba into a wealthy tourist's paradise. Then the re-opening of the Suez Canal in 1975 gave a big boost to the port again.

In this battle of bucks between boats and bathers the budget traveler unfortunately keeps being booted out on his butt. Aqaba today is swimming with outrageously expensive seaside hotels and restaurants, pampering Arabs who forgot to pack their modesty and hospitality, useless weapons in the contest of who can afford more luxury. The humble traveler in search of beautiful people and places may end up chatting with a clownfish at $20 a day.

Orientation and Practical Information

Between King Hussein's villa on the Israeli border and the huge fenced-in port facilities 4km away, Aqaba is one long beach. Super luxury hotels—the Holiday Inn, the Aquamarina, and the Coral Beach—have occupied vast plots of sand next to Hussein's villa, shrinking the accessible strip of no-man's-beach into manageable walking distance. This arrangement is fortunate, since there are no service taxis or buses. The remaining stretch includes the Aqaba Hotel, a military compound, the Palm Beach Hotel, Sinbad's Restaurant and the Al-Samaka Hotel and restaurant down to the port area. On the other side of the port is 10km of beautiful beach stretching to the Saudi border. Aqaba's **Visitors Center,** behind the old fort, has nothing to offer budget travelers and sometimes they don't even speak English.

Air-conditioned banks keep the crowds rolling in with regular business hours, but most shops play it by ear. Generally, they close between noon and 4 or 5pm, only to reopen for two or three evening hours. The **American Express** office is in the International Traders Travel Agency Office on Municipality Square (tel. 37 57), a short hike left of the Ali Baba Restaurant, and up from the Palm Beach Hotel. AMEX claims to be open 8am-1pm and 4pm-7pm but that too is flexible. Some folks, trying to save on the mileage surcharge, rent cars out of Aqaba, not Amman, to see Wadi Rum and the Kings Highway. But even group wallets feel the squeeze. **Kada Rent-a-Car,** charging about 6JD per day, plus 2JD for insurance and 40fils per km, is in the lobby of the large Aqaba Tourist Hotel (off the beach). On either side of the municipal park, three blocks up and a little east of the Palm Beach Hotel, are small bus plazas. From the upper one you can get daily minibuses to Amman for 3JD every few hours, or one to Petra for 1JD. Those to Petra leave when full—usually around 10am and 11am and never on Fridays. Full service taxis leave six days a week from the lower lot for about 1.500JD. A regular taxi offers groups quick transport to

Petra for around 20JD; the service taxi and minibus take three times as long due to stops, tire changes, naps, prayers, etc. Four daily air-conditioned luxury buses leave for Amman from a JETT station about four blocks to the east closer to the beach (mostly in the morning). 3JD buys you a morning departure, on-board bladder relief, and sometimes even a host or hostess for the 4½-hour trip. Boats to Suez in Egypt eventually set sail at least once each day, but are highly unreliable. Deck fare for the sixteen-hour trip is 21JD, third class is 23JD, second class is 28JD and first class, roughly 32JD. Although not officially honored, student ID cards can sometimes secure 5-10% discounts. To buy a ticket, contact an independent travel agent with information on all five companies, whose fifteen ships ply the Jeddah-Suez-Aqaba route. You can book passage in either Amman or Aqaba.

Aqaba is all beach, and almost all of Aqaba is restricted to hotshot hotel patrons. The Aqaba Hotel will let you pay 1JD for the privilege of burning your feet on its white sands. Righteously indignant, sun and coral worshippers often choose to walk southeast to the free pebble beach behind a "Restricted Area—No Camping" sign. Despite snobbish opinions, the water is exactly the same. The best beaches are far and free. The trek out past the port on the 10km strip leading to Saudi Arabia is long and the hitch difficult, but with a whole day to kill and a huge picnic, this is the place to go. Since the tankers are further away than they look and the sun is closer than it looks, watch out for the latter. Eilat in Israel is shockingly close too but there is no need to worry. Even biblical Elath and Etzion-Geber were separate cities which knew how to get along. Throughout the Middle East's wars, Jordan and Israel have kept their promises not to disturb each other's fancy hotels.

Accommodations

A riddle has long circulated among budget travelers: which is higher in Aqaba—temperatures, prices or tan lines? In between trying to sneak to exclusive beaches and discos, spend some time carefully choosing a hotel. Especially in summer, the stifling night time heat may preclude sleep without an air-conditioned pillow. The sleazy joints have fans, but all they do is noisily blow the hot air around. Although you forego the shower (however sleazy it is) camping out is the only way to expose yourself to outdoor breezes. It is legal but, inexplicably, frowned upon. The easiest place is beyond the port if you are careful with your belongings and plan to be up with the sun.

Al Absi Hotel, near the market a few blocks up from the beach. Clean with real toilets and showers. Obscene prices for only tiny fans to ward off the heat. Singles 5.500JD; doubles 7.500JD.

Palm Beach Hotel, on the beach (tel. 57 80). Actually a pension with its own stretch of sand and restaurant. Private bath and air conditioning included. Doubles 8JD; triples 12JD. With bargaining, you can reduce it by 1JD.

Al-Jamil, adjoining the mosque up from the Palm Beach Hotel (tel. 41 38). An arrogant little place with tiny beds and wimpy fans. Singles 3JD, doubles 5JD.

Red Sea Hotel, up from the Palm Beach to the west of Al-Jamil (tel. 21 56). Fans blessed with a crosswind. Fills up quickly, but quite safe—best cheap place for single women. Singles 2JD; doubles 3JD.

Nile Palace Hotel, near Red Sea. Clean rooms and toilet; toy fan. 200fils for salad, hummus, and tea breakfast. 2JD per person. Bargain down.

Al-Samaka Hotel and Fish Restaurant, on the beach. Cheapest, sleaziest, smelliest place in town. Small beachfront and good fish, though. 1.500JD per person.

But you came to Aqaba for a splurge, right? The **Coral Beach** and **Aquamarina** are four-star hotels on the beach, but the three-star **Aqaba Hotel** is the best deal. Singles are 6JD, doubles are 8JD and you can sometimes put four or five in a cottage for 10 to 12JD. The air conditioning on the water can't be beat.

Food

The fare of Aqaba is exactly what it claims to be: only fair. Fresh fish should be a welcome and obvious addition to the Arabic menu, but it's actually difficult to get here. Due to a low plankton content in the clear northern waters of the Gulf of Aqaba, there are few commercial fish here. Jordanians are not permitted to work Saudi waters further south. A few Lebanese have opened the embargo somewhat, and you certainly won't starve, but it's no wonder that Aqaba's the only city in Jordan where men and women are thin enough to feel comfortable in briefs and bikinis.

Ali Baba Restaurant, northwest of the Palm Beach Hotel. The "in" hang-out these days. Tasty, filling spaghetti and meat sauce 770fils, soups 2-300fils. Tea or beer (400fils) available all day.

The Chinese Restaurant, west of Ali Baba's near the Grindley's Bank. A few excellent dishes—try sweet and sour beef with rice, 1JD. Various thick soups are 3-400fils.

Sinbad's Fish Restaurant and next to it **Al-Samaka,** on the beach, offer good fish for 1.500JD. The salad and hummus (each 100fils) suffer from water floodage. Coffee and tea free with full meals. Good local wine at 1.500JD.

If you're just looking to fill up, fruit, bread, and cheeses are found on two streets leading away from the bus station parking lots to the east.

Sights

The only sights really worth seeing in Aqaba belong to the sea. Above all else, stick your be-snorkelled head underwater and breathe naturally for as much of your visit as possible. This **coral reef** ranks among the world's top five, and it's cool in more ways than one. Most fancy hotels and bikini barns rent snorkels, masks, and fins (always wear *some* foot covering). They'll take you out, but self-exploration is where it's at these days. Try to go near the Saudi border where the fish run on super-octane. Remember—no coral-snatching or spear-fishing allowed.

The **glass-bottom boat** rides available up and down the coast are cute but costly. If you've never been to a tropical pet fish store, they're definitely worthwhile. The fare is 6-10JD whether your group is two or twelve. Make sure you ask the helmsperson to zero in on a small shipwreck (there are lots).

Aqaba should thank its lucky starfish for aquatic splendors, because interesting sites above sea level don't really hold water. The military has made the remains of a Crusader castle on **Pharaoh's Island** (Isle de Graye, 7km offshore) off-limits. Baldwin I built it if you're still interested. The ruins of **Etzion-Geber** at Tel el Khalifa, a bit north of the King's villa, are pretty sparse and inaccessible. The **Middle Ages Fort** in a palm grove near the Visitors Center is almost always closed and, even when open, looks just like an empty fort, although the double-arched portico sports the Hashemite Coat of Arms—certainly nothing to sneeze at. It's not even so easy to find the store owners who meticulously fill little glass bottles with colored sand by hand any more. Ask around if sand's your bag.

Near Aqaba

Those who most appreciate the majestic grandeur of **Wadi Rum** revel in its inaccessibility. No buses or service taxis call it their destination and most Jordanians have never been here. Buses and service taxis along the Desert Highway will drop you off if you pay the full price of your seat, however, and it is easy to hitch from there. The service from Aqaba to Ma'an, or from Petra to Aqaba, costs 1JD. The only other option is to rent a car—cheaper from Aqaba than from Amman if you're only visiting Wadi Rum.

The sign on the Desert Highway points to Ram and to Mudawwara near the Saudi Arabian border. From an old 18km road you bear right onto a flat track for twelve more kilometers until you reach the fort of the Desert Camel Corps. They're descended from the Arab Legion organized by T. E. Lawrence of Arabia in 1920. In the history of his desert campaigns, Lawrence wrote of the rusty crags towering all around so that his "little caravan fell quiet . . . ashamed to flaunt itself in the presence of such stupendous hills" (from *Seven Pillars of Wisdom*).

The Desert Patrol, however, are proud to flaunt and be photographed on their ornamented camels and in their distinguished uniforms. Their full-length zabouns are crisscrossed by camel-leather cartridge straps and graced by bright red bandeliers, daggers and pistols. Stay on their good side. The red and white checked *kaffiyeh* with black cord *(egal)* is worn by all the male Howeitat Bedouins here, and their wives still embroider the colorful patterns on their long black dresses. Many of the men wear a *thobe,* a Bedouin version of the *jalabeya* and camelskin thonged sandals. If all this looks strangely familiar, you probably saw some of these very same Bedouins in *Lawrence of Arabia,* filmed here.

Beyond the ruins of the Nabatean temple behind the Bedouin tents, the great massif of Jebel Rum shoots up to 1754m. A jeep, or better, a camel can take you further through the sheer rust cliffs towering above the mudflats. These monstrous slabs of granite and sandstone thrust through the desert floor millions of years ago, and their striations in the bays and apses point toward magnificent vistas down the 130km-long wadi. The pale, almost purple mountains cast against a deep blue sky have inspired the name **Valley of the Moon,** seen on some of the tourist brochures. For 1-2JD, a Bedouin will lead you on camelback to a crack in the rocks where the springs that support all the wadi's life begin. Dark stains point out the conduits carved by the ancient Nabateans to conserve their precious water. The Bedouin can point to many places where huge boulders shoulder Thamudic graffiti thousands of years old. Such script, which evolved into modern Ethiopic rather than Hebrew or Arabic, can be seen from Mada'in Salih in Saudi Arabia to Ma'an.

Jeep and rented cars are granted permission to continue through Wadi el Yutm el Umran to Khirbet Kithara back on the Desert Highway near Aqaba. Be sure to leave yourself plenty of time to enjoy the fantastic Bedouin hospitality, especially if you opt for the camel ride. So far, no commercial stands have sprung up at Wadi Rum, so bring food and water with you. Camping is easy; if the Bedouins don't tender an invitation, the Desert Police will suggest places to camp. You are completely safe in the desert. Beneath the watchful eyes of the caverns cut into the cliffs by Allah, you are protected from everything but thirst.

The Kings Highway

Only the long, monotonous Desert Highway fills the gap between the Government Rest House at **Ras en Naqab**—from which you can see a vast expanse of wasteland flowing from the stormy sands of Wadi Rum—to the Roman reservoir at **Jiza** near Amman. To the west and parallel to the Desert Highway, however, the **Kings Highway** strings together ancient civilizations and their monumental mountainside castles. Except for the impatient holiday-maker rushing from Amman to Aqaba or the traveler with only three days in Jordan to be spent at Petra, this ancient route is the way to travel the length of Jordan.

The transportation system here is woefully inadequate and unreliable. Service taxis run only when full and then only a short distance. It's rarely worthwhile to sit for hours waiting for them nor to insist they tell you when they'll leave—they don't know. Either you buy the remaining seats or let your thumb do the walking. From Wahadat service taxis go to **Madaba** for 300fils (last return is 6pm, give or take 3 hours). If you will skip Madaba to do it in a separate daytrip from Amman, service from Amman to Karak is 1.700JD.

Despite light traffic and a preponderance of full cars, hitching along the Kings Highway is not so difficult—you can expect to wait up to two hours for a ride. Of course a light pack and lots of water are a must. On Highway 49, 18km south of Amman, is the junction for Naur, a tiny Circassian town. By the mini-obelisk marking the Kings Highway/Desert Highway fork, you often see a small group of hitchhikers waiting to see if their first offer will take them to Wadi Rum and Aqaba or Madaba, Karak, Shobak and Petra.

Madaba

The Government Rest House at Madaba is built on top of the Madabas of Moabites, Nabateans, Romans and Byzantines. There is little of interest in the Rest House, and only scant remains in the town. Although Madaba was a Roman provincial capital, only a cistern and a few mosaics still exist. The Rest House does have one specialty—its steak plates for 1.500JD. The town also has its specialty—the **Map of Madaba.** Discovered in 1824, it is the oldest map of ancient Palestine, dating to the sixth century. It stretches from Sidon (modern Lebanon) to Egypt, but centers on a road map of ancient Jerusalem.

The Rest House, just before the town's center circle, will direct you to the **Church of St. George,** where the map forms part of the floor. A guide will show you first where the mosaic, originally made of 2.3 million tiles, was broken to make it fit into its new place and then some Byzantine coins found here. The first right after the Rest House and then the first left take you to signs for the Museum (open weekdays 9am-5pm, Fri. and holidays 10am-4pm, closed Tues.). Some of the mosaics here are as colorful as the Map, with four shades of red, five of blue-green and other colors.

Near Madaba

Mount Nebo

On Mount Nebo Moses was granted a view of the promised land before he died. If you're hitching down the Kings Highway, explain Mt. Nebo's significance and ask if your ride is interested in the detour. Otherwise, traffic is too light for convenient hitching here; you may need to take a taxi to get to the site. 1JD round trip should do it, if you can't get a ride from the tourist police at the Rest House. In Madaba, the right turn after the Rest House passes a mosque en route to Mt. Nebo.

On the way, a beautiful tree-lined road offers vistas of the Jordan valley. On Jebel Nebo itself are only a few dolmens (tombs), but if you continue to the higher Mount Siyagha there is a huge illuminated cross marking the **Memorial of Moses.** This building, still under renovation, houses many local mosaics. Along the road you pass the **Ain Musa** from which Madaba gets its water. This is the biblical **Beth Peor** (also called **Pisgah**) opposite the secret cave where Moses was buried.

Zarqa Ma'in

Herod the Great, King of Judea in 40 B.C.E., frequently visited the hot mineral springs of Zarqa Ma'in to relieve his rheumatism. As he lay dying, he was carried here from his fortress at nearby **Mukawir** where John the Baptist was beheaded (Matthew 14:1–12). The road from Madaba descends southeast from a high escarpment to the Zarqa Ma'in river into which spring water cascades from the low cliffs. From here you can see the hills of the West Bank rising across the Dead Sea. If you can find the places (you'll have to ask around) you can join local Arabs in the hot indoor pool (**Hamman es Zerqa)** sunk in the cliff face or bathe under torrents of the hot waterfalls. The indoor pool is open to men only in the morning and women only in the afternoon and is, thus far, popular only among the Bedouin. About 5km further south are Herod's mineral springs and 4km further, the Dead Sea. It's possible to camp although there are no facilities or refreshments. Aside from a taxi, hitching is the only way to get here and leaving leaves your thumb no option. Stock up on fluids whenever the wandering vendor comes acallin'.

Karak

The Kings Highway from Madaba to Karak climbs a series of escarpments only to drop into their wadis en route to the Dead Sea. On one such escarpment is biblical **Dibon** where the Mesha Stele was found in 1868. The original huge tablet, engraved by King Mesha with the earliest Hebrew script found up to that time, is now in the Louvre. Ancient Roman mile markers appear on both sides of the road approaching the modern town of Dhiban, and after it falls away, the great **Wadi Mujib** opens up. This ancient border gorge between the Moabites to the south and the Amonites to the north is 4km across and 1100m deep. The view from either embankment is powerful, appropriate for an approach to Karak.

Karak itself is the largest in the long line of mountain-top Crusader castles stretching from Turkey to Aqaba. Baldwin I built it as the precise midpoint between Shobak and Jerusalem. If geometry leaves you cold as a castle stone, then stay at the Government Rest House in Karak. You can see the lights of Jerusalem clearly through the starry night, yet tomorrow's ride to Shobak is less than two hours. From the road up to Karak you have to bear right all the way around the town to reach the Rest House and the castle entrance. The thirteen doubles available at the **Rest House** cost 6.500JD each; extra beds run 3JD. You can eat steak (2JD), roast chicken (800fils) and mazza (250fils) out on a terrace overlooking the wadi leading down to the Dead Sea just across from Hebron. The main street in the town of Karak leads right out of the Castle to a small market and a number of cheap kebab stands.

Although the Castle is virtually destroyed, its building blocks are still large enough to leave you awed. Inside are large audience halls and smaller adjoining barracks. You can still see the bolt holes for mammoth stone doors which have since turned to dust or—worse—souvenirs. The upper story still has a few intact walls providing views into the deep dungeons and cisterns. To the west, across the moat, are battlements from which unwanted prisoners were cast to their deaths. The tower in the northwest corner was added in the thirteenth century by Baibar Sultans. Beneath it a 50m tunnel leads out of the town through an arched gateway. To the right of the castle entrance, you can descend a stone staircase to the **Museum,** open Sat.-Thurs. 9am-5pm, Fri. and holidays 10am-4pm, and offer a small donation. It has wonderful descriptions of the frightening archeological site of **Bab edh-Dhra,** the biblical cities of Buseirah and Rabbah (also on the Kings Highway), and Dhiban's Mesha Stele.

Near Karak

The road from Karak away from the Kings Highway follows Wadi Karak down 2km past Bab edh-Dhra towards the Dead Sea "port" of Mazra'ah at the head of the Al Lisan (Tongue) peninsula. The cemeteries at the ancient site seem to have held some twenty thousand tombs containing an unbelievable five hundred thousand bodies and well over three million pottery vessels. The size of the long bones indicate that average height in Bab edh-Dhra was a healthy 2m. Expect very little traffic whether you're thumbing between here and Karak or along the Wadi Araba Highway linking the Dead Sea to Aqaba. Stop in at the **Mazra'ah Police Post** 5km north of the junction if you need assistance.

Tremendous hospitality is assured in towns just north of Karak on the Kings Highway (Rabbah, Qasr) and just south (Mazar, Tafila). The surprisingly large mosque at **Mazar** houses a small **Islamic Museum** on the first floor. Only after you pass Mazar and descend into the great Wadi Hasa does Karak begin to fade from view.

Shobak

Shobak was the first of seven castles built by Baldwin I to control the triangular trade between Syria, Egypt and Saudi Arabia. From the road you'll see a concrete two-story structure on the right. At the dark tire marks on the road, turn onto the gravel track to the castle. If you miss it you'll come to the town of Nijil/Shobak with a Housing Bank on the right and then a gas station. Although most of the castle is gone, the view from the approach road across the natural moat is outstanding when the huge white stones are silhouetted against the sky and the desert brush. Villagers who lived inside the castle walls and depended on the water from the rock-hewn well, 375 steps deep, have recently abandoned the area.

Jarash

Amidst the many Arabic phrases you are unlikely to understand is a timeless Jordanian expression which may be translated for you when a host apologizes for what he perceives to be the sorry state of his country. "Like the ruins of Jarash" does not sound very complimentary, yet Jarash deserves a place among the outstanding ruins of the world. Called the Pompeii of the Middle East, it is the most extensive provincial Roman city left to us, and the only great Decapolis city with any significant remains. Because of its relative isolation in a remote valley among the mountains of Gilead, Jarash has survived long after the great Decapolis cities of Gadara (Um Qeis) and Philadelphia (Amman) were destroyed.

The Roman occupation of the site was extensive: very little pre-Roman evidence exists, even around the permanent water source. However, inscriptions calling the town Antioch on the Chrysoras River reveal that one of the Seleucid Kings Antiochus had a prominent outpost here. But, the Pompeii of the Middle East began teeming with life when the Roman Emperor Pompey conquered the area in 63 B.C.E. A self-governing democracy, Jarash joined the Decapolis and celebrated with a 250-year building spree. But, when the Syrian trading center of Palmyra was destroyed, when its Nabatean trading partners to the south began to decline, and when the Byzantines began using the stones of monuments for their churches, Jarash finally fell into ruins. The Persians sacked it in 635, and the great earthquake of 747 further shook things up. By that time, however, the Muslims had control. The Crusaders describe Jarash as uninhabited and it remained abandoned until it was rediscovered in the nineteenth century. After the invasion of Ottoman Turks, a Circassian community built the modern town just across the tiny river near the Rest House.

Since excavations begun in 1925 have uncovered so much, a visit to Jarash is like complete immersion in the Roman bath of antiquities. And while your imagination is spirited away by columns, theaters, temples and gates, remember that 90% of ancient Jarash still lies buried beneath your feet.

Orientation and Practical Information

About 50m beyond the Triumphal Arch, the **Visitors Information Center** is on the left of the main road entering the city from the south. Here groups of any size may hire guides for 2JD. You can also buy the comprehensive yellow pamphlet for 100fils. The tourist police, helpful if you need them, mostly fade into the ruins. From the South Gate down the Street of Columns to the North Gate, the entire city is barely 1 km long—eminently walkable.

Jarash offers no real accommodations, although people occasionally camp on the outskirts of town beyond the Synagogue Church. The **Government Rest House,** to the right of the Forum as you enter the South Gate, offers complete meals for 1.750JD. The tiny Chrysoras ("Golden") river separates the ancient city on the west bank from the new town on the east. By heading down from the Visitors Center to the Wadi and up the street on the other side you can walk two blocks to all the cheap sidewalk stands in the marketplace. Avoid the felafel here: the oil looks old enough to have anointed Herod's crusty old joints.

You can also enter the new town from where the Street of Columns meets the first intersection. From the Tetrapylon, walk right to the old Roman bridge which leads you to the market and the bus/taxi station. Minibuses and service taxis go to and from Amman (420fils), Ajlun (230fils) or Irbid (370fils). You'll have to be pushy to get a seat. Sparse accommodations and services should not present a problem, however. With an early start, the ruins at both Jarash and Ajlun can be seen in a day, leaving you time to get back to Amman or to Irbid for the night. If you're hitching to Amman, Dibbin or Ajlun, walk south from the Visitors Center to the major intersection less than 1 km away. The right turn goes to Dibbin National Forest (where camping facilities are being built) and Ajlun, while the left (or straight) road returns to Amman. For Irbid, do *not* go to the road exiting by the North Gate. This old road leads not north, but west. Instead walk southeast from the North Gate to the main road heading north which empties onto the west side of the Roman Bridge or the taxi stand due north.

Sights

Coming from the south, as Emperor Hadrian did in 129 C.E., you are greeted by the triple-arched **Triumphal Arch.** The city's multitude of columns and ruins are framed beyond this portico, built outside the city walls to accommodate further growth. The Persians city never quite reached the Arch before the Persian offensive. The Persians contributed but one monument: the polo goalposts seen in the **Hippodrome** through the Arch to the left.

Ahead, the South Gate opens into the **Forum of Ionian Columns,** formerly the site of a Roman marketplace and exhibitions. To the left you can climb into the **South Theater.** Behind its five thousand seats is the ruined **Temple of Zeus.** From the Forum to the North Gate is Gerasa's main drag, the **Cardo Maximus** (a.k.a. "Street of Columns"). The 260 columns on either side once were topped by aqueducts carrying water throughout the ancient city. At its first intersection, called **South Tetrapylon** since four slabs of stone outline it, you can turn right to the Roman bridge and new town or left to the **Mosaics Museum,** dedicated to preserving the few relics that escaped Caliph Yazid II's order to destroy all "images and likenesses" in 720 C.E.

Along the Cardo you can make out the grooves wild chariots wore into the huge paving stones. Ahead and to the left, the "crow-step" designs on the **Cathedral** and **Fountain Court** are similar to those found in Petra; they bear witness to the presence of Nabatean traders in Jarash. Nabatean coins have also been found here. In late Roman and Byzantine years, the fountains were used in an annual reenactment of the Miracle at Cana where water was changed into wine. Enjoying any excuse to drink, the bishop sat in the large stone chair between the staircases in the Fountain Court.

Before the second intersection stand four arches which used to support a central dome. To the left of this North Tetrapylon are the semicircular **Nymphaeum** fountains. One set of restored stairs leads to the **Propylaeum** and another stone staircase continues to the great **Temple of Artemis,** the patron goddess of Gerasa. The view from its monumental gate, built on the highest point of the ancient city, is magnificent. In honor of Hadrian's visit, Corinthian capitals replaced their Ionian predecessors on these 15m columns. Behind the Temple is the **North Theater** and across the street rests one of two important **Thermae,** or Roman baths, of the city. The **East Baths** are across the Wadi, just north of the mosque in the new town. Scattered around the western part of the city are the ruins of some thirteen churches of more recent vintage. They're of little interest today; even when first built, the stones were pillaged from the larger monuments and ornamentation was carelessly executed.

Near Jarash

Ajlun

A huge peak towers over the little town of Ajlun (pop. 4,700); at its base lies the town's main circle, which revolves around a large hena shade tree. Ajlun's mosque is actually only a minaret left over from an eighteenth-century mosque built on an abandoned Byzantine church. Below the spire is the sleepy marketplace where you can buy cheeses, fruits, breads and, if you're feeling holy, cheap clothing. Although the town could be visited for its picturesque setting alone, people usually come to climb the 1300m mountain crowned by the **Qalat Rabadh,** visible from all around. From the center circle, near a stone marker citing the construction of the castle in 1184, you can catch a taxi to the top for 500fils each way. It takes over an hour to walk up, perhaps a half hour to return. The driver will usually be glad to show you around if you'll take the trip down with him also. Saladin's cousin and local governor Izz Al-din Usamah built the castle in response to the construction of the Roman castle of Belvoir, which is in Israel's Jordan valley. From the high stones the view is breathtaking even if it's not quite clear enough to see Mt. Hermon on the northern edge of the Golan Heights or the Dead Sea. The Mamelukes used the castle to transmit messages either by beacon or by pigeon: from Baghdad to Cairo, day or night, the relay could be made in twelve hours. The drive from nearby

Jarash still takes almost an hour and from Irbid or Amman almost two. So far the only lodgings are the luxury **Rabadh Hotel,** with rooms for 6.600JD (the beds are big enough for two) and an overpriced terrace restaurant overlooking the castle and the valley. If a splurge means scenery to you, it's a steal.

Dibbin National Park

From the town of Dibbin, the National Forest extends some 20km to the south. It can get quite crowded on Fridays, which is family day, but this makes the hitching even easier than usual. Though the Aleppo pines, many oaks and generally fertile forest may be an incredible sight to Jordanians whose country is 80% desert, it is still just a forest, nothing more. Camping facilities will make this a convenient base for exploring Jarash and Ajlun. On the old road to Jarash near Dibbin, the government is now completing a Rest House to make accommodations and meals available. Rooms will be 5.500JD for singles, 6.500JD for doubles; extra beds for 3JD.

Irbid

North of Jarash, the main road passes through Husn, whose few remains indicate it was probably ancient Dion of the Decapolis, and then forks right to Ramtha and the Syrian border or left to Irbid. The latter, Jordan's capital of the north, is a fast-growing industrial center with a new University (Yarmoukh). For travelers, though, Irbid is but a pit stop on the way to Um Qeis and El Hemma. It's the only place in the north with accommodations (good if you miss the border closing beyond Ramtha). Other than this the town pulls out all the stops and is pure pit. The bus from Amman or service taxis from Jarash or Ajlun will let you off along the main drag. From here you must ask directions 1) to the North terminal for transit north, 2) to the University and the two respectable hotels or 3) to the one dive in town, **Al Armen.** This hotel is just a block to the right at a large intersection if you continue walking from where you were dropped off (ask for the Rivco stores and you're almost home). Singles are 1.500JD, doubles 2.500JD, and showers 250fils. If you're lucky, it will already be filled up by sorry-looking strangers. Ask to be led to the service taxi (150fils) to Yarmoukh University. (A private taxi is about 500fils.) The atmosphere here is a little more pleasant and the students helpful in directing you to one of the hotels. The **Al-Nasim Hotel,** a few minutes walk from the campus (tel. 74 31 0), has clean rooms for 4.500JD a single, 7JD a double. On the other side of the campus is the **Al-Razi Hotel.** Its clean, spacious rooms have private baths, but at 8JD for singles and 10JD for doubles, you'll probably only want to frequent the excellent restaurant here. Sitting outside among veiled students and *nargileh* water-pipes, you can order pizzas for under 1JD or a mini mensaf for 1.500JD. Some college bimmy from the U.S. must have taught them how to make pizza—it's great.

Near Irbid

Um Qeis and El Hemma

For archeological fanatics, the dark ruins at **Um Qeis** (Biblical Gedara) may prove interesting. For aquatics aficionados, the indoor pool there ranks as one of the most famous in the region, and the most bizarre in the world.

The Romans' use of strong black basalt stone infuses the rooms with an eerie atmosphere. The remains, depleted by plunder, belie the grandeur which greater Gedara achieved in its heyday as a Decapolis city. As a huge resort for Romans who wanted to live near El Hemma's hot springs, Gedara had several theaters and more temples even than Jarash. You can see Lake Tiberias on the clearest of days: greater Gedara once extended to those distant, verdant shores.

Head for El Hemma for the beautiful ride in sight of the Golan Heights and the Sea of Galilee. From Um Qeis you can hitch or wait for the next minibus from Irbid to El Hemma. While you wait on the road near where you first alighted from the bus, look for a woman garbed in the traditional black smock of the Irbid region: she bakes huge flatbreads on an open hearth, and for 100fils she'll serve you one with salty yogurt and a spice called *za'atar*.

Shortly beyond Um Qeis a soldier will ask to see your passport. Just after the military road block, the valley of the Yarmoukh River opens below. The high plateau across it—surprisingly near—is the Syrian Golan Heights, recently annexed by Israel.

Arriving in the tiny village of **El Hemma,** you should quickly resolve not to stay here overnight in the bright pink staircase-shaped hotel which charges 4.500JD for a small room. Although the horrendous sulfurous odor probably comes from the mineral springs, it seems to be just as strong at the hotel. At the springs compound, a shack on the right sells tickets; the cafe nearby sells sandwiches and watermelons.

Men swim on Fridays in the outdoor pool, despite rumors of tiny biting bugs lurking within. The rest of the week, 500fils buys entrance to the infamous indoor pool. Three bare bulbs transform the yellow room into a urine-tinted womb, while sulphurous minerals in the water make the air smell worse. The lukewarm water only adds to the Freudian nightmare. Don't complain or grimace: your delighted Arab co-bathers, unversed in aquatic arts, have probably never been in any other pool. If you swim, they'll think it well nigh miraculous.

To get to Um Qeis and El Hemma hop into a taxi or service taxi on Irbid's main street, and go to the North Terminal by asking for service Al Shamali (Al Moujama) ala Mabarrat Al-Husseini. There aren't many services for 150fils, and private taxis cost 400fils. Before you get in, ask both price and estimated time of departure. Once inside, be ready to leap into another vehicle revving its motor, and don't pay until you're in transit. Remember to bring a swimsuit and your passport. The last minibus back to Irbid leaves around 5pm and sometimes leaves you enough time to get an Arabella or Hijazi bus back to Amman.

Azraq and the Desert Castles

It is difficult for us to imagine the intensity with which the Bedouins worship Azraq. The springs here are the only permanent body of water in over fifty thousand square kilometers. The enchanting pools and marshes have yielded evidence of Paleolithic settlements, two hundred thousand years old. Today Azraq is home to some two thousand Druze and Circassians and a stop-off point for almost two hundred species of migratory birds. Over forty thousand Bedouins depend on it for personal drinking water and the grazing grasses for livestock; the Bedouins are also migratory as they roam from the southern slopes of Syria past Azraq and the Wadi Sirhan down deep into Saudi Arabia. They hold Azraq as precious, for, as Lawrence of Arabia said of the place, "numen inest"—the spirit of God is here.

The first Arab dynasty, the Umayyad Caliphs, had their roots in this same nomadic desert life. Once in power, they enjoyed all the urban comforts available in the eighth century. A deep love for the desert, however, fired their ritual of annual forays back to the lands and sands of their elders. To facilitate these month-long journeys, they built a series of beautiful palaces on the fringes of the desert. While these castles stretch from a cluster north of Damascus to Khirbet-al-Mafjar near Jericho, the finest examples are those in Jordan's slice of the Arabian Desert.

Orientation

A tourist's trip to Azraq and the desert castles is also somewhat of a migration filled with uncertainty and drama. Touring the desert is impractical without a car. If you cannot afford to rent one for the day (a sufficient duration), consider this: few Jordanians beyond the Bedouin have ever seen these castles and oases. If you can talk about them, you may well find yourself with car and company for the trip. Excluding Qasr el-Touba and Qasr el-Mushatta, Azraq and the castles lie on a 100km by 50km oval with a wide end touching Amman. Touba cannot be reached without a 4-wheel-drive vehicle and Mushatta, a bit off the track, was never really completed and offers little to see. Start out early on the southern loop and save the easiest stretch of driving for the late afternoon return. Bring enough water and food for the day, and a flashlight for inner chambers at Qasr Amra.

After leaving Amman you pass the tiny village of Sahab and soon Muwaqqar. The remains of an Umayyad castle here are too scant for archeologists to reconstruct even a floor plan. A Kufic inscription says it was built by Yazid II in 720 C.E.; beyond this you'll need an experienced guide to see more.

After the last Bedouin tents have receded, **Qasr Kharaneh** is visible in the distance. The Bedouin man from the hut who will bring you the keys will explain that the Bedouins have five different words for the twisters of sand that whirl all around on the horizon. The castle, well-preserved and strong, was possibly the only of these desert castles intended for defense. The Bedouin knows what interests foreigners and will mechanically point out the Greek inscription in the doorjambs. Its presence implies that the Umayyads built upon an earlier structure.

The road beyond Karaneh begins to deteriorate where the highway construction becomes visible, but who can dwell on difficulties when mystery and divinity straddle the road? Huge swamps to the right in the morning and to the left in the afternoon are called Lake Mirage in Arabic. Wadi Butm, the Valley of the Pistachio, is named for the great groves of trees that once grew here.

Qasr Amra draws nigh, and and at its side is another grizzled old Bedouin entrusted with the keys. This is the best-preserved of the desert palaces: mosaics grace most of the floors and painted frescoes enliven all the walls. As they are restored and freed from the soot of centuries of Bedouin camp fires, a picture of Umayyad life is unveiled. The men return from the hunt laden with gazelle, oryx, and deer. Musicians and dancers run out to greet them. The naked frolicking of the women in the *hammam* (baths) slowly calms as they prepare the spit for the evening roast. Remember to bring a flashlight as the ages of Arabic modesty have dimmed the light inside the chambers. An ancient form of sun dial lets just a few rays of light through the domed ceilings.

As you reach the Iraq-Saudi Arabia junction, the twin city of Azraq is spread out around you. Towards Saudi Arabia on the south is **Azraq Sheeshan,** a sleepy Circassian villagette.

North, towards Iraq, is **Azraq Druze,** with the Roman castle and nearby Government Rest House. Doubles here cost 6.600JD and triples, 8.800JD. Groups of five or more receive full room and board for 5.500JD, or room and two meals for 5JD per person. Otherwise breakfast costs 600fils, other meals 1.500JD. No transportation goes to either the town or the castle, and heatstroke is a real possibility for hikers. Every two or three hours, however, a bus passes between Azraq and Zarqa which will drop you off here, but makes no other stops.

The castle is cavernous as befits the headquarters of Lawrence of Arabia during the Arab Revolt. Situated on the edge of a vast lava flow, its basalt blocks give it a strange appearance. The individual boulder blocks are merely piled one on top of another; any mortar is long gone. The knowledgeable Druze gatekeeper will point out millwheels, grindstones, stables with stone hitching posts, and mammoth three-ton stone portals which still swing out. Greek, Roman and Byzantine inscriptions date the castle.

Just to the south the palm groves mark the springs where you can swim if you don't mind being watched. A few kilometers further south is the **Shaumari Nature Reserve,** which so far protects only the nocturnal hedgehog, shrew, and five-toed jerboa.

On the road back towards Zarqa, you can see the difference between the sand and limestone desert on your left and the hammada or volcanic desert to the right. Just off the road to the left is the **Hammam Sarah.** There is no doorkeeper or rather, no lock. Just go up to the gate, pick up a rock and knock the bolt to the right to open it. The road here looks like it's a thousand years old and the baths are ruined as well. The many stones thrown into the well over the last thousand years have not made it any shallower.

Beyond the baths, **Qasr Halabat** comes into view. Make the right turn onto the paved road and then turn left up the track to the gate. The Bedouin gatekeeper's tent is the closest one on the left. The castle's ruins lie in heaps all over the large site making it difficult to distinguish Nabatean ruins from Roman ones and the Byzantine monastery from the Arab mosque. Down the hill you can see the snakeline remains of a wall which was part of the outer defenses of the castle.

The road continues to Zarqa and then, through Jordan's worst speed trap, to Amman. The fine here for speeding is 50JD and the cops speak English.

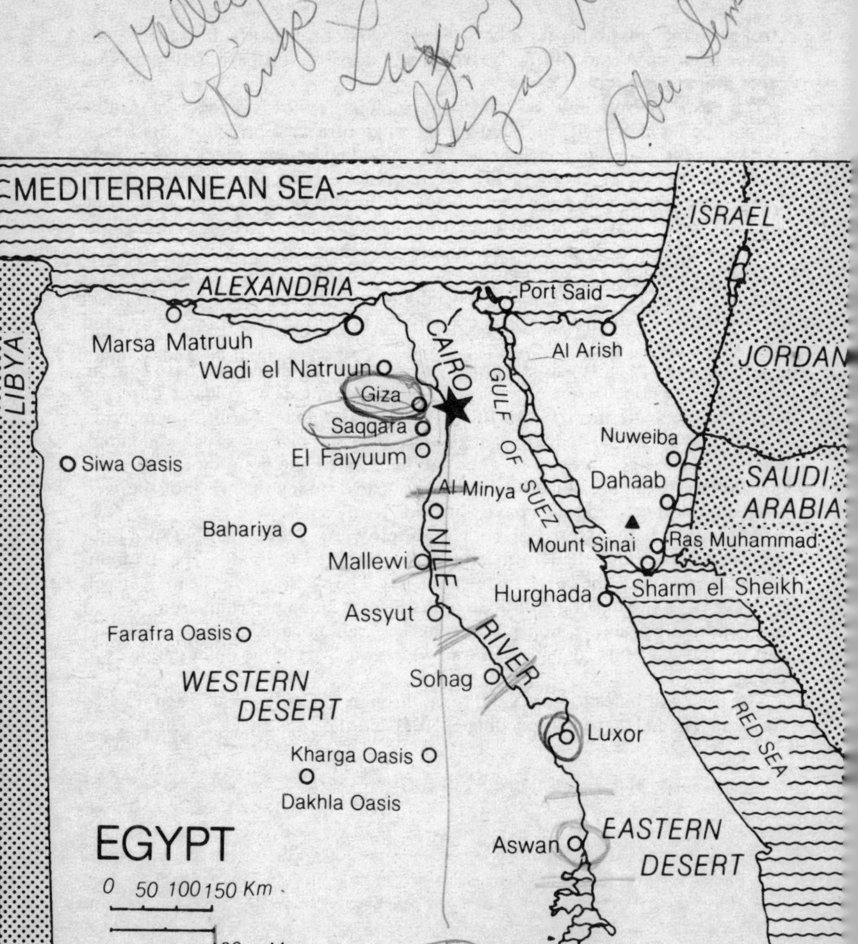
MEDITERRANEAN SEA
ISRAEL
JORDAN
SAUDI ARABIA
LIBYA
SUDAN
ALEXANDRIA
Port Said
Al Arish
Marsa Matruuh
Wadi el Natruun
CAIRO
GULF OF SUEZ
Giza
Saqqara
El Faiyuum
Siwa Oasis
Al Minya
Nuweiba
Dahaab
Bahariya
NILE RIVER
Mount Sinai
Ras Muhammad
Mallewi
Sharm el Sheikh
Hurghada
Assyut
Farafra Oasis
WESTERN DESERT
Sohag
RED SEA
Luxor
Kharga Oasis
Dakhla Oasis
EASTERN DESERT
Aswan
EGYPT
0 50 100 150 Km
0 50 100 M
Abu Simbel

EGYPT

$1 = .70 Egyptian Pounds (LE) **$1.43 = LE1 = 100pt**

Egypt broods on the distant edge of modern consciousness. Its ancient people inhabited the darkest realms of human history, and their religion, singularly preoccupied with death and the possibilities of an afterlife, stirred the deepest fears and hopes of mankind. Their art is archetypal; what remains are some of the most monumental works of the human imagination. Today, much of Egypt looms as part of the challenge of the Third World, struggling with the crippling problems of overpopulation, poverty, disease, and illiteracy. Any journey through Egypt traverses both these realms of past and present: ancient monuments inspire awe for sheer size and age, while crowded cities and the undeveloped countryside challenge the mind, the stomach, and sometimes the heart.

Passing through both worlds, the Nile *is* Egypt and has been since the introduction of agriculture to the area at least six thousand years ago. From the first cataract at Aswan to the Mediterranean Sea, the mighty African river flows 1200km through the countryside, bringing life-giving water to an otherwise parched land. Until the completion of the Aswan Dam in 1971, the annual flooding of the Nile dictated the rhythm of Egyptian life, inundating its valley and delta each summer with the water and silt which supported Egypt's large and concentrated population. The flow of the Nile is now regulated, with elaborate irrigation systems replacing the natural floods. But the river remains, as always, the lifeblood of the country and its still primarily agriculture-based populace.

Taken in its entirety, the expanse of Egypt's history swells so large that it reduces any single era or individual to insignificance. Few epochs in human history are as broad as the Pharaonic Age, which spans a period as wide as all of Western civilization since the Golden Age of Greece. After the passing of the Pharaonic Age, the most formative event in Egyptian history was unquestionably the arrival of Islam a thousand years ago. Unravished by the ages and almost completely neglected by most tourists, the Islamic architectural treasures of Egypt are among the finest in the world. Cairo, in particular, is a vast treasure-trove of medieval monuments, exploding with ornate mosques, towering minarets and stately Qur'anic schools.

Modern Egypt is a cultural, political, and economic battlefield between the established wisdom of the Islamic tradition and the more recent and abrupt influences of colonization and commercialism from the West. Alexandria and downtown Cairo represent the Arab world at its most cosmopolitan: Coca-Cola billboards, department stores, and advertisements for American movies abound. Arabs, especially from the Persian Gulf countries, flock here to enjoy their vacations. However, the signs of modernization have not succeeded in effacing their traditional counterparts. Camels and water buffalo stroll casually through traffic jams, and *muezzins* (prayer-singers) compete with the sounds of disco music. More significantly, many men still support several wives, many women never learn how to read or write, and most of the peasants still toil in the fields along the Nile in much the same manner as their ancestors four thousand years ago.

Ancient pyramids against a row of shiny modern hotels, a Qur'anic school adjoining a Kung Fu Cinema, peasants working their fields at the foot of the sleek Aswan Dam—these images mixed with smog, sphinxes, palm trees, petroleum, and papyrus create modern Egypt. An enigmatic, tightly-knit tangle of contradictions, Egypt will occasionally overwhelm you, and often force you to break into a smile. But, chances are, it will never cease to intrigue you. To invoke the one phrase of English that every Egyptian knows by heart: "Welcome to Egypt."

Orientation

Geography

Like a great brown package bound by the slender line of a single green ribbon, Egypt is defined geographically by vast deserts and a narrow strip of vegetation nourished by the Nile. Every visitor to Egypt is struck by the abrupt and dramatic contrast. On one side are lush groves of date palms, fig, banana, and mango trees; only a few feet away, desolate sand dunes stretch as far as the eye can see. These contrasts divide Egypt into four neat quadrants, plus the Sinai Peninsula. **Lower Egypt** consists of the Delta and Cairo vicinity, while **Upper Egypt** ("upper" because it is upriver) comprises the whole Nile Valley to the south. In other words, if you look at a map, the upper part is Lower Egypt and the lower part is Upper Egypt. To the east is the **Arabian Desert,** facing the Red Sea Coast and its ports, Suez and Hurghada. The western or **Libyan Desert** is characterized by ports of a different sort. If the camel is the "ship of the desert," then the oases of Kharga, Farafra, Dakhla, Bahariya, and far-away Siwa have for centuries been the sandy ports for dune-roving caravan traders and pirates.

During the Pharaonic Age, the shape of Egypt was said to resemble that of a flower: the Nile Valley formed the stem, the oasis of Faiyuum the bud, and the Delta the flower in full bloom. If the image appears to neglect a great deal, consider that even today virtually all of Egypt's population resides within the contours of this flower. Modern Egypt's territory extends nearly one million square kilometers—larger than any European country—and the population of Egypt is around fifty million and rapidly climbing. However, since most of the country is barren desert, only 4% of Egypt's land area is inhabited, and the Nile Valley and the Delta are among the world's most densely populated regions. This crucial factor contributes to much that is fascinating as well as much that is tragic about contemporary Egypt.

Climate

Though by no means the hottest place in the world, Egypt is certainly the hottest place regularly visited by tourists. Fortunately, it is probably also the driest, and the body's cooling system works miraculously well in the low humidity. Even in the middle of summer, air temperatures (which can reach 120 degrees Fahrenheit or higher in the south) should be no problem unless you are completely unaccustomed to hot weather. Even so, you must make some concessions to the weather; refer to the Health and Packing sections for suggestions.

Cairo is only marginally hotter than Tel Aviv or Amman, but the air pollution can make the afternoons uncomfortable. Alexandria is temperate year round, but what punch the climate loses in temperature it makes up for in higher humidity. Down south in Upper Egypt things really begin to warm up, especially around Luxor and Aswan. Afternoons here are best spent either sleeping, sipping lemonade in a cafe, or swimming in a pool.

You can avoid the heat by coming in the winter, but be *sure* to bring some warm clothes. Egypt can get downright cold in winter; this coolness has probably ruined the trips of more unprepared tourists than the summer heat.

Useful Organizations

While in Egypt, if you have any questions about accommodations, restaurants, transportation, sights, or anything else, go to the local tourist office. The offices in Cairo and Alexandria can give you a map and guidebook to their respective cities. Other offices of the **Egyptian General Authority for the Promotion of Tourism (EGAPT)** are located in Luxor, Aswan, Port Said, Suez, Hurghada, and the Sinai (St. Catherine). The **Tourist Police,** another source of aid, are established in Cairo, Alexandria, Luxor, Aswan, Port Said, and Suez. The officers, many of whom speak English, wear distinctive uniforms with the words "Tourist Police" printed on them.

You can gather much information about travel in Egypt before you reach the country from sources in North America. The **Egyptian Tourist Authority** offices in the United States are at 630 Fifth Ave., New York, NY 10111 (tel. (212) 246-6960) and 323 Geary St., San Francisco, CA 94102 (tel. (415) 781-7676). Write to the former for the very useful *Travel Guide to Egypt* booklet by Shawki Hussein. In Canada, the Egyptian Tourist Authority is at Place Bonaventure, Frontenac 40, P.O. Box 304, Montreal, Quebec H5A 1B4 (tel. (514) 861-4420).

Below is a list of Egyptian embassies and consulates, for more technical advice:

Embassy of Egypt, 2310 Decatur Place NW, Washington, DC 20008 (tel. (202) 234-3903).

Embassy of Egypt, 454 Laurier Ave., E. Ottawa, Ontairo K1N 6R3 (tel. (613) 234-4931).

Consulates:

New York, 1110 Second Ave., New York 10022 (tel. (212) 759-7120).

Illinois, 505 N. Shore Lake Dr., Suite 6502, Chicago 60611 (tel. (312) 670-2633).

California, 3001 Pacific Ave., San Francisco 94115 (tel. (415) 346-9700).

Quebec, 3754 Cote des Neiges, Montreal H3H 7V6 (tel. (514) 937-7781).

The main office for **EgyptAir** in the U.S. is at 720 Fifth Ave., New York, NY 10019-4168 (tel. (212) 581-5600).

Currency and Exchange

The currency of Egypt could bewilder any foreign visitor. Banknotes and coins come in a variety of colors and sizes, and some very old large ones have only Arabic numerals printed on them (English numerals are derived from Hindu-Arabic). Furthermore, the Egyptian government has recently brought into circulation a new, entirely different series of banknotes, making matters even more confusing. Both types are in use, so be careful. The *ginyh,* or **Egyptian pound (LE)** is divided into 100 *piasters* or *irsh* **(pt)** and 1000 *millims* (though the latter subdivision is rapidly becoming antiquated). The older banknotes are size-graded (the larger the denomination, the larger the bill) and color coded. Most have both Arabic and English numerals. These bills come as follows: LE20 (green); LE10 (red); LE5 (blue); LE1 (brown); 50pt (red and brown); and 25pt (green). The new series is not size-graded, but has been issued in the same denominations. The new LE1, 50pt and 25pt notes have replaced almost entirely those of the earlier series. There are also 10pt and 5pt notes (black and purple respectively) of which the older ones are marked only in Arabic numerals and a new LE100 note has recently been introduced. Coins can be even more confusing; they are printed with only Arabic numerals and lettering. But they are also size-graded and can be divided up, more or less, by color. 10pt (the largest) and 5pt coins are silver colored and have ridged edges, and these days are the most common; 2pt, 1pt and ½pt coins are aluminum or bronze colored, but the latter are very rare. Sums in pounds and piasters may be written either with or without a decimal point. For example, 9 pounds and 26 piasters may be written either as LE9.26 or as 926pt.

The black market in foreign currencies thrives in Egypt, particularly in Cairo, Alexandria and the touristed cities in the south. In the summer of 1983, the black market exchange rate was between 110 and 115pt per U.S. dollar. You will often be approached on the street to "change money." There is usually little risk in carrying out transactions with street salesmen, since most of them represent bazaar owners who run a side business in foreign currencies. But do shop around for the best rates; they will often quote lower rates if they think you don't know any better. You will get the best rate with large amounts of cash, although the black marketeers operating out of legitimate businesses will normally accept major travelers checks as well. Don't expect the top rate unless you change about $100; they'll knock their quoted rate down a few piasters for lower sums. Remember, though, that some large purchases in Egypt, including all airline tickets, require a bank receipt to prove that you changed your money legitimately; don't go into an airline office with a wad of black market bills and expect them to sell you a ticket.

When you first enter Egypt, you will be required to change US $150 at the official exchange rate, though if you arrive at Cairo Airport and already have an Egyptian visa, you may avoid the requirement. If you need to extend your visa while in Egypt, you may have to change another $180 at the official rate—when you go to the passport office you must bring a receipt to prove you have done so. The U.S. Embassy in Cairo changes money for U.S. citizens at a slightly preferred rate. You can cash a travelers check into U.S. dollars at any American Express office (provided that on that particular day they have dollars), but they charge a 1% commission for the service. They will also cash personal checks into U.S. dollars for cardholders. If you want to change money on the black market it's best to convert your travelers checks at American Express and change hard currency.

For information on sending money, see the General Introduction.

Business Hours and Holidays

The Muslim day of communal prayer is Friday (you shouldn't visit mosques during times of prayer), and most government offices, banks, and post offices are closed. Other establishments, such as restaurants, are open seven days a week. Store hours are normally Sat.-Thurs. 9am-1pm and 4-8pm (and many Fri. as well). Bank hours are Mon.-Thurs. 8:30am-12:30pm, Sun. 10am-noon. Foreign banks keep longer hours, but are closed on both Fri. and Sat.

The major religious holiday observed is **Ramadan,** a month in summer when Muslims fast during the day. Some restaurants remain closed for the entire month, and many others close during the day, but otherwise there are few disadvantages to visiting Egypt during Ramadan. During this month-long holiday, Muslims break the fast right after sundown—streets empty as everybody sits down to breakfast. (The Arabic word for the meal is *iftar*.) Then business resumes as usual; shops, closed at 3:30pm during Ramadan, reopen from 8-

11pm. (See Festivals for more on Ramadan.) In the middle of the night, around 2-3am, Egyptians sit down for the second daily meal of Ramadan (called *sahur*) before going to sleep. Especially in the Islamic parts of Cairo, the streets are quite active until long after *sahur*.

The major national holidays in Egypt are Labor Day (May 1), Evacuation Day (June 18), Revolution Day (July 23), Revolution of September 1, Armed Forces Day (October 6), Suez National Day (October 24), and Victory Day (December 23).

Telephones, Telegrams, and Mail

Making telephone calls in Egypt can be time-consuming and frustrating, depending upon where you are calling. There is a direct dial system in place for most of Egypt's important cities and towns. If you have problems getting through to a local number, dial 10 for the operator, who will help you make the connection.

Public pay phones are not a common sight in Egypt, but phones can be found in most small shops and cigarette kiosks. Most hotels allow you to use their phones for local calls either free or for a nominal fee. Be careful, however, of using a phone in a private hotel room; proprietors sometimes level exorbitant surcharges, even for local calls. Local calls usually cost 10pt (sometimes 5pt, sometimes 15pt). Dialing locally anywhere in Egypt requires a modicum of patience. Dial slowly and try several times. Even if you dial the number faultlessly, you will not necessarily get through to the correct party. So, if you dial and reach a number with no answer, don't immediately assume that your party is not at home.

For long-distance or international calls, go to one of the government telephone offices, but be prepared to wait (sometimes several hours) for connections to Europe or the United States. For international calls it is best to go to the main office either very late at night or early in the morning, when they can usually get you a line quite quickly. You cannot make a collect call from Egypt. The public telephone offices do have their drawbacks—you have to pay in advance for a specific number of minutes and you will be abruptly cut off once your time is up. Also, especialy at smaller telephone offices, it can be difficult to communicate your wishes if you do not speak Arabic.

The more convenient and more expensive alternative for international calls is to call from any one of the many large hotels around the country which provide the service. These hotels charge 50-100% more, but will save you the trouble of waiting in line and being cut off. (See Cairo Practical Information listing.)

The larger telephone offices usually provide telex and cable services as well. If you're in Cairo, it is best to go to the Ataba Square telegraph office, directly opposite the main post office. Cables to the U.S. cost about 60pt per word and to Europe 40-50pt per word. You can also send cables to Israel. If you want to send a telegram by phone, dial 124. It is not always possible to send an international telegram from even the main telegraph office in Egyptian cities outside of Cairo. However, there is usually at least one major hotel in town that provides the service.

Mail to and from Egypt is extremely unreliable: a great deal simply disappears. Mail that does make it can take anywhere from several weeks to several months. Don't send anything important by Egyptian mail if you can possibly help it. It is common practice among foreign residents in Egypt to carry mail for one another whenever they leave the country. If you do mail a letter from Egypt, it's a good idea to send a second copy. A letter to the U.S. or Europe costs 27pt air mail. The most reliable place from which to post letters is the mail box at the Nile Hilton, inside by the reception desk; when sending postcards, you will almost always have better success mailing them from a major hotel than from a post office. Most reception desks sell stamps. The best place to receive mail is the main American Express office (see Cairo Practical Information for address), though *poste restante* functions in most major cities. You can also have mail addressed to the American Consulate at 5 Latin America St., Garden City.

To send a package from Egypt you must first obtain an export license from the Ataba Sq. post office in Cairo. Since most souvenir shops will mail packages for a fee including the license and packaging, you may prefer to have them do so directly. In theory, all mail leaving the country is opened and checked.

Language

Because of Egypt's 150-year colonial history, but perhaps more directly because of its close association with the United States, more English is written and spoken here than in most other Arabic-speaking countries. Most educated Egyptians speak at least some English, and many are fluent. French is commonly spoken among the Egyptian upper classes, especially in Alexandria. Nevertheless, once you depart from the beaten track you will encounter almost everything written in Arabic. If you don't know Arabic, at least learn the characters for the Arabic numbers before you arrive. This will help you immensely when shopping and using public transportation (see below). And any Arabic you can pickup will make traveling in Egypt much easier. One good phrasebook is the Dover publication *Say It In Arabic—Egyptian Dialect*, available in bookstores. The Egyptians love it when foreigners take the trouble to learn even a few words of Arabic.

One expression you will encounter repeatedly is *maalesh,* which roughly translated means, "it doesn't matter," but also embodies an attitude towards life. If the cab driver pockets the change from your ten-pound note he may say *maalesh,* i.e., "don't worry about it." If there is a disagreement over something someone usually says *maalesh,* "it's not worth it," or "it doesn't matter." If you've been waiting over two hours for the bus, the response is usually *maalesh,* "calm down, relax, things take time." There is no other word that Egyptians seem to have more occasion to use when talking to tourists.

Other useful expressions include:

hello—*ahlan*
good-bye—*ma'a salama*
good morning—*sabah al kheir*
good evening—*masa' al kheir*
thank you—*shukran*
please (to a man)—*min-fadlak*
(to a woman)—*min fadlik*
excuse me (if you are a man)—*ana asif*
(if you are a woman)—*ana asfa*
excuse me (to call attention for e.g., in a restaurant)—*law samaht*
what's wrong with you? (if someone's bothering you)—*inta malak*
hotel—*fundug*
where—*feen*
you're welcome (in response to someone who says "thank you")—*afwan*
you're welcome (i.e., at this place)—*a'hlan wassa'hlan*
no—*le*
yes—*aiwa*

do you have (for a man)—*'andak*
(for a woman)—*'andik*
there is, is there—*fii*
there isn't—*ma fiish*
how much—*bikam*
what time is . . .—*issa'a kam*
the check—*il hissab*

The most difficult Arabic pronunciations are the *kh* sound (pronounced like the *ch* in the German *nacht*), the *gh* sound (similar to a Parisian *r*), the *ain* (similar to incipient vomiting) and the breathed *h* (as in Muhammad).

Arabic Numerals

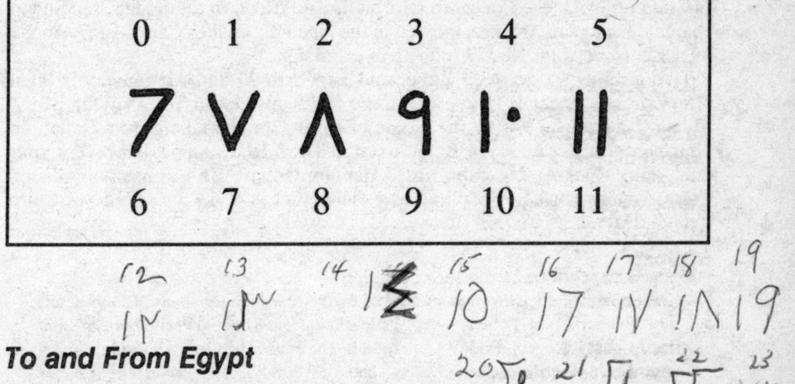

To and From Egypt

By Air

Direct flights between North America and Egypt, though expensive, are readily available; they are discussed in the Getting There section of the General Introduction. Flights from all over Europe, North Africa, and the Middle East make Egypt quick and easy to reach by air. Many airlines offer student discounts on intra-European travel; the standard student discount in Egypt is 55%. **EgyptAir** occasionally offers "special" fares to particular cities. Remember that when buying tickets for most airlines in Egypt, you must have a receipt to prove you've changed money officially (exceptions noted below). If you are planning to travel to neighboring countries from Egypt, you will find the embassies of those which require visas in the Cairo Practical Information listings. Note: it is impossible to obtain a Syrian visa in Egypt.

Two major carriers that offer comparatively inexpensive flights between Egypt and Europe are **Alitalia** and **Olympic Airways.** Alitalia flies Cairo-Rome for LE135 one way, with student discount. The standard student fare from Athens to Cairo is $87.50 one way; Olympic Airways fare Cairo-Athens costs LE79.40 one way, LE157 round trip. The Olympic Airways office in Cairo is at 23 Kasr el Nil St. (tel. 75 13 18 or 74 41 34). **Air France** flies Cairo-Paris for LE180, with student discount. **JAT** (Yugoslavian Airlines), 9 Sherif St., Cairo (tel. 74 21 66 or 74 20 54; also located in the courtyard of the Nile Hilton) offers cheap fares to European capitals, and does not require a receipt validating currency. Other Eastern European carriers also offer excellent deals between Cairo and Europe. The most important Cairo offices are **Aeroflot,** 8 Kasr el Nil St. (tel. 74 31 32); **Bulgarian Airlines,** 37 Abdel Khalek Sarwat (tel. 75 12 11); **Czechoslovak Airways,** 9 Talaat Harb St. (tel. 75 14 16); **Hungarian Airlines,** 15 Kasr el Nil St. (tel. 74 49 59); and **Polish Airlines,** 1 Kasr el Nil St. (tel.74 71 30).

To travel from Egypt to the rest of North Africa you must fly, and you will probably have to bypass Libya. Egyptian-Libyan relations are strained, and the border is usually closed; moreover, it is difficult for U.S. citizens to obtain a Libyan visa. The Cairo offices of the main carriers to North Africa are as follows; **EgyptAir,** at the Nile Hilton (tel. 75 97 71 or 75 98 06) or on Adley St. (tel. 92 24 44 or 90 05 54); **Tunis Air,** 14 Talaat Harb St. (tel. 74 07 26 or 75 34 20); **Royal Air Maroc,** 9 Abdel Salam Aref (tel. 74 29 56 or 75 05 61). If you wish to fly to the Sudan, contact **Sudan Airways,** 1 Abdel Salam Aref (tel. 74 71 45 or 74 72 99). For more information on travel to the Sudan, see Sudan chapter. **Ethiopian Airlines,** located in the Nile Hilton, flies Cairo-Addis Ababa for LE291 one way, LE379 round trip excursion.

Two airlines fly between Egypt and Israel, **El Al** and **Air Sinai.** Air Sinai offers slightly cheaper fares, with three flights a week to Tel Aviv for LE95. Flying to Israel saves you the hassle of getting an exit stamp from Rafiah on your passport as you leave Egypt to enter Israel (the stamp will prevent your entry into other Arabic countries). **Alia** (Jordanian Airlines) has daily flights Cairo-Amman for LE109.50 one way. The office is at 6 Kasr el Nil St., Cairo (tel. 75 09 05 or 75 08 75).

By Boat

Greece: In 1983 the *Odysseus Elitis,* run by the **Maritime Company of Lesbos,** left for Alexandria from Piraeus every Wednesday, from Rhodes every Thursday, and from Limassol every Friday year round. The return trip left Alexandria every Saturday for the above ports, Lesbos, and (very rarely) Chios. Main port agencies in **Piraeus,** 4 Astingos St. (tel. 41 19 544); **Rhodes,** 11-13 Amerikis St. (tel. 27 72 1); **Alexandria,** 63 Nebi Daniel St. (tel. 30 05 0); and **Limassol,** 636 Gladstone St. (tel. 63 16 1). Group One fare (cheapest berths): Piraeus-Alexandria 12,715dr low season, 14,670dr high season; Rhodes-Alexandria 11,420dr low season, 13,225dr high season; Limassol-Alexandria 6700dr low season, 7990dr high season. Low season deck class (sometimes unavailable) to Alexandria: from **Piraeus** 9075dr; from **Rhodes** 8200dr; from **Limassol** 4950dr. 20% student discount on all fares. On the more luxurious *Espresso Egitto* car ferry, run by **Adriatica Lines,** three berth cabins (E class) Piraeus-Alexandria cost $150 low season (Oct.-June), $154 high season (July-Sept.); with ISIC, $130 low season and $145 high season. Piraeus office at Gilvari Agencies Ltd., 97 Akti Miaouli and Favierou (tel. 45 24 580 or 45 22 679). Boats no longer run between Iraklion (Crete) and Alexandria.

Italy: Mena Travel Agency or **Mentours,** 14 Talaat Harb St., Cairo (tel. 74 32 13 or 74 33 82) sells tickets for Adriatica Lines between Italy and Egypt. In **Alexandria,** the office is at 28 El Ghourfa El Tagarich St. (tel. 80 84 07 or 80 69 09). In Egypt, you must purchase tickets 48 hours before departure. In **Venice,** Adriatica's office is at Adriatica di Navigazione, 1412 Zattere (tel. 29 13 3 or 30 30 6). E class three-berth cabins Venice-Alexandria: $305 low season, $335 high season; with ISIC, $285 low season, $295 high season.

Jordan: Egyptian Navigation Company sails Suez-Aqaba weekly (approximately nineteen hours). In **Cairo:** corner of Kasr el Nil and Sherif Sts.; in **Alexandria:** Misr Edco Shipping Co., 42 Abd al Qadir Ragab St., Rushdi (tel. 47 57 9). First-class double cabins LE77, with three beds LE71; second-class cabins with four beds LE55.50; third-class or deck LE46. Third- and deck-class are crowded, particularly going from Aqaba to Suez. All fares must be paid in officially changed pounds or by credit card.

Black Sea Shipping Co: In **Greece,** Transmed Shipping, 85 Akti Miaouli, Piraeus (tel. 41 31 402/3); in **Egypt,** Amon Shipping Agency, 3 Adib St., P.O. Box 60764, Alexandria; in **Cyprus,** Francoudi and Stephanou Ltd., New Port Rd., Limassol (tel. 55 33 1). Twice-monthly boats (May-Oct.) between Odessa, USSR and Alexandria, with stops in Varna (Bulgaria), Istanbul, Piraeus, Larnaca (Cyprus) and Latakia (Syria).

For information on boats to the Sudan, see Sudan chapter.

By Bus to Israel

Note: For information on travel from Israel to Egypt, see the Israel introduction. For details on a service taxi to the Israeli border from Cairo, see Cairo Transportation section.

A number of small private Egyptian companies run relatively inexpensive buses to Israel. Perhaps the best of the lot is the **Eastern Delta Transportation Co.** (or Delta for short), located just off Hoda Sharawi St. around the corner from Felfela Restaurant (see Cairo, Food). To reach their office, take two sharp rights as you step out of Felfela—they're actually in the same building as the restaurant on the third floor. There is no English sign. Delta, besides being slightly cheaper than the other companies, has a single bus from Cairo to Tel Aviv with no stops: you don't have to switch buses at the border. The Cairo-Tel Aviv fare is LE20 one way, LE38 round trip. During most of the year, you should reserve a seat several days in advance; in midsummer you can reserve a seat only 24 hours in advance. Make return reservations in Tel Aviv. Buses leave Cairo every day but Saturday from Sinai Station in Abusseiya at 7:30am. To get to Sinai Station take the shuttle bus that leaves from in front of the Nile Hilton at 6:30am (be there by 6am).

If you wish to travel directly Cairo-Jerusalem, the cheapest company is **Travco,** whose main office is at 9 Is-haq Ya'aqub St., near the Marriot Hotel in Zamalek. Buses leave daily (except Saturday) from the Cairo Sheraton in Dokki at 4:30am. Fares fluctuate with the season but are generally LE5-10 more than Delta. To reach Travco's office as you step onto Zamalek from 26 of July Bridge, walk straight down 26 of July Street, turn left after the first gas station, then turn left when you see their office on a small side street. **Holy Land Travel** also runs daily buses from Cairo to Tel Aviv (LE24 one way; LE48 round trip). The trip takes seven hours. Take the 6:30am shuttle bus to Sinai Station from in front of the Nile Hilton. The bus for Tel Aviv (via Rafah) leaves at 7:30am. Holy Land is the most professional of the operators to Israel and the staff speaks English. They switch buses at the border, which can sometimes involve a bit of waiting around. Their office is located just off of Talaat Harb Sq., at 13 Sabri Abu Alam St. in Cairo (tel. 74 01 53 or 75 74 89). Open 9am-7pm.

Getting Around

Travel Restrictions

Under Egyptian law, foreigners are not permitted to leave the main roads and the cities which fall on them. Travel in the Delta, the New Valley oases, the Sinai except for the coast and St. Catherine's, and other less touristed areas are officially restricted for foreigners. However, that does not mean that you cannot visit. If you explain where you want to go and why to the Travel Permits Department of the Ministry of the Interior, on the corner of Shaykh Rihan St. and Nubar St. in Cairo, they will usually grant you a permit. Mainly, they just want to keep track of you. In Alexandria, the office is located on Ferraana St., off el Honiyya St. No matter where you go, and particularly if you plan on traveling to an unusual area, you should always carry your passport with you.

Foreigners are required to have permits to travel in the following areas:

1. Secondary roads in the Delta.
2. Along the Suez Canal between Ismailiya and Suez.
3. Beyond Suez to Port Tewfik.
4. Coastal road to Libya beyond Marsa Matruuh.
5. Siwa Oasis.
6. All areas in the Sinai off the main roads and outside of the tourist zone.
7. The Farafra and Dakhla Oases and connecting roads within the Western Desert.

Enforcement of the laws concerning restricted travel is becoming less stringent throughout Egypt (except to Siwa, Farafra and Dakhla Oases). Difficulties are not likely to arise despite warnings posted throughout the country. Nonetheless, if you encounter a particularly vigilant police officer off a main road or in a restricted area, it is within his rights to confiscate your passport and hold you for questioning. This is the most dire consequence you are likely to suffer. Should such a circumstance arise, flattering, obsequious apologies and confessions of ignorance should put the matter to rest.

Train

Although the Egyptian railway system is hardly extensive, it does serve almost all the major towns and points of interest in the country. It is one of the easier ways of getting from city to city, particularly from Cairo to Alexandria, Luxor, and Aswan. The trains are relatively comfortable if you travel first or second class; try to travel third class only for short hauls. Trains are surprisingly inexpensive. Unfortunately, they are also one of the most popular ways of getting around, which might mean long lines and crowded cars. In spite of the inconveniences, you'll probably find that trains are the best way to travel long distances in Egypt. For shorter distances, however, alternative forms of transportation (most notably service taxis) are much faster and more reliable.

The Egyptian Railways run four major lines along the Nile river and into the Delta. The Cairo-Alexandria connection, which stops at several Delta towns en route, is probably the most efficient and most traveled line in the country. Another rail link of particular interest to tourists is that between Cairo and Luxor and Aswan. There is no more comfortable way to travel the same stretch for a comparable amount of money.

Between Cairo and Alexandria there are five trains a day with second- and third-class cars. In addition, ten other third-class trains normally make the trip in about three and a half hours, leaving Cairo between 0655 and 2130. Unlike first- and second-class trains, third-class trains do not take reservations. Advance ticket purchase is not required on these trains—just get on the train in the station and pay the ticket collector when he arrives. He'll charge the normal ticket price plus a small surcharge of 5pt to 10pt, but you'll avoid having to stand in the long ticket line. Although the cars nearest the entrance usually fill up first, you'll be amazed to find often virtually empty cars waiting for you at the far end of the platform.

Trains also run north from Cairo to Port Said and Suez, and along the north coast from Alexandria to Marsa Matruuh. The latter line, however, is unreliable; take a bus. Only one line extends south along the Nile to Luxor and Aswan. Many local trains serve the smaller towns of the Delta, but these trains are usually slow, crowded, and rather uncomfortable. Don't expect air conditioning and be prepared to stand. It might be advisable to take a bus or a service taxi instead.

The train schedule for the entire country has changed very little over the last several years. Since it is difficult to get precise comprehensive information on rail departures anywhere in the country, the timetables we have included in the Appendix (valid as of 1983) will prove invaluable.

Two trains a day travel directly between Cairo and Suez, departing Cairo at 5:50am and 3:35pm, and departing Suez at 9:40am and 7:15pm.

Cairo has a fairly efficient commuter train running from the center to the southeastern part of the city (as far as Helwan). Trains leave every fifteen minutes from Bab al-Luq Station, three blocks east of Tahrir Square. Fares are 5pt to Ma'adi and 10pt to Helwan in first class, half that in second class.

The 1983 train fares for major lines were, from Cairo to specified destinations:

Destination	1st class	2nd class
Luxor	LE11	LE5.05
Aswan	LE13.75	LE6.10
Alexandria	LE4.25	LE2.05
Assyut	LE7	LE3.35
Port Said	LE3.30	LE1.85
Dumyat	LE2.95	LE1.70
Tanta	LE1.90	LE.95

Student discounts on most of these major routes tend to be slightly shy of 50%, e.g., Cairo-Luxor first class LE 5.30, second class LE3.30; Cairo-Aswan first class LE8.40, second class LE4.20. If you are taking a night train, consider reserving a sleeper. Second-class sleepers from Cairo to Luxor or Aswan (or vice versa) are not a bad deal. The price includes dinner and breakfast. Second-class sleeper to Luxor is about LE12 and to Aswan about LE15, including meals. First-class sleepers are slightly more comfortable and much more expensive—to Luxor LE21 and to Aswan LE25. Student discounts on sleepers are less than on regular seats. Sleepers are usually in berths with two *couchettes*. If you are traveling with a member of the opposite sex and wish to share a single cabin, say you are married when buying the ticket; unmarried couples are not allowed to share a cabin. Much more expensive is the special first-class daily express train which features *wagon-lits* sleepers (LE33 from Cairo to either Luxor or Aswan); their redeeming virtue is that they are never booked. The first-class express leaves Cairo southbound at 7pm daily, and leaves from High Dam northbound at 5:20pm, from Aswan at 5:10pm, and from Luxor at 10:25pm. It makes no other stops.

Tickets can be bought and reservations made at the ticket office in any train station. Since you cannot make round-trip reservations at the point of origin, always take care of return reservations as soon as you reach your destination, particularly if you intend to take a sleeper. During the last week of Ramadan and the entire week thereafter, reserved seats on all Egyptian trains (especially to Luxor and Aswan) are completely booked. To travel during this period, you must book your tickets at least a full week in advance. At other times, reservations made several days in advance are sufficient. Note: if the train you wish to take is full and you don't have time to wait around, don't despair: just board the train without buying a ticket. The conductor will sell you a ticket on the train, and your only problems will be a small fine and trying to find a seat. If you are traveling from Cairo to Alexandria or the Delta, you might want to avoid the hassle of waiting in the ticket lines for reserved seating this way—the trip is short, you might find a seat anyway, and the fine for not having a ticket on these runs is only around 25pt. (The fine on the Luxor and Aswan trains may be as much as LE1.)

Don't be put off by the bustle at Ramsis Station. Though only a few signs are in English, trains are normally marked with Roman numerals to indicate their class. Northbound and southbound trains leave from separate sets of platforms (north from in the main station, south from off to the side). If you are confused, ask a conductor or a fellow passenger to send you to the right platform. The trains normally enter their berths at least a half-hour before departure time, so you should have time to find your place. If you get lost, don't hesitate to ask for assistance. The ticket office at Ramsis Station is open 8am-10pm; for information, call 75 35 55.

Finally, don't throw your money away in despair at the labyrinthine bureaucracy of Egyptian railways: it is possible both to return and to change tickets for very little extra cost. If you have bought reserved tickets and decide you don't want them, go to the station-master's office of the station from which you would have departed; you will be refunded your money minus a 15pt cancellation fee if you do so before the time of departure. If you miss your train and are left holding a ticket, immediately do the following. Go around to the back of the ticket windows and find the door to the ticket office, barge in, ask to see the director, get mildly hysterical, show them your tickets, explain you've just missed your train and you're a poor student, etc. You'll be amazed: the same lethargic, creeping bureaucracy that made you wait for hours to buy the ticket often acts like lightning, under such circumstances. If you're extremely lucky, you may be issued a ticket on the next train out—even if there are officially no seats available for at least a week! However, never try to bribe a train station official. If you try to throw your money around, all you'll do is offend someone and obstruct your own interest.

Bus

With a few exceptions, buses are an inexpensive and generally uncomfortable way of traveling in Egypt. A number of private lines serve the Delta, as well as other points in Egypt which do not have railway service, such as the oases, the Sinai (up to the border crossing at Rafiah and to Sharm el Sheikh), and the Red Sea Coast. Buses are the best means of transportation on the North Coast. Unfortunately, there is no single inter-provincial bus depot in Cairo, so you'll have to seek out the various points of departure. The most important stations in Cairo are:

Midaan Tahrir: directly behind the Nile Hilton. For Alexandria, Marsa Matruuh. Buy your ticket 24 hours in advance if you want to be assured a seat.

Midaan Ulali: across from Ramsis Station. For Port Said, Ismailiya.

Midaan Ahmad Hilmi: behind Ramsis Station. For Hurghada (LE5; 9 hours), towns south of Cairo, Rafiah, and Faiyuum.

Azhar Station: near intersection of al Azhar St. and Port Said St. For Kharga, Dakhla, and Bahariya oases. The buses cost practically nothing. Due to the heat and crowded conditions, by the time you reach the oasis you will feel like practically nothing. The trip to Bahariya takes seven hours, to Kharga and Dakhla considerably longer.

Sinai Station: in Abusseiya. For Israel and the Sinai. To get there, take the yellow and green bus that leaves from in front of the Nile Hilton from next to the yellow ticket booth with the green stripe (50pt).

Buses traveling between major cities leave frequently throughout the day, although buses to the Sinai, Hurghada, and the oases depart only early in the morning. If you can, go to the station the day before to confirm departure times. Special air-conditioned buses run regularly between Cairo and Alexandria (three hours), and in the morning between Cairo and Marsa Matruuh. These leave from behind the Nile Hilton (on the street between the Hilton and the municipal bus station at Tahrir Square) and are comfortable and efficient. Tickets should be purchased in advance from a small office next to the Iberian Airlines office on the east side of Tahrir Square; return tickets to Cairo should be purchased as early as possible at the ticket office adjacent to Ramli Station in Alexandria. Fares are normally LE3-3.50.

Municipal buses are another story. Cairo's buses during rush hours are something to behold and worth the trip, if only for the experience. Although some routes are hazardously overcrowded, on the whole the system is a very good way of getting around the city inexpensively.

One of the drawbacks of taking buses in Egypt is that the numbers and destinations are normally written only in Arabic. If you're in doubt about which bus to take, ask someone at the station to direct you to the right one. The conductors who sit in the little kiosks at Tahrir, Ramsis, and the other main terminals are usually extremely helpful (for more information, see Cairo Transportation).

Taxi

Private taxis *(taxis special)* differ from the usual shared variety not so much in shape or color as in function; in general, the shared taxis travel longer distances, and only along set routes. If you hire a private taxi to take you to a particular destination, you pay much more than you would for the equivalent distance in a shared taxi. Compared to buses and trains, both of which are dirt cheap and relatively quick, private taxis seem an exorbitant luxury, but they may be necessary for travel to out-of-the-way places or late-night travel. Keep in mind, however, that Egyptian taxi drivers are notorious for their insane driving and for milking inflated fares out of unsuspecting tourists. To decrease your chances of being ripped off, try to hail a private taxi on the street instead of finding one which is parked, particularly around popular tourist sights and large hotels. If a cabbie approaches you first, you know he's out to milk you.

A cheap alternative to hiring a private taxi in Cairo and Alexandria is to hop in one of the intra-city shared taxis buzzing about town. In Cairo, they're black and white, in Alexandria black and orange. Using these taxis, however, requires some practice. For further information on both kinds of taxis, see Cairo Transportation section.

Service Taxi (Inter-City Shared Taxi)

Although more expensive than all but first-class trains and buses, *taksi ugra*, or service taxis, are regular, convenient, and comfortable ways to travel. Their primary function is to travel fixed routes between cities; they are the ideal way to travel along the Nile. The cost of a trip, alway set, is split between seven or eight passengers. There is no advance purchase of tickets, and cars leave as soon as they fill up. Normally, you won't have to wait longer than ten or fifteen minutes to get started. Taxis to the Canal towns leave from Ulali Square across from Ramsis Station. Taxis to the Delta leave Ahmad Hilmi Square behind Ramsis Station, and taxis to Faiyuum and other points south depart from Midaan Giza. The fare from Cairo to Alexandria is LE2.50. (For information on taxis to the Cairo environs see Cairo Transportation section, and for more information on service taxis along the Nile, consult the introduction to the Nile Valley.)

Plane

EgyptAir is the official airline for all domestic flights in Egypt. They have flights from Cairo to Luxor (one hour; LE47.50); Cairo to Aswan (two hours; LE34); Cairo to Alexandria (thirty minutes; LE13); Cairo to Hurghada (LE34); and Aswan to Abu Simbel (forty minutes; LE40 round trip). There are also flights to the oases of the New Valley (Kharga and Dakhla). Make your bookings as far in advance as possible, particularly on the Luxor and Aswan routes. Outside Cairo, EgyptAir offices are located in New York (see Useful Organizations), Aswan (tel. 24 00), Luxor (tel. 20 40), and Alexandria (tel. 20 77 8 or 33 35 7). Many travel agencies will make reservations for you without charge. There are no student discounts or youth fares on domestic flights.

EgyptAir has several offices in Cairo, some of which are far more crowded than others. The following offices have staff members who speak English:

No. 6 Adley St., across from the Tourist Office (tel. 92 24 44 or 90 05 54).

Nile Hilton, by Tahrir Sq. (tel. 75 97 71 or 75 98 06).

Heliopolis Sheraton Hotel (tel. 98 54 08 or 98 30 00).

No. 22 Ibrahim El Lakani St. (tel. 96 53 05 or 96 05 52).

At the Cairo Airport (tel. 96 88 66 or 96 89 05).

EgyptAir's special flight information telephone number is 87 21 22/3.

Air Sinai flies from Cairo to Sharm el Sheikh for LE32 one way and from Cairo to St. Catherine's Monastery LE25.50 one way. (No student discounts.) Their office is in the courtyard of the Nile Hilton.

Boat

For information on travel by boat along the Nile see the introduction to the chapter on the Nile Valley and the Cairo Transportation section.

Car

Renting a car is a comparatively expensive way to get around Egypt, even when several people band together in a single vehicle. Fortunately gas is cheap (16pt per liter), so the cost of exploring remote regions only accessible by car, such as the oases or the Red Sea Coast, is not prohibitive. An **International Driver's License** will be accepted in Egypt, but any insurance you have will not cover you here. Plan to invest in proper coverage (the rates listed below include insurance unless otherwise indicated). If you are in an accident, be sure to obtain immediate documentation from the police and the first examining doctor; otherwise, your insurance may not pay the requisite fees. Your biggest headache on the road will be the traffic, which demands nerves of steel to negotiate no matter where you go. Finally, remember the travel restrictions on foreigners and obtain the necessary permits before driving to the Delta or the oases. In Cairo, the following rental agencies will rent you a car for anywhere from two days to two months:

Budget Rent-A-Car: 5 El Makrizi St., Zamalek (tel. 80 00 70 or 80 94 74). Located just off 26 July St. at the foot of the bridge joining Zamalek to the west bank. Cars can be obtained on short notice. LE24 per day plus 8pt per km over 100km per day. No age requirements.

Bita Car Rental: Champollion St., across from the Anglo Swiss Pensione (tel. 74 61 69 or 75 31 30). Usually a short wait (one or two days) for a car, but if you stop by the office in person the process speeds up. Open daily 9am-2:30pm and 5:30-8pm; closed during the afternoon Fri. and Sun. LE20 per day plus 7pt per km over 100km per day. Additional 10% service charge. Must be 25 or older.

Avis Rent-A-Car: 16 Maamal El Sukar St., Garden City (tel. 27 08 1 or 28 69 8). Also in the Nile Hilton (tel. 74 07 77 or 75 06 66). Usually a three-day wait for a small car. LE24 per day plus 8pt per km over 100km per day. Must be 25 or older.

Hertz Rent-A-Car: 15 Kamel el Shennawi St., Garden City (tel. 22 94 8 or 23 20 3). Often must book a week in advance. LE21 per day plus 8pt per km over 100km per day. Must be 25 or older.

Life in Egypt

Egyptians are a far more eclectic collection of peoples than most foreigners realize at first. Alexandrians are the most European of the lot: cosmopolitan, modern, and comparatively unhurried. Upper-crust Carienes also fit this description, but almost 70% of Cairo's population consists of *fellahin*, or peasant farmers, who have resettled from the countryside. In rural areas along the Nile, the *fellahin* pursue a mode of life unchanged for centuries amidst rumbling donkey-carts and ancient water-wheels. But Egyptian ethnicity involves more than the simple dichotomy between urbane city-dwellers and rural farmers. Scattered throughout the country are the Copts, the direct descendants of the mummy-making ancient Egyptians who today practice a form of Christianity established by St. Mark in Alexandria. The Copts, who use their own language for liturgical purposes, make up 5-20% of the country's population today—probably close to 14%.

Almost 85% of the country is Sunni Muslim. The European, Levantine, Turkish, and Jewish minorities that played a significant commercial and political role during medieval times now constitute less than 1% of Egypt's population. In the deep south, around Aswan, the Nubian and Bishari cultures pulse to distinctly African rhythms. And if you travel anywhere in the Libyan Desert or the Sinai, you're likely to encounter tribes of Bedouins. These desert nomads, living in tents and raising camels, goats, and sheep, manage to eke an existence out of one of the harshest environments on earth. Their mode of life is still that of the biblical Abraham and his descendants.

Despite regional differences, Egyptians all have one thing in common. Egyptians value hospitality above all else, feeling that the greatest honor is in being the host. For the traveler, always the "guest" in another's country, this is a rare treat indeed. You won't have been in Egypt long before someone invites you for tea, a meal, or an all-night wedding.

But from the Western tourist's point of view, a less positive feature seems to unite Egypt's peoples into an undifferentiated whole: their apparently unequivocal lack of concern for time. Travel in Egypt proves frustrating for those European and American visitors who approach the country with their own standards of efficiency; to enjoy Egypt without reservation, you must accept the fact that the most economically sound use of time is not a national priority. Slow down, don't cram too much into your schedule, and savor the relaxed atmosphere. If your bus is late, sit back and sip a glass of tea. Never set your mind so fixedly on your plans that you forget to attach to them the calming clause *"in sha 'allah"* (God willing).

Frustration is most likely to reach epileptic proportions in encounters with Egypt's mind-boggling bureaucracy. You may well feel that you spend more time buying train tickets than exploring ancient temples. Just try to laugh at the whole mess. Read the paper as you wait in line and try not to notice how a bureaucrat disappears to drink tea with his buddies just as you approach his window.

To Egyptians, the unifying feature of all tourists is money. No matter how poor you may feel and no matter how pressed for cash, in the eyes of those around you, you are rich. Cabbies will try to solicit business with you as you walk down the street; so will the sellers of tourist junk, shirt salesmen, and a few professional beggars. Children will frequently, seemingly just for the hell of it, ask for some *baksheesh*.

Baksheesh is the one word in the world more universal than "Coca-Cola." There are three general varieties of *baksheesh*. The most important and common is a tip in return for a favor performed—unlocking a door, parking your car, etc. Do not tip until the service has been rendered, and don't let yourself be railroaded into forking over huge sums. Something between 20 and 50pt will usually suffice. In special situations, such as getting to see something after hours, several pounds may be in order. Always carry small change with you, and don't expect change for large bills. *Baksheesh* is rarely expected in return for directions or advice: it would be highly inappropriate, for instance, to offer money to an Egyptian businessman who has helped you find your seat in a train. But *baksheesh* in the form of a tip is advisable in almost any situation where you would like to enjoy good service on repeated occasions.

The second type of *baksheesh* is the giving of alms. Everywhere you go you will encounter beggars who survive on *baksheesh* given to them in the spirit of generosity and unmotivated mercy. Unfortunately, tourists tend to confuse these two kinds of *baksheesh*. Consequently, in heavily touristed areas some characters either simply harass foreigners or thrust unwanted services upon them and then promptly demand *baksheesh*. Refuse all unwanted favors in a firm, unambiguous tone of voice. Giving people money in return for being hassled sets a precedent that will continue to haunt you.

The final form of *baksheesh* is simply a bribe, and not something you are well advised to attempt as a tourist. Bribery requires a great deal more delicacy, familiarity with the culture and language, and discretion than you will be able to exercise as an outsider.

Accommodations

At first glance, accommodations in Egypt seem to reflect the gap between the rich and the poor. The glistening new resort complexes in Cairo, such as the Meridien and the Sheraton, stand in stark contrast to the spartan dusty hotels along busy side streets. But don't let appearance deceive you; good cheap and moderately-priced hotels can be found if you spend some time looking for them. Prices vary considerably between high season and low season. The high season in Alexandria is June-August, in the Nile Valley October-April. If you visit in the high season, expect hotel rates for the Nile Valley (particularly Luxor and Aswan) to be anywhere from 10-50% higher than as listed here. In Cairo the high season is theoretically also in winter, but the discrepancy between seasonal prices tends to be less.

Most towns and cities have lower-range hotels with rooms for LE1-4 per person, as well as a number of middle-range hotels, those that fall below the high-priced tourist resorts and a bit above the down-and-outs, with rooms for LE5-7 per person. More comfortable hotels in the LE10-15 range have many of the services you'll find in the really expensive places. If you feel pressed for cash you can usually get by for about LE1 per night without having to look very far. Keep all your valuables with you if possible, and sleep with your passport and money close to your body, especially in hostels. In any hotel, ask to see the room before you pay, since price does not always indicate quality. Finally, be aware that hot water and private baths are luxuries in Egypt; you won't get them without paying for them. The same goes for air conditioning, private telephones, and other conveniences.

Egypt has twelve **youth hostels** which range somewhat in quality. Most are bearable, if grungy and crowded. The price can't be beat at 60-90pt per night. Advance reservations are not usually necessary, since they let almost everyone in, but you might arrive early just to be sure. Theoretically, Egyptian youth hostels require a valid IYHF card, but the rule is not enforced. Moreover, you save only 10-20pt per night with the card. If you do wish to purchase a membership card, you can do so at the **Youth Hostel Office,** 1 Abrahim St., Garden City, Cairo (tel. 30 32 9), next door to the Sudanese Embassy. Open Sat.-Thurs. 5-8pm.

Egyptian youth hostels are divided into two classes: large and small. The larger hostels, located in Cairo, Alexandria, and Port Said, charge 60pt per person for those under 21, 80pt for those over 21. The smaller hostels charge 40pt per person for those under 21 and 60pt for those over 21. They are located in Aswan, Assyut, Damanhour, Marsa Matruuh, Sohag, and Suez. The one hostel outside this classification system is the luxurious Sharm el Sheikh Hostel, in front of the bus stop in Sharm el Sheikh, which charges LE2 per person, including air conditioning. All hostels have kitchen facilities. For more information, write the Egyptian Youth Hostel Association, 7 Abdel Hamid-Said St., Cairo (tel. 75 80 99).

Food

The fare served in most Egyptian restaurants is influenced by Greek and Turkish cuisine. Since it often wreaks havoc with inexperienced digestive systems, rumors have been fostered that Egyptian food is strongly flavored and spicy. In fact, it tends to be colorless and rather bland. However, if you are reasonably careful about where and what you eat, you should be able to avoid getting sick. Major cities and towns have plenty of cheap and clean restaurants which serve plentiful helpings of Egyptian food for LE2 or less. It is wise to stay away from the extremely inexpensive street vendors, as uninitiated stomachs will almost certainly protest very energetically within a few hours. If you're in a hurry, it's a better idea to catch a quick bite at a snack bar or fast-food restaurant.

Egyptians generally prefer big hot meals, which are eaten with flat loaves of bread instead of silverware. *Kebab* is a familiar and popular evening meal, usually served roasted on a skewer with salad, *tahina*, and pita bread. Chicken is far less expensive and widely eaten by those who can't afford beef or mutton. Since meat of any sort is a luxury which the large majority of Egyp-

tians cannot afford on a regular basis, the most common Egyptian food is *fuul* (brown beans served mashed or whole with oil and sometimes an egg or small pieces of meat) and *kushari* (a mixture of macaroni, rice, lentils, and tomato sauce). For an exclusively Egyptian dish, try *mulakhiyya,* a thick spicy green stew made from a flat leaf (Jew's Mallow) cooked either by itself or together with pieces of rabbit, chicken or lamb. Like chicken, fish *(samak)* is an inexpensive alternative to red meat, and both salt water and fresh water types are available. Catfish from Lake Nassar is especially delicious. Pigeons *(hammama)* are also very tasty, although you will come away hungry unless you eat two or three.

You can grab a quick meal at one of the many small restaurants and stalls which line the streets of Egyptian cities and town. *Fuul mudamas* and *taamiyyas* (small fried patties or balls of mashed beans and vegetable paste), both served either by themselves or in a sandwich, are the main fare of these small restaurants. *Tahina,* a dip made of seasame-seed paste, and *baba ghanug,* a mixture of tahina and mashed eggplant, may also be available in these restaurants, and are generally eaten with pieces of pita bread.

Shopping for yourself in the market *(suq)* is the cheapest alternative, but you must select your food carefully. Bread, subsidized by the government, is cheap and available in three basic types: *aish baladi* (round unleavened loaves made with coarse flour); *aish shami* (similar to *baladi,* but made with processed white flour); and *aish* (leavened "French" style loaves). Street salesmen offer the flat or pita types while the leavened loaves must be bought directly from bakeries. Cheese comes in two locally produced varieties, *gibna bayda* (white feta cheese) and *gibna rumi* (a hard yellow cheese with a sharp flavor). You can also purchase imported cheeses at reasonable prices. Yogurt *(zabadi)* comes unflavored and makes a filling addition to any meal, as does *amar ad din* (apricot jello), which is served especially during Ramadan. Egyptian bakers produce a wide range of delicious pastries, including *baklava* (made with dough, honey, and nuts) and *fatir* (pancakes or flake pastry which may be filled with anything from eggs to apricot preserves). Although a luxury for Egyptians, fruit and fruit juices are some of the best values in Egypt by western standards. Small fruit juice stands abound in Egyptian towns, serving fresh juices in season (mango, strawberry, pomegranate, banana, orange, etc.), as well as perennial favorites such as *asab* (sugar cane juice), *tamar hindi* (tamarind), and *subiya* (a drink made from rice and sugar). After you've tried fresh Egyptian grape juice, you'll never be able to go back to Welch's. Fresh fruit is available all year round, but seasonal in variety: oranges, dates, and bananas, for instance, are plentiful during the winter, while melons, peaches, plums, and grapes are summer fruits. If you visit Egypt in August or September, try *tin shawki* (cactus fruit).

Egyptians are fanatic devotees of coffee and tea. Egyptian tea, similar to the western variety, is normally drunk with a lot of sugar and no milk. Though you can get western-style coffee, Egyptians prefer Arabic coffee *(ahwa)* which comes in three degrees of sweetness—*ahwa sada* (no sugar), *ahwa mazbut* (medium sugar), and *ahwa ziedda* (very sweet). Especially when you are in Upper Egypt, try *kirkaday,* a refreshing red drink made from brewing the flower of the fuscha plant and served hot or cold. Egyptian beer, with the brand-name *Stella,* is light and has a generally lower alcohol content than European beer. It normally costs between LE1.75 and LE2.50 in restaurants and bars. For wine enthusiasts, Egypt produces a selection of red and white wines which range between LE2 and LE5 a bottle. Try some before you buy a case—it's not the greatest wine in the world.

Although Egyptian popular cuisine reflects traditionally Arab tastes, the country's colonial history has left its impact on Egypt's food. Restaurants serving European food are common in Cairo and Alexandria. In recent years, several western fast-food chains have set themselves up in Egypt and a taste for hamburgers, french fries, and fried chicken is spreading among certain segments of the country's urban population. These chains (and their local imitations) are confined to the major cities and more traditional fare can be found almost anywhere.

Sightseeing

Admission tickets to most sights were printed up years ago and are completely out of date. As a consequence, they advertise a price one-tenth of what you paid. But generally speaking, the men who work at the ticket kiosks at archeological sites in Egypt are scrupulously honest; they are often the best people to ask about how much to pay for a hired taxi or camel. Admission to archeological sites costs LE1-5, but students with ISIC receive discounts up to 50%. The sites in Egypt are usually open 7am-6pm, though in summer the most important ones in the Nile Valley open at 6am. In summer, the very early morning is the only time of day when temperatures are comfortable—afternoons are unbearable. Try to adjust your schedule to the heat by taking a long afternoon nap.

When you set out sightseeing, bring plenty of water and avoid guides like the plague. If you must buy drinks at an archeological site, firmly offer 25pt and no more; the vendors will usually agree to your price. Guides are an unnecessary luxury. Most of them are uninformed and impossible to escape without paying them more than they deserve. An exception is the caretaker who shows you around mosques or related monuments in Islamic Cairo, without whom you won't have access to many places. Otherwise, only pay someone a little *baksheesh* if he unlocks a door or performs another service for you.

Shopping

Shopping in Egypt is almost always an adventure, and one that requires patience and discretion. Don't buy your souvenirs from the shops near the archeological sites and major attractions; save your money for village shops, popular folk markets, and the *suqs* in larger cities, particularly Cairo, Aswan, and Alexandria. Whether you are trying to buy jewelry or tomatoes, as a foreigner expect to be charged more than the average Egyptian. If you have a sense that a merchant is accustomed to overcharging naive tourists, move on to another shop. Don't start bargaining for an object unless a) you really want it, b) you know approximately what it's worth, c) you're prepared to pay any figure you utter, and d) you can purchase it without requiring change for a large bill. Don't allow yourself to be bullied, but come prepared to do verbal battle. Broken English is a remarkably expressive language; learn to enjoy the sport of sparring for a good price. Smile at the merchant's contrived stories to explain why you should pay more, and laugh when you are grossly overcharged.

Study/Work

The major option for study in Egypt is the **American University in Cairo** (AUC), located at 113 Sharia Qasr Al-Aini, just off Tahrir Square (P.O. Box 2511, Tel. 22 96 9). In addition to regular degree programs, the AUC has a Year Abroad Program through which students may spend a semester or a year at the AUC as non-degree candidates. AUC is licensed and chartered in the U.S. and has affiliations with many American schools; credits are normally transferrable to American universities. Further options at AUC include the year-long intensive Arabic Language Unit and a regular summer session with courses on

Middle Eastern history, society, and culture. Tuition for a full year is $4000, $4750 for the Arabic Language Unit; the summer session costs $990 for two courses (six credits). Guaranteed Student Loans can be applied to tuition. AUC has dormitories for eighty women and ninety men. For more information and details about application, write to the American University in Cairo, Office of Admissions (LG), 866 United Nations Plaza, New York, NY 10017. AUC is approved for the GI bill.

Several language institutes offer shorter-term studies in colloquial and classical Arabic. The **International Language Institute,** Mahmoud Azmy St., Medinet El Sahafeyeen, Cairo (tel. 80 30 87), offers morning and evening classes at all levels. The **Berlitz School,** 165 Muhammad Farid St. (tel. 91 50 96) specializes in colloquial Arabic.

If you want to work in Egypt, a good place to begin research is the nearest university library. Try to secure a job with an American or Canadian firm; knowledge of Arabic is a distinct advantage. Once you have an employer, you can obtain a work permit through any Egyptian consulate, or, in Egypt, from the Ministry of the Interior. If you are interested in teaching English, the **Institute of International Education** (see the General Introduction for address) puts out an excellent publication on opportunities called *Teaching Abroad.* The **International Association for the Exchange of Students for Technical Experience** (see General Introduction) sponsors traineeships for undergraduates and graduates in Egypt. Placement depends upon available openings, and applicants are expected to help locate prospective American employers. For more information, write or call IAESTE.

The **National Council for Youth and Sport** in Egypt runs voluntary workcamps each year. Unfortunately, they accept only five participants from the U.S. If you're interested in applying, contact either the Council at 10 Moderiet El Tahrir St., Garden City, Cairo, or the Egyptian Embassy.

Festivals

Aside from official national holidays, Egypt has few organized festivals (usually marked by little more than the closure of government buildings and schools). However, some religious and secular celebrations provide intriguing insights into Muslim and Egyptian culture. Most follow the Islamic rather than the Christian calendar; check with the tourist office for exact dates.

Ramadan is the most important month of the year for Muslims. During Ramadan, which will run from early June to early July in 1984, devout Muslims fast from dawn until dusk. Although many restaurants close for the month and the general pace of life slows down during the day, there are few disadvantages to visiting Egypt during this month. You'll probably like the relatively empty streets right after sundown, when most Egyptians are at home breaking their fasts. In some of the more traditional areas of Cairo and Alexandria, and in most provincial towns, the people hang colorful lanterns in the streets, some of them very elaborate constructions. Much of the romance, however, has been lost with electric light bulbs replacing the candles which for centuries illuminated the lanterns. The last day of Ramadan is the time reserved for the most enthusiastic celebrations. People dress up in their best clothes, and the final *iftar* (breakfast feast) is sumptuous; the festivities continue on well into the night. The celebrations, known as *Id-al-Fitr,* continue for three more days into the Muslim month of *Shawal* (the next after Ramadan).

Another important Islamic holiday is *Id-al-Adha,* which commemorates the offering of Ishmail by his father Abraham. It lasts four days and will fall in the first half of September, 1984. Sheep are traditionally slaughtered in remembrance of Abraham's sacrifice, and the occasion brings together families and friends for large meals and general festivities.

Several *mulids* (birthdays) are celebrated throughout Egypt. The most important of these is *Mulid an-Nabi,* or the birthday of the Prophet Muhammad, which will fall in the end of December in 1984. The celebrations include large processions in most of the major cities, particularly Cairo, where it is quite a spectacle. Other smaller, more localized *mulids,* for a variety of saints and religious figures are sometimes more interesting and bizarre than the formal *Mulid an-Nabi,* but you have to know when and where they take place to get in on the festivities. In Cairo, the more important *mulids* are those of *Sayyida Husayn, Sayyida Ruqqaya, Sayyida Nafisa,* and *Sayyida Zaynab.* They are generally localized to the areas of the respective mosques/shrines of these religious figures. Check with the tourist office for details. Similarly, you might visit the celebrations of the birthday of Rifa'i at the Rifa'i mosque, next to the Sultan Hassan mosque in Cairo. Some of the provincial towns also hold *mulids*—the festival of *Sayyida al-Badawi* in Tanta is probably the largest and most interesting.

If you visit a *mulid,* you are likely to witness the Sufi rituals of *Zikr* and *Zahr.* In the former, a rythmic group dance begins very slowly and builds to a frenzied climax, resulting in a state of mass hypnosis. The *Zahr,* another group dance generally reserved for women, is primarily an exorcism performed on one or more participants in turn by a male exorcist. Both of these rituals are practiced on Fridays in many populous areas.

Another holiday, *Sham an-Nissim,* falls on the first Monday after Coptic Easter (normally the middle of April). Though it traces its origins to a mixture of Coptic and Pharaonic influences, it has developed into a largely secular holiday. Egyptians traditionally take picnics with their families (the Pyramids are popular spots) and spend the day eating *fasikh* (a dried, salted fish difficult for most Western palates to appreciate). The evenings are spent either strolling quietly along the Nile or sipping tea or coffee in a cafe.

The Coptic celebrations of Easter and Christmas are tranquil affairs marked by special church services rather than public festivals. Perhaps more interesting to observe are Egyptian weddings. The bigger affairs come complete with golden thrones for the bride and groom, belly dancers, live bands, and Arabic singers. Weddings often take place on Thursday nights at the larger hotels. Go to the Hilton at 9-10pm to see what's happening—you may catch the procession coming down the steps.

Ancient Egyptian Culture

Behind the stability, success, and amazing longevity of Ancient Egyptian culture lurks an all-embracing and extremely conservative conception of the world. The social and political structure of Ancient Egypt was rigidly defined, and all aspects of Ancient Egyptian life uniformly strove to maintain the status quo. It is not surprising therefore that the Ancient Egyptians worshipped the events of nature which never failed to repeat themselves, such as the rising of the sun and the annual flooding of the Nile. Socially, everyone's place was defined within a caste system. The purpose of life was simply to fulfill the obligations of one's position in the social hierarchy. The Egyptians believed that the world was structured around a principle called *mat,* best translated as "order": sin to the Ancient Egyptians, consisted of what we might call "making waves."

Even the Pharoah, at the top of the social and political system, was expected to follow the demands of *mat.* His life was regulated to the most minute detail because the proper performance of his duties, it was thought, assured the prosperity of the land; life remained frozen in its ways until death took the Pharoah away. The original impetus behind the elaborate funeral rites and tomb building seems not to have been a desire to make the Pharoah happy and secure in the afterlife, but to protect society. If the Pharoah survived the natural transition of death, so might the society as a whole survive this disruption of its *mat*.

In art, this desire to maintain the status quo was translated into a crushing uniformity of style that spanned two millenia. Since all art was religiously oriented, originality was tantamount to heresy. The quest for stability also led to the self-confident monumentalism so prevalent in both their art and architecture. Bigger was better for most Ancient Egyptians, because it would last longer.

To the dismay of the casual tourist, this same sort of rigidity did not find its way into the pantheon of Egyptian gods. Religion was one aspect of Egyptian thought that shows some flux. Through the ages, gods exchanged names, shapes, and purposes; lesser deities rose to become greater deities, and the greater become lesser.

Yet, even in this chaos of divinities, some order can be found. As you learn quickly, the sun is almost a palpable presence in Egypt, and a sun god was almost always the top deity in mythology. Most of the other important gods were somehow descended from him. Originally called Ra, the sun god created a daughter and a son who, in the best Pharaonic tradition of marrying one's sibling, became husband and wife. Shu, the god of air, and Tefnut, the goddess of moisture, in turn engendered Gleb, the earth, and Nut, the sky. You should have no trouble identifying Nut: she is usually depicted stark naked and stretched out over the ceilings of tombs, sometimes with Shu lending necessary support beneath her mid-section. She creates night and day by swallowing the sun at dusk and giving birth to it in the morning. Gleb and Nut's offspring are the gods most closely associated with Egyptian beliefs in an afterlife: Nephus, Seth, Isis, and Osiris.

Osiris was originally a god of the Nile, and his sibling spouse Isis represented the alluvial planes which he inundated and brought to life yearly. Seth, the mortal enemy of Osiris, was a god of sterility and destruction, identified, logically enough, with the desert. Nephus seems to have been around solely for the sake of symmetry and to serve as Seth's consort. Seth, like the desert threatening to appropriate the fertile land, became intensely jealous of Osiris and wanted Isis for himself. He killed Osiris, cut up his body and buried it all over Egypt. Isis, in deep mourning for her beloved, sought out his parts, and Osiris was reborn. Isis conceived a child by the resuscitated Osiris; the god she gave birth to, Horus, subsequently killed Seth. Horus is the falcon god whose wings frequently wrap around the head of Pharoah's statues and coffins—he helps transport the Pharoah's body in death, his *ka*, to the afterlife. Osiris' is a cult of resurrection; he becomes its ruler, its Pharaoh, and in paintings and sculpture he is often shaped like a mummy, holding the Pharaonic staff and flail.

But entrance to the world of Osiris was not automatic at the moment of death. First, the deceased had to be judged worthy. Numerous ancient Egyptian paintings are concerned with this judgment scene. If one passed the examination, the very worldly realm of Osiris was his; if not, he met annihilation. Pictorially, annihilation was represented by a sharped-tooth creature that sat with its mouth open under the scales, poised to gobble up any miscreant. During the New Kingdom, passages from the Book of the Dead were written on the walls of tombs to tell the deceased how to respond to the examiners, and to inform him of magic formulas that would assure his immortality.

Despite their emphasis on an afterlife, the Egyptians *never* believed in a physical resurrection. Mummies were not thought to rise up suddenly to unbandage themselves like the invisible man. Rather, the preservation of the body of the deceased, it was believed, helped maintain the stability and full functions of the *ka*.

History

The seemingly endless age of Pharaonic civilization began to see its twilight in the sixth century B.C.E., when the great armies of the Persian Empire conquered the land of the Nile, establishing the twenty-seventh dynasty—the first truly foreign dynasty in Egypt. The struggle with Persia lasted for the next two hundred years, with Egypt at times loosening the conqueror's grip and at other times succumbing. From this time until Nassar's revolution in 1952, Egypt was ruled almost continuously by foreign powers.

In 332 B.C.E., Egypt suddenly plummeted into history at the hands of a young Macedonian. Alexander the Great presented himself as a liberator for Egypt; the military genius proved to be a political genius. After ousting the Persians he set off for the oracle of Amon in distant Siwa Oasis, who told him that he was truly the son of Amon and the Pharaoh in Egypt. Alexandria takes its name from the period of his rule, when it flourished as the political capital of the region. With his death in 323 B.C.E., Alexander's empire was divided into three parts, and Egypt fell under the authority of another Macedonian, Ptolemy I. For 275 years the Ptolemies ruled Egypt as pharaohs and gods until they inevitably came, as did all the kingdoms of the ancient Mediterranean world, under the yoke of the Roman Empire.

In 40 B.C.E., more than a century after Rome had made its presence known along the Nile, Julius Caesar came to Egypt in pursuit of his rival Pompey, and there met Egypt's queen, Cleopatra VII. So began the events which have come to mark (at least since Shakespeare wrote *Anthony and Cleopatra*) the end of the ancient pagan world. Cleopatra's liaison with Caesar, though amorous, was brief. When the emperor was assassinated four years later, the queen, shedding nary a tear, returned to Egypt and eventually met Marc Antony, sparking history's most glorified love affair. Their love and demise brought an end to both Republican Rome and the Ptolemaic dynasty. The Egypt that followed, the Egypt of Imperial Rome and then of Byzantium, was characterized by the political stability of an entrenched bureaucracy as well as the introduction and eventual predominance of Christianity. Coptic Christianity took root in Egypt and gave rise to a tradition of monasticism, which powerfully influenced subsequent developments in European Christianity deemed heretical by the Roman and Byzantine orthodoxy.

From the point of view of modern Egypt, the single most important event in the country's history occurred in 640 C.E. (the eighth year of the Muslim calendar) when the Arab armies sent by the Caliph 'Umar, swept into Egypt under the leadership of his general 'Amr ibn al-'As, bringing with them the faith of the prophet Muhammad. Islam did not conquer Lower Egypt as rapidly as its armies did, but by the end of the Umayyad Caliphate, which ruled Egypt from Damascus, Islam had become firmly established as Egypt's primary religion, and Arabic as its new language. The Umayyads succumbed to the Abassids in 750 C.E. and they to the Fatimids in 969. Under the Fatimids, a North African Shi'i dynasty who were opposed to the Sunni Abbasid caliphate of Baghdad, Egypt regained some of its ancient glory. The Fatimids founded the walled city of Cairo and adorned it with some of the finest Islamic monuments ever constructed. During their administration, Egypt became the center of culture and trade in the medieval world. Its influence extended as far west as Spain while Europe was languishing in the mire of the Dark Ages. This was the great age of tolerance in Islam when Christians,

Jews, and Muslims alike held high positions in government and carried the banner of ancient learning.

In 1169, Saladin, a Kurdish warrior from Syria, became vizier of Fatimid Egypt and set out to convert the country back from Shi'i to Sunni Islam. In the process he at least nominally reunited Egypt with the eastern Abbasid Caliphate. But the Ayyubid dynasty he established in 1171 was overthrown in 1250 when the Mamelukes, originally soldier-slaves of the earlier dynasty, came to power. They brought to Cairo a surviving member of the Abbasid family and established him as Caliph in Cairo. In 1258, the Mongols overran Baghdad and the eastern Islamic lands; Egypt, and specifically Cairo, emerged as the unrivaled political and cultural center of the Islamic world for the next 250 years. By the start of the sixteenth century, the Mameluke power was beginning to wane just as a new Muslim empire was arising in Anatolia. When the Mameluke regime fell to the Ottomans in 1517, Egypt became a province of the sublime Porte in what is now Istanbul. The country continued to prosper and to enjoy a substantial degree of local autonomy during the Ottoman period.

Egypt's modern history began with the arrival of a man who modeled himself after Alexander—Napoleon Bonaparte. The French occupation of Egypt, though brief (1798-1801) had an enormous impact on the country: it marked the entrance of the great western powers into the affairs of Egypt. Modeling himself after Napoleon, Muhammad Ali, a Circassian slave of Albanian origin, became the official ruler of Egypt in 1805 in the name of the Ottoman Sultan. Although the country was at least nominally ruled by Muslims, nineteenth-century Egypt really belonged to French and later British colonial interests. In 1869, the Suez Canal, built under the direction of the Frenchman Ferdinand de Lesseps, opened Asia to European domination. By the final decade of the nineteenth century, the British were firmly entrenched economically, politically, and militarily in Egypt. To perpetuate the guise of democratic self-rule, they allowed the formation of a nationalist political party called the *Wafd,* but soon discovered that the *Wafd* could not be contained effectively. The *Wafd,* the monarchists, and the British colonial administrators vied for influence among the people until the British, unable to control popular unrest, granted Egypt political independence and installed King Fu'ad as constitutional monarch in 1922. (Britain, however, retained most of its colonial economic interests in the country, including control over the Suez Canal.) The struggle between the nationalists and monarchists continued until both parties were left in disarray by the Second World War and, shortly thereafter, Egypt's humiliating defeat at the hands of newly-established Israel in 1948.

Into the vacuum stepped a group of young officers led by Colonel Gamal 'Abd an-Nassar, who overthrew King Farouk, Fu'ads's son, in a bloodless coup known as the "Revolution of 1952," and established the first Egyptian republic one year later in 1953. Abd an-Nassar became not only the symbol of the new revolutionary Egypt, but also of the entire Arab world. Together with Tito and Nehru he founded the Organization of Non-Aligned Nations, he organized and led the pan-Arab movement, and became the standard-bearer of the Arab commitment to the Palestinian people. His photograph still dominates the homes of Arabs throughout North Africa and the Middle East, though you don't see it much in Egypt anymore. It was Nassar who defied the western powers in 1956 when, in spite of military defeat at the hands of French, British, and Israeli troops, he nationalized the Suez Canal and won a major political victory. It was Nassar who, rebuked by the French, British, and Americans, turned to the Soviet Union to build the High Dam at Aswan and invited Soviet military advisors to Egypt; and it was Nassar who called for the withdrawal of the U.N. forces from Sinai in June, 1967, thereby providing the Israelis with the pretext to launch their invasion, which destroyed both his army and much of his prestige in the Arab World in six decisive days.

The last decade has witnessed more changes and initiatives. 'Abd an-Nassar died in 1970 and the banner of the republic was passed to Anwar al-Sadat. In the eleven years of his presidency, Sadat did much to command the world's attention. He dismissed the Soviet advisors whom 'Abd an-Nassar had welcomed, and soon thereafter broke through the "impregnable" Bar Lev Line in October 1973, thereby restoring to the Arabs and the Egyptians the dignity they had lost in 1967. In November of 1977, he commenced probably his most monumental venture—he journeyed to Jerusalem and offered the olive branch to Israel. Although Sadat's reconciliation with Israel, finalized by the Camp David Accords, isolated Egypt within the Arab world (and was likewise rejected by most socialist countries and much of the developing world), for many it was the promise of peace and prosperity in a country too long plagued by war and poverty. In September, 1981, Sadat was assassinated by a group of religious fundamentalists during a military procession near Cairo. They were opposed to his alignment with the west and to the large-scale arrests his secret police had carried out not too long before. Despite his popularity in the west, among Egyptians Sadat is not remembered with the same fondness and pride as his predecessor. Sadat's death and the succession to power of Husni Mubarak throw into question the future status of Egypt's position in the Middle East and the world at large. Mubarak is gradually attempting to reestablish Egypt's status in the Arab world and to broaden Egypt's international associations (he has achieved some success in both regards), while at the same time continuing Egypt's ties with Israel and the United States. Most Egyptians have adopted a wait-and-see attitude towards their new president, and hope that he will eventually commit himself in some positive and decisive direction.

Literature

Not all of the books listed below are available in bookstores, but they are available at the library of the American University in Cairo. All of them make good travel literature and (with the exception of Nagel's) were chosen for the ability to entertain as well as inform:

Cocteau, Jean: *Maalesh: A Theatrical Tour of the Middle East.* Peter Owen, London, 1956; written as a journal. One of France's greatest playwrights and most sardonic wits has some insightful and humorous things to say about Egypt.

Durrell, Lawrence: *The Alexandria Quartet.* Faber Press. The classic thing to read while in Egypt. Available in all of Cairo's English-language bookstores. It consists of four novels: *Justine, Balthazar, Mountolive,* and *Clea.*

Flaubert, Gustave: *Flaubert in Egypt,* edited by Francis Steegmüller. The Bodley Head, London, 1972. A travel journal detailing Flaubert's fascination with everything from the pyramids to local prostitutes.

Forster, E. M.: *Alexandria: A History and A Guide.* Another standard item in the Cairo bookstore repertoire. A literate person's guide to Alexandria. More entertaining is his *Pharos and Pharillon.* Hogarth Press, London, 1967. Vignettes set in Alexandria.

Freeman-Grenville, F. S. P.: *The Beauty of Cairo.* East-West Publications, London. Usually available at the Nile Hilton bookstore for LE8.85. A great little backpocket-size paperback of the sights of Islamic and Coptic Cairo. Good maps.

Lane, E. W.: *Manners and Customs of the Modern Egyptians*. East-West Publications, London, 1978. First published in 1836. Wonderful reading. An account of life in Cairo in the 1830s. A great companion for touring Islamic Cairo.

Mendelssohn, Kurt: *The Riddle of the Pyramids*. Sphere Books, 1977. An English physicist offers some interesting solutions to archeological puzzles.

Moorehead, Alan: *The White Nile*. Penguin, London, 1963. An account of early explorers first discovering the Nile. The companion volume focuses on the Sudan: *The Blue Nile*.London, Four Square, 1964. Both are easily obtained in Cairo bookstores.

Nerval, Gerard de: *Journey to the Orient*. Nerval was one of the first French surrealists. The book recounts his psychedelic images of Egypt in the late nineteenth century.

Nagel's Encyclopedia Guide to Egypt: The most thorough guide to Egypt's Pharoanic monuments that is easily available in English. Very expensive (LE40-50).

Parker,Richard B. and **Sabin,**Robin: *A Practical Guide to Islamic Monuments in Cairo*. American University Press in Cairo, 1974. Available throughout the city. This should be the bible of anyone who wishes to explore Islamic Cairo. Very informative; easy to use. Comes with an invaluable set of maps. LE5.50.

Sadat, Anwar: *In Search of Identity*. Harper and Row, New York, 1978. The autobiography of Egypt's second president. Not flawless history, but interesting reading.

Twain, Mark: *The Innocents Abroad*. New English Library, London, 1966. Highly recommended. Delightful witticisms on travel in the Mediterranean, Egypt, and the Holy Land. An iconoclastic review of sights and sightseeing—notes on the naive American abroad.

Vatikiotis, P. J.: *The History of Egypt from Muhammed Ali to Sadat*. Weidenfield and Nicholson, London, 1980. Don't be put off by the title. A readable and informative analysis of recent Egyptian history by a first-rate scholar.

Wilson, John: *The Culture of Ancient Egypt*. University of Chicago Press, Chicago. For the Pharoanic era freaks—an excellent and entertaining overview.

A considerable quantity of modern Egyptian literature is well worth reading and has been competently translated into English. Most of what is available in English is published by either Heinemann Press, Three Continents Press, or American University in Cairo Press. In the U.S. most of the books are distributed by **Three Continents Press,** 1346 Connecticut Ave. NW, Suite 1131, Washington, D.C. 20036 (tel. (202) 387-5809 or (202) 477-0288). They send books very promptly by UPS. All of the following authors' books come in paperback and cost between $1.95 and $5.95; all can also be found in Egypt at **Madbuli's** bookstore (see Practical Information, Cairo).

Taha Hussein: The towering figure in modern Egyptian literature. He has written a large number of novels, many of which are available in English. One of modern Egypt's most fascinating personalities: a blind man who married a French woman, he became famous as the country's minister of education. Although a devout Muslim, he felt that the educational system should be revamped and modernized to include much more than traditional Qur'anic instruction. He pushed through numerous reforms, shaping Egypt's educational system into its present form.

Naguib Mahfouz: Generally considered Egypt's premier contemporary novelist. If you're visiting Cairo definitely start with *Midaq Alley*—about life along the streets of the Fatimid neighborhood in northern Islamic Cairo in the 1960s. *Children of Jebelawi,* a much longer novel (600 pages), follows several generations in the lives of a lower-income Cairene family. *Miramar,* set in Alexandria, is about several tenants in a boarding-house and how they interact.

Yusuf Idris: Egypt's leading short-story writer. The collection *Cheapest Nights* deals with modern Egyptian middle-class urban life. Quite witty.

Sonallah Ibrahim: *The Smell of It* is perhaps the finest work by a contemporary Egyptian author. Interestingly enough, the only unabridged edition of the novel exists in English since the Arabic version has been censored. It deals with the experiences of a writer coming off of a five-year jail term and finding that he is unable to write. Vaguely autobiographical.

Tewfik Al Hakim: The Egyptian representative of the Theatre of the Absurd. One title should give you an idea: *The Fate of a Cockroach and Other Plays of Freedom.*

Fathy Ghanem: His finest novel, *The Man Who Lost His Shadow* (450 pages), is about a man who rises up in the world by becoming a journalist during the 1952 revolution in Egypt.

Tayyeb Salih: The Sudan's leading contemporary writer. *Season of Migration to the North* is an inverted version of Conrad's *Heart of Darkness*. It tells the story of a Sudanese man who is educated in London and then tries to return home. *The Wedding of Zein* is a very short tale in the fashion of traditional Sudanese folklore.

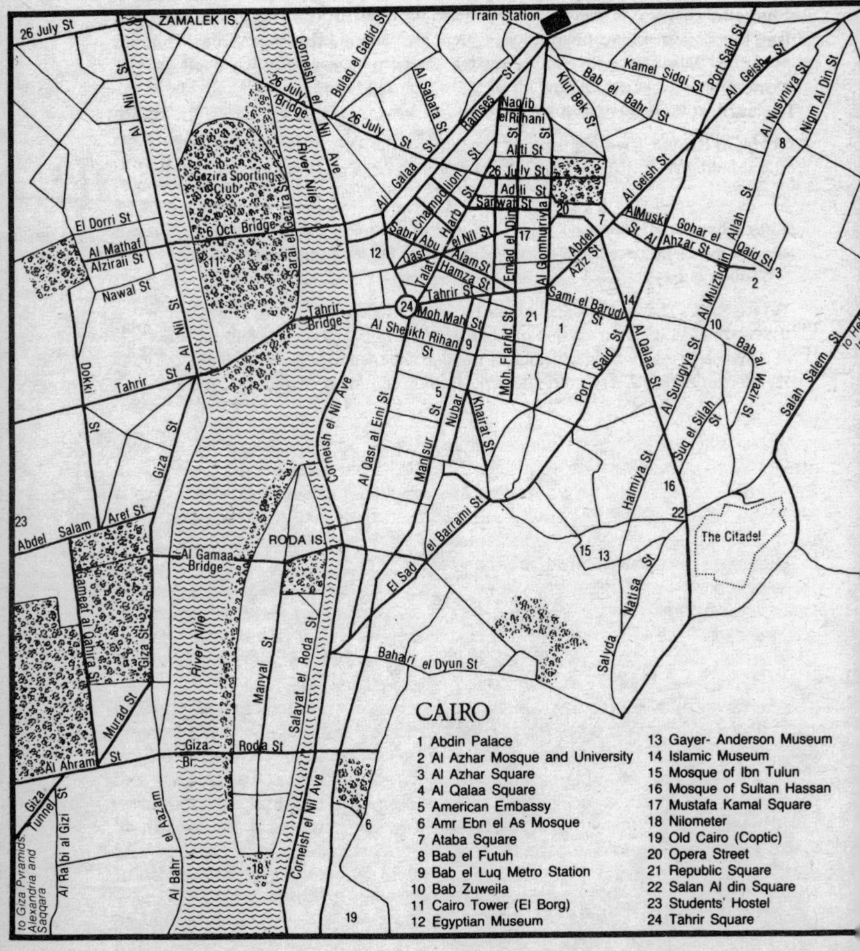
CAIRO
1 Abdin Palace
2 Al Azhar Mosque and University
3 Al Azhar Square
4 Al Qalaa Square
5 American Embassy
6 Amr Ebn el As Mosque
7 Ataba Square
8 Bab el Futuh
9 Bab el Luq Metro Station
10 Bab Zuweila
11 Cairo Tower (El Borg)
12 Egyptian Museum
13 Gayer- Anderson Museum
14 Islamic Museum
15 Mosque of Ibn Tulun
16 Mosque of Sultan Hassan
17 Mustafa Kamal Square
18 Nilometer
19 Old Cairo (Coptic)
20 Opera Street
21 Republic Square
22 Salan Al din Square
23 Students' Hostel
24 Tahrir Square
ZAMALEK IS.
Train Station
26 July St
Gezira Sporting Club
6 Oct. Bridge
Tahrir Bridge
26 July Bridge
River Nile
Corneish el Nil Ave
RODA IS.
Al Gamaa Bridge
The Citadel
Port Said St
Al Azhar St
Bab el Bahr St
Kamel Sidqi St
Tahrir St
Dokki St
Giza St
Al Ahram St
Bahari el Dyun St
to Giza Pyramids, Alexandria and Saqqara

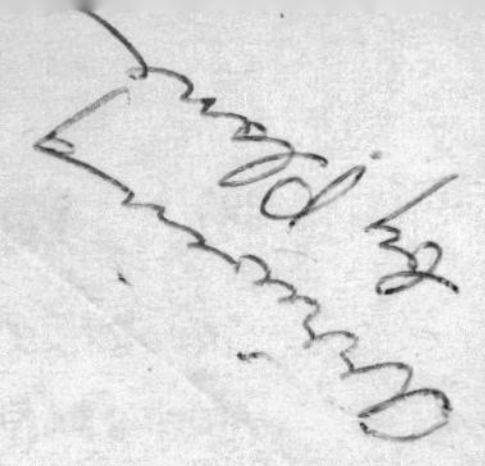

Cairo (Al-Qahira)

Intense, inscrutable and ingrown, Cairo is at the center of all that is Egyptian. The traveler will easily become immersed in the city's long love affair with archeology. Exploring Cairo can resemble excavating a pharaonic tomb—you have to sift through a lot of dirt before you get to the treasure. Cairo is a dense, loud, and sometimes squalid city, but for a budget traveler, it is an outstanding find. It is not only one of the world's least expensive capitals, but also one of the most intriguing.

The earliest Arab settlement, which would eventually give rise to the tenth-century walled city of al-Qahira, was founded by the conquering Muslim armies of 'Amr Ibn al'As in the middle of the seventh century. The walled city, known today as Medieval Cairo (or Islamic Cairo), was built several kilometers from the eastern banks of the Nile in order to protect it from the seasonal flooding of the river. By the fourteenth century, the city's population could not be contained within its walls. Expansion has continued intermittently ever since, and today the Cairo metropolis spreads for miles without interruption in all directions. At last count, the population was an estimated eleven million, making Cairo not only the home of one-fourth of the entire Egyptian population, but also the largest city on the African continent and in the Arab world. Above all, it is a crowded city, its huge population packed into a limited region of inhabitable territory and surrounded by a vast expanse of inhospitable desert.

As the ancient pyramids which press into the sky southwest of the city attest, Cairo's location just above the Nile Delta has long been a logical spot for human endeavor. The Egyptians of the Old Kingdom built their capital Memphis just south of the present city. They further enhanced the prestige of the area by constructing massive temples to their sun god Ra towards the north at Heliopolis. Although the Christian center of Egypt was Alexandria, the Muslims chose a site near modern-day Cairo as their first stronghold, returning to the area the importance it had enjoyed in ancient times. Though Memphis is now no more than a few scattered stones, and Heliopolis a fashionable residential district, successive invaders, recognizing its strategic and symbolic importance, have constructed fort after church after mosque in Cairo.

Countless traffic jams, leaking sewage pipes, and ever-present construction sites all reveal that Cairo has been modernized and industrialized at a frenetic pace over the past three decades. Visitors may find themselves assaulted by the unfamiliar and often threatening intensity of motion in Cairo. Cars and buses hurl recklessly down avenues, threatening life and limb, while pedestrian traffic swells off the sidewalks and into the streets. If the wealth of Cairo's privileged elite is conspicuous, so are the worn faces, tired bodies, and dirty rags of the poor. But though life may seem foul and destitute in much of Cairo, it is at the same time fascinating and rich in flavor. Dirty doorway passages frequently open up into tidy, well-swept private worlds complete with doilies and family portraits. Cairenes have a great deal of self-respect and take pride in their homes and families even when the world outside seems to be falling apart.

To the unprepared visitor, Cairo presents a strange and somewhat savage spectacle. It can be intimidating—as Ibn Khaldoun wrote in his autobiography, "What one can imagine always surpasses what one seeks, because of the scope of the imagination—except Cairo, because it surpasses anything one can imagine."

Orientation

Arriving by Plane

If you don't have a visa, you will be required to change $150 at the official rate (see Currency section of General Introduction) upon arrival at Cairo International Airport. As you pass out of customs at the airport, pick up a map of the city at the Tourist Office desk on the left. To reach the center of town, take bus #400 to Tahrir Square (the red and white bus towards the rear of the parking lot directly in front of the terminal); you should be able to get a seat. The ride into the town takes over an hour and the bus station in Tahrir Square is the last stop. Fare is 10pt. Bus #400 runs 24 hours a day, but it runs less frequently late at night and early in the morning. You can take a taxi or limo, but these cost at least LE3. Be prepared to do some bargaining.

Arriving by Train or Bus

All trains arrive at Cairo's Ramsis Station. To reach Tahrir Square, take either a black and white taxi (35-50pt, depending on traffic) or almost any bus headed southwards down Ramsis Street. (See Cairo Transportation section below for a list of buses from Ramsis to Tahrir.)

If you are arriving by bus, you are probably coming from Alexandria, the Sinai, or Israel. Buses from the Sinai and Israel usually deposit you at Sinai Station, a special bus station in the northern suburb of Abusseiya. To reach Tahrir Square from here, hop a southbound black and white cab (75-100pt) or a southbound bus down Ramsis Street. The terminus for all buses from Alexandria is in front of the Nile Hilton in Tahrir Sq. Some buses from Israel also let passengers off at Tahrir or at major hotels.

Downtown Cairo

Throngs of pedestrians, exhaust fumes, and the outstretched hands of beggars fill **Tahrir Square,** the confused and bustling hub of modern Cairo. Buses to every part of the city and its suburbs leave from the square's two bus terminals. To the northwest of the square is the pale blue and white Nile Hilton, where you can either pick up a free map at the reception desk or buy a good one with street indices in the bookshop for LE1. Flanking the Nile Hilton on one side stands the **Egyptian Museum,** downtown Cairo's premier tourist attraction, and on the other, the **Mugamma Building,** the appropriately monstrous central headquarters of Egypt's bureaucracy. You must register at the Mugamma within one week of your arrival. Across the street, the Old Campus of the **American University in Cairo** has a pleasant garden, usually crowded with both English-speaking Egyptians and Arabic-speaking Americans. To reach the main **Tourist Office,** walk up Talaat Harb St. (the one with the Air India office near the Square) past Suleyman Pasha Circle, and turn right on Adli Pasha St. The office is several blocks down on the left side of the street, at #5 (about 2km from Tahrir).

Suleyman Pasha Square, also known as **Talaat Harb Square,** forms the intersection of several major commercial arteries, in particular, Talaat Harb St. and Kasr el Nil St. Along the streets radiating outwards from the Square you will find many of Cairo's most noteworthy cinemas, travel agents, restaurants, budget hotels, and the city's few department stores (Omar Effendi is the largest chain). The best bookstores, clothing stores, banks and tourist shops are also here. Not surprisingly, this area is Cairo's noisiest and most crowded during business hours.

Due west of Tahrir Square, just before the Kasr el Nil Bridge, on Tahrir St., is the **Arab League Building.** Many buses and taxis leave for destinations to the west from here. Beyond the tourist office on Adli Pasha St., you will arrive at Opera Square, next to the site of the Ezbekiyya Gardens. Continuing straight alongside the gardens, you come to **Ataba Square,** a major transportation hub and the site of the central post office.

Metropolitan Cairo

Metropolitan Cairo consists of two administrative governorates: Cairo, on the East Bank of the Nile, and **Giza,** on the West Bank. To the south of Tahrir Square are the quiet residential streets of **Garden City.** This neighborhood contains many foreign embassies and banks as well as many of the city's best preserved nineteenth-century colonial mansions. Garden City flanks the west side of one of southern Cairo's main north-south avenues, **Kasr al-Aini St.** A large lower-income neighborhood sprawls to the east and south of Kasr al-Aini St., unbroken but for the area just south of the American University, which has been gentrified by student housing. As you continue south, the city becomes steadily more impoverished until you reach the squalor of **Old Cairo,** the historical and spiritual center of Coptic Cairo. Two and a half kilometers east of Tahrir Square lies **Islamic Cairo,** the dense germ of the modern city, full of museums, monuments, and mosques. No visit to Cairo is complete without at least a few days spent exploring this vast gold mine of architectural treasures. Here you will also find Cairo's main *suq* (market) and tourist bazaar. Yet farther east on the outskirts of the city lies the so-called **City of the Dead,** the northern half of Cairo's vast Islamic necropolis. Today, approximately two million inhabitants live in and around the mausoleums of the cemetery under extremely cramped conditions. The necropolis extends southwards to the **Southern Cemetery.** To the northeast, **Ramsis St.,** the road to the airport, passes through **Abusseiya** and then through the fashionable residential quarter of **Heliopolis,** replete with colonial architectural extravaganzas including the residence of President Moubarak. Due north of Downtown Cairo, beyond Ramsis St., the lower middle-class districts of **Bulaq** and **Shubra** gradually fade into the farmlands of the Nile Delta.

For the purposes of tourists, the most convenient bridge across the Nile is the **Kasr el Nil Bridge,** crossing from just west of Tahrir Square to the southern tip of **Zamalek** island. The island's green southern half consists of a large public garden and two private sporting clubs, while the northern forms a counterpart to Garden City—a neighborhood of foreign embassies, banks, fancy stores, restaurants, and upper-class residential streets. South of Zamalek in the Nile is **Roda Island,** site of Manial Palace and the Nilometer. Continuing on Kasr el Nil Bridge beyond Zamalek, you will find the Sheraton Hotel on the West Bank. You are now officially in Giza. This area of town is known as **Dokki,** a residential area with a handful of important embassies. North of Dokki begins **Mohandissin,** or "Engineer's City," designed in the late 1950s by President Nassar as a neighborhood for engineers and journalists, and now a middle-class residential area. Past Mohandissin to the north lies **Imbaba,** which hosts the weekly Camel Market, and beyond spreads a vast, crowded shanty-town. South of Dokki, just beyond the handsome campus of Cairo University and the Cairo Zoo at **Giza Square,** is the beginning of Pyramids Road, lined with sleazy overpriced nightclubs. The road culminates in the Pyramids of Giza. (For information on places of interest in the greater Cairo area, see the Near Cairo section.)

Books and Publications

The most comprehensive compendium of practical information on Cairo is *Cairo: A Practical Guide* which includes a superb set of maps of the city. It is published by American University in Cairo Press and is available at most good bookstores for LE6. For information on books about sights in Cairo, see Egypt introduction.

The daily English-language newspaper, *The Egyptian Gazette* (5pt), is weak on news but carries listings of current happenings, films, and entertainment. *Cairo by Night,* a free weekly periodical available in hotels, occasionally has some useful information. *Cairo Today,* a monthly magazine sold at newsstands (75pt), runs interesting articles on the city and attractions in the surrounding area.

Transportation

Getting around Cairo can be extremely confusing. There is no shortage of options: buses, private mini-buses, shared taxis, private taxis, streetcars and trains all contribute to the city's tightly-laced network of public transportation. Almost all of the options are very inexpensive. The following pages will help clarify some of the method underlying the madness.

Buses

The cheapest option, buses in Cairo are shabby, crowded, and uncomfortable, but they run often and everywhere. Most numbers and all destinations are written in Arabic, so you must know how to read Arabic numerals and be at least somewhat familiar with the layout of the city (see Arabic Numerals in Egypt Introduction). Most buses run from 5am until 11pm or midnight. Two of Cairo's central bus depots are located in Tahrir Square. The station opposite the American University and in front of the Mugamma serves points south, Giza, and southern portions of Islamic Cairo; the one in front of the Nile Hilton serves points north and the rest of Islamic Cairo. Once you get to the right station, ask someone to point out the correct bus. Most buses cost 5pt; some longer rides and specific routes are 10pt. The ticket takers on the metropolitan buses are generally honest; if they're slow to give you change, it is usually because they haven't got it. Try to have change handy. Outside the main stations, catching a bus is often simply a matter of running it down and timing one's leap properly, as they seldom come to a full stop. The rear doors have been ripped off most buses to facilitate this practice. The entrance is always the rear door (except at a terminus), although buses may come to a full stop for women if they attempt to enter the front door. To get out, pick a moment when the bus is not moving too rapidly and face the front of the bus as you jump off. If you want the bus to come to a full halt at an official bus stop, you must disembark through the front door. The front of a bus is generally less crowded than the rear, so it's worth the effort to push your way forward. The following are among Cairo's most important bus routes:

From in front of the Mugamma:

#8: Tahrir-Kasr al-Aini-Manial-Giza-Pyramids-Mena House Hotel.

#900: Tahrir-Kasr al Aini-Manial-Cairo University-Giza-Pyramids-Holiday Inn Hotel (except early in the morning, very crowded).

#83, 86, 182: Mausoleum of ash Shafi'i-Southern Cemetery.

#174: Sayyida Zeinab-Ibn Tulun-Sultan Hassan-Citadel.

From in front of the Nile Hilton:

#510: Heliopolis.

#400: Cairo Airport via Heliopolis and Midan Roxy (10pt).

#72: Sayyida Zeinab-Citadel-Mausoleum-of ash Shafi'i.

#173, 403: Citadel-Sultan Hassan.

#75: Islamic Museum-Bab Zuweila.

#66: Al Azhar-Khan el-Khalili.

Buses from Tahrir to Islamic Cairo are as a rule extremely crowded. For Ramsis Station, take any bus from the platform farthest from the Nile.

From in front of the Arab League Building (on Tahrir St., fifty yards before Kasr el Nil Bridge):

#13: Zamalek.

#110, 182 (and others): Dokki Square.

A general warning: when taking buses, keep your wallets and valuables securely buried on your person. Deft pickpockets abound.

Metro

If you are traveling to the southern part of Cairo, the commuter train is faster and more convenient than the bus. The point of origin is **Bab al-Luq Station,** located three blocks due east of Tahrir Square; stops include Old Cairo (Mari Girigs), Ma'adi, and Halwan. The Bab al-Luq metro begins running at about 5am, and usually stops around midnight. The fare is 5pt to Ma'adi and 10pt to Helwan in first class, half that in second class. Tourists will have little occasion to use the other trains throughout the city. The only possible exception is the metro to Heliopolis.

Black and White Taxis

The secret to happiness when traveling within Cairo lies in learning how to take a cab. Never take the large, unmetered, monochromatic Peugeot taxis within the city—they charge LE2-3 for a drive around the corner. Confine your attention instead to the metered black and white cabs that run passengers on a collective basis.

To catch a taxi from the right place, pick a major thoroughfare headed in the general direction in which you wish to travel. To hail a cab, stand on the side of the street, stretch out your arm as a taxi approaches, and scream out your destination as it goes by. If the driver is interested in your business, he'll stop and wait for you to run over. Jump in, but don't talk to the driver except to verify your destination. Don't be alarmed if, after you've confirmed the destination, the taxi doesn't seem to be going the right way. Drivers sometimes take circuitous routes to avoid traffic-jammed main arteries. Furthermore, cabs often take detours to deposit other passengers at some point. If a cab stops but the driver says he has to travel a long distance before reaching your destination, refuse the offer and wait for another cab.

Although you must take metered taxis, you should be concerned only that the cab *has* a meter, not that the driver use it. Arguing about whether he should turn on the meter is a waste of time—he'll probably tell you it's broken, and it probably is. The only way to avoid being ripped off is to act like you know what you're doing and how much to pay. Never try to negotiate the fare before the ride is over, for that implies that you don't know what you owe. Cairenes simply hail a cab, hop in, and pay what they think is adequate upon arrival. If you follow their example and are firm, the driver will just smile and wish you a nice day. If he starts screaming, let him.

Once you've used the taxis for a while you'll master the hidden logic of the fares. Until then, pay along the lines of the fares suggested below. For short journeys of 1km or less, 40pt is usually sufficient; for 1-2km, 50pt is fine. Add 15-25pt per kilometer thereafter.

If you wish to travel longer distances to points outside the city proper, you should negotiate a fare in advance. The following list is a representative sample of proper taxi fares from the downtown area to most important destinations (if you don't have precise change, plan on paying more):

Pyramids (one way)—LE2
Zamalek—35-50pt
Citadel—50-75pt
Northern Cemetery—LE1-1.50 (heavy traffic)
Al Azhar, Khan el-Khalili—50-75pt
Southern Cemetery—LE1-1.25
Heliopolis—LE1-1.50
Ma'adi—LE1.50-2
Ramsis Station—40-50pt
Old Cairo, Fustat—LE.75-1
Airport—LE3-5
Roda-Manial Palace—40-50pt
Roda-Nilometer—LE.75-1.25
Dokki—35-50pt
Mohandessin—40-50pt
Camel Market—LE.75-1
Abusseiya (Sinai Station)—LE.75-1

We quote an upper and a lower price because a number of variables affect the fare. If you get in a normal black and white cab with several people already in it, you can pay a little less than normal. If you travel with others as a closed group, you should pay a little more, as you are taking away possible business from the driver. And if you travel on side streets, or through heavy traffic, slightly higher fares are in order.

The cabs, even the black and white ones, that wait in front of major hotels (such as the Nile Hilton, the Ramses Hilton, and the Sheraton), run on a private rather than a collective basis. Expect to pay prices at least LE2-3 higher for them.

Private Taxis

There are only a few reasons to hire one of the expensive unmetered Peugeot taxis: if you have enough bags to need a luggage rack; if you want to go to a precise and difficult-to-locate spot (e.g., a street address in the suburbs); or if you want to hire a cab for the day instead of renting a car. The last venture will cost LE2-3 per hour after hard bargaining. Some of the larger cabs function as service taxis between Cairo and outlying areas, and therefore have fares inappropriate for intra-city travel. Others are simply private taxis designed to transport wealthy people who don't mind paying more for a cab to themselves.

If you are interested in hiring a cab for the day, Cairo has a limousine service that rents vehicles with drivers for a daily rate much lower than the cost of paying a private taxi by the hour. Contact **Limousine Misr** (tel. 83 13 58, 83 51 74, or 82 43 59).

Mini-Buses

You will see mini-buses (a sort of taxi-van) which carry 15-20 passengers and have the words "taxi" written on the side of them all around town. In

Arabic these mini-buses are called *arrabiya bil nafar*. They generally charge 10pt for shorter hauls and up to 25pt for longer trips. In many ways they function more like buses than taxis, running along fixed routes, often stopping only at certain places. To catch a mini-bus, go to a mini-bus stop and yell out your desired destination as the buses pass. Two of the main places to catch mini-buses in Cairo are **Ataba Square** (to Ramsis, Tahrir, Northern Cemetery, Zamalek, Islamic Cairo, Heliopolis), and **in front of the Arab League Building** (to Giza Square, Zamalek, Dokki). Mini-buses provide the only means of inexpensive transportation between Cairo and some of the outlying areas, most notably Sakkara.

Inter-City Taxis

The large monochromatic Peugeot taxis that sometimes function as private taxis within Cairo also run as service taxis to neighboring areas. They generally seat seven or eight passengers, but sometimes they pack in more. They leave from established places in Cairo for a variety of destinations, and there is usually a set fare (per person) for each route. If you don't know how much to pay, watch what other passengers pay upon arrival. Plan on paying more if you have a significant amount of luggage. Service taxis depart only when they're full, so plan to leave when other people are likely to travel. Mornings are the best time. Taxis make sense only from Cairo to certain destinations, most notably the Delta, Faiyuum, and the Canal cities. They also run frequently to Alexandria via the Delta Road, but you may find the bus (which also goes via the Desert Road) or the train more comfortable. Traffic jams and suffocating exhaust fumes on crowded roads make service taxis less enjoyable in the greater Cairo area than in the south.

Most service taxis leave from two stations near Ramsis Station—convenient if you should happen to miss your train. **Ulali Square** is across the street and to the west of Ramsis Station; **Ahmed Hilmi Square** is behind the station and to the north. Service taxis to the Canal cities leave from Ulali Square. Taxis to the Delta go from Ahmed Hilmi Square (most destinations cost twice as much as a third-class train fare; the farthest Delta destination should not exceed LE4-5 per person). Taxis for Alexandria leave from both squares, but more frequently from Ahmed Hilmi (250pt). To catch the service taxis to Faiyuum and other points south you have to go to **Midaan Giza** (Giza Square).

Service taxis also run from Ulali Square to Rafiah on the Israeli border. Generally, they are not a convenient option since they can only take you to the border. You have to find new transportation several kilometers across the border to Gaza, and then out of Gaza into Israel proper. However, taxis leave Cairo starting at 4:30am and reach Rafiah quickly; they are your best option if all the buses to Israel are booked and you want to go immediately. The fare shouldn't be much over LE10.

Ramsis Train Station

Perhaps the single most confusing spot in this most confusing of cities is Cairo's chaotic central train station at Ramsis Square, next to the towering statue of Ramses II. Everything is marked in Arabic, and most of the personnel speak only Egyptian Arabic. As you step into the station from the square, the platforms immediately to your left are for trains to **Alexandria** or the **Delta.** In order to buy reserved seats for these trains go to the ticket windows at the left-hand corner of the main hall. From the same ticket windows, signs (marked "WL") point the way to the separate ticket office for the special **Wagons-Lits Sleeper Cars** to Luxor or Aswan. The personnel at this office speak excellent English and there is almost never a line, but fare is a steep LE33 to either Luxor or Aswan. If you can't afford the Wagons-Lits, ignore the porters who try to steer you towards that window. From Ramsis Square, if you walk straight through the main entrance hall, you will be standing on platform #11. Most regular trains to **Luxor, Aswan,** and other points south along the Nile leave from here. To buy reserved seating for southbound trains, however, you have to go to the farthest part of the station. Take the steps from platform #11 down to the underpass that runs beneath all of the tracks, and walk all the way to the last platform on the other side. Off to the left of this platform are several ticket windows, where you can buy a reserved seat to Luxor, Aswan, or any other point south along the Nile. Along this same platform is the **Station-Master's Office,** where you should refund an unused ticket.

Ticket windows at Ramsis Station are open 8am-10pm. If you don't want to spend hours waiting in line, come a half-hour before the windows open. The line you must wait in depends upon whether you are reserving a seat in advance or trying to buy a ticket for the same day (often impossible). Women (and men traveling with women) can take advantage of the special "women's line" which forms at very crowded times and which is much shorter and faster than the corresponding "men's line." Always be sure you are in the right line so you don't end up wasting hours. If you give up one day and come back the next, don't assume that the same ticket window is the one you want. Depending upon the available personnel, one ticket window may take over the responsibilities of another.

The trains normally enter their berths at least a half-hour before departure time, so you should have plenty of time to find your place. If you get lost, don't hesitate to ask for assistance. For **information** at Ramsis Station, call 75 35 55. There is also an **Inquiry Desk** right next to the sleeper reservations window in the front of the station. (For a timetable of Egyptian trains, see the Egypt introduction.)

Walking

To experience Cairo properly, you have to get your shoes dirty. For example, it is almost impossible to get a car, let alone a bus, down many of the streets in Islamic Cairo. Until you get your bearings bring a good map. Don't be put off by the crowds; be adventurous, plunge in and move with the flow. But whatever you do, don't be in a hurry. Just about anywhere you go, traffic (vehicular and pedestrian) will be heavy. Never assume that you have the right of way: cars are king in Cairo, and the pedestrian is always expected to look after himself. Cars and buses swoop around corners and tear down avenues impervious to man, woman, or child. Until you get the characteristic Cairene knack of dodging cars, be extremely careful and cross busy streets only at properly marked intersections.

Note: sandals are not recommended for extensive walks; in some areas the garbage, leaking sewage, and donkey manure run deep.

Feluccas

A pleasant way to spend an evening in Cairo is to hire a *felucca* (sailboat) to take you out on the Nile. Most *feluccas* can take up to eight people comfortably. The more passengers the cheaper the cost, but you'll have to do some bargaining for a good rate. The *feluccas* for hire are just south of the Kasr el Nil Bridge on the East Bank. Across the Corniche (on the water) from the Meridien Hotel, a group of boats sail for LE5-7 during the day, for LE10 in the evening. Across the corniche from the Shepherd's Hotel, one agency is always ready to hire boats. You can even wake them up (they sleep there) at 4am and they'll happily take you out. Their price is LE10 during the day and LE12-15 at night, depending upon your bargaining powers. You can also hire a *felucca* (with pilot) for LE600 to take you to Aswan and back, stopping everywhere you please for a month. If you split the cost among six people, it comes to just over LE3 a day per person and covers at least some of your accommodations expenses. If you do hire a boat for a month and get a good *felucca* driver he will probably fish for you and cook up some great meals. One note about *felucca* etiquette: whether you hire a boat for an hour or a month, if you bring food on board for a picnic, share it with your driver. But don't go overboard sharing alcoholic beverages or *you* may go overboard.

New City

The more modern cosmopolitan quarters of Cairo do not possess any of the city's significant Islamic monuments or the slightest trace of romantic medieval atmosphere. Nonetheless, in the new parts of the city, especially around the downtown area, you'll find most of the budget hotels and restaurants; most tourists end up spending their time here. In addition, the more modern sections of Cairo feature a few interesting attractions of their own, most notably a handful of excellent museums, a weekly Camel Market and some scenic vistas of the Nile. (For an overview of the New City, see the Orientation Section.)

Practical Information

Note: The addresses of Cairo travel agencies, airlines, and other offices for boats and planes can be found in the Egypt introduction and at appropriate places in the text.

Tourist Office: Main office, 5 Adli Pasha St. (tel. 84 00 0). A low-key operation, but they know their facts and have current information on travel restrictions. English spoken. Open daily 8:30am-4pm; during Ramadan 8:30am-3pm. Other offices: Cairo International Airport (tel. 66 74 75), just inside the exit of the southern building; Giza Pyramids (tel. 85 02 59).

Banks: If you wish to have money wired to Egypt, these are the largest American banks: **Chase Manhattan**, 9 Gamal El Din Aboul Mahassan, Garden City (tel. 26 11 1); **Chemical Bank,** 14 Talaat Harb, second floor (tel. 74 07 07); **Citibank,** 4 Ahmed Pasha, Garden City (tel. 27 24 6); **Manufacturer's Hanover,** 3 Ahmed Nessim, Giza (tel. 98 82 66). All banks open Mon.-Thurs. 8:30am-1:30pm, Sun. 10am-noon. Foreign banks are closed on Sat., while most Egyptian banks are open. **Bank Misr** at the Nile Hilton open 24 hrs. Banking services in other major hotels are open until 8pm.

American Express: 15 Kasr el Nil St., just off Talaat Harb Sq., three blocks north of Tahrir Sq. (tel. 75 31 42). The place to have money sent. Open daily 8am-3:30pm; 9am-2pm during Ramadan. Client letter service closed Fri. Other American Express offices: Nile Hilton (tel. 74 33 83); Meridien Hotel (tel. 84 40 17); and Sheraton Hotel (tel. 98 80 00). All Cairo offices provide cash dollars for travelers checks. Hotel offices provide faster service, but sometimes run out of cash. The one in the Nile Hilton has the longest hours, 8am-10pm.

Central Post Office: Ataba Square. Open 24 hrs. Other post offices open daily except Fri. 8:30am-3pm; 9am-1pm during Ramadan.

Central Telephone Office: on Adli St. near Ataba Sq. Open 24 hrs. Other offices on Tahrir Sq., Alfi St., and Ramsis St.

Central Telegraph and Telex Office: Ataba Sq. opposite the main Post Office. Open 24 hrs. Other offices throughout the city: major offices at Tahrir Sq., Ramsis St., Adli St., and Zamalek near the bridge to Aguza.

Local Phone Calls: The Nile Hilton has several pay phones in the lobby that take 10pt coins. The cashier at the reception desk provides coins.

International Calls from Hotels: The two most convenient plces are the Sheraton and the Meridien Hotels, both along the Nile. The President Hotel in Zamalek, 22 Taha Hussein St. is the least crowded.

Police: In emergency, dial 122.

Ambulance: Dial 123.

Hospitals: Anglo-American Hospital, Gezira-Zamalek, next to the Cairo Tower (tel. 80 61 65). There are two expensive top-rate hospitals. **Cairo Medical Centre,** Midaan Roxy; and **El Salam Hospital,** on the Corniche on the way to Helwan.

Private Doctors: Specialist in tropical diseases: Dr. Zoheir Farid, 16 Abdel Khalek Sarwat St. (tel. 74 50 23); **Gynecologists:** Dr. Muhammad Fayad, 1103 Corniche el-Nil (tel. 33 52 3); Dr. Doreya Barsoum, 8 El Batal Ahmed Abd. El Aziz, Bab al Luq (tel. 75 64 82). **Dentist,** Dr. Mokim Ishauk (tel. 84 83 51), Dokki.

Immunizations: Public Health Unit in the Continental Savoy Hotel (on the left at the back of the lobby) in Opera Square (tel. 91 32 2). Cholera and yellow fever vaccinations, booster shots, immunization certificates. The unit is open for immunizations Sat.-Thurs. 10am-1pm and 6-8pm; Fri. 10am-noon and 6-8pm.

Travel Agency for the Disabled: Dr. Sami Bishara, ETAMS, 99 Ramsis St. (tel. 75 24 62 or 75 47 21). Organizes tours and advises handicapped travelers in Egypt.

English Bookstores: Some of the better ones are the **Anglo-Egyptian,** 165 Muhammad Farid St. (tel. 91 43 37); **Shady,** 29 Abdel Khalek Sarwat St. (tel. 74 86 18); and **Lehnert and Landrock,** 44 Sherif St. (tel. 75 53 24). If you are looking for books on Egypt, **Madbuli's,** 6 Suleyman Pasha Square (downstairs), has a good collection, as does the bookstore in the **Nile Hilton.**

Foreign Newspapers and Magazines: Available all over town. The largest collection can be found at the kiosks along Suleyman Pasha Sq., or at the intersection of 26th of July and Hassan Sabri St., Zamalek.

American Cultural Center: Just across from the British Embassy at 4 Ahmed Rageb St., also called Latin America St. (tel. 30 53 2 or 29 60 1, ext. 336). Bring passport for entrance. Library with English-language books and American newspapers. Usually, with an American passport they'll allow you to take books out of the library. Open Mon., Wed. 10am-8pm (4pm in summer); Tues. Thurs. 10am-4pm; closed Sat.

Passport Office: Mugamma Building (second floor), Tahrir Square. New passports must be stamped here. Follow the signs directing you off to the right and eventually up to the second floor. Go to window #50 for alien registration. You must also register every time you enter Egypt.

Xerox Service: 35 Muhammad Mahmud. 5pt per copy. Take three sharp rights as you step out and you will come to the more professional Artistic Xerox around the corner, where you can leave materials to be copied and/or bound.

Egyptian Youth Hostel Association: 7 Dr. Abdel Hamid Said St., Cairo (tel. 75 80 99). Entrance across the street from the Odeon Hotel (office on the second floor). Information on hostels, certificates for train reductions. Ask about the Youth Travel Bureau student tours. Open 9am-1pm and 6-9pm; closed Fri.

Ministry of the Interior: Corner of Sheikh Ridan St. and Nuban St. The place to apply for a permit to travel to restricted areas. You may have to wait.

Embassies

American Embassy: 5 Latin America St., Garden City (tel. 28 21 9 or 77 46 66). Open Mon.-Fri. 8:30am-2pm. American citizens with business in the embassy are admitted immediately. If your passport is lost or stolen, a new one can be prepared overnight for $42. They'll also help report the loss to the Egyptian police and give you instructions about how to get a new visa. If you get sick, they can give you a list of recommended physicians. (For more information on visas and passport replacement see General Introduction.)

Canadian Embassy: 6 Muhammad Fahmi el Sayed St., Garden City (tel. 23 11 0).

Israeli Embassy: 4 Ibn al Malek St., in Dokki. Cross over to Dokki from Roda Island on University Bridge. The street to the right of and parallel to the bridge is Ibn al Malek. Look up at the top floors for the Israeli flag or for the security guards by the entrance. The security guards will ask to see your passport.

Sudanese Embassy: 3 El Ibrahimi St., Garden City (tel. 25 65 8). For visas go two blocks away to the **Sudanese Consulate** at 1 Muhammad Fahmi el Sayed St., Garden City (tel. 25 04 3). From Tahrir, go down Kasr al-Aini, take the fourth right. Visa window open 9am-noon. Visas cost LE10 and take a minimum of three weeks to be processed. To apply, you need a letter of recommendation from your embassy.

Kenyan Embassy: 8 El Madina El Monawara, Dokki (tel. 70 44 55 or 70 45 46).

Ethiopian Embassy: 12 Midaan Bahlawi, Dokki. Travel in Ethiopia is restricted to Addis Ababa; you must enter the country there.

Jordanian Embassy: 6 Gohaina, Dokki (tel. 98 27 55 or 89 22 47). Technically the Jordanian Interests Section annex of the Pakistani Embassy. Open 9am-2pm. Visas are free of charge and take 24 hours. If you bring an application with three pictures at 9am, you may be able to get one by 2pm of the same day.

Tunisian Embassy: 25 El Gezira, Zamalek (81 69 40 or 80 49 62).

Accommodations

Most of Cairo's inexpensive hotels are hidden away on the upper floors of office buildings and apartment blocks downtown. Others are scattered throughout the more crowded areas of the city. The managers of these places, for the most part, receive high marks for friendliness and hospitality although in some cases (especially late at night) there may not be anyone on hand who speaks English. In summer, many of the least expensive hotels fill up, so don't be surprised if the first places you check have no room. The quality of the rooms varies, but many are shabby and not terribly clean.

Don't shy away from a hotel perched on the twelfth floor. Cairo's streets are noisy throughout much of the night and the extra height will make sleeping a lot easier. However, beware of the uppermost floors of downtown buildings; they are often without running water, especially at night. Verify that the taps are in service before checking in. Even during the dog days of summer, nights in Cairo are cool enough that air-conditioning really isn't needed, though it will enable you to close the windows and shut out the cacophony from the streets below. If it does get insufferably hot, some places rent fans at reasonable rates. Most hotels also serve tea, coffee, and soft drinks in their lobbies.

For dormitory accommodations, there is a **Youth Hostel** along the Nile only about a half-hour walk (or ten-minute bus ride) south of Tahrir Square. The Golden Hotel and Pensione Oxford also regularly set aside rooms for dorms (see below for details). Finally, there is a campground near the pyramids (see Giza Section).

Talaat Harb St. and Vicinity

Golden Hotel, 13 Talaat Harb, third floor (tel. 74 26 59). Very popular with young travelers, and not without reason. Perfect location about a block and a half from Tahrir Sq. The rooms are sometimes so jammed with people and backpacks that cleaning is impossible. Toilets and showers break down regularly. Irregular office hours. Singles LE2.85, doubles LE5.65, triples LE7.50. All rooms have private shower and toilet. Dorm accommodations available for slightly less. No breakfast.

Anglo-Swiss Pension, 14 Champollion St., sixth floor (tel. 75 91 91). Roomy with family boarding house atmosphere and clean white walls. Rooms are a bit on the drab side (especially bathrooms), but clean. Singles LE4.25, doubles LE6.20, triples LE8.20. All prices include breakfast.

Garden City House, 23 Kamal el Din St. in Garden City (tel. 28 40 0 or 28 12 6). From the southwest corner of Tahrir Sq., at the end of Tahrir Bridge, head down the street immediately east of the Foreign Affairs mansion and take your first sharp right (a two-minute walk). A very pleasant, clean pension in a quiet part of town. Popular with Cairo regulars. Half-board is obligatory. Singles LE11, LE14.50 with private shower; doubles LE17.70, LE22.60 with private shower; triples LE26. All prices include breakfast and one meal (either lunch or dinner).

Hotel Tulip, 3 Talaat Harb Sq., reception on the third floor (tel. 47 43 7 or 56 96 5). Rooms are small but clean, as are bathrooms. Friendly management. Singles with shower L6.85; doubles LE8.65, LE11 with private shower, triples LE11.85, LE14.45 with private shower. All prices include breakfast. Fans 50pt.

Hotel Beau Site, 27 Talaat Harb St., fifth floor (tel. 74 98 77). Look for the alleyway heading in off this block. Clean, airy rooms and pleasant management. Water sometimes runs only at night. Singles LE3, doubles LE5, triples LE7.50. Dorm rooms LE2 per person. Obligatory breakfast for 50pt each if more than one person, or LE1 if you're alone.

Hotel Regent House, 2 Sharaf Marrouf, off Talaat Harb St., same block as the Radio Cinema (tel 74 89 79). Entrance just around the corner from the Cinema to the west off of Talaat Harb. Small (seven rooms) family-run operation. Rooms are run down but generally clean, with the possible exception of the bathrooms. Singles LE2-3.50, doubles LE3-5, extra beds for LE1.50 each. Optional breakfast LE1.50.

National Hotel, 30 Talaat Harb St. (tel. 74 56 25 or 74 56 44). Large, hectic and shabby, with a pleasant cafe and gaudy nightclub in the same building. Singles LE4.50, doubles LE7, triples LE10. All prices include private shower and breakfast.

Hotel des Roses, 33 Talaat Harb St., reception on the fourth floor (tel. 75 80 22). Not a bad place. The triples are large and all the rooms and bathrooms are clean. Singles LE5.45, LE6.05 with private shower; doubles LE7.75, LE8.40 with private shower; triples LE10. All prices include breakfast.

Pensione Oxford, 32 Talaat Harb St., reception on the sixth floor (tel. 75 81 73). Entrance through the large doorway next to the Zeina Restaurant. A friendly dive. Normally very crowded with young backpackers. Good place to meet hard-core travelers just back from the Sudan. Singles LE2.04, doubles LE2.62, dorm rooms LE1.08 per person. You can flop on the floor for a few piasters. Bring your rolling paper.

Claridge Hotel, 41 Talaat Harb St., second floor (tel. 74 52 61 or 75 77 76). Rooms are old, clean, and large, but uniformly painted a nauseating shade of green. The toilets are not kept up, but the manager is a very pleasant chap. Singles LE4.85, doubles LE9.70, breakfast and service charges included.

Away From Talaat Harb

Select Hotel, 19 Adli St., eighth floor (tel. 75 95 13). Decent rooms with so-so bathrooms. Jolly manager named Hind. The elevator is usually broken, and it's a very long climb. LE3 per person for singles, doubles, and triples. Water can be scarce here in the daytime.

Pensione Roma, 169 Muhammad Farid St. one block east of Sharif St. off of Adli St. (tel. 91 10 88). A genuine step up. Gracious manager and clean rooms. Singles LE4.40, doubles LE8.50, triples LE10.70, extra bed LE3.20. All prices include breakfast.

Hotel Montana, 23-25 Sharif St., seventh floor, third alleyway on your left, two blocks south of Adli (next to the Robert House). Quiet and clean, though it shows its age. Singles LE5.50, LE7.20 with beautiful private shower; doubles LE8, LE9.50 with private shower; triples LE9.30, LE10.80 with private shower. Extra beds LE1.45. Optional breakfast for 85pt.

Orient Palace Hotel, 26 July St., 14, tenth floor (tel. 75 93 75/6). Rooms small but clean. Bathrooms a bit grungy. Singles LE2.50, doubles LE5 (LE7.50 with private shower), triples LE7.50. Prices include breakfast.

Omayad Hotel, 26th of July St., 22, on the corner of Talaat Harb St. (tel. 75 53 41 or 75 52 12). This place has seen better days, but the rooms are large and clean. Singles LE5.05, doubles LE7.30, triples LE10; private showers in all rooms. Breakfast included.

Everest Hotel, Ramsis Sq., on the fourteenth floor of the tallest office building immediately south of the train station, topped by a neon EgyptAir sign (tel. 74 25 06). Rooms are cheap, but not luxurious. Women should be careful in the hotel elevators. Singles LE2.70; doubles LE4.10, LE5 with private shower, LE6.50 with air-conditioning, and LE7.50 with both. Optional breakfast 90pt.

Fontana Hotel, Ramsis Sq., northeast of the station. Entrance just east of Ramsis St.; look for the sign (tel. 92 21 45 or 92 23 21). Comfortable rooms with a luxurious air. Singles LE10, doubles LE15, triples LE18, including private shower and breakfast. Air-conditioning LE1.50 extra. Swimming pool on eighth floor, open to non-guests for LE2.

Hamburg Hotel, 18 al-Bursa St., three blocks north of 26 July St. near Ramsis St. (tel. 76 97 99 or 74 44 47). From Ramsis Station head south on Ramsis St. and take your third left. Walk until you see the sign. Pleasant rooms and clean bathrooms, though a bit pricey. Singles LE12.80, doubles LE16.70, triples LE22.10. All prices include breakfast, private shower and air-conditioning.

Khan el Khalili Hotel, 7 Post (Busta) St., just north of Ataba Sq. (tel. 90 02 71 or 91 95 07). Classified as a three-star hotel, but don't believe it. The manager and staff are attentive and helpful. Singles LE8, LE11 with private shower; doubles LE11, LE16 with private shower. Prices include breakfast.

El Hussein Hotel, on el Hussein Sq. (tel. 91 80 89 or 91 84 79). Located on the edge of the Khan al Khalili bazaar and opposite the Mosque of Hussein. The best place to stay to see a more traditional side of Cairo in the evening. Singles LE7.50, LE10 with private shower; doubles LE11, LE14 with private shower. Prices include breakfast. Two-day advance reservation required before Islamic festivals and holidays.

Radwan Hotel, near the el Hussein Hotel off el-Hussein Sq. (tel. 90 13 11). A much cheaper, much dingier alternative to the El Hussein if the Khan al-Khalili is where you want to bed down. Singles LE4.15, doubles LE8. Extra beds and optional breakfast available.

Youth Hostel (IYHF), 135 Abdel Aziz al-Saud St., Manyal (tel. 84 07 29). From Tahrir Square, follow the river down along the Corniche. Cross the channel that branches from the river at the Meridien Hotel, and continue to the large bridge (University Bridge) over the main part of the river. Or take bus #8 or #900 from Tahrir Sq. and get off just before the University Bridge. From Ramsis Station take bus #95 or ask someone to put you on a bus to Manyal. The hostel will be one of the first buildings on your left (south) along the river. Wall-to-wall bunk beds in spartan rooms. Clean for the most part with pleasant balconies for watching the sun set across the Nile. Often crowded, but they rarely turn anyone away. Hostel cards LE12. Has kitchen facilities, breakfast, but no dinner. Closed 10am-2pm and 11pm-7am, as well as 6-8pm during Ramadan. 11pm curfew. Open all year. Beds cost 80pt, 60pt if you are under 21. Be extremely careful with your valuables; the hostel has had a history of thefts.

Food

If you just want to fill your stomach, you can do so in Cairo for as little as 10pt, though taste and sanitation may be wanting. The cheapest grub in town is probably *kushari,* a peppery mixture of macaroni, rice, lentils, and fried onions. *Kushari* shops are scattered all over the city and are easily picked out by the conical piles of rice displayed in the windows. Some are more hygienic than others. One good *kushari* restaurant is the **Lux** on Tahrir St. near the American University, about three blocks east of Tahrir Square. Another inexpensive alternative is the old standby of *fuul* and *taamiyya* (felafel). There are literally hundreds of *fuul* restaurants in Cairo. One of the best and most popular, is **Dumyati,** located on the north side of Tahrir St. at the pale blue pedestrian overpass leading to Bab al-Luq St. (about four blocks east of Tahrir Sq.). *Fuul, taamiyya,* salad, bread, and a dessert of *mahalabiyya* (a sort of rice pudding) should run about 50-60pt. If you want more expensive and sophisticated fare, try:

Felfela, 15 Hoda Sharawi St., just off Talaat Harb and a half block from the Golden Hotel. Has a "take-away" counter in the front that serves very good *taamiyya* sandwiches for only 4pt a piece; two make a lunch. Inside it's a genuine tourist trap; they ship them in by the busload here. The tacky decor has to be seen to be believed. The restaurant serves a variety of Egyptian cuisine with full meals running LE2 and up. *Foul* 30-45pt; *taamiyya* plain 15pt, with egg 35pt, with minced meat 45pt. Chicken soup 60pt. Spaghetti with minced meat 85pt. Rice with minced meat LE1.10.

Restaurant Shaheen, El Manial St. one street inland from the Youth Hostel. For those who tire of the hostel's gruel. Decent *kebab.* Full meals about LE2.

Roy Restaurant and Bar, on Talaat Harb, across the street and slightly north of the Metro Cinema. Clean and pleasant, with very good food at reasonable prices. Beer and liquor served. Kebab LE2-3; ½ chicken LE2.50. Good service.

Fu Shing, official address at 28 Talaat Harb St, but actually off the street in an alley (tel. 75 61 84). The best of the handful of Chinese restaurants in the downtown area. Normally (not during Ramadan) they stop serving around 9:30-10pm. Chicken curry LE3.50, deep fried shrimp LE4.20.

Restaurant Zaina, 34 Talaat Harb St. next door to the Oxford Guest House. A popular midtown eatery where you can get complete meals for LE1-2. If you stand and eat at the counter, you'll save the 10% service charge. The food is on display at the counter; make your choice there. Pastries and *shwarma* sandwiches also available. The food can sometimes be worth even less that it costs, especially with meat dishes. Make sure you get meat and not just fat.

Sofar, 21 Adli St. Lebanese food. Friendly and inexpensive. Same street as the tourist office. A dinner costs LE2-4. Roast dishes run about LE2.50; grilled dishes LE2.50-3. Try their *tabouleh* (bulgar and chopped tomatoes with meat) or their fried eggplant with yogurt. Open noon-10pm.

Rex, 33 Abdel Khalek Sarwat. Turn west of Talaat Harb onto Sarwat and it is 20m on your right. Small, homey atmosphere. Good food. Dinner will run LE3-5.

Estoril, 12 Talaat Harb; in passway between Talaat Harb and Kasr El Nil, near American Express. Very good food. Dinner LE4-6. Closed during Ramadan.

Ariston, off Talaat Harb St., north of intersection with Sarwat St. before Adli St., in a passageway on the west side of the street by the Cinema Miami. Greek and pseudo-Greek food. Huge salads. You can get dinner with a *moussaka* entree for LE4.

Coin Kebab, 28 Talaat Harb St. Walk down the passage way past the Fu Shing Restaurant to the back street and you'll see the place. The best *kebab* place in the downtown area. A very filling meat salad and *tahini* meal runs LE2.50-3.

Hag Mahmoud El Samak, Sharia Abdel Aziz. Between Ataba and Abain Squares, opposite Omar Effendi dept. store. One of the best inexpensive fish and shrimp places in town. Clean, simple; no alcohol. Food to go. Shrimp sells for LE8-11 per kilo, depending on the size. ¼ kilo per person is a big meal and will cost LE2-2.50.

Abou Shakra, 69 Kasr al-Aini. About a mile south of Tahrir Square, but worth the trip if you are in search of top-notch *kebab* and *köfte*. You can catch one of the Giza buses (#8 or 900 will do) and get off when it turns right to cross the bridge to Roda Island; this will put you in the right area. Order a quarter kilo of meat per person; meals run about LE3.

Hati-al-Gaysh, at the corner of Tahrir and Falaki Sts., three blocks east of Tahrir Sq. If you want a good *kebab*, this restaurant is a bit closer to the center of town. Very clean and courteous, with a quarter kilo of *kebab* and *köfte* for about LE2.50-3. Closed until after sunset during Ramadan.

Indian Tea Center, Talaat Harb St., opposite Radio Cinema, two blocks beyond Tahrir Sq. Sometimes a second entrance at 31 Borsa El Gedid St. is used. As the name implies, it is primarily a café; however, a variety of Indian dishes are served upstairs in the late afternoon and early evening. Curry, rice, *puri*, and a very large pot of tea will cost you less than LE2. No cold drinks; only tea.

El Tabie, 31 Sharia Orabi, between Midaan El Ramfikia and Ramsis St. Go straight up Talaat Harb until it becomes Orabi St.; it is about ¼ mile farther up.

The best place in town for *fuul, taamiyya,* and the like. You are served a set meal and the price is right at 30pt.

Restaurant Alfi Bey, Alfi St., one block north of 26 July St. Good *kebab* and other Egyptian food at reasonable prices. *Kebab* with salads and bread is around LE2.5.

Other Parts of Town

In Khan el Khalili, in front of the Hussein Mosque, restaurants serve only set meals (LE1.50-2). Each one has a different specialty from roast chicken to liver to brains. The best meal in the area is offered by the **Hussein Hotel.** The entrance is by Fishawi's Tea House; take the hotel elevator up to the rooftop cafeteria. No alcohol is served anywhere near the Hussein Mosque. A meal in the cafeteria will cost LE2.50-4. Try *tagin,* meat cooked in an earthen pot with vegetables. Good breaded veal, *köfte* or *kebab.*

Near the Giza Pyramids, three excellent restaurants are along Sharia el Maryutia. Turn at the second canal before the pyramid on the road to Kardassa. **Andrea,** a great place for barbecued chicken, is about 1 km down from the turn-off. Meals run LE3-4. Across the street, **The Farm,** 23 Maryutia, has an informal garden for eating outdoors in summer. The speciality is grilled lamb (a bit expensive); meals run LE5-7. Next door, **Bonito,** 25 Maryutia, is an *al fresco* fish restaurant also in a rural farm setting. Dinner costs LE4-6.

In Zamalek, on 26 of July St., two blocks west of the intersection with Hassan Sabri St., is a great *kebab* restaurant—**Ghanim**—where you can fill up on *kebab,* salad, and *tahina* for LE2.50. The management is friendly. The dining area upstairs is pleasant. Try **Pub 28** on Shargarat Al Dor. Walk west down 26 July St. beyond Hassan Sabri until you reach the theater, then take the first substantial street off to the right. The Pub is two blocks down, on the corner. Very good steak for LE4.50, club sandwiches for LE2.25. Alcohol served. You didn't come to Egypt for pizza, but you'll still like **Pizza Baffe** in the building next door to the President Hotel at 20 Taha Hussein St. Pizza costs about LE3. The best place around for Japanese food is **Tokyo.** As you step onto Zamalek Island from 26 of July Bridge, take your first right and then your first left onto Sayyid al Bakri St. A delicious meal runs LE4-6.

If you've tired of mediocre food, then splurge:

Arabesque, Kasr El Nil St., next to the Kasr el Nil Cinema, just off Tahrir Sq. Egyptian and Lebanese food of the highest quality. Dinner will run you LE8-13 depending upon what your budget can absorb. It's located in a tasteful complex with a bar and an art gallery. Serves until midnight.

After Eight, on the other side of the cinema from the Arabesque. The best quality meat in Cairo. Crowded Egyptian highbrow scene. Steak goes for at least LE8. Restaurant usually closes at midnight.

Moghul Room, in the Mena House Hotel. By the entrance to the pyramids in Giza. Fantastic Indian music and food. A full course meal with a beer costs LE11.

Tea Houses

Cairo has a number of tea houses and coffee/pastry shops which make excellent refuges from the city's noise and summer heat. If your stomach hasn't adapted to Egyptian fare or if you're feeling wiped out by the afternoon heat, the following shops provide beverages and light snacks in a cool environment.

Groppi: Taalat Harb Square; also Adli Pasha St. directly opposite the Tourist Office. Both have coffee, tea, cold drinks, ice cream, and a wide selection of pastries. The Groppi on Adli Pasha has a very relaxing outdoor section and is generally less crowded and hurried than the one on Taalat Harb Square. Their *cafe au lait* is excellent at 40pt a pot, enough for two people. If you go early in the morning, try their croissants. A 12% service charge is added to all bills. The one on Talaat Harb Square has a pleasant restaurant in back. In either Groppi you can get an omelette or grilled cheese sandwich for a reasonable price. Breakfast of cakes, croissants, and coffee LE1.

Lappas, Kasr El Nil St., one block northeast of Talaat Harb Square. Less expensive, less crowded, and more private than Groppi, but without ice cream. Pleasant atmosphere and excellent service. The air-conditioning is often on the fritz.

Fishawi's, in Khan el Khalili. A classic. A traditional teahouse with hammered brass tables where you can enjoy a pot of mint tea for 20pt. Nicknamed the "Cafe of Mirrors." From the square in front of the Hussein Mosque, go to the extreme left side of the Hussein Hotel (on your left). Walk down along the left side of the building and turn right into the first alley. Fishawi's is straight ahead.

Riche Cafe, 17 Talaat Harb. An outdoor cafe with pleasant atmosphere. Closed on Fridays and during Ramadan. A hangout for Egyptian intellectuals. The 1952 revolution is said to have been largely plotted here. Unlike at the above, you can get beer, ouzo, and other acoholic drinks here.

Ibis Cafe, ground floor of the Nile Hilton. Surprisingly enough, one of the best deals in town. From 6-11am they offer an all-you-can-eat buffet for LE2.30 (plus 12% service) that includes croissants, sticky rolls, yogurt, and melon. From 6-10am you also have free range over eggs, meats, and cheeses for LE5.50. With both buffets, you get all the coffee or tea and fruit juice you can drink. Their regular menu is quite expensive, but has a good selection of pastries. Open 24 hours.

Simonds, in Zamalek. On 26 July, just east of the intersection with Hassan Sabri St. Great for breakfast. *Cappucino* 20pt, *chocolat au lait* 20pt. Lemon or carrot juice 20pt, mango or grapefruit juice 25pt. Croissants, plain or sweet, 10pt. *Pâtés* 12-20pt. Open at 7:30am.

Le Poire. The best place in town for Egyptian or European pastries. Two blocks south of the American Embassy, turn left, and it will be on your left. Take-out only. Pastries run 25-50pt; croissants 15pt.

In the evening you might also try eating at one of the many "casinos" which line the Nile. Many middle-class Egyptian couples frequent these places. The **Casino an-Nil,** on the west side of Tahrir Bridge, is one of the best, but you can take your pick from dozens (some swank, others very simple). On Thursday nights they tend to be jammed.

Sights

Museums

The Egyptian Museum, known officially as the Museum of Egyptian Antiquities, more commonly as the Cairo or National Museum, is the world's unrivaled warehouse of pharaonic remains. Recently renovated, the museum is no longer the dark and cluttered maze it once was, but it still lacks the organization and careful displays one would expect to find in a museum of such unparalleled fame and quality. Don't try to digest the museum in too orderly a fashion or in too large a gulp. Come for a few short visits. However you approach the monster, one collection unquestionably outshines the rest—the objects from the tomb of Tut-Ankh-Amon, which occupy an entire quarter of the upper floor. If you only have a couple of hours to spare for the museum, come straight here. Even in the dim light the gold dazzles. Room #4, the most magnificent of all, flaunts the famous coffins and funeral mask, as well as a fabulous collection of jewelry. In rooms #7 and 8, you'll find the king's four lavishly decorated shrines of stuccoed and gilded wood. Designed to fit inside each other, the shrines represent the world's most precious collection of nested Chinese boxes. They originally encased the gold sarcophagus of King Tut-Ankh-Amon at their center.

The lower level of the museum follows a roughly chronological order as you enter the building; the displays proceed clockwise around the central domed court. If you tour the exhibits in order, you will gain a fairly comprehensive grasp of the development of pharaonic art. As you enter, the Old Kingdom rooms are to your left. Don't miss the famous statues of Zoser and Chephren, which were found near their respective pyramids, and are now on display in room #42. To bone up on your mythology, study the representations of the gods and goddesses of the ancient Egyptian pantheon in room #19. Farther down the hall are exhibits of the Middle Kingdom, with four superb granite sphinxes occupying room #16. In room #17 are particularly interesting papyrus sheets recording the secrets of the *Book of the Dead*. The Middle Kingdom statues show a harmony of form and a subtle control over detail that isn't found in the Old Kingdom works. At the back of the museum's lower floor is the section on the New Kingdom, whose art shows a greater concern for individuality than previous works. Especially noteworthy are the contents of the royal tombs displayed in room #12.

If you are beginning to think that all pharaohs look the same, go to the Akhnaton room (#3), which contains statues of the heretical pharaoh who some say introduced monotheism into the Middle East. Idealization is abandoned in these statues and the likenesses of Akhnaton are as hideously ugly as those of his wife Nefertiti are lovely and graceful. The trend towards naturalism climaxed in the later Ptolemaic period under the influence of classical art; the resulting works can be seen in rooms #24 and 25.

At the end of the first floor, circling back towards the main entrance, are the larger Greco-Roman and Byzantine exhibits. The finest pieces in this portion of the museum are the colossal bust of Serapis in room #34 and the wonderfully inscribed fragment of the coffin of Petrosiris. In the central courtyard of the museum is a mixture of pieces too large to display elsewhere, the highlight of which is the painted plaster floor from Tel al-Amarna.

In the summer of 1981, President Sadat issued an executive order which closed the museum's famous Mummy Room to the general public on the basis that it was both offensive and sacrilegious to display corpses for an admission fee. The decision was generally a popular one, and there are no plans at this time to reopen this section of the museum.

The National Museum is right in the center of town, just off Tahrir Square, northeast of the Nile Hilton. The museum is open Sat.-Thurs. 9am-3pm, Fri. 9-11:15am and 1:15-3pm; admission LE3, LE1 for students. Friday is not a good day to visit: if you wish to tour the museum for more than two hours you will have to purchase two admission tickets. If you plan to spend a good deal of time at the museum, it may be worthwhile to purchase the handy 300-page *Guide to the Egyptian Museum* which costs LE1.50 at the ticket window. Every artifact has a number which corresponds to its description in the book. In the Cairo English-language bookstores you can find several other good guides to the museum's collection.

Before plunging into Islamic Cairo and sampling the accomplishments of the city's Muslim architects and builders, visit the newly-renovated **Museum of Islamic Art,** located off Ahmad Mahar Square (the corner of Port Said St. and Muhammad Ali St.). The museum houses one of the world's finest collections of Islamic art. There's a little of everything here, from carpets, glassware, and metalwork to wood carvings, calligraphy, and pottery. If you buy a guide to the museum, make sure it has been thoroughly updated or it is unlikely to be very helpful. The museum is arranged largely by type of craft rather than period, so you can easily follow stylistic developments within a single medium. Since most tourists concentrate on Cairo's pharaonic attractions this superb museum is usually quiet and uncrowded. One of the most interesting exhibits features a magnificent collection of ancient Qur'anic scientific and philosophical manuscripts. Some of the Qur'ans are engraved in beautiful fluid Kufic script. Notice the stylistic influence of Chinese ceramic work on the Islamic crafts of medieval Persia in the ceramics collection. Open daily 9am-4pm; Ramadan 9am-3pm; admission LE2, LE1 for students. The museum is about ½km due west of Bab Zuweila, so you can easily incorporate it into your tour of the Islamic monuments. To get there from Tahrir Square, walk east down Tahrir St. all the way to Ahmed Maher Sq. on Port Said St. at the edge of Islamic Cairo. The museum dominates the northern half of Ahmed Maher Sq.

One of Cairo's best-kept secrets is on the northern edge of Roda Island, on your left after you cross the canal off Ali Ibrahim St. The **Manial Palace Museum** comprises the sumptuous interior of an early nineteenth-century palace built by Muhammad Ali. Though the southern half of the extensive structure now forms a posh Club Med Hotel, the more elegantly furnished northern rooms are on view to the public. Among the attractions are a reception palace, a private mosque, and Muhammad Ali's collection of hunting trophies, some of which have been crafted into unusual pieces of furniture. Open daily 9am-2pm; admission 50pt. The entrance to the museum is on Sharia Sayala. The museum is located right next to the Cairo Youth Hostel and is serviced by frequent buses (see Transportation).

In addition to the three discussed above, Cairo has an enormous number of smaller museums. Many of the most outstanding ones are located in Islamic or Old Cairo and are discussed in the sections on those parts of the city. In the New City, the most worthwhile of the smaller museums are:

The Folklore Center, 18 Borsa El Adima (tel. 75 24 60). Crafts and costumes from the oases in the western desert. Open daily 10am-1pm, except Fri.; admission free.

Mahmoud Khalil Museum, 1 Sharia El Sheikh Marsafy (tel. 81 86 97), in Zamalek. Opposite the exit gate of the Gezira Sporting Club. Works by the famous modern Egyptian sculptor and painter Muhammad Mahmoud Khalil. Open 9am-2pm and 5-8pm every day but Fri.; admission free.

Museum of Modern Art, 18 Sharia Ismail Abul Fetuhg, off Midaan El Sad El Aali, Dokki (tel. 81 53 69). Works by modern Egyptian artists. Open daily 9am-1:30pm, Fri. 9-11:30am; admission 50pt; students 25pt.

Palace of Arts, known in Arabic as *Mogamma el Fenoun,* corner of 1 Sharia El Maahad El Swissry and 1555 Sharia 26 July, in Zamalek, at the foot of the Zamalek Bridge. The first floor features works by modern Egyptian artists, while the second floor has paintings and sculptures by European notables such as Bonnard, Courbet, Degas, and others. Admission free.

Sights in the New City

While you should concentrate most of your sightseeing energies on Islamic Cairo and Old Cairo, the more cosmopolitan segments of the city merit some attention as well. The New City's most interesting attraction is the weekly **Camel Market** at Imbaba. The largest of its kind in the country, the market is held on Fridays 5am-10am and is liveliest 7am-9am. A few of the camels come from the Western Desert, but most of them are brought all the way from the Sudan. Some of the Sudanese Bishari tribesmen who bring their beasts to market wear traditional dress. Accustomed to a nomadic lifestyle on open desert terrain, they look noticeably uncomfortable in an urban environment. The camels look so lean because they've been en route a long time—first, a thirty-day march to Aswan, then a twenty-four hour ride (by truck) to Cairo. Adjoining the camel enclosure is a livestock market where sheep, goats, donkeys, and water buffalo are for sale. To reach the market, take a taxi to the Imbaba Airport, or make the forty-five minute trek from downtown via the 15th of May Bridge across the Nile, taking Mohandessin St. to Midaan Sphinx (Sphinx Square). To your left will be broad Ahmed Orabi St.; follow it to the end, turn left, take the first right, cross the railway tracks, turn left and the Imbaba Airport will be on your right. From here, just keep going straight until you cross some more railway tracks, then turn right; you'll soon see the market. As the market winds down, traffic throughout the shiny boulevards of Mohandessin comes to a standstill as camels and other creatures are herded through the streets.

You can pick up all sorts of used clothing and assorted junk for next to nothing at the large daily **flea market** in an area of Cairo called **Bulaq** behind the Radio/Television Building, north of the Ramsis Hilton. For still another sort of market, visit the **Army Surplus Suq** that takes place every day by Ahmad Hilmi Square behind Ramsis Station. This is a great place to get canteens, excellent military boots, khaki wear, belts, etc.—prices are unbelievably cheap. A strong pair of khaki pants should cost about 75pt.

While you're in the neighborhood you might as well absorb a little culture. Notice the towering **Statue of Ramses II,** in front of the train station, after which Ramsis Square is named. It was excavated in 1888 near the remains of the ancient city of Memphis. From Tahrir Square, a several-block walk due east down Tahrir St. will bring you to **Abadin Palace,** formerly the residence of the Egyptian Royal family; and since 1953 known as the "Kasr El Gomhuriya," which means the "Presidential Palace." The interior of the palace is closed to the public.

Cairo's two main islands both merit a short visit. The main tourist attraction on **Zamalek** (also known as **Gezira,** or "the Island"), the 200m **Cairo Tower,** provides a good overview of the central part of Cairo. For 50pt you can take an elevator to the observation platform. The view stretching from the pyramids to the medieval citadel and beyond is breathtaking. Drinks are available at the high-priced cafeteria at the top. Just south of where the Abu Alala Bridge meets the Island, the **Marriot Hotel,** a nineteenth-century palace, is one of Cairo's finest examples of colonial-period architecture. It was built for the reception of European guests upon the occasion of the completion of the Suez Canal. The interior, though often gaudy, is visually impressive and provides a dramatic sense of the lavish wealth of the pre-revolutionary Egyptian autocracy during the last century: Silvered mirrors, gilt-framed pictures, mahogany paneling, plush carpets, and imposing nineteenth-century canvasses combine in an aura of tremendous decadence. The hotel bar is a swanky place to hang out and enjoy the decor. Zamalek also has a handful of pleasant museums (see

Museums). At the intersection of the island's two main avenues, 26 of July and Hassan Sabri Sts., several kiosks sell a wide variety of European and American magazines and newspapers. The one block stretch around and along Hassan Sabri St. north of 26 of July St. is a lively area filled with colorful shops, grocery stores specializing in imported goods, and pleasant cafes.

On the southern tip of **Roda Island** stands one of Central Cairo's most noteworthy ancient monuments: the famous **Nilometer,** designed to measure the height of the river and thereby prophesy how the annual harvest would fare. The structure originally dates from the ninth century C.E., though it was restored and the conical dome added under Muhammad Ali's reign. The steps descend into a paved pit well below the level of the Nile, culminating in the graduated column that marks the height of the river. The entrance to the Nilometer is often locked, but the custodian lives nearby. Just express interest and one of the local children will run to fetch him. As the Nilometer lies quite far south, it might be most conveniently visited in conjunction with a tour of Old Cairo. Easier to reach is the **Manial Palace,** Roda's main tourist attraction, on the northeastern edge of the island (see Museums section for details). From the palace walk west across the island over the El Gamaa Bridge and you will find a lush green portion of the neighborhood of **Dokki.** Straight ahead, at the end of the broad boulevard, looms the handsome campus of **Cairo University.** Flanking the boulevard to the north stretch the city's **Botanical Gardens** (also known as El Urman Garden)—the best place in town to toss a frisbee or just sit under a shady tree. Flanking the full length of the boulevard to the south and facing the botanical gardens is the **Cairo Zoo.** Admission to either the gardens or the zoo is 5pt. Both are open daily 9am-4pm and both are extremely crowded on Fridays.

The posh district of **Heliopolis,** at the eastern edge of the city, has some fanciful colonial mansions and a few minor sights. This is the most ancient corner of Cairo; a few scanty pharaonic ruins remain, such as a fragment of a temple dedicated to Rē and the more substantial 20m-high **Obelisk of Sesostris I.** In the village of **Matariya,** just to the north, stands the sacred **Virgin's Tree,** an ancient sycamore under which the Holy Family reputedly rested during the Flight into Egypt. (For information on sights in the suburban Cairo area, see Near Cairo.)

Nightlife

B's Corner, in Zamalek, a bar with video, a host of board games (chess, backgammon, etc.), and a constant flow of rock'n roll, reggae, and jazz, is a popular hangout with foreigners who live in Cairo and a great place to meet people who know the city well. Open until 1am, it's located at 20 Taha Hussein St. To get there, take Hassan Sabri St. north of 26 July St. until you come to a square three blocks down, then take the fork that runs off at 90 degrees to the left; it's 100m down the second street, next to the President Hotel. In the same building is **El Capo,** a great place for live music. The act often changes nightly, ranging from rock'n roll to reggae to excellent live jazz. Most of the bands are foreign and occasionally quite well-known. It's not really a dancing spot, but sometimes the urge takes over. When big name groups play, you have to consume a minimum of LE10 of food and drinks. On most nights, however, LE2 worth of liquids will suffice. Most bands are scheduled to begin at 10pm, but as everywhere in Egypt, schedules exist to be ignored. Things often keep rolling until between 3 and 5am.

The **Sound and Light Show** at the Giza pyramids is interesting, although overrated and definitely overpriced. From 9:30-10:30pm in summer, 7:30-

8:30pm in winter, the story of the ancient pharaohs is narrated while the Sphinx and the three pyramids are illuminated. Tickets, costly at 400pt, go on sale at 6:30pm. If you want to be assured of a good seat, go early—there are occasionally crowds. On Mon., Wed., and Sat. nights, the performance is in English. Organized tours (from the American Express Office or the Hilton) cost 800-900pt, but you can easily take a taxi (about 150-200pt) or a bus (5pt) out to Giza and save the expense. It is also possible to see the show on the sly by paying a couple of pounds to one of the "guides" who saturate the area around the pyramids. He'll find you a place to watch within earshot of the narration. Occasionally, concerts are performed at the pyramids theater. Acts in the past have ranged from the Philadelphia Symphony Orchestra to the Grateful Dead. (For information on climbing the pyramids at night, see Near Cairo section.)

Other nightlife options include swank bars, nightclubs, and discotheques in most of the fancy hotels, but expect your wallet to be much lighter when you leave. You can gamble at **casinos** in the Hilton and Sheraton hotels, where you must show your passport to enter and do all your gambling in foreign currency. Egyptians are not allowed to enter. Cheesier nightclubs are scattered throughout the city, and if you want Middle Eastern bump and grind, a number of places on the road to the pyramids have nightly belly-dancing performances. Again, these places are not particularly cheap and are sometimes a bit on the seedy side.

Several theater and dance companies perform in Cairo. One of the best is the folk-dancing group called the **Rida Troupe,** which plays regularly at the Balloon Theater on al-Nil St. in Aguza, at the Zamalek Bridge. The troupe performs a series of traditional Egyptian dances and is well worth the trip to Aguza. The Balloon Theater also hosts occasional concerts by famous Arabic singers. The theater is open Oct.-March; check with the tourist office for upcoming events. The **Cairo Circus,** right next door to the theater, gives an entertaining one-ring show Sept.-May (Alexandria in summer), with lions jumping through burning hoops, scantily-clad female gymnasts, clowns, and the works. Performances are only in the evening. Check with the tourist office for details. There are also weekly performances by the **Arabic Music Troupe** and the **Cairo Symphony Orchestra,** and occasional appearances by other dance and musical groups at the **Sayyid Darwish Theater,** off Pyramids Road on Gamal al-Din al-Afghani St. in Giza. Finally, the **Cairo Puppet Theater** in Ezbekiyya Gardens, near Opera Square, offers nightly performances at 5:30pm Oct.-May.

A quiet and relaxed alternative, and one which many Egyptians prefer, is to spend your evenings sitting drinking tea or soft drinks at one of the many cafes which line the Nile. Or consider relaxing on the river itself on a sailboat (see *feluccas* section under Cairo Transportation).

In the downtown area, Cairo has a handful of cinemas that run foreign-language films. All are on or around Talaat Harb or 26 July St. Generally, they feature films that were first-run movies in the U.S. about a year ago. Representative prices are 85pt for armchairs, 70pt for balcony seats, and 60pt for orchestra seats. Remember that the predominantly Egyptian audience doesn't give a hoot about the sound since they can read the subtitles. Try to sit in the least popular and hence quietest part of the theater, usually the rear of the orchestra seats. Evening performances usually begin at 9pm. The *Egyptian Gazette* lists what is playing.

The American University in Cairo runs the **Wallace Theatre,** featuring plays performed in English, in the New Campus on Muhammad Mahmoud St. The University also hosts a variety of concerts from jazz to chamber music. Check bulletin boards anywhere in the buildings of the Old Campus. The **American Cultural Center** (see Practical Information) sometimes has free films on Friday nights. The Italian and French Cultural Centers, as well as the Goethe Institute show both foreign and particularly excellent Egyptian films, usually with French subtitles, free of charge. The **Italian Cultural Institute** is on Zamalek at 3 El Sheikh Marsafy St., behind the Marriot Hotel (tel. 80 87 91). The **French Cultural Center** is on the Madraset El Houqouq Al Frinsiyya Mounira, east of Kasr al-Aini St. (tel. 27 67 9 or 33 72 5). The **Goethe Institute** is at 5 Abdal Selem Arif St., formerly Buistan St. (tel. 75 98 77).

During Ramadan, nightlife takes on a whole new meaning in Cairo. All cinemas have performances starting at midnight. However, most Cairenes take to the streets at that hour, particularly around the Al Azhar and Hussein Squares. Starting at 10-11pm, there's street theater, magic shows, and general pandemonium. You can enjoy a drink with a panorama overlooking the Nile and the Cairo skyline from the top floor of the **Shepherd's Hotel,** where the small bar features an outdoor terrace. The hotel is in Garden City on the Corniche just south of the Kasr El Nil Bridge. The top floor of the Ramsis Hilton at **Club 36** offers a more elegant and more expensive alternative. Jeans and T-shirts are not allowed after 5pm. It's on the Corniche due north of the Nile Hilton, through a sea of parking lots from Tahrir. The most elegant center of Cairo's gay scene among both the city's foreign and Egyptian community is the **Taverne du Champs de Mars,** a *fin-de-siecle* Belgian bar transferred from Brussels, with good piano music, but high prices for food and drink. Located in the Nile Hilton. For more information on nightlife, consult the list of publications in the Cairo Orientation section.

Islamic Cairo

A walk through the medieval Islamic District, along with the Egyptian Museum, is top priority for sightseers in Cairo. The splendid mosques and other monuments represent some of the finest tenth- to seventeenth-century Islamic architecture found anywhere in the world; certainly Cairo's is the richest collection in any single city. But the monuments are only part of life in this section of Cairo. Once the unrivalled cultural and intellectual center of the Arab World, Islamic Cairo is now a crowded, poverty-ridden neighborhood built around the still-majestic landmarks of bygone eras. Its narrow streets will dazzle your eyes, jangle your ears, and offend your nose and standards of cleanliness.

Unlike Baghdad and Damascus, the other two great capitals of the medieval Islamic world, Cairo was spared devastation at the hands of the Mongol invaders. Nowhere else in the Arab World can you get such a sense of what life was like in the period of "one-thousand-and-one-nights." A fluke of history is largely responsible for the remarkable survival of Cairo's medieval heritage. The border between contemporary Islamic Cairo and the New City is the large north-south artery of Port Said St. Throughout the Middle Ages, the East Bank of the Nile stood where the present-day street is laid. The later westward shift of the Nile left ample room for expansion during the Colonial Period, thus saving the exquisite city from destruction.

In the early years of Islam, the city of Baghdad served as the cultural and political center of Islam. Beginning in the year 750 C.E., Cairo was governed by administrators appointed in Baghdad, including a governor named Ahmed Ibn Tulun, who secured a brief period of independence for the city (870-935 C.E.). Although Cairo soon fell under foreign rule again, there had been enough time to build the first and perhaps the most beautiful of the city's great sanctuaries, the **Mosque of Ibn Tulun.** The dawn of Cairo's golden age coincided with the arrival of the **Fatimids,** heralding from Mahdia in present-day Tunisia. Claiming to be descendants of the prophet Muhammad through his daughter Fatima (hence their name), they conquered Egypt in 969 C.E. At that time Cairo was still located at the site of al-Fustat (see Old Cairo section). The Fatimids set out to build Islam's first great Shi'ite city, which they christened *Al-Qahira* ("The Conqueror"), the name the city retains to this day. The Fatimid city was enclosed by a nearly-impregnable wall, stretching from the monumental gateways of Bab Al-Futuh to Bab Zuweila.

In 1171, the Fatimids fell to the army of Saladin, inaugurating the **Ayyubid Dynasty** (1171-1250). Saladin promptly set out to convert the citizens of Cairo back from Shi'i to Sunni Islam, and was eventually named by the Abbasid Caliphate in Baghdad to be ruler of all of Egypt, North Africa, Nubia, Western Arabia, and Syria, with his seat of power in the prospering city of Al-Qahira. Cairo began to grow into one of the great political capitals of medieval times. The Ayyubids' most outstanding addition to the city's skyline was the mammoth **Citadel,** which from its commanding site continues to dominate Islamic Cairo to this day. In 1250, Mameluke slave troops seized power, initiating a period of ruthless and repressive military rule that continued for over two and a half centuries. The Mameluke generals had a voracious appetite for ostentatious mosques and mausolea, culminating in their most impressive creation, the **Mosque of Sultan Hassan.** From 1517 until the arrival of Napoleon (1799) the city declined under Turkish Ottoman rule, as famine and disease gradually reduced a metropolis of eight million people to a desperate and starving community of two million, bringing to a close Cairo's preeminence in the Islamic world. A number of small, attractive residences within the walls of the Fatimid city represent the Ottoman period, but the most conspicuous Turkish contribution is the **Mosque of Muhammad Ali,** on top of the Citadel.

Orientation

In architectural terms, Cairo is to Islam what Rome is to Christianity. Try to pick up a copy of Parker and Sabin's *A Practical Guide to Islamic Monuments in Cairo,* whose superb set of maps of Islamic Cairo will save you many hours of fruitless searching. Also highly recommended is Freeman-Grenville's short guide. The following pages should prove helpful in selecting the most outstanding monuments, making it possible for the casual tourist to see the most important attractions if time is limited.

When visiting the mosques in Islamic Cairo, two distinctive architectural features merit special attention: the *mihrab* (prayer niche) pointing towards Mecca, and the *minbar* (pulpit)—both are often ornate, forming the primary focus of interior decoration in most mosques.

A note on dress: revealing clothing on either sex will attract a great deal of unsolicited attention in Islamic Cairo, and will bar admission to many conservative mosques. Women should bring something to cover their heads, and should wear at least knee-length skirts or long pants—and no sleeveless shirts. During prayers women are forbidden to enter many mosques; in most mosques tourists are generally not appreciated until the prayer session has ended—wait for a few minutes after they have finished before you enter. The only one of the five prayer sessions likely to conflict with your sightseeing is the mid-day prayer. On Fridays, the Muslim day of worship, the periods of prayer are considered particularly sacred. Friday afternoon prayers at major mosques take a full hour (noon-1pm). Cairo's principle "congregational mosques" (Sayyida Hussein, Sayyida Zenab, and Sayyida Nefisa), particularly venerated, are closed to tourists. Al-Azhar is an important congregational mosque, but because of its historical importance it remains open to tourists who are dressed with appropriate modesty. Most mosques are open all day long. Small palaces and museums usually close early (2pm) and during Ramadan are often open only in the morning.

Many of the more important monuments charge admission. None of them (with the exception of the Muhammad Ali Mosque) offer student discounts. If we do not list an admission price then admission is free. Caretakers usually serve as tour guides; for ordinary assistance, proffer a gratuity *(baksheesh)* of about 15pt. If a caretaker doesn't do anything for you, don't give him anything. If he holds your shoes or provides shoe-coverings, 25pt is in order; you can save money by taking your shoes with you. If you need to hunt down someone to unlock a door for you or someone shows you around in some detail, tip 50pt. Bring lots of small bills with you—getting change when you are supposed to be offering *baksheesh* is awkward, if not rude. When visiting smaller monuments or when trying to get through locked doors to see the interiors of tombs, don't be bashful about hunting down the custodian. Declare your interests to whomever is about and usually the caretaker will be fetched promptly. If you confine your tour of Islamic Cairo to unlocked doors, you are going to miss out on many of the city's most precious treasures.

Don't try to tour Islamic Cairo by car; it will be nothing but a nuisance. Streets are narrow, traffic molasses-slow, and parking nearly impossible. And don't be put off by the dirt, sewage, and garbage—once you penetrate the Islamic City's dingy exterior, you'll discover ornate decorative friezes, lovely arabesque stuccowork, finely carved wooden grillwork, and vaulted and domed interiors. The countless minarets are especially interesting; often it seems that an architect chose the most visible element of the building to make a fanciful flourish or pithy recapitulation of the structure below. Many can be climbed and utilized as an observation deck, providing a view of Cairo's splendor that is impossible to get while embroiled in its close, crowded streets. One good way to start your tour of Islamic Cairo is to acquire a good map of the city, walk to the mammoth south gate of **Bab Zuweila,** climb one of its two towering minarets, and try to match up your two-dimensional map with the three-dimensional array below. Once you've picked out the minarets and domes of the major monuments, you should be ready to begin your tour of Islamic Cairo. If you wish to plunge straight into the fray, take bus #63, 65, or 66 from Tahrir Sq. (see Cairo Transportation for buses to specific destinations). Alternatively, walk eastward from Opera Square (or Ataba Square) on Al Azhar St. Although Islamic Cairo begins when you reach Port Said St., continue on al-Azhar St. about a quarter-mile to Sharia El Muizz Al-Din Allah which runs north-south through the medieval city, connecting its northern and southern gates and providing an excellent place to begin your tour of the district. If you stand on the corner of Sharia El Muizz Al-Din Allah and Sharia Al-Azhar, Bab Al-Futuh will be to the north, Bab Zuweila to the south, and Al-Azhar Mosque one block due east.

Sights

The Northern Walls

Islamic Cairo is bordered on the north by substantial remnants of the Fatimid Walls, once vital to the city's security and the only protection against Mongol invaders. Built in 1087 C.E., the fortifications are the best surviving example of Arab military architecture dating from pre-Crusader times, and their colossal dimensions provided medieval Cairo with an impregnable defense. The city was never besieged after their construction. Medieval Europe, which borrowed most of its knowledge of siege warfare and fortification technology from the Arab world, could not boast anything comparable to Cairo's Fatimid walls at this period. Three of the fortified gates originally built into the ramparts have survived to the present day. **Bab An-Nasr** (located at the top of Sharia El Gamaliya) and **Bab Al-Futuh** (on Sharia El Muizz Al-Din Allah, just in front of the Al-Hakim Mosque) are connected by an uninterrupted stretch of wall so thick it accommodates a tunnel. You can still walk through the vaulted archway, entering via either one of the gates (admission 50pt). Exercise care, as the dark interior conceals unexpected holes and small steps where you can easily trip and injure yourself. The walls once wrapped all the way around the Fatimid City to Bab Zuweila, the only other surviving gate (it is located south down Sharia El Muizz). The northern bastions, whose domed roofs are the earliest of their kind in Egypt, were constructed with stones plundered from the ancient temple complex at neighboring Heliopolis, as the occasional hieroglyphics and reliefs on the interior walls indicate. Bab Al-Futuh offers the finest interior, consisting of a single large room connected by tunnel with the other gates. Troops were once garrisoned within the chamber. Although this arrangement provided the soldiers with uncomfortably-cramped living conditions, it was not without its advantages—especially during the rather frequent uprisings of the native population. As late as the nineteenth century, when Napoleon conquered the city, the walls were used to protect soldiers from hostilities originating within Cairo as well as outside the city. The Fatimid **Al-Hakim Mosque,** just inside the walls between the two bastions (entrance off Sharia El Muizz) was built between 990 and 1010 and remains the second largest mosque in Cairo. The structure was restored recently (amid great controversy) by the Ismaili Indian and Pakistani sect of Shi'i Islam, who view the Fatimids as their religious forefathers and who now regard the Aga Khan as their spiritual leader. Rather than restore the mosque according to its original plan, they chose to spice it up with a decidedly Indian accent. The spacious, bright interior gleams magically, and provides a peaceful and inviting haven from the noise and dirt outside. Scholars of art history and experts on Islam are disgusted and outraged by the liberal alterations, especially of the interior courtyard. For the less indoctrinated tourist, however, the mosque offers variety and an uplifting contrast to the brown weathered exteriors of Cairo's other mosques. Built in about 1000 C.E., the original tower was weakened by a series of violent earthquakes, so that in 1300 a huge, trapezoidal buttress had to be constructed around its base.

Cairo's best preserved medieval inn, the **Wakala of Qayitbay,** resides behind the Mosque of Al-Hakim, just inside Bab An-Nasr. Built in 1481, the caravanserai has never been restored. Its ground floor, like most medieval Cairene buildings, originally consisted of a row of shops and is now occupied by squatters. Outside the city walls, about a half mile to the north and well off the beaten track, stand the massive walls of the **Mosque of Baybars I,** often referred to as Fort Schulkowski. To reach the mosque from Bab Al-Futuh walk east (i.e., turn left as you step out) on Al Baghala St. along the walls, then continue until you reach Al-Gaysh St. Turn right, walk north, and you'll eventually see the walls of the Mosque on your left. Built in the mid-thirteenth century in the tradition of the great congregational mosques, its location outside of the Fatimid City walls was selected by Baybars I in order to avoid partisanship towards any of the political factions within the city. The marble was brought from Jaffa (near present-day Tel Aviv) after Baybars I captured the city from the Crusaders. The windows are richly framed by delicate Kufic inscriptions. Under Napoleon the mosque was turned into a fort, and today it forms part of a public garden.

Northern Sharia El Muizz Al-Din Allah

Between Bab Al-Futuh and the Al-Azhar Mosque, Sharia El Muizz is lined with a heavy concentration of Fatimid and early Mameluke structures. Exploring all the avenue's mosques, madrasas and palaces will take many hours, so you may want to make more than one trip. This area is called Bayn Al-Qasiayn, the Arabic for "between the palaces." The name derives from the two Fatimid palaces which housed 20,000 citizens on Sharia El Muizz. Running roughly parallel to Sharia El Muizz, from Bab An-Nasr past the Mosque of Hussein to the square in front of Al-Azhar, is Sharia El Gamaliya, on which several noteworthy buildings are located. Walking from Al Azhar up Sharia El Muizz, through both Bab Al-Futuh and Bab An-Nasr, and then returning by way of El Gamaliya is one way to minimize walking.

If you are coming from Al-Azhar Square, proceed west down Goher El Qaid St., and take a right on the first trafficked street. Then take Sharia El Muizz north toward Bab Al-Futuh, walking until you see the **Tomb and Madrasa of Al-Salih Ayyub,** with a nearly-square minaret and ornate doorway. Al-Salih Ayyub, the last ruler of Saladin's Ayyubid dynasty, was the husband of Shagarat Al-Durr, a Turkish slave-girl who rose to become ruler of Egypt, singlehandedly engineering the succession of the Mameluke dynasty to the throne after the Sultan's death in 1249. To see the remains of the structure, walk through the arched doorway and turn left into the open courtyard, where the madrasa was located. The domed mausoleum adjacent to the madrasa's facade is locked, but it is possible to enter if you can find the custodian who has the keys.

Diagonally across the street from the gate are located the **Tomb, Madrasa and Hospital of Qalaun,** in a single complex, dating from the late fourteenth century. Qalaun, a Mameluke Sultan who died on the way to Acre where he had planned to attack a Crusader fortress, sponsored the construction of this impressive grouping. Three high arched *liwans* of the original hospital structure remain, and the present building is still used for its original purpose. The ornate stuccowork on the interior is orginal, though the undersides of the arches have been restored. The Madrasa (college) of Qalaun, built in the late thirteenth century, had a curriculum of religious subjects. To gain access to the mausoleum, farther along, hunt down the guard and ask him to unlock the door for you—some *baksheesh* will be in order. The interior of the mausoleum is lavishly decorated, the work being especially fine around the entrance to the tomb. The exquisite wooden screen, separating the tomb from the rectangular forecourt, dates from the time of the structure's original construction. The jewel-like interior is particularly enchanting when viewed in the rainbow light of the stained-glass windows. Until the fourteenth century C.E., Egypt stood unrivalled as the world's premier center for glasswork; many of Cairo's older mosques have stained glass windows, though nowhere is this feature exploited to greater effect than at the mausoleum of Qalaun. This intricately-embellished tomb caused quite a bit of controversy at the time of its construction, for it presented a serious challenge to orthodox Muslim architectural practices. According to official Islamic doctrine, no distinctions in terms of a person's wealth are permitted at the time of burial. Ostentatious tombs were frowned upon as a sign of narcissism and vanity. Nevertheless, by 1000 C.E., the practice of building ornate tombs, especially for rulers, was not unheard of (the custom was probably imported from the east), and by the thirteenth century, such decorative burial sites were commonplace. The exterior of the mausoleum is reminiscent of the European Romanesque style; no doubt Qalaun's architects were influenced by the medieval European architecture of the Crusaders in Syria.

Approximately 50m in from Sharia El Muizz, on the left side of the street which begins directly opposite the mausoleum of Qalaun, look at the fragment of the **House of Uthman Katkhuda,** a Mameluke palace constructed in 1350. Its doorway is indicated by the small green and white plaque which marks Islamic monuments. The spacious interior contains some excellent fourteenth century woodwork as well as a good bit of the original decor.

Continuing north along Sharia El Muizz, next to the Mausoleum and Tomb of Qalaun, you will see the Gothic **Mausoleum of al-Nasir Muhammad,** constructed in 1304 by Sultan Qalaun's son. Al-Nasir Muhammad's forty-year reign marked the height of prosperity and culture in Egypt under Mameluke rule. Nasir's brother brought the mosque's doorway from a Crusader church at Acre after the city fell to the Mamelukes in 1291. The mausoleum and madrasa are in a ruinous state, but the facade and an ornately-decorated minaret survive. Next door, to the north along Sharia El Muizz, is the **Mosque of Sultan Barquq,** with silver-inlaid marble doors and a colorfully-striped, ornate exterior. Barquq, who came to power through a series of plots and assassinations, built the mosque as a madrasa in 1386. The inner courtyard is cruciform in shape, with four *liwans* (archways), the largest and most elaborate of which doubles as a place of prayer. Its timber roof has been beautifully restored, richly painted in blue and gold. The colorful ceiling is supported by four pharaonic columns made of porphyry, quarried in ancient times in the mountains near the Red Sea coast. The marble floor is typical of medieval Arab architecture. The round disks of which it is composed are sliced-up Greek and Roman columns, appropriated because Egypt itself possesses no marble.

From the mosque of Barquq, proceed up Sharia El Muizz until you reach a fork in the road. On the left are the remains of the **Qasr Beshtak,** a fourteenth-century palace which can be entered from the side alley (second door on your right). Finding someone with a key can take some time. Amir Beshtak, builder of the mansion, possessed virtually unlimited wealth. His palace originally stood five stories high, with running water on all floors. The grand entrance-foyer indicates the luxury in which Cairo's medieval aristocracy dwelt.

Further north along Sharia El Muizz another fork is created by a triangular patch of buildings. At the apex of the triangle is the delightful **Sabil Kuttab of Abdul Rahman Katkhuda.**This architectural combination of a *sabil* (public drinking fountain) and a *kuttab* (Qur'anic school for neighborhood children) housed within a single building dates from 1744, and presently shares the block with an apartment building constructed in about 1300.

Bearing left at the fork, you can continue north along Sharia el Muizz until at the far end of the next block, on the right, you reach the Mosque of Al-Aqmar, its marble facade heavily decorated with reams of Qur'anic script. *Al-aqmar* means "moonlit", and the light marble facade surely sparkles, even in dim light. The 6m slice out of the corner of the building (on the north side) was typical of subsequent Cairene architecture; the height of the cut is just about equal to that of a loaded camel, as the chink was intended to make the turn onto the side street easier to negotiate. The mosque is located below the present-day street, on the original level of Sharia El Muizz at the time of construction.

Proceeding north from Al-Aqmar Mosque, take the second right and follow the winding alley about 50m down, looking for the doorway on the left indicated with a monument plaque. This marks the entrance of Cairo's finest old house, the sixteenth-century **Bayt Al-Suhaymi** (admission 50pt), a charming domestic haven with an exquisite reception room on the second floor and a quiet interior courtyard complete with well and garden. Don't prowl around the premises without consulting the management first—a huge watchdog is often unleashed when the mansion is closed. Continuing along the same alley, away from Sharia El Muizz, you will eventually run into Sharia El Gamaliya. Across the street stands the rectilinear facade of the fourteenth-century monastery of **Baybars Al-Gashankir,** orginally where the Sultan kept monks in an effort to monitor their whereabouts and intellectual activity.

Al Azhar and the Khan Al Khalili

The oldest university in the world and the foremost Islamic theological center, the **Mosque of Al Azhar,** may be found just a few steps from the midpoint of Sharia El Muizz, at the end of Sharia Al-Azhar, facing onto the large square. Al-Azhar University was established in 970 C.E., rising to preeminence in the fifteenth century as a center for the study of Qur'anic law and doctrine, a position which it still enjoys today. The mosque has been heavily restored and is composed of bits and pieces from various periods. The facade dates from the eighteenth century, while the *mihrab* in the central aisle is original. Just left of the main entrance is a library which contains over 80,000 manuscripts. The core of the university's curriculum has remained virtually unchanged since the Mameluke era, although recently it has expanded to include peripheral faculties in mathematics, physics, and medicine. One can still witness the traditional instruction: groups of students, seated in a semicircle around a professor, engage in a process of Socratic questioning. Women must cover themselves completely in Al-Azhar (the front desk will provide a long wrap). It is not permitted to photograph the interior. Admission 50pt.

Across the square from Al-Azhar, like an Islamic imitation of a Presbyterian church, stands **Sayyida Al-Hussein,** Cairo's most sacred Muslim shrine. The mosque is revered throughout the Islamic world as the resting place of the head of Al-Hussein, the grandson of the prophet Muhammad. Al-Hussein was killed in the battle of Kerbala in Iraq in 680 C.E. The head is said to have been transported in a green silk bag to Cairo in 1153. As is the case with Cairo's other major congregational mosques, non-Muslims are not permitted to enter the premises. However, it is possible to view the interior of the mosque from any of the large entrance-ways. The present edifice is of recent construction and the gaudy interior has large green neon displays that glow with the name of *Allah.* Nonetheless, it is interesting to observe how the most devout Muslims worship the central shrine, which houses the sacred relic.

On *mulids* (feast days), the President of the Republic traditionally comes to pray at Sayyida Al-Hussein, while outside in the large square before the mosque, raucous festivities take place. This square is the nerve-center of modern Islamic Cairo. During Ramadan, it is the best place to witness the breaking of the fast, signalled by the advent of the evening prayers (around 8pm). All of the restaurants have the food laid out at least an hour before the prayers begin and famished patrons swarm to the tables. When everyone is satisfied, the square becomes the scene of festive celebrations.

Behind Sayyida Al-Hussein lies the eighteenth-century **Musafirkhana Palace,** a monument well worth visiting but rather difficult to locate. To reach the palace, walk north down Gamaliya Street (towards Bab An-Nasr) until you come to the little fourteenth-century **Mosque Gamel Al-Din Al-Ustudar.** 100m east of the mosque is the entrance to the palace. Built during the Ottoman period in imitation of the Mameluke style, the Musafirkhana Palace served as residence for the Egyptian royal family during the nineteenth and early twentieth centuries. Until the deposition of King Farouk, the palace was used to entertain dignitaries and foreign heads of state. The interior has been restored by some of Egypt's leading artists and today it is a favorite destination of Cairo's tour guides. If your arrival at the palace does not coincide with that of a tour group you may have difficulty gaining entry. Officially, it is open daily 9am-4pm; admission 50pt.

Stretching between Sayyida Al-Hussein and Sharia El Muizz is one of the largest tourist bazaars in the Middle East. Just turn down any of the little passageways leading west from Sayyida Al-Hussein and you'll immediately encounter the glittering alleys of the **Khan Al-Khalili.** The Khan, as it is known to Cairenes, is the city's most stereotypically Near Eastern, expensive, and tourist-infested bazaar. As you walk through the labyrinth of twisted alleys you'll see leather-dyers, furniture-makers, inlay workers, glass-cutters, and broom-makers. Most of all, however, you'll see literally hundreds of tourist shops selling everything from beautiful inlaid and wooden furniture to fake pharaonic antiquities. You'll also be accosted in English at every turn with offers to "change money," "smoke hashish," "get special guide," "just come in and look." Getting a good price on anything in the Khan requires patience and ferocious bargaining. The best strategy is to shuttle back and forth between shops and let the shopkeepers bargain each other down. Old maxims of haggling like splitting an initial offer by one-third are useless here. Many shopkeepers will quote a starting price that is fifty times an object's true value. Don't start bargaining for something until you have a sense of what its proper value is, and never name a price that you are not prepared to pay. Some stores post fixed prices that are nothing of the sort.

Far more colorful, far less touristy, far less expensive, and, alas, also less exotic is **El Meski**—the long bazaar avenue where Egyptians shop for pillowcases, tacky furniture, wedding portraits, and foodstuffs. El Meski stretches from Sharia El Muizz all the way to Port Said St., running parallel and one block north of Sharia Al-Azhar. If you want to walk between Islamic and Downtown Cairo, El Meski offers by far the most picturesque route.

Southern Sharia El Muizz

In the Fatimid period Sharia El Muizz was the main avenue of the city and ran straight through the heart of Cairo, meeting the city walls at Bab Al-Futuh and Bab Zuweila. Today, it is only a minor thoroughfare and is bisected by the much larger avenue Sharia Al-Azhar. Right at the southern corners of the intersection of Sharia Al-Azhar and Sharia El Muizz stand two impressive Mameluke structures. The building on the southwestern corner is the **Madrasa of Sultan Al-Ghouri** (ca. 1505), while across the street is the **Mausoleum of Al-Ghouri.** The interior of the *madrasa* is tranquil and soothing—a good place to get away from the noise and crowds. Admire the decorative work on the arches and the ceiling. Eventually a custodian will discover you and provide a tour, highlighted by a climb up to the roof and the fanciful minaret. The charge for the tour is usually LE1 per person, but you can point out that that's a bit steep and try to keep it to the standard of 50pt per person. The Mausoleum doubles as a community center, but can be explored whenever the doors are not locked.

Far easier to overlook is the **Wakala of Al-Ghouri**—from the mausoleum, turn left onto Sharia Al-Azhar. Then turn right (east) off the street and walk 100m down Sharia El Sheikh Muhammad Abdul. On your right, at #3, you will come to a magnificently preserved *caravanserai* (built in 1505) which has been transformed into a cultural center. Open 9am-5pm; admission 50pt. Inside is a center for handicrafts and folkloric arts, and the courtyard is often used as a theater and concert hall. Originally, the structure served as a commercial hotel—camels and donkeys were kept in the courtyard below, while merchants would set up shop in the rooms above.

Retracing your steps to Sharia El Muizz, head south, and on your left you will see the eighteenth-century **Fakahani Mosque.** It rests upon the site of a twelfth-century Fatimid mosque from which its beautiful wooden doors were taken. Down the narrow lane behind the mosque is a small doorway overlooked by all but the most vigilant of tourists. It leads in to the **House of Gamal Al-Din** (admission 50pt) an upper-class sixteenth- to seventeenth-century mansion. It is open sporadically 9am-5pm (hours are much shorter during Ramadan). It is easy to unhitch the latch and just walk in but be prepared to encounter the watchdog. The house is one of the most splendid of the surviving Ottoman residences in the city with beautiful wooden ceilings, striking mosaics, and a calm, quiet atmosphere. Continuing south down Sharia El Muizz at the corner of Sharia Ahmed Maher, on the left side you'll find the entrance to the **Muayyad Mosque** built between 1416 and 1420. Although not considered to be of great architectural significance, the interior and especially the ceiling is brightly painted and gilded, quite popular with tourists. As you enter the mosque, before reaching the prayer-hall, you'll pass through the mausoleum of Sultan El Muayyad with its austere vaulted dome. The *muezzin* (prayer-caller) will offer to show you the minaret. Before he does, he may take visitors aside and grant them a private performance singing the prayer. Once you return from climbing the minaret, give him some *baksheesh*. Admission to the mosque is 50pt. The mosque's most unusual feature is that its minarets are detached and imbedded into the Fatimid walls, seated upon the colossal southern gateway, **Bab Zuweila,** by far the most imposing of the three surviving Fatimid gates. Extending to the east for 100m, the remains of the adjoining wall reveal why Cairo was considered impregnable during the twelfth and thirteenth centuries.

Across the street from Bab Zuweila, the small, elegant **Mosque of Salih Talai,** built in 1160, is one of Cairo's best preserved Fatimid structures. The austere yet graceful courtyard is arranged in a compact symmetrical design, opening into a small prayer hall. The custodian (who will expect *baksheesh*) will show the way up to the roof. Continuing south, Sharia El Muizz passes by the Mosque and turns into a covered alley bazaar with wooden roofing, known as the **Street of Tentmakers,** followed a few blocks down by a similar covered alley called the **Street of Saddlemakers.** If you turn left as you step out of Bab Zuweila, you'll find yourself on Darb El Ahmar St. heading towards the Citadel. If you turn right, you'll be on Ahmed Maher St., lined with the shops of parasol-makers, carpenters, tombstone-carvers, and metalworkers. The street leads out to Ahmed Maher Square on Port Saïd St., across from the Museum of Islamic Art.

The Citadel

Dominating Islamic Cairo, the lofty Citadel was begun by Saladin in 1178 C.E. and has been expanded and modified under subsequent rulers all the way into this century. To enter the Citadel complex, walk all the way around to the far eastern side of the structure—follow the road along either the northern or southern walls. Don't be misled by the mammoth western gateway of Bab al 'Azab across from the Sultan Hassan Mosque—it is impossible to use this entrance which is kept locked because this part of the citadel is used today, as in times past, to incarcerate political prisoners. While making your way east, admire the walls, mostly Ayyubid and Turkish work. Enter through the eastern gate of Bab Al-Qulla, and follow the road up to the top of the Citadel to reach the main attraction, the distinctively Turkish **Mosque of Muhammad Ali.** (Open daily 8am-6pm, but closed Friday noon-1pm; admission LE2, students LE1.)

During his reign from 1805 to 1848, Muhammad Ali laid the foundations of the modern Egyptian state, sparked the trend towards Europeanization of the country, introduced education in the arts and sciences, and paved the way for an independent dynasty ruled by a monarch. Muhammad Ali leveled the western surface of the Citadel and built a structure that was intended to serve as a symbolic reminder of Turkish dominion. Modelled after the Nuri Osmaniye Mosque in Istanbul, it provides a delightful and striking contrast to Cairo's more somber and subdued Fatimid and Mameluke mosques. The edifice is more attractive from a distance; up close, the outline of the structures resembles a giant toad and much of the alabaster exterior is peeling and eroded. The interior is far more dramatic, however, especially just after prayers, when the large chandelier and all of the tiny lanterns are still illuminated. To your immediate right as you enter the prayer-hall is the gaudy gilt **Tomb of Muhammad Ali.** Undoubtedly the most enchanting architectural feature, a huge French gingerbread clock overlooks the courtyard. It was a gift of King Louis Phillipe of France in 1848 in return for Muhammad Ali's gift of the pharaonic obelisk that now stands in the Place de la Concorde in Paris. In the most notable alteration of the past year of active restoration, all of the little domes were repainted a brilliant fresh shade of silver, allowing the mosque to glisten on the Cairo skyline.

Directly across from the Muhammad Ali Mosque, merged with the interior fortificational walls, sits the fourteenth-century **Mosque of Al-Nasir Muhammad,** presently undergoing restoration. On the southeastern edge of the mosque, you'll find the steps leading down to Joseph's Well (also known as the Well of Saladin), descending 100m to the level of the Nile. The well was dug by Crusader prisoners who were attempting to escape from the Citadel. The **Military Museum** (open daily 9am-2pm), located in the northern part of the Citadel, has a large collection of medieval weaponry and military paraphernalia but is hardly worth the outrageous LE5 admission fee. There are no student discounts, but if you plead poverty and point out that they're charging more than any other monument in the entire country you can usually obtain some reduction. The eastern walls of the Citadel, mostly fifteenth- to seventeenth-century Ottoman work, feature a splendid view of the stark cliffs of the Moqqatam Hills, saddling the edge of the Islamic city and bringing it to an abrupt halt at the foot of their sheer walls.

Central Islamic Cairo

The one "must" in the central quarters of the Islamic city is the overwhelming **Mosque of Sultan Hassan,** Cairo's most celebrated Muslim edifice after the Ibn Tulun Mosque. It is considered the finest achievement of Mameluke architecture. Devotees of pharaonic art despise it, however, because many of the stones used in its construction originally served as the exterior casing-stones for the Pyramids at Giza. The mosque stands on Salah-Al-Din Square, facing the western gate of the Citadel (open 8am-6pm; admission LE1, no student discount). The easiest way to reach it from downtown is to take Muhammad Ali St. from the southern edge of Ataba Square and keep walking east for 2km. Frequent buses also run from Tahrir (see Cairo Transportaiton). Strictly speaking, Sultan Hassan is not a mosque but a combination of a *madrasa* and a mausoleum with a prayer-niche added. The ample interior courtyard belongs to the **Madrasa of Sultan Hassan,** surrounded by four enormous vaulted *liwans* (archways). A *madrasa* is a Qur'anic school and each of the *liwans* was reserved for instruction in a different one of the four separate traditional rites of Sunni Islam. Notice the beautiful Kufic inscription around the eastern *liwan* (directly across as you enter). Inside of the *liwan,* the *mihrab* is flanked by a pair of Crusader columns. On either side of the eastern *liwan,* bronze doors open into the **Mausoleum of Sultan Hassan.** The right-hand set of doors is particularly fine, still retaining much of its original inlaid gold. The huge cenotaph in the center of the mausoleum is frequented by devout Muslim women who beg Sultan Hassan's intercession and assistance in their personal difficulties.

Directly across the street from the Sultan Hassan Mosque is the enormous **Rifa'i Mosque** (open 8am-6pm; admission LE1, no student discount). Built between 1869 and 1912, this mosque is the most popular destination in Islamic Cairo for tour-groups. It's of little architectural or historical importance, but its gargantuan size and shiny polished interior draw crowds, and it is the resting place of many Egyptian monarchs including King Fuad, one of Egypt's last monarchs. It also contains the tomb of the Shah of Iran, who was ousted from power several years ago by the Ayatollah Khomeini. Both the Rifa'i and Sultan Hassan Mosques are illuminated at night, creating an imposing spectacle.

Just around the corner, the small **Mosque of Amir Akhor** has one of the most appealing exteriors of any of Cairo's mosques, with a rare double-pinnacled minaret and beautifully-carved dome. If you are facing the mosque, proceed to your right (east) along the walls of the Citadel and turn left (north) up Bab El Wazir Street. You will soon come to the fourteenth-century **Mosque of Aqsunqur,** more commonly known in guidebooks as the Blue Mosque, after its blue faience tiled interior. The tiles were imported from Damascus and added in 1652 by a Turkish governor who was homesick for the grand tiled mosques of Istanbul. Turn right as you leave and continue up the same street; the name of the street changes to Darb El Ahmar St., which means "the Red Way." It is named after Muhammad Ali's massacre of the Mameluke generals that took place here after he had had them to dinner at the Citadel. On your left you will come to the **Maridani Mosque.** The mosque receives few tourists and you are bound to attract some attention, but don't let it stop you. Notice the tastefully-restored *minbar* and *mihrab,* the granite columns which originally belonged to a pharaonic structure, and the large wooden screen that separates the courtyard from the prayer-hall.

Continue north along Darb El Ahmar Street; at the corner where the street veers to the left stands the simple and unobtrusive **Mosque of Qijmas Al-Ishaqi.** Don't be deceived by the unremarkable exterior. The light from the stained glass windows beautifully illuminates the inlaid marble and stucco work of the interior. The custodian is friendly and accommodating—ask him to lift the prayer-mats to reveal the underlying marble mosaic floor by the east *liwan.* As you step out notice the metal grillwork of the *sabil* (water dispensary) on your right.

Southern Islamic Cairo

If you see only one mosque in Cairo, let it be the **Mosque of Ibn Tulun,** the largest, oldest (879 C.E.), and the most harmonious of the city's major Islamic monuments. With huge sweeping contours and a vast courtyard, intricate inscriptions and lacy stuccowork, the mosque is a remarkable blend of overall simplicity and rich local detail. After Ibn Tulun freed himself from the Abbasid Khalif in Baghdad, he proceeded to build a new city north of Cairo's ninth-century site at al-Fustat. All that remains of the Tulinid city (868-905) today is its grand mosque. Although the mosque has undergone restoration on numerous occasions, no essential changes have been made in its overall design or character. (To reach the mosque, walk west along Saliba Street from Salsh Al-Din Square, by the western gate to the Citadel. Open 8am-6pm, admission LE1.)

The courtyard covers almost seven acres, with beautiful stuccowork inside and around the archways and a band of elegant Kufic inscription carved in sycamore that runs for over 2km. It is often said and widely believed (although it is far from true) that the entire Qur'an is inscribed on the walls of the mosque. Almost as interesting as the mosque is the idiosyncratic minaret, encoiled in an unusual external staircase. It was built in the thirteenth century to resemble the original Tulimid tower, which in turn was modelled after a similar minaret at the Great Mosque of Samerra in Iraq. The guard will permit you to ascend for a view of the courtyard, the city, and, in the distance, the Pyramids at Giza. Many tourists mistake the Madrasa and Mosque of Sarghatmish, which adjoins the northern side of the Mosque of Ibn Tulun, for Ibn Tulun's entrance. Sarghatmish is closed to non-Muslims. On the right as you step out of the main courtyard entrance, within the outer walls of the sanctuary, you will see the enchanting **Gayer-Anderson House** (also known as *Bayt al-Kritiliyya* or "The House of the Cretan Woman"). This pair of wonderful sixteenth- and eighteenth-century Turkish mansions was merged and refurbished in the 1930s by Major Gayer-Anderson, an English collector of artwork. After his death he donated the property to the Egyptian government and today it is a museum containing, among other exhibits, carved wooden *mashrabiyya* screens which allowed the women in the harem to see out without being visible to men in the streets. Open Sat.-Thurs. 9am-3:30pm, Fri. 9-11am and 1:30-3:30pm. Admission LE1, 50pt for students, ticket is valid for the Islamic Museum as well. A short walk to the west, the **Madrasa of Qayitbay** is considered by some experts to be the most beautiful of Cairo's Islamic monuments.

Continuing west down Saliba St., you will emerge at the foot of Port Said St., on the edge of Islamic Cairo, by the huge nineteenth-century **Mosque of Sayyida Zeinab.** Along with the Hussein Mosque, this is the most popular and spiritually vital of the city's places of worship. It is counted as one of Cairo's sacred congregational mosques because it houses the tomb of the prophet Muhammad's granddaughter, Zeinab. Non-Muslims are forbidden to enter, but it is worth glancing in the doorway, especially during prayers. Next to the mosque, you'll find the narrow alleys of the **Araz Bazaar,** less touristy but also less hygienic and polished than Khan El-Khalili. Also nearby, to the west of Port Said St. where the avenue bends sharply on Haret Monge St., **Beit Sennari** is a small museum of applied arts from the pharaonic period to the present, housed in an old Islamic house. Open daily in summer 9-11:30am and 1-2:30pm; in winter Sat.-Thurs. 9am-4pm, Fri. 9am-noon and 1-4pm.

Old Cairo

Some of Cairo's oldest architectural monuments are to be found in the southern sector of town known as Old Cairo. Nine hundred years before conquering Fatimids founded the city of Cairo, the Roman fortress town of Babylon occupied a position at the apex of the Nile Delta just 5km south of the later city site. This strategic outpost became a thriving metropolis during the Christian era, and a number of churches were built within the walls of the fortress. Many of these early Christian monuments have survived to the present day and are still revered as important places of worship by members of the surrounding community of Copts. Since it was outside the walls of the Islamic city, Old Cairo became the center for Cairo's Jewish, as well as its Coptic community. Although the Jewish population of the city has dwindled considerably in recent decades, a number of Jewish families still inhabit this quarter, worshipping at an ancient synagogue. In addition to a handful of lovely Coptic churches, Old Cairo offers one of the city's finest museums; while nearby are the recently-excavated remains of **Fustat,** Egypt's oldest Arab settlement and one of the first cities founded under the banner of Islam. To reach Old Cairo, take the crowded metro from Bab Al Luq Station and get off at **Mari Girgis,** the third stop on the line (fare 5pt.) Sharia Mari Girgis is the main thoroughfare running beside the walls which surround Coptic Cairo. You can also take bus #92, 134, 140, 201, or 94 from Tahrir Square to the end of the line. (This is probably the best way to *return* to downtown Cairo, since you're assured of a seat on the way back.) The bus stops directly in front of the Mosque of 'Amr. Finally, you can take a taxi to the outskirts of Old Cairo; tell the driver you want to go to **Masr Al-Qadima.**

Coptic Cairo

Many tourists tend to come away with a lop-sided view of Egyptian history. For most visitors, ancient Egypt is synonymous with the pharaonic age: the towering pyramids, jewel-covered mummies, hieroglyphics, Anthony and Cleopatra. This era is viewed as a mysterious isolated flowering of civilization which was then abruptly plunged into the Islamic age, characterized by mosques, medieval fortifications, and integration into the Arab world. What is often not realized is that for a crucial transition period of several hundred years, Christianity was the dominant cultural force in Egypt—beginning in the first century C.E. when Egypt became one of the first countries to embrace the new faith. Egyptian Christianity blossomed and spread, in its own distinctive form, through the Coptic Church, which split from the main body of the Christian Church in 451. Both culturally and intellectually, the Coptic age served as a link between the pharaonic and Islamic eras, and it has left its mark on modern day Egypt in a variety of ways. Although today the vast majority of Egyptians subscribe to the doctrines of Islam, nearly 15% of the population is Coptic Christian (the precise figures are a subject of heated controversy). "Copt" derives from the Greek word for Egyptian, *Aegyptos,* shortened in Egyptian pronunciation to *gibt,* the Arabic word for Copt. Usually, only the appearance of an occasional domed cathedral, or a tiny cross tatooed on the inside of a wrist indicate the presence of this populous tightly-knit religious minority. Persecuted for centuries under Islamic rule, the Copts have today emerged as an independent political and cultural force, giving rise to tension between the Coptic church and the Egyptian government. On a day-to-day basis, however, centuries of coexistence have instilled mutual tolerance: Egypt's Christians dwell happily side by side with their Muslim neighbors—especially in the towns of Upper Egypt: Assyut, Kift, Dendera, Luxor, and Esna.

The origins of the Coptic Church have never been explained adequately. After falling under Roman rule in 30 C.E., Egypt joined the rest of North Africa as part of the vast granary from which the empire drew its sustenance. By 188, several Christian patriarchs had established themselves in Alexandria, after the founding of a Christian university there in about 180. During the third century, the Bible was translated into Coptic, an Egyptian language which used the Greek alphabet. In 250, Paul of Thebes (St. Paul) became the first Christian monk, choosing a life of solitude in the Egyptian desert, thus initiating the austere tradition of Christian monasticism. During the next two centuries, monasteries sprouted up in all parts of Egypt and the practice of monasticism spread to other parts of the Roman empire. The new religion did not flourish without difficulty, however. Internal conflicts in the Christian church escalated as the Alexandrian patriarchs, guarding their power over the farming province of the Nile Delta, struggled against the Church leadership in Constantinople. A doctrinal dispute arose concerning the interpretation of the Trinity. Nestorius, bishop of Constantinople, maintained that there were two natures—human and divine—in the holy son, while the Alexandrians insisted that such a division was not in keeping with the teachings of Christ. The doctrine of the Coptic Church, monophysitism, recognizes only the divine nature of Christ. In 452, after an unsuccessful conciliatory meeting arranged by the Emperor Marcianus, the Alexandrian arm of the Church rebelled, declaring its theological and political independence from Constantinople. This challenge to the unity of the church met with a harsh response. Ascending to the throne in the wake of these developments, the Roman emperor Justinian sought to restore cohesiveness to the church by drastic measures. Condemning the Alexandrian patriarchs to internal exile, he compelled a large portion of Coptic clergy to retire to the isolated monasteries of the desert. These repressive edicts lost their significance only when the Byzantine Empire gradually declined under the pressure of internal decay and the external threat of the invading Mongols. When the Persians captured Egypt in 619, they were welcomed by the rebellious Copts as liberators. During the sixth through eighth centuries, the Egyptian Christians cooperated with their Muslim conquerors, participating in the local government and the arts. This collaboration eventually undermined the power of the Copts as, over the centuries, many Christians took up the banner of Islam. Beginning in the Tulumid period, many practical and political incentives were introduced to encourage further conversion to the Muslim faith. By the ninth century, the majority of Egyptians were Muslim and the Christians found themselves persecuted once again. Resuming their status as a threatened minority, the Copts at least managed to retain their language and culture. In medieval times the Coptic Church established some conciliatory ties with Rome, though doctrinal differences were never resolved and its independence was never surrendered. Today, liturgical services are still conducted in Coptic, the official language of the Church. Try to visit the celebration of the mass in one of the Coptic churches in Old Cairo on Sunday morning. When visiting any of the churches on any day of the week modest dress is required for both men and women.

Built on the site of the Roman **Fortress of Babylon,** the **Coptic Museum** possesses the world's finest collection of Coptic art. The museum is tastefully laid out, encompassing numerous peaceful courtyards and gardens. The floors are paved with colorful mosaics, while a host of elegantly-carved wooden *mashrabiyya* adorn the windows. The exhibits feature pieces dating from the third through seventh centuries C.E., tracing the development of Coptic art in its numerous forms. In the earliest works the predominant mood is clearly pharaonic, while in later pieces a Greco-Roman flavor begins to emerge. The most recent examples of Coptic art show the irresistible influence of their Islamic environment. It has been suggested that the tradition of the Christian cross as a dominant iconographic symbol owes its origins to the *ankh,* or pharaonic key of life. The *ankh* evolved into the crucifix shape in the course of the development of Coptic iconography. Coptic art may have exerted important influence on the evolution of Islamic architecture as well. For example, the elevated pharaonic throne of power seems to have provided the inspiration behind the first *minbar* (pulpit) erected in the Mosque of 'Amr at Fustat; the museum possesses one splendid Coptic precursor to the *minbar*. Unlike the earlier tradition-bound art of the pharaohs, Coptic art was a popular folk art; its fanciful and imaginative motifs represent a significant break with the severe styles of the period. The museum's collection also houses a variety of architectural fragments brought from the sanctuary of St. Menas at Maryut and the monastery of St. Jeremias at Sakkara. In addition the collection features colorfully-illuminated ancient manuscripts and numerous paintings, icons, and ivories. The finest exhibits are those of early Coptic textiles. The ancient Copts were weavers, embroidering garments, tablecloths, and curtains with intricately interwoven scenes of nymphs, centaurs, hunters, and animals of all kinds, as well as handsome stylized vine and leaf patterns. The museum is located directly across from the Mari Girgis stop on the metro line running from Bab al-Luq Station. If you arrive by bus or taxi, you'll be let off outside the walls of Old Cairo. Head directly south along the subway tracks and the museum will appear on your left. The museum is open Sat.-Thurs. 9am-4pm; Fri. 2-4pm. Admission LE2, LE1 with student I.D. Cameras are not permitted.

In front of the museum stands Cairo's only substantial classical ruin, the imposing **Roman Battlement,** which originally flanked the main entrance to the fortress of Babylon. Built in the first century C.E., the castle extended over a full acre and was virtually impregnable. It took invading Arabs over seven months to overpower the fortifications in the seventh century. The fortress was built directly overlooking the banks of the Nile (the river has subsequently shifted to the West). In ancient times, the castle's only surviving tower formed part of a massive harbor quay. Today a flight of stairs leads down to the foundation of the bastion; this lower area was closed to the public as of 1983.

Ensconced within the walls of the surrounding fortress, most of Cairo's Coptic churches do not face directly onto the street, and none of the older structures possess elaborate entrances, since the main gates were walled over long ago to protect against marauders. These early Christian structures are rectangular at one end, usually separated from the main hallway by a wooden *iconostasis* running the length of the room and serving as a partition, as in Byzantine basilicas. Upstairs, the gallery of the nave was reserved for women, who were separated from the male congregation. Today this upper level has fallen into disuse in most churches, though women and men are still segregated, sitting on opposite sides of the central aisle. Though none of the churches in Coptic Cairo charges admission, all contain donation boxes where you can leave a contribution if you wish. Generally speaking, the caretaker will not approach you for *baksheesh,* but if you are shown a secluded chapel or crypt, a small tip (10-25pt) is in order. Photographs are not permitted in any of the churches.

Just south of the Coptic Museum is the **Church of El-Muallaqa,** perhaps Coptic Cairo's loveliest church and the earliest known Christian place of worship in Egypt. Precariously sited atop the old gate house of the Babylon Fortress, this ancient structure is often known by its nickname, "The Hanging Church." The original suspended structure was erected in the late seventh century on a site occupied by a Roman place of worship. Repeated restoration has rendered this early structure all but invisible. Enter El Muallaqa through the doorway in the walls just south of the museum. A narrow vestibule ends in a flight of stairs leading up to a rectangular courtyard filled with icons dating from the eighteenth century. Adjoining the courtyard to the east, the church's facade is carved in intricate high relief. Inside, pointed arches and colorful geometric patterns enliven the main hallway. In the center, an elegant pulpit rests on thirteen slender columns—one for Christ and each of his disciples. The conspicuous black marble member of the group symbolizes Judas. The pulpit is used only once a year, on Palm Sunday. The ebony *iconostasis,* elaborately carved and inlaid with ivory, is one of the finest in Coptic Cairo, dating from the twelfth to thirteenth centuries.

North of El Muallaqa on Sharia Mari Girgis past the museum is the **Church of St. George,** a wide circular building erected over one of the towers of the ancient fortress of Babylon. A sixth-century Greek Orthodox church, St. George's has been renovated on several occasions. The present structure is not very old but it is one of the few remaining circular churches in the Middle East. The peaceful interior of the church contains a fine collection of icons and is illuminated by stained glass windows and candles.

North of St. George's Church, along Sharia Mari Girgis, a long stairway descends into Old Cairo proper. After entering the walled city, the first main doorway on your left will be marked with a marble plaque indicating the fourteenth-century **Convent of St. George.** A church stood on this site in ancient times, but has since been demolished. Venture farther into Old Cairo and continue straight down the main alley containing the entrance to the Convent of St. George until you reach the end. Bear right and directly ahead will be Coptic Cairo's most renowned structure, the **Church of Abu Serga,** also known as St. Sergius. According to tradition, the church marks the place where the Holy Family rested during their flight to Egypt. Sergius and Bacchus, to whom the Church was dedicated, were two Roman soldiers martyred in the early fourth century. The present structure, dating from the tenth to eleventh centuries, lies several feet below street level. A very low archway opens onto the main street leading into a narrow alley. The church is entered on the left. Inside, 24 marble columns flank the central aisle. A handsome twelfth-century iconostasis separates the sanctuary from the main chamber, crowned by a series of icons depicting the twelve Apostles. The sanctuary contains an onion-domed canopied altar, supported by four slender columns. (The original altar is on display around the corner in the Coptic Museum). Behind the left side of the iconostasis are a set of steps descending to the crypt, where the Holy Family is believed to have rested on their journey into Egypt. Each year on June 1, mass is celebrated in this tiny chapel to commemorate the event. Rising Nile waters have flooded the crypt in recent years and it is currently closed to the public.

Leaving the Church of Abu Serga, turn right and head eastward to the end of the alley. Immediately to the left lies the spacious **Church of St. Barbara,** constructed, like its neighbor Abu Serga, during the Fatimid era. Legend holds that when the Caliph discovered that these Christian churches were both being restored, he ordered the architect Yuhanna to destroy one of them. Unable to make up his mind about which church to demolish, Yuhanna paced back and forth between the two buildings until he died of exhaustion. Thc Caliph, moved by this tragedy, allowed both churches to survive. The interior of the Church of St. Barbara closely resembles that of its restored cousin. Though revered as a martyr, St. Barbara met her death in a rather unusual fashion. She was a little too vigorous in her attempts to convert her father to Christianity, and he finally responded by ending her evangelical career with a fatal series of blows. Her bones are said to rest in the tiny chapel reached through a door to the right as you enter the church. The bones of St. Catherine, for whom the monastery on Mount Sinai was named, are also rumored to lie in the chapel, though there is meager evidence to support this legend. An inlaid wooden iconostasis dating from the thirteenth century graces the church's ornate interior. The main sanctuary contains a series of seven marble steps decorated with black, white, and red stripes.

A few meters south of the Church of St. Barbara you enter the **Ben Ezra Synagogue** through a shady garden. During pre-Christian times, a Jewish temple occupied the site, but it was demolished in the first century C.E. to make room for construction of the Roman fortress. Later, a Christian church was built on the spot, and in the twelfth century this structure was transformed into the present synagogue. If you are fortunate enough to visit Ben Ezra when the caretaker is around, he will show you the distinctive Sephardic ornaments and a valuable collection of ancient manuscripts and sixth-century Torah scrolls. As of 1983, the synagogue was undergoing extensive repair. Though the building can be entered, most of the Synagogue has been roped off, and you have to content yourself with a limited glimpse of the lovely interior.

Fustat

Adjoining Coptic Cairo to the north are the recently excavated remains of Fustat, one of the oldest Islamic settlements in the world and the capital of Egypt for its first three centuries as an Arab nation. The foundations of this ancient city are currently being unearthed by an archeological team under the auspices of the American University in Cairo. In addition to a number of architectural fragments, several fine pieces of Islamic pottery and Chinese porcelain have been discovered here (the latter are currently on display in the Islamic Museum). Though none of the remains of Fustat is very substantial, a stroll through the site will reveal traces of mansions wih patios, cisterns, oil presses, water pipes, drains, and abandoned wells. In the northwest corner of the site, the heavily restored Mosque of 'Amr, Egypt's first Islamic place of worship, is still in use today. Nearby is a charming pottery district, where you can watch the artisans at work. To reach Fustat from Coptic Cairo, head north along Sharia Mari Girgis through a small square until you see the expansive Mosque of 'Amr on your right. The street just south of the mosque, Sharia Ain el-Sira, leads over a crossroad and left along a short lane to the site. The remains of Fustat consist of a labyrinth of tiny alleyways surrounded by a low wall. The walk to Fustat takes about twenty minutes. If you venture out to this district in the heat of summer, make sure to bring some water along. The ground around the site is unstable in places, since the entire area was used as a rubbish dump until quite recently.

The ruins are all that remain of a city once crucial in the development of Egyptian culture. In 641 C.E. the fortress city of Babylon, Byzantium's most strategic Nile outpost, fell to invading Arabs under the leadership of Umayyad general 'Amr Ibn Al-'As. The conquering soldiers of Islam did not use the existing city, but instead founded a new community of their own a few hundred meters north of the Babylon fortress. Egypt's first Islamic city and one of the earliest Arab settlements in the world, the fledgling garrison town was named "Fustat." Some historians maintain that the name derives from the Latin word for camp, "fassatum." A more romantic account of the founding of Fustat is well-known to every native of Cairo. The conquering general 'Amr, enchanted by the magnificent Roman port of Alexandria, sent word to the Caliph in Medina that the Mediterranean city would be the perfect place for the capital of Egypt. To 'Amr's dismay, the Caliph replied, "Will there be water between me and the Muslim army?" As a true master of the desert people, the Caliph preferred to establish his outposts in a sea of sand, connected by desert trade routes and invulnerable to naval attack from seafaring Christians. The dissappointed general reluctantly returned to Babylon, and to his surprise found that a white dove had nested in his tent during his absence. Interpreting this occurrence as a divine omen, 'Amr founded the new capital of Egypt on the site of his tent. The Arabic word for tent is "fustat," and the site was thus dubbed "Al Fustat," the "City of the Tent." Under the direction of 'Amr the encampment grew into a city and its position as the capital of Egypt was secured under Umayyad rule.

One of 'Amr's most significant and lasting contributions was a lovely mosque—the first in Egypt—erected in the center of the encampment. It served as a religious and cultural center, seat of government, post office, and *caravanserai* for travellers and visiting armies. In front of the mosque was a huge open square capable of holding nearly 12,000 worshippers (the size of 'Amr's army). After the death of 'Amr in 664, Fustat became even more sophisticated, acquiring a large treasury, numerous mansions, and an elaborate bath and sewage system, the likes of which was not seen in Europe until the eighteenth century. Although the city enjoyed a lengthy period of prosperity, the Umayyads concentrated most of their architectural efforts in Syria, Jordan, and Palestine. After the fall of the Umayyads, Fustat continued to prosper under the Abbasids of Baghdad, remaining capital of Egypt until conquering Fatimids established the neighboring city of Cairo in 969 C.E. By the middle of the twelfth century, however, the Fatimid dynasty was gradually weakening, and in 1168 Cairo was invaded by King Amalric of Jerusalem, who forcibly removed the Fatimids from their position of authority. During the battle Fustat was burned to the ground to prevent it from falling into the hands of the Crusader King. Except for the great mosque, little survived of the once thriving metropolis. Sparsely inhabited over the next few hundred years, by the end of the fourteenth century Fustat was virtually abandoned. The present day **Mosque of 'Amr** occupies the site of the original building of 642, which was a modest structure, barely one fourth the size of the present edifice. Its low roof consisted of thatched palm leaves on a series of palm trunks. One of 'Amr's first additions was a *minbar* (raised pulpit), from which he addressed the crowd. It is said that when the Caliph learned of 'Amr's addition, he ordered him to destroy it, for the general was not supposed to elevate himself to the rank of a spiritual guide for the other men. The oldest portion of the present-day mosque is its crumbling southeast minaret, added during the Turkish period. The eighteenth-century design of the mosque encompasses a single, spacious courtyard lined on four sides by stately white marble columns, plundered from local Roman and Byzantine buildings during medieval times.

Near the Mosque of 'Amr is **Deir Abu'l Sefrein,** a complex of three Coptic churches dating from the eighth century. From the mosque, head north and take the first left; follow the thoroughfare down to the railroad tracks and the wooden entrance to the churches will be slightly behind you to the north. Try to visit Deir Abu'l Sefrein between 8am and 1pm, when the churches are open, but if you arrive later, or if the doors are locked, knock as loudly as possible in order to rouse the caretaker. Ask for Gergus, a warm-hearted young artist in charge of the keys who speaks perfect English and will be glad to show you the churches. The main attraction is the **Church of St. Mercurius,** dating from the sixth century, but heavily restored during medieval times. The cathedral houses several early icons, as well as a delicate ebony iconostasis. In the northern side of the main chamber, an icon picturing St. Barsaum, "The Naked One," with a snake, marks the entrance to a tiny vaulted crypt, where the saint is said to have lived for twenty years with his pet snake. On September 10 a mass is celebrated in the crypt to honor St. Barsaum's feast day. Upstairs is another church comprising numerous tiny chapels.

Next door is the seventh-century **Church of St. Shenudi,** the most famous Coptic saint. This tastefully decorated chapel contains two fine iconostases—one of red cedarwood and the other of ebony, while an elegant wooden canopy crowns the altar in the central sanctuary. The smallest of the three main structures at Deir Abu'l Sefrein is the **Church of the Holy Virgin,** a tiny one-room chapel crowned with icons. Despite the proliferation of small paintings, the church is a peaceful haven from the noise and confusion outside.

As you leave Old Cairo, heading north by bus or taxi, you will pass the well-preserved fourteenth-century **aqueduct,** erected by Sultan Muhammad En-Nasr to transport water from the Nile to the Citadel.

Cities of the Dead

Stretching over a 6km area to the northeast and south of the Citadel, the Cities of the Dead, vast and forbidding necropolises, house hundreds of tombs and mausolea dating from the Mameluke era. The cemeteries were the burial site of the Mameluke sultans, who spared no expense in the construction of their final resting places. Elaborate tomb complexes, outfitted with domed mausolea, mosques, and adjoining *madrasas,* were erected for Cairo's despotic rulers, who excelled in the art of building despite—or perhaps by means of—their repressive and bloodthirsty tradition of autocracy. Along with these royal mausolea are many aristocrats' tombs, built for the families of Mameluke noblemen, and varying in size from tiny tottering tombstones to magnificent marble mausolea. Cenotaphs of all shapes and sizes dot the crowded thoroughfares of the royal necropolises. Despite the proliferation of funerary architecture, the Cities of the Dead remain very much alive. Doubling as a bustling residential district, the area serves as home for hundreds of thousands of Cairenes. In recent decades vast shanty-towns have grown up around the edge of both cemeteries. The modern residents of the medieval necropolises dwell amidst the marble tombs; many households have even incorporated the grave markers into their houses and yards. Labyrinthine networks of narrow alleyways are punctuated by an occasional open square or garden. Far from providing the deceased with a peaceful unmolested place of rest, the tombs often serve as clotheslines, soccer goals, and public benches. On Fridays these quarters come alive with visitors arriving to pay their respects to the deceased. Many of the grave plots are enclosed by high walls, encompassing an adjoining chamber and a small house where the family is expected to pray for their dead relatives on holy days. The Egyptian custom of picnicking at the family tomb on feast days may well be an ancient holdover from pharaonic times, when the body was believed to require nourishment and protection after death in order to ensure the spirit's well-being in the afterlife. The Cities of the Dead are particularly fascinating on holidays, although women may not be permitted into mosques on Fridays, especially during prayers.

The Mameluke necropolis is divided into two separate sectors. The **Northern Cemetery,** northeast of the Citadel, is characterized by wide boulevards, quiet gardens, and courtyards. It contains the finer monuments of the two necropolises, with structures dating from the later Mameluke period (fourteenth to sixteenth centuries). To reach the Northern Cemetery, take one of the several buses departing from Ataba Square for Dirasa, a large terminus situated directly west of the necropolis on Sharia Salah Salem, the road to Heliopolis. You can also walk to the cemetery from the Al-Azhar mosque. Head eastward around the north side of Al-Azhar until you reach Sharia Bab Al-Ghurayyib. Follow this avenue straight east until you hit Sharia Salah Salem. Dirasa lies ¼km north (look for the blue overpass). The **Southern Cemetery,** known to locals as *Al Khalifa,* is a far more crowded necropolis, housing the oldest Mameluke tombs (twelfth to fourteenth centures), including one particularly outstanding mausoleum (Imam Al Shaf'i). It is located due south of the Citadel. Take bus #182 from Tahrir, or #81 from Ataba to reach the main thoroughfare of the Southern Cemetery, Sharia Imam Al-Shaf'i. The metro also runs to this area from Ataba Square (5pt). You can reach the Southern Cemetery on foot from either Ibn Tulun or the Sultan Hassan Mosque, or the Citadel. From Ibn Tulun or Sultan Hassan, proceed eastward to Salah Al Din Square, just southeast of the Citadel. From here head directly south past the Manshiya Prison, to Sharia Al Imam Al Shaf'i. The Mausoleum of Imam Al Shaf'i is south of Salah Al Din Square.

The Northern Cemetery

Bordered on the west by Sharia Salah Salem, the Northern Cemetery is a splendid outdoor museum of Mameluke art, containing Cairo's finest architectural monuments from this period. Its most illustrious structure is the magnificent **Mausoleum of Qayitbay,** dating from the fifteenth century. The gently tapered minaret and ornately carved dome of the mausoleum stand directly west of the Dirasa bus stop, clearly visible above the peaks of the surrounding tombs. Admission to the mausoleum complex is 50pt. Approach the structure from the north, through the open square, in order to gain the best view of the facade, colorfully striped with polychromatic brickwork in a variety of geometric patterns. The finest flower of Mameluke architecture, Qayitbay's splendid mausoleum is familiar to every Egyptian as the towering monument pictured on the front of the one pound note. Qayitbay was a Mameluke slave purchased for LE130, who rose through the ranks of the army to become leader of Egypt during the closing decades of the fifteenth century. Reigning for 28 years—longer than any other Mameluke except Al-Nasir Muhammad—he was a ruthless and repressive sultan with a soft spot for beautiful buildings. Enter the complex through the northern doorway, passing first into a rectangular sanctuary, with four graceful *liwans* (archways), capped by an octagonal lantern-shaped roof. The mausoleum proper is an airy domed chamber housing the marble cenotaphs of Qayitbay and his two younger sisters (Qayitbay's is the largest of the three). Also housed in the tomb chamber are two black stones bearing the impressions of feet. Originally brought to Egypt from Mecca, the footprints are said to be those of the prophet Muhammad. A climb to the top of the triple-tiered minaret will be rewarded with a spectacular view of the Northern Cemetery's crowd of domed mausolea. From here you can also gain a close-up view of the elaborately carved dome of the mausoleum, one of the finest stone domes in Cairo. The pieces of the complex ornamental pattern fit together with an unbroken precision.

South of the Mausoleum of Qayitbay are two fourteenth-century monuments constructed for members of the royalty. To reach them, follow the main road south of the mausoleum through the **Gate of Qayitbay,** a stone archway which once guarded the entrance to the tomb complex. This thoroughfare intersects with a paved road; turn right, and head west toward Dirasa and Sharia Salah Salem. Just beyond the next main street are the remains of the **Tomb of Umm Anuk** (1348), a heavily ribbed dome adjoining a sweeping pointed archway. Umm Anuk was the favorite wife of Sultan Al-Nasir Muhammad, and her loving husband presented her with an appropriately lavish tomb. He also constructed the **Tomb of Princess Tolbay** across the way for his principal wife. Although he preferred Umm Anuk, Muslim law required him to treat the two women equally. The Sultan obeyed only the letter and not the spirit of Qur'anic law: judging from the inferior craftsmanship of the second tomb, it is clear where the sultan's genuine affections lay.

The remaining important tombs in the Northern Cemetery are situated north of the resting places of these two rival spouses. Follow the cemetery's main north-south boulevard which runs parallel to Sharia Salah Salem until you reach a pair of bulbous, pointed domes east of the street. One of the domes is carved with an energetic series of zig-zag stripes, the other with an intricate geometrical design vaguely resembling a tulip or other floral pattern. These are the **Tombs of Barsbay Al-Bagasi** and the **Amir Sulayman,** constructed about ninety years apart for two aristocratic noblemen. The earlier dome (decorated with the floral pattern), was erected in 1456 by Barsbay 'Ali Al-Bagasi, the Sultan's Grand Chamberlain and Master of the Horse Guards. The design is a variation on a Moroccan motif known as the *darj w ktaf* (the "cheek and shoulder"). In 1544, after the Turkish conquest, the Amir Sulayman constructed the neighboring dome.

Around the corner to the east is the imposing **Mausoleum of Barquq,** easily identified by means of its matching pair of ornately sculpted minarets. Built in 1400 for Sultan Barquq by his son, Nasir al-Din Farag, this enormous family plot encompasses a spacious inner courtyard containing the meager remains of a stone fountain and a tamarisk shade tree. The *minbar* (pulpit) beneath the western arcade was donated to the mausoleum by the Mameluke ruler Qayitbay. Three larger domes grace the western arcade. The smaller, central peak covers the richly decorated *minbar,* while two matching zig-zag domes—the earliest stone domes in Cairo—shelter the family mausolea located in either corner. Sultan Barquq is interred below the northeast corner of the complex and the remains of his two daughters occupy the chamber beneath the southeast dome. For a bit of *baksheesh,* the caretaker will show you around the mausolea and let you climb the minaret. In the northeast corner of the complex, the second story holds the remains of a large *kuttab* and numerous monastic cells which once housed dervishes—members of Muslim religious orders who engaged in devotional exercises and ritual body movements to achieve an altered state of consciousness. Admission to the Mausoleum of Barquq—not including the tomb chambers and minaret, is 50pt per person.

The **Mosque and Mausoleum of Sultan Ashraf Barsbay** are 50m south of the mausoluem of Barquq, along the cemetery's main thoroughfare. Originally intended as a monastery, the fifteenth-century mosque has meticulously executed marble mosaic floors—don't be bashful about lifting the protective mats to have a look at the colorful tilework. Adjoining the mosque to the north is the mausoleum, a domed chamber containing a white marble cenotaph, an elaborately-decorated *mihrab* and gleaming mother-of-pearl and marble mosaics. A local tailor has set up shop inside the tomb chamber.

The Southern Cemetery

The Southern Cemetery's most impressive edifice is the celebrated **Mausoleum of Imam Al-Shaf'i.** The largest Islamic mortuary chamber in Egypt, the mausoleum was erected in 1211 C.E. by Saladin's brother and successor, Al-Afdal, in honor of the great Imam Al Shaf'i, who had died in 820. Imam Al Shaf'i, founder of one of the four rites of Sunni Islam, was directly descended from Muhammad's uncle Abu Talib. In 1178 Saladin erected a large cenotaph over the grave of Imam Shaf'i which is now housed within the thirteenth-century mausoleum. In order to weaken the influence of Shi'i Islam, which had made gains under Fatimid rule, Saladin also constructed a small *madrasa* on the same site, the first such school in Egypt (no trace of the *madrasa* remains). Today, the Imam's revered mausoleum is often crowded with devout Muslims offering prayers. In addition to the tomb chamber, the complex contains two mosques, one dating from 1190 C.E. and the other from 1763. The earlier mosque is closed to non-Muslims. The more recent mosque is the one primarily used for prayers and is still a vital center for traditional worship. The mausoleum itself has a graceful dome crowned with a representation of a bronze boat, resembling a small weathervane. Popular legend holds that this ornament was intended for use as a bird-feeder. Traditionally, the tiny barque was filled with grain during an annual *muhlid* celebrating the Imam's birthday. Experts claim that the figure is a ceremonial boat symbolizing the Imam's passage into the afterlife—an interesting remnant of pharaonic traditions. Built in 1799, the dome consists of two nested wooden shells—about 30cm apart—painted with a layer of lead. Below, the original edifice houses the cenotaph and mortuary chamber. The interior of the mausoleum, comprising a single octagonal room, sparkles with a rainbow of colorfully decorated patterns. In the center is the exquisite teak cenotaph of Imam Shaf'i—one of the finest pieces of Ayyubid wood carving to survive to the present day. Women often come to the tomb to pray for assistance with personal difficulties and appeal for intercession on the part of Imam. Although lavishly decorated, the large original *mihrab* with the mausoleum is not correctly aligned with Mecca. A notice posted beside it indicates the deviance and nearby is a *mihrab* pointed in the proper direction. There is no official admission price to the Mausoleum of Imam Shaf'i but the local caretaker will probably approach you with a request for *baksheesh*. 25pt is a reasonable tip.

The **Mosque of Sayyida Nafisa,** Egypt's third-holiest Islamic shrine, is situated on the western edge of the Southern Cemetery not far from Al-Sultaniyya, an elegant fourteenth-century tomb. To get there, go to the main intersection southeast of the Citadel and take the main thoroughfare which follows the twelfth-century **Wall of Saladin** in a southwesterly direction. At the end of the wall, bear sharply right and weave your way westward through a short maze of side streets to reach the entrance. As one of Cairo's three Congregational Mosques, the mosque of Sayyida Nafisa is a center of Islamic worship and off-limits to non-Muslims. However, there is no reason you cannot pause in the entrance for a glimpse of the interior. As is the case with Cairo's other Congregational Mosques, Sayyida Nafisa houses a relic of a direct descendant of the prophet Muhammad. Sayyida Nafisa, the great granddaughter of Al-Massan, a grandson of the Prophet, was a widely venerated figure during her lifetime. After her death in 824 C.E., Sayyida Nafisa's tomb attracted throngs of pilgrims. By the tenth century, the original structure proved to be too small to contain the many devoted worshippers, so successively larger mosques were built. The present structure dates from the nineteenth century. So many mausolea were erected in the immediate vicinity of Sayyida Nafisa's tomb that historians suspect that the construction of this sacred shrine sparked the development of the Southern Cemetery. On Fridays you will see crowds making their way through the Southern Cemetery from all directions to converge on the mosque.

Adjoining the Mosque of Sayyida Nafisa on the eastern side are the thirteenth-century **Tombs of Abbasid Caliphs.** A large gate in the side of the passageway opens up into a spacious L-shaped courtyard. The brick and stucco facade of the Mausoleum lies on the courtyard's northern side, graced by three delicate pointed-arched doorways. At the peak of their authority, the Abbasid Caliphs ruled virtually the entire Muslim world from their seat of power in Baghdad. The last reigning Caliph fled from Baghdad in 1258 C.E. after invading Mongols toppled the regime. Arriving in Egypt, he was welcomed by the reigning Mameluke Sultan, who befriended and exalted the deposed Caliph in an effort to legitimize his own position. Subsequent Mameluke rulers continued to protect the succession of Caliphs in order to further their own political purposes, without ever allowing the Caliphate to gain any degree of effective power. Finally, the sultan in Istanbul declared himself to be Caliph in 1538, thereby consolidating the religious as well as the political authority of the

Ottoman Sultanate. At this time Egypt was under Ottoman rule so it was impossible for the regional government to protest the abolition of their local charade of religious authority. Though the Abbasid Caliphs have been fully deposed, their succession continues to present day, and members of the family are still buried within the walls of the thirteenth-century mausoleum. Inside are wooden cenotaphs marking the graves of the exiled Abbasid Caliphs.

North of the Tombs of the Abbasid Caliphs along Sharia Al Calipha, is the **Shrine of Sayyida Ruqayya** (1160), dedicated to the daughter of 'Ali, husband of the Prophet's daughter Fatima and the fourth great Caliph. The central niche of this popular place of worship is embellished with the name of 'Ali, elaborately recorded seven times in intricate Qur'anic script.

Across the street lies the **Tomb of Shagarat Al Durr,** the latest Ayyubid building in Cairo (1250 C.E.) and the final resting place of one of the few women ever to achieve political power in the history of Islam. Shagarat Al Durr (Arabic for "Tree of Pearls") was a slave who rose to a position of power after marrying Al Salih Ayyub, the final ruling member of Saladin's Ayyubid dynasty. After her husband's death in 1249, she was determined to maintain control of the kingdom and for three months successfully concealed the Sultan's death, ruling in his stead until her son, Turan Shah, returned from Mesopotamia to claim the throne. The wily queen soon realized that her frail son would never be able to command a following among Mameluke slave troops so she promptly engineered his murder. Proclaiming herself Queen-ruler, Shagarat Al Durr governed for eighty days until she married the leader of the Mameluke forces. The renegade couple managed to consolidate power over the next several years, but their happy rule ended when the queen discovered that her new husband was considering a second marriage. Overcome with jealousy, she arranged for the Sultan to be murdered. Not to be outdone, his prospective second wife avenged the death of her lover by beating Shagarat Al Durr to death with a pair of wooden clogs and then hurling her body from the top of the Citadel, where it was left to the jackals and dogs. Inside Shagarat Al Durr's mausoleum is a wooden band around much of the upper chamber wall, carved in heavy Kufic script. Below, the *mihrab* is sparked with a colorful glass mosaic in the Byzantine style.

Near Cairo

Most visitors to Egypt spend a few days in Cairo and then immediately head south for Luxor. If you have any time to spare, linger a while longer. The area around Cairo offers particularly worthwhile excursions: the **pyramids** at **Giza** and at **Sakkara,** the Coptic monasteries of **Wadi el-Natruun** and the sprawling oasis of **Faiyuum.**

The Pyramids at Giza

From a distance they look simple and benign, like the world's largest paperweights. As you approach, they gradually appear more ominous until you are seized by, as Napoleon said, "a sort of stupefaction, almost overwhelming in its effects." Even if you are not as short as Napoleon, the dimensions of the pyramids are sure to impress you. When completed in 2690 B.C.E., the Cheops Pyramid was a touch more imposing than it is now, at 140m, but four and a half millennia have taken their toll.

The most monumental human constructions, the pyramids at Giza testify to two of the ancient Egyptians' greatest obsessions: geometry and the afterlife. Labeled without hesitation by the ancient Greeks as one of the seven wonders of the ancient world, and drawing everyone from Alexander the Great to Napoleon, the pyramids have always been the world's greatest tourist attraction. Since the pyramids are the only surviving wonder of the original seven "wonders," it is hardly surprising that little has changed in this regard. Nowhere else in Egypt is evidence of the country's booming tourist industry so abundant. For a solid mile all around the pyramids souvenir shops, alabaster factories, papyrus museums, etc., all conspire to pawn off fraudulent ancient artifacts. At the foot of the pyramids is a sizeable army of hustlers offering to rent you everything from a student-price camel to an Arabian race horse. Even if you won't be treading virgin soil, you won't want to miss the chance to spend at least a few hours gawking at the pyramids.

Practical Information

To get to the pyramids (*El Haram* in Arabic), take bus #8 or 900 (5 pt) from in front of the Mugamma Building at Tahrir Square (see Cairo Transportation section). Bus #8 will leave you right near the entrance to the pyramids—stay on until the last stop. Bus #900, somewhat more crowded, goes down to Pyramids Road. You must get off at the turn-off for the Mena House Hotel. Don't jump off as soon as you see the pyramids; they look closer than they actually are. The mini-buses in front of the Arab League Building also go to the Pyramids (25 pt). If you are visiting in summer, go early—you'll beat half of the hustlers, most of the crowds, and all of the heat. The site is open 9am-4pm, but the interiors close at 3:30pm. Admission to the site is a steep LE3; no student discounts. The ticket admits you to the main pyramids and the Sphinx complex. It's actually easy to get into the site without paying for a ticket: just walk around and enter on the far side near the Sphinx. The only place tickets are checked is the entrance by the Cheops Pyramid. If you plan on climbing inside the monuments, however, you will need to buy a ticket. A separate ticket must be bought for the Cheops Barque Museum (open 9am-4pm; admission LE5, no student discounts).

Around the north side of Cheops Pyramid is a lot of tourist-oriented hoop-lah; Bedouin pretenders will hound you, telling you of the marvelous horses for rent, others will hawk tourist junk at inflated prices, and self-appointed "guides" will approach you at every turn. If you don't show any particular interest, they'll usually move along to a more promising victim. Renting horses is quite enjoyable; most of the stables have well-trained and exquisitely beautiful Arabian horses. The cost of a horseback riding venture is difficult to specify, as it depends upon when you go and how well you can bargain. To hire horses for a couple of people, including the expense of the guide who rides along, can run anywhere from LE15-30, and for one person LE10-20, depending on the length of the excursion. If you just want to ride the beautiful horses, go in the evening when the crowds are gone and the site is officially closed—it's cheaper and more pleasant. In order to get a good price, just stroll from one stable to the next and let them gradually bargain each other down.

For information on the nightly **Sound and Light Show** see the Cairo Evenings section.

If you're an Egyptology enthusiast, or merely enjoy bedding down amidst sun and sand, stay at **Pyramids Tourist Camp,** 416 Al-Ahram St., Giza (tel. 85 22 02), which has running water and electricity. There is not much else to do in the immediate area, however, and the restaurants around the pyramids are rip-off operations. (The exceptions are about 2 kms away; see Cairo Food section.)

Although it is illegal to climb to the top of any of the pyramids, tourists do so regularly; there is no chance of getting into serious trouble with the authorities. The best time to slip by the guard and make a dash for the top is in the late afternoon when things are beginning to quiet down. Be cautious, for the climb can be dangerous (people have been killed). The safest and fastest route up Cheops is from the northeast corner. At the top, a rather large flat surface provides a spectacular view of the surrounding area. Some *baksheesh* will be in order if you come back down and find the guard waiting for you. Guides offer to show the way up either Cheops or Chephren, but they're expensive and can be a nuisance. The nicest time to climb is on a moonlit night when it is cool and you can take your time.

The minor **Pyramid of Abu Roash,** 7km north of the Giza pyramids, can be reached by foot or by hired animal. Service taxis and minibuses also run to the nearby village of Abu Roash from Giza Square. The pyramid itself is a mound 9m high, only worth a visit to those with an extreme interest in Egyptology.

Sights

Each of the pyramids once adjoined its own funerary complex, complete with mortuary temple and riverside pavilion. In the mortuary temple, the pharaoh continued to be worshipped after his death, for the ruler was supposed to be a god on a par with the familiar animal-headed deities of pharaonic decorative art. A long, narrow causeway linked the mortuary temple with the neighboring waters of the Nile, culminating in the valley temple, through which the complex proper was reached. The mummy of the deceased ruler was conveyed by boat across the Nile, taken up the causeway in solemn procession and finally deposited in its sacred resting place at the heart of the giant pyramid. Unfortunately, most of the smaller structures surrounding the mammoth tomb in Giza proved unable to weather the centuries of quarrying, flooding, and looting. Better-preserved funerary complexes can be seen at neighboring Sakkara.

The first pyramids in Egypt were constructed during the thirtieth century B.C.E. Pyramid-building reached its zenith in the twenty-sixth century B.C.E., but rapidly declined during the following decades, as the pharaohs consolidated their power and became the uncontested rulers of Egypt. The Pyramid of Mycerinus, the smallest of the three main pyramids at Giza, was one of the last of these great tombs to be erected.

The trio of pharaohs interred beneath the three main pyramids are Cheops, Chephren, and Mycerinus—grandfather, father, and son respectively—all of whom reigned during the twenty-sixth century B.C.E. The **Pyramid of Cheops** is the first pyramid you will encounter upon entering the site. The total weight of Cheops is estimated at six million tons. To appreciate the pyramid's mass, crawl through the narrow passageways inside, which lead up to the King's Chamber in the center of the pyramid, probably the most popular place for spelunking in the world (not recommended for the claustrophobic). The highlight of the expedition is the tall and narrow **Gallery,** with nine-meter walls formed out of fourteen massive slabs of granite. **The King's Chamber** is a large square room containing only the cracked bottom half of the sarcophagus. Its most novel feature is the impressive collection of nineteenth-century graffiti adorning its walls. In the summer, the temperature at the center of the pyramid can soar incredibly high, especially when passageways are packed with profusely sweating tourists. Try to time your climb into the pyramid to avoid large groups. The passageway to the Queen's Chamber, which starts at the bottom of the Gallery, is closed off by an iron grille.

Once back outside, walk around to the northern face of the structure to see one of the most celebrated archeological finds of recent decades: an ancient **Solar Boat,** unearthed in 1954 near the base of the great pyramid. Probably the oldest boat in existence, it was buried near the Pharaoh in order to carry him over the ocean of death beneath the earth. It was most likely this vessel which transported Cheops across the Nile from the "land of the living" on the east bank to his final resting place in the "land of the dead." A plywood-and-glass structure which looks like a futuristic ski lodge houses the boat today. Unfortunately, the cost of providing a climate that will prevent Cheops' sacred barge from deteriorating has compelled the local authorities to charge a whopping LE5 admission fee to the museum. On the eastern side of the pyramid are the meager remains of the **Mortuary Temple of Cheops.** Besides a few sockets for columns, only the foundations remain.

The middle member of the trio, the **Pyramid of Chephren,** is only one meter shorter than the Cheops. Portions of the limestone casing that originally covered the monument still sheathe its sloping sides, making it Egypt's most beautiful pyramid. Another sacred boat was unearthed on its south side, but can be seen only with special permission from the Antiquities Service. The interior of Chephren's tomb is the finest of the three at Giza: the burial chamber still contains Chephren's sarcophagus, and the relatively spacious passageways make Chephren the coolest and most comfortable of the three. A long passageway switches back and leads out to the exterior of the pyramid to a lookout point commanding a view of the surrounding area. If you wish to climb Chephren, this spot (if unguarded) provides a good point of departure. However, owing to this practice, the passageway is intermittently closed to the public.

Third in line comes the **Pyramid of Mycerinus,** comparatively small at only 66m. Its burial chamber once contained a magnificent basalt sarcophagus covered with ornate decorative carving. Unfortunately, this rare treasure was lost at sea en route to the British Museum during the early nineteenth century. Outside, at the northeast corner of the temple, lie the quarried remains of the **Mortuary Temple of Mycerinus.** Further away, the ruins of the unexcavated Valley Temple of Mycerinus are submerged beneath a heavy blanket of sand.

The various smaller pyramids around the "big three" were constructed for the Pharaoh's wives and children. Demurely half-buried in the sand throughout the area are fascinating unmarked tombs of ancient Egyptian nobles. Hire one of the impromptu guides to show you the best ones, or just stroll around on your own.

The famed **Sphinx** is located downhill to the northeast of the Pyramid of Cheops. Hewn almost entirely from a solid piece of rock, the poised figure is 80m long and gazes out over the world from a height of 22m. Known as *Abu'l-Hul* ("father of terror" in Arabic), the mysterious feline man wears a serene and detached look. Opinion is divided concerning the Sphinx's identity: some believe the face is a portrait of Chephren, whose pyramid lies to the northeast behind it, while others maintain that the features represent a local deity named Hwran. Its expression and attitude are clearly discernible, though the soft limestone from which it was sculpted has been greatly weathered. Used for target practice during the Turkish occupation, the Sphinx has lost not only its nose (now in the British Museum), but also its beard. At the foot of the Sphinx, just around the corner to the south, is the **Valley Temple of Chephren**, discovered in 1853 by the French archeologist Mariette. Sixteen great pillars support the roof of this edifice, rising to a height of 15m each. Notice the fine grain of the stone, something you may be forced to do since guides invariably show it to you with a candle and expect some *baksheesh* in return.

Directly south, in a tourist complex which originally served as the rest house of King Farouk, is the **Sphinx House Cafe.** They charge LE1 for a very cold and welcome bottle of mineral water. The Sound and Light Show takes place in front of the rest house.

Kardassa

Coming from Cairo, a turn-off to the right at the second canal before the Giza pyramids leads to the village of Kardassa (8km). To get there by public transportation, take the minibus (25pt) from Giza Square or from the turn-off from Pyramids Road. You can also hire a taxi from Giza Square to take you there for LE2.50, and then catch the minibus back. The village of Kardassa is the door to the Western desert—the camel road to Libya begins here. Recently, it has become a popular destination for tourist buses because of the quantity of local crafts. Much of what you see for sale in the tourist shops of Cairo and in the Khan El-Khalili is made in Kardassa. The major products of the village are wool and cotton scarves, *galabayehs,* rugs, and Bedouin weavings. The shops are in a sand-lot across the canal from the village. The artisans' workshops are usually in the back of the shops or in the side alleys off the main tourist drag. Unfortunately, the influx of tourists to Kardassa has heavily inflated the prices in recent years. The villagers can also be very pushy; they've become used to tourists who throw money around carelessly. The village has become a hideout for Muslim brotherhood members, who are evading the government.

Sakkara

Many of Egypt's oldest pharaonic monuments are clustered 32km south of Cairo at Sakkara, burial ground of the pharaohs during the most glorious days of the Old Kingdom (2680-2260 B.C.E.). The ancient royal necropolis, spanning a 7km stretch of the arid Libyan desert, teems with a wealth of fabulous funerary monuments, including the world's oldest grand pyramid, erected by

King Zoser in 2700 B.C.E. Pyramids, subterranean tombs, and mortuary temples are here to be discovered. There is even a serapeum, where dozens of mummified Apis bulls were once interred in a communal grave. Although not quite as polished as their pointed cousins at Giza, (these have a stepped exterior), the pyramids at Sakkara have an equally powerful visage. They are less frequented by tourists and they are situated squarely in the desert with nothing but an endless waste of sand stretching in all directions.

Sakkara (accent on the second syllable) was the burial ground of the pharaohs who ruled at nearby Memphis. Memphis was the capital of Egypt during the Old Kingdom. This was the period of Egypt's great unification, a process begun by Menes, founder of the first of Egypt's thirty dynasties, and completed by Zoser, who ushered in the Third Dynasty.

Practical Information

What is loosely labelled as "Sakkara" is actually a cluster of several different archeological sites scattered over a large area. This cluster consists of five sites: **North Sakkara, South Sakkara, Abu Sir, Dahshur,** and **Memphis.** The primary destination for most tourists is North Sakkara, site of the funerary complex and the great Step-Pyramid of Zoser I. The three pyramids of Abu Sir lie 6km north of North Sakkara, only a few kilometers from the tiny village of Abu Sir. The two pyramids and the funerary complex of South Sakkara are located about 4km south of the site at North Sakkara; Dahshur lies yet another 3km to the south. The ruins of the ancient city of Memphis are farther from the necropolis of Sakkara, located next to the Nile just south of the village of Mit-Rahine. Despite their historical significance, the ruins of Memphis are scanty and will not interest most visitors to the area. The only catch in visiting the other sites is that it takes time to get around. In order to see as much as possible, try to get a very early start. If you are visiting in summer, the afternoon desert sun may immobilize you; be sure to bring water and wear a hat. Illumination inside some of the tombs is poor, so you may wish to bring a flashlight as well.

The place to start your tour of the ruins is North Sakkara. Short of hiring a taxi, however, there is no simple way to get there. The cheapest and most pleasant of the complicated ways is to take a minibus bound for the village of Abu Sir (25pt). The minibus starts running at 6am from Giza Square; catch it at the second canal before the Giza pyramids, where there's a turn-off marked with a sign that says "Sakkara 22 kilometers." About 6km before the entrance to the site of North Sakkara, the bus turns off the paved road. You can get off here and try to hitch a ride to the entrance. Alternatively, you can wait until the last stop, at Abu Sir—from there it is a pleasant 3km walk to the entrance. Walk south (to the left as you arrive) along the canal just before the village. You can't get lost—just keep following the dirt road by the canal until you reach a paved road. The walk takes you through farmland and you may be able to hitch a ride on one of the pick-up trucks for most of the way. Once you reach the paved road turn right and it's only a few hundred meters to the entrance of the site.

If money is not an obstacle and you want to get there without any waiting or walking, you can take an organized tour offered by one of the hotels or tourist companies for LE12-15 per person, but besides being very expensive, these prearranged tours leave out important sites and push you at a blistering pace. The most common way to reach Sakkara from Cairo is to take a local train from Ramsis Station to either Al-Badrshin or Dahshur and then catch a cab from there to Sakkara. Though you must schedule yourself around the trains, this is one way to stretch your Egyptian pounds. You can also catch the commuter train from Bab al-Luq Station, and get off at the main station in Helwan (the end of the line; 10pt), where you can get a cab across the river to al-Badrshin and then on to Memphis and Sakkara. This eliminates scheduling problems, as the Cairo-Helwan metro runs every fifteen minutes, beginning at about 5am. If you're in a large group, you might want to take a taxi; you'll save money if you hunt the cab down by the second canal before the pyramids (or at least at Giza Square).If you want the taxi to wait for you it will probably cost LE 15-20 depending upon how much of the day you spend there. (See Cairo Transportation for information on hiring private taxis and approximate costs.)

Getting back from Sakkara is slightly less difficult than getting there, since you can always hunt down a cab at the site (split one with other tourists) or hitch a ride from visitors at the site.

If you indulge in Lawrence-of-Arabia fantasies, you might want to hire a camel, donkey, or horse (the latter is far more comfortable) for the two-and-a-half hour ride from Giza to Sakkara. The desert ride will take you past **Zawiyyat Al-Aryan Pyramid,** the site of the sun temple of **Abu Gurab** (from the fifth dynasty), and the three ruined pyramids of Abu Sir. To rent a horse or camel, go to the stables between the Mena House Hotel and the pyramids in Giza and begin negotiating; if you take your time and don't seem too anxious to get on the road, you'll probably be able to get a reasonably good deal. A group of several people can get a good "package" price and split the added cost of the guide and his animal. The trip from the Giza pyramids to Sakkara should cost approximately LE10 per person by camel, and LE15 by horse. If you can find someone who is willing to rent you a donkey for the trip it can be as little as LE7 per person but this is a bit slow.

Admission to North Sakkara is LE3, 50pt for students; the ticket admits you to all sights in the area. The site is officially open from 9am-4pm, but you can always view the monuments from the outside. Most of the guards start locking up the doors at the antiquities (especially in summer and definitely during Ramadan) between 3 and 3:30pm. Save the pyramids of Abu Sir (if you wish to go there) for the end of your visit, since there's nothing inside them.

If you wish to visit Dahshur you need special permission from the Ministry of the Interior in Cairo, since it's a restricted military zone. Ignore the camel-rental characters who will tell you how wonderful Dahshur is and offer to rent you their animals. They take uninformed tourists out to Dahshur and feign astonishment upon arrival at the military establishment, kindly telling their clients the Arabic equivalent of "that's the way the cookie crumbles." The paved road to North Sakkara leads up through to the pyramid of Zoser, over to the Serapeum, onto South Sakkara, and then onto Dahshur.

If you are without wheels the only ways to get to South Sakkara, Dahshur, and Abu Sir are on foot and by hired animal. Contrary to what the boys who rent the camels will tell you, it is perfectly possible to walk from North Sakkara to either Abu Sir or South Sakkara. If you are at all athletically inclined either walk should take an hour to an hour and a half. The distance is a little longer than it seems because the desert terrain is very hilly. The experience can be very rewarding: the silent and spectacular desert landscape surrounds you and, as you approach, the pyramids gradually loom larger until they completely dominate your field of vision. Since both sets of pyramids are easily visible from the Serapeum, there is no chance of getting lost. If you hire an animal, bargaining is in order. The proper price per person from the Rest-House next to the Serapeum to Abu Sir and back is LE2-3 by donkey, LE5 by camel, and LE6-7 by horse. Prices to South Sakkara and back are approximately the same or possibly slightly less than to Abu Sir. Prices all the way to Dahshur including South Sakkara should be almost double. Chances are you will have the stamina to walk to only one place, so rent an animal to South Sakkara and make your desert hike to the pyramids of Abu Sir, since from there it is only a 2km hike to the village of Abu Sir where you can get a minibus (25pt) back to Giza.

To reach Abu Sir from the pyramids, just walk to the clearly visible green belt of fields. From there bear right along the canal to the canal village. The best way to pick up the road to the canal is to zero in on the dense grove of palm trees visible from the pyramids. The guards at the pyramids will point out the way. If you came through the village of Abu Sir on your way to North Sakkara, you walked south from the village to reach the entrance of North Sakkara; once you've made your way to the Pyramids of Abu Sir, however, you are *north* of the *village* of Abu Sir and have to walk south along the canal in order to return to it; at which point you will have come full circle. If you are finished touring South or North Sakkara and simply want to reach the village of Abu Sir, where you catch the minibus back to Giza, walk back to the entrance and along the paved road until you come to a bridge, cross the bridge, turn left and follow the dirt road along the canal (3km).

Sights

The dominant edifice of Sakkara is the mountainous **Step-Pyramid** built by Imhotep, chief architect to the Pharaoh Zoser, in about 2650 B.C.E. This was the first of Egypt's pyramids and the first stone structure in the world built on a grand scale. By breaking with the traditional pattern of constructing a small wooden tomb for the pharaoh, Imhotep paved the way for all of Egypt's subsequent architectural achievements, including the Giza pyramids, which followed less than a century later. Like most pharaonic structures, the Step-Pyramid was built as part of a funerary complex. Most experts believe the tomb began as a *mastaba* (literally "bench," the simple flat brick mortuary structure of the Old Kingdom) and was added to five separate times, until the present six-level building was completed.

The entrance to the Step-Pyramid complex is on the eastern side of the limestone **enclosure wall,** a bastioned, panelled barrier designed to reproduce the appearance of mud-brickwork, emulating the sort of fortifications typically used to surround cities and palaces of the period. Plunging into the complex itself, you will find yourself in a lengthy, forty-pillared **colonnade,** filled with flies but very impressive, though the walls and roof have been restored. The uniquely Egyptian pillars of the colonnade, known as "bundle columns," are ridged to create the stylized effect of a bundle of palm stems. This imposing corridor culminates in the Hypostyle Hall, a fledgling version of the great hallways found at Karnak and Abydos. Its roof is supported by four stately bundle columns slightly smaller than their counterparts in the adjoining colonnade. On the far side of this chamber is a stone simulation of a half-open doorway, carved so as to imitate the appearance of wood. Beyond this eccentric exit lies the **Great South Court,** a magnificent open yard flanking the southern side of Zoser's stepped tomb. A piece of cobra frieze which once adorned the upper portion of the enclosure wall has been restored in the court's corner. Beside the court, on the southern side, a large trench plunges 28m into the soft desert floor. This huge rectangular pit once contained an extensive collection of sacred funerary jars.

If you climb over the enclosure wall into the southern portion of the site, you'll see to the west the massive **Pyramid of Unas.** Unas was the last pharaoh of the Fifth Dynasty. You can spelunk around within the interior burial chamber of the ruined monument. If the door to the pyramid is closed when you arrive, you won't have to wait long before a guard comes to unlock it in the hope of receiving some *baksheesh.* Although the passage into the tomb is uncomfortably low at points, the central burial chamber is airy and light; its walls consist of huge slabs of white alabaster embellished with hieroglyphic inscriptions. These ancient carvings, known as the **Pyramid Texts,** were discovered in 1881, and constitute the earliest known example of decorative hieroglyphic writing on the walls of a pharaonic tomb chamber. Carefully etched into the shiny alabaster, the well-preserved texts record hymns, prayers, and articles necessary for the afterlife; on the western edge of the main chamber sits the basalt sarcophogus of Unas, its lid on the ground beside it. Above, the ceiling glows with a multitude of five-point stars, which still retain traces of their original bright blue coloring.

Outside and to the south, a tiny wooden hut stands isolated at the edge of the funerary complex. This unlikely looking shanty leads to three of Egypt's deepest subterranean burial chambers, the so-called **Persian Tombs,** constructed for three Persian aristocrats named Psamtik, Zenhebu, and Peleese. A dizzying spiral staircase drills its way 25m into the ground, terminating in the burial area, which consists of three vaulted chambers linked by narrow passageways. Inside, decorative carving covers the walls of the elegant tombs, enlivened with traces of brightly-colored paint. According to the ancient inscriptions, Zenhebu was a famous admiral and Psamtik a chief physician of the pharaoh's court. Unless you have brought your own source of light, a guard will have to show you around with a lantern.

To the west of the Pyramid of Unas, a 100m path leads out through the desert to the unfinished **Pyramid of Sekhemkhet,** a meager pile of rubble unearthed in 1951. This pyramid was originally intended as an imitation of its giant neighbor, the Pyramid of Zoser. Construction was abandoned after its walls had reached a height of only 3m. Underground passageways, one containing an unused alabaster sarcophagus, are buried beneath the rubble foundations but are closed to the public because of the tenuous structural condition of the roofing and corridor walls. To the east of the Pyramid of Unas, running down the hill, is a long, narrow **causeway,** smoothly paved and walled-in. Nearly 1 km long, the causeway originally linked the Pyramid of Unas with a lower valley temple at the banks of the river. Strewn by the sides of the causeway are the **Old Kingdom Tombs** of Sakkara. Over 250 *mastabas* have been excavated here, though only a few of the larger and best-preserved tombs are open to the public. Although the low, rectangular *mastabas* are dwarfed by the towering pyramids, the best ones are well worth visiting as they contain fascinating and delicate bas-reliefs. The lovely **Tomb of Idut,** adjacent to the southern enclosure wall of Zoser's funerary complex and just east of the Pyramid of Unas, comprises ten chambers, of which three are especially beautiful. An entrance chamber leads into a roomy apartment decorated with scenes of Idut watching a hippopotamus hunt. Next door, in the chapel, the eastern wall is embellished with a beautiful depiction of oxen, gazelles, and ibex, as well as the sacrificial slaughter of cattle. Nearby, the **Mastaba of Mehu** and the **Mastaba of Queen Nebet** both have delightful interiors painted with highly naturalistic scenes of birds, cattle, and other sacrificial animals. South of the causeway is a fabulous pair of enormous **Boat Pits,** side by side next to the causeway just 100m east of the Pyramid of Unas. Speculation exists as to whether these pits were intended merely to house the royal barques, as at Giza, or whether these finely-sculpted trenches of stone were meant as visible representations of boats. In either case these 44m banana-shaped pits are symbolic of the pharaoh's journey to the afterlife. Directly across from the causeway is the **Tomb of Nebkau-her,** a large, well-preserved structure with a beautiful interior, closed to the public as of 1983. If you round a slight bend in the causeway and continue east, you'll reach the **Mastaba of Nefer-her-ptah,** situated directly south of the causeway. Known as the "tomb of the birds," the *mastaba* contains remarkable half-completed scenes of birds, the sculptor having abandoned the project to a skillful painter half-way through. This tomb was also closed as of the summer of 1983.

Reaching the end of the substantial remains of the causeway, go uphill southward to the **Monastery of St. Jeremias,** located less than 150m away. Built in the fifth century C.E., this structure has been devastated several times, first in 960 when invading Arabs ransacked the entire edifice. More recently, the Antiquities Service removed all of its decorative carvings and paintings to the Coptic Museum in Cairo. Completing this process of effacement, the desert has begun to cover the scanty remains of the Monastery with a thick layer of sand. Little of the original structure remains visible. Head back up to the causeway and round the corner to return to the **Great South Court** of Zoser's mortuary complex. In the northern end of the Court, at the base of the great Step-Pyramid, are the remains of the *mastaba* that was the seed of Zoser's tomb. In the middle of the pyramid's south face is an entrance to the tomb's interior. This long passageway, known as the **Saite Gallery,** offers stunning views of the interior frame of the pyramid, but special permission from the Antiquities Services is required to gain entrance. To the east, the **Heb-Sed Court** runs the length of one side of the courtyard.

The more substantial **House of the South** is situated just next door, on the eastern side of Zoser's Pyramid. Its facade is enhanced by the presence of stately, proto-Doric columns. Inside, the walls are inscribed with the world's oldest known tourist graffiti, left by a visiting Egyptian in the twelfth century B.C.E. The messages, expressing admiration for King Zoser, are hastily splashed onto the walls with dark paint, scrawled in a late cursive style of hieroglyphics. Heading northward, you'll come to the **House of the North,** its facade similarly decorated with a row of three engaged papyriform columns. Nearby, located directly in front of the Step-Pyramid, is Sakkara's most haunting spectacle: the **Statue of King Zoser,** encased in a wooden coffin tilted slightly back to enable visitors to peer through two tiny apertures at the fixed stare of the Pharaoh. This small structure is known as the **Serdab,** and was originally constructed so as to enable the spirit of the pharaoh to communicate with the outside world. The striking figure is only a plaster copy of the original, which has been removed to the Antiquities Museum in Cairo. Just behind the Serdab is the original entrance to the Step-Pyramid (closed to the public as of 1983).

To the west, toward the edge of the Step-Pyramid complex, a raised patch of desert commands a clear view of the western edge of North Sakkara. If you have wheels, you may wish to go back to the entrance of Zoser's mortuary complex and drive around to the western portion of the site. Or you can hike a short distance across the desert in order to reach the **Tomb of Akhti-Hotep and Ptah-Hotep,** situated due south of the main road between the Step-Pyramid and the Rest House. This remarkable double tomb housed the bodies of two inspectors of the priests who served the pyramids. Father and son, respectively, Akhti-Hotep and Ptah-Hotep designed a mortuary complex for themselves, consisting of two burial chambers, a chapel, and a pillared hallway. The reliefs contained within the burial chamber are of superior quality, rivalling even the carvings housed in the celebrated neighboring Temple of Ti. The structure is entered through a long corridor, culminating in the burial chamber of Akhti-Hotep. Just around the corner is the undecorated pillared hall, leading on to a rather dim chapel covered with delightful scenes depicting Akhti-Hotep in various poses in the marshes: constructing boats, fighting off enemies, and fording a river. To the south of the pillared hallway is the tomb of Ptah-Hotep, containing the complex's finest reliefs. Animals cavort across the splendid walls as hunters attempt to catch up with them, fowlers cast their nets and people fishing enjoy a healthy meal.

Due west of the Tomb of Akhti-Hotep and Ptah-Hotep is a shady **Rest House,** where cold drinks can be purchased for 30pt. Hot tea costs an outlandish 40pt per glass. Farther along the highway, where the road jogs sharply to the west, a semicircular area has been cleared away to reveal some badly-weathered **Greek Statues,** said to represent a group of Hellenic thinkers: Homer in the center, Pindar at the west end, and Plato at the eastern end.

The **Serapeum,** located a few hundred meters west of the Rest House at the terminus of the main road, was discovered by the French archeologist Mariette in 1854. An eerie underground subway system, dimly lit with tiny lanterns, this surrealistic subterranean mausoleum houses the **Tombs of the Apis Bulls,** where 25 sacred oxen were embalmed and placed in enormous sarcophagi made of solid granite. Only one of the bulls was discovered *in situ* (the rest had been stolen); it is now located in the Agricultural Museum in Cairo. Mariette also discovered a meter-high golden statue of a bull which he sent to the Louvre in Paris. The Serapeum is the sole legacy of a mysterious bull-worshipping cult which apparently thrived during the New Kingdom, though little is known about its history or beliefs. Work on the main portion of the underground complex was begun during the seventh century B.C.E. by Psammetichus I and continued through the Ptolemaic era, though much older tombs adjoin this central set of chambers. In the oldest portion of the Serapeum, Mariette discovered two large gold-plated sarcophagi and several canopic jars containing human heads, as well as the undisturbed footprints of the priests who had laid the sacred animals to rest 3,000 years before; this portion of the tomb is no longer accessible. Nonetheless, the Serapeum remains Sakkara's most visually stunning monument. Cavernous recessed tomb chambers flank the main corridor on both sides, each containing a monolithic sarcophagus. It is difficult to imagine these mammoth coffins being transported to the confines of the cave, for their average weight is 65 tons. Even more puzzling to a twentieth-century observer are the preparations invested in the mummification and interment of the 25 bulls. When you arrive at the final tomb along the passageway, you'll come upon the largest sarcophagus of all. Hewn from a single piece of black granite, the great coffin is covered with hieroglyphic inscriptions. Clamber down into the chamber to get a close-up view. At the far end of the Serapeum an equally enormous pink granite sarcophagus is meticulously decorated with a number of fine reliefs.

The **Tomb of Ti,** 300m north of the Serapeum, was excavated by Mariette in 1865, and since then has been one of the primary sources of knowledge about both everyday and ceremonial life in ancient Egypt. It tells of life during the Fifth Dynasty (towards the end of the Old Kingdom, approximately 2400 B.C.E.), when Ti was a high-ranking court official. The Henry Kissinger of his day, serving under three pharaohs, Ti must have been quite a power-broker: his titles included Overseer of the Pyramids and Sun Temples at Abu Sir, Superintendent of Works, Scribe of the Court, Royal Counselor and even Lord of Secrets. His rank was considered so lofty that he was allowed to marry a princess, Nefer Hotep-S, and his children were ranked as royalty. In the representations in the tomb, the children wear the braided hairpiece, the sign of a contender for the throne. Note also how the children depicted on the bas-reliefs almost invariably have fingers in their mouths. This kind of stylization is used in the Tomb of Ti to great effect; the bas-reliefs here stand out as the artistic masterpieces of Egypt's Old Kingdom.

The ancient Egyptians believed that death was an extension of life, and that a dead person's soul (the *ka*) needed food and utensils just as it did when the body was alive. A large part of a dead person's estate, therefore, was used to insure that a given portion of land and livestock, plus a sufficient number of priests, would continue to supply the *ka* with food. It was not all that simple, however: first of all, because mummification had not yet been perfected during the Old Kingdom, the body could decompose, leaving the *ka* with nowhere to reside. Therefore statues of the deceased were placed in the funerary chambers with the hope that in the event the body should decay, the statue could take its place. Poorly-performed sacrifices on behalf of the *ka* were another potential problem; the Egyptians insured against lax performance of ceremonial duties by depicting sacrifices on the walls of the *mastaba*.

In keeping with the belief that the dead person has needs analogous to those of the living, there arose the practice of depicting scenes from the deceased's daily life on the walls of the funerary chamber. Experts are unsure whether the purpose was to comfort and entertain the deceased or to procure blessing on the practices requested. The walls of tombs such as the Tomb of Ti depict scenes of the hunt, battle, barter, athletic contests, and domestic life. No overtly funerary scenes are included; the Egyptians viewed the continued existence of the *ka* in the afterworld as more important than its passage from this world to the next. Altogether, the scenes from everyday life provide us with the most important store of information about life in ancient Egypt. From the eastern wall of the Tomb of Ti, for example, we learn about a typical harvest, as well as about shipbuilding; from the southern wall we learn about the various types of food consumed by wealthy Egyptians, as well as about the fairly harsh system of tax collections; in the northern wall we see how linen was woven and fish were caught. All around are charming scenes from upper-class family life featuring Ti, his wife, and his children. Many visitors are impressed by the delightful representations of birds of all sorts both at rest and in motion. During the Old Kingdom, the depiction of animals, and birds most especially, progressed to a far greater degree of elegance and realism than the depiction of human beings.

Although it is now entirely buried in sand, an **Avenue of Sphinxes** once ran the full width of the site, commencing near the Tomb of Ti and paving a straight course due east past the Step-Pyramid complex to culminate at the river's edge near the **Pyramid of Titi.** This somewhat weather-beaten pyramid can be reached today by following the east-west highway past the Rest House to the fork and heading a short distance north. The interior of Titi's tomb boasts some interesting sacred inscriptions, but is usually closed to the public. You should be sure to explore some of the thirty rooms comprising the magnificent **Tomb of Mereruka,** situated just next door to the Pyramid of Titi. As you enter, notice the hippopotamuses depicted on the opposite wall near the door. In some instances, the hippopotamus was worshipped as a benevolent goddess known as Thoeris, the ponderous patron of women in childbirth. Here, the hippos are not depicted as deities, but shown for what they are—the Nile's hefty river horses, complete with gaping jaws and curly tusks. The unstylized, naturalistic portrayal of wildlife found inside the Tomb of Mereruka has enabled scientists to reconstruct Egyptian fauna from the time of the pharaohs. Even the various species of fish can be differentiated thanks to the minutely detailed work of the ancient artists.

A bit further east is the neighboring **Tomb of Ankhma-Hor.** Inside this tomb, you'll see fascinating representations of surgical operations from the Sixth

Dynasty (about 2200 B.C.E.) like a Gray's *Anatomy* in stone. Among the operations shown are a circumcision and surgery on a man's toe. To the left after you enter are scenes of mourning, not very well preserved. One noted Egyptologist has asserted that the Sixth Dynasty tendency to include funerary scenes indicates a growing pessimism among Egyptians about the afterlife as the Old Kingdom went into its final decline.

South Sakkara

The most interesting funerary monument at South Sakkara is the **Mastabat Faraun** ("Pharaoh's Seat"), an enormous stone structure shaped like a sarcophagus and topped with a rounded lid. The great mausoleum was erected for Shepseskaf, the son of Mycerinus (whose pyramid sits at Giza). Apparently Shepseskaf reigned for only three or four years, but his brief stint on the throne was still long enough to qualify him for a magnificent tomb. Originally covering 7,000 square meters, the Mastabat Faraun is a unique pharaonic edifice, being neither a *mastaba* nor a pyramid. The interior of the tomb consists of a number of long passageways and a burial chamber containing fragments of a huge sandstone sarcophagus. Find a guard to let you in.

Just north of the Mastabat Faraun are the ruins of the **Mortuary Temple of Pepi II.** A central colonnade gives way to a tiny chamber housing five empty statue niches; beyond, the remains of the Sanctuary are still visible. This edifice originally adjoined the pyramid on the west end and was linked to the east with a large valley temple, of which little remains today. The **Pyramid of Pepi II** was the culmination of a long processional causeway which joined the valley and mortuary temples. Its interior contains some very fine hieroglyphic texts. Two other royal entombments, the **Pyramid of Queen Apuit** and the **Pyramid of Queen Neith,** are both situated immediately northwest of the Pyramid of Pepi II; both imitate in smaller scale the plans of the pharaohs' grand funeral complexes.

The **Pyramid of Djekare-Ises,** called by the locals *Haran esh-Shawaf* ("the Pyramid of the Sentinel"), lies north of Pepi II's Valley Temple. It rises to a height of 25m, and can be entered from the north side via a tunnel.

Dahshur

South of Sakkara on the new road from Giza, west of the village of Dahshur, are four more pyramids. The most important is the so-called **Bent Pyramid,** constructed by Snofru, the father of Cheops. Most of the Bent Pyramid's casing is still in place, and its shape is unique: halfway up the sloping sides of the 100m structure, the angle of ascent abruptly becomes less steep. Egyptologists offer competing theories to account for the pyramid's idiosyncratic shape. Some maintain that Snofru became convinced, in the course of the pyramid's construction, that the angle of inclination was so dangerously steep as to make the structure unsound. Others suggest that Snofru ran out of manpower halfway through, and abruptly scaled down the scope of his project, reducing the angle to save on labor and stone. Two kilometers to the north is the handsome **Red Pyramid,** also constructed by Snofru.

Two lesser pyramids also stand at Dahshur. The 30m **Pyramid of Amenemhat III,** 1km east of the Bent Pyramid, is perhaps best treated as a lookout from which to view the surrounding countryside. The truly fanatical pyramid-lover can brave the desert to reach the **Pyramid of Sesostris III,** 1½km northeast of the Red Pyramid. Once much larger, the tomb now stands only 27m high.

The Pyramids of Abu Sir

The Pyramids of Abu Sir are romantically isolated in the Eastern Desert just north of Sakkara. You can enjoy them in solitude without hordes of camera-clicking companions, since no tour buses can make it here. Accessible only on foot or on animal, the pyramids (6km from North Sakkara and 2.5km from the village of Abu Sir) are surrounded by an ocean of sand dunes. (For information on how to get there, see Practical Information above.)

The most imposing of the trio of pyramids, clearly visible from North Sakkara, is the **Pyramid of Neferirkare,** 45m high and one of the best-preserved monuments in the Sakkara area. Although the structure originally had an outer stone facing like its northern neighbors at Giza, the casing has completely deteriorated and the exterior now resembles a step-pyramid. The **Pyramid of Niuserre** is the most dilapidated of the group, but it possesses an interesting causeway running to the remains of a funerary temple to the southeast. It is possible to enter the **Pyramid of Sahure,** the northernmost member of the group, on its north face. One of the custodians at the site will show you the entrance, which is about a half meter high and 2m long and requires a challenging belly-crawl along the sand floor. Inside is a small chamber that served as the pharaoh's tomb. More pyramids are visible from here than from any other site in the country, including those at Giza, North Sakkara, and South Sakkara. You should be able to distinguish at least ten pyramids on the horizon.

There is no admission charge to the site, but the custodians are desperate for business and one of them will show you about with great enthusiasm. Some *baksheesh* is in order. In addition, the guards will offer you some water from an adjoining spring. If you intend to walk on to the village of Abu Sir, have the guards point out the way. Finding your way to North Sakkara is easy, thanks to the immense form of King Zoser's Pyramid. If you are traveling by animal en route between Abu Sir and Giza, have your guide stop off on the way at the **Sun Temple of Abu Gurab.** Located on the fringe of an area of cultivated fields, the temple was built by King Nuiserre in honor of the sun god Rē and features an impressive altar constructed from five huge blocks of alabaster.

Memphis

The funerary monuments of Sakkara were built for the rulers by the citizens of Memphis, the capital of the Old Kingdom. Although the city was eventually replaced as the political center of Egypt by Luxor during the Middle and New Kingdoms, it did not fall into decline throughout the pharaonic age, remaining a thriving metropolis all the way through the Ptolemaic period. Little remains of the city today, however. 500m south of the modern village of **Mit-Rahine,** near the road from the Nile to Sakkara, are the only substantial ruins, the outlines of a temple dedicated to Ptah. In particular, there are two huge statues, an eighty-ton alabaster statue of a sphinx and a towering figure of Ramses II, standing over 3m high. The latter was unearthed in 1912; nearby (in 1888) a somewhat smaller twin had been found that now stands at Ramsis Square in Cairo. (For information on how to reach Memphis, see the Practical Information section above.)

Greater Cairo

Except for the pyramids at Giza and Sakkara, the Greater Cairo metropolitan area does not have any outstanding monuments. However, it features a handful of minor attractions that may interest even the casual tourist. The suburb of **Helwan** is Egypt's most industrialized and polluted factory town, but it does possess a pair of eccentric sights. To reach Helwan take the commuter train (10pt) from Bab al-Luq Station (see Cairo Transportation). Only a few blocks from the Helwan station (to your right as you walk out), are the only **Japanese Gardens** in the Middle East. Although they are in a sad state of disrepair, it is evident that the gardens once must have been magnificent. Meandering paths take you by two ponds, several pagodas, numerous little statues of Buddha, and a small cafe where you can enjoy a drink. Only a few blocks farther away lies the **Wax Museum** (open 9am-5pm—admission free but a 20pt tip for the guide is in order) with its series of tableaus dramatizing important moments in Egyptian history from the reign of Ramses II to the presidency of Nassar. If you're feeling lazy you can hop a horsedrawn carriage from the station (25pt) to either the museum or the gardens.

The commuter train that runs to Helwan takes you through the upper-class residential area of **Ma'adi.** Most of the Americans in Egypt live in this stable community. The ACIC (American College in Cairo) Primary and Secondary School here educates the children of many of Cairo's wealthy Egyptian families as well as American children. On the Fourth of July, in a budget traveler's dream come true, the school holds a carnival at which American citizens are entitled to all the hot dogs, soft drinks, and pot luck food they can put away, free of charge. Just bring your American accent and an empty stomach. The surrounding part of Ma'adi is worth strolling through, with posh villas set amidst flowers and trees, but it's the furthest thing from a typical Egyptian neighborhood.

The Delta

The most scenic spot in the immediate vicinity of Cairo lies 15km north at the **Nile Barrages.** Delightfully designed with brightly-colored turrets and arches, the barrages were constructed during Muhammad Ali's reign in the first quarter of the nineteenth century. The banks of the Nile are full of outdoor cafes and casinos set in plush gardens where Cairenes and inhabitants of the larger towns in the Delta take refuge from the smog and noise of the city. Next to the barrages, where the Nile reaches one of its widest points, little bridges connect islets in the river. It is possible to rent *feluccas* and enjoy the scene from the Nile. Immediately past the barrages, the river splits in half into the Rosetta and Damietta branches, flowing into the Mediterranean at the two ports of Rosetta and Damietta. Qanater, at the fork, marks the official beginning of the Delta. Buses run to Qanater from in front of the Nile Hilton at Tahrir Square. A small passenger ferry also runs along the Nile between Cairo and Qanater (25pt, two hours)—catch it on the west bank of the Corniche north of the Ramses Hilton in front of the Television Building. It is also possible to hire a *felucca* but the journey to Qanater from Cairo is very time-consuming, since the mast of the boat must be lowered for the bridges.

Further to the north begin the rolling agricultural lands of the **Nile Delta,** reputed to be the most fertile region in the world. The larger towns tend to be unattractive and uninteresting for the casual tourist. However, the countryside features breathtaking green landscapes and pleasant farming villages. The best way to enjoy the region is to rent a car and drive along the canals and roads winding through the landscape. As a tourist you are not supposed to leave the main roads, but you probably won't be stopped if you do a little roaming. If you travel by train or service taxi you will catch some regional flavor but it won't be as scenic since both forms of transportation serve only the major cities. (For information on service taxis to the Delta see Cairo Transportation; for information on trains see the Egypt Introduction.)

The Old Kingdom was born and blossomed primarily in lower Egypt, and throughout the pharaonic period many fine monuments were erected in the Delta. However, today there is not much to see: due to the looseness and richness of the soil, the deployment of irrigation canals, and the natural fanning out of the river, almost all of the major pharaonic sites in the Delta have been obliterated. Just outside of **Zagazig,** one hour and twenty minutes from Cairo via any train bound for Port Said, or one hour by service taxi, lie the ruins of **Babustis,** one of Egypt's most ancient cities and the most accessible of the Delta's pharaonic sites. The name means "house of Bastet," referring to the handsome feline cat-goddess to whom the main temple was dedicated. Herodotus described the temple as the most pleasurable to gaze upon in all of Egypt. The same cannot be said today, as comparatively little remains of the sanctuary other than a scattered pile of inscribed blocks. Nearby (200m down the road) you can explore the winding underground passages of the **Cat Cemetery,** where numerous celebrated bronze likenesses of Bastet were uncovered. The region's most worthwhile pharaonic site is located far (four and a half hours by service taxi) from Cairo in the northeastern corner of the Delta's fertile triangle. Just outside of the village of **Sam El Hagar,** the ruins of ancient **Tanis** are scattered over an area of about four square kilometers, comprising a royal necropolis, the foundations of several temples, and a pair of sacred lakes.

Wadi el-Natruun

Like four arks floating in an endless sea of sand, the Coptic monasteries of Wadi el-Natruun have withstood the sieges of unbelievers and the ravages of time. The name Wadi el-Natruun is derived from the Arabic word for sodium carbonate *(natruun),* a mineral which the ancient Egyptians used in their mummy-making embalming process. Today, however, the valley is a center for Coptic monastic culture, not ancient Egyptian history. The four monasteries of Dayr Al-Suriani, Dayr Amba Bishoi, Dayr Baramus, and Dayr Makarius continue to serve the needs of pious Copts in search of blessings as well as adventurous tourists in search of interesting places off the beaten track. Although there are a few new buildings, the life of the resident monks has changed little since the monasteries were completed in the fourth century. Decked out in black hoods and robes, the bearded monks keep alive the traditions of the early Egyptian church. For them, fasting, solitude, and chanting a six-hour liturgy remain the essentials of a daily routine. If the buzzing crowds of downtown Cairo made you think that all of Egypt is a three-ring circus, come to Wadi el-Natruun to see the other side. The quiet, austere surroundings restore tranquility to even the most shattered nerves.

One warning: in a little-known battle, the late President Anwar el-Sadat exiled Pope Shenouda III, the 117th apostolic successor to Saint Mark, the bishop of Alexandria. He sent the patriarch to the monasteries of Al-Suriani and Amba Bishoi, and appointed a council of bishops to run the Church. Government troops guard the monasteries, and access is only possible with government permission. This situation will almost certainly last until the death of Shenouda III. Check with the Tourist Office in Cairo or Alexandria before heading out to Wadi el-Natruun.

Practical Information

To get to Wadi el-Natruun from Cairo, you must reserve a seat at least two days in advance on a bus going to Alexandria by the desert road. Don't take a train or service taxi since they travel by way of the Delta. About 102km southwest of Alexandria is the Rest House, which is where you will have to get out to go to Wadi el-Natruun. When you buy your ticket in Cairo, be sure to tell the ticket seller that you are only going as far as Wadi el-Natruun. Otherwise, you'll end up paying the full fare. Not all the Cairo-Alexandria buses stop here, so you might have to inform the driver yourself where you want to go. Once you're safely off the bus, at the Rest House, start looking around for a ride to the monasteries. Three of them, Al-Suriani, Amba Bishoi, and Baramus, are just 10km west of the Rest House; you can hire a taxi to take you out and back for LE5. The road leads out into the Wadi and branches to the right following the signs for Baramus. If you finish touring the Baramus and wish to see Makarius as well, you must catch a ride or taxi down the road towards Cairo, and turn off into the desert at the signpost, traveling another 5km from there. When you finish touring the Wadi, you can return to Cairo or Alexandria by bus from the Rest House, but you must remember to book the return trip in advance. If this is impossible, you may not want to risk making the trip.

It is best to start early and do as much of Wadi el-Natruun as you can (or care to) as a day trip, spending the night in either Cairo or Alexandria. If you wish to stay longer, you can stay over at the Rest House, which has singles for LE7, LE8.40 with bath, and doubles for LE8.40, LE12.60 with bath. The Rest House also has a restaurant with meals running about LE2. There are no other accommodations in Wadi el-Natruun. If you happen to have a special interest in monasticism or Coptic culture, men—but never women—are permitted to stay overnight within the monasteries (particularly at Dayr Baramus). If you want to stay overnight, it is imperative that you first get written permission from the office of the Patriarchate, either in Alexandria (at the Coptic Orthodox Patriarchate, Nebi Daniel St.—ask for His Grace Bishop Temothawis), or else in Cairo (at the Coptic Orthodox Patriarchate, Ramsis St., Anba Reuis Building—adjacent to St. Mark's Church—in Abusseiya). Remember, a monastery is not a hotel, and a certain sense of propriety and respect is required. If you are lucky enough to gain access, don't abuse the hospitality.

Sights

The Copts are the direct descendants of the original pharaonic Egyptians. The word "Copt" originally meant "Egyptian," but over time came to designate Christian Egyptians specifically. Six centuries before the coming of Islam, the apostle Saint Mark founded the church of Alexandria. The message of Christ spread throughout Egypt and the Coptic Orthodox Church was born. (The Coptic Orthodox Church is often, and mistakenly, called the Coptic Church.) The Church split from the rest of Christianity at the council of Chalcedon in 451, over the issue of whether Christ has two natures, one human and one divine, or one nature both human and divine. The Coptic Orthodox Church subscribes to the latter theory, while the rest of Christianity accepts the former. 1500 years later, the controversy still exists.

It was the Orthodox Copts who first developed the tradition of monasticism in Christianity. Believing that one could be closest to God by severing all ties with the world of earthly desires, the early monk, "seeking a life of prayer, fasting, and meditation, went alone into the desert, found some natural cave or dug one for his purpose and lived therein for the rest of his life; unknown, unsought, and completely by himself" (see I. H. Elmasri's *Introduction to the Coptic Church,* available at the Patriarchate in Cairo). Today four monks in Wadi el-Natruun still practice this most ancient and extreme form of monasticism. The first Christian monastery was established in the so-called Arabian, or Eastern, Desert of Egypt by St. Anthony the Great (250-355 C.E.). In 330 one of St. Anthony's disciples, St. Makarius, began monastic life in Wadi el-Natruun. His example inspired the establishment of over fifty monasteries in the Natruun valley, of which only the four still exist. The ascetic life has enjoyed varying degrees of popularity over the ages: the heyday of Coptic monasticism came in the fourth century. There were some seven thousand monks in Wadi el-Natruun alone. But when Pierre Sicard visited the area in 1712, he found only "three or four monks" living in the crumbling ruins. In the 1980s, strangely enough, Coptic monasticism is again on the upswing. Today the monasteries must continually build new cells in order to accommodate the over 340 monks living in the Natruun valley. The vast majority of these monks practice the cenobitic, or communal, monasticism. Although each monk has his own cell, or *laura,* and retreats to parts of the monastery for periods of complete seclusion, most eat their meals together at the refectory and attend daily communal prayer services. To be sure, there are still plenty of aged, desert Fathers wandering through the corridors, but nowadays most of the monks are young, college-educated, English-speaking Egyptians.

The monks begin their day in church at 3am. Amidst billows of incense, wide-eyed icons, and flickering candlelight, they chant the haunting Coptic liturgy for the next six hours. The service, at specified times, is punctuated by the rhythmic tingle of triangle and cymbal music. The atmosphere and ceremony are interesting, if a bit eerie, and definitely have an Oriental flavor. If you are intrigued by ritual, symbolism, and Church history, you may want to catch a glimpse of this early Christian ceremony. Come before 9am to attend the service. Non-Christians must sit in the non-believers section at the back; Christians may sit in front.

The monks are cloaked from head to foot in black. This signifies, as they will tell you, that they are dead—at least symbolically. When a new monk is initiated, he "dies" to his former self and the world of corporeal desires. The Copts also wear a black hood with twelve crosses embroidered on it, each cross representing one of Christ's twelve disciples. The hood is said to symbolize the "helmet of salvation" (see Ephesians 6).

Although each monastery is slightly different, all four conform to a general architectural plan. Each is surrounded by a massive wall some forty feet high and from nine to twelve feet thick, which once protected the inhabitants from frequent attacks. Inside the walls is the **keep**—a huge, block-like structure built in Roman style where the monks took refuge during sieges. Entered by a narrow wooden drawbridge which isolated it from the rest of the monastery, the keep consisted of storerooms, air-vents, wells, bakery, kitchen, and chapel. In the middle of the monastery is the church, frequently constructed in the shape of an ark, symbolizing Noah's Ark and its salvation of the faithful from a world flooded with sin. You enter the church and its various chapels through low doors—so low, in fact, that you must stoop to get inside, a sign of humility. Be sure to remove your shoes before going inside. Inside, Coptic Churches are divided into three chambers—another practice retained since the days of the early Christians. The **sanctuary,** or *haikal,* containing the altar lies behind a curtain or wooden screen inlaid with ivory. This always faces east. You are not permitted to enter the sanctuary, but ask the monk who shows you around if you can just peep inside. The next chamber, known as the **choir,** is the section reserved for Believers, i.e. Coptic Christians. Behind it is the **nave,** consisting of two parts, the first reserved for the *catechumens,* those who are learning church doctrine in preparation for conversion. The last chamber in the church is for the so-called Weepers, or Sinners. These Christians, having willfully transgressed, were formerly made to stand at the very back of the church.

All the churches have very interesting and historically important icons and beautifully carved iconostases. Three of the churches have frescoes reputed to date from the fourth and fifth centuries—many of them are so dark from centuries of accumulated candle smoke and soot, however, that you can barely make out the shapes and colors. At Dayr Al-Suriani, so called because of the many Syrian monks who at one time inhabited the monastery, be sure to ask to see the Door of Prophecies in the middle sanctuary of the **Church of the Virgin Mary.** The doors consist of eight ebony leaves, each inlaid with eight ivory panels. The uppermost panels depict disciples while the panels below depict the seven epochs of the Christian era. The domes of the church are covered with frescoes of the Annunciation, the Nativity, and the Ascension of the Virgin. On the floor of the nave stands a marble basin which the abbot uses to wash the feet of twelve other monks on Maundy Thursday in emulation of the acts of Jesus during Passion week.

At the back of the Church is a low, dark passageway leading to the private cell of St. Bishoi. The monks will show you an iron staple and chain dangling from the ceiling and explain that St. Bishoi would fasten it to the hair on his head, thereby maintaining himself in a standing position lest he fall asleep during his night-long prayer vigils. Next door, within walking distance from Dayr Al-Suriani is the monastery of **Dayr Amba Bishoi,** named after the aforementioned monk. In addition to having a sitting room where you can take a few minutes rest from your tour of the monasteries and cool down with some drinking water drawn from its own wells, Dayr Amba Bishoi is a perfect place to watch the sunset. If you happen to be there at the right time of day, cross the narrow drawbridge resting on the gatehouse and enter the fifteen-hundred year old keep built of burnt brick and limestone rubble. Climb up to the **Chapel of St. Michael;** from the rooftop you can watch the crimson sphere sink behind the dunes. Downstairs, in the monastery proper, the church (rebuilt in 444 after having been sacked by barbarians) is also worth a visit. Inside are the remains of St. Bishoi, believed still to perform miracles for the faithful.

Several miles away (you'll have to backtrack and take the other fork in the road) is **Dayr Baramus,** from the Coptic word meaning "two Romans." The name refers to Emperor Valentinus' two sons, Maximus and Domidius, who dwelt as monks here. The monastery was built by St. Makarius in 351 and, as such, is the oldest of the four monuments. The church is noted for its beautiful iconostasis of inlaid ivory. Tradition holds that a crypt under the altar holds the remains of Sts. Maximus and Domidius. The church also houses the relics of St. Moses the Black, an infamous Nubian murderer-turned-monk.

By this time you may have had enough of Coptic monasteries, but if you do go on to visit the monastery of **Dayr Makarius,** built in the eighth century, be sure to see the frescoes of St. Paul, St. Anthony, and St. Pachomius, as well as the depiction of the mounted "warrior saints" in the Church of Saint Michael.

Faiyuum

Sixty-five miles southwest of Cairo is the oasis of Faiyuum, an elaborately irrigated agricultural area at one time filled by the now shrunken Lake Qaruun. The development of this fertile and productive oasis began over 3800 years ago during the pharaonic Middle Kingdom. During the Twelfth Dynasty it became a resort for the pharoahs; the artistic and architectural remains from that period still spatter the area. Since that time, Faiyuum has been both an important Christian and Islamic center. The Greeks called the place Crocodiliopolis because they believed Lake Qaruun's crocodiles were sacred animals. A temple was built in honor of the crocodile-headed deity Sobek. Crocodile worship has since passed away, and little remains from the Greek or pharaonic ages, but agricultural methods, customs, and living conditions remain virtually unchanged since ancient times.

The historical sights of Faiyuum are generally disappointing. The view of the **Necropolis of Maidum** on the way to Faiyuum is impressive, however, as the pyramid is starkly outlined against the desert on one side and the oasis on the other. The desert comes right up to the western shore of Lake Qaruun, and sunsets on the lake are breathtaking. The city of Faiyuum itself is grimy and possesses many of Cairo's worst attributes, but the surrounding area is green and lush—a peaceful and welcome contrast to the heat and hectic pace of Cairo.

Near the city are a pair of pyramids and the meager ruins of a once spectacular temple complex known as **Labyrinth;** both are located near the road connecting Faiyuum with Bani Suef. Five miles from Faiyuum is the brick **Pyramid of Hawwara** and six miles further down the road is a second mud-brick **Pyramid of Lahun.** About fifteen miles west of Faiyuum city (near the southwest corner of the lake) is the Ptolemaic temple of **Qasr Qaruun,** and nearby are the ruins of the Roman city **Dionysias.** For the traveler on a limited itinerary, Faiyuum should not be a first priority; its main attraction is the greenery and the village life. Although you can stay overnight in Faiyuum, it's probably best to treat the area as a brief side trip on your journey south.

To take a bus to Faiyuum from Cairo, follow the footbridge in Tahrir Square to the Ahmed Hilm station (a crowded parking lot). To get a seat on one of the air-conditioned buses, you must purchase tickets in advance at the kiosks. One-way fare is 85pt. A cheaper mode of travel, and one which does not require advance planning, is the train from Ramsis station (via al-Wasta). The trip is three hours, however, and very hot and crowded. One-way fare is 30pt. Both bus and train deposit you in the center of Faiyuum town.

Once in Faiyuum, the wisest course of action is to take a taxi to **Ain Es-Siliin** or to **Bubaira Qaruun** (Lake Qaruun). Wave at the driver and shout your destination—he'll stop if he's going your way. The fare is 15pt; never pay more than 30pt. In Ain Es-Siliin, the **Ain Es-Siliin Hotel** offers rooms with showers for LE6.7 for single or double occupancy. A restaurant adjoins the hotel, but be careful not to be charged for meals or dishes you did not order. At the lake, the hotels range from the **Panorama,** with doubles for LE20.50 to the sleazy **Hunter's Cottages,** with doubles for about LE5. One warning: do not go to Faiyuum without mosquito repellent and malaria pills. Voracious hordes of the beasties will greet you at every corner.

The Nile Valley

No river has ever exercised a greater sway over either the human imagination or the course of history. Along the Nile's fertile columns of farmland, carved out of the endless sand of the Sahara, the seeds of Western society germinated, took root, and blossomed into a flower of culture that thrived for several thousand years. The fruits of this golden age line the entire length of the river. Monumental pharaonic remains are to be found at Abydos, Dendera, Luxor, Edfu, and Philae, with countless lesser sites on either bank.

The world's longest river starts its journey from remote Lake Victoria in present-day Uganda, winding its way through the Sudan and down the entire length of Egypt. From Aswan to Cairo the Nile irrigates a fertile valley; on either side of this delicate thread of farmland, the harsh terrain of the desert presents a dramatic contrast to the valley's agricultural wealth. At Aswan, the desert conquers and engulfs the farmland for a few kilometers. Just above the High Dam south of Aswan is enormous Lake Nassar, an artificial body of water.

Rather than hopping from one ancient temple to the next, try to devote some time to the beautiful rural regions of the Nile. Take local service taxis through farm country, or hire a *felucca* and watch the evening sun bathe the river in an orange glow. In summer, plan on doing most of your sightseeing between 6 and 11am before temperatures soar above 110°F. Luckily many of the pharaonic monuments consist of either tombs or well-preserved temples, so much of your actual sightseeing will take place out of the sun. Mid-afternoons are most comfortably spent within a short crawl of the edge of a swimming pool.

Transportation

In the bygone days of Edwardian Britishers' vacations, a slow, romantic cruise down the Nile was an aristocrat's indulgence. Times haven't changed. Many companies offer unforgettable luxury cruises, at unforgettable prices. Most of the steamers run between Aswan and Luxor, stopping briefly at the antiquities of Esna, Edfu, and Kom Ombo along the way, and charging at least a couple of hundred pounds per person. The most prestigious tours are run by the Hilton and Sheraton hotels; the alternatives are only a shade cheaper. **Pyramid Travel Agency** at 1 Talaat Harb St. in Cairo sends the *Ramses, Tut-Ankh-Amon,* and *Queen Cleopatra* between Luxor and Aswan for three-night cruises (LE350 for a double berth) or six-night cruises (LE580 for a double). Fares with **Eastmar** start at LE200 per person for a seven-day cruise, but they generally run only in winter.

If you're still set on rolling down the Nile, you can rent a *felucca* to sail between Luxor and Aswan for LE100—after some hard bargaining. If several people split the cost, this isn't a bad deal. The sail from Luxor to Aswan can be done in four days, but make it a five-day trip and leave some time for stops at Esna, Edfu, and Kom Ombo. Make up your mind about where you want to go before you start your search for a boat; otherwise bargaining is hopelessly complicated and sometimes ineffectual. Bring food and plenty of water.

The Cairo-Aswan train stops at points all along the Nile Valley (see Egypt Introduction for timetable). The train is the most comfortable alternative for traveling the full distance between either Luxor or Aswan and Cairo. For shorter distances, trains are slow, unreliable, and less convenient than service taxis. Most tourists don't take advantage of the taxis because they fear they'll be ripped off by the drivers. But if you know the proper fare from one town to the next, you can simply pay the appropriate amount upon arrival. We list the correct fares for most connections; for others, find out at the tourist offices in Luxor and Aswan, or ask others what they paid as they get out of the cab, and then pay the same. Don't travel in a taxi *special* (private taxi) or you'll end up paying ten times as much. The best time to travel is early in the morning; by mid-afternoon you have to wait an hour or more before a service taxi going your way fills up with the requisite seven passengers. Once underway, the taxis are remarkably cool.

Mallawi

Life in the little Upper Egypt town of Mallawi, along the banks of one of the Nile's slow-moving canals, seems to glide along amidst an endless stream of donkey carts, *feluccas,* and sun-baked farmers. Trucks move through the town 24 hours a day on the way to Cairo or Aswan, carrying everything from potatoes to porcelain. Everything seems to move past Mallawi, but if you wish to see the antiquities at Tel el Amarna, Hermopolis, Tuna al Gabel, or Beni Hassan, you must go against the current and make a stop.

Practical Information

You can reach Mallawi by train from Cairo or Luxor. The trip takes a little over four hours on the air-conditioned second-class train (fare LE2.80 or LE1.90 with student ID). The last train back to Cairo is at 1am. Service taxis leave regularly for Mallawi from Giza Station; one-way fare is LE3, and the 300km trip takes around seven hours, depending on traffic. Avoid the service taxis unless you're within 150km of Mallawi (i.e., Minya, Assyut or Sohag); the fare should be around 1pt per km.

The **train station** in Mallawi is on the eastern bank of the canal across from town. South of the terminal is the **taxi station** serving points south of Mallawi; a few hundred meters north of the train station, across the canal, past a white mosque on the bank of the canal, is another **taxi station** serving points north. A small bridge spans the canal, leading over to the main paved strip of the town running alongside the waterfront: Sharia Essim. Most of the town's few hotels and restaurants are located along this main thoroughfare. The **police station** is a few blocks down Sharia Bank al Misr, just north of the second taxi station. A tiny **Archeological Museum** nearby houses artifacts unearthed at the local sites. Open Thurs. and Sat.-Tues. 9am-1pm; admission 50pt, 25pt with student ID. Show the gatekeeper the Arabic on the back of your ISIC card to receive a student reduction.

The **Samir Amis Hotel and Restaurant,** on Sharia Essim (tel. 29 55), just north of the train station and across the canal, has singles for LE1, doubles for LE1.50. The rooms aren't bad, but the toilets are abysmal. Ask the manager to give you a room on the back side of the hotel, away from the noisy street. The restaurant downstairs offers the most filling meals in town: meat dishes are LE1.70, chicken LE1.60, rice 25pt, vegetables 30pt, and beer LE1.50. Various cafes and shish kebab places are sprinkled throughout town, especially along Sharia Bank al Misr. If you sup at these places be sure that your intestines have already been initiated into the often unpredictable outcome of curbside cuisine.

Tuna al Gabel and Hermopolis

The ancient Egyptians explained the earth's origins by saying that the sun god sprang from a cosmic egg on the hillock at Hermopolis. Although the mound no longer exists, remains of Hermopolis survive 10km northwest of Mallawi. Twelve kilometers farther, beyond the Nile's protective strip of vegetation and isolated in an arid plain at the foot of the western desert hills, lie the ruins of Tuna al Gabel. This necropolis features a bizarre collection of funerary remains, including an enormous underground burial area where thousands of sacred baboons and ibises were mummified and interred.

Hermopolis and its eerie necropolis can be visited in a single trip. Since Tuna al Gabel is a desert site, bring plenty of water and wear a head covering; otherwise, the blistering sun and scorching desert heat will overwhelm you. Try to bring a flashlight—some of the most important tombs are unlit, and you'll have to dish out extra *baksheesh* for a guide with a light. The local transportation consists of small open pickup trucks which charge only a few piasters to carry you throughout the countryside. Vehicles depart every ten minutes or so from the small station on Sharia al Masguid al Erfang, a side street off Sharia Bank al Misr across from the Archeological Museum. The fare to Ishmunin, near the antiquities at Hermopolis, is 15pt; to the tiny village of Tuna al Gabel, it's 15pt more. You can flag down these pickup trucks at any point along the way, or try to hitch rides from the locals or tour buses visiting the sites. Remember that most locals have never heard the name "Hermopolis," so ask for the vehicle to Tuna al Gabel.

A twenty-minute drive from Mallawi will bring you to the rural village of **Ishmunin**—a tiny farming community especially interesting on Sundays, when the local *fellahin* arrive to do business at the town market. Just outside Ishmunin is the turn-off for Hermopolis, which is 1 km from the main road. Stick to the paved road which curves to the left before entering the site, marked by a yellow sign which reads "To the Baboons."

The two huge stone baboons straight ahead are all that remain of the ancient city of Khmun, called **Hermopolis** by the Greeks. The apes once supported the ceiling of a great temple; the unfortunate creatures had their prominent erect phalluses hacked off by later generations of prudish Egyptians. The temple served as cult center for Thoth, an enigmatic god who chose the ibis and baboon as his sacred animals. Thoth had the body of a man and the head of an ibis, and is often depicted holding a wooden scribal palette. He was revered as the scribe of the divine court, the inventor of writing, and the patron of wisdom and learning. A fragmentary papyrus known as "The Adventure of Setne-Khaemwese and the Mummies" mentioned the cryptic *Book of Thoth*. According to British Egyptologist T.G.H. James, he who possessed this book held "the power to charm heaven and earth, night, the mountains and water; to understand the language of birds and reptiles, to see into the depths of the sea, and, greatest spell of all, to resurrect the dead from the tomb." The Greeks, arriving in the fifth century B.C.E., associated this learned deity with their own messenger god, Hermes, and named the metropolis in his honor.

A short distance away, across a lush green field, are the slender columns of a well-preserved **Roman agora** dating from 420 C.E. Archeologists have discovered important Greek and Byzantine papyri buried below its ancient pavement. An earlier temple to Thoth once stood on the site.

To continue on to Tuna al Gabel, flag down the next northbound pickup truck from the intersection at the main road. The necropolis lies 5km beyond the village of Tuna al Gabel. Some of the local trucks continue on past the village into the desert to bring workers to a local quarry. Don't pay more than 25pt per person to get from the village to the antiquities, and less if there are workers sharing the truck with you.

The necropolis of Tuna al Gabel is currently under excavation by an Egyptian team under the auspices of Cairo University. Most of the ruins date from

300 B.C.E. to 300 C.E. The most unusual attraction is **Al Sarad-eb** (the Galleries), a series of gloomy underground catacombs where thousands of baboons, ibises, and ibis eggs were buried. The practice of mummifying sacred animals and placing them in special burial chambers was a custom typical of the Ptolemaic and Roman periods. The caretaker will unlock the chamber housing the *cynocephali* (mummified baboons) in exchange for a bit of *baksheesh*. Above the cemetery are the remains of a small enclosure where the sacred ibises were housed.

Farther into the desert on the narrow stone walkway is the **City of the Dead,** or necropolis, filled with royal mausolea laid out like a small city with houses, streets, and walkways. Most of the tombs in the City of the Dead show the influence of Hellenistic style. The finest structure in this portion of the necropolis is the **Tomb of Petosiris;** inside, a vestibule opens up into the central tomb chamber, where a square shaft plummets straight down to the burial chamber (closed as of 1983). Petosiris' coffin is currently on display in the Cairo Museum. The decorative bas-reliefs on the walls of the tomb, dating from around 300 B.C.E., depict pharaonic deities in poses typical of Hellenic art. Behind this edifice sits the lovely **Tomb of Isadora,** erected in 120 B.C.E. for a young woman from Antinopolis. Isadora's mummy is on display inside a glass case: teeth, fingernails, and even traces of hair can still be detected on the corpse—quite an accomplishment for the embalmers, considering that Isadora drowned and her body has endured the dust and heat of the desert for two thousand years.

Slightly south of the Tomb of Isadora, a stone walkway branches northward toward the **Well,** a huge circular brick shaft which once supplied the necropolis and its sacred aviary with fresh water. Built in 300 B.C.E., the water wheel pumped water up from 70m below the desert floor. The walkway to the ancient well passes through the remains of a great **Temple to Thoth** which once dominated the entire necropolis. A few of the massive columns of its facade remain, along with a series of pillars that once enclosed the forecourt to the temple.

A yellow and brown Rest House, just inside the main entrance to the site, has lukewarm mineral water for LE1.25 and cold drinks 50pt each. The site is open daily 6am-6pm; admission LE1 (no student discount), plus a 25pt toll to enter the desert area. To return to Mallawi from the site walk 1 km to the intersection of the desert road and the turn-off for the neighboring quarry, and hitch into the town of Tuna al Gabel on one of the trucks going back from the quarry. From the town, the local taxi trucks will take you back to Mallawi.

Tel el Amarna

Twelve kilometers south of Mallawi is the beautiful necropolis of Tel el Amarna, housing fine rock tombs from the fifteenth century B.C.E. Tel el Amarna served as the necropolis for the heretical Pharaoh Akhnaton, his wife Nefertiti, and their royal court. Akhnaton broke with centuries of pharaonic tradition by abandoning the Great Temple at Karnak and the worship of Amon. Instead of adhering to orthodox polytheism, he introduced a monotheistic creed venerating a single god named Aton. Aton was pictured as a brilliant sun-disk whose life-giving rays terminated in benevolent outstretched palms. Frequently the hands of the sun-disk are shown holding an *ankh*—the circle-topped cross symbolizing life. Akhnaton chose not to be buried at Thebes alongside the other pharaohs of the Middle and New Kingdoms, and the rock-hewn tombs at Tel el Amarna remain a testimony to his religious rebellion.

To reach Tel el Amarna, take one of the local pickup trucks from the depot south of the Mallawi train station (10pt). The trucks leave from the parking lot at the end of the bridge crossing into town; they'll drop you off at the bank of the Nile where you can take a *felucca* across to the site for 25pt (with a bit of negotiating). Avoid taking the motorboats since they cost LE2. On the other side you must hire a donkey or a tractor to bring you to the antiquities. The prices are fixed and posted at the boat landing on the east bank. A full tour of the site by donkey will take at least four hours; tractors take less time, but cost more and provide a less picturesque mode of transport. The site is open 7am-4pm; admission LE1, no student discount. Be sure to bring along a flashlight; the watchmen have only sun reflectors.

The tombs of Tel el Amarna cover an area of over 15 sq. km and sit at the base of the towering rock cliffs of the desert. The northern tombs are far better preserved than their counterparts to the south. Don't miss the **Tomb of Haya** (#1), constructed for the superintendent of the royal harem. Its decorative reliefs depict King Akhnaton with his family and closest friends. One of the largest tombs at Tel el Amarna is the **Tomb of Meri-Re** (#4), the high priest of Aton. The scenes embellishing its walls have enabled Egyptologists to deduce the appearance of the city's official buildings. The **Tomb of Panehsy** (#6) was converted into a church by early Christians, but its original decorative carvings survive in reasonably good condition. Of the southern group of tombs, only two are worth touring. The **Tomb of Mahn** (#9), Akhnaton's chief of police, contains several levels of chambers, connected by a winding stairway and adorned with various scenes of the deceased with royal personages. The striking **Tomb of Ay** was constructed for the secretary and groom to the King, who was Queen Nefertiti's nurse and later became Tut-Ankh-Amon's successor as pharaoh. Although Ay abandoned his designs on this resting place before its completion in order to excavate a more elaborate tomb for himself in the Valley of the Kings at Thebes, the structure was intended to be the finest tomb in the necropolis at Tel el Amarna, and its hypostyle hall is still imposing. The wall inside the main entrance is covered with scenes depicting the bustling street life of the ancient city, complete with soldiers, visiting officials, and dancing women.

Beni Hassan

Thirty kilometers north of Mallawi at one of the widest points of the Nile lies the pint-sized town of Minya. It serves as the stopping point for visitors wishing to view the antiquities at Beni Hassan, just a few kilometers away. The rushing waters of an angry mountain stream apparently destroyed the ancient village of Beni Hassan, but the neighboring necropolis, housing 39 pharaonic rock tombs, remains securely on the map as one of the finest Middle Kingdom sites in Upper Egypt. Dating from the Eleventh and Twelfth Dynasties (2000-1800 B.C.E.), most of the tombs contain paintings which still retain a touch of their original vibrancy, though the ruinous effects of four thousand years of earthquakes and vandalism are evident.

To reach Beni Hassan from Mallawi, hop a northbound local train or service taxi and ask to be let off at Abu Qurgas, a tiny village just south of Minya on the west bank of the canal. Look for the sign indicating the road to the antiquities—from Abu Qurgas it's a 3km walk or taxi ride east to the Nile riverbank. From here, you must hire a *felucca* or motorboat to ferry you to the opposite shore and then proceed on foot or hired donkey to the Rest House at the edge of the site. You can reach the tombs by a steep rocky path leading up from here.

Of the three dozen tombs in the necropolis, only four are of particular interest. The **Tomb of Kheti** (#17) originally contained six lotus columns hewn from solid rock. Two of the graceful supports still adorn the interior, and decorative scenes on the southern wall depict Kheti accompanied by his various servants: fan-bearer, sandal-bearer, and even a gnarled dwarf. In the Old Kingdom all citizens except the pharaoh were forbidden to keep dwarves, but by the time of the Middle Kingdom the law had changed. Kheti's father Baket was responsible for the construction of one of the necropolis' most lavish burial places: the **Tomb of Baket** (#15) features scenes of various citizens at work—hairdresser, laundryman, painter, goldsmith, fisherman. The **Tomb of Khnumnotep** (#3) was built for one of the province's most prestigious officials—ruler of the *nome* (province) of Antelope and governor of the Eastern Desert. In the neighboring **Tomb of Amenemhat** (#2), a checkerboard pattern enlivens the vaulted ceiling, while the upper walls display wrestlers and fighting soldiers. A badly damaged statue of Amenemhat with his wife and mother rests at the rear of the tomb chamber.

If you wish to spend the night near the antiquities at Beni Hassan, Minya has a handful of hotels. The best for both money and quality is the two-star **Lotus Hotel** (tel. 23 78), a modern pink structure north of the station on Sharia Port Said. All rooms have air conditioning and adjoining bath; doubles start at LE6. The **Ibn Khasib Hotel** on Sharia Ragheb (first right as you leave the station) and the **Beach Hotel** (three blocks from the station near the river) have good food but are a bit overpriced for one-star hotels—both are run by the same family and charge LE10 for singles and LE16 for doubles including breakfast and dinner. In the off season you can bargain them down and get out of the mandatory meals.

Assyut and Sohag

"Every beautiful vision requires an eye that is able to see it." These are the words of the Neo-Platonist thinker Plotinus (205-270 C.E.), Assyut's most famous native son. In **Assyut** (80km south, two hours by train and one hour by service taxi from Mallawi) the philosopher's words take on a particular irony, since there's nothing at all beautiful about it—it's noisy, crowded, and unattractively urban. But Assyut remains the major embarkation point for visitors heading on to Kharga and the other oases of the Western Desert. The cheapest bed in town is available at the **Youth Hostel** (tel. 48 46), Lux Houses, El Walidiya Building #503; 60pt per person over 21 and 40pt per person under 21. Near the train station, in the American College, is a tiny collection of artifacts with a long name: the **Museum of Pharaonic and Coptic Antiquities.** Adjoining the museum is a small carpet-making school also open to the public. From the train station, follow Sharia el Mahatta to get to the center of town and the lively *suq*. Assyut's most famous pharaonic remnant is very difficult to reach and hardly worth the effort. Outside of town, at the top of a steep winding trail and accessible only by foot, the **Tomb of Hapi-djefa** dates from the reign of Sesostris I and consists of a handful of subterranean chambers.

About 12km northwest of **Sohag,** on the edge of the desert, the Red Monastery and the White Monastery are among the finest Coptic monuments in Upper Egypt, and (if you don't have a car) are most easily reached by hiring a private taxi in Sohag for LE3 to 4, round trip. The **White Monastery** is named for its white limestone blocks, many of which originally belonged to a pharaonic temple, as the various ancient inscriptions and designs testify. The Monastery was founded in 400 by the Coptic St. Shenoudi and is known in Arabic as Dayr Amba Shnouda. The interior still possesses some Coptic frescoes. Nicknamed for its dark red Roman brick exterior, the smaller **Red Monastery** is called Dayr Amba Bishoi in Arabic, also after its founder, St. Bishoi—a thief who converted to Christianity and repented his sins through a strict regimen of fasting and prayer. You can discern the outlines of a tenth-century fresco of the Pantocrator on the apse of the central altar. This region of the Nile still supports a thriving Coptic community: across the river from Sohag is the Christian town of **Akhmim,** renowned for its cotton weavings, particularly shawls and batik crafts. If you wish to spend the night in Sohag, you can stay at the **Youth Hostel,** 5 Sharia Port Said, for 60pt, 40pt if you're under 21.

As well as the usual rail connections, frequent service taxis run between Sohag and Qena (142km), passing by al-Balyana en route. The quickest inexpensive way to reach al-Balyana (near the ruins of Abydos) is to take a service taxi from Sohag. From Assyut, change taxis in Sohag.

Abydos

The ancient city of Abydos, one of the oldest in Egypt, has all but vanished, except for the imposing **Temple of Osiris** built by the Nineteenth-Dynasty Pharaoh Seti I. Although not as imposing as its gargantuan cousins at Luxor and Karnak, the Temple is the greatest work of the New Kingdom, and is noted particularly for its delicately-painted murals and magnificent bas-reliefs. Abydos was a cult-center for Osiris, one of the most important and pervasive deities of the whole Egyptian pantheon. Egyptians of the New Kingdom hoped to make the pilgrimage to the temple, either in life or in the afterlife.

Practical Information

Since there are no accommodations in the area, most people visit Abydos as a long daytrip from Luxor. You can also stop en route between Luxor and points farther north. The closest town to the ruins is **al-Balyana,** easily accessible and on the main north-south rail line. Eight of the ten daily Luxor-Cairo trains stop at al-Balyana. From Cairo the best strategy is to take the train (11 hours). From Luxor, it's much faster to go by service taxi: take a service taxi to Qena (60pt) and change for al-Balyana (LE1.35). For the return trip, take a service taxi to Nag Hammadi (75pt); from there you can usually catch one to Qena without difficulty. The service taxi station in al-Balyana is one block east of the railway station. From there you can also catch a service taxi to Abydos for 20pt. An infrequent and crowded bus also runs from town to the ruins and costs 10pt. The proper fare for a private taxi to Abydos is LE3, though it requires some hard-headed bargaining. The site is open 7am-6pm; admission LE1, 50pt with student ID. The ticket covers everything so there's no need to fork over any *baksheesh.*Near the entrance to the ruins, a refreshment stand sells freshly-pressed sugar cane juice for 5pt a glass.

Sights

According to Egyptian mythology, Osiris, the god of the Nile, was slain by his evil brother Seth—god of storms, violence, and the desert—dismembered and scattered throughout Upper and Lower Egypt. Osiris' wife Isis recovered all but one of the pieces and reconstituted his body. (She later had a son by him, so we know what wasn't missing.) Still, poor Osiris was in no condition to reign over the land of the living, so he reconciled himself to being the lord of the afterlife. Osiris' resurrection was his greatest achievement, and dead pharaohs throughout Egypt's history came to be identified with him.

Abydos became the site for the cult of Osiris because, according to legend, his head was buried here. The myth of Osiris was reenacted annually at Abydos. First, a statue of Osiris was borne to the temple in a triumphant procession. During the approach to the temple, a horde of evil characters attacked the entourage, and were repulsed by the statue's bearers. Next, the statue was conveyed into the temple where secret rituals were performed, simulating the death and dismemberment of Osiris. The following morning, a funerary procession marched with the statue to Osiris' tomb and, in the final act of the drama, Osiris' son Horus avenged his father by killing the evil Seth. Osiris, brought back to life by Horus' deed, returned to the temple in triumph, retiring alone to the inner sanctuary until the following year's enactment.

The temple is constructed in three stages: the visitor passes first from light into semi-darkness, and finally into the dark interior where the gods dwelt, and mortals were forbidden to set foot. During the approach, the ceiling becomes lower and the floor slopes gently upward, in order to create the effect of greater depth and isolation from the world of light.

Approach the great **Temple of Seti I,** which is devoted to Osiris, through the rubble remains of the First Court, once planted with trees and flowers. Only three of the original seven doors remain to the **Portico of Twelve Pillars,** which guarded the entrance of the temple proper. The central doorway leads to the **First Hypostyle Hall,** lined with 24 colossal papyriform columns. This grandiose entrance gives way to the magnificent **Second Hypostyle Hall,** which contains some of the finest bas-reliefs ever carved in Egypt, colorfully-illuminated in striking tones of orange and blue. On the right hand wall as you enter, Seti I is displayed offering incense to Osiris and other deities. At the opposite end of the Second Hypostyle Hall, a long, narrow corridor known as the **Gallery of the Kings** leads off towards the southeast. This simple passage houses one of Egyptology's most treasured finds: the **Kings' List,** which although incomplete, mentions the names of 76 Egyptian rulers from Menes of Memphis to Seti I. Correlating this list with prior knowledge, scholars have pinpointed the sequence of the Dynasties. The Gallery of Kings ends in a series of small unfinished chambers, probably intended for use as storerooms and sacrifice areas.

The remains of the **Osireion,** a great *cenotaph* (empty tomb) for Seti I, are below the main temple in a swampy depression. (The actual tomb of Seti I is in the Valley of the Kings in Western Thebes, alongside the burial places of the other pharaohs of the Middle and New Kingdoms.) Unfortunately, the sodden earth prohibits visitors from seeing the interior, so the most you can do is climb up to the roof of the neighboring main temple to view the Osireion's layout. Nearby is the largely destroyed **Temple of Ramses II,** built by the illustrious son of Seti I.

Retrace your steps to the temple's Second Hypostyle Hall, through the Gallery of the Kings, to view the southern wing of the great Temple of Abydos. Beside the entrance to the Gallery of the Kings is another doorway, yielding to a chamber with two tiny chapels adjoining it. The right-hand chapel contains a graphic relief showing the mummy of Osiris impregnating his sister Isis, who has transformed herself into a falcon.

Return to the Second Hypostyle Hall before proceeding into the temple's interior. **Seven sanctuaries** dedicated to various deities—Horus, Isis, Osiris, Amon, Horakhti, Ptah, and the patron Pharaoh Seti I—line the hallway. In a number of the small sanctuaries and throughout the rear portion of the temple many of the figures have been defaced. Osiris' sanctuary, naturally, is more elaborate than the others, opening into the **Inner Sanctuary of Osiris,** a chamber still possessing most of the original painted scenes of Osiris' life. Only a few of the fine reliefs adorning the walls have suffered abuse by Yahoo travelers. The sanctuary is flanked by three small chapels, housing the best-preserved reliefs in the temple: brilliantly-colored scenes of rituals surrounding Osiris.

Qena and Dendera

The main transportation hub for the part of the Nile Valley between Assyut and Luxor, Qena is a bustling agricultural town usually visited by tourists either to catch a bus or service taxi to destinations such as Abydos or Hurghada, or to visit the Ptolemaic Temple of Dendera, only 8km west of town. Dendera is best visited as a daytrip from Luxor.

Practical Information

For a town its size the transportation situation in Qena couldn't possibly be more complicated than it is. The best way to get from one of the five terminals to another is to hail one of the horse carriages (don't pay more than 20pt per person), and tell the driver which terminal you want.

Train Station: Dominates the center of town. Nine trains a day in either direction. 11-13 hours to Cairo.

Northbound Service Taxis: Ask for a service taxi to Sohag, the farthest north that the service taxis go. To reach Abydos, say you want to go to al-Balyana (LE1.35), the closest town. Don't mention Abydos or you'll have to refuse offers for a special taxi.

Southbound Service Taxis: At the southeast corner of town. From the train station cross the canal and walk south along its eastern bank. Frequent connections to Luxor (60pt) and Aswan (LE2.50). To reach Esna change at Luxor. To reach Edfu or Kom Ombo by service taxi, you'll have to pay the full fare to Aswan.

Bus Station: Behind the town's main congregational mosque. Look for the cluster of towering minarets at the western edge of town. As many of the buses are slow and crowded they are recommended only for the Qena-Hurghada run, there being no real alternative (see below).

Taxi to Dendera: From the local taxi station, near the bus station and between Qena's two largest mosques. There are seldom service taxis to Dendera. With some earnest bargaining a taxi can be hired to Dendera for LE3. If you plan to keep the driver waiting several hours pay him LE4. One way should cost LE1.50.

The road between Qena and Hurghada is the major overland connection between the Nile Valley and the Red Sea. Most tourists wandering through Qena are en route to Luxor or Hurghada and trying to figure out what they're supposed to do in order to get the hell out of Qena. The best way to get to Luxor is to head for the southbound service taxi station. To go from Luxor to Hurghada, start as early as possible. Take a service taxi or a bus to Qena (60pt, 45 minutes), hop a horse carriage to the bus station (15-20pt), and try to buy a ticket immediately, as the most comfortable buses (when they're running) have reserved seats. In 1983 buses ran three times a day in the morning from Qena to Hurghada, and some were reputed to have air conditioning (fare LE2, four hours).

To reach Dendera in winter, you have two options: you can walk the pleasant 8km across the Nile and through agricultural lands, or you can hire a special taxi. In summer, probably only the latter will have much appeal. Try to hook up with other tourists headed for Dendera to minimize the cost; the taxi driver is not supposed to charge on a per person basis. Take your time and bargain assiduously with the taxi drivers, as there is no great rush to beat the sun: the temple is in excellent condition which means much of a visit is spent indoors and out of the sun. Open sunrise-6pm; admission LE2, LE1 with student ID.

The **New Palace Hotel,** on the main square by the station, has doubles for LE3.50-4.

Sights

The **Temple of Hathor** is in great shape: its roof, walls, and inner sanctuary remain largely intact. Only the colossal Temple of Horus at Edfu is better-preserved. Hathor, the city's patron deity, was worshipped in the Old Kingdom, but this temple dates from the first century B.C.E. The late Ptolemies and the Romans found it politically expedient to associate themselves with the worship of Hathor, and sponsored the decoration of the temple during the reigns of Cleopatra, Augustus, Claudius, and Nero. A benevolent goddess, Hathor was usually depicted as a cow-headed woman, or as a woman wearing a crown of two horns cradling the sun-disk of Ra. Hathor, "the Golden One," was identified by the Greeks with Aphrodite because of her patronage of love and joy. During an annual festival, a statue of Hathor was conveyed in a sacred procession from Dendera to Edfu, site of the Temple of Horus, to be joined with her falcon husband in a ritual union.

During the summer a large colony of bats inhabits the more secluded portions of the temple. If this makes you squirm, you may wish to glance up at the ceiling before entering some of the temple's smaller chambers. At any time of year, a flashlight will come in handy as a supplement to the rather weak interior illumination.

As you approach the temple from the main entrance to the site, before you looms the magnificent facade of the **Great Hypostyle Hall,** its eighteen columns surmounted by haunting capitals in the form of the cow-goddesses' heads. A cat-like quality comes through Hathor's bovine features: the pharaohs merged three goddesses during the later years of the New Kingdom, Hathor, Sekhmet the lioness, and Bastet the cat. On the ceiling, protective birds, both the vulture of Upper Egypt and the winged disk of Lower Egypt, outstretch their wings in a bold pattern. Farther into the temple's inner sanctum, wall paintings depict the embalmer's art, while the ceiling is decorated with pictures of Nut, the sky-goddess. In the **Second Hypostyle Hall,** also known as the "Hall of Appearances," six columns march in double formation up the central aisle of the temple, complemented by six small chambers on either side. The function of these chapels (other than as bat nests) is indicated on their interior walls: perfumes used during sacred rituals were kept in the **laboratory** and across the hall is the temple's **treasury.** The Second Hypostyle Hall gives way to the Hall of Offerings, where daily rituals were performed. A staircase leading up to the roof of the temple is decorated with processional figures carved in elegant relief. From the top, enjoy the view that encompasses farmland and desert. At the lovely kiosk (southwest corner of the roof) priests performed the ceremony of "touching the disk," in which the soul of the sun-god Ra appeared in the form of light.

Return to the Hall of Offerings via a second staircase running down the eastern side of the temple and proceed into the **Hall of the Ennead,** immediately preceding the inner sanctuary of the temple. The chamber to your left as you enter is the **wardrobe,** and opposite, a doorway leads through a small treasury into the **Court of the New Year,** where sacrifices were performed during the

New Year festival. On the ceiling of the portico, the goddess Nut gives birth to the sun, whose rays shine upon the head of Hathor. Retracing your steps to the main temple, proceed to the most sacred portion of the temple, the sanctuary, once the site of the cult statue of Hathor. Its interior is adorned with a series of carvings depicting various scenes of offerings. The sanctuary is actually a room within a room; its exterior surface is decorated with a frieze of ninety squatting divinities just below the upper cornice. The "Mysterious Corridor" surrounds the sanctuary on three sides, opening off into eleven chapels, each with a peculiar religious function. One of them, the **Per Naser Chapel,** is dedicated to Hathor in her most terrifying form, that of a lioness. A small chamber known as the "Throne of Ra" adjoins the Per Naser Chapel. A miniscule opening in its floor leads to the **crypt,** a fascinating subterranean hallway embellished with reliefs. Officially, the crypt is closed to the public, but unofficially it is not. The guard will be more than happy to give you a guided tour in exchange for a little *baksheesh*.

Of the relief work outside the temple, the scene on the southern end portraying the son of Julius Caesar making offerings to the gods with his mother Cleopatra is the most notable. To the southwest of the temple some stone steps lead down to the enclosed, overgrown **Sacred Lake,** and around the corner, directly south of the temple, are the scanty remains of the **Temple of Isis,** built by Augustus to commemorate the birth of the pharaoh. Festivals celebrating a god's or pharaoh's birth took place at these *mammisis* (birth houses). Just southwest of the main entrance gate to the temple are two other *mammisis*. Although the **Mammisi of Nectanebo** is in ruins, the **Roman Mammisi,** built during the reign of Nero, offers more to see. Reliefs display Hathor in various poses on both the interior and exterior walls, and beside the *mammisi,* to the north, some bits of an interesting cobra-head frieze lie on the ground.

Luxor

One of Egypt's most popular modern songs begins with a sequence of rhymed couplets that translate roughly as follows: "Luxor is our land and the land of the tourists, everyone enjoys themselves here, and no one wants to go home." Indeed, comparatively clean, quiet, and hospitable, the town of Luxor provides a haven on the sometimes-trying Egyptian itinerary: the townspeople are long accustomed to the sight of European faces, the pace of life is relaxed and slow, and prices are low despite the heavy influx of tourists. Built on the site of ancient Thebes, capital of united Egypt during the New Kingdom (Eighteenth to Twentieth Dynasties, 1555-1090 B.C.E.), the town of Luxor is custodian of some very impressive monuments: the Temples of Karnak and Luxor  alone affect even the most jaded world traveler with their overwhelming array of gateways and towering masses supported by forests of gigantic columns. And these temples are only a part of Luxor's historical and artistic wealth. On the other side of the Nile are still more monuments and Luxor's famous tombs, chiseled deep into bleak limestone outcroppings. Luxor's location is also well-suited to daytrips encompassing the antiquities at Abydos, Dendera, Edfu, and Esna. Plan to spend at least a couple of days in Luxor to explore Egypt's most treasured monuments.

Orientation and Practical Information

Although there are only a few street signs in town—and even fewer maps—you should not have any trouble finding your way around Luxor as long as you learn the three main streets: Station Street (**Sharia al Mahatta**) runs east-west, perpendicular to the Nile, from the train station to Luxor Temple; River Street (**Sharia al Bahr**) runs north-south along the east bank of the Nile; and Karnak Street (**Sharia al Karnak**) runs parallel to and one block away from the Nile between Luxor Temple and Karnak Temple.

Tourist Information Office: in the tourist bazaar next to the Old Winter Palace Hotel, just south of the Luxor Temple (tel. 82 21 5). Helpful English-speaking staff. Open every day (including Ramadan) 8am-2pm and 4:30-7:30pm.

American Express: inside the New Winter Palace Hotel, south of Luxor Temple on the Nile (tel. 82 22). Open daily 8am-9pm, but closed 2-5pm during Ramadan.

Post Office: half way down Sharia al Mahatta. Sporadic hours.

Telephone, Telex, and Telegram Office: next door to the New Winter Palace Hotel. Place international calls here. International telegrams must be sent from the Savoy Hotel, also along the Nile.

Train Station: at the head of Sharia al Mahatta. If you're returning by train to Cairo, make your reservations the day you arrive. Six trains a day to Aswan and points south (4-7 hours to Aswan), ten times a day to points north (12-16 hours to Cairo).

Bus Station: at the intersection of Sharias al Karnak and al Mahatta in front of Luxor Temple. Six buses a day leave for Aswan (LE2), Kom Ombo (LE1.60), Edfu (LE1.10), and Esna (60pt). Buses cost 50% more if air-conditioned. You can't tell whether a bus will be air-conditioned until you get onto it. Daily buses to Cairo leave between 5 and 6am (LE5.50, 15 hours), and are not recommended unless the train is completely booked. Buses to Qena (60pt, one hour) leave twice a day in the morning.

Collective Taxi Station: on Sharia al Karnak, one block up from the Luxor Museum on the Nile. During early morning and late afternoon hours, service taxis leave every fifteen minutes for Qena (60pt, 45 minutes), Esna (60pt, 45 minutes), and Aswan (LE2, 3 hours). Special taxis cost about ten times more.

Hospital: Sharia al Bahr, next to the Luxor Museum.

Foreign Books and Newspapers: Gaddis Bookstore, next to the tourist office, has a large collection of books in English on Egypt. **Hachette Bookshop,** in the arcade of the Etap Hotel, specializes in French-language books. A variety of publications is available from the kiosk in the train station.

Swimming Pools: The only comfortable way to survive a summer afternoon in Luxor. The **Etap Hotel,** several blocks north along Sharia al Bahr from Luxor Temple, often does not charge admission. If things start getting crowded, they charge a steep LE5. The Luxor Hotel always charges admission, although their official rate of LE2.50 can often be negotiated down to LE1.50.

Accommodations

Choose your hotel carefully in Luxor since this is probably where you will stay while you explore the surrounding Nile Valley. Rates listed below are off-season (May-September). High-season rates can be 10 to 50% higher. Most of the budget hotels cluster around the station and line both Sharia al Mahatta and Sharia al Karnak, but most also leave a lot to be desired. If your standards of cleanliness and comfort are minimal, just start knocking on the doors of these hotels and it won't be long before you find a room for LE1 per person or less. Be sure to look at the room before you take it to see if it is acceptable. The following listings are more comfortable and more expensive. If you can't survive without air conditioning consult the last two selections.

Youth Hostel (IYHF), Sharia el Manshia (tel. 21 39). The hostel is quite new and its location is a bit inconvenient—about halfway between Luxor and Karnak Temples (visible from Sharia al Karnak). Closed daily 10am-2pm and 11pm-6am. Rates for a bed in a dorm room: over 21 without card, LE1; over 21 with card, 80pt; under 21, 60pt. They will also house you in a private room: LE6.40 for a double, LE6.60 for a triple.

Negem el Din Pension, Sharia Ramses (tel. 23 52). Basic rooms, moderately clean, and very inexpensive. Next to railway tracks, so get to like the midnight train horns. Off-season LE1.50 per person including breakfast (omelette, bread, cheese, butter, jam, and tea). Peak season 75pt extra for breakfast. Room includes fan. Hot showers. If you want breakfast before 7am tell the management the night before.

El Salam Hotel, Sharia Sitiel Awal. Look for their sign on Sharia al Mahatta, on your right as you walk towards Luxor Temple. Clean, reasonably-priced rooms, including fan and shower, LE1.50 per person. Breakfast 75pt extra.

New Karnak Hotel, opposite the train station. Plain, relatively clean, good location. Very popular and can fill up quickly at any time of year. Singles LE2, doubles LE3, doubles with private shower LE4. Dorm-style rooms LE1 per person. Breakfast 35pt.

Horus Hotel, Sharia al Karnak (tel. 21 65). Immediately to the right of the end of Sharia al Mahatta, facing Luxor Temple. Comfortable, clean rooms. Friendly, sincere, English-speaking staff. Singles without shower LE2.50, with shower LE4; doubles without shower LE3.35, with shower LE5. Unfortunately, next to the mosque. Try to get a room on the opposite side of the hotel, away from *muezzin*.

Radwan Hotel, around the corner from the New Karnak (tel. 22 14). Take the second left as you leave the station. Friendly management, clean dorm-style rooms let in the off-season as private accommodations. Beds go for about LE2, including breakfast, shower, and fan.

Grand Hotel, Sharia Muhammad Fared. Take second left after leaving the station, walk past the Radwan, and turn left three blocks farther down by their sign. Decent singles and doubles, all with fans, for LE1.50 per person. 20% service charge. Breakfast 75pt.

Salah el Din, el Manshia Square. Walk past the Radwan and keep walking for ten minutes. Cheap, but not overly clean. Pretty good bathrooms, fans. Rooms without shower LE1.50 per person. Doubles with shower LE5.

Dina Hotel (tel. 82 42 0). Follow their signs from Sharia al Karnak. Once a very nice hotel, now beginning to deteriorate. Still a step up from all of the above. Large rooms with fans and adjoining baths. Singles with breakfast LE6.50, doubles with breakfast LE9.50. In the low season you should be able to negotiate at least LE1 off of these rates.

Ramoza Hotel, Sharia al Mahatta (tel. 82 27 0). On your right as you walk away from the station. Better chance of getting an air-conditioned room. Spotless, cleaned daily. Hot water. Singles LE12, doubles LE16, including breakfast and private shower. In the off-season you may be able to chip anywhere from LE2 to LE6 off rates.

Nile Hotel. Follow the signs from Sharia al Bahr for the Philip Hotel; the Nile is next door. In the off-season, clean air-conditioned doubles with adjoining showers go for LE11.

Camping: Free of charge in the garden in front of the Luxor Hotel.

Food

Most of the inexpensive restaurants in Luxor huddle around the train station. The cheapest filling meal in town is the *kushari* joint (15pt for a regular plate, 30pt for a large), on your left as you walk down Sharia al Mahatta from the station. If you arrive in the middle of the night by train, the only place open is the outdoor *köfte* grill to the right as you walk out of the station—LE2 for *köfte,* salad, bread, and *tahina*.

New Karnak Restaurant, next to the hotel of the same name. Excellent place for snacking. Prompt service, unbeatable prices. Eggs (scrambled, fried, or boiled) 25pt, rice or potatoes with tomato sauce 15pt, spaghetti with tomato sauce 20pt, chicken soup 15pt, a quarter of a roast chicken 85pt, chocolate milk, or lemon juice 20pt.

Radwan Restaurant, in the inner courtyard of the Radwan Hotel. Quiet except during prayers. Decent food and generous portions. Full dinner menu for LE1.50 features soup, choice of chicken, *köfte* or goulash, pasta, vegetable, and dessert. Best dinner bargain around.

Restaurant Limpy, Sharia al Mahatta. Across from the New Karnak. Come here if you get tired of the above. Well-prepared full-course menu for LE1.50, but small portions, often slow service, and rip-off beverage prices.

Nile Casino, Sharia al Bahr. On the Nile across from Luxor Temple. Nice cafe with earthen floor—perfect for sipping *kirkaday* and watching the *feluccas* glide by. Full dinner menus feature ample portions—beef entree LE1.50, chicken or fresh fish entree LE2. Menu includes appetizer, vegetable, and pasta. Drinks are more expensive when there's music. Below the restaurant is a cool riverside garden.

Chez Farouk Restaurant, on the Nile, a shade north of Luxor Temple. A cut above our other listings. Indoor dining room overlooking the river. Their four-course menu, with a choice of beef or fresh carp, makes a nice splurge at LE2.85 plus 40pt service charge.

Sights

Within the town of Luxor itself, on the east bank of the Nile, there are two outstanding attractions: the mammoth Temples of Luxor and Karnak.

The graceful columns of Luxor Temple, visible from Sharia al Mahatta, are just several blocks west of the train station. The first work on the temple was done by the New Kingdom Pharaoh Amenophis III, who built on the site of a small Middle-Kingdom temple to Amon and rededicated the place to Amon, his wife Mut, and their son the moon-god Khonsu. The unfinished work of Amenophis was completed by Tut-Ankh-Amon. The most significant later contributions were those of Ramses II, who added an enormous colonnaded court, a pylon, two obelisks, and six large statues of himself to guard the entrance. The sanctuary was later restored by Alexander the Great, and when Christianity came to Luxor, part of the complex was used as a church. Only an altar and a few mosaics are left from this period, but the **Mosque of Abu'l-Hagaf,** added much later by the Muslims, still stands in the court of Luxor

Temple and remains in active use; in 1968, it was even added to by the local Muslims while the Egyptologists were away on summer vacation.

Luxor was the site of an annual festival honoring the god Amon. A great procession accompanied a statue of the deity from Karnak Temple along the river to Luxor Temple. The entire 3km distance between the two great temples was connected by the sacred **Avenue of the Sphinxes**—a paved boulevard lined on both sides by hundreds of majestic human-headed lions, each holding a statuette of Ramses II between its paws. The final stretch of the Avenue remains, complete with two rows of sphinxes, culminating at the main entrance to the temple. The doorway to the interior of the temple is cut through the enormous **Pylon of Ramses II,** nearly 24m tall. Flanking the main doorway are two of the six original colossi of Ramses II, plus a pink granite obelisk with four praying apes on one side. (There were originally two such obelisks, but the other was removed in 1836 and now stands in Paris.) Carved reliefs on the pylon describe Ramses' battles against the Hittites.

The open **Court of Ramses II** is surrounded by double rows of monumental papyriform columns with lotus-bud capitals. Huge statues of Ramses II, with the smaller figure of his wife carved at the foot, are placed between each pillar. The more sacred **Temple of Amon, Mut, and Khonsu** lies in the northwest corner of Ramses II's court. Continue through the court to reach the **Colonnade of Amenophis III,** with its fourteen pillars crowned by Egyptian lotus-bud capitals. From here, proceed into the **Court of Amenophis III.** Notice the traces of the original coloring on the architraves; it is likely that much of the temple complex was originally painted in this manner. Beyond this second court rises the **hypostyle hall,** or antechamber, with its 32 enormous columns set in four rows. Latin inscriptions to Julius Caesar adorn an altar in one of the rooms to the south of the pillared hall. Alexander appears before Amon and other deities in some bas-reliefs in the **Sanctuary of Alexander the Great** at the end of the corridor.

Visit at night if possible, when the dark silky Nile moves silently by the completely illuminated interior. Daytime temperatures are almost unbearable anyway. An early-morning visit will complement the nocturnal one by revealing details of the temple as well as its overall structure. Open in summer daily 6am-8pm, in winter daily 7am-9pm, during Ramadan 6am-6:30pm and 8-11pm. The lights go on year-round at 7:30pm. Admission LE2, LE1 with student ID, but there is no student discount in the evening.

Like the Temple of Luxor, the even more sumptuous **Karnak Temple** was originally a much smaller shrine to Amon. By the Eighteenth Dynasty (fifteenth century B.C.E.), both Amon and Thebes were at the peak of their careers as the supreme authorities over a united Upper and Lower Egypt; the Temple of Karnak was the most confident expression of their popularity. It is a melange of additions and alterations spanning millenia, but because of the traditionalism of pharaonic architecture, all seem of a piece. The deeper you proceed from the entrance on the west, the farther back you go in time: the first pylon is Ptolemaic (second century B.C.E.), and the eighth is Queen Hatshepsut's contribution (fifteenth century B.C.E.). The double row of ram-headed sphinxes before the temple entrance is the other end of the great Avenue of the Sphinxes which once extended all the way to the Temple of Luxor. The ram was traditionally associated with Amon. The largest single portion of the complex at Karnak, and the area you will encounter when you emerge from the first pylon, is the **Great Court,** built during the Twenty-second Dynasty (tenth century B.C.E.). The lone column is all that remains of the row that once surrounded the court. On the left are three chambers dedicated to

Amon, Mut, and Khonsu, adorned with bas-reliefs depicting the deities. Karnak's oldest structure, the **Pavilion of Sesostris I,** lies to the north of the Great Court. The reliefs inside are exquisite. Special permission is required to gain entrance to the nineteenth-century B.C.E. pavilion.

Leave the temple and walk eastward along the dirt track for five minutes in order to reach the **northern gateway** and **Temple of Ptah.** The entrance to the three chapels of the temple's interior is locked, but for a bit of *baksheesh* the guard will open the door. In the central chamber lies the elegant but headless cult statue of Ptah, while a memorable statue of his consort, the lion-headed divinity Sekhmet, survives in near-perfect condition in the room on the right. Make your way back to the Great Court and continue through the second pylon to the overwhelming **Great Hypostyle Hall,** a convocation of 134 colossal papyrus columns. The hall, with its original roof, would have been large enough to accommodate Paris' Notre Dame; each of the great capitals has enough room for one hundred people to stand on it. Many of the pillars still exhibit their bright paint, especially in the upper portions, and every square centimeter of the ceiling, walls, and columns is carved with inscriptions. The mammoth proportions, lavish decoration, and gentle, extended contours make the Great Hypostyle Hall one of the pinnacles of pharaonic architecture. Don't follow the example of passing tour groups and simply do a quick two-step around the pillars. Slow down and sense the subtle life of this granite forest.

Beyond the Great Hypostyle Hall lies the **Central Hall,** where you can make a foray through the fourth, fifth, and sixth pylons, or turn south toward the seventh through tenth pylons. The latter section is officially closed and often under excavation, but some *baksheesh* will allow you in to see the six large statues of royal personages (carved in limestone and granite) near the eighth pylon. By heading eastward toward the fourth pylon, you will encounter a small colonnade in the center of which stands the **Obelisk of Queen Hatshepsut,** carved in pink granite. Passing on through the rubble of the fifth pylon and the granite sixth pylon, enter the **Hall of Records,** where two elegantly-proportioned granite pillars stand, one decorated with carvings of the lotus of Upper Egypt, the other with the papyrus of Lower Egypt. The **Sanctuary of the Sacred Boats** is a double-chambered chapel famous for its exquisite carvings, many still retaining their original color. The outside wall of the southernmost chamber is particularly well-preserved, depicting the sacred boats of Amon's annual procession.

Straight ahead, the **Festival Hall of Thutmose III** dominates the eastern edge of the Karnak complex—the roof of the Hall survives intact, supported by 52 pillars which taper downward, becoming narrower at the bottom. Some of the column bases were actually shaved off even further in order to make room for large processions. In Christian times, the Hall was converted into a church, and frescoes of haloed saints still adorn the interior walls and column shafts.

The limpid waters of the **Sacred Lake,** south of the Festival Hall, contrast with the angular monuments surrounding them on three sides. Priests would purify themselves in the holy waters of this rectangular pool before performing ceremonies within the temple. A small **cafe** next to the lake offers refreshments at outlandishly high prices. Outside the main complex, to the southwest, is the Twentieth-Dynasty **Temple of Khonsu,** and about a quarter of a mile south is the lavishly-decorated **Temple of Mut,** seldom visited.

It will take at least 1½ hours to see the entire complex, so in summer it is advisable to bring bottled water and come early. With a bit of arguing you can purchase a bottle of mineral water for 75pt in front of the site. Soft drinks should be 25pt. Don't pay more than 50pt for the sun hats being peddled. The temple lies 3km north of Luxor Temple at the end of Sharia al Karnak, one block east of Sharia al Bahr. Walk along the Nile or take a horse carriage (don't pay more for a carriage ride than 20pt per person—and definitely not the standard tourist price of LE1). A local bus runs between Karnak and the station (fare 5pt). Unfortunately it does not start until 8am, which is too late for sun-shy visitors. Open sunrise-6pm; admission LE3, LE1.50 with student ID. To understand and appreciate these vast ruins, it can't hurt to tag along with a guided tour group, or equip yourself beforehand with Jill Kamil's book, *Luxor* (LE5 in bookstores; see Practical Information.)

A ninety-minute **Sound and Light Show** plays at Karnak Temple every night of the week at 8:30pm, with a second show at 10:30pm on some nights. The first show on Mondays, Wednesdays, and Saturdays, and the second show on Fridays, are in English. The narration is melodramatic, but these fanciful pharaonic ruins take nicely to souped-up lighting. Admission LE3, LE1.50 for students.

Luxor Museum, on Sharia al Bahr halfway between Luxor and Karnak Temples, is Egypt's most aesthetically pleasing museum, and the collection, although small, is of extremely high quality. Treasures from the neighboring temple complexes, as well as from the Valley of Kings, including the celebrated tomb of King Tut-Ankh-Amon, beckon visitors away from the sites themselves. Open daily 5-10pm in the summer and 4-9pm in winter; last ticket sold a half hour before closing. Admission LE2, LE1 with student ID. The museum is air-conditioned. Across the street from the Luxor Museum on a large houseboat is the **Papyrus Museum of Dr. Ragab.** Open 9am-2pm and 4-10pm; admission free.

Evenings in Luxor, especially in summer, are most pleasantly spent relaxing aboard a *felucca* on the Nile. A worthwhile nearby destination is **Banana Island,** 3km upriver from Luxor—an isolated palm-studded islet where you can eat all the bananas you want for free! Local *feluccas* will take you there for about LE2 per person, though you may be able to negotiate a lower price if you have a group of four or more people, particularly if you arrange the trip a day in advance. Due to the recent influx of naive tourists, *felucca* fares are inflated and tenacious bargaining is called for. The *felucca* drivers along the Nile north of Luxor Temple tend to be rip-off artists; instead, work on the boaters south of Luxor Temple. The excursion to Banana Island takes two to three hours, and if you leave Luxor in the late afternoon you will return in time to enjoy a brilliant Egyptian sunset from the Nile. A shorter trip shouldn't cost more than LE2 per hour, regardless of the number of passengers. Don't set out for an excursion too late, since the local government prohibits *feluccas* from sailing after sunset.

West Thebes

The west bank of the Nile overflows with a fabulous array of Egyptian tombs, temples, and treasures, just across the river from Luxor, dispersed over seven square kilometers of mountainous desert landscape. The Necropolis ("City of the Dead") of Thebes is possibly the world's most richly endowed graveyard. Though robbers and archeologists have, over the course of centuries, pilfered much of the original treasure, the Necropolis still sparkles with an unparalleled collection of Egyptian funerary art.

The richness of the facilities at Thebes derives only in part from purely aesthetic criteria; mundane considerations of security were actually the primary motive for Middle-Kingdom (ca. sixteenth-century B.C.E.) rulers establishing the sort of tombs here that they did. Robbers had become so adroit at entering the pyramids at Memphis, the capital of the Old Kingdom, and making off with the articles meant to accompany the pharaohs into the afterlife, that the royal mummies were barely cold before suffering mutilation and blasphemy at the hands of intruders. Clearly, a radical change in burial practices was essential if piety and proper treatment of the dead were to be salvaged.

The western edge of Thebes, capital city of the New Kingdom, was selected as the site for all subsequent tombs. A deceased pharaoh would be interred, and workers would begin immediately to construct the tomb destined for the succeeding monarch. In order to conceal information on the location, contents, and design of the tomb, the work was carried out in utmost secrecy, by a team of laborers who dwelled within the necropolis itself. Perfecting techniques of tomb construction, decoration, and mummification, this tiny community of craftspeople devoted itself to the City of the Dead over the course of generations, handing their knowledge down to their own children. (Remains of the workers' walled city have been excavated near the Temple of Dayr el Medina.) Tomb design reflected the new emphasis on secrecy. Instead of a single ostentatious pyramid, there were pairs of funerary monuments: an underground grave was lavishly outfitted with the precious articles needed for a journey into the afterlife, and sequestered in an obscure recess of the desert, while a grandiose mortuary temple supplied the setting where the monarch would be worshipped throughout eternity. Inside the tomb, false passages, fake sarcophagi, and hidden doorways were designed to foil even the most cunning of robbers. A deep square shaft, plummeting to a depth of over 5m, prevented entrance to the innermost chamber in nearly every tomb. One spot, in particular, presented itself as ideal for the purpose of entombment: a narrow, winding valley ringed on three sides by jagged limestone cliffs and approached by a single rocky footpath. This isolated canyon, known as the

Valley of the Kings, became the burial place of New Kingdom pharaohs. It all sounded wonderful on the drawing board, but the grave-robbers were not deterred. Few of the tombs managed to escape vandalization.

Eventually, queens and favored consorts were also accorded ceremonial burial with full honors and security precautions in a separate corner of West Thebes, the **Valley of the Queens.** The highest members of the Theban aristocracy also subscribed to this custom. Numbering over three hundred in all, several of the **Tombs of the Nobles** rival the royal burial chambers in quality of craft and design. There are over four hundred tombs all told in West Thebes. While the dry desert climate preserved the painted walls from the elements, the elaborate subterfuges did protect some tombs from incursion. As a result, many of the burial chambers boggle the mind with their untouched state upon being exposed to the eyes of the world.

Sights

Practical Information

If you are visiting in the summer take the following piece of advice to heart: start early in the morning. Summer afternoons on the west bank of the Nile are brutally hot and most of the guards close up the antiquities and head home after 2pm. Your tour of West Thebes will be far more pleasant if you shift your schedule and start at sunrise (5am). Explore the area in a series of early-morning visits, as the sun doesn't really get cooking until about nine in the morning, which is about when most tourists finish breakfast and invade the area. All the sites open at 6am, offering about three hours of peace and pleasant temperatures. Drinks are sold at some of the ruins but usually for extortionate sums—bring plenty of water.

Assuming you are without a car of your own, you have three transportation options: bicycle, taxi, or donkey. The first of these is the most practical and the most economical. The correct rental fee for a bike is LE1 per day; don't pay more. Rent before crossing the river, as bikes are harder to find on the west bank. In winter bicycling allows you to determine your own pace and your own routes. In summer, however, when temperatures sometimes approach 115°F, riding a bicycle is not a sensible thing to do unless touring is strictly confined to the early morning. Be aware that the ride to the main complex of antiquities is uphill, a fact made easier to swallow when you realize that the tough haul takes place during the cool early morning while the return trip in the afternoon is all downhill.

Hiring a taxi for the day is surprisingly economical, allows you to cover more ground, and reduces the hassles of mobility to a minimum. The correct fare for a small cab (1-4 passengers) is LE7 and for a large cab (5-8 passengers) LE10.50. Approach tourists in Luxor (try the New Karnak Restaurant) and ask if they would like to share the cost of the taxi, then come early and bargain hard with the cab drivers who wait at the ferry dock on the other side of the Nile. Ignore any prattle about government rates and per-person charges. You must state not only your price, but also the period of time for which you will require the driver's services.

Plodding along on the back of a donkey is a novel way of sightseeing. Don't pay more than LE1.50 for a donkey; with some looking around and bargaining, you can find one for LE1. You may have to pay extra for a guide, in which case the bigger your party the better, since the price for the guide should be the same regardless of how many are in his charge. (If you are stuck with a guide, make sure you like him. Some of Luxor's less charming donkey boys have developed the nasty habit of attempting to extort money from tourists and knocking them off their donkeys if they don't comply.) Although slow, the donkeys do offer more versatility in that they can take the spectacular, if precipitous, paths that criss-cross the limestone ridges on which the various sights are scattered.

The business of **admission tickets** is complicated. The ticket booths are located by the river, far away from the archeological sites, which means tickets must be purchased at the beginning of the day. Hence, decide which antiquities you want to visit and get the appropriate tickets. The more homework you've done, the more pleasant will be your visit. There are two ticket kiosks: the one for non-students is on the west bank of the Nile next to where the tourist ferry docks, while the student kiosk is 3km inland past Qurna village and just beyond the Colossi of Memnon. If you are in a mixed group of students and non-students, go to the student kiosk—each student can purchase two student tickets for each monument. The student discount is 50%—ISIC card required. The following is a list of admission tickets and their respective (non-student) prices:

#1	Valley of the Kings	LE5
#2	Dayr el Bahri (Temple of Hatshepsut)	LE2
#3	Medinet Habu (Temple of Ramses II)	LE2
#4	Ramasseum	LE1
#5	Asasif Tombs	LE1
#6	Tombs of Nakh and Mena	LE1
#7	Tombs of Rekh, Mina, and Sennofer	LE1
#8	Tombs of Ramose, Userhet, and Khaemt	LE1
#9	Dayr el Medina (Temple and Tombs)	LE1
#10	Valley of the Queens	LE1
#11	Seti Temple	LE1

When purchasing tickets, bear the following in mind: a ticket is valid only for the day on which you buy it; you won't be reimbursed for unused tickets; it is impossible to buy tickets anywhere except at the ticket kiosks; it is impossible to enter a site without an admission ticket; and you probably will not be permitted to buy (and won't have time to use) more than five separate tickets. Most tourists buy more tickets than they can use. Make the Valley of the Kings your first priority and try to take in one or two minor sites as well. If you're staying for more than one day, break your visit of West Thebes into geographical segments that eliminate doubling back. This requires some prior research about the various ruins. The best inexpensive guidebook to the area is Jill Kamil's paperback *Luxor,* available for LE5 in the bookstores in town (see Luxor Practical Information). The most thorough, though far more expensive, coverage readily available in English is *Nagel's Encyclopedic Guide to Egypt*.

Try to bring a flashlight when visiting West Thebes. Especially in the Tombs of the Nobles, though also to a lesser extent in the Valley of the Kings and the Valley of the Queens, a flashlight will save you the necessity of paying *baksheesh* to guards and will enable you to see much more than you would otherwise.

In order to get to West Thebes from Luxor, take one of the ferries that leave from points all along the riverside. There are two different types of ferry. Tourist ferries operate frequently but cost more (25pt). Two local ferries (10pt) are more picturesque but sometimes wait around for as much as thirty minutes before leaving; one docks just north of Luxor Temple, the other (which carries cars) at a well-marked spot halfway down Sharia al Mahatta towards Karnak Temple.

Valley of the Kings

To reach the Valley of the Kings from the non-student kiosk, backtrack to the fork near the ferry landing and turn westward to the village of New Qurna just across a wide irrigation canal. Bear westward past the Colossi of Memnon and the student ticket kiosk and then follow the signs which clearly mark the way to the Valley of the Kings and all the other antiquities. There are over 64 known tombs in the Valley, many of which are not open to the public at any given time. Each tomb is numbered; the most worthwhile are #2, 6, 8, 11, 15, 17, 34, 35, 57, and 62. Even some of these may be closed when you visit. These are described below.

The twelfth-century B.C.E. **Tomb of Ramses IX** (#6), on the left upon entering the valley, has weathered the centuries well. Most of the decorative carving adorning the interior walls depicts scenes from the Book of the Dead, describing the spirit's journey to the underworld after death. A lengthy, sloping corridor descends to a large anteroom, covered with a proliferation of demons, serpents, and wild animals. Beyond, through a pillared room and corridor, the burial chamber retains traces of Ramses IX's sarcophagus. Nut, goddess of morning and evening, embellishes the ceiling, soaring above constellations and boats full of stars.

Just around the corner, in front of the Rest House, is West Thebes' most renowned and anticlimactic tourist attraction, the **Tomb of Tut-Ankh-Amon** (#62). Its celebrated discovery in 1922 unearthed the cache of priceless pharaonic treasure which has toured the world several times and is now on exhibit in the National Museum of Cairo. Archeologist Howard Carter, convinced that the young Pharaoh Tut-Ankh-Amon had been buried near his ancestors in a splendidly-outfitted tomb, set out for Egypt to uncover "King Tut's" grave. For many decades, Egyptologists had believed that the undiscovered tomb of

Tut-Ankh-Amon contained little of interest because the Pharaoh had reigned only a short time when he died. The experts scoffed at Carter's optimism, but the determined archeologist, ignoring professional censure, toiled for six long seasons in the Valley of the Kings. Finally, after more than 200,000 tons of rubble had been moved, Carter began to lose heart. Even his sympathetic patron, the wealthy Lord Carnarvon, reluctantly decided to cut off funding for the project. But before admitting that the entire venture had been in vain, Carter made one last attempt. The final unexplored possibility for the tomb's location was a site beneath the tomb of Ramses VI, in an area covered with workers' huts. Beneath these shanties an ancient door was found. Preparing for the final assault, Carter wired Lord Carnarvon in London, who journeyed to Egypt for the tomb's opening. This sensational event revealed a breathtaking store of riches, vindicating Carter beyond his wildest dreams. The tomb had remained intact, undisturbed by robbers for centuries: it was crammed full of decorated furniture, jewelry, and utensils—even several royal walking sticks—and three mummies, including that of King Tut himself. Carter, underemployed for so long, was now kept busy for ten years cataloguing the contents of the tomb.

The innermost mummy case of solid gold, studded with decorative jewels, remains *in situ,* along with the exquisitely-carved sarcophagus of Tut-Ankh-Amon. The interior walls of the burial chamber, perfectly preserved, depict colorful scenes from the *Book of the Dead.*

The **Tomb of Ramses VI** (#9), situated directly behind the Tomb of Tut-Ankh-Amon, is best known for its unusual and imaginative ceiling. An elongated bright gold portrait of the goddess Nut extends along the ceiling from the third main corridor, through a fourth hallway, curving around into a pillared chamber. Her severely-attenuated midriff is filled with a long row of stars. As goddess of morning and evening, she has eaten the stars in an effort to transform night into day. Farther along, on the ceiling of the tomb chamber Nut is pictured again, in two figures symbolizing the morning and evening skies. Below are the remains of Ramses VI's sarcophagus, smashed to pieces by impatient grave-robbers.

From Ramses VI's Tomb, walk east up the hill past the Rest House and behind it to reach the **Tomb of Seti I** (#17), the Theban necropolis' largest and most superbly-decorated tomb. Three long corridors decorated with scenes from the underworld give way to a pillared chamber adorned with an enchanting mural depicting the Pharaoh with deities. In the adjoining room, portions of the relief work remain unfinished, yet the sketched outlines were doubtless applied by a master carver. Descend the staircase to a series of sloping hallways terminating in a large chamber, from which a short ramp leads to the burial area of Seti I. The Pharaoh's mummy was found in the front chamber, inside a remarkable sarcophagus carved from a single piece of alabaster (since removed to the Soane Museum in London). In the rear portion of the mummy shaft, the vaulted ceiling is embellished with a group of astrological figures, depicted on a black background in an unusually asymmetrical, unrepetitive arrangement. On the rear wall, the opening to another shaftway has been blocked off. This passage reputedly terminates in another chamber, but has never been fully excavated. Archeologists uncovered 90m of undecorated passageway before abandoning the project, afraid that the hundreds of workmen needed for hauling out rubble would damage the priceless interior of the tomb proper. Only speculation remains regarding the possibility of any contents. If you have limited time in the Valley of the Kings, try to concentrate your attention on the resting place of Seti I.

Known as the "Tomb of the Harp Players," after a pair of musicians adorning one of its interior chambers, the **Tomb of Ramses III** (#11) is just west of the Rest House. The third corridor of this otherwise perfectly linear tomb abruptly ends, jogging sharply to the right to avoid intersecting with the adjacent tomb of Amenmeses. Such apparent haphazardness has led Egyptologists to speculate as to whether there was a master plan for the Valley of the Kings. It is possible that individual construction projects were so secret that the architects were always taking their chances as regards such mishaps as this one. Despite its flawed plan, however, the tomb of Ramses III has a pleasing interior, decorated with scenes of the afterlife. Off the second corridor, the fourth tiny chamber on the left contains the unusually expressive harp players.

West Thebes' most dramatically situated burial site is the **Tomb of Thutmose III** (#34), reached via a long, steep staircase across a precipitous ravine sandwiched between towering limestone cliffs. To reach this spectacular tomb, follow the dirt road which commences beside the Tomb of Ramses III, leading southwest up the hill (look for the signs). In summer, brave the short walk through the desert heat: it's worth the visit. One of the first pharaohs to be interred in the Valley of the Kings, Thutmose III's primary concern was secrecy, and he chose as inaccessible and uninviting a spot as possible for his tomb. In no other tomb in the Valley of the Kings was greater care taken to camouflage the grave's location; subsequent pharaohs soon learned that these precautions were futile and saved themselves the trouble of hauling stone up and over cliffs. Instead, they decided to site all tombs in one area that was placed under armed guard. Thutmose III's resting place is admirable in large part because of the measures taken to increase security, such as having passages adjoin one another at odd and haphazard angles. An astonishingly sudden and deep rectangular shaft also serves as an obstacle to robbers; it's now traversed by a small and somewhat harrowing footbridge.

The tomb chamber is an oval room with remarkably innovative yet restrained ornamentation. The usual assortment of bright tempera colors is lacking, and the light salmon-colored interior is varied only with touches of black. Simplified hieroglyphic writing, dashed somewhat speedily onto the walls, complement elegant human figures drawn entirely in outline.

In 1898, some local Egyptians directed France's most eminent archeologist, Loret, to the **Tomb of Amenhotep II** (#35). The names of these *felahin* have been forgotten, but they immediately catapulted Loret to international recognition. Although thieves had relieved the tomb of its most valuable riches, the interior was essentially undisturbed, containing, besides the untouched mummy of Amenhotep II, nine other sacred mummies and a burial chamber decorated with a complete, unspoiled set of texts from the *Book of the Dead*. Moreover, the burial chamber is one of the most beautiful in the Valley of the Kings. Only rare touches of bright color enliven the figures of deities, outlined in black, which adorn its muted yellow walls. The decorators apparently intended to create the effect of wallpaper, since the coloring closely resembles that of papyrus paper. The tomb is located down the road from that of Ramses III, due west of the Rest House beyond the fork leading off up the hill toward the Tomb of Thutmose III.

Next door, the **Tomb of Harmhab** (#57) has an unimpressive entrance, opening up into a small well-room, covered with a series of festive reliefs, all of superior quality. The well-room leads into a false burial chamber, its roof supported by two pillars. Grave-robbers were not fooled, however. They unearthed the stairway leading down from this room into the real tomb and made off with the Pharaoh's stock of articles for the afterlife, leaving behind only a handsome red granite sarcophagus which remains *in situ*. The decorations in Harmhab's burial chamber are unfinished. Apparently the Pharaoh passed away before his tomb could be completed.

In addition to the above, the only other tombs likely to be open to the public in 1984 are those of Seti II and Ramses IV. The **Tomb of Seti II** (#15) is located southwest of the Rest House. Take the road leading up the hill toward Thutmose III's tomb and bear right at the first opportunity. This grave consists of a series of long, descending corridors culminating in a small burial chamber which houses a statue of the Pharaoh. Although the painted decorations on the corridor walls are in a fairly good state of preservation, their crafting is inferior to that of the neighboring tombs. The **Tomb of Ramses IV** (#2) is situated outside of the main entrance to the Valley of the Kings. Walk 100m down the paved road away from the entrance booth and the tomb is on the left. Since it is seldom visited, you might have to request that the guard turn on the interior lights. Like the tomb of Seti II, the painted interior carvings retain most of their original color, but lack the vitality and the expressiveness found in many of the other tombs. Closed in 1983, the **Tomb of Merneptah** (#8), north of the Rest House, is worth visiting if it opens in 1984. From the main entrance to the Valley of the Kings, pass the Tomb of Ramses IX and bear right, across the open area. The road to the tomb leads off from here. The descent into the tomb of Merneptah stretches about 80m and the burial chambers contain some huge granite sarcophagus lids.

The **Rest House,** serving expensive refreshments, closes around 1 or 1:30pm in summer.

Mortuary Temples

Treated as gods while living, the pharaohs continued to be worshipped after death, and the mortuary temples of Thebes were intended to provide a setting in which the pharaoh's cult could thrive. With the exception of Dayr el Bahri, the mortuary temples afford very little shade and during the summer months are best visited before the onslaught of the afternoon sun.

The largest mortuary temple, that of Amenhotep III, has been destroyed, except for an impressive pair of statues known as the **Colossi of Memnon,** seated in magnificent isolation on the northern side of the entrance road to the Necropolis. Towering to a height of 20m, these figures of Amenhotep III were Thebes' greatest tourist attraction during the Roman era. Several pharaohs had used them as a quarry for their own mortuary temples, and the figures were in a ruinous state, but they still attracted hordes of the curious. At night, an eerie whistling sound could be heard emanating from the stones, which the Romans interpreted as the voice of Memnon, the legendary son of Aurora, goddess of dawn, greeting his mother at sunrise each day. The sound was actually produced by grains of sand splitting off from the statues as the sun-baked rocks contracted in the cool night air. Unfortunately, the colossi ceased to sing after they were repaired during the reign of Septimus Severus.

Medinet Habu is a series of well-preserved edifices constructed in several stages by various pharaohs. It is located southwest of the Colossi of Memnon. The largest, most impressive structure in the complex is the **Mortuary Temple of Ramses III,** decorated with reliefs of the Pharaoh's numerous successful military campaigns. Ramses III's status as the richest pharaoh of all time is evident throughout. The temple is approached through an elaborate entranceway known as the Pavilion. Two small watchtowers and a massive battlement guard the first doorway, leading through a single gate into an outer courtyard. To the north lies the original temple complex, constructed by

Amenhotep I and Queen Hatshepsut (in ruins), and beyond, the remains of a Sacred Lake. On the court's southern side is the Shrine of Amenertais.

Entering the Temple of Ramses III through the imposing First Pylon, you will reach the First Court. A series of columns runs the length of the south side, while caryatids representing the king once supported the roof to the north. Early Christians converted the Second Court into a church, covering the walls with a layer of mud to obscure the representations of gods and pharaohs. To the Christians' chagrin, the carvings are in all the better condition for having been covered. The Great Hypostyle Hall adjoins this courtyard, and numerous small chambers, originally used to store jewels and valuables, abut. Beyond the Great Hypostyle Hall lie three chambers, in varying states of deterioration, surrounded by small chapels dedicated to a variety of deities.

The **Mortuary Temple of Hatshepsut** rises up from the desert floor against a backdrop of sheer limestone cliffs, hugging the terrain in colonnaded terraces which seem carved out of the mountainside itself. Architecture is spectacularly integrated with environment at Dayr el Bahri (the temple's Arabic name, meaning "Most Splendid of All"). The site is located in the center of the Necropolis, just west of the Tombs of the Nobles off the main north-south road. At a distance, it is difficult to believe that you are looking at an ancient Egyptian temple, for the long, majestic porticoes of the structure have a lean, geometrical form which seems modern. It is not until you glimpse the colorful interior, decked with hieroglyphics and Egyptian deities, that you are convinced of the Temple's authenticity.

Queen Hatshepsut spared no expense in the construction of her mortuary temple, and may have helped design it as well. After the death of her father Thutmose II, Hatshepsut assumed the role of monarch, the only woman ever to have done so in ancient Egypt. She obstinately refused to acknowledge that law forbade a woman from becoming pharaoh, and wore a traditional pharaonic costume and ceremonial beard. Her closest consort was the architect Senmut, a man who exercised considerable influence over the Queen. The structure, currently being excavated by a team of Polish archeologists, has been restored, yet retains much of its original grandeur.

The complex is entered through the Lower Court, where two colonnaded wings abut the northern and southern sides. Pass between these colonnades to reach the Central Court, from which a ramp ascends to the Upper Court. Badly defaced by Christians, it is currently undergoing restoration (closed to the public as of 1983). Pass from the Central Court into two wide colonnaded porticoes on the west side, where the best-preserved carvings remain. To the south of the ramp stands the **Colonnade of the Expedition of Punt,** commemorating an expedition organized by Hatshepsut to the land of Punt, in Africa, to procure valuable myrrh and incense trees for planting in front of the temple. On the southern wall, the eccentric Queen of Punt, her legs swollen with elephantiasis, greets Hatshepsut's Egyptian envoys.

To the south of this magnificent portico is the lovely **Shrine of Hathor,** entered through two covered colonnades with Hathor-headed columns. Unfortunately, the chapel's interior is not illuminated, so bring a flashlight or candle with you to Dayr el Bahri. In the first chamber, Hatshepsut is depicted with several deities, and the ceiling is painted a rich shade of blue inhabited by tiny stars. Though the figure of Hatshepsut was unfortunately scraped off by early Christians, the relief picturing the Queen making offerings to Hathor in the second chamber remains. You can see Hatshepsut drinking from the udder of the cow-goddess Hathor in the shrine's innermost room.

The important **First Colonnade** on the northern side of the main ramp is decorated with a series of reliefs narrating the birth of Hatshepsut. These were intended to counter opposition to Hatshepsut's rule. The Queen is depicted as a boy, and gods bless the mother before recording her divine birth. By associating herself with divinities and assuming male dress and behavior Hatshepsut hoped to win over her opponents.

The **Shaft of Dayr el Bahri,** located north of the Temple of Hatshepsut at the foot of the towering cliffs, was the site of the greatest mummy find in history. In 1876, the local director of antiquities began receiving reports that a steady flow of unknown ancient articles was appearing on the Luxor market, and became convinced that a pharaonic tomb was being plundered. Rounding up the local antique dealers, he questioned them thoroughly concerning the possibility of a newly-discovered tomb, but received no new information. Finally, however, the eldest brother of Luxor's most prominent antiquities merchant, after fighting with his sibling, admitted to the authorities that a grave had been found, and directed them to the spot. The site consisted of a shaft descending 12m into the earth and literally crammed with royal mummies. Amenhotep I, Thutmose II, Thutmose III, Seti I, Ramses I, and Ramses III were all laid to rest in this single shaft. Apparently the high priests, realizing that even the most elaborate precautions failed to prevent grave robbers from disturbing the bodies of deceased pharaohs, made a final successful attempt to hide the mummies by moving their remains to this secret communal grave. In all, there were forty mummies unearthed at Dayr el Bahri, all currently on display in the National Museum in Cairo. Strangely, the body of Hatshepsut was not among them. Though the Queen constructed two tombs for herself, one in the Valley of the Kings, and the other south of Dayr el Bahri, her remains have never been found.

Southeast of Dayr el Bahri, across the highway, is the **Mortuary Temple of Ramses II,** better known as the Ramasseum. It is most conveniently visited in conjunction with the nearby Tombs of the Nobles. Ramses II, who reigned for 67 years during the thirteenth century B.C.E., was an admirer of sculpture who prized size above all other consideration. His favorite statues were those of himself, especially when they were executed in mammoth proportions. The Ramasseum once housed two of the largest of Ramses II's fanatical exercises in narcissism. Though only a shadow of its original 17m, 1000-ton bulk (only the chest, shoulder, and one foot remain), the **Colossus of Ramses II** is considered by many the most awesome remnant of the entire Theban Necropolis. Located in the scanty remains of the Temple's First Court, the beautifully-carved ancient torso looms forcefully, dwarfing the neighboring statues of Osiris. The forefingers alone measured over 1m long. This monolith was transported in one piece from the Pharaoh's granite quarries at Aswan to Thebes. Originally, this colossus and a twin flanked the passageway leading into the Second Court, a colonnaded square whose pillars were carved with representations of Osiris. The Second Court is reputedly that identified by the Roman historian Diodorus as the Tomb of Ozymandias. The connection with this pharaoh arises from speculation that Ramses II's second names, "User-ma-re," when corrupted might sound like Ozymandias. This story, as well as the magnificent Colossi of Ramses II, provided Shelley with the inspiration to pen his famous poem "Ozymandias."

The westernmost portion of the temple is completely ruined, though bits of relief work, expertly sculpted, still poke out of the rubble.

Seti I, father of Ramses II, was a great warrior who enlarged the Egyptian empire to include the island of Cyprus and parts of Mesopotamia. The **Mor-**

tuary Temple of Seti I contained some of the priceless treasure brought back by the Pharaoh from his successful campaigns, as well as some of the finest relief work ever executed in ancient Egypt. Though the treasure is gone, the carvings remain, despite the condition of the temple. The quality of craft in these traditional temple decorations is unparalleled. The best-preserved section of the edifice is the **Hypostyle Hall,** its roof ornamented with winged sun-disks; eight small chambers open onto it. Here Seti I is depicted before various deities, offering incense and performing sacred rites. At the west end, the goddesses Mut and Hathor suckle the infant Pharaoh. Beyond the Hypostyle Hall is a **sanctuary,** where the sacred boat of Amon was housed. The sanctuary's walls are ornamented with equally splendid reliefs of Seti I. The overall structure of the temple presents an imposing spectacle. The large, original entrance remains, possessing attractively-inscribed decorative work.

Tombs of the Nobles

Situated just a few hundred meters southeast of Dayr el Bahri is West Thebes' most crowded burial site. There are over 300 Tombs of the Nobles, and although many of these aristocratic graves are closed, a good number of the most interesting tombs are usually open. The area is divided up into five regions, for each of which a separate ticket must be procured: the Tombs of Rekhmire (#100) and Sennofer (#96); the Tombs of Ramose (#55), Userhet the Scribe (#56), and Khaemt (#57); the Tombs of Nakht (#52) and Menna (#69); the Tombs of Asasif; and the Temple and Tombs of Dayr el Medina. Tombs near those listed on the ticket are also open on occasion; when you reach the site, keep your eyes open for accessible tombs. As in the rest of West Thebes, it is advantageous to come equipped with a flashlight or candle, since many of the tombs are unlit. You don't need a guide in order to tour the tombs; adjacent to a village, the site is always full of local Egyptians who will point out the way for you. Nonetheless, if you can get your hands on it, a map of the area can be useful.

Throughout the New Kingdom, Theban aristocrats held *de facto* control over much of the pharaoh's empire. Even the most petty court cases officially fell under the pharaoh's jurisdiction, since according to tradition it fell to the ruler to decide upon all matters pertinent to the destiny and well-being of Egypt. However, since one person was hardly in a position to make informed decisions concerning every trivial matter, the pharaoh was typically surrounded by a barrage of advisers who supplied him with information and recommendations regarding matters of state. Depending on the personality and acuity of the ruler, these secretaries of state could wield a great deal of power or very little. The pharaoh often remained ignorant of the most crucial political developments, as individual members of the elite, thirsting for power, fought among themselves for control of the kingdom. Given this state of affairs, some aristocrats grew wealthy and influential, if not always respected in all quarters. They affected pharaonic status by amply providing themselves with luxuries for the afterlife and devising well-hidden underground tombs. Unlike the divine pharaoh, who would live among the gods after his death, the Theban aristocrats needed more assurance that a comfortable existence awaited them in the afterlife. Accordingly, every facet of life on earth which they wished to retain in the hereafter was carefully recorded on the walls of their tombs. The decoration is thus more naturalistic than the reliefs found in the tombs of self-satisfied pharaohs. Artists freely followed their inclinations, limning scenes of everyday Egyptian life. Owing to the fact that the limestone in this portion of the Necropolis was inferior, artisans were prevented from carving in relief. Instead, mural ornament was painted on a white-washed stone surface in intricate detail.

Starting at the northwest portion of the site, tomb #100 belongs to Rekhmire, a governor of Thebes who was an advisor of Thutmose III and prided himself on his breadth of learning and administrative genius. The **Tomb of Rekhmire** is comprised of biographical narratives. You'll see a trial of tax evaders by Rekhmire, who sits with a set of rolled papyrus texts strewn at the foot of his judgment throne. This painting indicates that written law existed as early as 1500 B.C.E. In the second chamber, Rekhmire is seen supervising the delivery of farm produce and overseeing the construction of an entrance portal to the great Temple at Karnak.

Proceed to #96, the **Tomb of Sennofer,** also known as the "Tomb of the Vines," after the filigreed grapevine that creeps along the ceiling. A delightful lattice of purple and green simulates the cool repose of a shady arbor. Sennofer, overseer of the royal gardens of Amon under Amenhotep II, apparently wished to have his occupation known in the hereafter. The plan of the tomb is as unusual as its decor—a curving wall leads into the first room, which in turn leads straight on into the pillared burial chamber. In the rear right hand corner as you enter the tomb, a priest robed in leopard skin purifies Sennofer and his wife, as they make offerings to the gods of the underworld. A single ticket admits you to the Tombs of Rekhmire and Sennofer. A flashlight is needed for the Tomb of Sennofer; otherwise, the guard will show you around by lantern.

The **Tomb of Ramose,** southeast of the tombs of Rekhmire and Sennofer down a short dirt road, was built during a time of religious transition from the polytheism of the Old Kingdom to monotheistic worship of Ra, the sun-god. Ramose attained preeminence during the reigns of Amenhotep III and Akhnaton, and was apparently one of the first converts to the new monotheism. His unfinished tomb is decorated with both conventional carved figures in the Old Kingdom style and the more naturalistic paintings characteristic of the new period. The sun-worship introduced by Akhnaton transformed the great god Amon into nothing more than a local deity, broke sharply with ancient beliefs, and upset the status quo of the priesthood. Akhnaton's religious reforms swept Egypt swiftly, the Tomb of Ramose being remarkable testimony to the new devotion to Ra. The tomb's main hypostyle chamber remains unfinished, and is decorated in both the old and new styles. The eastern walls (to the left as you enter), carved in unpainted relief, reflect the stiffer, more tradition-bound tastes of the Old Kingdom, with scenes of Ramose making offerings to the gods. In contrast, the figures on the rear wall are more realistic and expressive; the Pharaoh and his wife hold before them the symbols of life and happiness, bathed in fourteen rays of the sacred sun.

Continue on from the Tomb of Ramose to the **Tomb of Userhet the Scribe** (#56), only a few meters to the south. Although an early Christian destroyed most of the female figures adorning the walls (after making his home within the confines of its burial chamber) the Tomb's decor still has a festive quality, which the interior frescoes accomplish by the use of unusual pink tones. Amenhotep II's royal scribe, Userhet chose to adorn his resting place with scenes from everyday life. The left-hand entrance wall narrates scenes from rural life: farmers brand their cattle, and grain is collected for the royal storehouse. The refined figures are executed in remarkable detail. Opposite, a line of men awaits haircuts as the barber carefully trims the locks of a client. The inner corridor holds the tomb's most engaging scene: Userhet in a chariot chases a herd of fleeing jackals, gazelles, and hares, his bow drawn taut and the reins tied behind his back.

Just south of this beautiful tomb, off the main dirt road, is the **Tomb of Khaemt,** an aide-de-camp who supervised the granaries of Upper and Lower Egypt during the reign of Amenhotep III; many of the murals in his funeral chamber recall this important occupation. On the rear wall is an exquisite portrait of Renenet, the snake-goddess of the granaries, and farther along corn-laden boats dock at the busy port of Thebes. The subjects are carved in extraordinary detail. In the second chamber, notice the remarkable portrait of the jackal-headed Osiris, with Hathor beside him. The third chamber contains a plaster cast of a bust of Khaemt; the original is now in Berlin. Admission to the Tombs of Ramose, Userhet the Scribe, and Khaemt is by a single ticket.

Slightly north of the Tomb of Ramose a trail leads off the main dirt road, winding east a short distance to the **Tomb of Nakht.** The warm, vivid paintings in its interior chamber memorialize the life of Nakht, scribe of the royal granaries under Thutmose IV. Notice the portrait of Nakht and his wife at the rear of the first chamber. Their son presents them with geese and flowers, and below Nakht's chair, a large cat eats contentedly. An aging photograph on display in the second chamber is all that remains of an exquisite statue of Nakht lost at sea on its way to America during World War I.

Check whether the **Tomb of Userhet the Prophet** is open. (Walk due south from the Tomb of Nakht along the dirt road). Though the Tomb is in a poor state, it contains a fine painting of Userhet with his wife and sister, seated beneath a fig-laden tree drinking the water of life from a golden vessel. Before them, reflected in a small pond, the souls of Userhet and his spouse, represented as human-headed birds, also sip the precious fluid.

From the Tomb of Nakht, you can head north a short way and bear west toward the **Tomb of Menna,** mainly of interest for the naturalistic frescoes depicting wildlife. Menna, the land steward under Thutmose IV, is seen fishing and fowling. Birds take flight from the swaying papyrus thickets, while crocodile and fish swim about in the waters below. The tomb did not belong originally to Menna; in the first corridor to the right as you enter the tomb, a patch of stucco has flaked off, revealing an older set of decorations. Apparently, Menna stole his burial place from another noble, a practice not unheard-of in these times. The Tombs of Nakht and Menna are covered by a single admission ticket.

Southwest of Dayr el Bahri, east of the Tombs of Nakht and Menna lies **Asasif,** a region of the Tombs of the Nobles which became the most popular aristocratic burial area during the Twenty-fifth and Twenty-sixth Dynasties (ca. tenth century B.C.E.). The finest aspect of this portion of the necroplis is the well-known **Tomb of Kheruef** (#192), constructed during the fourteenth century B.C.E. for one of Amenophis III's most powerful and influential stewards. Enter the burial site through an outer courtyard containing other tombs, where a series of well-wrought reliefs stands against a protecting wall. To the left of the doorway as you enter, look at the ceremonial dance in which a jumping bird and monkey are accompanied by flautists and drummers. On the right is a striking portrait of Amenhotep III surrounded by his sixteen princesses.

The other Asasif tomsbs are sporadically open to the public. Particularly noteworthy are the **Tomb of Pabasa** (#279), with a grand staircase leading down to the first chamber; the **Tomb of Pedmenopet** (#33), the largest tomb in the Theban Necropolis (a good flashlight or the assistance of a guide is required to negotiate the ladders); and the **Tomb of Ibi** (#36). In the latter, a steep staircase descends to some austere chambers. All of the Asasif Tombs are part of a single ticket. Several of them are kept locked and you have to hunt down the guard in order to be admitted.

To get to the scanty remains of the **Tomb Workers' Walled City,** start from the Ramasseum and follow the small road west to Dayr el Medina. Nearby, the small **Temple of Dayr el Medina** ("Monastery of the Town") is an elegant shrine dating from the Ptolemaic era. Dedicated to Hathor, the goddess of love, and

Maat, the deity of justice, the temple was named during Christian times, when monks constructed a monastery next door. The temple is entered through a vestibule adorned with two palm columns. The doorway leading into the center chapel (of three) is flanked by seven heads of Hathor and inside, each shrine is enhanced by relief carvings depicting scenes from the *Book of the Dead*. A number of aristocratic tombs are situated near the temple; the finest is the **Tomb of Sennutem** (#36). This prominent noble held the esteemed title of "Servant in the Place of Truth." His burial chamber is oval, enlivened by an enchanting, well-preserved mural. Osiris is shown enbalming Sennutem's mummy. Across the room are agricultural scenes, with wheatfields, flowers, and fruit. Scenes from Sennutem's journey to the underworld, including the opening of his tomb, ornament the unusually low, curved ceiling. The Temple and Tombs of Dayr el Medina and the Workers' Walled City fall under a single admission ticket.

Valley of the Queens

During the later years of the New Kingdom, a special burial area was chosen for the wives and children of the pharaohs. In the southwest corner of West Thebes, directly west of the Colossi of Memnon at the end of the main road, the Valley of the Queens contains fewer than thirty royal tombs, but its most important burial sites are beautifully-decorated and worth visiting. A single ticket will admit you to all the tombs in the Valley of the Queens, although only a few will be open to the public on a given day. Illumination in the tombs is sometimes poor, so try to bring a flashlight.

Closest relations of the pharaoh traditionally had been buried beside the monarch. This arrangement changed during the reign of Ramses I (fourteenth century B.C.E.): princes, consorts, and wives from this time on were buried in the Valley of the Queens. The quality of these tombs varies enormously—some are little more than large holes in the ground, while others sparkle with a profusion of ornament.

The **Tomb of Amon-Hir Khopshef** (#55), who died at a very young age, is nonetheless richly decked with low-relief carvings. In the large entrance hall, the young prince, as a nine-year-old boy, is introduced by his father Ramses III to each of the gods. In the rear chamber, the sarcophagus which once held the mummy of the royal infant remains *in situ*. Nearby, the modest **Tomb of Queen Titi** (#52) houses some striking murals. Titi was the mother of Akhnaton and a consort of Amenhotep III. Two corridors give way to a tomb chamber, abutted by three small chapels where the finest reliefs are to be found. In one, the goddess Hathor is shown changing from a cow into human form in order to bless the Queen with water from the Nile. The rear chamber depicts Titi praying to a group of gods seated about offering-tables. South of the Tomb of Titi is the **Tomb of Prince Kha-em-Waset** (#44), another son of Ramses III buried in the Valley of the Queens at a young age. It is not an exceptional tomb but does have some traditional relief work in good condition.

Although it is officially closed to the public and cannot be visited without special permission, the **Tomb of Queen Nefertari** (#66) is the most beautiful tomb in the Valley of the Queens and worth the trouble to visit. Nefertari (Arabic for "Beautiful Companion"), wife and closest consort of Ramses II, not surprisingly was provided with a sumptuous place of rest. The Pharaoh devoted considerable attention to provisions for her afterlife. In the entrance hall, to the left as you enter, the soul of Nefertari worships the sun rising between two lions, symbols of past and future. The side chamber is graced with a fine representation of Nefertari adoring seven sacred cows.

Esna and Edfu

South of Luxor and easily visited together in a single daytrip are two Ptolemaic/Roman temples at Esna and Edfu. The first-century B.C.E. Temple of Khnum at Esna is a relatively small but charming structure, while its counterpart, the Temple of Horus at Edfu is the largest and best-preserved temple in all of Egypt.

Transportation

Esna and Edfu are generally visited either en route to Luxor or Aswan or as a daytrip from Luxor. It is possible to visit Edfu as a daytrip from Aswan. Nine trains run daily in each direction between Luxor and Aswan, stopping at Esna and Edfu. They take twice as long as service taxi: Luxor-Esna 1½-2 hours, Esna-Edfu 2 hours. For Hurghada, take the train to Qena (LE1.80 second class) and then a bus. If you pick up the bus en route to Luxor or Aswan, there will probably be no seats. But the bus is a reasonable choice for the first leg of the journey to Esna or Edfu. Buses leave Luxor from in front of Luxor Temple (see Luxor for departure times and fares).

Probably the most efficient and sensible option is to travel by service taxi. Luxor-Esna should cost 60pt, Esna-Edfu 75pt, Edfu-Luxor LE1.35. Luxor-Edfu costs LE2 since you have to take an Aswan-bound service taxi and pay full fare to Aswan. Luxor-Esna takes 45 minutes, Esna-Edfu one hour. A private taxi is only a sensible option for 5 to 7 people en route between Luxor and Aswan. Probably the best price you can get for the trip with stops at Esna and Edfu is LE20 for the entire venture. As long as you are paying the money, you might as well stop at Kom Ombo (see below) in addition and make it a very full day of sightseeing.

Esna

The Great Hypostyle Hall, built during the reign of the Roman Emperor Claudius, is all that remains of the magnificent **Temple of Khnum** at Esna. The temple lies nearly ten meters below the street level in an open pit in the middle of the busy agricultural community of Esna. Esna itself remains untainted by the trickle of foreigners who come to view its only pharaonic monument. The short walk through town to the site traverses winding alleys, passing some beautiful *mashribiya* (wooden-screen) windows and small medieval mosques. There is a vista of the Nile from near the temple and a small tourist bazaar to visit. The amiable townspeople are more than obliging about showing you the way. To reach the temple from the service taxi station, walk south along the main street for about five minutes. The site lies just a couple of blocks east of the road. From the Nile, head south along the river about ½km past the bridge connecting Esna with the east bank. The temple is located just a few hundred meters in from the river. Open 7am-6pm; admission LE1, 50pt with student ID.

Khnum was a ram-headed creator god who moulded the first human on a potter's wheel. Although begun in the Eighteenth Dynasty, the Temple of Khnum is largely a Roman creation—in many ways a feeble imitation of the technical and artistic achievements of the legacy which they inherited. As one of the largest communities south of Luxor along the Nile, Esna was an important regional center, and the pharaohs of the Eighteenth Dynasty, desiring stronger popular support, dedicated this temple to the local deity. At one point the grand portico was used as a house, then the temple was covered with sand, and served as foundation for peasant homes. Archeologists who unearthed the magnificent hallway found it to be in excellent condition. Today the temple forms an incongruous spectacle in Esna; as if in revenge for the centuries it spent as sub-basement to the humble neighborhood, Khnum threatens to engulf the tiny houses.

Many of the interior carvings are of an inferior quality. The Romans, in an effort to decorate the temple in a traditional pharaonic manner, produced a forced and uncomfortable result. A procession of stiff, strangely-deformed figures marches solemnly across the walls of the hallway; traditionally stylized bodies combine with life-like limbs, a strange amalgam of naturalistic and orthodox styles. Roman leaders Septimus Severus, Caracalla, and Julia Domna are seen paying a visit to Esna. Another scene near the exit illustrates a potter's wheel being offered to the god Khnum. Outside, on the side walls of the Temple, the King seizes his enemies by the hair. In front of the Temple are the ruins of an early Christian chapel.

Edfu

Egypt's largest and best-preserved pharaonic temple is the magnificent **Temple of Horus** at Edfu, a massive labyrinth of dark chambers and towering pillars. Beyond the entrance of the imposing pylon and the Great Court retires an inner sanctuary hewn out of granite. Like the Temple of Khnum at Esna, the Temple at Edfu was one of the last great Egyptian efforts at monument-building. Dedicated to Horus, the falcon-headed son of Osiris who avenged his father's death, the Ptolemaic structure took over 200 years to construct and was completed only in 57 B.C.E. If you've visited the temple at Dendera, you'll be struck by the remarkable similarity of design between that temple and the one at Edfu.

The colossal pylons of the Temple of Horus are visible from the center of Edfu. From the main service taxi station, walk two minutes inland (away from the Nile) to reach the site. Open 7am-6pm; admission LE2, LE1 with student ID. Next door to the temple, the **Andrea Rest House** sells cold mineral water for a steep 75pt, and has public restrooms.

In ancient times Edfu was the site of a number of important religious festivals centering around the life and death of the falcon-god Horus. During the annual "Union with the Solar Disk," Horus' earthly form was brought to the roof of the temple to be rejuvenated by the rays of the sun. This rite was generally performed in conjunction with the celebration of the New Year. Another important ritual was the "Coronation Festival." In this, a falcon was selected from the sacred aviary to become the living symbol of Horus during the following year. After secret rites were performed, the bird was crowned in the temple's main court and then triumphantly paraded to the interior of the temple, where he reigned in darkness for one year.

From where you enter the site, by the ticket kiosk, walk the full length of the structure in order to enter the walls of the temple complex through a wide entrance at the far end. The entire temple is surrounded by a massive exterior wall, closed off at one end by a pylon through which the temple proper is entered. The main doorway through the pylon is flanked by two battlements rising to a height of 36m and guarded by two noble granite falcons. Enter the temple through the twelve mammoth columns of the **Great Hypostyle Hall,** continuing on to the **Second Hypostyle Hall,** outfitted with a similar arrangement of somewhat smaller pillars. Doorways on either side head out to the **Corridor of Victory,** a narrow exterior passageway running between the temple and its protective wall. Note the progressive narrowing of the temple as you proceed toward the end containing the inner sanctum. Several elegant lion's heads jut from the otherwise smooth brick surface to survey the narrow corridor.

Two staircases lead up to the roof (closed in 1983) from the Hall of Offerings, which follows the Second Hypostyle Hall. Next comes the Central Hall, flanked on two sides by small chapels. To the right as you enter, a doorway leads to the **Court of the New Year,** where the sky-goddess Nut is curved into a slender L-shape on the ceiling. Beyond the central hallway is the sanctuary, where the cult statue of Horus was once housed (only the foundations of the figure remain). Fully enclosed within the outer shell of the main temple and surrounded by a corridor on three sides, the sanctuary is inscribed with scenes depicting Horus and other deities. Eight smaller chambers open off the corridor. The central one at the rear of the temple houses a modern reconstruction of the sacred barge used to convey the cult statue during important ceremonies. Outside the temple, directly in front of the main entrance pylon, is a well-preserved **Roman mammisi** (birth house), where the birth of Horus was reenacted each year amidst festive celebration. Next to the village of el Mahemid, about 15km north of Edfu along the east bank of the Nile, are the scanty pharaonic ruins of **el Kab.**

Kom Ombo

A short jaunt north of Aswan by service taxi or train will bring you to Kom Ombo—the site of an Egyptian temple as unique for its location as for its rigorously symmetrical construction. Unlike most other temples in Egypt, Kom Ombo is still situated along the banks of the great green Nile, giving much the same visual impression today as it did when completed during Ptolemaic times. The sanctuary's real peculiarity, however, lies in the fact that every architectural element has a twin. Double doorways lead into double chambers and sanctuaries after passing through double halls and past double colonnades. The temple was dedicated to two gods: Sobek, the toothsome crocodile god, and Haroeris, the winged, falcon-headed sun-disk. The priests were diplomatic even when it came to supernatural matters; not wanting to offend either god, they ordered everything to be built in tandem.

Practical Information

Most people visit Kom Ombo as a daytrip from Aswan. However, the town is easily accessible as a stop-off between Aswan and Luxor. One hour (40km) north of Aswan by rail, Kom Ombo receives all but one of the regular Aswan-Luxor trains, and all of the buses between Aswan and Luxor. Coming from Aswan, however, the most efficient connection is provided by frequent service taxis (50pt, thirty minutes) which leave from the taxi station next to the main bus station in Aswan. If you are traveling in summer, it is a good idea to get up early (6-7am), when most of the locals travel by service taxi.

The remains of the Temple are 4km from the center of town. The bus, train, and service taxi stations in Kom Ombo are all next to each other along the main street. A covered pickup truck (5pt) runs all day long between the river near the ruins and the center of town. If you wish to hire a private taxi, don't pay more than LE1 one way, LE2 round trip. To catch the 5pt truck to the ruins, look for the minaret of the large mosque on the main street; the truck leaves from behind the mosque, one block off of the main street. From where the truck lets you off it is a 1 km walk along the river to the temple. Open 7am-6pm; admission LE1, 50pt with student ID.

Sights

Although a temple has stood at Kom Ombo since the time of the Middle Kingdom, the oldest portions of its ruins have been removed to the Louvre and the Cairo Museum. What you see now dates from the Ptolemaic and Roman periods. The **main temple** dominates the site from a hill overlooking the Nile. After its abandonment during the decline of the Roman Empire, the rising waters of the river inundated the site, and left the temple almost completely submerged in sand when they receded. In later years the portions of the temple still above ground were used as a quarry for a neighboring edifice and as a result the side walls have vanished. Somehow, though, the temple exhibits much of its original magnificence. Enter the structure through the paved court, whose columns retain their original coloring. In the center sits the foundation of a granite altar once used for ritual ceremonies. Pass from the court into the **pronaos,** with carvings strung across the far wall. The figures near the top were located above the concealing layer of sand and were consequently defaced by unappreciative Christians. In the interior of the temple are the less substantial remains of the **Hall of Offerings** and the inner sanctuaries dedicated to Sobek and Haroeris.

Adjoining the northern edge of the temple are the Roman **water supply tanks,** comprised of two wells joined to a stepped vat, and to the west the remains of a Roman mammisi. The **Chapel of Hathor,** located directly south of the main temple, houses a remarkable collection of crocodile mummies, unearthed near the road leading away from the site (closed to the public in 1983).

Daraw

The village of Daraw resounds with the gurgling and farting of camels every Tuesday morning as Sudanese merchants and Bishari tribespeople convene for the camel market. The Bishari are traditional Saharan nomads with a unique language and culture. Some of the men conduct business in full dress: flowing pants, fighting sword and dagger, and a cloak draped over their shoulders. Some of the men also wear a gold ring in their nose, and long hair dressed with camel oil. One of the most appealing things about the camel market is that it has been almost entirely neglected by the local tourist industry.

Service taxis go to Daraw from Kom Ombo, 8km to the north (10pt, five minutes) and Aswan, 32 km to the south (50pt, twenty minutes). The camel market runs from 5-10am; towards the end things begin to peter out. A good strategy would be to rise very early in Aswan, visit the camel market, and then move on to see the temple at Kom Ombo. To reach the camel market, you have to walk through an equally large **fruit and vegetable market** where the Nubian women do their weekly shopping. Flanking the camel market is a livestock market where cattle, water buffalo, sheep, and goats are traded and sold. In case you are interested, the price for a large strong camel is LE500.

Aswan

Situated just downstream from the first cataracts of the Nile, Aswan grew and flourished as the frontier town of Egypt. The alluvial plains north of the city succumb to the desert, and the fertile land expires just at Aswan's doorstep. Having prospered as the trading center between Egypt and the rest of Africa, Aswan remains a gateway to the desolate lands of the Sudan and of Nubia, the latter now inundated by Lake Nassar. More recently, Aswan emerged as Egypt's premier winter resort offering a warm and dry climate along with a host of ruins—pharaonic, Coptic, and Islamic—to explore. The High Dam outside of town may change all this, as immense and eerie Lake Nassar adds moisture to the air while the dam powers Aswan's burgeoning industry. For the time being, though, Aswan is still a city of only 200,000 inhabitants, small enough to be pleasant, yet of sufficient size to have a distinctive character, history, and style. The long riverside Corniche is Egypt's most beautiful and spotless boulevard, situated directly across from an archipelago of small islands huddled together to form one of the most beautiful settings along the entire length of the Nile.

Orientation and Practical Information

You are almost never more than two blocks from the river in Aswan, making it the only town in Egypt in which you'll never get lost. Most of the city lies along or between three long avenues running parallel to the east bank of the Nile. By far the most handsome and prominent of the trio is the riverside **Corniche el Nil,** featuring most of the fancy hotels, travel agencies, public services, restaurants, etc. Two blocks in, Aswan's busiest and most picturesque lane, **Sharia el Souk** features a little of something for everyone with everything from sellers of towering aromatic mounds of spice to tacky tourist trinket stands with pseudo-marble busts of Queen Nefertiti. Last and perhaps least, running between the Corniche and the market street, **Sharia Abtal el Tahrir** starts at the youth hostel and culminates in its own little cluster of overpriced tourist bazaars.

Tourist Information: Corniche el Nil (tel. 32 97). Not directly on the Corniche. Walk north of the Abu Simbel Hotel. You should not walk along the Nile side of the street (the building is obscured by a small park). On the other side of the park is a large arcade containing the tourist office. Open Sun.-Thurs. 8am-2pm, Fri. 5-7:30pm.

American Express: Corniche el Nil. Next door to the entrance to the Grand Hotel. Open 9am-5pm and 7-9pm. Not a banking service. You can't get U.S. dollars here.

Post Office: Next door to the Municipal Pool (see below). Your mail will fare better if you send it from a major hotel. All the reception desks sell stamps.

Telephone, Telegram, and Telex: Two doors south of EgyptAir. Comparatively efficient for international calls.

Train Station: Northeast corner of town, at the start of Sharia el Souk. Ten trains a day to Luxor and Cairo. The ticket window is open for several different two-hour stretches daily. The least crowded time for buying tickets is the last shift from 8-10pm. Reserve seats for Cairo several days in advance. Southbound trains run nine times a day for the High Dam where boats for Wadi Halfa and Abu Simbel depart.

Bus Station: Three blocks south and one block west of the train station. Four to six buses daily to Kom Ombo, Edfu, Esna, and Luxor, sometimes air-conditioned.

Service Taxi Station: Just north of the bus station and one block south of the Ramses Hotel. Frequent connections to Daraw (50pt) and Kom Ombo (50pt) and sporadic service to Luxor (LE2). In summer come early.

EgyptAir: Corniche el Nil. At the southern edge of town, before the Cataract Hotel. Frequent flights to Abu Simbel. Book in advance.

Nile Navigation Company: Next door to the tourist office. Erratic hours. They're supposed to know when what boats go to Abu Simbel (see Abu Simbel).

Sudanese Nile Navigation: Sharia Abtal el Tahrir (tel. 20 39). Details on the boat to Wadi Halfa. (See Sudan chapter for details.)

Hydrofoil to Abu Simbel: Out of commission in 1983. Should be running again by 1984. Ask at tourist office. Fare LE10. Six-hour journey.

Local Ferry to Elephantine Island: across from EgyptAir—just before the park, next to the Cataract Hotel, climb down the steps to the Nile. Runs every fifteen minutes; 10pt per person. There are other ferries but they tend not to be very keen on tourists.

Hospital: at the eastern edge of town. Extremely crowded and understaffed. If you need treatement, return to Cairo if at all possible.

Municipal Swimming Pool: Corniche el Nil. Across from the Rowing Club Restaurant. Admission 50pt. Very crowded. Sometimes uncomfortable for foreign women.

Hotel Swimming Pools: The **New Cataract** and the **Oberoi Hotels** both officially charge LE2 admission but neither consistently enforces the fee. The former is located at the southern edge of the Corniche, while the Oberoi has its own ferry (no charge) that runs to the hotel located on the northern half of Elephantine Island.

Accommodations

Nowhere in Egypt is the difference between high season and low season as pronounced as in Aswan, especially regarding accommodations. During high season (October to April) expect to pay between 10 and 50% more than the rates listed here. In the low-season luxury hotels sit empty and become desperate for business, sometimes lowering their rates by as much as 60%. There are fewer very cheap hotels in Aswan than in Luxor, as the city favors slightly more comfortable "middle-class" hotels, with rooms that always have fans and sometimes air conditioning, often at reasonable prices. The area around the train station is pleasant to stay in, while the center of town is best for more impecunious travelers. Rooms are available in the city center, but they cost more. A campground is in the park opposite the Tourist Office, where you can put up a tent free of charge.

Youth Hostel (IYHF), Sharia Abtal el Tahrir, by the train station (tel. 21 3). Entrance to the section for foreigners on the side of the building. Crowded large rooms that are difficult to sleep in—people are getting up at all hours to catch trains. Not too clean. Amuse yourself in the evenings by watching movies for free, as the hostel has a direct line of view onto an open-air movie theater. Kung Fu movies seem the most popular, though you might be able to catch spaghetti Westerns. If you have little interest in grade B cinema, you may find the soundtrack, which runs until 2am, a bit hard to sleep through. Exceedingly hot in summer. Dorm-style accommodations, segregated by sex. 60pt with IYHF card, 70pt without. If you tire of the hostel scene but are pinched for piasters, the **Merwa Hotel,** across the street and next to the cinema, offers shabby but adequate rooms for LE1.50 per person.

Ramses Hotel, one block east and two blocks south of the train station. Entrance just off Sharia Abtal el Tahrir. Off-season rates for large spotless rooms with air-conditioning and good bathrooms are quite low: rooms on the far side (near the noisome cinema) LE3 per person, rooms on the near side LE4 per person. In the middle of peak season rates a flat 50% higher. Rooms cleaned and sheets changed daily. Management very helpful in arranging taxi rentals. Optional breakfast a rip-off for LE1; you can order sandwiches from the bar by the lobby for 10-15pt and tea for 20pt.

Hotel Continental Aswan, Corniche el Nil, across from el Shati Restaurant (tel. 23 11). Simplest and cheapest rooms in town. Informal atmosphere. Good place to meet fellow backpackers. Wear shoes when you go to the bathroom. Singles LE1, doubles LE1.50, triples LE2.25.

Hathor Hotel, Corniche el Nil, 1 km south of the tourist office (tel. 25 90). Entrance on the alley leading off the Corniche just south of the market area of Sharia Shawarbi. Very clean rooms with cramped adjoining bathroom and shower. Some rooms have a nice view of the Nile and the island. Off-season, rooms go for as little as LE6 for a single, LE8 for a double. Even in shoulder season you may have to pay about 20% more, in high season up to 60% more. Air conditioning LE1.50 extra. All prices include breakfast, but it is not served until 7am, which can be inconveniently late in summer.

Rosewan Hotel. Turn right as you leave the station, head past a gas station, and take the next left. The hotel is on the right in the middle of the following block. Clean and hospitable, though slightly overpriced. Good-sized, if very plain and somewhat dusty rooms. Owner-manager Farouk Nassar is friendly and looks after his guests. Low season: singles LE2, singles with shower LE4; doubles LE4, doubles with shower LE6; triples LE7.50. High season (Oct.-April): all rates a flat 50% higher. If full, try the **Saffa Hotel** next door which is dark and a little dingy but at least has sinks in each room; singles LE3, doubles LE4.

Abu Shelib Hotel, corner of Sharias Abas-Farad and el Souk (tel. 30 51). Good location in the center of town, one block from the Nile. Simple rooms; management not very friendly. Official off-season rates: singles LE5, singles with bath LE6; doubles LE6, with bath LE7. Between June and August you should have no difficulty chipping LE1 off any of these rates.

Food

The restaurant situation parallels the hotel situation in Aswan: there is little that is both good and rock-bottom cheap, but for just a little more you get a lot more.

Gomhoreya Restaurant, next to the train station—on the left as you exit. Excellent reasonably-priced food. Delicious and very large full-course menu for LE2 including salad, bread, *tahina,* vegetables, pasta, and a choice of chicken, *köfte,* or roast beef. The *köfte* features some of the best meat you're likely to eat in Egypt as a budget traveler. The menu-dinners are so large you might consider splitting one between two people. You have to sit indoors if you wish to order beer. Two doors down, across from the hostel, the nameless **snack bar** has excellent fresh yogurt for 20pt (15pt to go) and simple sandwiches for 15pt.

El Shati Restaurant, Corniche el Nil, beneath the Eastmar sign directly on the Nile. A delicious selection of fruit juices: banana 30pt, mango 55pt, lemon, very fresh grape, or *guave* juice, or *kirkaday* 25pt. Try the pineapple juice with milk for 25pt. Decent full-course menu for LE1.50 with a choice of beef, chicken, or steak entree. Complete menu with fish entree LE1.30.

Restaurant el Nil, across from the above and only two doors down from the Continental Hotel. Good place for fish. Full menus with fish or meat entree LE2.

The nicest place for tea or a soft drink is down the Corniche in the park just north of the Cataract Hotel. Full of Egyptians, the cafe here has almost no mark-up, with tea only 8pt.

Sights

Know from the beginning: Aswan is not, like its northern cousin Luxor, a city of great sights. Although there are pharaonic, Coptic, Islamic, and modern monuments, none of these attractions are outstanding treasures. The noteworthy exception is the Temple at Philae (see below). Aswan's real charm lies in its inviting market streets and its beautiful situation on the Nile. Around Aswan the river suddenly ceases to be sandwiched by green fields, and courses through the stark landscape of the desert. On the west bank of the Nile, directly across from the city, the wind-blown sand forms dunes with elegant razor-sharp edges and peaceful sweeping contours. In between lie a host of tiny islets upon which rest most of the city's official attractions. The largest of these, **Elephantine Island,** is the only island which is connected by regular ferries (10pt; leaves from the spot across from EgyptAir—see Practical Information). As you disembark from the ferry, you'll see the **Aswan Archeological Museum,** with its modest collection of local finds, on the left. Open in winter daily 9am-5pm, in summer Sun.-Thurs. 8:30am-1pm, Fri. 8:30-11:30am; admission LE1, 50pt for students with ID. The employees will serve you tea for 20pt.

If you walk past the museum's entrance to the water's edge, you come to a sycamore tree. Directly beneath the tree, carved into a rock by the water is the celebrated **Nilometer,** a long cylindrical shaft that measured the height of the Nile. In ancient times nothing was of greater practical significance than the testimony of the Nilometer. When it proclaimed that the river was high the annual flooding of the Nile would be profuse and the harvest correspondingly bountiful. When the Nilometer indicated a dearth of water, it foretold times of hunger and misery. The Nilometer is hollowed out of the stones of an ancient **harbor quay,** best viewed by *felucca* from the water. The upper stones of the quay date from the Roman period, while the lower stones stem from pharaonic times and still bear large inscriptions and cartouches from the reigns of Thutmose III and Amenophis III.

Elephantine Island was the original site of the city of Aswan. All of the surviving remains have been excavated on the southeast corner of the island, directly behind the museum. The ruins are comparatively uninteresting and consist of traces of an ancient city, including the remains of the large **Temple of Khnum** and a small stone **Temple of Heqa-Ib,** dedicated to one of the island's ancient rulers. On the other side of the ruined city, at the very southeastern tip of the island (particularly delightful when viewed from the Nile) is a little Ptolemaic temple that has been reconstructed by German archeologists. Obviously, many of the blocks are not original, but its situation peacefully facing the water compensates for what it lacks in authenticity. Most visitors confine themselves to a brief tour of the ruins at the southeastern end of Elephantine Island. The western edge of Elephantine, however, has three Nubian villages, whose residents are friendly and whose alleys are interesting to explore. The entire northern half of Elephantine Island is taken up by the Oberoi Hotel, surrounded by a tall *cordon sanitaire* which keeps the tourists away from the Nubians. To reach the hotel, take their own ferry from the Aswan Corniche.

Behind Elephantine Island and not visible from Aswan, **Kitchener's Island** (known to the Arabs as Geziret el Nabatat—Island of the Plants) is Aswan's most enchanting spot. The entire island is one unbroken Botanical Garden where African and Asian species grow and blossom in profusion. The bizarre plant life also attracts a variety of exotic flamboyant birds. Lord Kitchener, the British general of both the Sudan and the Boer War, served at the turn of the century as Her Majesty's Consul-General in Egypt and lived on the island. In his leisure time Kitchener pursued his interest in botany with fanatical passion, planting and overseeing the botanical garden which has since fully taken over the island. White ducks inhabit a lake at the southern end of the island that belongs to a biological research station. Also at this end of the island is an overpriced **cafe** which provides a wonderful spot to rest. The semi-circular lower terrace of the cafe features an exquisite view. Mineral water goes for a steep LE1.25; the cheapest offering is a glass of tea for 25pt.

The island is open to tourists 7am-7pm; admission 25pt. To reach Kitchener's Island, you can rent a *felucca* and combine an island visit with stops along the west bank. It is also possible to reach the island without the expense of a *felucca* by hiring a rowboat from the west side of Elephantine Island. Nubian boys of Elephantine spend much of their day bathing in the river on the western shore of the island. Without too much negotiation you should be able to arrange with them for a rowboat to take you over to Kitchener's Island for no more than 75pt for any number from one to five passengers. If you wait until 7pm, when all of the Egyptians who work on the island head home, you can catch a rowboat back for even less.

To reach the sights on the west bank of the Nile, hire a *felucca*. You'll have to negotiate with the *felucca* pilots, some of whom are unprincipled thieves. Practically all will tell you they are charging the official government rate; the official government rate for a three-hour trip to Kitchener's Island, the west bank, and around Elephantine is LE4 for a small boat regardless of the number of passengers. In practice, it often takes earnest bargaining to get such a rate; it is not too difficult to get a boat for LE6 for the entire trip. Be very explicit in advance, however, about where you want to go (especially if you wish to visit St. Simeon's Monastery) and how much time you plan to take, or the pilot will cut your tour of the west bank short. It is not too difficult to meet other tourists who wish to share a *felucca* at one of the cafes along the Corniche. If you wish to visit the Tombs of the Nobles in addition to the usual itinerary, plan on at least a five-hour trip and a couple more pounds for the *felucca*. If you don't mind spending the money to rent a *felucca* twice, though, it is more relaxing to visit the Tombs of the Nobles on a separate trip.

The most accessible attraction on the west bank of the Nile is the **Mausoleum of Agha Khan,** just a short climb from where the *felucca* docks. Agha Khan is the hereditary title of the ruler of the Ismaili, a Shi'ite sect of Islam. The Agha Khan used to rule from Pakistan, the spiritual home of the Ismaili, but political exile has since compelled them to take up residence elsewhere. Aswan became the favorite wintering place of Muhammad Shah Agha Khan (1899-1957), the 48th Imam of the Ismaili. Upon his death, the Begum (Agha Khan's wife) oversaw the construction of the mausoleum. She still spends her winters in the large villa overlooking the Nile and adjoining the steps up to the mausoleum. The exterior of the shrine is less impressive than its interior, modeled after the traditional Fatimid tombs of Cairo. (The Ismailis view the Shi'ite Fatimids as their spiritual ancestors.) The mausoleum is entered through a massive pair of brass doors. At the opposite end of the structure in the small domed tomb chamber stands the marble sarcophagus inscribed with passages from the Qur'an. Each day a red rose is laid upon the sarcophagus, and several contemporary legends tell of the distances across which a red rose has been flown when there were none available in the area. Open 9am-5pm; admission free. *Baksheesh* for the guards is supposedly forbidden. Both male and female visitors may be refused entrance if they are wearing shorts.

Standing isolated and majestic in the desert, directly inland from the mausoleum, is the Monastery of St. Simeon. Built in the sixth and seventh centuries C.E. and abandoned in the thirteenth, the monastery sits on a terrace carved into the steep hill. No one is really quite sure who St. Simeon was or what he did. Arabs remember him by the name Amba Hadra, and hence the monastery is known in Arabic as **Dayr Amba Samaan.** With its turreted walls rising to a height of 6m, the monastery has more the appearance of a fortress than of a place dedicated to the religious life. Indeed, it was eventually abandoned partially owing to repeated attacks by desert Bedouins, as well as to the difficulty of maintaining a supply of water. The original walls of the complex stood 10m high, enclosing a community of 300 resident monks, accommodations sufficient for several hundred pilgrims, and a church. Some of the original frescoes of the church can still be made out. Open 9am-6pm; admission LE1. The monastery is clearly visible from the Mausoleum of Agha Khan. To reach it walk through the desert (one hour, bring water), hire a camel by the *felucca* stop, or make arrangements for a camel in Aswan.

The **Tombs of the Nobles** are neglected by most visitors to Aswan. They lie farther north along the west bank of the Nile, honeycombed into the face of the desert cliffs and beautifully illuminated at night. The tombs, dedicated to governors and dignitaries, date primarily from the end of the Old Kingdom and the First Intermediate Period before the ascension of the New Kingdon. Unfortunately, most of the tombs are in a sad state of repair.

The **Tomb of Sirenput I** (#31), ca. 1920 B.C.E., possesses some frescoes as does its namesake the **Tomb of Sirenput** (ca. 1980 B.C.E.). Indeed, the latter is considered to be the most finely-decorated of the collection, containing handsome effigies of Sirenput, and, on the rear wall, scenes depicting him relaxing, hunting, and fishing. Finally, also of interest, the **Tomb of Heqa-ib** (unmarked, just north of #35) boasts an attractive facade and some excavated relief work in the interior.

Nightlife

None of it is cheap and most of it is trash. The two main nightclubs are in the Kalabsha and Oberoi Hotels. The latter is on Elephantine Island and their routine usually features Nubian music and a competent belly dancer. Cover charges vary according to season; drinks are very expensive. In winter the Aswan Cultural Center, on Corniche el Nil between the Abu Simbel and Philae Hotels, features genuine Nubian dancing (ask the tourist office). They also sell Nubian handicrafts. However, by far the best way to enjoy an evening at Aswan is to hire a felucca and sail arond Elephantine Island at sunset (see above for details). Join the citizens of Aswan just after sunset for a promenade down the full length of Sharia el Souk from the train station.

Near Aswan

The sights around Aswan are all a little difficult to reach, but worth the effort. The best strategy is to view all of the sights within the space of a single day by hiring a private taxi and splitting the expense among several people. The proper fare for renting a small taxi (1-4 persons) for four or five hours is LE6.60; the proper fare for one large taxi (5-8 people) is LE10. Small taxis that are willing to oblige for the official fee can be a bit difficult to find, but most large taxis can be obtained without too much argument for LE10. A full itinerary for this fare includes: the High Dam, the Old Dam, Philae Temple, the Unfinished Obelisk, and the Quarries. You may wish to omit Philae Temple and go there by public transportation another time in order to have a more relaxed visit. A taxi driver will probably be reluctant to wait for much over an hour at the ruins. In order to visit Kalabsha Temple you will have to pay a few more pounds. The best place to pick up a taxi for hire is at the **service taxi station** (see Practical Information). The best place to meet tourists for such a venture is in one of the cafes by the train station. If you don't mind spending a little more, another way to see all the sights except the Temple of Kalabsha is to take one of the taxi tours that the youth hostel occasionally organizes by special request at the cost of LE4 per person. Though you'd save money by getting your own group together, the tour has the advantage of leaving at 5am sharp, allowing you to be the first to reach all the sights. The driver is taciturn, and the group rarely grows larger than four. Inquire at the Youth Hostel at least two nights before you want to go.

The most notorious of the attractions in the area is Egypt's contemporary essay in monumentality: the High Dam, completed in 1971. Over 4km wide and 115m high, the dam has been a mixed bag: on the negative side, it inundated Nubia with waters as deep as 200m, requiring the relocation of thousands of people and the removal of a number of ancient monuments to high ground by UNESCO. The dam also interrupts the flow of silt which is critical to the fertility of the land. Finally, there looms the potential devastation should the dam break; almost the entire country would be flushed away into the Mediterranean. On the positive side, the dam does produce a large proportion of Egypt's electricity, and for now at least, greatly enhances agricultural productivity. Egypt's surface area of arable soil has been increased by 30%. The implications of the massive project are still unfolding; for example, a rise in the Sahara's water table has been noticed as far away as Algeria. The most conspicuous consequence of the High Dam is Lake Nassar, the world's largest artificial lake, stretching 500km across the Tropic of Cancer and into the Sudan. The beauty of the Lake—long slender fingers probing into the desert—is tempered by remembering the dispersion of an entire people followed by the slow death of their culture, and the loss of priceless antiquities beneath its waters.

The history of the High Dam at Aswan has had significant international repercussions. The plans for the construction of such a dam were unfolded after World War II when it became apparent that Egypt had achieved maximum agricultural output and was in no position to feed its rapidly increasing population. In addition, it was desirable to take some steps to obviate the unpredictable flooding of the Nile that had blessed and tormented the inhabitants of Egypt since time immemorial. When the United States suddenly refused to provide the financial backing for the High Dam project in 1956, President Nassar ordered the seizure and nationalization of the Suez Canal as a means of generating the necessary financial resources. This triggered the Suez Crisis in which France, Britain, and Israel simultaneously threatened to invade Egypt and were restrained by the United Nations. The Soviet Union provided the necessary loans and technology for the project and work began on the dam in 1960.

Before you visit the dam, on the east bank you pass a **Visitor's Pavilion,** containing a large model of the dam and a variety of exhibits. The most interesting are numerous plaques and sculptures featuring a harmonious blend of Soviet socialist-realist motifs with traditional pharaonic figures and symbols. Another remnant of the Soviet period, on the west bank at the foot of the dam, is a large stone monument in the form of a stylized lotus blossom, intended as a symbol of Soviet-Egyptian friendship. Admission to the top of the High Dam is supposed to be 60pt but it is often possible to gain access free of charge. A cafeteria by the entrance sells soft drinks for 25pt. The top of the dam features excellent views of the islands to the north and Lake Nassar to the south.

It is possible to reach the High Dam via public transportation. All Cairo-Aswan trains terminate at **Sadd-el-Ali,** the High Dam (20pt from Aswan). If you just need to go to the High Dam in order to catch the boat to Wadi Halfa or to Abu Simbel definitely take the train. The train station usually presents a colorful spectacle, crowded as it is with Sudanese (largely Bishari) tribespeople camping out, waiting for the next boat homewards.

Less spectacular than the High Dam, but also much more picturesque, the **Old Dam,** a few kilometers to the north, merits a brief visit. Built by the British between 1898 and 1902, the dam supplied most of Egypt's power for many years. The Old Dam can also be reached by public bus from the Aswan bus station—ask for the bus to Hazan (departures every hour, 10pt). The area known as the **First Cataract** is extremely fertile, and one of the most pleasant spots in the Aswan area. Just beside the dam on the east bank of the Nile the water gushes forth dramatically, filling the air with cool spray, while the surrounding trees grow heavy with peaches and mangoes. Situated just below the waters of the First Cataract, the island of **Sehel** attracts remarkably few tourists. Its claim to immortality lies in some scanty ruins and a variety of incriptions ranging from the Fourth Dynasty to the Ptolemaic period. Nonetheless, if you're interested in a longer *felucca* ride from Aswan, the island makes a perfect destination.

If you're traveling by taxi, on your way back to Aswan after touring the High Dam and/or Philae ask the driver to stop at the following cluster of adjacent sights: the **Unfinished Obelisk;** the **Fatimid Tombs,** a collection of early Islamic shrines; and the **granite quarries,** which supplied all of ancient Egypt with the raw material for pyramids and temples.

Some of the best pharaonic ruins in the Aswan area are to be found at **Kalabsha Temple.** Of all the Nubian monuments rescued from the encroaching waters of Lake Nassar, many Egyptologists consider Kalabsha to be second only to the unparalleled treasures of Abu Simbel. The Temple of Kalabsha was the first pharaonic structure to be saved from the onslaught of the Nile waters. The temple's original site was 50km south of Aswan. It's worth negotiating the necessary bureaucratic hurdles to reach the site of Kalabsha, dramatically situated amid the sparkling waters of Lake Nassar at the top of the High Dam. Dedicated to the Nubian god Mandulis, the temple was erected primarily during the reign of Augustus and subsequently served as a church during the Christian era. The structure survived its journey north remarkably well.

Unfortunately, visiting Kalabsha requires cutting several layers of red tape. The temple is located on the west bank of the Nile, just south of the High Dam. Immediately south of the dam stands a military checkpoint; the temple, only a few hundred meters beyond, lies in a restricted military zone. Any tourist can gain permission from the military authorities to visit, but it does take time. The first step is to find a taxi driver who is authorized to drive to Kalabsha. If you wish to include Kalabsha on an itinerary with the other sights in the area, do not pay the driver more than an extra LE4 for the visit to the temple. The taxi driver will help you make the necessary arrangement with the military authorities. Bring your passport (the stamp for the permit costs 40pt) and be prepared to wait around. Securing a permit in Aswan does not guarantee that you will be able to get to the temple, since there may not be a boat available to take you out to the little island. The least expensive of these operates from the west bank. The more common and expensive option is to hire a *felucca* from the east bank by the train station for several pounds. Sometimes, however, there is no *felucca* available, and then the attempt to see Kalabsha can be declared a failure.

Perhaps the most worthwhile excursion in the Aswan area is to any one of the numerous **Nubian villages** in the surrounding region, particularly on the occasion of a wedding ceremony. Usually, several weddings are celebrated simultaneously at a single village in a huge festival featuring dancing and tons of food. Getting yourself invited to such an affair is not as difficult as one might expect since it is considered a mark of honor to have foreign guests attend one's wedding ceremony. The village of **Abu Simbel,** 30km north of Aswan, is particularly given to inviting guests to its wedding ceremonies. If you do receive such an invitation, you will suddenly find yourself in the predicament of being lavished with a great deal of attention and not being permitted to pay for any of it.

Philae

If you're making daytrips from Aswan, make the island of Philae, situated in the backwaters of the original Aswan dam, a high priority. The collection of romantic ruins used to be flooded for most of the year, but was recently moved to higher ground. The major ruin is the Temple of Isis, one of the latest Egyptian temples to be built, started in the Ptolemaic period. Though smaller than the monsters around Luxor, the temple is a stunning, balanced collection of pylons and colonnades that focuses on a small inner sanctum. You can visit Philae by taxi as part of an itinerary including the High Dam, or you can reach the island by public transportation by taking a bus to the Old Dam from the Aswan bus station—ask for a bus to Hazan; departures every hour, fare 10pt. From the last bus stop walk 1 km south along the Nile to reach the dock where the boats leave for the island. Whether you come by bus or by taxi, you have to hire a motorboat to reach the island. Usually, not too much bargaining is required. The proper fee for a small motorboat is LE4-4.20 (one to five persons); for a large, LE5 (six or seven people). It is easy to find other visitors to join in a rental on the motorboat docks at any time of year since Philae is a popular tourist destination. The fare is for the round trip; don't pay until you're back on the east bank. The boat pilot is obliged to wait for you as you tour the site, so don't allow yourself to be rushed. Open 7am-6pm; admission LE3, LE1.50 for students. Tickets are purchased on the east bank.

Sights

Circumstances have conspired to perpetuate the aura of romance which has long surrounded the island of Philae. One of Egypt's legendary tourist attractions during the nineteenth century, Philae became almost completely submerged beneath water six months out of the year after the completion of the Old Dam in 1902. Archeologists feared that the temple eventually would be destroyed by the river's strong current. The construction of the High Dam in the 1960s sealed the island's fate. Over the course of three years Philae's pharaonic structures were dismantled and pieced together on higher ground. The buildings on Philae comprise Egypt's most spectacularly-situated pharaonic ruins, clinging to the tiny desert island amidst a shimmering stretch of the widened Nile.

Dominating the island's western edge is the **Temple of Isis,** who was the sister-wife of the legendary hero Osiris, mother of nature, protector of humans, and goddess of purity and sexuality. Her following was so strong that her cult continued long after the establishment of Christianity, dying out only in the sixth century during the reign of the Emperor Justinian. Nearly all the structures on Philae date from the Ptolemaic and Roman eras, after the beginning of artistic decline in Egypt. Hence the quality of their decorative relief work is comparatively poor. Nevertheless, all of the buildings display the influence of the Greco-Roman style, a harmonious blend of classicism and pharaonic traditionalism. A fascinating collection of antique graffiti is inscribed on the ancient walls, testifying to Philae's long history of tourism.

From the landing at the southern tip of the island, climb the short slope leading to the temple complex past Philae's oldest structure, the **Portico of Nectanebo.** The paved Portico once formed the vestibule of an ancient temple, but the larger edifice has been washed away. The eastern side of the colonnade remains unfinished, and the capitals crowning its handsome columns all differ from one another. At the **First Pylon,** towers rise to a height of 18m on either side of the main entrance into the temple. Pass through this entrance into the **Central Court** on whose western edge sits a **Roman mammisi,** its elegant columns emblazoned with the face of the cow-goddess Hathor. To the north is the slightly off-center Second Pylon, marking the way to the Temple's inner sanctum. The first area you will encounter is the pronaos, which was converted into a church by early Christians who incised Byzantine crosses on the chamber walls. Proceed on to the naos, the Temple's innermost sanctuary. Just inside the doorway is an amusing piece of ancient graffiti etched into the granite wall in capital letters: "B. Mure Stultus Est." ("B. Mure is stupid.") The Naos terminates in three small chapels, decorated with representations of Isis and other deities. A staircase leads from the western side up to a set of apartments known as the **Osiris Chambers,** which contain some excellent reliefs depicting various subjects mourning Osiris (closed to the public in 1983).

Retrace your steps to the second court to explore the island's western edge. Beyond the Roman mammisi are a series of ruined structures, and at the foot of the quay an ancient **Nilometer.** Slightly to the north is **Hadrian's Gateway,** with a relief showing the Nile god, wrapped in the coils of a serpent, pouring water from two vessels below the solemn gaze of a vulture and a falcon. At the northern tip of the island are situated the **Temple of Augustus** and the **Roman Gate.** Nearby is a somewhat grimy restroom (bring your own toilet paper). Return to the landing via the island's eastern edge. About half-way down, directly east of the temple's Second Pylon, is the charming **Temple of Hathor;** fanciful representations of flautists, harp players, and lyre-playing monkeys adorn its columns. Farther south, clinging to a steep slope leading down to the water's edge, is the enchanting **Kiosk of Trajan.** The elegant raised pavilion commands a view of rugged arid mountains above a serene lake of sapphire green. South of the Kiosk of Trajan is a tented **Rest Area,** where drinks are sold for 50pt.

Abu Simbel

At the southernmost end of Upper Egypt lies one of the most awe-inspiring monuments in the country. Four 22m-tall statues of Ramses II, carved out of a single slab of rock, greet the sunrise over Lake Nassar each day from the massive **Great Temple of Abu Simbel.** The son of Amon, Ramses II built this

Be sure to see

great sanctuary and the Temple of Hathor nearby more than 3500 years ago.

When the rising waters of Lake Nassar threatened to engulf one of Egypt's greatest treasures, the nations of the world pulled together and moved the two great temples at Abu Simbel 200m to higher ground. At a cost of $36 million, teams of engineers from six countries cut the temples into over 2000 pieces ranging from ten to forty tons in weight. The pieces were moved, reconstructed, and a hollow mountain built around the two temples. They were carefully oriented to face the same direction as before, and the earlier landscape was recreated.

Try to view the smaller **Temple of Hathor** first. Six statues of Ramses and his wife Nefertari as the goddess Hathor adorn the facade. The temple was constructed in the traditional three-room fashion: the first chamber containing six columns was open to everyone; the second chamber was open to nobles and priests, and the third inner sanctuary was reserved for the pharaoh and the high priest. The beauty of this temple lies in its harmony and completeness.

Outside, across the compound, stand the four **Colossi of Ramses.** From the interior of the Great Hypostyle Hall, six more statues of Ramses stare out ominously under artificial light. Etched on the walls are some of Egypt's most beautiful murals. Notice the double-image technique used to portray motion. Deeper inside lie antechambers, libraries, and the inner sanctum. The statues of four gods originally encased in gold and diamonds—Ramses, Amon, Re-Horachto and Ptah—wait with divine patience for the moment twice a year (February 22 and October 22) when the first rays of the sun reach 100m into the Temple to bathe them in light.

Practical Information

Abu Simbel is 50km from the Sudanese border and 274km south of Aswan. Throughout most of 1983 the only way to visit was by plane via EgyptAir. Two flights a day from Cairo and Aswan serve Abu Simbel (round-trip Aswan-Abu Simbel LE40.80). If you fly, EgyptAir provides free bus service to the temple. After a whirlwind tour, you'll be driven back to the airport for the return flight to Aswan.

In 1984 there may be one or two alternatives to flying. Boat service, interrupted by a tragic accident in 1983, may resume—ask at the Nile Navigation Office in Aswan (see Aswan Practical Information). The fare and schedule should be comparable to what they were before: the boat left Aswan on Saturdays and returned three days later; fare was LE6. The discomfort of three days in 130°F temperature with no shade, food, or water makes this mode of transport worthwhile only for the most adventurous. Bring your own sustenance. A hydrofoil may begin service to Abu Simbel in 1984 (See Aswan Practical Information).

Entrance fees to the site are LE6, LE4 for students. During the winter, you can stay overnight at Abu Simbel at the **Nefertari Hotel** (LE20 for a double).

Alexandria and Mediterranean Coast

Alexandria (Iskandariya)

As Egypt's second largest city, with possibly as many as five million inhabitants, Alexandria faces many of the same problems as Cairo. Yet despite certain similarities, Alexandria has a more distinctly European character. Its waterfront cafes, temperate weather, and relative cleanliness—no dust and no trash clutter up the city's streets—combine to make a colorful, attractive metropolis. Ten or fifteen degrees cooler than Cairo in the summer, Alexandria looks out on 18km of public and private beaches that make it a popular summer vacation spot for tourists and natives alike; and in the winter, when the city's population is reduced by half, it becomes an even more compelling vacation site.

Alexandria was founded by Alexander the Great in 332 B.C.E. He determined the site for the city on a journey to the oracle of Amon at Siwa, and envisioned it as the future capital of his empire. But he didn't live to see its completion. The city saw its heyday under the leadership of Ptolemy, one of Alexander's most trusted generals, who became heir to the Egyptian Empire after the death of Alexander's son. The Greek Ptolemaic dynasty ruled Alexandria for nearly three hundred years, during which the city prospered. The famous library symbolized the city's role as the most vital center of Greek learning in the Hellenistic Age (the fourth to the first centuries B.C.E.). The lighthouse of Pharos, standing 125 meters high, was also built during the Greek period, and was counted one of the seven wonders of the world.

When the young emperor Octavian Augustus defeated Queen Cleopatra and her consort Marc Antony in 31 B.C.E., Alexandria became a Roman outpost. The city fell into a 1000-year decline; the library burned during Roman times, and the lighthouse was destroyed by an earthquake several centuries later. But Alexandria continued to be Egypt's most important city throughout the Roman and Byzantine periods. After the Islamic conquest of Egypt in the seventh century C.E., the country's political center was established at Cairo, but Alexandria remained one of Egypt's most lively economic and intellectual centers.

A cultural rejuvenation occurred in Alexandria following Napolean's brief occupation of the city at the end of the eighteenth century. This period marked a major turning point in the history of the modern Middle East. The French influence is still seen in the small French cafes and restaurants along the port; even today, the Egyptian elite speaks French and looks to France for cultural leadership. Since its military significance was realized in World War II, Alexandria has grown and re-established itself as a major port city.

Orientation

As during ancient times, when a causeway linked the island of Pharos to the mainland, Alexandria has two harbors: an eastern and a western one, separated by a peninsula which now incorporates the former island of Pharos. The smaller Eastern Harbor is by far the more attractive and is used today almost exclusively by fishermen and private pleasure boat owners. The main Western Port handles almost all of Alexandria's heavy shipping traffic, including passenger lines. It is a busy, industrialized area with crowded and dirty harborside neighborhoods. At the tip of the peninsula separating the two is a fort cut out of the stones of the ancient lighthouse, built by the Mameluke Sultan Qayitbay in the fifteenth century.

The city of Alexandria is laid out as a narrow strip along the Mediterranean coast, about fifteen kilometers long and an average of only two or three kilometers wide. It is an easy city to navigate simply because it is almost impossible to lose your way. If you're not quite sure where you are you can always reorient yourself by walking down to the coastline where you can easily catch a bus or taxi on the Corniche, the main boulevard along the sea, which will deposit you back in the center of town. And because Alexandria follows the coastline in a narrow strip, the main transportation arteries all run east-west, so even if you happen to hop on the wrong tram or bus, you won't have to worry about being dropped off somewhere out in the sticks.

To take the bus from Cairo to Alexandria, you must buy tickets in one of three locations in Cairo: Tahrir Square, Ramsis Station, or Ismailiya Square. Tickets can also be purchased outside of Cairo, in Giza. The fare varies from LE2 to LE5, since the buses are privately owned. The buses drop you off at Ramli Station, located at Midaan Sa'ad Zaghluul (Sa'ad Zaghluul Square) in the center of Alexandria, about a block from the sea. To take the train, reserve tickets in advance at Ramsis Station. See transportation section in Egypt introduction. Alexandria's main railway station, Mahattat Misr, is located about five or six blocks southeast of Ramli Station, just beyond the Roman Amphitheater. Finally, service taxis *(taksi ugra)* run between Giza and Alexandria (2½ hrs; LE2.50); take care not to be overcharged by unscrupulous drivers. Taxis will drop you off at either Misr station or Alexandria's smaller Sidi Gabr Station, located several kilometers east of the center of town; from there you can take any one of Alexandria's double-decker electric trams going west to Ramli Station.

Ramli Station, at Midaan Sa'ad Zaghluul, is the center of the municipal bus system, which serves all of Alexandria as well as many outlying areas such as Ma'amura, Montaza, and Agami. Only a few lines depart from Midaan Orabi (Orabi Square), about a quarter mile west of Ramli. The buses in Alexandria are normally less crowded and less hazardous than those in Cairo, and can be a reliable way to get to areas not served by the tram system. Some of the more important bus and tram lines are:

#129: Midaan Orabi—Montaza—Abu Qiir.
#120, 220, and 25: Up and down the Corniche.
#500: Ramli—Orabi—Agami.
Tram #15: Ramli—Fort Qayitbay.
Tram #16: Orabi—Pompey's Pillar.

Midaan Sa'ad Zaghluul is in the center of Alexandria's commercial district. Most hotels and restaurants are within easy walking distance of the square.

One warning: due to the large numbers of tourists in Alexandria, con men abound. While Egyptians are naturally hospitable, occasionally generosity can cover up a clever ruse in which the visitor can lose his shirt. Do not allow casual acquaintances to change money for you. According to the tourist office, there have been numerous incidents of travelers being duped by Alexandrian shysters.

Practical Information

Tourist Office: Midaan Sa'ad Zaghluul (tel. 80 76 11). The office is open daily 8am-6pm; during Ramadan 9am-4pm. Branch offices (with the same hours) are at the train station (tel. 25 98 5) and at the port (tel. 25 98 6). The people here are friendly, so don't hesitate to go to them for information. You can pick up a free copy of *Alexandria by Day and Night,* which has a bad map of the town. A better map, published by Lehnert and Landrock of Cairo, sells for LE1 and is available in many of the foreign language bookstores in Alexandria.

Tourist Police: Main office at Montaza Palace (tel. 96 86 61). There's a branch office above the Tourist Office (tel. 80 79 85). Open daily 8am-8pm, Fri. 8am-2pm.

American Express: 26 Al-Horriya Road, in the Eyres Travel Office. The American Express sign is hard to find; look for Eyres Travel, which has a brown granite front. Open 9am-1pm and 5-7pm. Closed Fri. and Sat. afternoons, all day Sun.

Hospital: Al Moassat, on Al-Horriya Road (tel. 72 88 8), in the Hadra district. For most illnesses, ask for help at a five-star hotel or at the consulate.

U.S. Consulate: 110 Al-Horriya Road (tel. 80 19 11, 25 60 7, 22 86 1, or 24 85 8). Of limited use. All important business should be done at the embassy in Cairo. Open Mon.-Fri. 9am-noon.

British Consulate: 3 Mena St., in the Rushdi district (tel. 84 71 66 or 84 94 58).

Accommodations

Accommodations in Alexandria tend to be cleaner, more cheerful, and less expensive than those in Cairo. If you want an inexpensive room with a view of the sea, there are a number of small guesthouses and hotels on 26 July St. (the Corniche) and the streets which run off it. However, some of them are crowded, dirty, and no bargain at about LE2 per person. Remember to check your bed for fleas and ticks at any of these places. Otherwise, try the following:

Hotel Leroy, 25 Sharia Talaat Harb [Talaat Harb St.] (tel. 80 90 99). Like many of Alexandria's hotels, located on the top floors of an office building. The rooms are clean and have balconies. Both the bar and the restaurant have beautiful harbor views. Singles LE6.60, doubles LE8.10. Doubles with bath LE9.25.

Hotel Acropole, 1 Rue Gamal el Dine Yassine, 4th floor (tel. 80 59 80), one block west of Ramli Station. One of the best deals in Alexandria; clean, pleasant, and centrally located. Some rooms have a view of the sea. Singles LE2, doubles LE4, triples LE5, including breakfast. Bathrooms down the hall.

Hotel Union, 12 Rue Mohammed Talaat Nooman, 6th floor (tel. 80 75 37). Clean and friendly; most rooms have an ocean view. No singles. Doubles range from LE8 to LE12, including tax and breakfast.

Hotel Picadilly, 11 Al-Horriya Road, 8th floor (tel. 24 49 7), at Nabi Daniel St. Don't be put off by the building's grim lobby; the rooms are a bit decrepit, but clean. Singles with bath LE6, doubles with bath LE7 or LE8.

Hotel Ailema, 21 Sharia Amiin Fakry, 7th floor, south of Midaan Sa'ad Zaghluul. Don't get your hopes up too high when you pass through the revolving door to the reception area. The rooms are clean, but simple. Singles LE2.50 to LE5.25, doubles LE3.70 to LE7. Prices do not include a 12% service charge.

Hyde Park Hotel, 21 Sharia Amiin Fakry, one floor up from the Ailema. Same prices and conditions.

Food

The French tradition has bequeathed a number of reasonable French restaurants to Alexandria. Otherwise your best bet is *fuul* and *taamiyya* sandwiches. Some of these, however, are only recommended for those with a strong palate. For dining out, try the following:

Al Ekhlaas, 40 Sharia Safia Zaghluul. Very good Egyptian food in a quiet, unhurried atmosphere. Air conditioned. Full menus run LE3 to LE5.

Restaurant Elite, 43 Sharia Safia Zaghluul, across from Santa Lucia. Inexpensive, with reasonably good seafood and pleasant ambience. LE1 to LE5.

Gad, Midaan Sa'ad Zaghluul and Sharia Safia Zaghluul opposite the Amir cinema. Fuul and taamiyya sandwiches go for 5pt each. These little shops have a reputation for being the best in all Egypt; they are sometimes so crowded that you can't get in.

Muhammad Ahmed Fuul, just one block south of Midaan Sa'ad Zaghluul. Very famous, and similar to "Felfallas" in Cairo. An Alexandrian landmark.

Restaurant Denise, 1 Ibn Basaam St., three blocks east of the tram station. Famous for its fresh seafood, pulled daily from the Mediterranean. You pay by weight; light eaters can dine for LE2 to LE3.

Santa Lucia, 40 Sharia Safia Zaghluul. Bavarian decor with French food and French-speaking waiters. Excellent food. Meals run LE4 to LE6.

Tikka Grill, on the waterfront near Abuul Abaas Mosque. Fantastic view and elegant decor. LE3 to LE5, including a fine salad bar.

Zephyrion, on the coast near the main square. If you can round up a group of five or six people, order a few kilos of shrimp and two or three types of fish. The restaurant is perched on the edge of the ocean and you'll stuff yourself with absolutely wonderful seafood for about LE3-LE4 apiece. You may think the price a bit steep, but it's worth it. If you go alone, the shrimp is definitely the best deal.

If you want excellent fish, you should definitely make the trip out to Abu Qiir, which has seafood far superior to anything you will find in Alexandria. When you get off the bus at Abu Qiir, keep walking east until you come to the gulf. There, on the beach, is a row of tables. The fishermen will come in from the boats anchored offshore and cook the fish you select beside your table. This place is practically unknown to tourists, but Alexandrians flock here on the weekends.

Sights

All that remains of ancient Alexandria is a single granite column known as **Pompey's Pillar.** It survives from a huge temple called the Serpeum—the religious center in ancient Alexandria in which the rites of the cult of Serapis, a deity descended directly from the ancient Egyptian bull god Apis, were conducted. Not surprisingly, the temple was levelled once the Roman Empire became Christian, save for the still-standing isolated pillar that has a few sphinxes and pieces of sculpture strewn around it from an ancient library (not to be confused with the famed Library of Alexandria). The name of the pillar, by the way, is a mistake of the Crusaders, who thought that it marked the spot of the tomb of Pompey the Great. To get to the pillar from the main square, go west on Al-Horriya Rd. for about six blocks, then turn left at the tram tracks.

The site is open 9am-4pm, 9am-2pm during Ramadan; admission 50pt, 25pt with student ID.

Venturing into this part of Alexandria may not be worth it for the sake of seeing a single pillar (the area is crowded and very Egyptian; the kids just love to hassle foreigners), but it is most definitely worthwhile to visit the three-tiered **Catacombs of Kom Al-Shofaga,** located next to the pillar. These Roman tombs descend in three levels down to a depth of about 35m., and are remarkable for the bits of sculpture and reliefs that show Egyptian gods with unmistakably Roman bodies. Don't miss the jackel-headed Anubis that has a torso like Charles Atlas by the entrance to the innermost burial chamber. As you enter the central rotunda, the large room to your left is where the funeral feasts were held, a creepy place for a meal if there ever was one. The catacombs are open daily 9am-4pm, 9am-2pm during Ramadan; admission 50pt, 25pt with student ID.

Alexandria also has an excellent **Greco-Roman Museum,** located just north of Al-Horriya Rd. with an entrance at 5 Al-Mathaf al-Romani St. (Rue du Musee). Be sure to take a look at Room #9, which holds a mummified crocodile and other relics from the cult of the crocodile god Phepheros in Faiyuum (a pretty kinky cult even by modern standards). The museum also contains an astonishing collection of Greek alabaster head casts, and in Room #16, some impressive, life-like sculptures. Look out for Emperor Vespasian, whose "cold sneer of cruel command" (Shelley) surpassed even that of Ozymandias. Perhaps the most interesting exhibit is the collection of terracotta figurines *(tanagra)* of Greek everyday life. The abundance of see-through robes in Greek times was astounding. A huge bust of the pop-eyed Emperor Augustus bids you adieu as you leave the museum. Open daily 9am-4pm, Fri. 12:30-2pm; admission LE1, 50pt with student ID.

Between the Greco-Roman Museum and the main railway station is the beautifully-preserved white marble Roman Amphitheater—the only one of its kind to be discovered in Egypt. Still under excavation, the Polish archeological team working there has also discovered a Roman-period bath complex and an array of residential structures in the immediate vicinity of the amphitheater. The gate to the amphitheater is at Kom El-Dika. The site is open daily 9am-5pm, 9am-3pm during Ramadan; admission 50pt, 25pt with student ID.

Alexandria has two "summer palaces" of the former royal family of King Farouk: **Ras El-Tin,** in the west near Fort Qayitbay, and the **Montaza Palace,** at the eastern edge of the city. The palaces and their museums have been closed to the public indefinitely but the grounds are open. The gardens of the Montaza Palace are particularly beautiful, and are a favorite picnic and gathering spot for Alexandrians. Farouk's architect must have been a bit crazy; the palace is fanciful and entirely pink. Take bus #120 or 220 east along the Corniche. The 75pt admission fee lets you wander freely in the gardens; an additional LE1 admits you to a semi-private beach west of the palace with sheltered waters and a view of the palace tower across the bay.

The Islamic **Fort Qayitbay** is worth a visit. Located on the top of the peninsula separating the eastern and western harbors, the fort is visible from almost any point along the Alexandrian Corniche. Take tram #15 from Midaan Sa'ad Zaghluul, and get off at the corner of the peninsula. The first door in the fort leads to a rather pathetic oceanographic museum; the second gate is the entrance to the fort and naval museum. The fort is reputedly built from the stones of the lighthouse of Pharos, which stood on the same promontory. Inside, a scale model of the lighthouse gives you an idea of the dimensions of one of the seven wonders of the world. Note the pro-Nassar captions that appear throughout the museum. Admission is 5pt; the 25pt guidebook is unfortunately useless. For a brief side trip, follow the peninsula road from the fort and turn onto Sharia Ras El-Tin. To the left of the Palace is a gate leading to the **Catacombs of Kom El-Anfushi.** Entrance is free; the rubble of human skulls and bones makes a glance inside worthwhile. If you follow the tram tracks from the catacombs, you will find yourself in the midst of a crowded street bazaar full of vendors hawking food and assorted merchandise.

The **Mosque of Abuul Abaas,** with its four domes and tall minarets, is located about a half-mile south of the fort and is Alexandria's most interesting example of Islamic architecture. Inside, it is a peaceful oasis where Muslims relax and pray all day long on green mats. If you don't speak Arabic, you may be refused entrance. Better not to ask—just remove your shoes and walk in quietly.

Alexandria's biggest perennial attraction is its beaches. During the hot summer months, Cairenes flock here on weekends to get away from the noise, dirt, and heat of the capital. Most of the beaches along Alexandria's Corniche are family oriented—women in bikinis are rarely seen. Westernized Egyptians and foreigners tend to congregate at **Montaza, Ma'amura,** and **Agami,** where more typically European standards of beachwear apply. Ma'amura is cheaper than Montaza, though much more crowded. West of Alexandria, Agami can be reached by taking bus #17 from Midaan Sa'ad Zaghluul. Hotels and restaurants there run cheaper than in Alexandria proper.

Nightlife

A reasonable selection of censored English movies can be seen at the **Amir, Royal,** and **Zaghluul** theaters. In late summer, an international film festival presents uncensored films in all of the city's theaters. Otherwise, most entertainment centers around the string of nightclubs along the Corniche, which feature live music. **Crazy Horse,** just east of Midaan Sa'ad Zaghluul, is the best known among them. A minimum charge of LE5 to LE10 is enforced at each of these hotspots.

After the high season begins (July 1), the **Reda Dance Company** performs nightly at the Firqit Reda Theater in the Chabwi district. And the Cecil and Palestine hotels both have casinos, where you can gamble away your foreign currency at an alarming speed. Thriftier travelers can join the majority of Egyptians for an evening stroll down the crowded downtown streets, or a drink at one of the seaside cafes.

Mediterranean Coast

If you are interested in more secluded beaches, head west of Alexandria towards the Libyan border. Countless miles of sun, surf and sand are interrupted only by an occasional oasis or town. Foreigners are allowed to go as far as Marsa Matruuh, 170 miles from Alexandria. On the way you'll pass through some interesting desert settlements: El-Alamein, where Rommel and the Afrika Corps clashed with the British 8th army led by Montgomery, and the lovely beach town of Sidi Abdur Rahman.

El-Alamein

The name "El-Alamein," which means "two worlds," certainly is apt. History and geography have conspired to create an eerie town at the intersection of desert and sea, where the Axis and Allied forces clashed during World War II. In 1942, the Allies were reeling back from their defeat at Tobruk. Just 63 miles from his headquarters in Alexandria, General Montgomery chose to make a last stand. He mounted his defense at the point where the massive Qattara depression meets the Mediterranean. On October 23rd and November 4th, the 8th army held the line against Rommel's Afrika Corps. These battles proved to be the turning point in the North African war, but the cost in human lives was staggering. Over 80,000 men from both sides died in action. The barren desert now whips the sand in clouds over the tiny, desolate town, making the visitor feel incomprehensibly alone with the dead.

To get to El-Alamein, take a bus from Tahrir Square in Cairo or Midaan Sa'ad Zaghluul in Alexandria. Ask the driver to stop at El-Alamein. The fare from Alexandria is LE1.20. A train also runs from Misr Station in Alexandria, but the town is 2km beyond the station through the desert.

Upon arrival, try to see the war sites and move on to Sidi Abdur Rahman before nightfall. Transportation out of El-Alamein in either direction is difficult to come by; buses won't pick passengers up in the town. You must either walk to the train, flag a service taxi or hitch a ride from the occasional friendly tourists who pass in rental cars (the latter is your best bet). For those who want to stay, the El-Alamein Resthouse offers singles for LE3.97 and doubles for LE5.30, plus a 12% tax. You can buy a meal at either the Resthouse or the cafe at the bus stop.

Sights

On the eastern side of town, towards Alexandria, lies the **British War Cemetery.** 7,000 headstones wreathed in purple flowers and framed against the desert plains make this a moving sight. As you walk through the shaded halls of the entrance building, read the names on the wall. Units from east and west Africa, India, Malaysia, New Zealand, Australia, South Africa, Greece, France, and Great Britain participated in the battle here; their presence attests to the global nature of the war. Run by the War Graves Commission, the cemetery is almost always open, and entrance is free of charge.

The **War Museum**, on the western side of town, contains detailed displays on Rommel, Montgomery, and the battle of El-Alamein. One room is dedicated to Egypt's victories in the 1973 war with Israel. The smashing of the Bar Lev Line remains a point of great pride for all Egyptians. Open daily 9am-5pm, 9am-3pm during Ramadan; admission 25pt. Ten kilometers west of town are the German and Italian war memorials. The Italian monument is a massive structure framed by the Mediterranean: another impressive tribute to the thousands who died here.

Sidi Abdur Rahman

If you're looking for a perfect, unspoiled white sand beach lining the turquoise waters of a lovely bay, Sidi Abdur Rahman is the place to go. This lonely beach is one of the finest in Egypt, and runs for unbroken miles. The quiet, windswept village of Sidi Abdur Rahman lies 3km inland; only one hotel disturbs the peace and isolation of the beach.

Aside from the beach, the **Qattara Basin Project** is all that puts Sidi Abdur Rahman on the map. The goal of this grandiose scheme is to dig a channel from the Mediterranean to a massive depression in the desert that dips four hundred feet below sea level. The Qattara depression is so large that this project would create a vast inland sea; the project's planners hope eventually to change the entire climate of lower Egypt.

Although the beach at Sidi Abdur Rahman is breathtaking, food and accommodations are very expensive. The El-Alamein Hotel charges LE20 for a single and LE25 for a double. Villas with room for eight people can be rented for LE115 a day. The hotel also rents tents for LE11 a single, LE13 a double. The only available food is in the hotel restaurant and costs LE8 for lunch or dinner, so you should bring your own food and water.

Departing from Sidi Abdur Rahman is currently next to impossible, but as of late 1983 bus service should be starting up. Buses will run to and from Tahrir Square in Cairo and to Marsa Matruuh.

Near Sidi Abdur Rahman

You've heard of towns you will miss if you blink? You'll miss **Fuka** even if you prop your eyelids open with toothpicks. Nothing is there: no houses, no dung-heaps, no grimy shepherds. Just sand swirling around the peeling Fuka sign.

Marsa Matruuh

Built around a perfect white sand bay, the small city of Marsa Matruuh is one of the cleanest and most charming places in Egypt. But although tremendously popular among Egyptians, Marsa Matruuh is seldom visited by foreign tourists; its wealth of natural wonders remains a well-kept secret, jealously guarded from outsiders.

Orientation and Practical Information

You need only know two streets to find your way around Marsa Matruuh. The **Corniche** stretches the length of the bay, and **Alexandria St.** runs perpendicular to it from the Matruuh Governate to the hill behind the town. Shops and restaurants are located on or just off Alexandria St. Transportation around town is by foot or by donkey cart (about 25pt for most rides).

Buses to Marsa Matruuh leave Alexandria's Midaan Sa'ad Zaghluul every morning (LE2.50 one-way). You must reserve a place in advance at the ticket office across the street from the Tourist Office in Alexandria. Usually one bus a day leaves from Tahrir Square in Cairo as well. Again, it is essential that you reserve a seat in advance. Due to the condition of the tracks, train service to Marsa Matruuh, while it does exist, is abominably poor. To leave Marsa Matruuh, reserve a seat at the office next to Omar Effendi on Alexandria St.

Accommodations

Marsa Matruuh has forty or fifty hotels or *fundugs* (pronounced with the *u* in *put*). For a bed costing only LE1, walk up Alexandria St. and ask for a fundug. For the price, you will share a room with many others; this option is not open to women. If you are willing to pay more, try the following:

Hotel des Roses, next to the Rommel Hotel (tel. 43 20). Run by Greeks, it is clean and pleasant. Singles LE3.30, doubles LE6, both without bath. Breakfast LE1.20.

Hotel Awaam, next to Awaam Mosque on the Corniche. Some rooms are more than usually moldy. Women are not permitted to stay here. Singles LE2, doubles LE4, both with bath.

Hotel Rio, in the center of the town square (tel. 20 23). Clean, but noisy. Singles LE3.64, doubles LE5.60.

Hotel Beau Site, on the western end of the Corniche (tel. 20 66). Many Egyptians and foreigners living here swear this is the best hotel in all of Egypt. Unfortunately, compulsory full board boosts up the prices. Singles LE12.35 with bath, LE9.30 without; doubles LE16 with bath, LE12.35 without.

Food

Alexandria Tourist Restaurant, on Alexandria St. downtown. Fantastic *tahina* for 25pt. A full meal with salads, fish, and rice goes for about LE2.50.

Panayiots Tourist Restaurant, opposite the Alexandria Tourist Restaurant. Same bill of fare for about LE3. The *tahina* doesn't compare.

Hotel Beau Site, on the Corniche. For a splurge, try their superb lunches for about LE6; you'll get an incredible buffet plus three more courses.

Sights

A number of fascinating spots lie within Marsa Matruuh itself. The **Rommel Museum,** to the east as the Corniche continues around to Rommel's Isle, contains exhibits built into a series of caves which Field Marshal Rommel used as headquarters in the North African war. Farther east, just past the Marine Fouad Hotel, is **Rommel's Beach,** where, according to legend, he swam each day. On the ocean side of Rommel's Isle, the wreck of an old U-boat juts out of the water. Locating it can be difficult, since few locals know its whereabouts. A second sunken U-boat lies in the bottom of the bay. You can rent a surf kayak at the Hotel Beau Site for LE3 to get to the wreck. Head straight out to the red buoy on your left. The sub lies parallel to the beach 20m towards the mosque from the red buoy; you'll need a diving mask to see it under 3m of water.

Marsa Matruuh's most famous attractions are its magnificent beaches. To the east lie the almost unknown beaches of **Hashiisha** and **Alam El-Ruum.** According to local legends, the wrecks of several Roman galleys rest in the water off these beaches. The **Beach of Lovers** is easily reached by surf kayak across the bay. Farther east on the ocean side of the bay, is **Cleopatra's Beach,** on the far right hand side of which lies **Cleopatra's Bath.** Reputedly, the queen and Marc Antony frolicked here. Still farther down the coast lies a wide, flat sand beach called **Ubayyad.** Unfortunately, it is scarred by the barbed wire and tented villages of Cairo bureaucrats. Tents can be rented for LE7 per night. The furthest and most spectacular spot of all is **Agiiba.** On the way, stop at the ruins of the tiny **Temple to Ramses II,** which lies neglected in the sand. Agiiba itself is an inlet in a series of rocky cliffs. The view of the turquoise Mediterranean waters from the cliff tops is fantastic. Below, the sea is cool and inviting. In front of the cliffs there is a huge stretch of open sand beach, also called Agiiba. To get to any of these beaches, you must take a taxi. Fares run between LE10 and LE20.

Don't be alarmed by the enormous military presence in Marsa Matruuh. It is not uncommon to see men walking along the beach with machine guns and an occasional six-foot bazooka.

Sinai, Suez, and Red Sea Coast

The Sinai Peninsula will whet any hardened traveler's thirst for adventure. Dramatic mountainous terrain, reminiscent of the American Southwest, fills the southern interior. The area is riddled with bizarre, brightly-colored rock formations and hidden pools. The Red Sea Coast and the Gulf of Aqaba offer some of the world's best diving as well as fabulous beaches and fishing. Monasteries and religious centers hide away in the mountains of the Sinai and Egypt's Eastern Desert. Despite the often brutal sun and temperatures that hover between 105° and 110°F in the summer, few places possess such spectacular natural beauty.

History

A thriving tourist mecca during the Israeli occupation, the Sinai is once again isolated and ignored in the benevolently inefficient hands of the Egyptians. For decades, the Sinai has served as battleground for Arab-Israeli enmity. Four wars were fought between Israel and Egypt on the peninsula; remnants of these battles litter the now-peaceful desert.

The borders of the Sinai were first demarcated by the British in 1903; they were drawn from Rafiah on the Red Sea to Eilat, to keep the Turks and Germans a safe distance away from the Suez Canal. After World War I, the Rafiah-Eilat line became an international border and, after the bloodshed of the 1948 war for Israeli independence, it became the official border between Egypt and Israel. The only access to the Red Sea granted to Israeli vessels at the time was the tip of the Gulf of Eilat. Since the Suez Canal was barred to Israeli vessels, Eilat naturally grew into an important port, Israel's only link to Asia and Africa.

The fate of the Sinai took another turn in 1956, when Egypt tried to block the Gulf of Eilat, thus triggering the 1956 war, in which Israel promptly captured all of the Sinai. Foreign pressure and a United Nations promise to keep the Gulf open to Israeli ships persuaded Israel to return the Sinai to Egypt, but eleven years later the scenario was repeated. In 1967, Egypt called for the withdrawal of U.N. troops, and to the dismay of many, the troops were withdrawn. Egypt again tried to block the Gulf with the avowed intention of provoking an Arab-Israeli war, and succeeded. By the fourth day of the conflict, Israel had recaptured the Sinai. This time Israel ignored foreign pleas to accept peace terms that involved returning the Sinai, and held onto the territory as a buffer against Egyptian attack. In 1973, Egyptian forces crossed the Suez in a surprise offensive to recapture the Sinai. Again the result was a decisive Israeli victory: Israeli ground units penetrated into Egypt proper and were finally brought to a halt at a spot 101km before Cairo, thanks largely to a cease-fire agreement. Israeli forces subsequently retreated to the Red Sea, but maintained complete control of the Sinai until the signing of the 1978 peace treaty by Egyptian President Anwar Sadat and Israeli Prime Minister Menachem Begin. Under the terms of the agreement, the Sinai was returned to Egypt in two stages, the first half in 1979, the second in 1982.

Orientation

Only a few paved roads and a handful of permanent settlements spatter the Sinai. The peninsula can logically be divided into three distinct regions: the **Aqaba Coast,** stretching from Taba at the Israeli border to the southern tip, Ras Muhammad; the **Mediterranean Coast** from Rafiah to the Suez Canal, dominated by El Arish, the capital of the Sinai; and the interior of the **desert,** highlighted by Mt. Sinai and the Monastery of St. Catherine.

Buses are the only practical way to get around the Sinai; taxis are almost non-existent and very expensive. Traffic is meager, making hitching impractical, though once a car comes by, your chances of getting a lift are good. One bus daily runs from the Israeli border at Taba to Sharm el Sheikh (LE3) at 1pm Israeli time. En route to Sharm el Sheikh, the bus stops at Nuweiba (LE1, 1 hour), Dahaab (LE2, 2½ hours), and Na'ama (LE3.75, 4 hours). The bus leaves Sharm el Sheikh for Taba once daily; an evening bus goes only as far as Nuweiba. Two buses a day leave Sharm el Sheikh for Cairo (LE6.50), passing Ferran crossroads (LE2) for connections to St. Catherine's. Both buses pick up passengers in Na'ama a half hour before departure (50pt extra), but if you want to be assured of a seat, buy your ticket in advance in Sharm el Sheikh. Two buses a day run from the Israeli border at Rafiah to Cairo (LE5.25). Four buses a day go from El Arish to Cairo (LE4.50). Sheruts travel frequently from Rafiah to El Arish (LE2) and Cairo (LE10), and from El Arish to Cairo (LE5).

Buses for the Sinai leave from the Abusseiya station in Cairo to Sharm el Sheikh twice daily (LE7); to St. Catherine's once daily (LE6.50); to El Arish three times daily (LE4.50); and to Rafiah and the Israeli border. To get to the station from Midaan Abusseiya, walk alongside the elevated highway and under the overpass; the station is then on the right. The booking office is open 6am-4pm; it's wise to buy tickets in advance.

Practical Information

Climate. Refer to the Health section of the General Introduction for suggestions regarding travel in the desert.

Formalities. Though many travelers visit the Sinai on a regular tourist visa while in transit to or from Israel, the Egyptians have introduced a new Sinai-only visa in an effort to promote tourism on the peninsula. Though only valid for one week and limited to the Aqaba Coast and the St. Catherine's area, the visa does have one advantage: travelers are not obligated to meet the $150 currency exchange requirement. Unlike much else in Egypt, the process is quite simple—you receive your visa at the Taba border station, and need only pay the LE4.10 "tourist fee" which *all* tourists must pay. You *cannot* sneak into Cairo—there is a checkpoint about 30km south of the tunnel to the mainland.

If you enter the Sinai from Israel on a regular tourist visa, you must leave by the same port. For example, if you enter at Rafiah, you can't leave at Taba. You can, however, leave from the Cairo airport or from Alexandria—the rule only applies to the Sinai.

Accommodations. Inexpensive accommodations are essentially nonexistent in the Sinai, so be prepared to camp or sleep under the stars. The police are completely indifferent to free-lance camping, and may even help you by accepting your valuables for safekeeping. It's extremely unlikely that anyone will be energetic enough to cart off your entire backpack, but as always, never leave your valuables unattended (especially toilet paper, as it is never available in the Sinai).

Food. Food can be a problem in the Sinai. During the summer, restaurants throughout the Sinai serve meals for LE1-4, but in the winter months, budget travelers and Egyptian tourists are scarce, and some of the restaurants close down. The canned fish, canned fruit, and poorly-baked bread available in the Sinai are uniformly depressing. It is therefore advisable to bring food with you from Israel or Cairo. Don't leave your edibles unattended—goats and camels are surprisingly quick and efficient scavengers.

Tap water in the Sinai is generally safe to drink—much more so than in Egypt proper. If you plan to be cautious, expect to pay 60pt per bottle of mineral water.

Water sports. If you plan to spend any time on the Aqaba Coast, you may consider buying your own snorkeling equipment (very easy in Eilat; more difficult in Cairo). Since such equipment can't be bought anywhere in the Sinai, you should have little trouble reselling your gear before you leave.

Red Sea snorkeling is such an exciting experience that it is easy to abandon all caution. Wear sneakers or fins to protect your feet from sharp rocks, coral formations, the painful spikes of the black sea urchin, and the lethal bite of the less-common stonefish. Despite popular fears, there is very little danger of shark attack. Sharks are attracted by blood; never enter the water with an open wound. Panic tends to excite sharks—if you see one while snorkeling, calmly climb onto the reef and leave the water, and of course spread the word.

You must have a license to rent scuba equipment, but shops for diving equipment throughout the Sinai will take you on an introductory dive (a safe, shallow dive with a professional guide), or give you a full certification course for about $150. If you have an accident while diving, decompression centers are in the dive shop at Dahaab and at the Red Sea Divers shop in Na'ama.

Communications. Except in El Arish, no private telephones are in the Sinai. Mail is very slow, and only possible to and from Sharm el Sheikh.

Aqaba Coast

The Gulf of Aqaba stretches from Sharm el Sheikh to the Israeli border at Taba and features 250km of some of the most stunning coastline in the world. Moving from south to north, the main road runs slightly inland from Sharm el Sheikh to Nuweiba; from there it hugs the coast until the Israeli border. At the beaches, don't waste time padding around looking for bits of coral—ask people where the good reefs are. Although the coral is certainly magnificent, it is still a sideshow. The primary attraction are the oddly-shaped and -colored fish, which conveniently hang out near the coral reef.

Nuweiba

Though one of the most popular beaches south of Eilat, Nuweiba is actually the least attractive of the Aqaba Coast's trio of beach towns. The long, mostly barren strand is usually crowded with Israeli tourists, Egyptians working for the Taba border section, and a handful of MFO soldiers from one of the coast's three bases. The beach looks much the worse for wear. In fact, it's filthy. The camels you see trucking through town will assure you that you haven't landed in Miami Beach, but you'll be distressed to notice that their graceful necks are often buried in one of the underused garbage bins. The sizeable Bedouin population is also learning to exploit tourists; enterprising locals occasionally wander the beach trying to sell hashish or a camel ride.

The spectacular coral reefs, however, save Nuweiba from being just another beach. To reach the best snorkeling territory, walk south from the main beach and enter the water where you see the waves breaking. More secluded diving may be found farther south, at what locals refer to as the "Stone House," about 500m beyond the point visible from the main beach. The latter is also popular with nude sunbathers.

The dive shop is fully operative, but masks (LE1.50 per day), snorkels (LE1) and fins (LE2) are dispensed from the windsurfing booth at the northern end of the public beach. Scuba prices at Nuweiba are quite reasonable—LE35 includes all equipment, two boat dives, and guide.

The hotel at Nuweiba is outrageously expensive—sleep on the beach. The restaurant next to the kiosk is worth a splurge, however. For LE3.50, feast on fresh fish, spaghetti, salad, watermelon, and ice water. If you want meat or poultry instead of fish, it's LE1 more. An old sign above the door says the place is open 10am-9pm, but in fact it's open for lunch and dinner, and remains open until people stop coming (usually quite late).

Making your own meal from the selection at the kiosk and the bakery at the entrance to town is a miserable alternative, unless you have a keen appetite for canned tuna, canned mackerel, and canned jam.

A shower and restroom pavilion is at the far end of the parking lot. To use it, buy a ticket at the kiosk (25pt) good for the entire day (don't let the attendant keep your stub). The pavilion is usually open from about 10am to 6pm; if it's closed, climb through the small hole to the right of the entrance.

Behind the kiosk is the police station, where you can usually register between late morning and early evening. If you've avoided the $150 exchange requirement and are in the black market for pounds, Nuweiba is not the place to shop. None of the Egyptian workers will serve you; try approaching one of the few Westerners working in Nuweiba.

The modern buildings on the road into Nuweiba, once the Israeli *moshav* of Neviot, now house Egyptian government attachés. The *moshav* is fairly interesting to see—the houses contrast starkly with the plywood-and-plastic Bedouin shacks 2km to the north or those 4km to the south.

Dahaab

Going to Dahaab is like stepping into a Gauguin painting. Suddenly you are in an enchanting milieu of meandering goats, plodding camels, and dark-skinned children roaming about the encampment's palm-frond shanties. Most of the Bedouins live in houses sheltered in the palm grove, strung together out of driftwood, cardboard boxes, plastic, old sheets, and other detritus of the twentieth century. The villagers live, for the most part, off the fish they catch and the dates they harvest from the palms. They play checkers on a board drawn into the sand, using stones and bottlecaps as pieces.

Almost never seen by more than a handful of travelers, Dahaab is blessed with a stupendous mountain backdrop and even more startling underwater scenery. Dahaab means "gold" in Arabic, and this village is the Sinai's precious quantity, a great place to luxuriate.

Don't be fooled by the ugly modernity of the area around the bus stop. The Bedouin village and the best coral are 2½km away. This Israeli-built settlement, formerly the *moshav* of Di Zahav and an affiliated tourist camp, still has a number of conveniences, but is a noisy, glaring, and uninteresting place to sleep. The **dive shop,** the white building near the sea, rents mask, snorkel, and fins for LE4. Scuba excursions cost $35 for equipment, transportation, and guide, less if you pay in pounds. The adjacent restroom pavilion is no longer functional, but the dive center will allow customers to use their facilities. The "official" showers and restrooms are in the holiday village. The hotel charges an astronomical 50pt per usage, but since the facilities are never attended you may want to disregard this measure—go to the far right-hand corner of the complex. It costs LE2 per person to sleep on the hotel beach (no mattresses, blankets, or sheets), LE10 per person in a 6-bed dorm (breakfast included), or LE37 for a double room (breakfast and lunch or dinner included).

The kiosk where the bus unloads sells standard Sinai fare—canned fish, canned fruit, mineral water, and, occasionally, bread. None of the other advertised services are available (i.e. blanket rental, luggage storage, etc.). Behind the kiosk is the hotel restaurant, which serves breakfast for LE1, lunch and dinner for LE3. Open 7-10am, 1-3pm, and 8-10pm. The police station, for registration, is near the main road in the old *moshav*. If you want to camp near these various comforts, walk around the hotel beach fence and pitch anywhere between the fence and the dive shop. A far more interesting place to stay is in the Bedouin village. To get there from the bus stop, walk back across the parking lot and head straight for the two white water towers of the MFO base. On the inland side of the base, the asphalt road ends and a rough dirt track begins—follow this and aim for the *far* palm grove, barely visible from the base. If you don't have a tent but want some privacy or shelter from the wind, move into one of the uninhabited palm huts and a Bedouin will eventually come along to collect LE1. If you'd like a cooked meal as well, let the owner of the cafe know in the afternoon, and he will close up shop and go fishing for you. Fish and whatever else he has handy (usually rice) will cost about LE1-1.50.

The best of Dahaab's splendid reefs begin at the northern edge of the cove, but a smaller, equally brilliant shelf of coral is at the southern edge of the inlet (you'll see the waves breaking). To find reefs closer to the modern village, check the map at the dive shop.

If you do stay in the Bedouin village, remember that there are no toilets or drinking water and no electricity. Enjoy the rare experience of seeing stars undiluted by the haze of surface lights. Be respectful of your neighbors. The moment you see the Bedouin men in their long flowing white robes and the women in their austere black garb you will want to take a picture of them, but the Bedouins do not like to be photographed. Their religion prohibits making images of people, and they have a number of superstitions to the effect that they lose control of their souls when images are made of them. The women are far touchier on the subject than the men, which is unfortunate, for their embroidered garments are quite beautiful. If you can't resist the temptation, proceed at your own risk—but be warned, for you won't be the first to have a watermelon thrown at you.

Finally, don't expect anything from the Americans at the MFO base. Though quite friendly and overjoyed to meet Yanks, they cannot invite you onto the base, and can offer you little more than a heavily chlorinated refill of your water jug or use of their latrine (a small white box outside the compound on the bus stop side). They're paid in dollars and won't be interested in changing money—a very difficult undertaking in Dahaab.

Na'ama Bay

The Aqaba Coast from Tiran Island to Ras Muhammad conceals some of the best snorkeling and scuba diving in the world, and Na'ama is the perfect place from which to explore the area.

You'll have no trouble sleeping or camping on the beach at Na'ama; as is the case throughout the Sinai, the police are actually happy to have dozens of foreigners spending money.

Two amazing dive sites are within walking distance of Na'ama. Coral, fish, and undersea foliage await divers in the seductive **Near Gardens,** on the northern side of the cove, while the **Far Gardens,** farther along around the point, are even more exquisite. If you've had enough of both of these (this may take several months), you can also tag along with one of the dive shops' almost-daily trips to more distant sites. Trips by car (ninety minutes) cost $5. Boat trips are more expensive ($20), but the all-day excursion goes to Tiran Island or Ras Muhammad, the two best diving sites in the area. Wherever you go, you can get mask, snorkel, and fins for LE4.50 from any of the three dive centers at Na'ama (Red Sea Divers, at the far southern end of the cove; Aquanaut, halfway around the cove; or Aquamarine, in the Aquamarine Hotel). Trips for certified divers are offered by these shops almost daily at a cost of $45, including equipment, transportation, and accompaniment.

If you need a bed to sleep in, avoid the Marina Sharem Hotel (doubles LE37), and try the cheaper **Aquamarine Hotel,** on the opposite side of the bay (LE16.50 for bed and breakfast for two). A free shower and rest room pavilion (open 7am-8 or 9pm) is next to the tourist police station, so there is almost no reason not to sleep on the beach. If the sands aren't too crowded, the tourist police will usually let you leave your gear inside or in front of their office.

Food is better in Sharm el Sheikh (see below), but you can survive on Na'ama's offerings. The **Red Sea Dive Shop** operates a commendable restaurant where dinner runs LE4.50. The **Beach Front Snack Bar** next door serves soft drinks and small sandwiches for 25pt each. The snack bar in the same building as the police station sells tins of fish and fruit.

If you want to change money in Na'ama, tactfully approach one of the many Westerners working there. Registration formalities can only be carried out in Sharm el Sheikh. To get from Na'ama to Sharm el Sheikh and back, try hitching, or take the yellow, open-sided *tof-tof,* which runs about every hour until 7pm between the two settlements (25pt one way). Since the bus is unreliable and hitching quite good (low volume but high yield), a wise strategy is to begin thumbing and flag the bus down if it happens to come by. If you are American and decide to hitch, don't curse compatriots for not giving you a lift—MFO personnel are forbidden to pick up civilians.

Sharm el Sheikh

Sharm el Sheikh is a town with no sights to see, but it does have a members-only IYHF Youth Hostel and some decent food. After stocking up on food, you'll find there's nothing to do except follow the crowds to beautiful Na'ama Bay.

Sharm el Sheikh first made world headlines in 1956, when the Egyptian naval units stationed there began to bar the passage of Israeli vessels through the straits between the Sinai coast and the island of Tiran. This triggered the 1956 war. In 1967, President Nassar of Egypt made the remote port of Sharm el Sheikh front page news for a second time by trying to block the Tiran Straits again, leading to the Six Day War. After fifteen years of Israeli control, this strategic southernmost Sinai town was returned to Egypt in 1982, in accordance with the Camp David Agreement. Egypt has installed a large bureaucracy here, thus decreasing even further the town's chance of becoming interesting.

All of Sharm el Sheikh can be navigated from the only crossroads in town, where the road from Taba and Na'ama meets the road to the West Coast and Cairo. To the left, halfway up the hill, is the **tourist police** station and the **booking office** for buses to Cairo (and booking *is* recommended).

To register with the police, walk southward around the bay, and at the port, take the left fork. After about 100m, you'll see the office (technically open only 9am-5pm, but often staffed at other times as well).

Most necessities can be found on the main square: a small fruit and vegetable stand selling nearly inedible produce (open 8am-10pm), a **telephone and telegram office** (open 7am-10pm), and what Sinai residents call a supermarket—actually a small room containing the same canned junk available in other Sinai towns, but in larger quantity (open 9am-2pm and 7-9pm; closed Tues., and sometimes Fri.). Another store is around the building to the back. In the same square you'll find several banks. Straight on from the crossroads is the **bakery** (open 24 hours), where you can buy pita bread (1pt each), baked with a liberal measure of hair, sand, and occasionally insects. A sizable cluster of buildings to the right of the junction includes a **hospital** (facing the Cairo Road; look for the flags and ambulances), and a **post office,** facing the Na'ama Road (open Sat.-Thurs. 10am-3pm). Two places serve fish and rice for approximately LE1-1.50. Around the corner from the post office is the town's best **restaurant,** where you'll find a wide selection at similar prices, often in an air-conditioned environment (spaghetti 75pt, rice 50pt, steak LE2.25).

Food and other basic services are more available here than in Na'ama, but there is no beach appropriate for swimming or camping. The **IYHF Youth Hostel,** at the top of the hill in town, is air-conditioned, equipped with a kitchen, and fairly clean. Despite its perpetually mediocre occupancy rate, it is open to IYHF members only. Dorm-style accommodation costs LE2; the hostel is closed 9am-2pm with a curfew of 10pm in winter, 11pm in summer. The only alternative to curfew and dorms is the **Cliff Top Village** next door, with singles for LE15 and doubles for LE23.

Near Sharm el Sheikh is the diver's paradise of **Ras Muhammad.** Reputed to be one of the most spectacular dive sites in the world, this extreme southern tip of the Sinai offers, on clear days, a spectacular and rare view of two continents at once—on clear days you can see Asia to the east and Africa to the west. Unfortunately, the point is exceedingly difficult to reach. Dive shops in Na'ama make boat trips there on an irregular schedule ($20), but if you want to visit for more than a day you must hitch to the turn-off about 20km west of Sharm el Sheikh, and walk 10km from there, unless you can find a taxi willing to take you for an acceptable price (there are very few taxis in town and this route is almost never used). You must have a full Egyptian visa to pass the Egyptian Army checkpoint. There is a divers' camp at Ras Muhammad; if you want to make use of it, try to convince one of the dive shops at Na'ama to radio ahead for you.

The Desert

The interior of the Sinai, with the notable exception of the Mt. Sinai area, is technically off limits to tourists. This, however, should not necessarily stop the adventurous soul from exploring this ocean of mountains. All the roads are manned by soldiers, but Bedouins in Nuweiba and Dahaab regularly escort the intrepid on a camel trek in the desert for LE10 per person per day, food and camel included. To find a guide (if one doesn't find you first), ask around in either of these towns, especially at one of the Bedouin cafes. If you do happen to have a run-in with the army, plead ignorance and apologize profusely; such entanglements, however, are rare, since the Bedouin is likely to get in much more trouble than you, and is consequently circumspect.

Saint Catherine's Monastery and Mount Sinai

At the foot of Mount Sinai, on top of which Moses received the Ten Commandments, stands the majestic Monastery of Saint Catherine. Despite their remote location, the monastery and the nearby mountaintop remain the Sinai's prime tourist attractions. The cloister had its start in 342 C.E. when Helena, the mother of Constantine the Great, had a small chapel built next to a bush, believed to have been the famous Burning Bush through which God first spoke to Moses. In the sixth century, Emperor Justinian ordered the construction of a splendid basilica and monastery within the walls of a fortress to enable Christians to live in the desert without fear of persecution. Tradition has it that he ordered the execution of the monastery's architect when he learned that the monastery had not been built on the summit of Mount Sinai. In a way, it was fortunate that the architect ignored the emperor's directions and chose the foot of the Mount—it is not only well-protected but also close to an abundant water supply. Saint Catherine's is believed to be the oldest unrestored example of Byzantine architecture in the world. The monastery once housed hundreds of monks but its population has now dwindled to about a dozen. The monastery abounds in delightful sights. The museum exhibits jewel-studded crosses, handcarved wooden furniture, and exquisite icons dating back to the fourth century. Also found here is one of the finest libraries of ancient manuscripts in the world. The macabre Charnel House contains the bones of all the monastery's former residents. Christian pilgrims have primarily come to Saint Catherine's to visit the **Tomb of St. Catherine,** a martyr who lived in Alexandria and was persecuted for her belief in Christianity. Unfortunately, all of these were closed as of the summer of 1983, and it is not known when they'll be reopened. Only the chapel, which contains what is supposed to be part of the original Burning Bush, is open to the public, and then only Mon.-Thurs. and Sat. from 9:30am-12:30pm. Modest dress is required.

The Sinai peninsula owes its name to the towering 2285m peak of Mount Sinai (*Gebel Musa* in Arabic) revered by Jews, Christians and Muslims alike as the site where Moses had his famous conversations with God and received the Ten Commandments. According to the Bible, Moses climbed up Mt. Sinai not one but three times: on the first, God revealed to him his desire to make a covenant with the people of Israel; on the second, God delivered the Ten Commandments; and finally, on the third, Moses was told to build the tabernacles, i.e., a place of worship where people could commune with God. (Not surprisingly, Mt. Sinai became known as the "Mount of God.") But Moses was not the only one to ascend the Mount in those days; a few hundred years later, the prophet Elijah also made a trip to have a little talk with the Almighty. You too can climb Mt. Sinai (though there's no guarantee you'll encounter a burning bush) by either of two ascents. The shorter of the two is the **Steps of Repentance,** which number some three thousand steps, and is actually the harder route to climb. It is said that the steps were built by a single monk in order to fulfill his pledge of penitence. The steps are treacherous by night and extremely arduous by day, so it is recommended that you take the Camel Path (two hours by foot), which begins directly behind the monastery, and reserve the steps for the way down. The path is clearly marked by stone curbs on either side, except at one confusing juncture about two-thirds of the way up, where the path nearly doubles back about 30m beyond a narrow stone corridor. A short distance on, downhill from where the Camel Path connects with the steps—about 750 steps before the top—is a five-hundred-year-old cypress tree dominating a small plain known as **Elijah's Hollow.** Here the prophet Elijah heard the voice of God (I Kings 19:9ff). Two small chapels now occupy the site, one dedicated to Elijah and the other to his successor Elisha.

The best time to make the two- to three-hour journey is in the late evening or at night, so as to avoid the midday heat. Such a plan allows you to wake up on the summit to experience the sunrise and Mt. Sinai's unforgettable view, extending to the mountains of Africa and Saudi Arabia, the Red Sea, and the Gulf of Aqaba. The summit holds a small chapel, built in 1937 over the remains of a Byzantine church. In the cave below, Moses hid himself when he first came face-to-face with God. The chapel is almost always unattended and closed, but if you're lean and able you can climb through the loosely barred windows on the south side of the church.

A few preparations are in order if you plan to make a night trek. Be sure to dress warmly and bring a sleeping bag, whether or not you plan to sleep, as the summit is cool even in summer and there's no room to pitch a tent. If you don't have a flashlight, wait at the start of the path for someone who does. Even if you arrive late, make a detour to the town to store your luggage. If the police won't watch it for you, the Bedouin hotel will take care of it for 25pt (see below for directions). You don't need a guide—the path is not difficult to find, the way is not dangerous, and the self-professed "guides" know nothing about the history of the mountain. The starting point of the path lies 50m directly behind the monastery enclosure's rear wall. If it's dark, search for the lighter-colored sand framed by a stone curb. Those who decide to negotiate the steps can find them behind the monastery on the right side. Six kilometers to the south of Mt. Sinai looms **Gebel Katherina,** the highest mountain in Egypt at 2642m. It is named after St. Catherine, whose remains were reportedly discovered on its summit in the seventh century by monks from the nearby monastery. The path to the top, more secluded and beautiful than the Mt. Sinai highway, begins in the village itself—get a local to show you where the way begins.

Getting to and from St. Catherine's can be quite a hassle, and should not be attempted if you have only a few days left on your visa. Getting into the area, seeing the points of interest, and getting back to a border can easily take three to five days, assuming you don't get stranded. There is a direct bus from Cairo to St. Catherine's, which leaves from the Abusseiya station at 10am. If you're coming from Sharm el Sheikh, you must take the 11am bus bound for Cairo as far as the Ferran crossroads (LE2; slightly over 2 hours) and wait until the bus from Cairo comes, any time after 2pm. There is a sunshade, and soda, tea, and canned food are available. You may consider spending the interim hitching, since the bus has been known to arrive already packed. If you are pressed for time and want to be sure of getting to St. Catherine's in one day, consider taking the 6am Cairo-bound bus, as the junction is livelier in morning.

Two kinds of nomads mingle in the village at St. Catherine's: those from the West, bound for the monastery and mountains, and the native people who seem oblivious to the hordes of *hawaget* (tourists). Accommodations are scanty. The monastery operates a shower-less **hostel;** but at LE5 it is a disappointment. Moreover, Western women traveling independently may be turned away. The hostel is often full, especially in summer, and there is no way of making reservations. The **St. Catherine Hotel,** opposite the turnoff for the monastery, is more likely to be empty, but the rates are LE12 for a single, LE18 for a double, and LE24 for a triple (no black-market pounds accepted). The third alternative in the town itself, equally bland, is the **Bedouin hotel.** It's only LE1 for a piece of foam rubber on a sand floor, but be warned that there are effectively no toilets, no showers, and the rooms are extremely hot and stuffy at night. You'll be much more comfortable if you simply choose any suitable place in or around town and sleep outside. To get to the Bedouin hotel, follow the *second* dirt road on the right past the gas station. If you don't mind sleeping 4km away from the town and the monastery, the best place to stay in the area is **Zeitouna Camping.** For LE3 per person per night, you get a bed in a large tent, and access to the showers and restrooms.

Thankfully, there is a cheap **restaurant** at St. Catherine's. It's located on the only road in town, just beyond the bakery (pita bread 1pt each). Rice, potatoes, spaghetti, and beans are all 30pt each. Next to it is a small grocery.

Slightly farther along the road is the **police station,** and in front of that, the **bus station.**

A rough desert road connects St. Catherine's to the Aqaba Coast, but there is *very* little civilian through-traffic, and ordinarily you need military clearance. Hitching is not recommended. If you can gather a group of ten or so people, you'll have little trouble finding someone in St. Catherine's who has a large vehicle to take you for about LE100 (and they'll help you take care of the travel restrictions). Split ten ways, the cost is not much more than the bus, and provides a shorter trip with better opportunities to view the scenery. If you do choose to try your luck hitching, the road begins at the St. Catherine's Airport and emerges on the Aqaba Coast at a point between Nuweiba and Dahaab.

El Arish

El Arish, capital of the Sinai Peninsula, has little in common with the towns to the south. Lacking the isolation and natural splendor of the Aqaba Coast or the Desert, El Arish is a rather uninteresting Egyptian city of 30,000 inhabitants. For the traveler fresh out of Israel, it provides a healthy and enjoyable transition to chaotic Cairo.

If the city seems unaffected by the twelve-year Israeli occupation, it is because the vast majority of its residents stayed through the turmoil. These days, El Arish is preparing for another invasion—by tourists: new buildings are sprouting up all over town like worms after a thunder-storm, and glossy posters depicting the town's palm-lined beach can be seen in travel offices all over Egypt. The palms do in fact stretch for miles, but what postcards and posters fail to show are the hundreds of tents erected every summer as seasonal homes by locals trying to escape the sweltering city. Surprisingly, these free-lance residents keep the beach clean—something that can't be said for the city itself. If you care to join these shore dwellers, be discreet about your campsite, since the police like to keep tourists confined to the official **El Arish Camping,** 7km west of town (LE4.50 for 2 beds in a spacious, lit tent, LE1.50 if you have your own equipment). In addition, *do not* walk on the beach after dark—the police are extremely strict about this, as part of a crack-down on drug smugglers.

To find the **police station** (tel. 12 0, 12 1, or 12 2) and the **hospital** (tel. 77), walk east on Sharia Gish from Midaan Suq, the first square inland from the shore road on 23 July St. The **central post office** (open Sat.-Thurs. 9am-3pm) and the **telecommunications office** (open 24 hours) are in the same building on a secondary thoroughfare named 23 July St., actually the third side street on the east side of the main 23 July St.

For those who decide not to sleep on the beach, El Arish does have more conventional accommodations, but the two hotels in town are fairly disgusting, and those along the beach, expensive. The **El Salaam Hotel** (tel. 21 9), above the Aziz Restaurant on 23 July St., seaward from the bus/taxi station in Baladiya Square, has doubles for LE4, and triples and quads for LE6. If you arrive alone, they'll give you a bed in a larger room for LE1.50, but only if other foreigners are also staying there. Farther along 23 July St., take the third left after Baladiya Square to find the **Crossing Hotel.** It is cheaper at LE2.40 for a double, LE4.20 for a triple, and LE4.70 for a quad, but also shabbier. On the beach, try the **Moon Light Hotel** (tel. 36 2), where beds go for LE4.80 per person in rooms with private bath, or LE3 in those without.

Fresh produce, bread, and good canned food are more readily available in El

Arish than in the rest of the Sinai. The **Aziz Restaurant,** on 23 July St., or one of the many Egyptian food stands elsewhere on 23 July St. provide cooked meals.

To get to and from thc beach and 23 July St. (city center), take a taxi (10pt) or a minibus (5pt).

Port Said (Buur Sai'id)

The most interesting of the cities along the Suez Canal, Port Said is a busy Mediterranean port unspoiled by tourism. Rows of tankers, freighters, and cruise ships dock next to the white colonnade of the port authority here, where the Suez Canal widens to meet the Mediterranean. The main attraction of Port Said is certainly the canal itself, the reason for the city's establishment.

Flanking the far side of the canal is Port Said's sister town, **Port Fouad (Buur Fouad).** Buses for the Canal cities depart from Ulali Square in Cairo and drop you at the **Firial Garden.** There you'll find a ticket office where you can buy a return ticket. You can also reach Port Said by train from Cairo: five trains leave Ramsis Station daily for the 135km trip (4½ hours, LE1.85 second class). When leaving Port Said, all visitors must pass through the Customs House (near Firial Garden). Because Port Said is a free port, you must pay a 12% tax on anything bought there. Be sure to come early to catch your bus or train, since customs processing can take an inordinately long time.

You'll find everything you need, including most important services, along the canal or along the beach at right angles to the canal. **Palestine Street** follows the canal; at #43 you'll find the **Tourist Office,** where you can pick up a copy of *Canal by Night and Day,* which contains a good map of the city. The number for the **Tourist Police** is 31 70. The **American consulate** at Tarh El Bahr St. (tel. 23 88 6) deals with shipping concerns and little else.

For accommodations, try the **Palm House Hotel,** 23 July St. #34 (tel. 26 39 2), which overlooks the beach. It's a charming old building with singles for LE3.23, LE3.88 with bath, and doubles for LE4.30, LE5.17 with bath. The **El Ghazli Hotel,** next door to the Palm House at #23, has reasonable rooms and the same view. Singles LE3.02, LE3.60 with bath; doubles LE4.03, LE4.81 with bath. Finally, there's the popular **Hotel de la Poste** on Gomhuria St. (tel. 24 04 8) across from the Holiday Hotel. Singles or doubles with bath LE8.70. There is also an **IYHF Youth Hostel** in Port Said on El Amin and Korneish Sts. (tel. 32 02); at 60pt per person for those under 23, 80pt for those over 21, it should be a last resort.

Port Said has a limited selection of restaurants. Try **Soufar,** on the corner of Degla and Gomhuria Sts., or **Seahorse,** on the Corniche. Both run about LE3 for dinner. Avoid the tourist traps nearer the boats.

The best view of the canal is at the white-colonnaded, blue-domed Canal House. The guard will let you in if you give him a few piasters. Take advantage of the free ferry ride across the canal to Port Fouad; the crossing gives you a magnificent view and the chance to wander around the less touristed shops of the smaller port. Port Said's **Military Museum,** on 23 July St., holds displays depicting ancient Pharaonic and Islamic battles, but concentrates on the victories of the 1973 war against Israel. Detailed maps show how the Bar Lev line was smashed in six hours. Admission 25pt. In front of the museum, the beach runs west to the Canal; for 50pt you can rent a chair to sit and watch the passing ships.

Ismailiya (Ismai'iliya)

Ismailiya, named after Egypt's ruler at the time of the Canal's construction, is the cleanest of the newly built Canal cities. Laid out in a checkerboard pattern of gardens, malls, and magnificent avenues lined with flame trees, the city is quiet and peaceful. Its main attractions are the few sandy beaches dotted along **Lake Timsah** (Crocodile Lake) and the Canal.

The town center consists of a few blocks around **El-Thowra St.** The bus station is grim, but if you walk back along the canal, the outlook improves. Bus fare from Cairo is LE2.50, from Port Said LE1. In addition, the train from Cairo to Port Said stops in Ismailiya (five trips a day, three hours). The **Tourist Office** is located in the governate building (tel. 20 71).

The best lodgings in town are at the **Nefertari Hotel,** which charges LE8 for a double with bath and air conditioning. It's located in the center of town at El-Thowra St. (tel. 28 22). The **Minerva Hotel,** 20 Omar Ibn Aas St. (tel. 34 73), has singles for LE4 and doubles LE8. All rooms have a bath and fan. It's also possible to camp on the beaches. You can buy food from street vendors, or eat at **George's,** down from the Nefertari, or **Groppi's** across the street.

The **museum** at Ismailiya covers the history of the Canal from ancient times to the present. Exhibits include a plaque of Darius the Persian declaring the opening of a canal from the Red Sea to the Persian Sea (today known as the Mediterranean). Admission 25pt. Other sights include the **House of Ferdinand de Lesseps,** the director of the Canal's construction, on Sharia Port Said, and the **Garden of the Stelae,** north of town, containing Sphinxes from the age of Ramses II. Otherwise, spend the day relaxing on the beaches. Access to the resort clubs requires payment of a stiff fee (LE5).

Suez (Suwiis)

Where the Red Sea meets the Suez Canal, the city of Suez sprawls like a sluggish animal; its oil refineries and myriad ships spew out smoke and fumes, the beast's malodorous breath. Through the smog, red cliffs behind the city contrast with the blue of the bay. Suez has very few hotels or restaurants and little to attract the tourist—most travelers simply pass through the city en route to the Sinai by way of the new tunnel 30km north of town or on their way south along the Red Sea Coast.

Suez can be reached by bus from Cairo (LE3) or Ismailiya (LE1), or by service taxi for roughly the same prices. The Arba'iin bus station is a few blocks from the bay. There are two train routes from Cairo to Suez, one via Port Said and Ismailiya and one express. The express trains leave Ramsis Station twice a day at 5:50am and 3:35pm, and take just under three hours. For more travel information, try the **Tourist Office** at 16 Sharia El-Shohadaa (tel. 23 89; office hours are rather sporadic). The **Tourist Police** can be reached by telephone at 23 81.

The town's few hotels and restaurants line Sa'ad Zaghluul St. and the Corniche (El Galaa St.). **San Stefano,** at 18 El Galaa St. (tel. 32 90), offers singles for LE3 and doubles for LE4.50. The rooms, though dirty, have a decent view. Other cheap hotels on Sa'ad Zaghluul St. identify themselves with bright neon signs. The **Suez Youth Hostel (IYHF),** on Tarik El Horreya St., charges 40pt per person under 21, 60pt over 21. **El-Magharbel** restaurant, next to the White Hotel on Sa'ad Zaghluul, has meals for LE3.

The only sights in Suez are the Canal and the bay. Three American tanks stand along the Corniche as a reminder of Egypt's victories in the 1973 war with Israel. A trip to the beach at **Ain Sukhna,** 60km south along the Red Sea, can be arranged with some ingenuity, as buses and service taxis run down the coast from Suez. The beach, desolate and windy, is quite peaceful.

Monasteries of Saint Paul and Saint Anthony

Two isolated outposts, the monasteries of St. Paul and St. Anthony, lie 82km apart near the edge of the Red Sea. These centers of faith, hidden high among the red cliffs, have come to represent the beginnings of the Christian monastic tradition. In the fourth century, St. Paul and St. Anthony first dedicated their lives to prayer and solitude; a few years after they entered the desert, communal monasteries sprang up around St. Paul's cave and St. Anthony's spring. Today, St. Paul's and St. Anthony's each harbor twenty-five monks and five novices, who lead a monastic life similar to that of their predecessors over the last sixteen centuries.

The Bishop assigns each monk a specific duty; since 1979, Father Sarabamon has guided visitors to **St. Paul's Monastery.** His English is excellent, as are his tours. To enter, just ring the bell at the gate. The **Church of St. Paul,** built in the cave where St. Paul is said to have lived for ninety years, is the most fascinating part of the monastery. Many of the frescoes date from the fourth and seventh centuries. Ostrich eggs, a Christian symbol of the Resurrection, hang from the roof. The candles used to illuminate the altars and murals heighten the mystery of the sanctuary. Above the church is the **fortress,** to which the monks retreated when the Bedouins attacked. A secret canal from the spring ensured their survival through long sieges.

Unfortunately, access to the monasteries is limited to private cars and tour buses from Cairo. Regular buses from Suez or Cairo will drop you off 12km from the Monastery of St. Paul; in the desert heat the walk is dangerous to undertake. Return buses are even less feasible, since drivers usually won't stop to pick you up. Without a private car, you could be stranded for a week.

The Monastery of St. Paul offers free lodging, including food and water, to any visitor who asks. This hospitality appears especially generous when you consider that the meager spring provides only four cubic meters of water a day. The supplies at **St. Anthony's Monastery** are more ample, but their guest facilities are restricted to Coptic Orthodox men. Before you visit either monastery, try to obtain permission from the Coptic Patriarch at St. Mark's Church on Ramsis St. south of Abusseiya Sq. in Cairo.

Hurghada (Ilgharda'a)

Buff-colored mountains, turquoise water, and powder-soft sand beaches greet the visitor in Hurghada. Tucked away in a bay on the coast of the Red Sea, the little fishing-village-turned-resort-town is now known by skin divers and fishermen the world over. Unlike the barren desert which stretches its lifeless fingers right down to the shore, Hurghada's brilliant underwater world teems with life. The off-shore coral reefs are home for some of nature's most colorful and exotic creatures. Buck-toothed trigger fish, stingrays with blue polka-dots, iridescent parrot fish, sea cucumbers, giant clams, and a million others perform in this briny, ocean-going circus. Always warm and crystal clear, the sparkling water invites even the most ardent land-lubber. If you want a break from crumbling temples and stuffy tombs, come to very un-pharaonic Hurghada.

Orientation and Practical Information

Hurghada, hardly the isolated fishing village it once was, can be reached by several routes. Buses run daily from Suez, as do service taxis, which take eight hours and cost LE7. Buses and service taxis also run from Qena in the Nile Valley. The taxis cost about LE3 per person (LE2 to Port Safaga and another LE1 to Hurghada). Flights from Cairo (six weekly) cost LE36.80; winter flights from Luxor cost LE14.

In order to accommodate an increasing number of international tourists, Hurghada is growing rapidly. Consequently, the town is rather spread out, with no visible street signs. Still, you can find your way around easily. At the far end of town, near the larger of the town's two mosques, is the **Telephone and Telegraph Office,** open 24 hours a day. The **Tourist Office** is on Governorate St. (tel. 826/43 93 37).

Accommodations and Food

You can camp for free at the beach or bed down in one of the Government Bungalows for LE10 per day. The cheapest and most popular places to stay are the various "tourist flats" scattered around town. You don't have to worry about finding these, since the totes will gladly escort you and your backpack to their humble establishment. The **Hurghada Happy House,** El Dhar Mosque Square near the bus station, has clean bathrooms and large rooms for LE1.50 per person. The retired sea-captain Muhammad Awad, a friendly, ever-smiling fellow, rents masks and snorkels for LE1.50 per day and arranges snorkeling trips to the reefs. Ask about his special trip to "The House of the Sharks." Even if you don't want to buy any of the seaside knick-knacks in his Red Sea Wonderland Shop or stay at his place, stop by for a chat. He knows the reefs, the water, the fish, and will gladly answer questions. **Luxor Tourist Flat,** on the main paved road coming into town near the military school, costs LE1 per person and is run by a courteous English-speaking family. They also arrange diving trips and rent snorkeling equipment. The **Sunshine House** next door to the Luxor Tourist Flat charges LE1.50 per person.

If you plan to do extensive scuba diving or snorkeling, buy a voucher from Misr Travel in Cairo for the **Club Med** at Maguawish for LE38; the price includes two dives plus equipment, food, and an air-conditioned room. Elsewhere, one dive will cost this much alone. The daily rate of LE18 entitles you to two snorkel dives and a superb buffet.

Immediately off the main road leading into the town are three or four inexpensive restaurants, all situated right next to each other. Chicken or shish kebab goes for LE1.50, fish for 90pt, and spaghetti for 50pt. Back on the main paved road leading to the Telephone and Telegraph Office you'll find the **Cafeteria** and the slightly more expensive **Restaurant Happyland.**

Sights

Obviously, Hurghada's main attractions are underwater. Red Sea creatures come in a dazzling display of colors, shapes, and sizes. To enjoy the beach in safety you need to take a few precautions, however. The desert sun can deliver a painful burn—all but the most deeply tanned should wear a protective sunscreen (or clothing). To walk near the reefs, you'll need tennis shoes or flipflops; the coral can easily make shish kebab out of your feet. If you see something that looks like an aquatic pin cushion, it's probably a sea urchin or blowfish, both of which are better left alone. Avoid the feathery lionfish as well—its harmless-looking spines can deliver a paralyzing sting.

Although there is some coral at the beach to the left of the Sheraton and another small patch along the seashore behind the Cafeteria, you must take a boat to get to Hurghada's interesting coral reefs. The Sheraton and the Club Med both rent reliable scuba and snorkel equipment. Stay away from rental snorkels, as they can transmit severe throat infections. The boat trip to **Geftun Island,** the most popular excursion, costs LE5 per person including lunch. The all-day affair allows you to snorkel around some spectacular reefs; one in the middle of the bay and one off the Island itself. Make arrangements the night before with the manager of your "tourist flat." Other boat trips can be arranged; be sure to haggle over prices.

Four kilometers outside of town are a mediocre (but free) **museum and aquarium.** Bus fare is 10pt.

Oases

The country's five major oases—**Bahariya, Farafra; Dakhla, Kharga,** and **Siwa**—reveal Egypt at its most Middle Eastern. Colorfully-clad peasant women, dramatic desert landscape, verdant rolling groves of endless palm trees, and remote oasis wells with delicious spring water all lie sprinkled throughout Egypt's vast Western Desert. If you've tired of the bustle and noise of Cairo and Alexandria, the oases are the perfect escape: quiet, unspoiled and beautiful.

These oases are Egypt's only patches of fertile land away from the banks of the Nile, with ruins dating from the Pharaonic, Roman, Christian, and islamic eras. The local Bedouin and *fellahin* who dwell along the fields and palm groves of the oases are, on the whole, friendly and generous, and still unaccustomed to tourists. Strangers are treated with the same hospitality these people have always extended to travelers in the desert. Nonetheless, a journey to the more remote oases is only recommended for the most adventurous of travelers. Getting around is improbable without a car, tourist facilities are almost non-existent, and almost no one speaks any language other than Arabic or a native dialect (usually Berber).

Orientation

Winter (October to April) is unquestionably the best time to visit the oases. It is not unusual for summer temperatures, especially at Kharga, to soar as high as 125 degrees Fahrenheit. Even at night, summer temperatures persist in the mid-eighties. There is no air-conditioning.

Permits

In order to visit Siwa, Farafra or Dakhla, a special permit is required from the Ministry of Interior in Cairo (see Cairo, Practical Information). The best time to apply is at 8:30pm on any evening except Friday. The applicant must appear in person with his/her passport and one passport-size photo. With a little luck it is possible to obtain permits by 10:30pm on the same evening. If you are applying for a permit for transit to either Farafra or Dakhla and therefore planning to pass through Bahariya and/or Kharga, you must apply for special permission for travel to these oases as well. If your permit is issued by the Ministry of the Interior in Cairo, it must outline your entire itinerary and mention any oases you plan to pass through. When applying for a permit leave plenty of leeway in estimating when you will arrive at the oases and how long you plan to stay. It is possible to apply for permission to travel to Farafra at the police station in Bahariya, and then for permission to travel to Dakhla at the police station in Farafra, etc., without going to the Ministry of the Interior in Cairo. This course of action, however, is not recommended; ultimately it will prove more time-consuming than getting a single permit in Cairo, and the language barrier may be insurmountable at small regional police stations. If you attempt to visit one of the restricted oases without a permit you will be intercepted at the military checkpoint along the desert road and sent back.

Transportation

Buses run from Al Azhar Bus Station in Cairo to Bahariya, Kharga, and Dakhla. (For more information see the bus section in general information). Inexpensive buses also run from the town of Assyut, halfway down the Nile, to Kharga, but they are slow, crowded and uncomfortable. Kharga is also serviced by plane: Wednesday and Saturday **EgyptAir** Cairo-Aswan flights stop off at the oasis. Otherwise, there is no public transportation to any of the oases. It is possible to hitchhike from one oasis to the next, but you may find yourself waiting as long as a week or more for a ride, especially from Farafra or Dakhla. Of course, if you enjoy the desert and are in no great hurry then, as the locals will tell you, *maalesh*—it doesn't really matter. For those who have a less Zen approach to travel, the only convenient and comfortable way to get to and around the oases along the Great Desert Road—i.e., Bahariya, Farafra, Dakhla, and Karga—is to rent a car. (For more information on getting to Siwa see below). This mode of oasis-hopping is rather expensive for most budget travelers, if still eminently worthwhile. The most popular itinerary is to begin in Cairo, (the best place in Egypt to rent a car), drive through the desert to Bahariya, then continue on to Farafra, Dakhla, and Kharga, and return via Assyut along the Nile passing by the archeological sites near Mallawi and Minya.

If you wish to rent a car and drive on to Farafra and Dakhla a number of caveats are in order. The road was just completed in 1980, so there are no gas stations anywhere along the Great Desert Road between Bahariya and Kharga. The only gasoline in Farafra and Dakhla is in the hands of the military, and they are usually very reticent about selling it to tourists. It is therefore necessary to procure a metal jerry-can from a gas station in Cairo or Assyut and fill it with at least 20 liters of gasoline. You should also bring several large containers filled with drinking water in case an accident leaves you temporarily stranded in the desert. The desert roads, by and large, are long, uneventful affairs stretching straight ahead for hundreds of kilometers. The monotony of the driving makes it remarkably easy to lose concentration, drive off the road into the desert, and flip your car over. For longer hauls, especially in summer, it is cooler and more comfortable to drive at night.

Accommodations

Siwa, Kharga, and Farafra oases have government rest houses, and Bahariya has a handful of simple hotels. Otherwise, the best alternative is to bring a tent and camp. Most of the fertile land belongs to farmers, but generally no one will mind if you put up a tent. The ideal spot is usually just outside of the main town of an oasis, where it's quieter and where you'll often find a sulphur spring or a small pool of water.

Literature

An excellent three-volume series has been written on the oases that offers a detailed coverage of the culture and the monuments of the region. *Siwa Oasis, Bahariya and Farafra Oases,* and *Kharga and Dakhla Oases,* all by Ahmed Fakhri, are published by AUC Press. The first two are available in the American University Bookstore in Cairo on the university's Old Campus, as well as at several of Cairo's English-language bookstores. All three volumes are in the American University library on the New Campus.

Bahariya

Bahariya is a large inviting oasis, a sea of agricultural lands dotted with tiny peasant villages. Groves of date palms stretch for miles, beckoning the visitor to explore the lush green carpet they cut across the desert's sandy floor. The main village of **el-Bawiti** is unattractive, with two seedy and inexpensive hotels along its single main thoroughfare. Slightly more expensive and far more comfortable than these, the **Hotel Alpin Blick,** just off the main drag, is never full and is the usual spot for foreigners to stay in town. If you wish to continue on to Farafra and do not have a permit, apply at the **police station** along the main drag. Fill up on gasoline before continuing on to Farafra. A bus leaves Bahariya every morning for Cairo.

Bahariya's Pharaonic remains are modest at best. El Bawiti has scattered fragments of an ancient settlement, including the remains of a temple dating from the time of the Seventeenth Dynasty, while the smaller village of **el Binaty** has a painted subterranean tomb. Less historic, but far more irresistible is the sulphur spring just outside of the main village along the road to Cairo—ask natives or look for the turn-off for Mataar. The water (potable) pours out of a viaduct into a small cement pool, surrounded by a tranquil velvet-green oasis landscape. This is an ideal spot to pitch your tent. The spring is slated for tourist development, so the situation may have changed by 1984.

As you approach Bahariya from Cairo, you'll notice that the entire landscape becomes drenched in a dark reddish color. This is due to the region's vast deposits of iron ore which are quarried by a huge iron mine just off the highway.

Farafra

Only recently accessible by paved road, Farafra remains isolated and remarkably unspoiled. With a population of one thousand, Farafra is the smallest of Egypt's major oases, and has so far remained unaffected by the government's attempts to beef up the agricultural productivity of the oases. The oasis has virtually no ancient monuments, but a visit is well worth your while. The road from Bahariya to Farafra features spectacular dramatic canyons, windswept mesas, and rugged desertscape. The oasis itself is perhaps the most picturesque in all of Egypt. The compact explosion of lush foliage perches on an elevated summit like a single large bright green fortress. The ancient wooden doorways of Farafra village are protected by fascinating old peg-locks that are opened by long slender keys, and several of the villagers have painted the outer walls of their houses with beautiful murals narrating their pilgrimages to Mecca. The local inhabitants are, as a rule, extremely hospitable; it is not unlikely that you will be invited for a meal. Outside of the community, in a quiet desert location off the road just before the police station, the small **Government Rest House** offers spartan accommodations, including a small kitchen for LE1 per person.

Near Farafra

Ten kilometers south of the village proper along the road to Dakhla you'll come to a tiny uninhabited oasis officially considered part of Farafra. The land here is cultivated by the villagers; occasionally, a handful of farmers can be seen. Otherwise, however, the spot is blissfully deserted and quiet, and unquestionably the best place in the area to pitch a tent. Nearby, in the desert, is an ancient well which you can climb down into (ask one of the farmers to show you). Don't drink the water.

Still further down the road towards Dakhla, about 50km from Farafra, is the tiny, sparsely-inhabited **Oasis of Sheikh Merzuq.** Here you'll find a sulphur spring with a viaduct carrying water into a concrete pool. If you don't mind drawing some attention, the pool is a refreshing spot to take a dip or a sip. Women are strongly advised not to swim here. The hospitable local Bedouins will show you the way to an ancient **Roman Well** which has delicious fresh water bubbling up from a spring deep within the bowels of the desert.

Kharga and Dakhla

The most accessible and the most developed of the oases, **Kharga** is the closest thing in Egypt to Phoenix, Arizona—a veritable desert boomtown. In 1958 the Egyptian government unveiled its New Valley Project. Studies revealed considerable stores of water below the desert floor; the series of oases scattered through the desert mark the trail of a prehistoric branch of the Nile. The New Valley Project was designed to harness the underground water to irrigate and fertilize the desert by boring wells deep within the desert floor. In order to cultivate the fields a mass transfer of population was slated to take place: landless *fellahin* from the crowded Delta were to be relocated to the New Valley. The original outline of the plan, not surprisingly, proved far too ambitious and expensive. But deep water wells have enabled vast regions of desert around the oasis to be opened for cultivation. Consequently, Kharga's population has mushroomed to more than 20,000 and model villages have sprung up on all sides to begin work on the new fields. Like much of Phoenix, sadly, Kharga's boomtown neighborhoods are not particularly interesting for the visitor. But even if the main village lacks an exotic ambience, the oasis is well worth a visit. It features worthwhile Pharaonic, Christian and Islamic ruins.

Practical Information

The best place to stay is the **Government Rest House,** where the rooms cook to a toasty temperature during Kharga's sizzling summer afternoons, and never quite manage to cool off. Each room has an adjoining bath with showers that oscillate between being very weak and not running at all; singles LE6, doubles LE8. Electricity is a recent and fragile commodity at Kharga, and blackouts are frequent.

One bus daily connects Kharga to Assyut, and two EgyptAir flights every week (Wednesday and Saturday) stop en route between Cairo and Aswan. The road between Kharga and Assyut is extremely good and takes about three hours by private car or five hours by bus. A rest house halfway between Assyut and Kharga offers water and refreshments. (For information on accommodations in Assyut, see Nile Valley chapter.) Procuring gasoline can sometimes be difficult at Kharga. If you're driving, bring as much as possible with you.

Sights

Kharga's major tourist attraction is the **Temple of Hibis,** 3km north of the Government Rest House. Built by the mighty Persian warlord Darius I (521-486 B.C.E.) and dedicated to Amon, the walls of the temple are rich with inscriptions. On one of the entrances a Greek inscription from the year 69 C.E. continues for 62 lines, while nearby a string of hieroglyphics date from the reign of Nectanebo, one of the last of the pharaohs. The structure has been reconstructed so visitors can climb on the roof and tour the remains of the upper chambers of the edifice. The temple is in a delightful setting, nestled in a grove of palm trees that insulate it completely from the desert.

In the seventh century C.E., the oasis served as the home of a sizeable Christian community. The only surviving traces of this period are the domed mud-brick mausolea of the Christian **Cemetery of el-Bagawat,** just northwest of the Temple of Hibis. The interior frescoes predate the development of Egyptian art and are still painted in the early Alexandrian style. At the southern edge of the main village are the remains of a ninth-century Islamic Community. In order to avoid the heat much of the town consisted of vast and elaborate underground chambers, connected by a series of tunnels.

Extremely remote, but accessible by road, the secluded and picturesque oasis village of **Baris** lies 95km south of the main village of Kharga. Far removed from the beaten tourist track, it is possibly the hottest place in Egypt during the summer.

Unfortunately, there are no accommodations at the oasis of **Dakhla,** three to four hours' drive (180km) from Kharga. However, you can camp here or visit Dakhla as a daytrip or en route between Farafra and Kharga. Daily buses run to Dakhla from Kharga and Cairo. If you do wish to visit Dakhla and do not have a permit, apply for one at the main police station at either Farafra or Kharga. Nicknamed the "pink oasis" after the pink cliffs that line the horizon, Dakhla boasts some luxuriant fruit orchards and, at the village of **Deir el Hagar** (near the main village of Dakhla), some remains of a Pharaonic temple. Like its neighbor Farafra, Dakhla has only recently been serviced by a road, and the sight of foreign tourists remains a remarkable and unusual phenomenon for the local villagers.

Siwa

The Siwa oasis is probably the most mysterious and certainly the most inaccessible place in Egypt. Alexander journeyed here to consult the oracle of Amon; here, too, Rommel planned the taking of Alexandria. Due to Siwa's proximity to the militarily sensitive Libyan border, obtaining a permit to visit the region entails more than the usual inconvenience. First you must secure written permission from military intelligence in Cairo, which requires at least ten days. If you manage that, you must then submit the documents, along with three photos and your passport, to the military Governor in Marsa Matruuh. Permission may or may not be granted: simply stated, the army does not care much for visitors. If you overcome these obstacles, land rovers can be rented in Marsa Matruuh at rather exhorbitant rates (up to LE50 per day). The sand track to the oasis is good, but a guide is necessary. Buses occasionally make the trek; the ride is ten hours one way, and often only standing room is available. However, the situation is likely to improve as the present government has declared its intention to open the oasis to tourism in the next few years.

Sights

Since ancient Pharaonic times Siwa has been the site of an important temple dedicated to the sun deity Amon. The oasis' most illustrious guest was Alexander the Great. In 331 B.C.E. the young conqueror led an eight-day pilgrimage through the desert to Siwa, after having defeated the Persian general Darius I and captured Egypt. Upon his arrival at Siwa, the oracle of the temple is said to have revealed that the great Macedonian general was the son of Amon, thereby conferring legitimacy on Alexander's rule and raising him to the status of a god in the eyes of the Egyptian people. It is not surprising that Alexander's visit had such a momentous impact on the local mythology of Siwa: after a visit by the Greek traveler Pausanias in 160 C.E., the remote oasis was not visited again by a European until 1792. The sight of foreign faces remains a rare occurence and usually inspires lavish exhibitions of Bedouin hospitality. Located on the hill of **Aghurmi,** the remains of the **Temple of Amon,** though not very extensive, are nonetheless interesting. North of the hill, at the foot of the oddly-shaped desert bluff of **Gebel Motu,** lie a handful of **Pharaonic Tombs** with ornate interiors.

Siwa's greatest attractions, however, lie in the unspoiled traditions of the indigenous people and in its rich wealth of tropical vegetation. A vast network of palm and fruit orchards encompasses bubbling streams, grassy meadows, and an abundance of bird-life, including falcons and quails. The local women dress with brightly-colored garments in the fashion of the Berbers of the Saharan plains of Libya, Tunisia and Algeria, adorning their neck, head, and all of their limbs with heavy silver jewelry. They also braid their hair in elaborate styles. Unfortunately, according to ancient Berber custom, the women are kept extremely secluded and rarely wander far from their homes. The natives of Siwa have embraced Islam (though they were converted relatively late) and Arabic is widely spoken. Among themselves, however, they still converse in the Berber dialect known as Siwi, which may be related to the native tongue of the Tuareg people of Southern Morocco.

SUDAN

Due south of Egypt, forming the bridge between the Arab lands north of the Sahara and the Black nations to the south, lies Africa's largest state, the Democratic Republic of Sudan. Nurtured by the waters of the Nile, Sudan and Egypt have been sisters since the pharaohs built temples along the river as far south as the fourth cataract, and imported slaves from the tribal lands in the deep south. Under British rule, the Sudan and Egypt were united under a single colonial provincial governor, and in recent decades their respective governments have toyed with the idea of reuniting the countries. Despite the lack of good overland connections, travel south to the Sudan is becoming more and more popular among budget travelers. Although getting around the country is an exhausting and time-consuming affair, it is well worth the effort.

The Sudan stretches 2000km from its northern border on the twenty-second parallel, just south of Abu Simbel, to its irregular southern border with Zaire, Uganda, and Kenya along the fourth parallel. The southern border, especially to the west, is roughly defined by the line between the Nile River watershed and that of the Congo River. From its western border with Libya, Chad, and the Central African Republic, Sudan extends eastward for nearly 1600km to the mountains of Ethiopia and the Red Sea in the far northeast, encompassing a total land area of 6,500,000 square km. Its population of approximately twenty million people speaks 100 different languages and forms 160 distinct ethnic groups. Cutting through the heart of it all is the Nile—a single mighty stream formed by the waters of the Blue and White Niles which flow through the east and south until they merge at the capital city of Khartoum, just north of the sixth Nile cataract.

Sudan (known as Kush in ancient times) is traditionally divided into two regions, north and south, whose vague boundary is formed by the large marsh and swamp lands known as the **Sudd.** To the north lies predominantly Muslim Sudan, populated by Arabs, as well as Fur tribespeople in the far western provinces of Darfur, concentrated in the Jebel Marra Plateau, and the Nuba people in the Nuba Mountains of Southern Kordufan. Both of these latter tribes inhabit exquisite mountain terrain and continue to live traditionally. Jebel Marra is considered the most beautiful area of Sudan. To the south live Nilotic- and Niger-Congo-speaking people. The former live predominantly in the Sudd itself and consist primarily of Dinka people as well as Nuer and Shilluk tribes. Mostly fishers and herders, the Dinka are exceptionally tall (average height for men is well over 2m) and slender. Farther to the south and west along the Central African Republic and Zaire borders lies the land of the Zande people. The Zande once controlled a vast forest empire spanning the Congo and Nile watersheds from Central Africa to Uganda; today, they're a farming people. Except for Arab traders from the north, the southern Sudanese are not Muslim, but follow the animistic practices of their individual tribes. However, continuous missionary incursions in the last two hundred years have, to some extent, Christianized or at least affected the animistic beliefs of the people.

The north/south distinction marks political as well as ethnic and religious differences. Significantly less developed than the north, the Southern Sudan has always viewed itself as the object of northern indifference if not exploitation. These resentments were unleashed two years after Sudan gained independence in 1956, in the outbreak of a fourteen-year civil war. The Treaty of Addis Ababa, which granted the three southern provinces political and economic autonomy, was signed in 1972 by Sudanese President Jaffor al Nerneiry and the southern rebel forces. Occasional outbreaks of violence may force the government to close the south to travelers without notice.

Notwithstanding local variations in the Red Sea Hills to the northeast and the Jebel Marra Plateau in the far west, Sudanese climate also divides neatly into northern and southern varieties. The north and west tend to be reasonably pleasant in winter with temperatures averaging 25°C during the day. North of Khartoum, the land is primarily desert, while farther south it passes into dry plains and savannah. As a result, summers north of the Sudd can only be described as grueling and brutally hot with temperatures easily rising into the high 40s and low 50s°C (110-120°F). As one travels south towards the Sudd and beyond the seasonal temperature, fluctuations diminish to a more or less constant annual average of 25°C. Unlike the arid north, the south has an unmistakable wet season from April to October, making travel in the region all but impossible.

Orientation

Currency

The Sudanese pound (LS), like its Egyptian counterpart, divides into 100 piasters (pt). The official exchange rate between the U.S. dollar and the Sudanese pound is mercurial; everyone changes money on the black market anyway. The black-market exchange rate between U.S. dollars and Sudanese pounds in 1983 was $1=LS1.80. The official rate is usually around $1=LS.80. There is an official black market in the Sudan, carried on out of store-front offices called "free markets." It is not at all illegal to use the official black market. Black-market exchanges that take place on the street are illegal but frequently and openly conducted. If you can bargain well, the street rate is slightly better than at the free markets, and provides a helpful service on afternoons, evenings, and Fridays when the free markets are closed.

Visas and Health

If you decide to travel from Egypt to the Sudan, there are a number of things which you will have to take into consideration. First and foremost, American citizens need a visa in order to enter the country. You can obtain one in the U.S. by applying to the Sudanese Embassy at 2210 Massachusetts Ave. NW, Washington, DC 20008; you must produce three passport photographs, have a valid passport, current yellow fever and cholera vaccinations, some indication that you have the means to leave the Sudan (such as a ticket to any destination outside the country), and a letter from your bank proving you have sufficient funds to support yourself in the Sudan. Visas take two or three weeks to process, generally, but sometimes they can take as long as two months, since applications are sent all the way to Khartoum for approval. Visas through the Sudanese Consulate in Cairo (see Cairo Practical Information) take three to six weeks to process. Your application must include three passport photos and a formal letter of recommendation issued by the U.S. Embassy. These can be obtained without difficulty and free of charge. Visas cost LE10 per person. You cannot obtain a visa if your passport contains an Israeli visa, an Egyptian visa obtained in Tel Aviv, or an Egyptian stamp from any border crossing into Israel. If your passport contains any of these blemishes, get a new one in Cairo; if the Sudanese officials ask you why you have a new passport, earnestly inform them that your old one was lost or stolen. They have been known to refuse visas to holders of new passports on the mere suspicion that they've been in Israel. And even if you obtain a visa, there is no absolute assurance that you will be allowed across the border.

Before you depart for Sudan several health precautions are in order. You should get a gammaglobulin shot as well as a cholera vaccine either in the U.S. or in Cairo at the Savoy Continental Hotel (see Cairo). Highly recommended, but not essential, is a tetanus vaccine. Most countries require travelers coming from the Sudan to be vaccinated for yellow fever, so you need the shot in order to leave the country. You can get the vaccine in the U.S., at Cairo International Airport, or from a major hospital. The vaccine is good for ten years. Finally, anti-malaria pills are a must, since there is a great deal of malaria in Sudan (especially the South Sudan). In the U.S. a prescription is required for anti-malarial pills; in Egypt, no prescription is necessary, but be sure you know the proper dosage for the brand of pills you have purchased—excessive dosage may kill you and insufficient dosage will not protect you against malaria. Also be sure to bring diarrhea and water-purification tablets. Given the paucity of medical supplies in the Sudan, a well-stocked first aid kit is also advisable. There is no protection against sleeping sickness (which is communicated by *tsetse* flies) and green monkey disease, but if you avoid swampy regions of the country, especially in the rainy season, and stay well-fed, you have little to fear from either of these maladies.

Before you leave for the Sudan, load up on items not readily available within the country to use as *baksheesh,* or for bartering or returning favors. Recommended items are cigarettes (especially American brands), liquor, and Western clothing.

To and From Sudan

Sudan Airways (fondly known as *Insha'allah* Airways), 1 Abdel Salam Arel St. in Cairo (tel. 74 71 45 or 74 72 99) and **EgyptAir** (see Egypt Introduction) run daily 14- to 30-day excursion flights for LE205 round-trip (official money change required). EgyptAir generally offers the better service.

Egyptian Navigation Company boats (offices at the corner of Kasr el Nil and Sherif Sts. in Cairo) have recently begun to run boats between Port Suez and Port Sudan. (Port Sudan is connected to Khartoum by one of the only good intercity paved roads in Sudan.) This service may be discontinued for lack of passengers by 1984. A small Sudanese boat leaves the Aswan High Dam for Wadi Halfa on Thursdays. First- and second-class tickets on the Sudanese boat are available at the **Sudanese Nile Navigation Company,** in Cairo at Ramsis Station or downtown at 8 Kasr el Nil St. (tel. 75 34 44). Third-class tickets are sold only in Aswan at offices on Abtal el Tahrir St. (tel. 20 39). An even smaller Egyptian boat leaves the Dam on Mondays; for tickets, go to the Egyptian Navigation Company (see above). The boats are crowded and it is often impossible to get on.

Egyptian Railways has a direct Cairo-High Dam line that operates on Wednesday and Sunday nights, connecting with the boats. You can also buy a through ticket from Cairo all the way to Khartoum (train-boat-train) at Ramsis Station. Immigration into the Sudan takes place on a temporary barge attached to the bank of Lake Nassar, several kilometers from the train station at New Wadi Halfa (Old Wadi Halfa was covered by the lake). When you have made it successfully across the border, there is an extremely erratic train running to Khartoum which will probably be waiting in the station. Reservations are practically impossible to make in advance and may not be honored anyway—

there is always a terrible crush of locals trying to get a seat. The best way to get a seat is to be aggressive and use a bit of common sense; since you will have to buy a ticket at the Wadi Halfa station, be realistic and go straight for the second-class window so you won't waste your time in the first-class line simply to be told that they are sold out. Sometimes the Sudanese officials save an entire second-class car for foreigners, so you'll probably get a seat anyway. The only way to get a first-class ticket is to camp out in Wadi Halfa for three or four days and wait for the next train, which is an incredible waste of time. Lots of people ride on the roofs of the train cars, particularly during June and July when Sudanese students in Egypt are returning home for the summer vacation, but this mode of travel is not nearly as appealing as it may sound; not only is it very dangerous, but you'll also get covered with soot and dust within a matter of minutes. Unless you decide to travel first class, be prepared for an incredibly long and tiring journey. The trip from Cairo to Khartoum normally takes about five days, so you might consider stopping off at a few places along the way.

Think twice about driving to Khartoum; for most of the distance between Wadi Halfa and Khartoum there is no road (regardless of what you may have heard elsewhere), just desert with a series of posts to keep you going in the right direction. You must have sand ladders and be an expert car mechanic. The alternative of driving from Suez to Port Sudan along the Red Sea coast is much easier, but requires sheaves of military clearances from both the Egyptian and Sudanese sides which will probably take you months to get.

You can take a lorry along the Nile from Wadi Halfa to Khartoum. The journey takes about ten days and may be the best reason for traveling from Aswan since the train ride traverses uninhabited desert lands far from the Nile. To secure a ride, just ask around when you arrive at Wadi Halfa. The trip is very difficult and is only for the hardy and adventurous traveler.

With an **ISIC Student ID,** or with special authorization accrediting your student status from the Ministry of Youth in Khartoum, you can get student reductions of up to 50% on boat and train fares in the Sudan. Sudan Airways offers a youth fare reduction if you are under 26 years of age.

Trains and Trucks

Book your seats as far in advance as possible. All trains in the Sudan are chronically overcrowded and booked ahead of time. There is generally little difference between first and second class; use second class. During the dry season trains run more or less on time, but when the rains begin delays can be very long.

For more remote parts of the country, travel by truck presents the only viable option if you don't have a land rover. Trucks carrying large quantities of merchandise frequently take on a virtually unlimited number of passengers en route. If you want to be one of them, you may find yourself crowded and uncomfortable. Merchants sometimes travel with the drivers so the trucks stop at each village while the merchant attempts to sell goods. You don't need to stay near the truck—just tell the boys working the truck where you're waiting and don't wander too far. Trucks usually stop first at the police station and then proceed to a town center. You may be asked to register with the police at some villages as a formality. Drivers stop for four to five hours each night to camp. Bring flashlights and food; bread is available only in major villages. A stove is handy but the truck will make a wood-gathering stop before dark so you can join in to get your own firewood. Nights can be cold.

Khartoum

If you arrive by plane, go to the tourist office at the airport to procure a map of Khartoum and obtain a small initial black-market exchange (the rate is not favorable at the airport) so you can have some pocket money. Taxis from the airport into town are at least LS3, but buses are just as easy. Walk down the main road from the airport until you reach Africa Road, turn right, stand on the corner, and flag down any bus that passes by (fare 10pt). In Khartoum, you must register within three days at the **Ministry of the Interior** (also the **Police Headquarters for Aliens**), near Nile Ave., down from the Sudanese Airways office. The registration office is officially open until 2pm, but usually shuts down by noon. Another formality can be taken care of at the same office; you can obtain an official permit for traveling in areas outside of Khartoum (two photos are required). Travel permit and registration each cost 15pt. If you wish to take pictures anywhere in the Sudan (but especially in the south) a special photography permit is required; get it at the Ministry of Culture, on Gamaa Ave., between the Sudanese Airways office and the Ministry of the Interior. If you violate the regulations governing photography, your film and possibly your camera will be confiscated.

The main tourist office is the **Sudan Tourist and Hotels Corporation,** east of United Nations Square, just off Saleh Pasha el Mek St. The staff is extremely helpful; they'll provide train and boat schedules and fares, as well as information on traveling to Dinder Game Reserve. "Free Markets" for changing money in Khartoum are concentrated along Gamhuriyya Ave. (Khartoum's main drag), especially near the Sudanese Airways office. This is also the main neighborhood for black-market street exchanges. A couple of blocks southeast of the tourist office, on Ali Abdul Latif Ave., is the **U.S. Embassy.** The **British Embassy** is on Bar Laman Ave., near the intersection with Al Qasr Ave. If you're a Yank and homesick, head for the **American Cultural Center** across the street from the Meridien Hotel. The Khartoum Train Station is at the end of Al Qasr Ave., south of the Meridien Hotel. Make reservations as far in advance as possible.

Coming into town by bus, tell the ticket-seller that you want to get off at the Meridien Hotel. This is not where budget travelers will want to stay, but the neighborhood is full of cheap hotels. They are particularly abundant along Sayed Abdul Rahman Ave. just off Al Qasr Ave. The **Royal Hotel** on Sayed Abdul Rahman Ave., two blocks east of the Meridien, has a friendly proprietor named Ahmed who will let you sleep on the terrace for LS1.60. The cheapest place in town is the **Youth Hostel** (in the southeast corner of the city) while **El Nahrein Hotel,** near the hostel, and the **Port Sudan Hotel,** on Killiget At Tibb St., are both comparatively inexpensive.

Khartoum actually consists of two separate cities, situated on opposite sides of the confluence of the White and Blue Niles; Khartoum proper is the more modern commercial side. Though not much happens here from the tourist's point of view, a promenade along Nile Ave. is a pleasant way to spend a few hours. Even if seemingly bereft of activity, Khartoum can be a bewitching place, especially in winter. One- or two-story buildings, dusty windblown streets, general stores, and raised and porticoed sidewalks all combine to create the atmosphere of an Old West frontier town, exuding tranquility. Across the water, **Omdurman,** Khartoum's more African sibling, is a tangled cluster of tall scarified tribespeople; ivory, gold, and junk bazaars; and cars and buses driven into the shallows of the river for a wash. The community is deeply Arab, too. **Mahdi's Tomb** and the adjoining **Khalifa's House,** now a museum, recall the fifteen glorious but doomed years of the Mahdist Empire—the beheaded Gordon, the patchwork *galabiyya* of the poverty-cult of the *ansaris* (dervishes), Kitchener's march to Khartoum, and the final fateful battle when Omduram was filled with the great cry of 10,000 massacred dervishes as their army charged the British guns. Romance still resonates from those bloody *jihad* (holy war) days.

To reach Omdurman from Khartoum, go to the El Kebir Mosque, Khartoum's main Islamic shrine, two blocks south of the Sudanese Airways office. Buses leave from here for Omdurman (10pt), depositing you at **Suq el Raisi.** The bazaars in this neighborhood are well worth exploring.

A good way to spend an evening in Khartoum is on the terrace of the **Grand Hotel,** overlooking the confluence of the Blue and White Niles. The bar is a bit pricey. A good place to meet other travelers is the **Athenae Cafe,** next to the British Embassy. One block down Gamhoriyya Ave. is the **Sudan Club,** the last bastion of the British Empire—one-week membership costs LS2.50. It's a good place to meet British officials with valuable contacts in the countryside.

Northern Sudan

If you're traveling overland from Wadi Halfa to Khartoum via train you'll miss everything. If you are traveling upriver along the Nile by truck and thumb (count on at least two weeks), you will pass a handful of pharaonic and Nubian monuments. Among these are (from north to south) the **Temple of Amara,** near the town of Abri; the **Temple of Suddenga** and the **Temple of Sulb,** right next to each other; and the **Temple of Sesibi,** near the village of Delgo. Heading south of Delgo, beyond the third cataract of the Nile, you'll come to the regional center of the Dongola—nearby is the **Temple of Kawa.** From Dongola a Nile steamer runs south all the way to Karima (see below). The ride between Wadi Halfa and Dongola via truck is brutal—be prepared for a long tough haul. Continuing south, the archeological site of **ancient Dongola** is just before the village of El Debba. From here, the Nile switches back to the north and leads to the local center of Merowe. In this area are three small archeological sites: **El Nurru, Jebel Barkal,** and **Nuri.** From here, it is sometimes possible to catch a train from the village of Karima, across the river from Merowe, directly to the Wadi Halfa-Khartoum rail line. Otherwise, continue northeast along the river to the city of **Abu Hamed**—you can catch the Wadi Halfa-Khartoum train here. Abu Hamed is also the main place to pick up rides on trucks in the area, bound either north for Dongola or south towards Atbara. In **Atbara** you can stay at either the **Hotel Atbara** or **Hotel Astoria** for LS1. Bicycles can be rented for 40pt per day. From Atbara both a road and a train line fork east to Port Sudan.

If you travel to the Sudan via Red Sea ferry you will arrive at **Port Sudan.** The best road in the country connects Port Sudan to Khartoum and there are also comparatively reliable rail connections. The port is relatively expensive for the Sudan and is very crowded during the time of the *Haj*—annual pilgrimage to Mecca—as the port is the jumping-off point for Muslims throughout Africa to take ferries to Jeddah, across the Red Sea in Saudi Arabia. You can stay in Port Sudan for LS1-1.50 at the **Hotels Sinkat, Africa,** or **Olympia Park.** The **Red Sea Club** will sell you a temporary membership card for 25pt entitling you to use their swimming pool and bar. Some folks enjoy heading south to **Suakin,** an old Red Sea port, where you can enjoy the water in peace and quiet. The **Government Rest House** charges LS1 per night. Halfway between Port Sudan and Khartoum on the main highway is the wonderful town of **Kassala,** where members of a variety of local tribes converge to sell their crafts. The **Hotels El Watania, Shark Abu Tayar,** and **Africa** all run between LS1 and LS1.50.

Very popular among tourists, the **Dinder National Park,** south of Kassala and southeast of Khartoum, is a protected wildlife reserve. Dinder is everything it is reputed to be: African wildlife abounds. You will see water buffalo, gazelles, giraffes, monkeys, many species of exotic and lovely birds, and, on occasion, lions. Furthermore, the savannah of the reserve is exquisite. The trip is a very expensive undertaking, however. If you can afford it, rent a land rover. Public transportation by train or preferably by truck is easily available as far as **Sennar.** By truck the ride from Khartoum to Sennar costs about LS7 per person and takes about five hours. The drive takes you along the Blue Nile and features some lovely scenery. For the trip from Sennar to **Galegu,** inside the National Park, you can rent a land rover, which accommodates seven people plus a driver for LS300. The exorbitant price at least enables you to keep your land rover and driver for as long as you please. Gas is included in the price. If you can't afford to go by land rover, try and see if you can hook up with some tourists who have a vehicle in Sennar and are headed for the park. It is not permitted to tour the park without a vehicle. Admission to the park is LS8 per person, plus LS10 per camera; you must also hire a guide at a cost of LS3 per person per day. Accommodations at Galegu are available in traditional *tukul* (African hut) compounds, composed of three bedrooms, a common room, a shower, a pit toilet, and an enclosure for fires. The charge per compound is LS20 per night. Little food is available at Galegu—bring your own or be prepared to be overcharged.

Western Sudan

The **Jebel Marra Plateau,** inhabited by the Fur tribespeople, looms in the far western section of the country, near the Chad border. This region is the most beautiful corner of the Sudan—wild, well-irrigated, enchanting, and rarely visited by tourists. The jumping-off point for treks in the Jebel Marra is the town of **Nyala,** which has some interesting *suqs*. There are three ways to get there: Sudan Airways runs three (frequently canceled) flights a week from Khartoum to Nyala (two hours) on Sundays, Wednesdays, and Thursdays for LS127 per person. A train also runs from Khartoum to Nyala (a four-day journey); fare is LS39 (first class), LS27 (second class). Trucks depart from Al Hillal Stadium in Omdurman; the trip takes two to four (or more) days. In Nyala the **Hotel Danfur** charges 30pt per night. To continue to the plateau, you have to hunt down a private car or truck. Once you get close to the Jebel Marra region you can easily hire a donkey to complete the journey. Jebel Marra peak (over 3000m) is the country's second highest mountain and presents a breathtaking spectacle. To get to the base of the mountain, take a truck from the *suq* in Nyala to the village of **Nyertate** (LS2, eight hours). The last half of the journey is very tough going.

Nyala is also the rail terminus for Danfur province and is the place to head if you wish to travel on to Chad, if the civil war there should end. If you travel to Nyala via truck, you may have to change rides at **El Obeid.** The journey from Khartoum to El Obeid through the desert is very rough, takes two days, and costs about LS4. Trucks from El Obeid to Nyala take four or five days and cost LS7 per person. In El Obeid the **Hotel Liban** charges 40pt per night. If you stop off at El Obeid, you might consider a detour south to Kadugli to explore the lovely terrain of the **Nuba Mountains.** The views from the higher mountain ridges are stunning.

If you make it to Nyertete, at the foot of Jebel Marra, you can purchase a donkey for LS15-20 and wander around. The local tribespeople are wonderfully hospitable, and will haul you into their homes and insist that you share their meals. Otherwise, food is difficult to procure so stock up in the *suqs*. You can usually resell your donkey without difficulty. Don't worry about getting lost on the trails, as people are glad to straighten you out and even go out of their way to put you on the right track.

Central Southern Sudan

The south is Sudan at its most exotic. Some of the African continent's most fascinating indigenous peoples live in the Southern Sudan, which has long been the site of anthropological and ethnographic research. To reach the south, you can head directly to Juba, the capital, by taking one of Sudan Airway's Monday or Wednesday morning flights from Khartoum—LS163 per person. Don't take the train from Khartoum to Kosti—it takes a very ciruitous route requiring at least 24 hours. Buses from Khartoum run to Kosti via Wadi Medani; but trucks offer the fastest alternative. Trucks and buses for Kosti depart from Suq Sha'bi in Khartoum around 7am daily (about 12 hours). Boats can be taken upstream; the boat to Juba does not leave from Khartoum itself, but rather from the town of Kosti. Two different types of boats, "new boats" and "old boats," run from Kosti to Juba, but schedules are extremely unreliable. The new boat allegedly departs every Saturday, taking four to five days to reach Juba. The boat has sleeping accommodations for 100 people and sleeper reservations are strongly advised. You must make reservations in Kosti, so you might find yourself stuck there for a few days. Fares on the new boat are LS63 (first class), LS55 (second class), and LS39 (third class). A new boat theoretically leaves Juba every Saturday morning for Kosti; the return journey is about 24 hours shorter. An old boat leaves Kosti for Juba on Wednesday (and Juba for Kosti on Wednesday as well)—the trip takes ten to eleven days; sleeping accommodations for 200. Old boat fares are LS50 (first class), LS36 (second class), LS15 (third—roof—class). For either of the boats, bring plenty of food and water. The boats tend to be very crowded. A gas stove and a mosquito net come in handy.

A more interesting route than the one directly south to Juba is the trip southwest via train to Wau. From Khartoum the journey takes three to four days; the train leaves every Saturday at 11pm; fares are LS42 (first class), LS28 (second class), LS12 (third class). Food and water are available on the buffet car for moderate prices; tea, nuts, and some other food can be bought cheaply at stations along the way. Beyond the stop at Babanoosa, water must be purchased at the station platforms. If you wish to forego this expense and get at enough water to clean yourself, walk into town at one of the larger stations (keep alert for the train whistle) and find the local water pump. The Khartoum-Wau trip is crowded and exhausting, but, nonetheless, exhilarating. Aside from the direct connection from Khartoum to Wau, the Khartoum-Nyala rail link passes through Babanoosa, where you can change trains for transit between Nyala and Wau.

Wau itself is a relatively pleasant town and provides a more hospitable introduction to the south than Juba. The community is home to a variety of international aid workers and Christian missionaries. Wander over to the **Suq el Jo** where the people sell crafts, wooden carvings, and ivory. The Jesuit seminary in the neighboring village of **Nazareth** has a friendly English-speaking staff and makes for a nice hike from Wau. Don't wander around the outskirts of town after dark, though, as you may no longer be welcome. Wau has an attractive little Christian cathedral. For accommodations, try the **Nilien Hotel,** LS2 per bed in common rooms, but the place is most unsavory. The **Barbara Hotel** offers more inviting private rooms for LS6 per person including breakfast. The **Riverside Hotel** charges LS3 and is somewhere between the above two in quality. The **Youth Hostel** charges 50pt.

There are two ways to travel from Wau to Juba. The faster northerly route via Rumbek, though quicker, is desolate and uninteresting (two to three days by truck). This route is impassable in the wet season. The slower, more uncomfortable alternative via Yambio will take you through some of the country's most beautiful scenery. Trucks leave the central square of Wau for Yambio at sporadic intervals—fare LS15 per person.

The first village along the road from Wau to Yambio is **Bousheri,** where the truck crosses the river. During the rainy season the bridge here may be washed out, resulting in extended delays. Continuing south, you'll come to **Tambura,** near the border of the Central African Republic. The road from Wau to Tambura has deteriorated and will tire even the most sturdy travelers. From Tambura, the road forks into two routes to Yambio. One hugs the Sudanese border next to the Central African Republic and Zaire. If your truck takes the border route, you might want to disembark at **Source Jubu,** a paradise of mango orchards and colorful gardens. A Government Rest House provides reasonably-priced accommodations. This is the official crossing into the Central African Republic. The road improves, continuing along the border route; at Izo you'll be required to register with the police since the town is on the border. One and one-half to three days from Wau is **Yambio,** one of the most wonderful places in the Southern Sudan. Mango and palm trees line the town's roads and a small commercial center with a fine restaurant is enclosed by a cane screen—all is surrounded by extensive hilly savannah whose woods are laced with foot trails and dirt tracks leading far in all directions. Yambio is home to the Zande tribe, and the capital of Sudan's pineapple country—the fruit can be found in abundance in season. Try to stay a few days here to hike through the countryside, swim in the nearby lake, enjoy the Zairean beer, and take in the peacefulness of the place and its people. The Anglican Church of Yambio offers a **rest house** for travelers about 2km up the road to the left of the police station. Just ask for the cathedral. A well about 400m behind the rest house has good drinking water; it can be used for washing if you haul the water away from the well—ask the canon to let you in. As of 1983, the clean rooms remained unfurnished and cost LS2.50 per night; with furnishing, the price may rise to LS6 or so.

The road from Yambio to Juba leads through the town of **Maridi.** Your truck will probably stop here to do business; take the opportunity to enjoy a bath in the river amidst the tranquil scenery. From Maridi, the road forks leading to Juba either via Amadi or Yei. The latter route is traveled far less frequently, but is the more exciting of the two. **Yei** is, along with Yambio, one of the great paradises of the south; the Zande people are friendly and the lands are lush and green. The **Agricultural Research Station** often allows travelers to sleep on the premises for free. If you can't get to Yei from Yambio or Maridi, don't despair. Save it for later; there is frequent traffic on the road between Yei and Juba. The more direct route to Juba from Yambio via Amadi costs LS12 per person in back of the truck and LS20 for a seat in the cab of the vehicle (one day if you leave in the morning, otherwise two days).

Juba and the Deep South

Juba is the capital and the tourist center of the Southern Sudan. It also serves as the headquarters for all international aid organizations in the region. For such a remote town it has an astonishingly large European population. Like Khartoum, Juba consists of two separate towns: Juba and Malakia, **Malakia,** 4km from Juba, is the more traditional of the twin communities, with a large regional market featuring native crafts.

When you arrive in Juba you must register within 24 hours at the Immigration Office, down the street from the Sudan Airways office. The best place to stay in Juba is the **Multi-Trading Centre,** usually known as the MTC. Located by the Juba football stadium, halfway between Juba and Malakia, the MTC charges LS2.50 per person in a triple room, or LS1 to camp on their grounds. Electricity and running water are provided, but the drinking water is suspect. Though cheap, the **Africa Hotel** (LS1) is an awful place. Juba has two good restaurants. The **Greek Club** serves cold food and cold beer, while the adjacent **Unity Gardens** has warm food and warm beer. These are the places to meet resident foreigners in Juba. If you are short on money, you can eat very cheaply at the **People's Restaurant.**

If you wish to head on from Juba to Uganda or Kenya, stop off at the international aid agencies in town—you might be able to get a free lift.

South of Juba, on the Ugandan border, lies the village of **Nimule.** This is the entrance to the Nile Gorge and Game Reserve, where the Nile passes through a narrow gorge from Uganda into the Sudan. Trucks from Nimule depart from the bridge crossing the Nile outside of Malakia (seven-hour journey). One mile before Nimule is the game reserve **Rest House** with accommodations. More difficult but eminently worthwhile is the trip to **Mount Kinyeti,** the country's highest peak, in the Imetong Mountains. The best place to try for a ride is the bridge crossing the Nile outside of Malakia where you can catch a truck or hitch the seven-hour journey to the village of **Torit.** The **Norwegian Church Relief** in the village sometimes puts up travelers. From Torit, try for a lift to **Katire, Gilo,** or **Upper Talanga.** All three villages are surrounded by the spectacular mountain range and offer fabulous hiking opportunities, as well as abundant rivers and a refreshingly cool climate. No accommodations are available in Katire, but you can sleep comfortably on the sawdust hill behind the town saw mill. Gilo and Upper Talanga both have **Rest Houses** with running water (LS2.50 per person). The Gilo Rest House is particularly charming—an old British colonial outpost which was looted during the civil war. In addition, Upper Talanga has **camp sites** for travelers which include running water. All three villages are within hiking distance of one another (Katire-Gilo six miles uphill; Katire-Upper Talanga, 10 miles uphill). You won't lose your way since there is frequent pedestrian traffic along the trails.

The road to Kenya continues from Juba to Torit and then on to **Kapoeta.** At Kapoeta you may run into Europeans panning for gold in the river. To leave the Sudan via this route you need an exit stamp from the Sudanese police. The journey to the border from Juba takes three or four days but rides are hard to come by, and the road is virtually impassable in the rainy season. In these far reaches of the Southern Sudan, along the Kenyan border, you will encounter the **Masai** people. Masai men undergo extensive scarification after traditional puberty rituals initiate them into manhood. The men and women of the tribe paint their faces and perform elaborate dances on festive occasions. Westerners are sometimes welcome at such events.

Travel overland from the Southern Sudan to Uganda is not recommended until the political climate in Uganda improves. You cannot legally enter Ethiopia overland from the Sudan—the only official port of entry for the country is at Addis Ababa. To reach Ethiopia you must fly from Khartoum.

A Final Note

The history of *Let's Go* is as motley as the crew that produces it and the styles that go into its far-from-seamless prose. Older now than most of the current staff members, *Let's Go* began in 1960 as a pamphlet issued to passengers on a student charter flight. It featured a comprehensive four-page section on France. The 1968 edition included a section on "The Traveling Girl" and suggested that the reader take underwear to Europe. Over the years, *Let's Go* has expanded from a single book on Western Europe to nine books, covering all of Europe and the United States as well as parts of Asia and North Africa. Those original four pages on France have ballooned into a four-hundred-page regional guide, and a tenth book, on Mexico, is well into production.

Of the fifty-odd Harvard students who compile the guide, thirty are traveling researchers, masters of ferry-boat and picnic-table prose. These harried correspondents scribble out manuscripts while dashing across counties, countries, and occasionally continents. Editors select researchers every March from a pool of over one hundred applicants on the basis of solo travel experience, linguistic flair, and *chutzpah*.

In 1983, one bout with a Greek surgeon, two automobile accidents, three con jobs, four tropical diseases, and five counts of grand larceny brightened the lives of the *Let's Go* researchers while the editorial staff sequestered itself in a remote basement office. In the space of three months, some thirty thousand pages of manuscript (nearly twenty thousand of which were legible) flooded the underground headquarters. A platoon of ardent editors and intrepid typists reduced this imposing mass to about twelve thousand pages of text.

Labor Day travelers on the People Express flights between Boston and New York may encounter an exhausted courier clutching an over-large suitcase, headed for the Flatiron Building.

APPENDIX

Guide to Hebrew pronunciation

The alphabet

Here are the characters which comprise the Hebrew alphabet: capital letters do not exist. The left-hand column shows the handwritten characters, the middle column printed characters, and with the right-hand column you can pronounce their names in Hebrew. Five characters (צ, פ, נ, מ, כ) take a different form when appearing at the end of a word, as shown.

א	א	alef	ל	ל	lamed
ב	ב	bet	מ, ם	מ, ם	mem
ב	ב	vet	נ, ן	נ, ן	nun
ג	ג	gimel	ס	ס	samekh
ד	ד	dalet	ע	ע	ain
ה	ה	he	פ	פ	pe
ו	ו	vav	פ, ף	פ, ף	fe
ז	ז	zain	צ, ץ	צ, ץ	tzadi
ח	ח	het	ק	ק	kof
ט	ט	tet	ר	ר	resh
י	י	yod	ש	ש	shin
כ	כ	kaf	ש	ש	sin
כ, ך	כ, ך	khaf	ת	ת	tav

From the Berlitz phrase book "Hebrew for Travellers", by permission of Editions Berlitz.

Cairo-Ismailiya-Port Said

Cairo	dep.	6 25	1150	1530	1845	2140
Benha	arr.	7 02	1238	1607	1922	2222
	dep.	7 06	1244	1610	1927	2228
Zagazig	arr.	7 45	1315	1648	2000	2300
	dep.	7 56	1324	1700	2015	2113
Ismailiya	arr.	9 15	1435	1825	2127	0 40
Suez	arr.	1205	1715	2205	—	
Qantara	arr.	1002			2212	
Port Said	arr.	1055			2305	

Port Said	dep.		5 15	1250	1650	
Qantara	dep.		6 16	1345	1751	
Suez	dep.		—	1035	1505	
Ismailiya	dep.	5 10	7 00	1430	1838	2105
Zagazig	arr.	6 56	8 25	1546	2003	2218
	dep.	7 10	8 35	1552	2008	2223
Benha	arr.	7 42	9 07	1623	2039	2254
	dep.	7 56	9 17	1633	2048	2037
Cairo	arr.	8 40	9 55	1710	2125	2350

Cairo-Nile Valley

Cairo	dep.	3 10	7 30	7 40	1000	1200	1225	1610	1620	1900	2000	2040	2105	2250
Wasta	dep.	4 34	—	9 21	—	—	1348	—	1803	—	2123	2226	2251	0 14
Beni Suef	dep.	5 18	9 24	1005	1154	1355	1426	1804	1846	—	2201	2310	2336	0 54
Maghada	dep.	6 16	—	1105	1238	—	—	—	1934	—	2247	0 09	1 33	2 43
Minya	dep.	7 31	1056	1224	1339	1534	1600	1939	2057	—	2345	1 24	1 46	2 44
Abu Qerkas	dep.	7 51	—	1245	—	—	—	—	2171	—	—	1 45	2 06	—
Assyut	arr.	9 54	1229	1444	1525	1706	1733	2114	2321	—	1 27	3 49	4 03	4 34
	dep.	1010	1246	1502		1720	1745	2129	2337	—	1 44	5 05	4 17	4 50
Sohag	dep.	1215	1413	1720		1840	1938	2310	2 07	—	3 22	8 05	6 20	7 00
Girga	dep.		1455	1822		1925	2024		3 05	—	4 08	9 30	7 06	7 51
El Baliana	dep.		—	1900		1947	2047		3 27	—	4 31	1000	7 29	8 26
Nag Hammadi	dep.		1556	2014		2052	2201		4 23	—	5 26	1115	8 50	9 45
Qena	dep.		1705	2248		2203	2341		5 36	—	6 37	1309	1004	1059
Luxor	arr.		1814	0 50		0 20	1 20		7 04	5 38	8 10	1457	1135	1235
	dep.		1830						7 35	6 06	8 25	1517		1255
Esna	dep.		1954						8 48	—	9 47	1657		1430
Edfu	dep.		2110						9 54	—	1049	1851		1600
Kom Ombo	dep.		2223						1109	—	1202	2112		1745
Aswan	arr.		2320						1212	1000	1258	2235		1930
	dep.								1232	1037	1327			
Sadd el Ali	dep.								1255	1100	1350			

Sadd el Ali	dep.				1600	1720		1800						
Aswan	arr.				1623	1743		1823						
	dep.	5 40		1015	1638	1810		1840				5 15		
Kom Ombo	dep.	7 00		1203	1738	—		1949				6 15		
Edfu	dep.	8 45		1345	1852	—		2108				7 31		
Esna	dep.	1042		1526	1951	—		2213				8 49		
Luxor	arr.	1220		1655	2054	2200		2317				9 54		
	dep.	1242	1510	1719	2114	2225		2336	5 15	4 15	4 25	1014		
Qena	dep.	1433	1638	1856	2238	—		1 02	7 04	6 05	6 39	1126		
Nag Hammadi	dep.	1638	1805	2013	2353	—		2 18	8 15	7 29	8 50	1232		
El Baliana	dep.	1749	1857	2107	0 45	—		3 53	9 06	8 20	1003	—		
girga	dep.	1823	1930	2131	1 09	—		4 31	9 28	8 42	1035	1332		
Sohag	dep.	1943	2050	2229	2 10	—	4 30	5 32	1022	9 37	1147	1424	1440	
Assyut	arr.	2215	2243	0 20	3 25	—	6 08	7 12	1127	1145	1326	1529	1628	
	dep.	2230	2258	0 32	3 42	—	6 24	7 27	1134	1205	1338	1545	1642	1830
Abu Qerkas	dep.	0 33	0 58	—	—	—	—	9 25	—	—	1534	—	1857	—
Minya	dep.	0 59	1 25	2 28	5 35	—	8 04	9 50	1311	1348	1558	1728	1921	2022
Maghaga	dep.	2 11	2 36	3 26	6 30	—	—	1043	—	—	1707	—	2031	2120
Beni Suef	dep.	3 13	3 38	4 21	7 22	—	9 39	1133	1446	1525	1809	1903	2133	2210
Wasta	dep.	3 39	4 14	4 52	7 52	—	—	1202	—	1602	1843	—	2209	—
Cairo	arr.	5 35	6 00	6 20	9 20	9 45	1130	1330	1635	1730	2010	2055	2335	2400

INDEX

SEND US A POSTCARD

We'd like to hear your reaction.
Did you make any discoveries?
Did we steer you wrong?

Let us know.